Lecture Notes in Computer Science 15933

Founding Editors

Gerhard Goos
Juris Hartmanis

The series Lecture Notes in Computer Science (LNCS), including its subseries Lecture Notes in Artificial Intelligence (LNAI) and Lecture Notes in Bioinformatics (LNBI), has established itself as a medium for the publication of new developments in computer science and information technology research, teaching, and education.

LNCS enjoys close cooperation with the computer science R & D community, the series counts many renowned academics among its volume editors and paper authors, and collaborates with prestigious societies. Its mission is to serve this international community by providing an invaluable service, mainly focused on the publication of conference and workshop proceedings and postproceedings. LNCS commenced publication in 1973.

Ruzica Piskac · Zvonimir Rakamarić
Editors

Computer Aided Verification

37th International Conference, CAV 2025
Zagreb, Croatia, July 23–25, 2025
Proceedings, Part III

 Springer

Editors
Ruzica Piskac
Yale University
New Haven, CT, USA

Zvonimir Rakamarić
Amazon (United States)
Seattle, WA, USA

ISSN 0302-9743   ISSN 1611-3349 (electronic)
Lecture Notes in Computer Science
ISBN 978-3-031-98681-9   ISBN 978-3-031-98682-6 (eBook)
https://doi.org/10.1007/978-3-031-98682-6

This Springer imprint is published by the registered company Springer Nature Switzerland AG
The registered company address is: Gewerbestrasse 11, 6330 Cham, Switzerland

If disposing of this product, please recycle the paper.

Preface

It was our privilege to serve as the program chairs for CAV 2025, the 37th International Conference on Computer-Aided Verification. CAV 2025 was held in Zagreb, Croatia, on July 23–25, 2025, and the pre-conference workshops were held on July 21–22, 2025.

CAV is an annual conference dedicated to the advancement of the theory and practice of computer-aided formal analysis methods for hardware and software systems. The primary focus of CAV is to extend the frontiers of verification techniques by expanding to new domains such as security, quantum computing, and machine learning. This puts CAV at the cutting edge of formal methods research. This year's program is a reflection of this commitment.

CAV 2025 received 305 submissions. We accepted 24 tool papers, 4 case-study papers, and 51 regular papers, which amounts to an acceptance rate of roughly 25.9% overall. The accepted papers cover a wide spectrum of topics, from theoretical results to applications of formal methods. These papers apply or extend formal methods to a wide range of domains such as concurrency, machine learning and neural networks, quantum systems, as well as hybrid and stochastic systems. The program featured keynote talks by Corina Păsăreanu (Carnegie Mellon University, USA), Emina Torlak (Amazon Web Services and University of Washington, USA), and Roderick Bloem (Graz University of Technology, Austria). In addition to the contributed talks, CAV 2025 also hosted the CAV Award ceremony, and a report from the Synthesis Competition (SYNTCOMP) chairs. Furthermore, we continued the tradition of Logic Lounge, a series of discussions on computer science topics targeting a general audience. This year's Logic Lounge speakers were Moshe Y. Vardi (Rice University) and Henry Shevlin (University of Cambridge) who invited us to examine the nature of mind itself and whether artificial intelligence met its defining criteria.

In addition to the main conference, CAV 2025 hosted the following workshops: Verification Mentoring Workshop (VMW), Workshop on Synthesis (SYNT), Workshop on Verification of Quantum Computing (VQC), Workshop on Automated Reasoning for Tensor Compilers (AR4TC), International Workshop on Trustworthy Cyber-Physical Systems (TACPS), Workshop on Hyperproperties: Advances in Theory and Applications (HYPER), Symposium on AI Verification (SAIV), Meeting on String Constraints and Applications (MOSCA), Workshop on Horn Clauses for Verification and Synthesis (HCVS), and Workshop on Verification of Probabilistic Programs (VeriProP). Furthermore, CAV 2025 also included the following events dedicated to two prominent members of the CAV community: Ken McMillan Celebration and Allen Emerson Memorial.

Organizing a flagship conference like CAV requires a great deal of effort from the community. The Program Committee for CAV 2025 consisted of 122 members and two co-chairs—a committee of this size ensures that each member has to review only a reasonable number of papers in the allotted time. In all, the committee members wrote 958 reviews while investing significant effort to maintain and ensure the high quality of the conference program. We are grateful to the CAV 2025 Program Committee for their outstanding efforts in evaluating the submissions and making sure that each paper got a fair chance.

Like recent years in CAV, we made artifact evaluation mandatory for tool paper submissions, but optional for the rest of the accepted papers. This year we received 68 artifact submissions, all of which received at least one badge. We rejected 5 tool papers because the associated artifacts did not meet the functional badge criteria. The Artifact Evaluation Committee consisted of 83 members and two co-chairs, who put in significant effort to evaluate each artifact. The goal of this process was to provide constructive feedback to tool developers and help make the research published in CAV more reproducible. We are also very grateful to the Artifact Evaluation Committee for their hard work and dedication in evaluating the submitted artifacts.

CAV 2025 would not have been possible without the tremendous help we received from a number of individuals, and we would like to thank everyone who helped make CAV 2025 a success. First, we would like to thank our area chairs Anthony Widjaja Lin, Azadeh Farzan, Erika Ábrahám, Eva Darulova, Guy Katz, Peter Müller, Philipp Rümmer, and Roderick Bloem. Moreover, we would like to thank Matthias Heizmann and Tanja Schindler for chairing the Artifact Evaluation Committee. We also thank Grigory Fedyukovich for chairing the workshop organization. Ferhat Erata and Hadar Frenkel for leading publicity efforts, Ning Luo as the fellowship chair, Borzoo Bonakdarpour and Jana Hofmann as sponsorship chairs, and Jordan Schmerge as the website chair. Steve Siegel helped prepare the proceedings, while Alan Jović spearheaded the local organization. We also thank Grigory Fedyukovich, Mukund Raghothaman, Elizabeth Polgreen, Kaushik Mallik, and Thom Badings for organizing the Verification Mentoring Workshop. Last but not least, we would like to thank the members of the CAV Steering Committee (Kenneth McMillan, Aarti Gupta, Orna Grumberg, and Daniel Kroening) for helping us with several important aspects of organizing CAV 2025.

We hope that you will find the proceedings of CAV 2025 scientifically interesting and thought-provoking!

June 2025   Ruzica Piskac
                                                    Zvonimir Rakamarić

Organization

Steering Committee

Orna Grumberg	Technion, Israel
Aarti Gupta	Princeton University, USA
Daniel Kroening	Amazon, USA
Kenneth McMillan	University of Texas at Austin, USA

Conference Co-chairs

Ruzica Piskac	Yale University, USA
Zvonimir Rakamarić	Amazon Web Services, USA

Artifact Evaluation Co-chairs

Matthias Heizmann	University of Stuttgart, Germany
Tanja Schindler	University of Basel, Switzerland

Local Chair

Alan Jović	University of Zagreb, Croatia

Area Chairs

Anthony Widjaja Lin	Technical University of Kaiserslautern, Germany
Azadeh Farzan	University of Toronto, Canada
Erika Ábrahám	RWTH Aachen University, Germany
Eva Darulova	Uppsala University, Sweden
Guy Katz	Hebrew University of Jerusalem, Israel
Peter Müller	ETH Zurich, Switzerland
Philipp Rümmer	University of Regensburg, Germany
Roderick Bloem	Graz University of Technology, Austria

Workshop Chair

Grigory Fedyukovich   Florida State University, USA

Fellowship Chair

Ning Luo   University of Illinois Urbana-Champaign, USA

Publicity Chairs

Ferhat Erata   Yale University, USA
Hadar Frenkel   Bar Ilan University, Israel

Publication Chair

Stephen Siegel   University of Delaware, USA

Website Chair

Jordan Schmerge   Yale University, USA

Program Committee

Aarti Gupta   Princeton University, USA
Ahmed Bouajjani   Université Paris Cité, France
Aina Niemetz   Stanford University, USA
Alan J. Hu   University of British Columbia, Canada
Alberto Griggio   Fondazione Bruno Kessler, Italy
Alessandro Cimatti   Fondazione Bruno Kessler, Italy
Alexander J. Summers   University of British Columbia, Canada
Alexander Nadel   Technion & Intel, Israel
Alfons Laarman   Leiden University, Netherlands
Aman Goel   Amazon Web Services, USA
Anastasia Isychev   TU Wien, Austria
Anastasia Mavridou   KBR/NASA Ames Research Center, USA
Anca Muscholl   LaBRI, Université Bordeaux, France

Andreas Pavlogiannis	Aarhus University, Denmark
Andreas Podelski	University of Freiburg, Germany
Anna Lukina	TU Delft, Netherlands
Anne-Kathrin Schmuck	Max Planck Institute for Software Systems, Germany
Anthony Widjaja Lin	TU Kaiserslautern, Germany
Anton Wijs	Eindhoven University of Technology, Netherlands
Arie Gurfinkel	University of Waterloo, Canada
Armin Biere	University of Freiburg, Germany
Azadeh Farzan	University of Toronto, Canada
Barbara Jobstmann	Cadence Design Systems, Switzerland
Benjamin Kaminski	Saarland University, Germany
Bernd Finkbeiner	CISPA Helmholtz Center for Information Security, Germany
Bettina Könighofer	Graz University of Technology, Austria
Borzoo Bonakdarpour	Michigan State University, USA
Burcu Kulahcioglu Ozkan	Delft University of Technology, Netherlands
Cesar Sanchez	IMDEA Software Institute, Spain
Christoph M. Wintersteiger	Imandra, UK
Christoph Matheja	University of Oldenburg, Germany
Clark Barrett	Stanford University, USA
Claudia Cauli	Huawei Ireland Research Center, Ireland
Corina Pasareanu	NASA Ames Research Center, USA
Cristina David	University of Bristol, UK
Damien Zufferey	NVIDIA, Switzerland
Daniel Kröning	Amazon, USA
Daniel Stan	LRE EPITA Research Laboratory, France
Dirk Beyer	LMU Munich, Germany
Dominik Winterer	ETH Zurich, Switzerland
Đorđj e Žikelić	Singapore Management University, Singapore
Dorra Ben Khalifa	ENAC – University of Toulouse, France
Duc-Hiep Chu	Google Research, USA
Elizabeth Polgreen	University of Edinburgh, UK
Elvira Albert	Complutense University of Madrid, Spain
Enrico Magnago	Amazon Web Services, Germany
Erika Ábrahám	RWTH Aachen University, Germany
Eva Darulova	Uppsala University, Sweden
Gidon Ernst	LMU Munich, Germany
Guowen Xu	University of Electronic Science and Technology of China, China
Guy Amir	Cornell University, USA
Guy Katz	Hebrew University of Jerusalem, Israel

Hadar Frenkel	Bar Ilan University, Israel
Haoze (Andrew) Wu	Amherst College, USA
Harald Ruess	SRI International, USA
Hari Govind Vediramana Krishnan	University of Waterloo, Canada
Hazem Torfah	Chalmers University of Technology, Sweden
He Zhu	Rutgers University, USA
Hossein Hojjat	Tehran Institute of Advanced Studies, Iran
Ichiro Hasuo	National Institute of Informatics, Japan
Jana Hofmann	Max Planck Institute for Security and Privacy, Germany
Ji Guan	Institute of Software, Chinese Academy of Sciences, China
Jianan Yao	Amazon Web Services, USA
Jingbo Wang	Purdue University, USA
Jocelyn (Qiaochu) Chen	New York University, USA
Joey Dodds	Amazon Web Services, USA
Joost-Pieter Katoen	RWTH-Aachen University, Germany
Jorge A. Pérez	University of Groningen, Netherlands
Junkil Park	Aptos Labs, USA
Kaushik Mallik	IMDEA Software Institute, Spain
Kedar Namjoshi	Bell Labs, Nokia, USA
Kshitij Bansal	Google, USA
Kyungmin Bae	POSTECH, South Korea
Laura Kovacs	TU Wien, Austria
Magnus Myreen	Chalmers University of Technology, Sweden
Marco Faella	University of Naples Federico II, Italy
Marieke Huisman	University of Twente, Netherlands
Mark Santolucito	Barnard College, Columbia University, USA
Michael Emmi	Amazon Web Services, USA
Mihaela Sighireanu	University Paris-Saclay, France
Mirco Giacobbe	University of Birmingham, UK
Natasha Sharygina	University of Lugano, Switzerland
Nian-Ze Lee	National Taiwan University, Taiwan
Ning Luo	University of Illinois Urbana-Champaign, USA
Ondřej Lengál	Brno University of Technology, Czech Republic
Pablo Castro	Universidad Nacional de Río Cuarto - CONICET, Argentina
Pavithra Prabhakar	Kansas State University, USA
Peter Müller	ETH Zurich, Switzerland
Philipp Ruemmer	University of Regensburg, Germany
Qinxiang Cao	Shanghai Jiao Tong University, China
Ravi Mangal	Colorado State University, USA

Rayna Dimitrova	CISPA Helmholtz Center for Information Security, Germany
Roderick Bloem	Graz University of Technology, Austria
S. Akshay	Indian Institute of Technology Bombay, India
S. Krishna	Indian Institute of Technology Bombay, India
Shaobo He	Amazon Web Services, USA
Shibashis Guha	Tata Institute of Fundamental Research, India
Soham Chakraborty	TU Delft, Netherlands
Stefan Leue	University of Konstanz, Germany
Stefan Zetzsche	Amazon Web Services, UK
Stephen F. Siegel	University of Delaware, USA
Subhajit Roy	Indian Institute of Technology Kanpur, India
Sylvie Putot	Ecole Polytechnique, France
Sébastien Bardin	CEA List, Université Paris Saclay, France
Tachio Terauchi	Waseda University, Japan
Tatjana Petrov	University of Trieste, Italy
Thomas Wahl	Trusted Science and Technology, Inc., USA
Tim King	Amazon Web Services, USA
Timos Antonopoulos	Yale University, USA
Tom van Dijk	University of Twente, Netherlands
Tomas Vojnar	Masaryk University, Czech Republic
Vijay Ganesh	Georgia Tech, USA
Viktor Kunčak	EPFL, Switzerland
Wenxi Wang	University of Virginia, USA
William Hallahan	Binghamton University, USA
Xi (James) Zheng	Macquarie University, Australia
Yakir Vizel	Technion, Israel
Yedi Zhang	National University of Singapore, Singapore
Yu-Fang Chen	Academia Sinica, Taiwan
Yuting Wang	Shanghai Jiao Tong University, China
Yuxin Deng	East China Normal University, China
Yuyang Sang	Alibaba Cloud, USA

Artifact Evaluation Committee

Abdalrhman Mohamed	Stanford University, USA
Abhishek Kr Singh	National University of Singapore, Singapore
Adwait Godbole	UC Berkeley, USA
Akshatha Shenoy	Università della Svizzera italiana, Switzerland
Alejandro Hernández-Cerezo	Complutense University of Madrid, Spain
Ameer Hamza	Florida State University, USA

Amit Samanta	University of Utah, USA
Anna Becchi	Fondazione Bruno Kessler, Italy
Annelot Bosman	Universiteit Leiden, Netherlands
Avaljot Singh	University of Illinois Urbana-Champaign, USA
Avraham Raviv	Bar Ilan University, Israel
Benjamin F. Jones	Amazon Web Services, USA
Bruno Andreotti	Federal University of Minas Gerais, Brazil
Calvin Chau	Technische Universität Dresden, Germany
Cayden Codel	Carnegie Mellon University, USA
Chenyu Zhou	University of Southern California, USA
Christoph Weinhuber	University of Oxford, UK
Clara Rodríguez-Núñez	Universidad Complutense de Madrid, Spain
Daniel Ajeleye	University of Colorado, Boulder, USA
Diptarko Roy	University of Birmingham, UK
Ehsan Kafshdar Goharshady	Institute of Science and Technology, Austria
Enrico Magnago	Amazon Web Services, Germany
Filip Cano	Graz University of Technology, Austria
Filip Macák	Brno University of Technology, Czech Republic
Filipe de Arruda	Universidade Federal de Pernambuco, Brazil
Florian Sextl	TU Wien, Austria
Frédéric Recoules	CEA LIST, France
Geunyeol Yu	Pohang University of Science and Technology, South Korea
Guangyu Hu	Hong Kong University of Science and Technology, China
Hichem Rami Ait-El-Hara	Université Paris-Saclay, France
Idan Refaeli	Hebrew University of Jerusalem, Israel
Jacqueline Mitchell	University of Southern California, USA
Jaime Arias	CNRS, LIPN, Université Sorbonne Paris Nord, France
Jiong Yang	Georgia Institute of Technology, USA
Joseph Tafese	University of Waterloo, Canada
Kadiray Karakaya	Paderborn University, Germany
Konstantin Britikov	University of Lugano, Switzerland
Konstantin Kueffner	Institute of Science and Technology, Austria
Leni Aniva	Stanford University, USA
Lutz Klinkenberg	RWTH Aachen University, Germany
Mahboubeh Samadi	Tehran Institute for Advanced Studies, Iran
Mahyar Karimi	Institute of Science and Technology, Austria
Marek Chalupa	Institute of Science and Technology, Austria
Mário Pereira	NOVA School of Science and Technology, Portugal

Mathias Fleury	University of Freiburg, Germany
Mehrdad Karrabi	Institute of Science and Technology, Austria
Miguel Isabel	Complutense University of Madrid, Spain
Mihai Nicola	Stevens Institute of Technology, USA
Mihály Dobos-Kovács	Budapest University of Technology and Economics, Hungary
Mikael Mayer	Amazon Web Services, USA
Muqsit Azeem	Technical University of Munich, Germany
N. Ege Saraç	Institute of Science and Technology, Austria
Neea Rusch	Augusta University, USA
Nicolas Koh	Princeton University, USA
Omar Inverso	Gran Sasso Science Institute, Italy
Omkar Tuppe	IIT Bombay, India
Omri Isac	Hebrew University of Jerusalem, Israel
Oyendrila Dobe	Amazon Web Services, USA
Pablo Gordillo	Complutense University of Madrid, Spain
Patrick Trentin	Amazon Web Services, USA
Pei-Wei Chen	UC Berkeley, USA
Peixin Wang	Nanyang Technological University, Singapore
Philipp Kern	Karlsruhe Institute of Technology, Germany
Pinhan Zhao	University of Michigan, USA
Po-Chun Chien	LMU Munich, Germany
Rajarshi Roy	University of Oxford, UK
Sankalp Gambhir	EPFL, Switzerland
Sascha Klüppelholz	Technische Universität Dresden, Germany
Shantanu Kulkarni	IIT Bombay, India
Simon Guilloud	EPFL, Switzerland
Stefan Zetzsche	Amazon Web Services, UK
Timo Lang	Huawei Ireland Research Center, Ireland
Xuan Xie	University of Alberta, Canada
Yanju Chen	University of California, Santa Barbara, USA
Yannik Schnitzer	University of Oxford, UK
Yibo Dong	East China Normal University, China
Yizhak Elboher	Hebrew University of Jerusalem, Israel
Yogev Shalmon	Technion, Israel
Yuning Wang	Rutgers University, USA
Yusen Su	University of Waterloo, Canada
Zhengyang John Lu	University of Waterloo, Canada
Zhiyang Chen	University of Toronto, Canada
Zunchen Huang	CWI, Netherlands

Additional Reviewers

Abha Chaudhary
Adam Husted Kjelstrøm
Adam Rogalewicz
Alejandro Luque-Cerpa
Alejandro Villoria Gonzalez
Alex Ozdemir
Alexander Bork
Alexander C. Wilton
Alexander Stekelenburg
Andoni Rodriguez
Andrew Reynolds
Anja Petkovic Komel
Anton Varonka
Antonina Skurka
Antonio Casares
Arend-Jan Quist
Áron Ricardo Perez-Lopez
Arshia Rafieioskouei
Ashwani Anand
Benedikt Maderbacher
Benjamin Monmege
Che Cheng
Chia-Hsuan Su
Christian Lidström
Christina Gehnen
Christophe Chareton
Christopher Brix
Christopher Watson
Corto Mascle
Cruise Song
Daniela Kaufman
David Boetius
Dimitrios Thanos
Fabio Mogavero
Faezeh Labbaf
Felix Stutz
Filip Cano
Gianluca Redondi
Grigory Fedyukovich
Grégoire Menguy
Hangcheng Cao
Henrik Wachowitz
Igor Walukiewicz

Irmak Saglam
Iwo Kurzidem
Jan Martens
Jannick Strobel
Jasper Nalbach
Jia Hu
Jingyi Mei
Jinhua Wu
Johannes Haring
Joonhwan Yoo
Konstantin Britikov
Ling Zhang
Lutz Klinkenberg
Marc Farreras I Bartra
Marek Jankola
Marian Lingsch-Rosenfeld
Marvin Brieger
Massimo Benerecetti
Mathias Preiner
Matthew Davis
Matthias Kettl
Matthieu Bovel
Matthieu Lemerre
Michal Hečko
Milad Rabizadeh
Min Wu
Mingyu Huang
Muhammad Mahmoud
Pengzhi Xing
Pierre Ganty
Piyush Jha
Po-Chun Chien
Pranshu Gaba
Prithwish Jana
Rachel Cleaveland
Rafael Dewes
Raffael Senn
Ritam Raha
Robert Mensing
Roy Hermanns
Satya Prakash Nayak
Simon Guilloud
Steef Hegeman

Stefan Pranger
Subhajit Bandopadhyay
Thomas Hader
Thomas Lemberger
Tian-Fu Chen
Timm Spork
Tobias Winkler
Tomas Kolarik
Tomáš Dacík
Tzu-Han Hsu

Valentin Promies
Xieting Chu
Xin Hong
Xinyuan Qian
Yanis Sellami
Yicheng Ni
Yizhou Mao
Zhengyang Lu
Zhengyu Li
Zihao Li

Keynote Talks

Through the Looking Glass: Semantic Analysis of Neural Networks

Corina Păsăreanu

Carnegie Mellon University, USA

Abstract. Neural networks are known for their lack of transparency, making them difficult to understand and analyze. In this talk, we explore methods designed to interpret, formally analyze, and even shape the internal representations of neural networks using human-understandable abstractions. We review recent techniques including the use of vision-language models to investigate perception modules, the application of probing and steering vectors to identify vulnerabilities in code models, and an axiomatic approach for validating mechanistic interpretation of transformer models.

Bio. Corina Păsăreanu is an ACM Fellow working at NASA Ames. She is affiliated with KBR and Carnegie Mellon University's CyLab. Her research interests include model checking, symbolic execution, compositional verification, AI safety, autonomy, and security. She is the recipient of several awards, including an ETAPS Test of Time Award and an ACM Impact Paper Award. She has served as Program/General Chair for several conferences, including CAV in 2015, and more recently ICSE in 2025. More information can be found on her website: https://www.andrew.cmu.edu/user/pcorina/.

Cedar: A New Language for Expressive, Fast, Safe, and Analyzable Authorization

Emina Torlak

Amazon Web Services and University of Washington, USA

Abstract. Authorization is the problem of deciding who has access to what in a multi-user system. Every cloud-based application has to solve this problem, from photo sharing to online banking to health care. This talk presents Cedar, a new language for authorization that is designed to be ergonomic, fast, safe, and analyzable by reduction to SMT. Cedar's simple and intuitive syntax supports common authorization use-cases with readable policies, naturally expressing concepts from role-based, attribute-based, and relation-based access control models. Cedar's policy structure enables authorization requests to be decided quickly. Its policy validator uses optional typing to help policy writers avoid mistakes, but not get in their way. Cedar's design has been finely balanced to allow for a sound, complete, and decidable logical encoding, which enables precise policy analysis, e.g., to ensure that policy refactoring preserves existing permissions. We have implemented Cedar in Rust and used Lean to formally verify important properties of its design. Cedar is used at scale in Amazon Verified Permissions and Amazon Verified Access, and it is freely available at https://github.com/cedar-policy.

Bio. Emina Torlak is a Senior Principal Scientist at Amazon Web Services and an Affiliate Professor at the University of Washington. Emina works on new languages and tools for program verification and synthesis. She received her Bachelors (2003), Masters (2004), and Ph.D. (2009) degrees from MIT. Emina is the creator of Rosette and Kodkod, and leads the development of Cedar. Rosette is a solver-aided language that powers verification and synthesis tools for all kinds of systems, from radiation therapy control to Linux JIT compilers. Kodkod is a solver for relational logic, used widely in tools for software analysis and design. Cedar is an expressive, fast, and analysable language for authorization, used at scale at Amazon Web Services and beyond. Emina is a recipient of the Robin Milner Young Researcher Award (2021), NSF Career Award (2017), Sloan Research Fellowship (2016), and the AITO Dahl-Nygaard Junior Prize (2016).

Side Channel Secure Software: A Hardware Question

Roderick Bloem

Graz University of Technology, Austria

Abstract. We will present a method to prove the absence of power side channels in systems that are protected using masking. Power side channels may allow attackers to discover secret information by measuring electromagnetic emanations from a chip. Masking is a countermeasure to hide secrets by duplication and addition of randomness. We will discuss how to formally prove security against power side channel techniques for circuits. We will then move on to software running on a CPU, where hardware details can have surprising effects. We will present some vulnerabilities on a small CPU and how to fix them, and we will talk about contracts that take side channels into account.

Bio. Roderick Bloem is a professor at Graz University of Technology. He received his M.Sc. degree in Computer Science from Leiden University, the Netherlands, in 1996, and his Ph.D. degree in Computer Science from the University of Colorado at Boulder in 2001. From 2002 until 2008, he was an Assistant at Graz University of Technology, Graz, Austria. From 2008, he has been a full professor of Computer Science at the same university. He is a co-editor of the *Handbook of Model Checking* and has published over 140 peer reviewed papers in formal verification, reactive synthesis, Safe AI, and security.

References

1. Bloem, R., Gigerl, B., Gourjon, M., Hadzic, V., Mangard, S., Primas, R.: Power contracts: provably complete power leakage models for processors. In: Yin, H., Stavrou, A., Cremers, C., Shi, E. (eds.) Proceedings of the 2022 ACM SIGSAC Conference on Computer and Communications Security, CCS 2022, Los Angeles, CA, USA, 7–11 November 2022. pp. 381–395. ACM (2022). https://doi.org/10.1145/3548606.3560600
2. Bloem, R., Gross, H., Iusupov, R., Könighofer, B., Mangard, S., Winter, J.: Formal verification of masked hardware implementations in the presence of glitches. In: Nielsen, J., Rijmen, V. (eds.) EUROCRYPT 2018. LNCS, vol. 10821, pp. 321–353. Springer, Cham (2018). https://doi.org/10.1007/978-3-319-78375-8_11

3. Hadzic, V., Bloem, R.: COCOALMA: a versatile masking verifier. In: Formal Methods in Computer Aided Design, FMCAD 2021, New Haven, CT, USA, 19–22 October 2021, pp. 1–10. IEEE (2021). https://doi.org/10.34727/2021/ISBN.978-3-85448-046-4_9
4. Haring, J., Hadzic, V., Bloem, R.: Closing the gap: Leakage contracts for processors with transitions and glitches. IACR Trans. Cryptogr. Hardw. Embed. Syst. 2024(4), 110–132 (2024). https://doi.org/10.46586/TCHES.V2024.I4.110-132

Contents – Part III

Automated Reasoning

Polyregular Model Checking

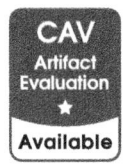

Aliaume Lopez$^{(\boxtimes)}$ and Rafał Stefański

University of Warsaw, Warsaw, Poland
ad.lopez@uw.edu.pl

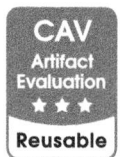

Abstract. We introduce a high-level language with Python-like syntax for string-to-string, polyregular, first-order definable transductions. This language features function calls, boolean variables, and nested for-loops. We devise and implement a complete decision procedure for the verification of such programs against a first-order specification. The decision procedure reduces the verification problem to the decidable first-order theory of finite words (extensively studied in automata theory), which we discharge using either complete tools specific to this theory (MONA), or to general-purpose SMT solvers (Z3, CVC5).

1 Introduction

String manipulating programs of low complexity are ubiquitous in modern software. They are often used to transform data and do not perform complex computations themselves. In this paper, we are interested in verifying Hoare triples for such string manipulating programs, i.e. specifications of the form $\{P\}$ code $\{Q\}$, where P and Q are pre- and post-conditions, meaning that whenever the input satisfies property P, the output of the program satisfies property Q.

Regularity Preserving Programs. One particularly interesting class of specifications in the case of string-to-string functions are *regular languages*, which can be efficiently verified using automata-based techniques. We say that a function f is *regularity preserving* if it preserves regular languages under pre-image, i.e. if $f^{-1}(L)$ is regular for all regular languages L. For regularity preserving functions, the verification of a Hoare triple $\{L_P\}\, f\, \{L_Q\}$ can be reduced to the nonemptiness problem of the language $L_P \cap f^{-1}(L_Q)$, where L_P and L_Q are regular languages. This is a well-studied problem in the literature, and is at the core of several more involved techniques [2,13,18]. The key challenge of this approach is that there exist uncomputable regularity preserving functions, so such approaches will only work on classes of functions for which pre-images of regular languages are (relatively) efficiently computable. Usually, these classes come from generalisation of automata models to functions, also known as *string-to-string transducers*.

A. Lopez—Supported by the Polish National Science Centre (NCN) grant "Polynomial finite state computation" (2022/46/A/ST6/00072).

R. Stefański—Supported by the European Research Council (ERC) under the European Union's Horizon 2020 innovation program (grant PROCONTRA-885666).

⬚ This document uses knowledge: notion points to its *definition*.

String-to-String Transducer Models. There is a wide variety of models for string-to-string transducers [24], and one of the most prominent ones is called *linear regular functions*, that are equivalently defined using two-way finite transducers (2DFTs) [26], streaming-string-transducers (SSTs) [1], or linear regular list functions [9]. Notably, Alur and Černý have proven that SSTs have a PSPACE-complete model checking problem when the functions are given as SSTs, and the specifications are given as automata [2, Theorem 13]. This was used for instance by Chen, Taolue, Hague, Lin, Rümer, and Wu to study *path feasibility* in string-manipulating programs [13].

A similar approach was used by Jeż, Lin, Markgraf, and Rümmer, who leveraged the *rational functions* (a strict subclass of linear regular functions) to study programs manipulating strings with infinite alphabets [19]. Remark that in the setting of infinite alphabets, the landscape of automata and transducers is much more complex: In partcicular, the class of languages recognised by two-way automata is stronger that the class of languages recognised by one-way automata, and has undecidable emptiness [8, Figure 1.1].

One limitation of the linear regular functions is that they only allow for linear growth of the output, excluding many useful string-manipulating programs. The class of *polyregular functions* is an interesting generalisation of linear regular functions that allows for polynomial behaviour, and is much closer to real life string manipulating programs. The model is relatively old, first introduced in [16], and has recently gained a lot of traction now that several other characterizations have been obtained [6,7].[1] However, the proof of the regularity preserving property for polyregular functions is of theoretical nature (no implementation or complexity bounds are given), and writing programs using any of the existing equivalent definitions of polyregular functions is cumbersome and error-prone. Because polyregular functions can succinctly encode formulas in first-order logic on words, and since the satisfiability problem for such formulas is known to be TOWER-complete [27, Theorem 13.5], one can expect that verifying polyregular functions to be quite complex.

MSO vs FO. Instead of using the full power of regular languages (defined equivalently using finite automata, monadic second order logic (MSO), finite monoid recognition, or regular expressions [11,21,28,30]), we will use specifications written in first-order logic (FO) on finite words. A cornerstone result of the theory is establishing the equivalence between languages described in this logic, *star-free languages*, and *counter free automata* [22,25,29]. The advantage of using this weaker specification model is twofold: first, it allows us to focus on a simpler class of star-free polyregular functions[2], which are easier to work with in practice. Second, it allows us to reduce the satisfiability of a Hoare triple to

---

[1] Note that for this extended model, being regularity preserving is tightly connected to being closed under function composition [17, Proposition III.3], and this closure under composition was one of the surprising conclusions of [7].

[2] The notion of being *star-free* has been extended to various classes of transducers, see [7,9,12,24].

the satisfiability of a *first-order* formula on finite words, for which one can use general purpose SMT solvers, in addition to automata based tools (MONA) which also work for the MSO logic on words. Even though the SMT solver are *incomplete*, they can, in some cases, lead to faster decision procedures. Indeed, the satisfiability problem for first-order logic on finite words, while decidable, is TOWER-complete [27, Theorem 13.5].

Contributions. In this paper, we introduce a high-level programming language for implementing star-free polyregular functions in a Python-like syntax, including features such as boolean variables, index variables, immutable list variables, function calls, and nested for-loops. The language was carefully designed not become too expressive – this is ensured by a number of syntactic restrictions and a novel type system for index variables. We show that this language can be compiled into one of the equivalent definitions of polyregular functions (namely, simple for-programs), which does not allow for function calls nor list variables. We also provide an implementation of the previously known abstract result stating that polyregular functions are regularity preserving (in the case of star-free functions and languages), being careful about the complexity of the transformations. Finally, we reduce the verification of Hoare triples to the satisfiability of first-order formulas on words. Since we are using first-order logic as a target language, we are not restricted to using automata based tools like *MONA* [20], but can also employ general purpose SMT solvers like *Z3* [23] and *CVC5* [32], generating proof obligations in the SMT-LIB format [3].

All the steps described above have been implemented in a `Haskell` program, and tested on a number of examples with encouraging results.[3] While this is not a tool paper, we believe that the proof-of-concept implementation is a good starting point to demonstrate the viability of our approach, and we believe that there is a potential for further investigations in this direction.

Outline. The structue of the paper is as follows. We introduce our high-level language in Sect. 2. In Sect. 3, we recall the theory of polyregular functions by introducing them in terms of simple for-programs and FO-interpretations. We will also provide an efficient reduction of the verification of Hoare triples to the satisfiability of a first-order formula on words in Sect. 3.4. In order to verify for-programs, we compile them into simple for-programs in Sect. 4, and then compile simple for-programs into FO-interpretations in Sect. 5. Then, in Sect. 6, we present tests of our implementation on various examples, discussing the complexity of the transformations and the main bottlenecks of our approach. Finally, in Sect. 7, we discuss potential optimizations and future work.

---

[3] An anonymized version of our code is available at https://github.com/AliaumeL/polyregular-model-checking.

2 High Level For Programs

In this section, we introduce our high-level language for describing list-manipulating functions which can be seen as a subset of `Python`, which we call *(high-level) for-programs*. Our goal is to reason algorithmically about the programs written in this language, so it needs to be highly restricted. To illustrate those restrictions, let us present in Fig. 1 a comprehensive example written in a subset of `Python`.[4]

```python
def getBetween(l, i, j):
    """ Get elements between i and j """
    for (k, c) in enumerate(l):
        if i <= k and k <= j: ①
            yield c ②

def containsAB(w):
    """ Contains "ab" as a subsequence """
    seen_a = False ③
    for (x, c) in enumerate(w):
        if c == "a": ④
            seen_a = True ⑤
        elif seen_a and c == "b":
            return True
    return False

def subwordsWithAB(word):
    """ Get subwords that contain "ab" """
    for (i,c) in enumerate(word): ⑥
        for (j,d) in reversed(enumerate(word)): ⑦
            s = getBetween(word, i, j) ⑧
            if containsAB(s):
                yield s
```

Fig. 1. A small Python program that outputs all subwords of a given word containing ab as a scattered subword

For the sake of readability, we implicitly coerce generators (created using the `yield` keyword) to lists. Our programs will only deal with three kinds of values: booleans ($\mathbb{B}$), non-negative integers ($\mathbb{N}$), and *(nested) words* ($\mathcal{W}$), i.e. characters ($\mathcal{W}0$), words ($\mathcal{W}_1$), lists of words ($\mathcal{W}_2$), etc. These lists can be created by *yielding*

---

[4] The corresponding program in the syntax accepted by our solver is given in the full version of this paper.

values in a loop, such as in ② of Fig. 1. In order to ensure decidable verification of Hoare triples,[5] we also will enforce the following conditions, which are satisfied in our example:

(I) **Loop Constructions.** We only allow `for` loops iterating forward or backward over a list, as in ⑥ and ⑦. In particular, `while` loops and recursive functions are forbidden, which guarantees termination of our programs.

(II) **Mutable Variables.** The only mutable variables are booleans. The values of integer variables are introduced by the `for` loop as in ⑥, and their values are fixed during each iteration. Mutable integer variables could serve as unrestricted counters, resulting in undecidable verification. Similarly, we prohibit mutable list variables, as their lengths could be used as counters. However, we still allow the use of immutable list variables, as in ⑧.

(III) **Equality Checks.** We disallow equality checks between two nested words, unless one of them is a constant expression. This is what happens in point ④ of our Fig. 1. Without this restriction, verification would also be undecidable. More generally, classical string *algorithms* (edit distance, string matching, longest common subsequence, etc.) should not be expressible in our language, since one can easily derive an equality check from them.

(IV) **Integer Comparisons.** The only allowed operations on integers are usual comparisons operators (equality, inequalities). However, we only allow comparisons between integers that are indices of the same list. Every integer is associated to a list expression. For instance, in points ⑥ and ⑦ of our example, the variables i and j are associated to the same list variable `word`. Similarly, for the comparison of point ① to be valid, the variables k, i, and j should all be associated to the same list variable l.

To ensure this compatibility, we designed the following type system, containing Booleans, nested words of a given depth (characters are of depth 0), and integers associated to a list expression (the set of which is denoted by LExpr):

$$\tau ::= \mathsf{Bool} \mid \mathsf{Pos}_o \mid \mathsf{List}_n \quad n \in \mathbb{N}, o \in \mathsf{LExpr} \quad .$$

These types can be inferred from the context, except in the case of function arguments, in which case we explicitly specify to which list argument integer variables are associated. Without this restriction, the equality predicate between two lists can be redefined.

(V) **Variable Shadowing.** We disallow shadowing of variable names, as it could be used to forge the origin of integers, leading to unrestricted comparisons .

(VI) **Boolean Arguments.** We disallow functions to take boolean arguments, as it would allow to forge the origin of integers, by considering the function `switch(b, l1, l2)` which returns either `l1` or `l2` depending on the value of `b` .

---

[5] Using first-order logic on words as a specification language.

(VII) **Boolean Updates.** Boolean variables are initialized to `false` as in ③, and once they are set to `true` as in ⑤, they cannot be reset to `false`. We depart here from the semantics of Python by considering lexical scoping of variables; in particular a variable declared in a loop is not accessible outside this loop.

This restriction allows us to reduce the verification problem to the satisfiability of a first-order formula on finite words. This problem is not only decidable but also solvable by well-engineered existing tools, such as automata-based solvers (e.g., MONA) and classical SMT solvers (e.g., Z3, and CVC5). Without this restriction, the problem would require the use the monadic second order logic on words which is still decidable but not supported by the SMT solvers.

Formal Syntax and Typing. We extend the typing system to functions by grouping input positions with the list they are associated to. For instance, the function `getBetweenIndicesBeforeStop(l, i, j)` has type $(\mathsf{List}_2, 2) \to \mathsf{List}_2$, that is, we are given an input list l together with two pointers to indices of this list. Similarly, the function `containsAB(w)` has type $(\mathsf{List}_1, 0) \to \mathsf{Bool}$, while the function `subwordsWithAB(word)` has type $(\mathsf{List}_1, 0) \to \mathsf{List}_2$. We implemented a linear-time algorithm for the type checking and inference problems.

The formal syntax of our language is given in the full version of this paper. They define the syntax of *boolean expressions* (BExpr), *constant expressions* (CExpr), *list expressions* (LExpr), and *control statements* (Stmt). For readability, we distinguish boolean variables $\mathbb{V}_{\mathrm{bool}}$ $(b, p, q, \ldots)$, position variables $\mathbb{V}_{\mathrm{pos}}$ $(i, j, \ldots)$, list variables $\mathbb{V}_{\mathrm{list}}$ $(x, y, u, v, w, \ldots)$, and function variables $\mathbb{V}_{\mathrm{fun}}$ $(f, g, h, \ldots)$. A *for-program* is a list of function definitions together with a *main* function of type $\mathsf{List}_1 \to \mathsf{List}_1$.

Semantics. Given an *evaluation context* that assigns values (functions, positions, booleans, nested words) to variables, the semantics of boolean expressions into booleans $\mathbb{B}$, constant expressions into nested words, and list expressions into nested words pose no difficulty. For the control statements, there is a crucial design choice regarding the semantics of backward iteration. While the semantics of forward iteration is unambiguous, the backward iteration $\mathrm{for}^{\leftarrow}(i, x)$ in l do s could be understood in two different ways, provided that l evaluates to a list $[x_0, \ldots, x_k]$:

- Executing the statement s for pairs $(k, x_k), \ldots, (0, x_0)$. This corresponds to Python's `for (i,x) in reversed(enumerate(l))` ;
- Executing the statement s for pairs $(0, x_k), \ldots, (k, x_0)$. This corresponds to Python's `for (i,x) in enumerate(reversed(l))`.

As shown in our example program, we use the first interpretation (see ⑦). In fact, the second interpretation would allow us to define the equality predicate between two lists, leading to undecidable verification.

3   Polyregular Functions

To obtain a decision procedure for the verification of Hoare triples for for-programs, we will prove that they can be compiled to *first-order polyregular functions*– a class of transductions introduced in [7] whose model checking problem is decidable [7, Theorem 1.7]. We provide two equivalent definitions of the first-order polyregular functions: one using first-order simple for-programs [7, p. 19] and one using the logical model of first-order string-to-string interpretations [6, Definition 4], the equivalence of which was proven in [7].

To make the models more suitable for large alphabets (such as the Unicode characters), we present them in a symbolic setting (which uses a simplified version of the ideas presented in [15] or in [5, Section 3.1]). This will dramatically reduce the size of the first-order string-to-string interpretations, and in turn, of the first-order formula that we will feed to the solvers. We will prove in Sect. 5 that every first-order simple for-programs can be transformed into a first-order string-to-string interpretation in the symbolic setting. We believe that the other inclusion should also hold, but do not prove it, as it is out of this paper's scope.

3.1   Symbolic Transductions

Consider the program in Fig. 2, which swaps all as to bs in a string. Even though it operates on the entire Unicode alphabet, it only distinguishes between three types of characters: a, b and the rest. To formalize this observation, we model the Unicode alphabet as an infinite set $\mathcal{D}$, and we define a function $T : \mathcal{D}^* \to \mathcal{D}^*$ to be *supported by* a set $A \subseteq \mathcal{D}$, if for every function $f : \mathcal{D} \to \mathcal{D}$ that does not *touch* elements of A (i.e. $\forall_{a \in A}, f^{-1}(a) - \{a\}$), it holds that:

$$\forall_w \quad T(f^*(w)) = f^*(T(w)) \quad ,$$

where f^* is the extension of f to $\mathcal{D}^*$, defined by applying f to every letter.

Functions defined by for-programs (of type $\mathsf{List}_1 \to \mathsf{List}_1$) are supported by the finite set A of letter constants that they use. This is also going to be the case for the simple for-programs that we introduce in Sect. 3.2. In Sect. 3.3, we will define a version of the first-order string-to-string interpretations in a way that only depends on the size of their support A, and not on the number of the Unicode characters.

```
1   def asToBs(w):
2       for (i, c) in enumerate(w):
3           if c == 'a':
4               yield 'b'
5           else:
6               yield c
```

Fig. 2. The swapAsToBs program.

3.2 First-Order Simple For-Programs

First-order simple for-programs—originally introduced in [7, p. 19]—can be seen as simplified[6] version of the for-programs. The main difference is that the simple for-programs only define transductions of type $List_1 \to List_1$. Here is an example in a Python syntax:

```
1    # The program reverses all space-separated words
2    # in the input string. e.g
3    #         "hello world" -> "olleh dlrow"
4    seen_space_top = False ①
5    # first we handle all words except of the final one
6    for i in input: ②
7        seen_space = False ③
8        if label(i) == ' ': ④
9            for j in reversed(input): ⑤
10               if j < i:
11                   if label(j) == ' ':
12                       seen_space = True
13                   if not seen_space:
14                       print(label(j)) ⑥
15           print(' ') ⑦
16
17   # then we handle the final word
18   for j in reversed(input):
19       if label(j) == ' ':
20           seen_space_top = True
21       if not seen_space_top:
22           print(label(j))
```

We disallow constructing intermediate word-values, there are no variables of type $List_n$ for any n, and it is not possible to define functions (other than the main function). As a consequence, the for-loops can only iterate over the positions of the input word as in ① and ②. The character at a given position can be accessed using the keyword label, whether when testing it (⑤) or when printing it in (⑥). As we are considering a restriction of for-programs, we only allow comparing labels to constant characters (R. III). Finally, we only allow introducing boolean variables at the top of the program (①) or at the beginning of a for loop (③).

3.3 First-Order String-To-String Transductions

First-order string-to-string interpretations forms an other model that defines functions $\mathcal{D}^* \to \mathcal{D}^*$. It is based on the *first-order logic on words* (FO), the

---

[6] Actually, the for-programs were designed as an extended version first-order simple for-programs.

syntax of which we recall in Fig. 3. To evaluate such a formula φ on a word $w \in \mathcal{D}^*$ we perform the quantifications over the positions in w. The predicates $x = y$ and $x < y$ have the natural meaning, and $x =_L$ a is checks if the x-th letter of w is equal to a. Let us recall that the *quantifier rank* of a formula is the maximal number of nested quantifications in it.

$$\varphi, \psi := \forall_x \varphi \mid \exists_x \varphi \mid \varphi \wedge \psi \mid \varphi \vee \psi \mid \neg\varphi$$
$$\mid x = y \mid x < y \mid x =_L \text{a, where a} \in \mathcal{D}$$

Fig. 3. First-order logic on words.

An important property of FO, is that it has decidable *emptiness*, i.e. given a formula φ, one can decide if there is a word w such that φ holds for w. For finite alphabets, this property is well-know [11], and for the infinite alphabet $\mathcal{D}$ it is the consequence of the finite-alphabet case.

Having discussed the first-order logic on words, we are now ready to define the first-order string-to-string interpretations.

Definition 1. *A first-order string-to-string interpretation* consists of:

1. *A finite set of* character constants $A \subset_{fin} \mathcal{D}$.
2. *A finite set T of* tags.
3. *An* arity function $\text{ar} : T \rightarrow \mathbb{N}$.
4. *An* output function $\text{out} : T \rightarrow A + \{1, \dots, \text{ar}(t)\}$.
5. *A* domain formula $\varphi^t_{\text{dom}}(x_1, \dots, x_{\text{ar}(t)})$ *for every tag* $t \in T$.
6. *An* order formula $\varphi^{t,t'}_{\leq}(x_1, \dots, x_{\text{ar}(t)}, y_1, \dots, y_{\text{ar}(t')})$ *for every* $t, t' \in T$.

The order and domain formulas should only use constants from A.

The interpretation's output for a word $w \in \mathcal{D}^*$ is obtained as follows:

1. Take the set $P = \{1, \dots, |w|\}$ of the positions in w, and construct the set of *elements* as the set $T(P) = (t : T) \times P^{\text{ar}(t)}$ of all tags from T equipped with position tuples of the appropriate arity.
2. Filter out the elements that do not satisfy the domain formula.
3. Sort the remaining elements according to the order formula. Typically, we want the order formula to define a total order on the remaining elements of $T(P)$ – if this is not the case, the interpretation returns an empty word.
4. Assign a letter to each element according to the output function: For an element $t(p_1, \dots, p_k)$, we look at of out(t): If it returns $a \in A$ the output letter is a. If it returns $i \in \{1, \dots, k\}$, we copy the output letter from the p_i-th position of the input.

For example, let us present a first-order word-to-word interpretation for the function swapAsToBs in Fig. 4. It has two tags printB and copy, both of arity 1. The element printB(x) outputs the letter b and copy(x) outputs the letter of x-th position of the input word. The element printB(x) is present in the output if x is labelled with the letter b in the input, otherwise the element copy(x) is present: The tags are sorted by their positions, with ties resolved in favour of printB.

$$\text{out}(\textbf{printB}) = \textbf{b} \quad \text{out}(\textbf{copy}) = 1$$

$$\varphi_{\text{dom}}^{\text{printB}}(x) : x =_L \textbf{b} \quad \varphi_{\text{dom}}^{\text{copy}}(x) : x \neq_L \textbf{b}$$

$\varphi_\leq$	printB(x_1)	copy(x_1)
printB(x_2)	$x_1 \leq x_2$	$x_1 < x_2$
copy(x_2)	$x_1 \leq x_2$	$x_1 \leq x_2$

Fig. 4. The swapAsToBs interpretation.

3.4 Hoare Triple Verification

We say that the Hoare triple $\{\varphi\}$ F $\{\psi\}$ is valid if for every word w that satisfies φ, the output $F(w)$ satisfies ψ. An important property first-order string-to-string interpretations is that they admit a direct reduction of the *first-order Hoare triple* verification problem to the emptiness problem for the first-order logic on words [7, Theorem 1.7]. However, the resulting construction is not efficient. We provide a direct construction of a first-order formula $\chi(\phi, F, \psi)$ that is unsatisfiable if and only if the triple $\{\phi\}$ F $\{\psi\}$ is valid. Moreover, the size and the quantifier rank of χ are bounded by the following low-degree polynomials:

$$\text{qr}(\chi) \leq \max\left(\text{qr}(\phi), \text{qr}(\psi) \cdot (\text{ar}(F) + 1) + \text{qr}(F)\right) \quad |\chi| = \mathcal{O}(|\phi| + |F| \cdot |\psi|)$$

Here $|F|$ denotes the sum of the sizes of formulas in F, $\text{qr}(F)$ denotes quantifier depth of the deepest formula in F, and $\text{ar}(F)$ denotes the maximal arity of the tags in F.

To construct the formula χ, we introduce a *pullback operator* $\pi(F, \psi)$ that transforms the formula ψ applied to the output F, to a formula $\pi(F, \psi)$ that can be applied directly the input word, corresponding to a form of *weakest precondition* [31, Chapter 7]. The pull-back operation is defined in such a way that $F(w)$ satisfies ψ if and only if w satisfies $\pi(F, \psi)$. Once we have the pull-back operation, we can define $\chi(\phi, F, \psi)$ as $\phi \wedge \neg\pi(F, \psi)$. In the rest of this section, we show how to efficiently construct $\pi(F, \psi)$.

Naïve Pullback Definition. Let us start with a simple but inefficient construction of the pullback operation. Every position from $F(w)$ corresponds to a tag t and a tuple of $\text{ar}(t)$ positions of the input word w, so we can replace each quantification in ψ with a conjunction or disjunction over the tags, and use respectively the order formula and output function to implement the predicates over positions of $F(w)$. For example:

$$\forall_x, \psi \quad \rightsquigarrow \quad \bigwedge\nolimits_{t_x \in T} \forall_{x_1, \dots, x_{\text{ar}(t)}} \left(\varphi_{\text{dom}}^t(x_1, \dots, x_{\text{ar}(t)}) \Rightarrow \psi_t'\right)$$

A similar transformation can be done for the existential quantifications. Then, one can implement the $\leq$ predicate by consulting the order formula:

$$x \leq y \quad \leadsto \quad \psi_{\leq}^{t_x,t_y}(x_1, \ldots, x_{\mathsf{ar}(t_x)}, y_1, \ldots, y_{\mathsf{ar}(t_y)})$$

Similarly the $=_L$ predicate can be handled by consulting the output function, and $x = y$ predicate can be handled by comparing equality of the tags and the positions of x and y. This construction, although correct, is unfortunately inefficient: Replacing each quantification with a disjunction or conjunction over tags, results in an exponential blow-up of the formula.

Efficient Pullback Definition. Let us introduce an additional finite sort T to the logic, which allows us to quantify over the tags using $\forall_{t \in T}\varphi$ and $\exists_{t \in T}\varphi$. This does not add expressive power to the logic, as the new quantifiers can be replaced by a finite conjunction (resp. disjunction) that goes through the tags. However, this new sort will allow us to construct the pullback operator in a more efficient way, that can be understood by the solvers (we discuss it in more details at the end of this section). With the new sort of tags, we can pull back the quantifiers in the following way:

$$\pi(F, \forall_x \psi) \quad = \forall_{t_x \in T} \; \forall_{x_1, \ldots, x_{\mathsf{ar}(F)}} \left(\mathsf{dom}(t_x, x_1, \ldots, x_{\mathsf{ar}(F)}) \Rightarrow \pi(F, \psi) \right)$$

where dom is the following predicate based on the domain formula:

$$\mathsf{dom}(t, x_1, \ldots, x_{\mathsf{ar}(t)}) := \bigvee_{t' \in T} \left(t = t' \wedge \varphi_{\mathsf{dom}}^{t'}(x_1, \ldots, x_{\mathsf{ar}(t')}) \right)$$

In order to implement the atomic predicates, we use formulas similar to dom, but based the order formula and output function:

$$\pi(F, x \leq y) = \bigvee_{t_1, t_2 \in T} \left(t_x = t_1 \wedge t_y = t_2 \wedge \varphi_{\leq}^{t_1,t_2}(x_1, \ldots, x_{\mathsf{ar}(t_1)}, y_1, \ldots, y_{\mathsf{ar}(t_2)}) \right)$$

$$\pi(F, x =_L \mathsf{a}) = \left(\bigvee_{t \in T \wedge \mathsf{out}(t) = \mathsf{a}} t = t_x \right) \vee \left(\bigvee_{t \in T \wedge \mathsf{out}(t) \notin A} (t = t_x \wedge x_{\mathsf{out}(t)} =_L \mathsf{a}) \right)$$

This way, we push the disjunction over tags all the way down in the formula, thus avoiding the exponential blow-up of the naïve approach.

Encoding Tags. Finally, let us briefly discuss how we handle the tags in the formulas fed to solvers. For the SMT-solvers, we use the smtlib v2.6 format with logic set to UFDTLIA [3], which allows us to add finite sorts and quantify over them. For the MONA solver, which only supports the sort of positions, we encode the tags as the first $|T|$ positions of the input word. The pertinence of this choice of encoding will be discussed in Sect. 6.

4   From High Level to Low Level For Programs

In this section, we provide a compilation from high-level for-programs to simple for-programs. To smoothen the conversion, we introduce *generator expressions* to the language, as a way to inline function calls. We distinguish between nested-word generators $\langle s \rangle_l$ and boolean generators $\langle s \rangle_b$.

Generator Expressions. Let us briefly discuss the new typing rules and semantics of these generator expressions. The meaning of $\langle s \rangle_l$ is to evaluate the statement s in the current context and collect its output. For instance, $\langle \text{return } x \rangle_l$ is equivalent to x, and $\langle \text{yield } x \text{ ; yield } y \rangle_l$ is equivalent to $\text{list}(x, y)$. Similarly, $\langle s \rangle_b$ is used to evaluate a boolean statement and return its value. The type of a generator expression is equal to the type of the statement s it contains. Importantly, when evaluating the statement s in a generator, we hide all boolean variables from the evaluation context. In particular, let mut b = false in return $\langle \text{return } b \rangle_b$ is an *invalid program*, because the variable b is undefined in the context of the generator expression $\langle b \rangle_b$. The formal typing rules of generator expressions can be found in the full version of this paper.

Hiding the booleans from the context, ensures that the evaluation order of the expressions is irrelevant, allowing us to freely substitute expressions during the compilation process.

Rewriting Steps. We will convert for-programs to simple for-programs by a series of rewriting steps listed below. While most of the steps make can be applied to any for-program, some of them only apply to programs of type $\text{List}_l \to \text{List}_l$.

(A) *Elimination of Literal Equalities*, i.e., of expressions $c =_{\text{lit}} o$ where $c \in \text{CExpr}$ and $o \in \text{LExpr}$. This is done by replacing those tests with a call to a function that checks for equality with the constant c by traversing its input. We define these functions by induction on c. Note that this is only possible because equalities are always between a variable and a constant (R. III).

(B) *Elimination of Literal Productions*, i.e., of constant expressions in the construction of LExpr, except single characters. This is done by replacing a constant c by a function call. For instance, $\text{list}(\text{char}(a_1), \text{char}(a_2))$ is replaced by a call to a function with body yield $\text{char}(a_1)$; yield $\text{char}(a_2)$.

(C) *Elimination of Function Calls*, by replacing them with generator expressions. Given a function f with body s and arguments $x_1, \ldots, x_n$, we replace a call $f(a_1, \ldots, a_n)$ by $\langle s[a_1/x_1, \ldots, a_n/x_n] \rangle_l$ (or $\langle \cdots \rangle_b$ for boolean functions). This is valid because functions do not take booleans as arguments (R. VI).

(D) *Elimination of Boolean Generators.* Note that $\langle s \rangle_b$ can only appear in a conditional test, and let us illustrate this step on an example. Consider the following statement: if $\langle s_1 \rangle_b$ then s_2 else s_3. We replace it by let mut b_1 = false in $(s_1'$; if b_1 then s_2 else $s_3)$, where s_1' is obtained by replacing boolean return statements (return b) by assignments of the form (if b then $b_1 \leftarrow$ true else skip).

(E) *Elimination of Let Output Statements*, i.e., of statements of the form let $x = e$ in s. This is done by textually replacing let $x = e$ in s by $s[x \mapsto e]$.

(F) *Elimination of Return Statements* for list expressions. First, to make sure that the program does not produce any output after the first return statement, we introduce a boolean variable `has_returned`, and guard every yield statement by a check on this variable. Then, we replace every statement return e by a for loop for$^\rightarrow$ (i, x) in e do yield x. This is not possible if the return statement is of type List_0, and for this edge case, we refer the readers to our implementation.

(G) *Expansion of For Loops*, ensuring that every for loop iterates over a single list variable. This is the key step of the compilation, and it will be thoroughly explained later in this section.

(H) *Defining booleans at the beginning of for loops*. This is a technical step that ensures that all boolean variables are defined at the beginning of the program or at the beginning of a for loop. Thanks to the no-shadowing rule (R. V), we can safely move all boolean definitions to the top of their scopes.

Theorem 1. *The rewriting steps (Step A— Step H) all terminate and preserve typing. Moreover, normalized for-programs of type $\mathsf{List}_1 \to \mathsf{List}_1$ are isomorphic to simple for-programs.*

Forward For Loop Expansion. We now focus on the expansion of for loops, that is, Step G. The case of forward iterations is simpler and will illustrate a first difficulty. We replace each loop of the form for$^\rightarrow$ (i, x) in $\langle s_1 \rangle_1$ do s_2 by the statement s_1 where every statement yield e is replaced by $s_2[x \mapsto e]$. This rewriting is problematic because it leaves the variable i undefined in s_2. The key observation allowing us to circumvent this issue is that the variable i can only be used in *comparisons*, and can only be compared with variables j that are iterating over $\langle s_1 \rangle_1$ (thanks to R. IV). It is therefore sufficient to order the outputs of s_1 to effectively remove the variable i from the program.

One can recover the ordering between outputs of s_1 by storing the position of the yield e responsible for the output, together with all position variables visible at that point. Let us illustrate this in a simple example:

$$(\text{for}^\leftarrow\ (j, y)\ \text{in}\ e\ \text{do}\ (\text{yield}\ y\ ;\ \text{yield char}(a)))\ ;\ \text{yield char}(b)$$
$$\underbrace{\qquad\qquad\qquad}_{p_1(j)\quad p_2(j)}\qquad\qquad p_3$$

In this example, there are three yield statements at positions p_1, p_2 and p_3. We can compute the *happens (strictly) before* relation between outputs of the various yield statements:

$$\mathsf{before}(p_1(j), p_2(j)) = \mathsf{true} \quad \mathsf{before}(p_2(j), p_3) = \mathsf{true} \quad \mathsf{before}(p_1(j), p_3) = \mathsf{true}$$

$$\mathsf{before}(p_1(j), p_1(j')) = j > j' \qquad \mathsf{before}(p_2(j), p_2(j')) = j > j'$$

$$\mathsf{before}(p_1(j), p_2(j')) = j \geq j'$$

In the case of $j = j'$, the output of $p_1(j)$ happens before the output of $p_2(j')$, because p_1 is the first yield statement in the loop. When $j > j'$, the output of $p_1(j)$ happens before the output of $p_2(j')$ because the loop is iterating in reverse order.

Backward For Loop Expansion. The case of backward iterations adds a new layer of complexity, namely to perform a non-reversible computation s in a reversed order: indeed, in the for loop $\text{for}^{\leftarrow} (i, x)$ in $\langle s_1 \rangle_1$ do s_2, s_1 can contain the command $b \leftarrow \text{true}$ which cannot be reversed.

Let us consider as an example $\text{for}^{\leftarrow} (i, x)$ in $\langle s \rangle_1$ do yield x, where the statement s is defined to print all elements of a list u except the first one, namely:

$$s := \text{let mut } b = \text{false in } \text{for}^{\rightarrow} (j, y) \text{ in } u \text{ do if } b \text{ then yield } y \text{ else } b \leftarrow \text{true}$$

The semantics of $\text{for}^{\leftarrow} (i, x)$ in $\langle s \rangle_1$ do yield x is to print all elements of u in reverse order, skipping the last loop iteration. To compute this new statement, we will use the following *trick* that can be traced back to [7, Lemma 8.1 and Fig. 6, p. 68]: we will use two versions of the statement s, the first one s_{rev}, will be s where all boolean introductions are removed, if statements if e then s_1 else s_2 are replaced by sequences $s_1 ; s_2$, every loop direction is swapped, and every sequence of statements is reversed. Its intended semantics is to reach all possible yield statements of s in the reversed order. In our case:

$$s_{\text{rev}} := \text{for}^{\leftarrow} (j', y') \text{ in } u \text{ do yield } y'$$

Some yield statements are reachable in s_{rev}, but not when iterating over s in reverse order. To ensure that we only output correct elements, we replace every yield $\cdot$ statement in s_{rev} by a copy of s, leading to the programs $s' = s_{\text{rev}}[\text{yield} \cdot \mapsto s]$. In our case:

$$s' := \text{for}^{\leftarrow} (j', y') \text{ in } u \text{ do } s$$

It is now possible to replace every yield statement in this new program by a conditional check ensuring that the output would actually be produced by the original program s.

$$s'' = s'[\text{yield } e \mapsto \text{if } i = j' \text{ then yield } e]$$

s_{rev}

```
for← (j′, y′) in u do
    for→ (j, y) in u do
        let mut b = false in
        if b then
            if j = j′ then
                yield y
        else
            b ← true
```
yield guard

Fig. 5. Backward for loop expansion.

In our case, the final program is described in Fig. 5. This rewriting can be generalised to any program of the form $\text{for}^{\leftarrow} (i, x)$ in $\langle s_1 \rangle_1$ do s_2 combining the construction illustrated here with the one taking care of position variables in the case of forward loops.

5   Simple For Programs and Interpretations

In this section, we show how to compile a simple for-program into a first-order interpretation in the symbolic setting. Recall that this is already known to be theoretically possible in the non-symbolic case [7]. However, this existing construction is not efficient: It requires computing a normal form of the simple for-program ([7, Lemma 5.2]), and goes through the model of pebble transducers [7, Section 5]—both of these steps significantly increase the complexity of the generated formulas.

To transform a simple for-program into a first-order interpretation, we use as transduction tags the set of all print statements in the program, remembering their location in the source code. The arity of a print statement is the number of the position variables present in its scope. The output function of a print statement is easy to define: if the print statement outputs a fixed character c, then the output function returns c; otherwise, if the print statement outputs label(i), then the output function returns the De Bruijn index [10] of the variable i. For the ordering formula between two print statements, we use the technique for comparing addresses of the print statements, described in the for loop expansion procedure: In order to compare of two print statements, we compare their shared position variables, breaking the ties using their ordering in the source code. Observe that such ordering formulas do not use quantifiers.

The hardest part is the domain formula. This difficulty is akin to the one of the for loop expansion procedure for the reverse loop: given a print statement $p(i_1, \ldots, i_k)$, where $i_1, \ldots, i_k$ are the position variables in the scope of the print, we need to check whether it can be reached. This amounts to taking the conjunction of the if-conditions, or their negations depending on the if-branch, along the path from the root of the program to the print statement. The only difficulty in defining this conjunction is using the first-order logic to compute the values of the boolean variables used in the if-conditions. We do this, by defining program formulas, which are first-order formulas that describe how a program statement transforms the values of its boolean variables.

5.1   Program Formulas

A *program formula* is a first-order formula where every free variable is either: an *input boolean variable* $\mathrm{in}_\mathbb{B}(b)$, an *output boolean variable* $\mathrm{out}_\mathbb{B}(b)$, or an *input position variable* $\mathrm{in}_\mathbb{N}(i)$. In order to accommodate the boolean variables, we introduce a new two-element sort $\mathbb{B}$. We handle it in the same way as the tag sort from Sect. 3.4.

Given a fixed word $w \in \mathcal{D}^*$, a program formula φ defines a relation between the input boolean variables $\mathrm{in}_\mathbb{B}(b_1), \ldots, \mathrm{in}_\mathbb{B}(b_n)$, input position variables $\mathrm{in}_\mathbb{N}(1), \ldots, \mathrm{in}_\mathbb{N}(k)$, and the output boolean variables $\mathrm{out}_\mathbb{B}(b_1), \ldots, \mathrm{out}_\mathbb{B}(m)$. We are only interested in the program formulas that define *functions* between the input and output variables, for every w.

In this section we show how to compute program formulas for every program statement s, that describes how the statement transforms its state. The formulas are constructed inductively on the structure of the statement. We start with the simplest case of b := True, whose program formula is defined as $\Phi_{\text{setTrue}} := \text{out}_{\mathbb{B}}(b)$. Similarly, the program formula for a print statement is defined as $\Phi_{\text{print}} := \top$ (as it does not input or output any variables). For the induction step, we need to consider three constructions: conditional branching, sequencing, and iteration.

Conditional Branching. Given two program formulas Φ_1 and Φ_2 and a formula φ that only uses input variables (position and booleans), we simulate the if then else construction in the following way:

$$\Phi_{\text{if } \varphi \text{ then } \Phi_1 \text{ else } \Phi_2} := (\varphi \wedge \Phi_1) \vee (\neg \varphi \wedge \Phi_2) \quad .$$

This construction only works if Φ_1 and Φ_2 have the same output variables. If this is not the case, we can to extend Φ_1 and Φ_2 with identity on the missing output variables, by adjoining them with conjunctions of the form $\text{in}_{\mathbb{B}}(b) \iff \text{out}_{\mathbb{B}}(b)$ for each missing variable.

Composition of Program Formulas. Let us consider two program formulas Φ_1 and Φ_2, and denote their input and output boolean variables as $B_1^{\text{in}}, B_1^{\text{out}}$ and $B_2^{\text{in}}, B_2^{\text{out}}$. Let us start with the case where $B_2^{\text{in}} = B_1^{\text{out}} = \{b_1, \ldots, b_n\}$. In this case, we can compose the two program formulas in the following way:

$$\Phi_1 ; \Phi_2 := \exists_{b_1 : \mathbb{B}} \cdots \exists_{b_n : \mathbb{B}} \quad \Phi_1[\text{out}_{\mathbb{B}}(x) \mapsto x] \wedge \Phi_2[\text{in}_{\mathbb{B}}(x) \mapsto x]$$

If the sets B_1^{out} and B_2^{in} are not equal, we can deal with it by first ignoring every output variable b of Φ_1 that is not consumed by Φ_2. Interestingly, this requires an existential quantification: $\Phi_1' := \exists_{b' : \mathbb{B}} \Phi_1[\text{out}_{\mathbb{B}}(b) \mapsto b']$. Then, for each variable b that is consumed by Φ_2 but not produced by Φ_1, we add the identity clause $(\text{in}_{\mathbb{B}}(b) \iff \text{out}_{\mathbb{B}}(b))$ to Φ_1' obtaining Φ_1''. After this modification, we can compose Φ_1'' and Φ_2 with no problems.

This definition of composition requires us to quantify over all variables form $B_1^{\text{out}} \cup B_2^{\text{in}}$, which influences the quantifier rank of the resulting program formula. In our implementation, we are a bit more careful, and only quantify over the variables from $B_1^{\text{out}} \cap (B_2^{\text{in}} \cup B_2^{\text{out}})$, obtaining the following bound:

$$\text{qr}(\Phi_1 ; \Phi_2) \leq \max(\text{qr}(\Phi_1), \text{qr}(\Phi_2)) + |B_1^{\text{out}} \cap (B_2^{\text{in}} \cup B_2^{\text{out}})| \quad .$$

Iteration of Program Formulas. The most complex operation on program formulas is the iteration. We explain this on a representative case of a program formula Φ which has a single input position variable $\text{in}_{\mathbb{N}}(i)$, and whose output boolean variables are the same as the input boolean variables ($B^{\text{in}} = B^{\text{out}}$).

Given a word $w \in \mathcal{D}^*$, evaluating a forward loop over i in the range 0 to $|w|$ amounts to the following composition:

$$\Phi[\text{in}_{\mathbb{N}}(i) \mapsto 0]; \Phi[\text{in}_{\mathbb{N}}(i) \mapsto 1]; \cdots ; \Phi[\text{in}_{\mathbb{N}}(i) \mapsto |w|] \quad , \tag{1}$$

The main difficulty is to compute this composition independently of the length of the word w, while keeping the formula and its quantifier rank small.

To that end, we observe that Φ uses a finite number of boolean variables, and that each of those variables can only be set to `True` once (R. VII). As a consequence, in the composition in Equation (1), there are at most $|B^{\text{out}}|$ steps that actually modify the boolean variables. Based on this observation, one can *accelerate* the computation of the composition by guessing the sequence of those steps $(p_1, \ldots, p_{|B^{\text{out}}|})$. The resulting program formula Φ^* is given below (we assume that Φ contains at least 3 boolean variables, and we denote their set as $\{b_1, \ldots, b_n\}$ – the cases for $n \leq 2$ are either analogous or trivial):

$$\Phi^* := \exists_{p_1 \leq \cdots \leq p_n : \mathbb{N}} \tag{2}$$

$$\exists_{b_0, b_1, \ldots, b_{n+1} : \mathbb{B}^n} \tag{3}$$

$$\bigwedge_{1 \leq j \leq n} \Phi(p_j; b_{j-1}; b_j) \tag{4}$$

$$\bigwedge_{1 \leq j \leq n+1} \forall_{p_{j-1} \leq p \leq p_j : \mathbb{N}} \Phi(p; b_{j-1}; b_{j-1}) \tag{5}$$

$$\bigwedge_{1 \leq i \leq n} (b_0)_i = \text{in}_{\mathbb{B}}(b_i) \tag{6}$$

$$\bigwedge_{1 \leq i \leq n} (b_{n+1})_i = \text{out}_{\mathbb{B}}(b_i) \quad . \tag{7}$$

The structure of this formula is as follows: In Eq. (2), it guesses the steps $p_1, \ldots, p_n$ that actually modify the boolean variables. In Eq. (3), it guesses the intermediate values of the boolean variables (b_j's denote vectors of n boolean variables). In Eq. (4), it asserts that the guesses where *correct*, i.e., that the program formula Φ applied to position p_j and the boolean variables b_{j-1} produces the boolean variables b_j. In Eq. (5), it ensures that no position different than the p_i's modifies the boolean variables. (In this equation, p_0 and p_{n+1} denote the first and the last position of the word.) Finally, in Eq. (6) and Equation (7), it ensures that the initial and final values of the boolean variables are correctly set to the input and output values. The formula for the reverse loop is similar, but guesses the positions p_i in a decreasing order.

Our construction ensures the following bound on the quantifier rank of the resulting program formula, which shows that the number of modified boolean variables is a crucial parameter for the complexity of the overall procedure:

$$\text{qr}(\Phi^*) \leq \text{qr}(\Phi) + |B^{\text{out}}|^2 + |B^{\text{out}}| + 1 \quad . \tag{8}$$

6   Implementation

We implemented all the transformations expressed in this paper in a `Haskell` program. To measure the complexity of these transformations, we associated to a high-level for-program the following parameters: its *size* (number of control flow statements), its *loop depth* (the maximum number of nested loops),

Table 1. Results for the transformations. Here FP is a for-program, S.FP is a simple for-program, and FO-I is a first-order interpretation. The columns **l.d.**, **b.d.** and **q.r.** stand respectively for the loop depth, boolean depth and quantifier rank.

filename	FP			S.FP			FO-I	
	size	l.d.	b.d.	size	l.d.	b.d.	size	q.r.
identity.pr	3	1	0	2	2	0	1	0
reverse.pr	3	1	0	2	2	0	1	0
subwords_ab.pr	24	2	1	15	4	3	956	14
map_reverse.pr	36	2	1	18	4	1	285	5
prefixes.pr	6	2	0	5	3	0	2	0
get_last_word.pr	18	1	1	23	4	2	8553	15
get_first_word.pr	22	1	1	5	2	0	103	4
compress_as.pr	12	1	1	12	3	2	209	10
litteral_test.pr	29	1	1	129	3	12	3.2×10^4	82
bibtex.pr	110	2	1	802	6	29	13.7×10^6	136

and its *boolean depth* (the maximum number of boolean variables visible at any point in the program). We compute the same parameters for the corresponding simple for-program. In the case of first-order interpretations, we only compute its *size* (number of nodes in the formula) and its quantifier rank. This allowed us to estimate the complexity of our transformations on a small set of programs that we present in Table 1. Then, we used several existing solvers to verify basic first-order Hoare triples for these programs. We illustrate in Table 2 the behaviour of the solvers on various verification tasks, with a timeout of 5 seconds for every solver. These test offer only initial insight into the performance of our implementation, so developing our implementation into an actual tool would require systematic benchmarks and comparison with already existing tools.

Table 2. Verification of first-order Hoare triples over sample for-programs. We specify the preconditions and postconditions as regular languages, writing $\mathcal{L}_{ab}$ as a shorthand for $\mathcal{D}^* ab\mathcal{D}^*$, and similarly for $\mathcal{L}_{aa}$, $\mathcal{L}_{ba}$, etc. In the columns corresponding to the solvers, a checkmark indicates a positive reply, a cross mark indicates a negative reply, and a question mark indicates a timeout or a memory exhaustion. We indicate the size and the quantifier rank (**q.r.**) of the first-order formulas that are fed to the solvers.

Name	Pre.	Post.	q.r.	size	MONA	CVC5	Z3
compress_as.pr	$\mathcal{L}_{ab}$	$\mathcal{L}_{ab}$	16	763	✓	?	?
reverse_add_hash.pr	$\mathcal{L}_{ab}$	$\mathcal{L}_{ba}$	9	380	?	✓	?
get_last_word.pr	$\mathcal{D}^*a$	$\mathcal{L}_{aa}$	27	28274	?	?	✗
subwords_ab.pr	$\mathcal{L}_{ab}$	$\mathcal{L}_{ab}$	26	3276	?	?	?
map_reverse.pr	$\mathcal{D}^*a$	$a\mathcal{D}^*$	13	801	?	?	?

Compilation to FO-*Formulas.* Looking at Table 1, we observe that the generated simple for programs have reasonable size and boolean depth. The generated first-order interpretations still have reasonable quantifier ranks, but their size grows significantly. In the simplest cases of Table 1, our compilation procedure is able to eliminate all boolean variables, thus producing a *quantifier-free* formula. This is the case for `identity.pr`, `reverse.pr` and `prefixes.pr`. Moreover, we observe that the boolean depth of the simple for-program is a good indicator of the quantifier rank of the generated first-order interpretation. Furthermore, the tests indicate that elimination of literals is responsible for a significant increase of the formulas size and quantifier rank (`literal_test.pr` and `bibtex.pr`). This is explained by the fact that the elimination of literals introduces (non-cyclic) counters, simulated by a number of boolean variables. Finally, we observe that the size of the generated formulas differs significantly for the programs `get_first_word.pr` and `get_last_word.pr`. This is somewhat surprising, as the two programs are symmetric with respect to reversing the input words, and indicates some room for improvement in handling the reversed iteration.

Solver Performance. We can observe in Table 2 that the different solvers are complementary. This might seem surprising, as the MONA solver is a complete decision procedure. However, since it solves a problem that is TOWER-complete [27, Theorem 13.5], it is understandable that it underperforms the SMT solvers on some instances, even though we use them with the undecidable UFDTLIA theory. Let us justify this choice of the SMTLib theory: (a) *Uninterpreted Functions* (UF) are used to represent the word, which is treated as a function from positions to characters, (b) *Data Types* (DT) is used to represent finite sets of tags and characters, (c) *Linear Integer Arithmetic* (LIA) is used to deal with the order of the positions in the word. This choice might not be optimal, but we believe that it is a good trade off between ease-of-use and performance for our proof-of-concept implementation. We can also observe that no solvers was able to deal with `subwords_ab.pr` and `map_reverse.pr` within the 5 seconds timeout. Understanding the complexities that arise in those cases, might be helpful for improving the performance of our implementation.

7   Conclusion

We have show that the theory of star-free polyregular functions can be used to verify close to real-world programs, and have implemented a prototype tool that can discharge simple verification goals to existing solvers.

Benchmarks. It would be interesting to systematically benchmark our implementation against existing tools for verifying linear regular functions, in the case of first order specifications. Since our approach allows for polynomial size transformations, it would also be interesting to devise a set of benchmarks for this broader class of functions.

Optimizations. The preliminary tests indicate that one of the most promising source of optimizations is managing the boolean depth of the generated simple for-programs during compilation. This can be achieved by post-compilation optimizations (constant propagation, dead code elimination), or by improving the code generation mechanism itself, which are low-hanging fruits for future work. One source of the boolean variables seems to be the elimination of Literal Equality step (Step B), which could be mitigated by adding explicit successor and predecessor predicates to the language of simple for-programs.

At the level of first-order interpretations, we have identified several directions for improving their efficiency. One optimization is computing the sequential composition of programs in a way that minimizes the number of quantified boolean variables. Similarly, there seems to be potential for performing direct substitutions instead of quantifying over the variables in a lot of cases. Finally, our current approach for handling loops introduces universal quantifiers, whose number could be reduced by exploiting the monotonicity of the state transformations.

Solver Integration. There is a lot of potential for optimizing the input and parameters of the solvers for our particular use-case. An interesting research direction would be to reduce the verification problem to emptiness of LTL formulas, allowing us to use LTL solvers such as SPOT [14].

Modular Verification. The benchmarks show that one of the main bottlenecks of our approach is the expansion of loops (whether in the translation to simple for-programs or in the translation to first-order interpretations). For this reason, the ability to verify statements of the form `for (i, e) in enumerate(f(x)) do s done`, based on a specification of f given as a Hoare triple, would be a significant improvement. However, it remains unclear how to integrate such modular verification in our current approach.

Language Design. As mentioned in Sect. 2, for-programs extended with unrestricted booleans also enjoy a decidable verification of Hoare triples. However, the verification algorithm uses of monadic second-order logic (MSO) over words instead of first-order logic. While this prohibits the use of traditional SMT solvers, this logic can be handled by the MONA solver, and it might be interesting to implement and test the unrestricted version of the language.

Another interesting extension of the language would be to allow the use of complex types, such as pairs and records. This would make the language closer to real use cases such as configuration management and data processing. It would require extending the specification language to structured data types, bypassing the current limitation that we can only verify string-to-string transformations.

Integration with Existing Tools. It would be a natural next step to integrate our results inside frameworks for program verification or testing. This could be by checking goals generated by a tool such as Why3 [4], or by verifying properties of Python programs using decorated functions. We would also like to point out that verification methods based on a regularity preserving property (such as done in [13]) can transparently use our more general class of programs as input, instead of the more traditional linear regular functions.

Acknowledgements. We would like to thank Arnav Garg and Ojas Maheshwari for their participation in the early stage of this project.

References

1. Alur, R.: Streaming string transducers. In: Beklemishev, L.D., de Queiroz, R. (eds.) WoLLIC 2011. LNCS (LNAI), vol. 6642, pp. 1–1. Springer, Heidelberg (2011). https://doi.org/10.1007/978-3-642-20920-8_1
2. Alur, R., Černý, P.: Streaming transducers for algorithmic verification of single-pass list-processing programs. In: Proceedings of the 38th Annual ACM SIGPLAN-SIGACT Symposium on Principles of Programming Languages, POPL '11, pp. 599–610. Association for Computing Machinery, New York (2011). https://doi.org/10.1145/1926385.1926454
3. Barrett, C., Fontaine, P., Tinelli, C.: The SMT-LIB Standard: Version 2.6. Technical report, Department of Computer Science, The University of Iowa (2017). www.SMT-LIB.org
4. Bobot, F., Filliâtre, J.C., Marché, C., Paskevich, A.: Why3: shepherd your herd of provers. In: Boogie 2011: First International Workshop on Intermediate Verification Languages, Wrocław, Poland, pp. 53–64 (2011). https://hal.inria.fr/hal-00790310
5. Bojańczyk, M.: On the growth rates of polyregular functions. In: 2023 38th Annual ACM/IEEE Symposium on Logic in Computer Science (LICS), pp. 1–13. IEEE (2023)
6. Bojańczyk, M., Kiefer, S., Lhote, N.: String-to-string interpretations with polynomial-size output. arXiv preprint arXiv:1905.13190 (2019)
7. Bojańczyk, M.: Polyregular functions (2018). https://arxiv.org/abs/1810.08760v1
8. Bojańczyk, M.: Slightly infinite sets (2019). https://www.mimuw.edu.pl/~bojan/paper/atom-book
9. Bojańczyk, M., Daviaud, L., Krishna, S.N.: Regular and first-order list functions. In: Proceedings of the 33rd Annual ACM/IEEE Symposium on Logic in Computer Science, LICS '18, pp. 125–134. Association for Computing Machinery, New York (2018). https://doi.org/10.1145/3209108.3209163
10. de Bruijn, N.: Lambda calculus notation with nameless dummies, a tool for automatic formula manipulation, with application to the church-rosser theorem. Indagationes Mathematicae (Proceedings) **75**(5), 381–392 (1972). https://doi.org/10.1016/1385-7258(72)90034-0
11. Büchi, J.R.: Weak second-order arithmetic and finite automata. Math. Log. Q. **6**(1–6), 66–92 (1960). https://doi.org/10.1002/malq.19600060105
12. Carton, O., Dartois, L.: Aperiodic two-way transducers and FO-transductions. In: Kreutzer, S. (ed.) 24th EACSL Annual Conference on Computer Science Logic (CSL 2015). Leibniz International Proceedings in Informatics (LIPIcs), vol. 41, pp. 160–174. Schloss Dagstuhl – Leibniz-Zentrum für Informatik, Dagstuhl (2015). https://doi.org/10.4230/LIPIcs.CSL.2015.160

13. Chen, T., Hague, M., Lin, A.W., Rümer, P., Wu, Z.: Decision procedures for path feasibility of string-manipulating programs with complex operations. Proc. ACM Program. Lang. **3**(POPL) (2019). https://doi.org/10.1145/3290362. http://www.philipp.ruemmer.org/publications/atva2020.pdf
14. Duret-Lutz, A., et al.: From Spot 2.0 to Spot 2.10: what's new? In: Proceedings of the 34th International Conference on Computer Aided Verification (CAV'22). Lecture Notes in Computer Science, vol. 13372, pp. 174–187. Springer, Heidelberg (2022). https://doi.org/10.1007/978-3-031-13188-2_9
15. D'Antoni, L., Veanes, M.: The power of symbolic automata and transducers. In: Majumdar, R., Kunčak, V. (eds.) CAV 2017. LNCS, vol. 10426, pp. 47–67. Springer, Cham (2017). https://doi.org/10.1007/978-3-319-63387-9_3
16. Engelfriet, J., Maneth, S.: Two-way finite state transducers with nested pebbles. In: Diks, K., Rytter, W. (eds.) MFCS 2002. LNCS, vol. 2420, pp. 234–244. Springer, Heidelberg (2002). https://doi.org/10.1007/3-540-45687-2_19
17. Filiot, E., Reynier, P.A., Lhote, N.: Lexicographic transductions of finite words (2025). https://arxiv.org/abs/2503.01746
18. Jeż, A., Lin, A.W., Markgraf, O., Rümmer, P.: Decision procedures for sequence theories. In: Computer Aided Verification: 35th International Conference, CAV 2023, Paris, France, July 17–22, 2023, Proceedings, Part II, CAV'23, pp. 18–40. Springer, Cham (2023). https://doi.org/10.1007/978-3-031-37703-7_2. https://anthonywlin.github.io/papers/cav23.pdf
19. Kaminski, M., Francez, N.: Finite-memory automata. Theor. Comput. Sci. **134**(2), 329–363 (1994). https://doi.org/10.1016/0304-3975(94)90242-9
20. Klarlund, N., Møller, A.: MONA Version 1.4 User Manual. BRICS, Department of Computer Science, University of Aarhus (2001), notes Series NS-01-1. http://www.brics.dk/mona/
21. Kleene, S.C.: Representation of events in nerve nets and finite automata. Automata Stud. **34**, 3–42 (1956). https://doi.org/10.1515/9781400882618-002
22. McNaughton, R., Papert, S.A.: Counter-Free Automata. The MIT Press, Cambridge (1971). https://doi.org/10.5555/1097043
23. Microsoft Research: Z3 theorem prover (2008). https://github.com/Z3Prover/z3, swh:1:dir:d6e5b24a3751b89fb1a4844c5a80a6393c2c1fa6
24. Muscholl, A., Puppis, G.: The many facets of string transducers. In: Niedermeier, R., Paul, C. (eds.) 36th International Symposium on Theoretical Aspects of Computer Science (STACS 2019). Leibniz International Proceedings in Informatics (LIPIcs), vol. 126, pp. 2:1–2:21. Schloss Dagstuhl – Leibniz-Zentrum für Informatik, Dagstuhl (2019). https://doi.org/10.4230/LIPIcs.STACS.2019.2. https://drops.dagstuhl.de/entities/document/10.4230/LIPIcs.STACS.2019.2
25. Perrin, D., Pin, J.É.: First-order logic and star-free sets. J. Comput. Syst. Sci. **32**(3), 393–406 (1986). https://doi.org/10.1016/0022-0000(86)90037-1. https://www.sciencedirect.com/science/article/pii/0022000086900371
26. Rabin, M.O., Scott, D.S.: Finite automata and their decision problems. IBM J. Res. Dev. **3**(2), 114–125 (1959). https://doi.org/10.1147/RD.32.0114
27. Reinhardt, K.: The complexity of translating logic to finite automata. In: Grädel, E., Thomas, W., Wilke, T. (eds.) Automata Logics, and Infinite Games. LNCS, vol. 2500, pp. 231–238. Springer, Heidelberg (2002). https://doi.org/10.1007/3-540-36387-4_13
28. Schützenberger, M.P.: On the definition of a family of automata. Inf. Control **4**(2–3), 245–270 (1961). https://doi.org/10.1016/S0019-9958(61)80020-X
29. Schützenberger, M.P.: On finite monoids having only trivial subgroups. Inf. Control **8**(2), 190–194 (1965). https://doi.org/10.1016/S0019-9958(65)90108-7

30. Trakhtenbrot, B.A.: Finite automata and the logic of one-place predicates. Am. Math. Soc. Translat. **59**(2), 23–55 (1966). https://doi.org/10.1090/trans2/059/02
31. Winskel, G.: The Formal Semantics of Programming Languages: An Introduction. MIT Press, Cambridge (1993). https://doi.org/10.7551/mitpress/3054.001.0001
32. Barbosa, H., et al.: cvc5: a versatile and industrial-strength SMT solver. In: Fisman, D., Rosu, G., et al. (eds.) TACAS 2022. LNCS, vol. 13243, pp. 415–442. Springer, Cham (2022). https://doi.org/10.1007/978-3-030-99524-9_24

Veil: A Framework for Automated and Interactive Verification of Transition Systems

George Pîrlea[1], Vladimir Gladshtein[1], Elad Kinsbruner[2],
Qiyuan Zhao[1], and Ilya Sergey[1(✉)]

[1] National University of Singapore, Singapore, Singapore
ilya@nus.edu.sg
[2] Technion, Haifa, Israel
https://verse-lab.github.io/

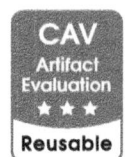

Abstract. We present Veil, an open-source framework for automated and interactive verification of transition systems, aimed specifically at conducting machine-assisted proofs about concurrent and distributed algorithms. Veil is implemented on top of the Lean proof assistant. It allows one to describe a transition system and its specification in a simple imperative language, producing verification conditions in first-order logic, to be discharged automatically via a range of SMT solvers. In case automated verification fails or if the system's description requires statements in a higher-order logic, Veil provides an interactive verification mode, by virtue of being embedded in a general-purpose proof assistant. We have evaluated Veil on a large set of case studies from the distributed system verification literature, showing that its automated verification performance is acceptable for practical verification tasks, while it also allows for seamless automated/interactive verification of system specifications beyond the reach of existing automated provers.

1 Introduction

Over the years, the research community has developed a spectrum of tools for formal reasoning about transition systems, ranging from interactive verification frameworks to fully automated tools. For distributed protocols in particular, formal verification has traditionally been carried out in interactive proof assistants [13,16,23,40,43,44,46–48,54,60], as the expressivity of their logics allows specifying and proving arbitrary properties, and their foundational nature [2], in which proofs are given only in terms of well-accepted axioms and are machine-checked, provides a high degree of assurance. The downside of interactive proofs, however, is that large systems take months-to-years of effort to verify [55].

At the other end of the spectrum, tools such as Ivy [37], UPVerifier [30], and mypyvy [53] use decidable fragments of first-order logic and advanced automated

---

E. Kinsbruner—Work done during a research visit to National University of Singapore.

R. Piskac and Z. Rakamarić (Eds.): CAV 2025, LNCS 15933, pp. 26–41, 2025.
https://doi.org/10.1007/978-3-031-98682-6_2

theorem provers [3, 32] to automatically verify properties of distributed protocols and thus reduce the manual proof effort to zero. Such tools, however, are not foundational and are limited in terms of the properties that can be naturally encoded, often requiring contorted specifications designed by experts in decidable reasoning to keep verification automated [36]. Whilst this has been shown to be a viable approach for many real-world distributed protocols, certain properties of interest are simply not expressible in a decidable logic. To work around this limitation, some tools of this nature provide an escape-hatch to allow the user to interactively prove difficult properties [21, 28, 50]. These escape-hatches tend to be much less usable than interactive proof assistants, however, often lacking visibility into the goals that need to be proven or advanced tactic support.

In this paper we present Veil, a verification framework embedded in the Lean 4 proof assistant [31] that delivers the best of both worlds—providing both push-button verification for decidable fragments of first-order logic and the full power of a modern higher-order proof assistant for when automation falls short.

Importantly, Veil is *foundational*: its verification condition (VC) generator is proven sound with respect to the semantics of its specification language. It is also *lightweight*: Veil is implemented as a library using Lean metaprogramming [39], its specification language and VC generation can be easily extended to support new constructs, along with their soundness proofs. Finally, Veil allows for *seamless* interaction between automated and human-assisted proofs, all done in Lean, allowing one to establish system specifications that are not expressible in first-order logic, and, thus, are beyond the reach of existing automated tools.

2   A Tour of Veil

This section gives a tour of Veil's features and its advantages over existing tools.

2.1   Case Study: Suzuki-Kasami Algorithm

As a running example, we consider an implementation of the Suzuki-Kasami protocol for ensuring mutual exclusion [49, 58]. An implementation of the protocol in Veil is shown in Fig. 1. Some boilerplate has been removed for brevity.

A Veil specification consists of three parts: a state definition and initialisation (lines 1–34), action definitions (lines 36–83) and invariants (lines 84–98).

State. The state is comprised of uninterpreted sorts, as well as constant, relation and function symbols. As Veil is embedded in Lean, it supports most Lean types, including structures and numbers. Veil supports both *mutable* and *immutable* constants, relations and functions. Mutable fields represent the state of the algorithm, while immutable fields cannot be modified and represent symbols from a background theory. To encode persistent facts about immutable values, Veil supports a notion of *assumptions*, which behave like axioms in Ivy and can be used to define a background theory for the immutable symbols. In Fig. 1, all values are implicitly mutable except for `init_node` (line 21).

```
1   type node
2
3
4   --- Requests
5   relation reqs : node → node → Nat → Prop
6
7   --- Tokens
8   relation t_for : Nat → node → Prop
9   relation t_q : Nat → node → Prop
10  function t_LN : Nat → node → Nat
11
12  --- Critical section
13  relation crit : node → Prop
14
15  --- Nodes
16  relation n_privilege : node → Prop
17  relation n_req : node → Prop
18  function n_RN : node → node → Nat
19  -- seq num of the most recently granted req
20  function n_seq : node → Nat
21  immutable individual init_node : node
22
23
24  after_init {
25    n_privilege N := N = init_node
26    n_req N := False
27    n_RN N M := 0
28    n_seq N := if N = init_node then 1 else 0
29    reqs N M I := False
30    t_for I N := I = 1 ∧ N = init_node
31    t_LN I N := 0
32    t_q I N := False
33    crit N := False
34  }
35
36  action exit (n : node) = {
37    require crit n;
38    crit n := False;
39    n_req n := False;
40    let token : Nat := n_seq n
41    t_LN token n := n_RN n n;
42    t_q token N := n_RN n n N = t_LN token N + 1;
43    if m : (t_q token m) then
44      t_q token m := False;
45    n_privilege n := False;
46    let k : Nat := token + 1
47    t_for k m := True;
48    t_LN k N := t_LN token N;
49    t_q k N := t_q token N
50  }
```

```
51  action enter (n : node) = {
52    require n_privilege n
53    require n_req n
54    -- enter critical section
55    crit n := True
56  }
57  action rcv_privilege (n: node) (t: Nat) = {
58    require t_for t n;
59    require (n_seq n) < t;
60    n_privilege n := True;
61    n_seq n := t
62  }
63  action request (n : node) = {
64    require ¬ n_req n;
65    n_req n := True;
66    if (¬ n_privilege n) then
67      let k := (n_RN n n) + 1
68      n_RN n n := k;
69      reqs N n (n_RN n n) := N ≠ n
70  }
71  -- node 'm' requesting from 'n' with seq. number 'r'
72  action rcv_request (n : node) (m : node) (r : Nat) = {
73    require reqs n m r;
74    let token : Nat := (n_seq n)
75    n_RN n m := if r ≤ (n_RN n m) then n_RN n m else r;
76    if (n_privilege n ∧ ¬ n_req n ∧
77        (t_LN token m) + 1 = (n_RN n m)) then
78      n_privilege n := False;
79      let k : Nat := token + 1
80      t_for k m := True;
81      t_LN k N := t_LN token N;
82      t_q k N := t_q token N
83  }
84  safety [mutex] (crit N ∧ crit M) → N = M
85  invariant [not_request_self] (reqs N M I) → N ≠ M
86  invariant (n_privilege N ∧ n_privilege M)
87          → N = M
88  invariant (crit N) → (n_privilege N ∧ n_req N)
89  invariant ((t_for I N) ∧ (t_for I M)) → N = M
90  invariant ((n_seq N) ≠ 0) → t_for (n_seq N) N
91  invariant ((n_privilege N) ∧ N ≠ M)
92          → (n_seq M) < (n_seq N)
93  invariant ((n_privilege N) ∧ (t_for I M))
94          → I ≤ (n_seq N)
95  invariant ((t_for I N) ∧ ((J + 1) = I) ∧ (t_for J M))
96          → N ≠ M
97  invariant ((t_for I N) ∧ (t_for J M) ∧ I < J)
98          → I ≤ (n_seq N)
99
100 #check_invariants
```

Fig. 1. An implementation of the Suzuki-Kasami locking protocol in Veil.

The state is initialised before every execution using the `after_init` block (lines 24–34). In Veil assignment statements, variables starting with a capital letter are implicitly ∀-quantified, *i.e.*, `n_RN N M := 0` means "set `n_RN N M` to `0` for all N, M".

Actions. Actions in Veil define the possible transitions between states of the protocol. They may take parameters and may have a return value. They can make assumptions using `require` statements (*e.g.*, line 58), which behave as preconditions for invoking the action. Actions can comprise of any Lean code, including constant (`let`) and variable (`let mut`) definitions and calling other actions. Actions can use *demonically non-deterministic values* using the ∗ symbol.

Invariants and Safety. Invariants are defined using the `invariant` keyword, and may optionally be given a custom name (*e.g.*, line 85), which will be used in generated theorems and Veil output. It is also possible to explicitly document an invariant as a safety property using the `safety` keyword which has the same semantics as `invariant` (*e.g.*, line 84). In invariants (and safety properties), variables starting with a capital letter are also implicitly universally quantified at the beginning of the formula, *i.e.*, the invariant (`crit N` ∧ `crit M`) → `N = M` will be interpreted as the Lean proposition $\forall N\ M, (\text{crit } N \wedge \text{crit } M) \rightarrow N = M$.

2.2   Bounded Model Checking

Once a protocol specification is defined, one might wish to verify that it is not vacuous, *i.e.*, that it produces non-empty execution traces.

This is done with the `sat trace` command with a series of action calls, as seen in lines 1–8 in Fig. 2. This generates a Lean goal that asserts that there are parameter values and nondeterministic choices such that this trace could be a viable trace of the specification. The generated goal can be resolved interactively with standard Lean tactics, or automatically using Veil's `bmc_sat` tactic which searches for executions via SMT-based symbolic bounded model checking (BMC) [4,15,53]. If a satisfying trace is found, it is displayed to the user. One can also verify that specifications *do not* admit certain executions. This is done using the `unsat trace` command, as seen in lines 10–14 of Fig. 2. This, too, produces a goal that can be discharged either interactively or automatically using Veil's `bmc` tactic,

```
1   sat trace {
2     request
3     enter
4     exit
5     request
6     enter
7     exit
8   } by bmc_sat
9
10  unsat trace {
11    enter
12    enter
13    any 2 actions
14  } by bmc
```

Fig. 2. BMC in Veil

which tries to prove that no such executions exist by invoking an SMT solver. `unsat trace` commands may involve `any action` or `any N actions` statements (*cf.* line 13) that will nondeterministically choose actions for a trace.

2.3   Automated Safety Proof

After specifying the protocol, the user can use the `#check_invariants` command (line 100 of Fig. 1) to try to automatically verify the protocol using SMT. Veil can use either Lean-auto [42] or Lean-SMT [29] to translate the Lean goal to SMT, and can use either cvc5 or Z3 to solve the goal automatically. The full details on Veil's SMT encoding can be found in Section 3.1. By default, if Veil cannot succeed with solving the goal automatically using one solver, it will try the other solver. After issuing the command, the user is met with the output shown below, where a result of either success, failure or unknown is reported for the initialisation of each invariant and for the preservation of each invariant under each action.

Initialization must establish the invariant:	The following set of actions must preserve the invariant:	
	request	exit
mutex ... ☑	mutex ... ☑	mutex ... ☑
not_request_self ... ☑	not_request_self ... ☑	not_request_self ... ☑
inv_2 ... ☑	inv_2 ... ☑	inv_2 ... ☑
inv_3 ... ☑	inv_3 ... ☑	inv_3 ... ☑
inv_4 ... ☑	inv_4 ... ☑	inv_4 ... ☑
inv_5 ... ☑	inv_5 ... ☑ ...	inv_5 ... ☑
inv_6 ... ☑	inv_6 ... ☑	inv_6 ... ☑
inv_7 ... ☑	inv_7 ... ☑	inv_7 ... ☑
inv_8 ... ☑	inv_8 ... ☑	inv_8 ... ☑
inv_9 ... ☑	inv_9 ... ☑	inv_9 ... ☑

With its default settings of a timeout of 5 s per SMT query and cvc5 as the solver, Veil can automatically verify that the invariant clauses are inductive in the specification in Fig. 1 and thus that the safety property holds.

2.4 Interactive Proof Mode

Sometimes, fully automated verification is not possible as SMT solvers time out and return unknown on the query. This can happen frequently when queries fall outside the decidable fragment. In these cases, because Veil is embedded in Lean, users can leverage Lean's theorem proving capabilities to interactively discharge these goals. In order to verify an invariant interactively, the user can ask Veil to generate the corresponding theorem statement. When one emits the #check_invariants? command, the IDE will automatically suggest to create a template (with proof to be filled in interactively) for *every* theorem needed to verify the safety of the system. Veil also supports #check_invariants!, which only suggests templates for the theorems that could not be proven automatically.

An example statement generated by #check_invariants? is shown in lines 1–3 of Fig. 3. The theorem expresses that given that the assumptions and invariants hold on a state st, all subsequent states st' reachable from st by taking the enter transition satisfy the invariant mutex, *i.e.*, mutex is preserved under enter. This statement relies on a relational semantics, which we discuss in Sect. 3.1. To discharge this goal, the user can use any native Lean tactics, as well as Veil-specific tactics (not shown in the example).

```
1  theorem enter_mutex : ∀ (st st' : State),
2      assumptions st → inv st → enter st st'
3      → mutex st' := by
4    intros st st' _ inv
5    simp [enter, invSimp] at *
6    rcases inv with ⟨allowed_crit, one_priv, _⟩
7    rintro n priv req ⟨⟩ N M critN critM
8    simp at *
9    apply one_priv
10   . by_cases h : (N = n)
11     <;> simp [allowed_crit, h, priv, critN]
12   . by_cases h : (M = n)
13     <;> simp [allowed_crit, h, priv, critM]
```

Fig. 3. Interactive proof that mutex is preserved by the enter action.

In Fig. 3, the user uses the Lean intros tactic to bring the states and the invariant into the Lean context, and then simplifies the action definition (enter) and unfolds the invariant definition (using the invSimp lemma set introduced by Veil). The proof only uses two invariant clauses, allowed_crit and one_priv, which are extracted from the invariant conjunction via the rcases tactic. The proof is concluded using the by_cases tactic to case-split on whether the considered node is n, the argument to enter, with the subgoals discharged by using implications from the action definition (`critN`, `critM`, `priv`), an invariant clause (`allowed_crit`) and the case assumption (`h`).

Veil also supports semi-automatic verification: sometimes, for a query that falls outside of the decidable fragment and cannot be decided automatically, it is possible to decide essentially the same query automatically after changing its structure slightly using tactics. Therefore, Veil introduces the `solve_clause` tactic, which automatically tries to discharge the current goal using SMT in the same manner as `#check_invariants`. Running `solve_clause` can result in three possible outputs: (i) either the verification succeeded and the goal is admitted;[1] or (ii) the goal is found to be false and a minimised model is presented as a counterexample (*cf.* Sect. 3.4); or (iii) the query returns `unknown` and no verdict can be reached. This lends itself to a style of *solver-guided interactive verification*, in which users write interactive proofs and occasionally invoke `solve_clause` to see if the goal can be discharged automatically, if they went on the wrong path and the goal is false, or if they have to keep going (solver returned `unknown`).

3   Implementing Veil in Lean

Veil is implemented in Lean 4 [31], a dependently-typed programming language and theorem prover, which offers monad comprehensions with local mutation [51].

3.1   Language Embedding

At the core of Veil lies a domain-specific language (DSL) for writing and specifying transition systems. The DSL is inspired by Alloy [14], Ivy [37], and mypyvy [53]; it adopts a standard first-order logic approach for specifying *properties* (*e.g.*, assumptions and safety), while the *transitions* (actions) are encoded as Lean's native monadic computations, embracing the full power of its do-notation [51].

Protocol states σ in Veil are represented by Lean structures with fields corresponding to the `relation`, `function`, and `individual` declarations in the specification. The type of the protocol's transitions is, thus, dependent on the type of its states. For a fixed type σ, each transition is encoded as an instance of a two-state relation of the form **BigStep** $\sigma \rho \triangleq \sigma \to \rho \to \sigma \to Prop$, which relates an input state with the possible outcome result of type ρ and an output state.

A naïve approach to reuse Lean's do-notation for Veil actions would be to simply provide a monad instance for **BigStep** $\sigma \rho$, defining the corresponding `bind` and `pure` operations. Unfortunately, a canonical definition of `bind` for **BigStep** $\sigma \rho$ as the composition of transition relations is not well-suited for SMT-based proofs. For a relation tr_1 : **BigStep** $\sigma \rho$ and a continuation $tr_2 : \rho \to$ **BigStep** $\sigma \rho'$, the composition is $\lambda s\ r'\ s',\ \exists(t : \sigma)(r : \rho'),\ tr_1\ s\ r\ t \land tr_2\ r\ t\ r'\ s'$. That is, an input state s is related to an output state s' and the return value r'

---

[1] Currently, proof reconstruction (provided by Lean-SMT) is off by default in Veil.

if there *exist* an intermediate state t and a result r that serve as an output of tr_1 and an input to tr_2. This encoding introduces higher-order quantification over the elements of the structure σ (*i.e.*, the relations describing the protocol state) in the respective VCs, which makes it impossible to discharge them via SMT solvers. Although Veil implements heuristics for quantifier elimination, running them for each `bind` operation severely impacts its performance.

To avoid the higher-order quantification introduced by such a definition of `bind`, Veil features an alternative encoding of transitions. We first define each atomic Veil command as an instance of type $\mathbf{WP}\,\sigma\,\rho \triangleq (\rho \to \sigma \to Prop) \to (\sigma \to Prop)$. This type is a weakest-precondition predicate transformer [8] that takes an assertion over a transition result ρ and state σ and returns the weakest pre-condition on the pre-state σ which must be satisfied in order to guarantee that the assertion holds in all post-states. The `bind` operation for $\mathbf{WP}\,\sigma\,\rho$ can then be expressed simply via nesting: given $tr_1 : \mathbf{WP}\,\sigma\,\rho$ and $tr_2 : \rho \to \mathbf{WP}\,\sigma\,\rho'$, their composition is defined as $\lambda post,\ tr_1\,(\lambda r',\, tr_2\,r'\,post)$. Following this approach, the `enter` action from Fig. 1 is first expanded into `enter.wp` (lines 1–6 of Fig. 4), where `get` and `modify` operations are standard monadic operations for state reading and writing, and `WP.req` is a monadic operation for the `require` statement (lines 7–8 of Fig. 4).

Given the weakest precondition semantics of a transition $tr : \mathbf{WP}\,\sigma\,\rho$, our encoding of Veil DSL derives its more traditional relational counterpart as follows:

$$tr' : \mathbf{BigStep}\ \sigma\,\rho \triangleq \lambda st_0\ res_1\ st_1,\ \neg tr\,(\lambda res\ st,\ \neg(res = res_1 \wedge st = st_1))\ st_0$$

Observe that $tr\,(\lambda res\ st,\ \neg(res = res_1 \wedge st = st_1))$ expresses the weakest precondition for the action tr under the postcondition that *excludes* result res_1 and state $post$ as reachable outcomes. The definition of tr', thus, ensures that the state st_0 transitions to st_1 with result res_1 only when such weakest pre-condition *does not hold* for st_0, *i.e.*, when st_1 and res_1 are reachable from st_0. We formally prove that this way of deriving tr' from tr is equivalent to the definition of tr' as a relation using standard big-step semantics for language constructs (bindings, assertions, *etc.*) for all actions tr with no failing assertions.

```
1  def enter.wp (n : ℕ) : WP σ Unit :=          7  def WP.req (P : Prop) : WP σ Unit := fun st post ⇒
2    get ▷.bind fun (st : σ) ⇒                   8    P → post () st
3    WP.req (st.n_have_privilege n) ▷.bind fun _ ⇒  9  def enter (n : ℕ) : BigStep σ Unit := fun st r st' ⇒
4    WP.req (st.n_requesting n) ▷.bind fun _ ⇒   10   st.n_have_privilege n ∧
5    modify fun st ⇒                             11   st.n_requesting n ∧ r = () ∧
6      { st with crit := fun x ⇒ st.crit x ∨ x = n }  12   st' = { st with crit := fun x ⇒ st.crit x ∨ x = n }
```

Fig. 4. Expansion steps for `enter` action from Fig. 1.

By applying this transformation and unfolding and simplifying all $\mathbf{WP}\,\sigma\,\rho$ definitions, Veil generates a two-state formula for the `enter` action (Fig. 4, lines 9–12). The result is used in the VC that is passed as a query to SMT solvers.

3.2 Soundness of the Verification Condition Generator

The main Veil soundness theorem states the equivalence of the two transition semantics from Sect. 3.1: $\forall s\ post, tr\ post\ s \Leftrightarrow (\forall s'r',\ tr's\ r's' \Rightarrow post\ r's')$ for all actions tr with no failing assertions. In other words, the weakest precondition of an action tr with a postcondition $post$ holds on a state s *if and only if* the two-state formula tr' relates the input state s to s' and r' from the postcondition *post*. A proof of this theorem is generated by Veil for each action declaration using Lean's type class resolution mechanism.

3.3 Interaction with SMT

All proof obligations Veil generates are Lean proof goals, which users can choose to either prove interactively using Lean's native tactics, or discharge via Veil's built-in automation that leverages the cvc5 [3] and Z3 [32] SMT solvers.

Since Veil is embedded in a higher-order logic and our verification condition generator (VCG) can emit goals that employ higher-order quantification (*e.g.*, to model non-deterministic assignment to relations), the main challenge in discharging Veil-generated goals with SMT is to reduce them to first-order logic. To this end, we developed a suite of custom tactics and `simp` procedures to (a) automatically destruct higher-order structures into first-order components, (b) hoist higher-order quantification to the top-level of the goal (where SMT supports declaring relations and functions), and (c) change the structure of the goal to make it easier for SMT solvers to discharge (*e.g.*, by recursively case-splitting `if`-statements and invoking the SMT solver separately on each sub-branch).

To translate Lean goals to SMT-LIB queries, Veil employs the Lean-SMT [29] and Lean-auto [42] libraries: Smt generates small, readable queries, but has longer translation time, whereas Auto is fast but generates larger queries. Veil uses Auto by default, but users can configure which translator to use on a per-query basis.

3.4 Model Minimisation

When the SMT solver provides a counter-example (model), *e.g.*, if an invariant provided by the user is not inductive, Veil can minimise the counter-example by issuing further incremental SMT queries to first reduce the sort and then the relation cardinalities, similar to the approach taken by mypyvy [53]. The counter-example is then displayed to the user in a human-readable format. In our experience, minimisation was crucial to make protocol models understandable.

4 Evaluation and Case Studies

Veil is available online [41].[2] We evaluated it w.r.t. the research questions below:

---

[2] https://github.com/verse-lab/veil.

RQ1: Can Veil automatically verify complex distributed protocol specifications?

RQ2: Can Veil automatically verify distributed protocol specifications that are encoded outside of Effectively Propositional Logic (EPR)?

RQ3: Is Veil expressive enough to supplement automation with interactive proofs?

The experiments in this section were run on a 2024 MacBook Pro with the M4 chip, 32GB of RAM, with cvc5 version 1.2.1, Z3 version 4.14.0, Lean version 4.16.0, and Lean-auto revision 918a699. We use Ivy revision dbe45e7.

4.1 Automated Verification of Distributed Protocols

To test RQ1, we collected 16 case studies from the following sources:

– 9 case studies from IvyBench [11], with manually added invariants,
– 2 case studies from the work of Padon *et al.* [36] on verifying Paxos [18], and
– 5 case studies from various other sources [6,26,38,58].

The case studies in our set total 1704 non-empty, non-comment lines of Lean code (average 100 lines per file), 85 actions and 185 invariants. All benchmarks have an equivalent formulation in Ivy. We attempted to prove each of them automatically using #check_invariants, without any interactive proof. We ran Veil on each of them separately and timed the execution by using Lean's profiler. For every benchmark, we also ran Ivy on the original formulation (with the complete=fo flag when required). Veil's timeout was its default of 5 s per SMT query for all benchmarks except Rabia, where it was set to 120 s. To the best of our knowledge, Ivy does not support per-query timeouts, so we set its overall timeout to 300 s. Times are an average over 5 runs.

Our results are summarised in Fig. 5. It splits the total time taken by Veil into simplification time (*cf.* Sect. 3.3), time taken for translation using Lean-auto, and time taken by SMT solver calls. The time taken by Ivy is also displayed. Veil successfully verified all benchmarks in the set, while Ivy has failed to verify two benchmarks, which are marked with * in Fig. 5.

Veil verifies all but 2 benchmarks in under 15 s (87.5%), and all but 4 benchmarks in under 10 s (75%). Ivy times out for 2 of the benchmarks. We conclude that Veil can verify a variety of distributed protocol specifications without the need for user effort, and its performance in doing so is acceptable.

4.2 Beyond EPR-Encoded Protocols

To test RQ2, we examine Veil's performance on benchmarks whose encoding to SMT is outside of the Effectively Propositional (EPR) fragment of first order logic, which is known to be decidable [24]. SMT solvers use heuristics and specialised techniques to try to decide first-order non-EPR queries, which may yield unknown. Nonetheless, it is often convenient to write protocols and algorithms in general FOL, as substantial work is often needed to restate them in EPR [36].

We will examine four case studies from the benchmark set of Section 4.1:

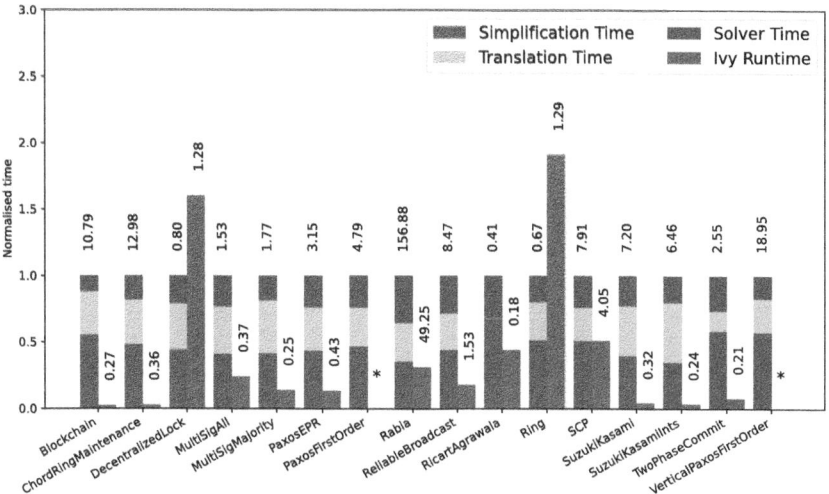

Fig. 5. Results of running Veil and Ivy on the benchmark set. The bar heights are normalised w.r.t. Veil verification times. All absolute times are in seconds.

- two variants of the Paxos protocol that are discussed in Padon *et al.* [36]: the Single-Decree Paxos [18], as well as Vertical Paxos [20],
- the Suzuki-Kasami algorithm with positive integer indices (Sect. 2), and
- the Reliable Broadcast protocol [6].

These four benchmarks are expressed in unconstrained first-order logic, and their encoding falls outside of EPR. Veil manages to verify all of them.[3] When running Ivy on these benchmarks (with the `complete=fo` flag to force Ivy to ignore that they are outside of the decidable fragment), it succeeds in verifying Reliable Broadcast and Suzuki-Kasami and times out for Paxos and Vertical Paxos.

From our results, we conclude that Veil is successful in verifying protocols whose encodings are even outside of EPR, which increases its versatility.

4.3 Combining SMT Automation with Interactive Proofs

For the RQ3, we considered two case studies, which have theorems established in interactive theorem provers, in addition to Ivy specifications. We ported these theorems and their proofs into Veil, and report our findings below.

Stellar Consensus Protocol (SCP). [25] features a formally defined model that includes several higher-order components, which, for example, involve quantification over sets. To encode SCP into Ivy, Losa and Dodds [26] abstracted these components by stating their required properties in FOL as assumptions; the

---

[3] For SuzukiKasamiInts, we disable the `-finite-model-find` option of cvc5, which Veil enables by default. With it enabled, verification takes around 120 s.

soundness of the abstraction w.r.t. a concrete higher-order model is then manually proven in Isabelle/HOL [52]. In our case, we bundle the assumptions as a type class and assume the existence of its instance during automated verification, so that the assumptions can be utilised by SMT solvers. We further ported the proofs from Isabelle/HOL to Veil and validated the abstraction soundness by deriving an instance of the assumptions type class from the concrete model. Compared with the combination Ivy + Isabelle/HOL, our approach allows the abstract model, the concrete model, and their correspondence to be verified in the same framework, without relying on a trusted manual assumption translation.

Rabia protocol [38] comes with a formalisation in both Ivy and the Rocq Prover, where the Rocq one only differs in that it (1) interprets the type of *phases* (a notion in Rabia) as the natural number type, (2) admits all invariants to be checked by Ivy as axioms, and (3) proves several more properties to be invariants of Rabia. To manually prove an invariant P in Rocq, it suffices to show that the established invariants (either checked separately by Ivy and admitted in Rocq, or proven in Rocq) entail P. Those additional invariants are proven in Rocq since they cannot be proven in pure FOL, *e.g.*, some require induction on phases. Thanks to Veil's support for manual invariant reasoning, we successfully verified all additional invariants proven in the Rocq formulation, for the Veil encoding of Rabia. Notably, during the porting process, we spotted one discrepancy between an invariant in the Ivy formulation and the corresponding admitted one in the Rocq code, since our Veil formulation was faithfully translated from the Ivy one, and Lean complained when we attempted to use that invariant as it is used in the original Rocq proof. Such nitpicking would require careful examination for the original Ivy + Rocq combination, which, again, shows the benefits of having a unified framework for both automated and interactive proofs.

5   Related and Future Work

Alloy [14] and the TLA $^+$ toolbox [19] are de-facto the most popular tools to date for prototyping and modelling state-transition systems in general and distributed protocols in particular [1,35]. Alloy only allows for bounded verification, assuming that each sort is finite. TLA $^+$ is most commonly used for concrete-state model checking of protocol designs [57], but also offers a proof system for deductive verification, TLAPS [7]. Unlike Veil, TLAPS does not offer easy extensibility via metaprogramming and relies on a *trusted* translation to the languages of its backend provers, Zenon [5] and Isabelle/HOL [52], to discharge its proof obligations.

The language of Veil is almost a verbatim port of RML, the specification language of Ivy [37], while its bounded model checking capability is inspired by a similar feature of mypyvy [53]. Unlike these tools, Veil is a foundational verification framework with a formal soundness proof of its VC generator, offering the full power of interactive proofs in Lean, its extensibility, and libraries.

Veil is a spiritual successor of Jahob [17] and Why3 [9], tools that provide rich specification languages and rely on third-party provers to discharge verification conditions, automatically or interactively. More recent frameworks RefinedC [45], RefinedRust [10], and Diaframe [33] are foundational embeddings of mostly-automated verifiers into the Rocq Prover (formerly known as Coq). Those tools target general-purpose programming languages and rely on custom tactic-based automation rather than general-purpose first-order logic solvers, making them not immediately suitable for effective reasoning about transition systems.

We believe our initial prototype of Veil opens several avenues for exciting future work. In particular, we are planning to explore the integration of state-of-the-art approaches for inferring system invariants in first-order logic [12,27,56,59] into Veil. Given the available higher-order specification composition mechanisms of Lean, we are also planning to explore ways to compose properties of individually verified protocols, in the style of the recent Bythos framework [60]. Finally, going beyond simple transition systems, we are hopeful that our experience of implementing Veil will pave the way for embedding general-purpose SMT-based program verifiers [21,22,34] into a foundational proof assistant.

Acknowledgements. We thank Peter Müller for his feedback on a draft of this paper. We also thank the reviewers of CAV'25 for their insightful comments. Mark Yuen has implemented the initial version of Suzuki-Kasami algorithm in TLA $^+$ and Ivy as a part of his Capstone thesis [58]. This work has been supported by a Singapore Ministry of Education (MoE) Tier 1 grant T1 251RES2108 "Automated Proof Evolution for Verified Software Systems", MoE Tier 3 grant "Automated Program Repair" MOE-MOET32021-0001, by Stellar Development Foundation Academic Research Grant, and by Sui Academic Research Award. The work of Elad Kinsbruner has been supported by the European Union (ERC, EXPLOSYN, 101117232). Views and opinions expressed are however those of the author(s) only and do not necessarily reflect those of the European Union or the European Research Council Executive Agency. Neither the European Union nor the granting authority can be held responsible for them.

Disclosure of Interests. The authors have no further competing interests to declare that are relevant to the content of this article.

References

1. TLA+ Examples. https://github.com/tlaplus/Examples. Accessed 30 Jan 2025
2. Appel, A.W.: Foundational proof-carrying code. In: LICS, pp. 247–256. IEEE Computer Society (2001). https://doi.org/10.1109/LICS.2001.932501
3. Barbosa, H., et al.: cvc5: a versatile and industrial-strength SMT solver. In: TACAS. LNCS, vol. 13243, pp. 415–442. Springer (2022). https://doi.org/10.1007/978-3-030-99524-9_24
4. Biere, A., Cimatti, A., Clarke, E.M., Strichman, O., Zhu, Y.: Bounded model checking. Adv. Comput. **58**, 117–148 (2003). https://doi.org/10.1016/S0065-2458(03)58003-2
5. Bonichon, R., Delahaye, D., Doligez, D.: Zenon: An Extensible Automated Theorem Prover Producing Checkable Proofs. In: LPAR. LNCS, vol. 4790, pp. 151–165. Springer (2007). https://doi.org/10.1007/978-3-540-75560-9_13

6. Chang, J., Maxemchuk, N.F.: Reliable broadcast protocols. ACM Trans. Comput. Syst. **2**(3), 251–273 (1984). https://doi.org/10.1145/989.357400

7. Chaudhuri, K., Doligez, D., Lamport, L., Merz, S.: A TLA+ proof system. In: Proceedings of the LPAR 2008 Workshops. CEUR Workshop Proceedings, vol. 418. CEUR-WS.org (2008). https://ceur-ws.org/Vol-418/paper2.pdf

8. Dijkstra, E.W.: Guarded commands, non determinacy and formal derivation of programs. Commun. ACM **18**(8), 453–457 (1975). https://doi.org/10.1145/360933.360975

9. Filliâtre, J., Paskevich, A.: Why3 - where programs meet provers. In: ESOP. LNCS, vol. 7792, pp. 125–128. Springer (2013). https://doi.org/10.1007/978-3-642-37036-6_8

10. Gäher, L., Sammler, M., Jung, R., Krebbers, R., Dreyer, D.: RefinedRust: a type system for high-assurance verification of rust programs. Proc. ACM Program. Lang. **8**(PLDI), 1115–1139 (2024). https://doi.org/10.1145/3656422

11. Goel, A., Sakallah, K.A.: ivybench: Collection of Distributed Protocol Verification Problems. https://github.com/aman-goel/ivybench. Accessed 29 Jan 2025

12. Hance, T., Heule, M., Martins, R., Parno, B.: Finding invariants of distributed systems: it's a small (enough) world after all. In: NSDI, pp. 115–131. USENIX Association (2021). https://www.usenix.org/conference/nsdi21/presentation/hance

13. Hawblitzel, C., et al.: IronFleet: proving practical distributed systems correct. In: SOSP, pp. 1–17. ACM (2015). https://doi.org/10.1145/2815400.2815428

14. Jackson, D.: Software Abstractions - Logic, Language, and Analysis. MIT Press (2006). http://mitpress.mit.edu/catalog/item/default.asp?ttype=2&tid=10928

15. Konnov, I., Kukovec, J., Tran, T.: TLA+ model checking made symbolic. Proc. ACM Program. Lang. **3**(OOPSLA), 123:1–123:30 (2019). https://doi.org/10.1145/3360549

16. Krogh-Jespersen, M., Timany, A., Ohlenbusch, M.E., Gregersen, S.O., Birkedal, L.: Aneris: A Mechanised Logic for Modular Reasoning about Distributed Systems. In: ESOP. LNCS, vol. 12075, pp. 336–365. Springer (2020). https://doi.org/10.1007/978-3-030-44914-8_13

17. Kuncak, V.: Modular Data Structure Verification. Ph.D. thesis, Massachusetts Institute of Technology (2007). https://dspace.mit.edu/handle/1721.1/38533

18. Lamport, L.: Paxos Made Simple. ACM SIGACT News (Distributed Computing Column) 32, 4 (Whole Number 121, December 2001), pp. 51–58 (2001). https://www.microsoft.com/en-us/research/publication/paxos-made-simple/

19. Lamport, L.: Specifying Systems, The TLA+ Language and Tools for Hardware and Software Engineers. Addison-Wesley (2002). http://research.microsoft.com/users/lamport/tla/book.html

20. Lamport, L., Malkhi, D., Zhou, L.: Vertical paxos and primary-backup replication. In: PODC. pp. 312–313. ACM (2009). https://doi.org/10.1145/1582716.1582783

21. Lattuada, A., et al.: Verus: a practical foundation for systems verification. In: SOSP, pp. 438–454. ACM (2024). https://doi.org/10.1145/3694715.3695952

22. Leino, K.R.M.: Dafny: an automatic program verifier for functional correctness. In: LPAR. LNCS, vol. 6355, pp. 348–370. Springer (2010). https://doi.org/10.1007/978-3-642-17511-4_20

23. Lesani, M., Bell, C.J., Chlipala, A.: Chapar: certified causally consistent distributed key-value stores. In: POPL, pp. 357–370. ACM (2016). https://doi.org/10.1145/2837614.2837622

24. Lewis, H.R.: Complexity results for classes of quantificational formulas. J. Comput. Syst. Sci. **21**(3), 317–353 (1980). https://doi.org/10.1016/0022-0000(80)90027-6

25. Lokhava, M., et al.: Fast and secure global payments with Stellar. In: SOSP, pp. 80–96. ACM (2019). https://doi.org/10.1145/3341301.3359636
26. Losa, G., Dodds, M.: On the formal verification of the stellar consensus protocol. In: 2nd Workshop on Formal Methods for Blockchains, FMBC@CAV 2020. OASIcs, vol. 84, pp. 9:1–9:9. Schloss Dagstuhl - Leibniz-Zentrum für Informatik (2020). https://doi.org/10.4230/OASICS.FMBC.2020.9
27. Ma, H., Goel, A., Jeannin, J., Kapritsos, M., Kasikci, B., Sakallah, K.A.: I4: incremental inference of inductive invariants for verification of distributed protocols. In: SOSP, pp. 370–384. ACM (2019). https://doi.org/10.1145/3341301.3359651
28. McMillan, K.L., Padon, O.: Deductive verification in decidable fragments with ivy. In: SAS. LNCS, vol. 11002, pp. 43–55. Springer (2018). https://doi.org/10.1007/978-3-319-99725-4_4
29. Mohamed, A., et al.: LEAN-SMT: An SMT tactic for discharging proof goals in Lean. In: CAV. LNCS. Springer (2025), to appear
30. Mora, F., Desai, A., Polgreen, E., Seshia, S.A.: Message chains for distributed system verification. Proc. ACM Program. Lang. 7(OOPSLA2), 2224–2250 (2023). https://doi.org/10.1145/3622876
31. de Moura, L., Ullrich, S.: The lean 4 theorem prover and programming language. In: CADE. LNCS, vol. 12699, pp. 625–635. Springer (2021). https://doi.org/10.1007/978-3-030-79876-5_37
32. de Moura, L.M., Bjørner, N.S.: Z3: an efficient SMT solver. In: TACAS. LNCS, vol. 4963, pp. 337–340. Springer (2008). https://doi.org/10.1007/978-3-540-78800-3_24
33. Mulder, I., Krebbers, R., Geuvers, H.: Diaframe: automated verification of fine-grained concurrent programs in Iris. In: PLDI, pp. 809–824. ACM (2022). https://doi.org/10.1145/3519939.3523432
34. Müller, P., Schwerhoff, M., Summers, A.J.: Viper: A Verification Infrastructure for Permission-Based Reasoning. In: VMCAI. LNCS, vol. 9583, pp. 41–62. Springer (2016). https://doi.org/10.1007/978-3-662-49122-5_2
35. Newcombe, C., Rath, T., Zhang, F., Munteanu, B., Brooker, M., Deardeuff, M.: How Amazon web services uses formal methods. Commun. ACM 58(4), 66–73 (2015). https://doi.org/10.1145/2699417
36. Padon, O., Losa, G., Sagiv, M., Shoham, S.: Paxos made EPR: decidable reasoning about distributed protocols. Proc. ACM Program. Lang. 1(OOPSLA), 108:1–108:31 (2017). https://doi.org/10.1145/3140568
37. Padon, O., McMillan, K.L., Panda, A., Sagiv, M., Shoham, S.: Ivy: safety verification by interactive generalization. In: PLDI, pp. 614–630. ACM (2016). https://doi.org/10.1145/2908080.2908118
38. Pan, H., et al.: Rabia: simplifying state-machine replication through randomization. In: SOSP, pp. 472–487. ACM (2021). https://doi.org/10.1145/3477132.3483582
39. Paulino, A., et al.: Metaprogramming in Lean 4 (2024). https://leanprover-community.github.io/lean4-metaprogramming-book/
40. Pîrlea, G., Sergey, I.: Mechanising blockchain consensus. In: CPP, pp. 78–90. ACM (2018). https://doi.org/10.1145/3167086
41. Pîrlea, G., Gladshtein, V., Kinsbruner, E., Zhao, Q., Sergey, I.: Veil: a framework for automated and interactive verification of transition systems. Software Artefact. (2025). https://doi.org/10.5281/zenodo.15208271
42. Qian, Y., Clune, J., Barrett, C., Avigad, J.: Lean-auto: an interface between lean 4 and automated theorem provers. In: CAV. LNCS, Springer (2025), to appear

43. Qiu, L., Kim, Y., Shin, J., Kim, J., Honoré, W., Shao, Z.: LiDO: linearizable byzantine distributed objects with refinement-based liveness proofs. Proc. ACM Program. Lang. **8**(PLDI), 1140–1164 (2024). https://doi.org/10.1145/3656423

44. Rahli, V., Vukotic, I., Völp, M., Veríssimo, P.J.E.: Velisarios: byzantine fault-tolerant protocols powered by Coq. In: ESOP. LNCS, vol. 10801, pp. 619–650. Springer (2018). https://doi.org/10.1007/978-3-319-89884-1_22

45. Sammler, M., Lepigre, R., Krebbers, R., Memarian, K., Dreyer, D., Garg, D.: RefinedC: automating the foundational verification of C code with refined ownership types. In: PLDI, pp. 158–174. ACM (2021). https://doi.org/10.1145/3453483.3454036

46. Sergey, I., Wilcox, J.R., Tatlock, Z.: Programming and proving with distributed protocols. Proc. ACM Program. Lang. **2**(POPL), 28:1–28:30 (2018). https://doi.org/10.1145/3158116

47. Sharma, U., Jung, R., Tassarotti, J., Kaashoek, M.F., Zeldovich, N.: Grove: a separation-logic library for verifying distributed systems. In: SOSP, pp. 113–129. ACM (2023). https://doi.org/10.1145/3600006.3613172

48. Sprenger, C., et al.: Igloo: soundly linking compositional refinement and separation logic for distributed system verification. Proc. ACM Program. Lang. **4**(OOPSLA), 152:1–152:31 (2020). https://doi.org/10.1145/3428220

49. Suzuki, I., Kasami, T.: A distributed mutual exclusion algorithm. ACM Trans. Comput. Syst. **3**(4), 344–349 (1985). https://doi.org/10.1145/6110.214406

50. Taube, M., et al.: Modularity for decidability of deductive verification with applications to distributed systems. In: PLDI, pp. 662–677. ACM (2018). https://doi.org/10.1145/3192366.3192414

51. Ullrich, S., de Moura, L.: 'do' unchained: embracing local imperativity in a purely functional language (functional pearl). Proc. ACM Program. Lang. **6**(ICFP), 512–539 (2022). https://doi.org/10.1145/3547640

52. Wenzel, M., Paulson, L.C., Nipkow, T.: The Isabelle Framework. In: TPHOLs. LNCS, vol. 5170, pp. 33–38. Springer (2008). https://doi.org/10.1007/978-3-540-71067-7_7

53. Wilcox, J.R., Feldman, Y.M.Y., Padon, O., Shoham, S.: mypyvy: a research platform for verification of transition systems in first-order logic. In: CAV. LNCS, vol. 14682, pp. 71–85. Springer (2024). https://doi.org/10.1007/978-3-031-65630-9_4

54. Wilcox, J.R., et al.: Verdi: a framework for implementing and formally verifying distributed systems. In: PLDI, pp. 357–368. ACM (2015). https://doi.org/10.1145/2737924.2737958

55. Woos, D., Wilcox, J.R., Anton, S., Tatlock, Z., Ernst, M.D., Anderson, T.E.: Planning for change in a formal verification of the raft consensus protocol. In: CPP, pp. 154–165. ACM (2016). https://doi.org/10.1145/2854065.2854081

56. Yao, J., Tao, R., Gu, R., Nieh, J.: DuoAI: fast, automated inference of inductive invariants for verifying distributed protocols. In: OSDI, pp. 485–501. USENIX Association (2022). https://www.usenix.org/conference/osdi22/presentation/yao

57. Yu, Y., Manolios, P., Lamport, L.: Model Checking TLA$^+$ Specifications. In: CHARME. LNCS, vol. 1703, pp. 54–66. Springer (1999). https://doi.org/10.1007/3-540-48153-2_6

58. Yuen, M.: Verifying Distributed Protocols: from Executable to Decidable. Capstone thesis, Yale-NUS College, Singapore (2022), accompanying code available at https://github.com/markyuen/tlaplus-to-ivy/

59. Zhang, T.N., Hance, T., Kapritsos, M., Chajed, T., Parno, B.: Inductive invariants that spark joy: using invariant taxonomies to streamline distributed protocol proofs. In: OSDI, pp. 837–853. USENIX Association (2024). https://www.usenix.org/conference/osdi24/presentation/zhang-nuda

60. Zhao, Q., Pîrlea, G., Grzeszkiewicz, K., Gilbert, S., Sergey, I.: Compositional Verification of Composite Byzantine Protocols. In: CCS, pp. 34–48. ACM (2024). https://doi.org/10.1145/3658644.3690355

Decision Heuristics in MCSat

Thomas Hader[1], Ahmed Irfan[2]([⊠]) [iD], and Stéphane Graham-Lengrand[2] [iD]

[1] TU Wien, Vienna, Austria
thomas.hader@tuwien.ac.at
[2] SRI International, Menlo Park, CA, USA
{ahmed.irfan,stephane.graham-lengrand}@sri.com

Abstract. The Model Constructing Satisfiability (MCSat) approach to Satisfiability Modulo Theories (SMT) has demonstrated strong performance when handling complex theories such as nonlinear arithmetic. Despite being in development for over a decade, there has been limited research on the heuristics utilized by MCSat solvers as in Yices2. In this paper, we discuss the decision heuristics employed in the MCSat approach of Yices2 and empirically show their significance on QF_NRA and QF_NIA benchmarks. Additionally, we propose new ideas to enhance these heuristics by leveraging theory-specific reasoning and drawing inspiration from recent advancements in SAT solvers. Our new version of the MCSat Yices2 solver not only solves more nonlinear arithmetic benchmarks than before but is also more efficient compared to other leading SMT solvers.

Keywords: SAT · SMT · MCSat · Decision heuristics

1 Introduction

Satisfiability modulo theory (SMT) is the backbone for countless verification and synthesis techniques that require expressive logical theories like real/integer arithmetic [4,28]. Modern SMT solvers rely on the combination of Boolean level reasoning with theory-specific methods through the Conflict-Driven Clause Learning with theory support (CDCL(T)) paradigm [30] or the Model Constructing Satisfiability (MCSat) approach [23,26]. The former employs off-the-shelf Boolean satisfiability (SAT) solvers as its core reasoning engines that aims to enumerate Boolean assignments, which are subsequently checked for theory compliance by independent theory algorithms. The latter lifts the Boolean-level Conflict-Driven Clause Learning (CDCL) algorithm to the theory level, incrementally building theory assignments alongside Boolean assignments, enabling a closer integration of theory reasoning in the Boolean search process. This approach is particularly effective for handling complex arithmetic theories, e.g. nonlinear arithmetic.

During the last couple of decades, SAT solving has gained impressive performance improvements by various techniques [7], many of which are arguably related to heuristics. These improvements of SAT solvers had positive impact

© The Author(s) 2025
R. Piskac and Z. Rakamarić (Eds.): CAV 2025, LNCS 15933, pp. 42–56, 2025.
https://doi.org/10.1007/978-3-031-98682-6_3

on SMT solvers. For CDCL(T) solvers, performance gains in SAT engines translates to improvements in the propositional core of the SMT solver [18]. However, as theory engines are decoupled from SAT solving, improvements in SAT do not directly translate to better theory engines in general (except for the theories that can be reduced to SAT, e.g. bitvectors [16]). In contrast, MCSat-based SMT engines perform theory reasoning similarly to how SAT solvers handle Boolean reasoning, making them more adaptable to heuristics from SAT solving with minimal modification.

A family of such heuristics are *decision heuristics*. Whenever a decision is to be made to continue the search, the decision heuristic selects a yet unassigned variable and a value to assign it to. Those decisions have a fundamental influence on how the search proceeds. In SAT solving, decision heuristics have had a substantial part in the success of modern solvers [7]. By tuning decision heuristics in MCSat, we show that the performance of MCSat solver can be improved without any changes to the actual theory solving techniques.

Contributions. In this work we present (i) a detailed summary on how well-established decision heuristic techniques from SAT can be adapted to the MCSat-based SMT approach (Table 1) and (ii) solutions for additional challenges and opportunities that arise for domains beyond the Boolean domain. We also (iii) show detailed experimental results on the performance implications for different heuristics in the MCSat engine in Yices2 on the SMT logics QF_NRA and QF_NIA– benchmarks taken from the SMT-LIB [3].

Related Work. The MCSat implementation in Yices2 that powers non-linear integer reasoning [22] has already been utilizing some heuristics discussed in this work (particularly exponential Variable State Independent Decaying Sum (VSIDS) (EVSIDS) and value cache). However, the specifics were not discussed and also no empirical evaluation of their impact was provided in [22]. This paper addresses this gap. Besides Yices2, different MCSat variable selection heuristics in the SMT-RAT [1,14] solver have been presented in [29] for the theory of non-linear reals.

The work of [18] proposed an enhanced interface from CDCL(T)-based solvers to off-the-shelf SAT solvers, which improved the performance of cvc5 [2, 33] by tightly integrating the state-of-the-art SAT solver CaDiCaL.

Table 1. Established SAT technologies and their MCSat version

SAT	MCSat	Section
VSIDS	Theory-based VSIDS	3.1
Reason side bumping	Boolean Scaling	3.1
Phase Saving	Value Cache	3.2
Target Phases	Target Cache	3.2
Rephasing	Recaching	3.2

MathSAT5 [11–13], which is a CDCL(T)-based SMT solver, allows for the use of different pluggable SAT solvers as the core SAT solver. However, the authors reported in [13] that there were no significant performance improvements from using external pluggable SAT solvers.

2   MCSat Overview

MCSat applies CDCL-like mechanisms to perform theory reasoning either as a dedicated theory solver (e.g., for non-linear real arithmetic: Z3/nlsat) or as a fully-fledged stand-alone engine (Yices2, SMT-RAT) that is capable of handling multiple theories. The MCSat architecture consists of a *core solver*, an *assignment trail*, and *plugins* for theory reasoning.

Core Solver. The core solver explicitly and incrementally constructs models with Boolean and first-order variable assignments – maintained in the assignment trail – while maintaining the invariant that none of the constraints evaluate to false. Figure 1a shows high-level pseudo-code for the MCSat search procedure. The core solver propagates the trail information by calling the propagation function of each plugin (line 3). If a conflict is found during propagation, it checks if there is any decision to backtrack over (line 9). If so, it learns a lemma, backjumps (line 11) and continues the loop. If not, it returns UNSAT (line 13). One of the key steps in MCSat is performing conflict analysis when a plugin detects a conflicting state. The lemmas learned via conflict analysis are based on theory-specific explanations, provided by the plugins, of conflicts and propagations. Note that Fig. 1a shows the restarting (lines 4–5) and variable scoring (line 10) mechanisms, which we will discuss in the next section. Furthermore, like SAT solvers, MCSat also performs clause database cleaning, which is not shown in the code for simplicity.

Plugins. They provide assignments for decisions, perform propagations, detect conflicts, and produce explanations. In modern MCSat engines, propositional reasoning is handled like any other theory by a dedicated plugin. When the core solver asserts a formula during search, each plugin (incl. the Boolean plugin) scans the formula and reports to the core solver all sub-terms that are *relevant* to the plugin's theory, namely those sub-terms that "appear as variables" to the theory, a.k.a. *theory variables* (actual variables or terms whose head symbols are not in the theory's signature), and such that a value assignment to those sub-terms would uniquely determine the truth value of the formula according to the theory. Relevant terms are then treated as MCSat variables—the core solver can decide or propagate value assignments for them. Plugins typically keep a set of feasible values for their theory variables. Whenever one of these sets gets empty, a conflict is raised and the plugin provides a conflict *explanation clause* that excludes the current trail and may even contain new terms.

```
1    int mcsat_solve():
2       while (true):
3          if (propagate()):
4             if (restarting())
5                restart()
6             else if (!decide()):
7                return SAT
8          else:
9             if (explain()):
10               bump_vars()
11               backjump()
12            else:
13               return UNSAT
```

(a) mcsat_solve method

```
1    bool decide():
2       variable var = vsids_pop_unassigned()
3       if (var != null):
4          feasible = false
5          if (has_value_cache(var)):
6             feasible = try_value_cache(var)
7          if (!feasible):
8             pick_new_value(var)
9       return (var != null)
```

(b) decide method

Fig. 1. MCSat search pseudo-code

Trail. The *trail* is the key data-structure in MCSat. It holds value assignments for relevant terms, functioning as a partial model during the search process (and turning into a complete model when the search concludes SAT). A term t can be *evaluated* (or is *evaluable*) in the trail M if t has an assignment in M, or if all closest relevant sub-terms of t have been assigned values in M. Evaluation-consistency is maintained in the trail, ensuring that no term evaluates to different values within it. Assignments on the trail can either be *propagated* or *decided*.

Example 1. Assume a search problem with integer ($\mathbb{Z}$) variables x, y, and z and boolean ($\mathbb{B}$) terms in the input formula $\mathcal{F}$.

$$\mathcal{F} = (\neg(x \geq 1) \vee (xy = 1)) \wedge (\neg(xy = 1) \vee (x + 2yz > 0)) \wedge (z^2 > 1)$$

A possible trail is $M = [\![(z^2 > 1) \mapsto \top, x \mapsto 1, (x \geq 1) \mapsto \top, (xy = 1) \mapsto \top, y \mapsto 1]\!]$. It consists of a $\mathbb{B}$-propagation, a $\mathbb{Z}$-decision, a $\mathbb{Z}$-propagation, a $\mathbb{B}$-propagation, and another $\mathbb{Z}$-propagation, respectively. The choice to select x was made arbitrary; any variable – Boolean or integer – which was not already on the trail could have been chosen. A different choice, say z, or a different value, say -1, would have led to different propagations and the search in a different direction.

Decision Heuristic. The purpose of this heuristic is to pick (i) a variable to decide, and (ii) a value to assign to the variable. The former is part of the MCSat core as the decision is made over *relevant terms* of all involved theories. Theory plugins can, nevertheless, influence the heuristic by increasing the weight of a variable and make it more likely to be picked. This process is called *bumping* a variable. Selecting a value is done by the relevant theory plugin. In Example 1, the variable x was picked by the central selection heuristic and the value 1 was chosen by the dedicated plugin for integer reasoning. As we will show in the following section, decision heuristics have a crucial impact on solver performance.

3   MCSat Decision Heuristics

In this section, we discuss the decision heuristic for variable and value selection that have been implemented in the MCSat scheme of the Yices2 SMT solver. The importance of these heuristics is demonstrated through experiments, which have not been previously explored in earlier Yices2 MCSat papers [19–22]. Additionally, we introduce new ideas on how to further improve the heuristics by incorporating theory-specific reasoning and insights from the SAT community. Finally, we evaluate the effectiveness of each proposed change through our experiments. For the experiments,[1] we used the benchmarks of quantifier-free logics of nonlinear real and integer arithmetic, namely QF_NRA and QF_NIA, from the SMT-LIB [3] release 2024 [32].

3.1   Variable Selection Heuristics

In SAT solving, heuristics for selecting the next variable usually follow the principle that variables which often appear in learned clauses are central to the problem structure and, thus, should be assigned early. This principle is reflected in the VSIDS variable selection heuristic, which was originally presented in the SAT solver Chaff [25]. An adaption named EVSIDS, originally implemented in the MiniSAT solver [17], is implemented in many state-of-the-art SAT solvers (e.g. CaDiCaL [5]) and has been crucial for their high efficiency [7,8]. Modern MCSat engines (e.g. Yices2, SMT-RAT) have adapted a variant of the VSIDS variable selection heuristic [23,29]. While in the SAT community other variable selection heuristics – like variable-move-to-front (VMTF) – have been proposed in the meantime [8,34] and modern solvers use heuristics-switching strategies on the fly [5], EVSIDS remains the state-of-the-art in MCSat engines.

EVSIDS Heuristic [Baseline]. In EVSIDS each variable x_i gets an activity score s_i. Whenever x_i gets bumped, s_i is increased by g^n where $g > 1$ and n is an integer that is increased at each conflict. At a decision, the variable with the highest score (efficiently determined using a priority heap), is chosen. In SAT solving, variables are bumped when they appear in conflict resolutions and different bumping strategies have been proposed. For further details we refer to relevant publications in the area of SAT solving [8,17].

In the MCSat implementation of Yices2, variables are bumped whenever they occur in a conflict resolution, i.e. either in the conflict clause or a resolution step. All variables are bumped once for each term they occur in, as long as the term is not assumed to be false on the trail by Boolean reasoning. Note that, in general, this favors non-propositional variables as they occur in many different propositional terms. Previous research on the SMT-RAT solver in the QF_NRA theory indicates that this behavior is beneficial for performance [29].

---

[1] The experiments were conducted on a 96-core 2.3 GHz AMD-CPU server running Ubuntu 24.04.1 LTS. Timeout per instance 5 min; memory limit 8 GB.

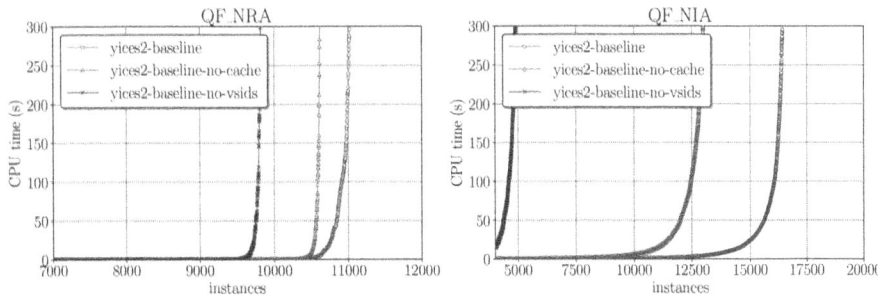

Fig. 2. Evaluation of state-of-the-art heuristics: EVSIDS and value cache

Example 2. Given a trail M and a conflict resolution containing $C_1 = x^2 y + 1 > 0$, $C_2 = x + z \geq 0$, and $C_3 = y^4 > 0$. Assume M contains a Boolean assignment mapping C_2 to false. Then all related terms C_1, C_2, and C_3 are bumped (once) and the variables x and y are bumped 1 and 2 times, respectively.

Theory Bumping. Theory plugins can influence the search by bumping variables using additional, theory-based heuristics. The following examples of theory-based bumping are implemented in Yices2:

- Whenever the *real or finite field plugins* detect a new term, they bump all variables according to their polynomial degree.
- The *bit-vector plugin* bumps (certain) variables of new terms once.
- The plugin for *uninterpreted functions and arrays* bumps sub-terms of conflicts in the equality graph.

What Performance Benefit does EVSIDS Provide in MCSat? We have evaluated the influence of EVSIDS with theory bumping against the baseline without EVSIDS, i.e. using a random, fixed variable order. The results are shown in Fig. 2. They clearly show that all EVSIDS is giving a huge performance boost over the fixed variable ordering.

Extending EVSIDS with Boolean Scaling [New Heuristic]. We could confirm that EVSIDS is a leading technique for dynamic variable selection [29]. Although we did not recreate all experiments presented, the reader can refer to [29] for a further evaluation on different variable ordering. However, the uniform bumping strategy in Yices2 can potentially reduce the chances of selecting a Boolean variable as the next decision. To mitigate this scenario, we introduce the *Boolean scaling* constant to increase the bumping of Boolean terms. It builds upon another idea from SAT solving, where state-of-the-art solvers put emphasis on literals of resolved clauses, instead of the conflict clause directly [5]. This idea was first presented in [24] by accounting for the *reason side rate*. In Yices2, whenever the conflict clause C is resolved with another clause D, all literals in $D \setminus C$ are bumped by the Boolean scaling factor. We use a factor of 20 for the Boolean scaling. The results comparing different Boolean scaling are in Sect. 3.3.

```
 1   mcsat_solve():                          1   bool decide():
 2     while (true):                         2     variable var = hints_pop_unassigned()
 3       if (propagate()):                   3     if (var != null):
 4         if (restarting()):                4       var = vsids_pop_unassigned()
 5           clear_hints()                   5     if (var != null):
 6           update_cache()                  6       feasible = false;
 7           restart()                       7       if (has_target_cache(var)):
 8         else:                             8         feasible = try_target_cache(var)
 9           if (recaching())                9       else if (has_value_cache(var)):
10             recache()                    10         feasible = try_value_cache(var)
11           if (!decide())                 11       if (!feasible):
12             return SAT                   12         pick_new_value(var)
13       else:                              13     return (var != null);
14         if (explain()):
15           bump_vars()
16           backjump()                         (b) Modified decide method
17           clear_hints()
18           update_cache()
19         else:
20           return UNSAT;
```

(a) Modified `mcsat_solve` method

Fig. 3. Modified MCSat search pseudo-code (italicized and green colored) (Color figure online)

Theory-Guided Variable Selection [New Heuristic]. While theory plugins can influence EVSIDS scoring with theory bumping, there are situations in the search where bypassing EVSIDS and directly suggesting a next variable is beneficial. Increasing the score of a variable substantially to ensure its selection is not wise, as this would destroy scoring for later decisions. We introduce a mechanism that enables theory plugins to suggest the next decision variable, so called *variable hints*. Hinted variables have precedence over EVSIDS and are guaranteed to be selected as soon as possible. Figure 3b shows the modified MCSat decide method: note that on line 2 hinted terms are selected before the terms suggested by EVSIDS, shown on line 4. As hints are intended to react on specific search states, they are cleared on backtracking. Theory plugins can hint a variable to the core solver whenever they detect, by theory-specific reasoning, in the current search state that the variable is a good candidate for the next decision. This is usually the case when a plugin has a "good" choice for a variable's value, i.e. the number of feasible assignments for a variable is limited or assigning a specific value is expected to have a significant impact on the search.

Example 3. Assume a trail M and two yet unassigned real variables x and y. A new term C is added to M that reduces the set of feasible values for x to a single value via theory reasoning, e.g. in the case of reals, using root isolation. However, $y \in (-\infty, \infty)$ still holds. Then assigning x before y avoids potential incorrect guesses on y when there is another term $D(x, y)$.

In practice, hinting is used whenever the set of feasible assignments for a variable is small or a singleton. Note that even if the set is a singleton, propagating the variable with the singleton value is not generally feasible because it involves generating a term that only contains already assigned variables (cf. [23]). The

```
1  recache():                                1  update_cache():
2    num_recaches = get_num_recaches()       2    if (trail_size > target_depth):
3    clear(target_cache)                     3      target_cache = trail
4    target_depth = 0                        4      target_depth = trail_size
5    if !(num_recaches % 2):                 5    if (trail_size > best_depth):
6      value_cache = best_cache              6      best_cache = trail
7      clear(best_cache)                     7      best_depth = trail_size
8      best_depth = 0
```

(b) **update_cache** method

(a) **recache** method

Fig. 4. MCSat `recache` and `update_cache` methods

term is substituted for the propagated variable when building a lemma out of conflict analysis. In the theories of reals and integers such a term cannot always be found and hinting the next decision is a promising alternative in such cases.

A feasible set interval is an interval that (tightly) over-approximates the feasible set. When its size is small, the associated variable is a good candidate for decision because the possible values are limited. In Sect. 3.3 we evaluate a modification to the reals/integers plugin that hints a real variable whenever its feasible set is unit or its *feasible set interval* size less or equal to 1.

3.2   Value Selection Heuristics

Whenever a variable is chosen for a decision, the theory plugin responsible for its type needs to find a value. While this is a theory-specific choice, there are theory-independent caching heuristics that improve performance in all evaluated theories.

Value Caching [Baseline]. The idea of value cache is to retain the value of a variable when its assignment is undone. When a decision is to be made for a variable, the previously cached value is used, if it is still feasible. The value caching is a generalization of *phase saving* [31] in SAT solving. This approach is based on the idea that solvers tend to revisit similar parts of the search space repeatedly. In MCSat we use the term *value* instead of *phase* to reflect the bigger space of potential assignments. The MCSat search loop's `decide` method, as shown in Fig. 1b, first attempts the previously assigned value (lines 5–6) by calling the appropriate theory plugin. If the cached value is not valid (lines 7–8), the `decide` method uses a new feasible value provided by the theory plugin.

Does the Value Caching Heuristic Provide Performance Benefits? Figure 2 shows plots of Yices2 with and without value caching. They show that Yices2 with value caching solves more benchmarks and is a lot faster than the version without value caching. Clearly, the value caching heuristic seems crucial for performance, in particular for the integer benchmarks.

Target, Best Caching, and Recaching [New Heuristic]. While phase saving has been standard for many years in SAT solving, more recent work [6,10] has indicated that different strategies for phase selection are beneficial. Inspired by the success of these caching strategies and the importance of value caching in the MCSat procedure, we have extended the MCSat search procedure to include two additional caches: *target* and *best*, along with a recaching mechanism.

Similar to the concept in SAT, the target cache stores cached values of variable assignments. However, unlike the value cache where values are updated after each decision, which is frequently, the target cache focuses on maintaining a *promising partial assignment* that does not lead to a conflict after propagation. The target cache is updated when the MCSat core solver discovers a 'more promising assignment'. A (partial) assignment is considered 'more promising' than earlier saved assignments if it assigns more variables/terms than the earlier assignments. The target cache update occurs before a restart (when in a non-conflicting state) and after back-jumping during conflict analysis and lemma learning. The updated MCSat search loop is illustrated in Fig. 3a: line 6 and line 18 execute the target cache update before a restart and after back-jumping, respectively.

When making a decision, the value stored in the target cache takes precedence over the value cache when selecting a value for a variable assignment. If the target cache does not have a variable assignment, then the value from the value cache is chosen. The revised `decide` method is depicted in Fig. 3b: lines 7–8 attempt the value from the target cache first, and lines 9–10 try the value from the value cache if needed.

As the target cache is favored for selecting variable assignments and is updated based on an objective function defined by the number of assigned terms, there is a risk of the target cache trapping the search in a local maximum state. To address this issue, we periodically *recache* both the target cache and the value cache, as also done is modern SAT solvers. Recaching is invoked during the main search loop when the recaching limit is reached, as indicated in lines 9–10 in Fig. 3a. Recaching clears the target cache but makes use of another cache, the *best* cache, to retain the most promising assignments. Similar to the target cache, the best cache is updated when a more promising assignment is

Table 2. Evaluation of different Boolean scaling

Scaling factor	Total (37512) solved	QF_NRA (12154) solved	sat/unsat	QF_NIA (25358) solved	sat/unsat
1	28777	11197	5522/5675	17580	11964/5616
5	28946	11240	5534/5706	17706	12098/5608
10	29039	11280	5541/**5739**	17759	12099/5660
20	**29101**	11290	**5556**/5734	**17811**	**12143/5668**
30	29062	**11293**	5554/**5739**	17769	12119/5650

found: Fig. 4b shows how this is done by tracking the number of assigned terms as `target_depth` and `best_depth` for the target and best caches, respectively. The target cache and the best cache differ at the point of recaching (Fig. 4a): the target cache is cleared at every recaching and the best cache is copied to the value cache at every other recaching.

3.3   Evaluation of New Heuristics

In Table 2, a comparison of Yices2 using hints with different Boolean factors (1, 5, 10, 20, 30) is shown. The table indicates that a Boolean scaling factor of 20 provides the best performance overall (when looking at the QF_NRA and QF_NIA benchmarks in total) among the tested factors.

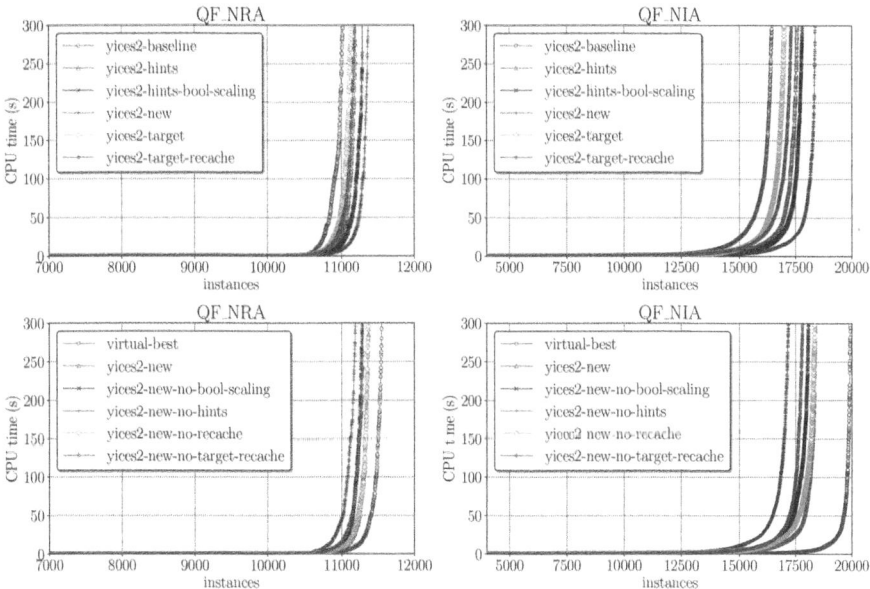

Fig. 5. Evaluation of new heuristics

In Fig. 5, the top row compares the novel heuristics introduced in this work for variable (Boolean scaling, variable hinting) and value selection (target caching and recaching) against the baseline Yices2 (including EVSIDS and value caching). The baseline Yices2 is represented by `yices2-baseline`, with additional features added on top: `yices2-hints` for variable hinting, `yices2-hints-bool-scaling` for hinting with the Boolean scaling factor 20, `yices2-target` for the target cache, `yices2-target-recache` for the target cache with recaching, and `yices2-new` representing the configuration with all techniques.

In the bottom row of Fig. 5, various plots compare `yices2-new` with one heuristic turned off (`yices2-new-no-heuristic` refers to the `yices2-new` configuration without the `heuristic`). Additionally, the virtual best solver for these

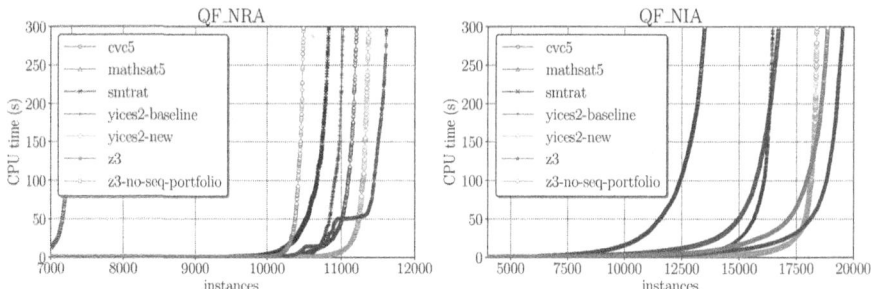

Fig. 6. Solver performance comparison

configurations is plotted as virtutal-best. The plots reveal that all techniques have a positive impact on performance in QF_NIA and QF_NRA. Interestingly, they contribute to solving different benchmarks, as demonstrated by the virtual best solver, especially in the case of QF_NIA.

We have also evaluated, under the same experimental conditions, the performance improvements on the combined theories QF_UFNRA and QF_UFNIA, which add uninterpreted functions. In the former, we can solve all benchmarks; in the latter we improved by almost 15%, solving 677 out of 806 with `yices2-new` compared to `yices2-baseline`.

4   Comparison Against Other SMT Solvers

We have compared our new solver `yices2-new` against the Yices2 [15] baseline `yices2-baseline`, cvc5 [2] (version 1.2.0), `mathsat5` [13] (version 5.6.11), smtrat [14] (version 24.06), and z3 [9,27] (version 4.13.3). We noticed that z3 implements a sequential portfolio approach for nonlinear arithmetic [9] which can clearly be observed in the step-shaped cactus in Fig. 6. Since Yices2 does not (yet) exploit sequential portfolio techniques, we have included in our comparisons a version of z3 with portfolio solving disabled (`z3-no-seq-portfolio`), making it algorithmically much closer, and comparable, to Yices2 MCSat. (The z3 commands used for i) QF_NRA: z3 tactic.default_tactic="(then simplify propagate-values solve-eqs elim-uncnstr simplify qfnra-nlsat)", and ii) QF_NIA: z3 tactic.default_tactic="(then simplify propagate-values solve-eqs elim-uncnstr simplify smt)".) The results are presented in Table 3 and Fig. 6.

When comparing `yices2-baseline` to `yices2-new`, it is evident that the latter is hugely improved, especially on the QF_NIA benchmarks. `yices2-new` can now solve a much larger number of benchmarks in less time than `yices2-baseline`. In comparison to other non-portfolio SMT solvers, `yices2-new` excels in performance on the QF_NRA benchmarks. While slightly behind z3 (both versions) on the QF_NIA benchmarks, `yices2-new` outperforms the other solvers. We believe that by exploring other heuristics in Yices2 MCSat, as well as sequential portfolio techniques, the gap between z3 and `yices-new` can be further reduced.

Table 3. Comparison with other SMT solvers. Solved benchmarks within 5 minutes and 8 GB RAM. Total number of benchmarks in top row.

Solver	QF_NRA (12 154)			QF_NIA (25 358)		
	solved	sat/unsat	time(s)	solved	sat/unsat	time(s)
Yices2-baseline	11 022	5 394/5 628	28 829	16 436	11070/5366	141 928
Yices2-new	**11 370**	**5 626**/5 744	23 462	18 387	**12 774**/5 613	98 871
cvc5	11 207	5 428/**5 779**	36 306	13 484	8 922/4 562	312 345
MathSAT5	7 292	2 742/4 550	23 677	16 689	11 451/5 238	314 851
SMT-RAT	10 828	5 345/5 483	47 833	-	-/-	-
Z3-no-seq-portfolio	10 489	5 453/5 036	18 844	**18 861**	12 364/**6 497**	305 923
Z3	11 612	5 761/5 851	67 633	19 507	12 991/6 516	264 204

5 Conclusion

In this work, we have demonstrated the importance of decision heuristics in the MCSat search procedure. Our empirical results have shown that dynamic variable ordering is crucial for having a performant MCSat solver. Additionally, we have shown that value caching is also vital for the performance of an MCSat solver based on our experiments.

We introduced a theory-guided hinting mechanism that enhances the variable selection and improves value selection techniques through the combination of value and target caches with recaching. Our evaluation indicates that theory-guided hinting provides the most significant performance boost, followed by target caches with recaching, and then Boolean scaling. With these new heuristics integrated, Yices2 is now more efficient and solves more benchmarks than other state-of-the-art solvers.

Our work is inspired by the recent advancements in propositional SAT solving. The positive results of our work suggest the potential for applying well-established SAT heuristics in the MCSat context.

In the future, we would like to conduct a more comprehensive empirical evaluation by including additional theory benchmarks. Moreover, we would explore other SAT heuristics like the VMTF decision heuristic, chronological backtracking, dynamic restart and clause database cleaning strategies based on the literal block distance (LBD) concept.

Acknowledgments. The authors thank Mathias Fleury for interesting insights into SAT solving techniques as well as Laura Kovács and Daniela Kaufmann for valuable feedback. We acknowledge funding from ERC Consolidator Grant ARTIST 101002685, the TU Wien SecInt Doctoral College, the NSF award CCRI-2016597, and from SRI Internal Research And Development funds. Any opinions, findings and conclusions or recommendations expressed in this material are those of the author(s) and do not necessarily reflect the views of the US Government or NSF.

Disclosure of Interests. The authors have no competing interests to declare that are relevant to the content of this article.

References

1. Ábrahám, E., Davenport, J.H., England, M., Kremer, G.: Deciding the consistency of non-linear real arithmetic constraints with a conflict driven search using cylindrical algebraic coverings. J. Log. Algebraic Methods Program. **119**, 100633 (2021)
2. Barbosa, H., et al.: cvc5: A Versatile and Industrial-Strength SMT Solver. Presented at the (2022). https://doi.org/10.1007/978-3-030-99524-9_24
3. Barrett, C., Fontaine, P., Tinelli, C.: The Satisfiability Modulo Theories Library (SMT-LIB) (2016). www.SMT-LIB.org
4. Barrett, C.W., Sebastiani, R., Seshia, S.A., Tinelli, C.: Satisfiability modulo theories. In: Biere, A., Heule, M., van Maaren, H., Walsh, T. (eds.) Handbook of Satisfiability - Second Edition, Frontiers in Artificial Intelligence and Applications, vol. 336, pp. 1267–1329. IOS Press (2021). https://doi.org/10.3233/FAIA201017
5. Biere, A., Faller, T., Fazekas, K., Fleury, M., Froleyks, N., Pollitt, F.: CaDiCaL 2.0. In: International Conference on Computer Aided Verification, pp. 133–152. Springer (2024)
6. Biere, A., Fleury, M.: Chasing target phases. In: Workshop on the Pragmatics of SAT (2020)
7. Biere, A., Fleury, M., Froleyks, N., Heule, M.J.: The SAT museum. In: POS@ SAT, pp. 72–87 (2023)
8. Biere, A., Fröhlich, A.: Evaluating CDCL variable scoring schemes. In: Heule, M., Weaver, S. (eds.) SAT 2015. LNCS, vol. 9340, pp. 405–422. Springer, Cham (2015). https://doi.org/10.1007/978-3-319-24318-4_29
9. Bjørner, N.S., Nachmanson, L.: Arithmetic solving in Z3. In: CAV (1). Lecture Notes in Computer Science, vol. 14681, pp. 26–41. Springer (2024)
10. Cai, S., Zhang, X., Fleury, M., Biere, A.: Better decision heuristics in cdcl through local search and target phases. J. Artif. Intell. Res. **74**, 1515–1563 (2022)
11. Cimatti, A., Griggio, A., Irfan, A., Roveri, M., Sebastiani, R.: Experimenting on solving nonlinear integer arithmetic with incremental linearization. In: Beyersdorff, O., Wintersteiger, C.M. (eds.) SAT 2018. LNCS, vol. 10929, pp. 383–398. Springer, Cham (2018). https://doi.org/10.1007/978-3-319-94144-8_23
12. Cimatti, A., Griggio, A., Irfan, A., Roveri, M., Sebastiani, R.: Incremental linearization for satisfiability and verification modulo nonlinear arithmetic and transcendental functions. ACM Trans. Comput. Log. **19**(3), 19:1–19:52 (2018)
13. Cimatti, A., Griggio, A., Schaafsma, B.J., Sebastiani, R.: The MathSAT5 SMT solver. In: Piterman, N., Smolka, S.A. (eds.) TACAS 2013. LNCS, vol. 7795, pp. 93–107. Springer, Heidelberg (2013). https://doi.org/10.1007/978-3-642-36742-7_7
14. Corzilius, F., Kremer, G., Junges, S., Schupp, S., Ábrahám, E.: SMT-RAT: An Open Source C++ Toolbox for Strategic and Parallel SMT Solving. In: Heule, M., Weaver, S. (eds.) SAT 2015. LNCS, vol. 9340, pp. 360–368. Springer, Cham (2015). https://doi.org/10.1007/978-3-319-24318-4_26
15. Dutertre, B.: Yices 2.2. In: CAV. Lecture Notes in Computer Science, vol. 8559, pp. 737–744. Springer (2014)
16. Dutertre, B.: An empirical evaluation of SAT solvers on bit-vector problems. In: SMT. CEUR Workshop Proceedings, vol. 2854, pp. 15–25. CEUR-WS.org (2020)

17. Eén, N., Sörensson, N.: An extensible SAT-solver. In: International Conference on Theory and Applications of Satisfiability Testing, pp. 502–518. Springer (2003)
18. Fazekas, K., Niemetz, A., Preiner, M., Kirchweger, M., Szeider, S., Biere, A.: Satisfiability modulo user propagators. J. Artif. Intell. Res. **81**, 989–1017 (2024). https://doi.org/10.1613/JAIR.1.16163
19. Graham-Lengrand, S., Jovanovic, D., Dutertre, B.: Solving bitvectors with MCSAT: explanations from bits and pieces. In: Peltier, N., Sofronie-Stokkermans, V. (eds.) Intl. Joint Conf. on Automated Reasoning (IJCAR), Part I. LNCS, vol. 12166, pp. 103–121. Springer (2020). https://doi.org/10.1007/978-3-030-51074-9_7
20. Hader, T., Kaufmann, D., Irfan, A., Graham-Lengrand, S., Kovács, L.: MCSat-based finite field reasoning in the yices2 SMT solver (short paper). In: IJCAR (1). Lecture Notes in Computer Science, vol. 14739, pp. 386–395. Springer (2024)
21. Irfan, A., Graham-Lengrand, S.: Arrays reasoning in MCSat. In: SMT@CAV. CEUR Workshop Proceedings, vol. 3725, pp. 24–35. CEUR-WS.org (2024)
22. Jovanović, D.: Solving nonlinear integer arithmetic with MCSAT. In: Bouajjani, A., Monniaux, D. (eds.) VMCAI 2017. LNCS, vol. 10145, pp. 330–346. Springer, Cham (2017). https://doi.org/10.1007/978-3-319-52234-0_18
23. Jovanovic, D., Barrett, C., de Moura, L.: The design and implementation of the model constructing satisfiability calculus. In: Intl. Conf on Formal Methods in Computer-Aided Design (FMCAD), pp. 173–180. IEEE (2013). https://doi.org/10.1109/FMCAD.2013.7027033
24. Liang, J.H., Ganesh, V., Poupart, P., Czarnecki, K.: Learning rate based branching heuristic for SAT solvers. In: Creignou, N., Le Berre, D. (eds.) SAT 2016. LNCS, vol. 9710, pp. 123–140. Springer, Cham (2016). https://doi.org/10.1007/978-3-319-40970-2_9
25. Moskewicz, M.W., Madigan, C.F., Zhao, Y., Zhang, L., Malik, S.: Chaff: engineering an efficient SAT solver. In: Proceedings of the 38th Annual Design Automation Conference, pp. 530–535 (2001)
26. de Moura, L., Jovanovic, D.: A model-constructing satisfiability calculus. In: Giacobazzi, R., Berdine, J., Mastroeni, I. (eds.) Intl. Conference on Verification, Model Checking, and Abstract Interpretation (VMCAI). LNCS, vol. 7737, pp. 1–12. Springer (2013). https://doi.org/10.1007/978-3-642-35873-9_1
27. de Moura, L., Bjørner, N.: Z3: An Efficient SMT Solver. In: Ramakrishnan, C.R., Rehof, J. (eds.) TACAS 2008. LNCS, vol. 4963, pp. 337–340. Springer, Heidelberg (2008). https://doi.org/10.1007/978-3-540-78800-3_24
28. de Moura, L.M., Bjørner, N.S.: Satisfiability modulo theories: introduction and applications. Commun. ACM **54**(9), 69–77 (2011)
29. Nalbach, J., Kremer, G., Ábrahám, E.: On variable orderings in MCSAT for nonlinear real arithmetic. In: SC-square@ SIAM AG (2019)
30. Nieuwenhuis, R., Oliveras, A., Tinelli, C.: Abstract DPLL and abstract DPLL modulo theories. In: Baader, F., Voronkov, A. (eds.) Intl. Conf. on Logic for Programming, Artificial Intelligence, and Reasoning (LPAR). LNCS, vol. 3452, pp. 36–50. Springer (2004). https://doi.org/10.1007/978-3-540-32275-7_3
31. Pipatsrisawat, K., Darwiche, A.: A lightweight component caching scheme for satisfiability solvers. In: Marques-Silva, J., Sakallah, K.A. (eds.) SAT 2007. LNCS, vol. 4501, pp. 294–299. Springer, Heidelberg (2007). https://doi.org/10.1007/978-3-540-72788-0_28
32. Preiner, M., Schurr, H.J., Barrett, C., Fontaine, P., Niemetz, A., Tinelli, C.: SMT-LIB release 2024 (non-incremental benchmarks), April 2024. https://doi.org/10.5281/zenodo.11061097

33. Reynolds, A., Tinelli, C., Jovanović, D., Barrett, C.: Designing theory solvers with extensions. In: Dixon, C., Finger, M. (eds.) FroCoS 2017. LNCS (LNAI), vol. 10483, pp. 22–40. Springer, Cham (2017). https://doi.org/10.1007/978-3-319-66167-4_2
34. Ryan, L.: Efficient algorithms for clause-learning SAT solvers (2004)

The VAMPIRE Diary

Filip Bártek[1], Ahmed Bhayat[4], Robin Coutelier[3], Márton Hajdu[3],
Matthias Hetzenberger[3], Petra Hozzová[1], Laura Kovács[3(✉)],
Jakob Rath[3], Michael Rawson[5(✉)], Giles Reger[4], Martin Suda[1(✉)],
Johannes Schoisswohl[3], and Andrei Voronkov[2,4(✉)]

[1] Czech Technical University in Prague, Prague, Czech Republic
martin.suda@cvut.cz
[2] EasyChair, Manchester, UK
andrei@voronkov.com
[3] TU Wien, Vienna, Austria
laura.kovacs@tuwien.ac.at
[4] University of Manchester, Manchester, UK
[5] University of Southampton, Southampton, UK
michael@rawsons.uk

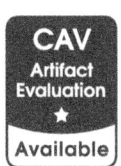

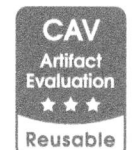

Abstract. During the past decade of continuous development, the theorem prover VAMPIRE has become an automated solver for the combined theories of commonly-used data structures. VAMPIRE now supports arithmetic, induction, and higher-order logic. These advances have been made to meet the demands of software verification, enabling VAMPIRE to effectively complement SAT/SMT solvers and aid proof assistants. We explain how best to use VAMPIRE in practice and review the main changes VAMPIRE has undergone since its last tool presentation, focusing on the engineering principles and design choices we made during this process.

1 Introduction

Automated reasoning has become indispensable for certifying the correctness of software systems and services [54], from Boolean satisfiability (SAT) through satisfiability modulo theories (SMT) to automated theorem proving (ATP) in first-order and higher-order logic. This tool paper describes major developments in saturation-based theorem proving, bringing our VAMPIRE system to bear on modern software certification. VAMPIRE now reasons efficiently in a polymorphic first-order logic with theories, induction and quantifiers, which is realized through (i) combining satisfiability solving with first-order theorem proving using the AVATAR framework [47,67]; (ii) native support for quantified reasoning with mixed arithmetic using extensions of superposition with quantifier elimination [37,55]; and (iii) embedding second-order induction schemata as inference rules in proof search [22,40]. Furthermore, (iv) VAMPIRE has evolved to support higher-order logic [9], program synthesis [27], and finding counterexamples [49].

Our advances in saturation-based reasoning *proved to make a difference.* VAMPIRE outperforms or complements many other state-of-the-art reasoners,

© The Author(s) 2025
R. Piskac and Z. Rakamarić (Eds.): CAV 2025, LNCS 15933, pp. 57–71, 2025.
https://doi.org/10.1007/978-3-031-98682-6_4

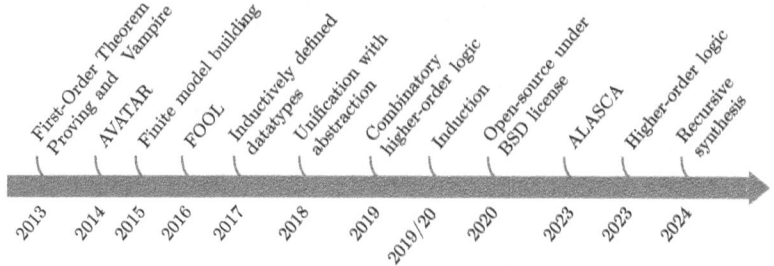

Fig. 1. VAMPIRE timeline since our 2013 tutorial tool paper [41].

including leading SMT solvers and inductive theorem provers. For example, in CASC-J12, the most recent world championship in theorem proving, VAMPIRE proved more problems than any other system in every competition division [63]. We believe that the increasing demand on efficient reasoning with quantifiers, theories and induction turns VAMPIRE into a powerful solver in the automation of mathematics [17], verification of logic programs [42], ensuring system security [32], and many other areas.

This paper details the aforementioned advances in VAMPIRE. It aims to explain how to use VAMPIRE (Sect. 2) and to give an overview of the reasoning techniques used under the hood in order to allow for reasoning in more expressive logics (Sect. 4) and more efficient reasoning in general (Sect. 5). With these new features, a new permissive license, and unprecedented performance, we believe that a tool demonstration after more than a decade of continuous development is overdue. Our diary of improvements since our 2013 tutorial paper demonstration [41] is summarized in Fig. 1. The present paper serves as a self-contained tool demonstration, describing the many new features VAMPIRE supports and users can exploit. Our paper contains typical usage guidance, properly instructing readers/users interested in VAMPIRE. For details on VAMPIRE's calculus, inferences processes and proof search algorithms we refer to [41].

2   User Guide

VAMPIRE ingests an input problem in either the TPTP [62] or SMT-LIB 2 [3] formats. It then attempts to show unsatisfiability[1] of the input by deriving falsum through application of its logical calculus. If it succeeds, VAMPIRE halts and prints a step-by-step refutation. In some cases VAMPIRE can also show satisfiability. This happens either by finding a finite model (Sect. 5.2) or by *saturation*: detecting that a refutation cannot be derived with a complete calculus.

Licensing. VAMPIRE is now open-source and available online[2] under a 3-clause BSD license. This has completely changed the Vampire team dynamics and coding culture: the development team grew, code became fully shared, and external

---

[1] TPTP allows the user to supply a `conjecture`: this formula is automatically negated.
[2] https://github.com/vprover/vampire/

contributors can improve VAMPIRE. The new license has increased the user base of Vampire in teaching, research and development.

VAMPIRE uses external code for specific tasks, including the MINISAT [18] and CADICAL [11] SAT solvers, the Z3 SMT solver [16] (optional), the VIRAS quantifier elimination routine [55], and `mini-gmp` [20] for arbitrary-precision arithmetic.

Installation. VAMPIRE is written in C++17 [30] and uses the CMake [35] build system. Since the previous tool demonstration over a decade ago [41], a series of patches have improved portability and VAMPIRE now runs on a variety of modern architectures and UNIX-like operating systems. We provide pre-compiled binaries for UNIX-like systems, and it is generally straightforward to compile VAMPIRE from source on such systems. Support for other operating systems is more experimental, but users report success with compatibility layers such as the Windows Subsystem for Linux [43], Cygwin [45], or Cosmopolitan Libc [66].

Quick Start. It is possible, but *usually undesirable*, to invoke VAMPIRE directly on an input file. This will cause it to run a single proof attempt, which will likely not be well-suited to the input. Instead, users should *schedule* an execution of a *portfolio* of many different *strategies*, which is achieved with the invocation

```
vampire --mode portfolio --schedule <schedule> --cores 0 <problem>
```

where `<problem>` is the input problem, `--cores 0` instructs VAMPIRE to use all available CPU cores, and `<schedule>` should be selected from VAMPIRE's list of built-in schedules (Sect. 5.4), depending on the input.

Understanding the Output. VAMPIRE prints status messages as new strategies are launched or old strategies fail, until either a strategy succeeds or the time limit is reached. When a strategy succeeds, by default VAMPIRE reports an SZS status [64] and then, assuming that the input is unsatisfiable, a human-readable proof. The most common SZS statuses VAMPIRE reports are:

`Satisfiable`: input does not contain a conjecture and is satisfiable
`Unsatisfiable`: input does not contain a conjecture and is unsatisfiable
`CounterSatisfiable`: conjecture present, after negation the input is satisfiable
`Theorem`: conjecture present, after negation the input is unsatisfiable
`ContradictoryAxioms`: conjecture present, but axioms alone are unsatisfiable

Controlling Output. VAMPIRE by default uses the SZS standards for output and reports a compact, human-readable proof. The VAMPIRE output can be changed with the *output mode* (`-om`) and *proof format* (`-p`) flags. For example, `-om smtcomp` produces a very terse output suitable for SMT-COMP [4], while `-p tptp` produces machine-readable TSTP [65] proofs. Some more exotic formats such as LaTeX (`--latex_output`) or Dedukti [1] are under development.

Setting Resource Limits. VAMPIRE can be configured to limit the amount of time (`-t <seconds>`), memory (`-m <MB>`), and on recent Linux systems the

number of userspace instructions retired (`-i <MI>`[3]). The value 0 means no limit.
Exploring Options. VAMPIRE has many, many options. A complete list can be generated with `--show_options on`, and a particular flag can be examined with `--explain`, e.g. `--explain output_mode`. Most options only affect a single strategy's behavior, but some affect the global behavior of VAMPIRE, such as the proof format or the time limit. Single strategy options are not usually controlled by the user but automatically set by portfolio schedules (more on this in Sect. 5.4).

2.1 Looking Under the Hood

It is sometimes useful for users to inspect the internal state of VAMPIRE, such as when debugging or optimizing an encoding. Here we sketch the internal mechanisms of VAMPIRE and explain how to inspect them during operation.

VAMPIRE works in two phases. First, the input is parsed, the conjecture — if present — is negated, and the resulting formulas are converted to clause normal form (CNF) and preprocessed. Then VAMPIRE tries to derive the empty clause (witnessing contradiction) in order to refute the CNF of the input problem. New clauses are derived from old by applying generating inferences in VAMPIRE's proof calculus, *superposition* [41]. The search space is partitioned into three sets of clauses: *new* clauses have been freshly derived; *passive* clauses survived VAMPIRE's simplification efforts but have not yet participated in inference, and *active* clauses have themselves participated in inferences generating new clauses. VAMPIRE allows inspection of these processes. To show the clauses resulting from an input, use

```
vampire --mode clausify <problem>
```

which causes VAMPIRE to stop after preprocessing < problem > and print the resulting CNF. The CNF may be surprising at times as VAMPIRE's preprocessing will happily eliminate parts of the input that it can detect will not help reaching a refutation. To inspect the progress of the preprocessing pipeline users may `--show_preprocessing on`. Once proof search begins, `--show_new on` displays new clauses (analogously, `show_passive` and `show_active`). Not all new clauses will make it to *passive*: use `--show_reductions on` to see the simplifications that VAMPIRE applies.

3 Demonstration: Arithmetic and Induction

Consider the proposition "the sum of two lists of real numbers is equal to the sum of their concatenation". While clearly true, a formal proof requires reasoning about arithmetic, algebraic datatypes, recursive functions, polymorphism, and at least one inductive step. When given the natural first-order formalization of the

---

[3] Millions of instructions [60]. Instruction limits tend to more stable than time limits across hardware and operating system conditions.

problem (Fig. 2) encoded into version 2.7 of SMT-LIB, VAMPIRE is able to find a proof immediately. We show a distilled version of the proof in mathematical notation in Fig. 3.

$$\frac{\begin{array}{c} \forall x : \mathbb{R}.\ \forall xs : [\mathbb{R}]. \\ \Lambda\alpha.\ \forall ys : [\alpha]. \\ \Lambda\alpha.\ \forall x : \alpha.\ \forall xs, ys : [\alpha]. \end{array} \quad \begin{array}{c} \mathrm{sum}(\epsilon) = 0 \\ \mathrm{sum}(x \,\#\, xs) = x + \mathrm{sum}(xs) \\ \epsilon \,+\!\!+\, ys = ys \\ (x \,\#\, xs) \,+\!\!+\, ys = x \,\#\, (xs \,+\!\!+\, ys) \end{array}}{\forall xs, ys : [\mathbb{R}].\ \mathrm{sum}(xs) + \mathrm{sum}(ys) = \mathrm{sum}(xs \,+\!\!+\, ys)}$$

Fig. 2. Motivating example in polymorphic first-order logic with uninterpreted functions sum : $[\mathbb{R}] \to \mathbb{R}$, $+\!\!+ : \Lambda\alpha.\ [\alpha] \times [\alpha] \to [\alpha]$, algebraic datatypes and real arithmetic.

The proof displays some new features of VAMPIRE, in particular the use of structural induction (Sect. 4.2) and superposition-based arithmetic reasoning via the ALASCA calculus (Sect. 4.1). These features are key to VAMPIRE's success on this problem. The need for our unique blend of induction, arithmetic and polymorphism is supported by the fact that other solvers such as CVC5 [2] or Z3 [16] cannot, to the best of our knowledge, yet process or prove problems such as this one.

4 New Capabilities

Here we present the most significant new capabilities implemented in VAMPIRE since 2013 [41]. Improvements to existing capabilities are in Sect. 5.

4.1 Arithmetic Reasoning

Reasoning about arithmetic in the presence of quantifiers is highly desirable. To this end, VAMPIRE implements the Abstracting Linear Arithmetic Superposition Calculus (ALASCA) [37] that combines ideas like inequality chaining, unification with abstraction [51], and rewriting modulo linear arithmetic. Equality reasoning in ALASCA can be seen as applying the superposition calculus modulo the axioms of linear arithmetic. For example, take step 18 of Fig. 3. There, the literal $0 = x + \mathrm{sum}(y) - \mathrm{sum}(x \,\#\, y)$ is used to perform a rewrite $\mathrm{sum}(x \,\#\, y) \rightsquigarrow x + \mathrm{sum}(y)$ instead of a rewrite $x + \mathrm{sum}(y) - \mathrm{sum}(x \,\#\, y) \rightsquigarrow 0$, which would be the only permissible rewrite in standard superposition. In addition, ALASCA uses inequality chaining and dedicated factoring rules to deal with inequalities, and combines variable elimination rules with unification with abstraction to efficiently perform unification, modulo linear arithmetic.

Non-linear Reasoning. ALASCA itself supports reasoning in linear real arithmetic with uninterpreted functions and quantifiers. Nonlinear problems are also supported by treating nonlinear multiplications as uninterpreted functions, automatically adding the relevant axiomatization.

1. $0 = \text{sum}(\epsilon)$ assumption 1 (cnf)
2. $0 = x + \text{sum}(y) - \text{sum}(x \,\#\, y)$ assumption 2 (cnf)
3. $\epsilon \!+\!\!+\, x = x$ assumption 3 (cnf)
4. $y \,\#\, (z \!+\!\!+\, x) = (y \,\#\, z) \!+\!\!+\, x$ assumption 4 (cnf)
5. $0 \neq \text{sum}(\sigma_1) + \text{sum}(\sigma_0) - \text{sum}(\sigma_1 \!+\!\!+\, \sigma_0)$ conjecture (cnf)
6. $0 \neq \text{sum}(\sigma_3 \,\#\, \sigma_4) + \text{sum}(\sigma_0) - \text{sum}((\sigma_3 \,\#\, \sigma_4) \!+\!\!+\, \sigma_0)$ structural induction 5
    $\lor\; 0 \neq \text{sum}(\epsilon) + \text{sum}(\sigma_0) - \text{sum}(\epsilon \!+\!\!+\, \sigma_0)$
7. $0 = \text{sum}(\sigma_4) + \text{sum}(\sigma_0) - \text{sum}(\sigma_4 \!+\!\!+\, \sigma_0)$ structural induction 5
    $\lor\; 0 \neq \text{sum}(\epsilon) + \text{sum}(\sigma_0) - \text{sum}(\epsilon \!+\!\!+\, \sigma_0)$
8. $0 \neq \text{sum}(\sigma_0) - \text{sum}(\sigma_3 \,\#\, (\sigma_4 \!+\!\!+\, \sigma_0)) + \text{sum}(\sigma_3 \,\#\, \sigma_4)$ forward demodulation 6,4
    $\lor\; 0 \neq \text{sum}(\sigma_0) + \text{sum}(\epsilon) - \text{sum}(\epsilon \!+\!\!+\, \sigma_0)$
9. $0 \neq \text{sum}(\sigma_0) + \text{sum}(\epsilon) - \text{sum}(\sigma_0)$ forward demodulation 7,3
    $\lor\; 0 = \text{sum}(\sigma_0) - \text{sum}(\sigma_4 \!+\!\!+\, \sigma_0) + \text{sum}(\sigma_4)$
10. $0 \neq \text{sum}(\epsilon)$ ALASCA normalization 9
    $\lor\; 0 = \text{sum}(\sigma_0) - \text{sum}(\sigma_4 \!+\!\!+\, \sigma_0) + \text{sum}(\sigma_4)$
11. $0 \neq \text{sum}(\sigma_0) + \text{sum}(\epsilon) - \text{sum}(\sigma_0)$ forward demodulation 8,3
    $\lor\; 0 \neq \text{sum}(\sigma_0) + \text{sum}(\sigma_3 \,\#\, \sigma_4) - \text{sum}(\sigma_3 \,\#\, (\sigma_4 \!+\!\!+\, \sigma_0))$
12. $0 \neq \text{sum}(\epsilon)$ ALASCA normalization 11
    $\lor\; 0 \neq \text{sum}(\sigma_0) + \text{sum}(\sigma_3 \,\#\, \sigma_4) - \text{sum}(\sigma_3 \,\#\, (\sigma_4 \!+\!\!+\, \sigma_0))$
13. $0 = \text{sum}(\sigma_0) - \text{sum}(\sigma_4 \!+\!\!+\, \sigma_0) + \text{sum}(\sigma_4)$ subsumption resolution 10,1
14. $0 \neq \text{sum}(\sigma_0) + \text{sum}(\sigma_3 \,\#\, \sigma_4) - \text{sum}(\sigma_3 \,\#\, (\sigma_4 \!+\!\!+\, \sigma_0))$ subsumption resolution 12,1
15. $0 \neq \text{sum}(\sigma_0) + \text{sum}(\sigma_3 \,\#\, \sigma_4) - (\sigma_3 + \text{sum}(\sigma_4 \!+\!\!+\, \sigma_0))$ ALASCA superposition 2,14
16. $0 \neq \text{sum}(\sigma_0) - \sigma_3 + \text{sum}(\sigma_3 \,\#\, \sigma_4) - (\text{sum}(\sigma_0) + \text{sum}(\sigma_4))$ ALASCA superposition 13,15
17. $0 \neq \sigma_3 - \text{sum}(\sigma_3 \,\#\, \sigma_4) + \text{sum}(\sigma_4)$ ALASCA normalization 16
18. $0 \neq \sigma_3 - (\sigma_3 + \text{sum}(\sigma_4)) + \text{sum}(\sigma_4)$ ALASCA superposition 2,17
19. $\square$ ALASCA normalization 18

Fig. 3. VAMPIRE's proof output of the problem from Fig. 2 in mathematical notation. The symbols σ_i are fresh Skolem constants. The induction steps are detailed in Sect. 4.2.

Mixed Integer-Real Arithmetic. While the original ALASCA work is limited to real arithmetic, our current implementation in VAMPIRE lifts these restrictions. We support reasoning in mixed integer-real arithmetic, using a tailored quantifier-elimination procedure [55], as well as various new inference rules[4] to handle the combination of mixed arithmetic and uninterpreted functions by natively supporting the rounding (floor) function.

Simplifications and Generalizations. In addition to ALASCA, VAMPIRE also provides lightweight arithmetic reasoning [48]. This includes arithmetic subterm generalization rules that complement ALASCA reasoning, and other simplification rules entailed by ALASCA. Although these simplification rules are not as widely applicable as ALASCA, they provide for more lightweight and therefore efficient arithmetic reasoning, sufficient for many practical problems. The generalization rules include transformations like turning $\forall x, y : \mathbb{R}.\ P(3x + y)$ into the equivalent clause $\forall x : \mathbb{R}.\ P(x)$.

Integrating SMT Solvers. VAMPIRE sometimes hands off *ground*, that is quantifier-free, arithmetic reasoning to the Z3 SMT solver [16]. This is done

---

[4] The work on this inference system has not been published yet.

either by invoking AVATAR modulo theories [47] (see Sect. 5.2) or by *theory instantiation* [51]. Theory instantiation uses an SMT solver to find possible instantiations of clauses based on their purely arithmetical literals. To illustrate, consider the clause $\forall x : \mathbb{Z}.\ P(x) \vee 0 > 3x \vee x \geq 1$. The SMT solver is queried for a model satisfying $\neg(0 > 3x \vee x \geq 1)$, which is only the case for $x = 0$. The clause is instantiated with $\{x \mapsto 0\}$ and simplified to $P(0)$. Such integration of SMT solvers enables using state-of-the-art developments in SMT and is particularly beneficial for problem areas such as non-linear reasoning, for which VAMPIRE does not yet have dedicated calculi.

4.2   Inductive Reasoning

VAMPIRE supports inductive reasoning [40] over literals with up to one free variable.[5] It applies induction by generating theory lemmas, triggered by deriving an eligible induction goal. VAMPIRE supports structural induction over inductively-defined datatypes [52], induction over bounded intervals of integers [29], and well-founded induction principles generated from recursive function definitions [26]. Immediately after VAMPIRE generates the induction lemmas, it uses them to resolve their corresponding goals.

A distinctive feature of VAMPIRE is that it seamlessly interleaves induction with other inferences, efficiently handling hundreds of thousands of induction formulas. This makes it possible to use more explosive lemma generation techniques essential for solving some inductive problems. To synthesize lemmas, VAMPIRE can generalize over terms and term occurrences [23] or over multiple literals and clauses [24], use function definitions [26] and perform general rewriting [25].

Let us highlight some key steps of the automated induction in VAMPIRE using the proof from Fig. 3. First, when VAMPIRE sees clause 5, it detects that induction might be in order, as clause 5 corresponds to a universally-quantified goal using an inductively-defined datatype. Therefore, VAMPIRE uses clause 5 to instantiate the structural induction axiom for lists,

$$L[\epsilon] \wedge \forall x : \alpha, y : [\alpha].(L[y] \rightarrow L[x \# y]) \rightarrow \forall z : [\alpha].L[z],$$

by setting $\alpha := \mathbb{R}$ and $L[t] := 0 = \mathrm{sum}(t) + \mathrm{sum}(\sigma_0) - \mathrm{sum}(t + \sigma_0)$. Note that $L[\sigma_1]$ is set to be complementary to the literal from clause 5.

The instantiated axiom concludes that $L[z]$ holds for any $z : [\mathbb{R}]$, while clause 5 expresses that $L[\sigma_1]$ does not hold. To use this, VAMPIRE converts the axiom into CNF, obtaining clauses $\neg L[\epsilon] \vee L[\sigma_4] \vee L[z]$ and $\neg L[\epsilon] \vee \neg L[\sigma_3 \# \sigma_4] \vee L[z]$, where σ_3, σ_4 are Skolem constants corresponding to x and y, respectively. These clauses together express that either the antecedent of the axiom does not hold (the base case $L[\epsilon]$ does not hold, or for some σ_3, σ_4 we have $L[\sigma_4]$ but not $L[\sigma_3 \# \sigma_4]$), or the conclusion that $L[z]$ is true for any z must hold. Then VAMPIRE applies binary resolution on these two clauses with clause 5, resolving

---

[5] This covers the cases of a universally-quantified conjecture, and a conjecture with any number of universally-quantified variables and one existentially-quantified variable.

away $L[z]$, and deriving clauses 6 and 7. Clauses 6 and 7 are exactly $\neg L[\epsilon] \vee L[\sigma_4]$ and $\neg L[\epsilon] \vee \neg L[\sigma_3 \# \sigma_4]$, spelled out in full in Fig. 3. The rest of the proof then covers the refutation of these two clauses.

4.3   Polymorphic Logic

VAMPIRE now supports rank-1 polymorphic types [8] in the tradition of Standard ML [44]. This represents a trade-off between expressivity and ease of implementation. Note that VAMPIRE does *not* presently implement a sort inference routine and all sorts in non-variable terms must be explicitly given as sort arguments [12], which may themselves be variables. For example, the axiom $\text{sum}(\epsilon) = 0$ is actually represented as `sum(nil($real)) = 0`, and $\epsilon \mathbin{+\!\!+} ys = ys$ as `concat(A, nil(A), Ys) = Ys`. The original motivation for introducing polymorphic logic was supporting combinatory higher-order logic [7], but it has also proved useful for supporting polymorphic theories such as arrays, and for verifying programs that use parametric polymorphism.

4.4   Beyond First-Order Logic

VAMPIRE supports extensions of first-order logic useful for software analysis and verification. In particular, VAMPIRE implements FOOL [38], a conservative extension of many-sorted first-order logic with *if-then-else* and *let-in* expressions, which can be used to capture the next-state relation of loop-free programs [39]. As such, VAMPIRE also supports first-class *Boolean sorts*, by encoding the axiom $\forall x : o. \ x = 0 \vee x = 1$ as a new inference rule. The rule exploits the two-element domain property of the Boolean sort without blowing up proof search.

Higher-Order Logic. In addition, a branch of VAMPIRE [6]implements a superposition-based calculus tailored for higher-order logic [10], while still using the general saturation framework from first-order logic. As higher-order unification is undecidable, our implementation bypasses eager unification by performing bounded-depth unification and introducing constraints for remaining unification terms. This technique of constraint introduction has also been used in pure first-order reasoning as delayed unification [9] and in arithmetic reasoning as unification with abstraction [6,37].

4.5   Synthesis

We further utilize VAMPIRE's powerful proving capabilities to extend it to a program synthesizer [27,28]. VAMPIRE works with a relational input-output specification expressed in first-order logic, capturing "for all inputs x there exists an output y such that a given relation between x and y holds". In parallel to proving this conjecture, VAMPIRE constructs a program which computes the value of y for any given value of x. To switch on synthesis mode, use `-qa synthesis`.[7]

---

[6] https://github.com/vprover/vampire/tree/hol

[7] While synthesis of recursion-free programs is available in the mainline VAMPIRE, synthesis of recursive programs is currently in the branch `synthesis-recursive`.

5   Making It Work

Taking the above extensions into account, VAMPIRE must now prove theorems in a substantially richer logic with a much greater number of possible inferences. We now describe improvements to VAMPIRE's core that we consider most important for meeting this challenge and maintaining good performance in practice. This adds to the observations of our previous tutorial paper [41], which remain valid. We hope to provide useful information here for those readers who develop their own reasoning systems.

5.1   Preprocessing

Computing normal forms and preprocessing remain of vital importance: the right normal form can eliminate much search space or drastically shorten the required proof. To this end VAMPIRE has grown a new top-down clausal normal form routine [50], lifted the *blocked clause elimination* technique [34] from SAT [31], and adapted a highly effective goal-oriented rewriting technique from Twee [57]. As a general rule of thumb, preprocessing techniques have linear-time complexity, and avoid recursion to prevent stack overflow on large inputs.

5.2   Integrating SAT and SMT

One of the tricks for efficiently tackling real-life problems in rich formalisms such as first-order logic with theories is to look for sub-problems in simpler logics and offload them to dedicated tools. In this spirit, VAMPIRE implements the AVATAR architecture for clause splitting [67], which allows a prover to delegate the "propositional essence" of the given problem to a SAT solver. In AVATAR modulo theories [47], VAMPIRE uses a finer abstraction[8] and delegates ground *theory* sub-problems to an SMT solver.

SAT solving is also applied within VAMPIRE to find counterexamples to false conjectures. VAMPIRE now provides a MACE-style finite model building mode, using a translation to SAT [14,49]. This is often a useful complement to theorem-proving modes (provided that a small counter-model exists), which helps terminate futile searches early and delivers useful insights in the form of bug traces.

5.3   Redundancy and Proof Search

Redundancy elimination is key to efficient proof search. Intuitively, a clause is redundant if it is a logical consequence of smaller clauses from the search space: checking whether a first-order clause is redundant is therefore undecidable in general. VAMPIRE implements cheap conditions for detecting some cases of redundancy. The central technique used to implement these checks efficiently is *term indexing* [46] and here in particular *substitution trees* [19] and *code trees* [53].

---

[8] We remark that quantifiers are always handled natively by VAMPIRE.

Code trees are used for rewriting clauses by unit equalities [25, 26] and eliminating duplicate clauses, while substitution trees are used for other inferences. To efficiently solve term ordering constraints in redundancy elimination, VAMPIRE uses *term ordering diagrams*, which offer runtime-specialized implementations of simplification orderings [21]. Finally, VAMPIRE also uses SAT solving to check some redundancy conditions that can be modeled as at-most-one ground constraints over the Boolean structure of clause sets [15].

5.4   A Sea of Options, Strategies, and Schedules

By *strategy* we mean a particular configuration of VAMPIRE's option values. Since the behavior of VAMPIRE is controlled by more than 200 options, the number of available strategies is vast. Although expert users may sometimes have an idea of which options could be well suited to tackle a problem, the prover's behavior tends to be so chaotic [60] that even expert hunches often fail. For this reason, VAMPIRE provides *schedules* of pre-selected strategies executed sequentially, possibly adapting to the given problem's features.

Creating powerful schedules is a challenging problem. Since 2010, VAMPIRE has employed a dedicated support tool *Spider* [68] to construct schedules from a set of training problems. Spider trials random strategies to solve as many training problems as possible and eventually selects those strategies that *complement* each other particularly well and lead to a schedule with good coverage and a short overall runtime. Techniques have recently been developed to encourage the generalization of the constructed schedule to unseen problems [5].

Actively maintained schedules include `casc` and `casc_sat`, for general first-order theorem proving and disproving, resp., referring to the famous championship [61]. Similarly, `smtcomp` has its origin in another competition [70] and is optimized to work well on problems requiring theory reasoning. The higher-order branch (Sect. 4.4) provides schedules for reasoning in higher-order logic and the *Sledgehammer* [17] use-case. Finally, there is also `induction` and more.[9]

5.5   Branches

Some extensions to VAMPIRE would have violent and extensive impact on the code base. This is true of VAMPIRE's higher-order logic (HOL), for example. Integrating the HOL extension into VAMPIRE would be a significant amount of work and impose a burden on all VAMPIRE developers: but we would like it to continue, as it is a world-leading system for higher-order logic. The way we are currently dealing with this tension is by keeping this kind of feature on `git` branches, which are periodically synchronised with mainline VAMPIRE. When a branch is widely-used enough, stable, and has a clear path to be integrated cleanly with mainline VAMPIRE, we may consider merging it: this has happened in the past with rank-1 polymorphism and a previous approach to HOL [7].

---

[9] Use `--explain_option schedule` to list schedules available from your VAMPIRE.

6   Related Work and Conclusion

We have explained how best to use VAMPIRE, discussed new features of VAMPIRE that better align saturation-based first-order theorem proving with software verification, and described engineering required to make it work in practice.

As a first-order theorem prover with support for theories, induction and higher-order logic, VAMPIRE has been influenced by, competes with, and might be variously compared to: SMT solvers such as cvc5 [2] or Z3 [16]; first-order ATPs such as E [56], SPASS [71], iProver [36], or Twee [57]; inductive theorem provers such as ACL2 [33], HipSpec [13], or Zeno [58]; and higher-order ATPs such as Zipperposition [69] or Leo-III [59]. VAMPIRE distinguishes itself with its native support for quantifiers combined with calculus extensions to reason about theories, induction and higher-order logic, all tied together by highly-efficient adaptive data structures and algorithms. Naturally, VAMPIRE integrates SAT and SMT solving for ground reasoning tasks.

This paper overviewed the main reasoning engines and practices VAMPIRE offers in order to assist users in understanding the many ways VAMPIRE can be integrated in other technologies. The system is under continuous development, with new applications towards proof checking and extracting system code from formal proofs. Further advances in creating tailored VAMPIRE proof schedules for proof assistants, for example in Isabelle's *Sledgehammer* [17], are also under active development.

Acknowledgements. We would like to thank all users and prior developers who contributed to VAMPIRE. We acknowledge the valuable VAMPIRE contributions made by Daneshvar Amrollahi, Ioan Dragan, Bernhard Gleiss, Bernhard Kragl, Kryštof Hoder, Evgenii Kotelnikov, Alexandre Riazanov, Martin Riener, Simon Robillard, Boris Shminke, and Eva Maria Wagner.

This research was funded in whole or in part by the ERC Consolidator Grant ARTIST 101002685, the ERC Proof of Concept Grant LEARN 101213411, the TU Wien Doctoral College SecInt, the FWF SpyCoDe Grant 10.55776/F85, the WWTF grant [ForSmart Grant ID: 10.47379/ICT22007], and the Amazon Research Award 2023 QuAT. Martin Suda was supported by the project CORESENSE no. 101070254 under the Horizon Europe programme and by the Czech Ministry of Education, Youth and Sports under the ERC CZ project POSTMAN no. LL1902. Petra Hozzová was supported by the European Union under the project ROBOPROX (reg. no. CZ.02.01.01/00/22_008/0004590).

Disclosure of Interests. The authors have no competing interests to declare that are relevant to the content of this article.

References

1. Assaf, A., et al.: Dedukti: a Logical Framework based on the $\lambda\Pi$-Calculus Modulo Theory. CoRR abs/ arXiv: 2311.07185 (2023)
2. Barbosa, H., et al.: cvc5: a versatile and industrial-strength SMT solver. In: TACAS, pp. 415–442 (2022)
3. Barrett, C., Fontaine, P., Tinelli, C.: The Satisfiability Modulo Theories Library (SMT-LIB). www.SMT-LIB.org (2016)
4. Barrett, C., de Moura, L., Stump, A.: SMT-COMP: satisfiability modulo theories competition. In: CAV, pp. 20–23 (2005)
5. Bártek, F., Chvalovský, K., Suda, M.: Regularization in Spider-style strategy discovery and schedule construction. In: IJCAR, pp. 194–213 (2024)
6. Bhayat, A., Korovin, K., Kovács, L., Schoisswohl, J.: Refining unification with abstraction. In: LPAR, pp. 36–47 (2023)
7. Bhayat, A., Reger, G.: A combinator-based superposition calculus for higher-order logic. In: IJCAR, pp. 278–296 (2020)
8. Bhayat, A., Reger, G.: A polymorphic VAMPIRE (short paper). In: IJCAR, pp. 361–368 (2020)
9. Bhayat, A., Schoisswohl, J., Rawson, M.: Superposition with delayed unification. In: CADE, pp. 23–40 (2023)
10. Bhayat, A., Suda, M.: A higher-order VAMPIRE (short paper). In: IJCAR, pp. 75–85 (2024)
11. Biere, A., Faller, T., Fazekas, K., Fleury, M., Froleyks, N., Pollitt, F.: Cadical 2.0. In: CAV, pp. 133–152 (2024). https://doi.org/10.1007/978-3-031-65627-9_7
12. Blanchette, J.C., Paskevich, A.: TFF1: The TPTP typed first-order form with rank-1 polymorphism. In: CADE, pp. 414–420 (2013)
13. Claessen, K., Johansson, M., Rosén, D., Smallbone, N.: Automating inductive proofs using theory exploration. In: CADE (2013)
14. Claessen, K., Sörensson, N.: New Techniques that Improve MACE-style Model Finding. In: WS on Model Computation - Principles, Algorithms and Applications (2003)
15. Coutelier, R., Rath, J., Rawson, M., Biere, A., Kovács, L.: SAT solving for variants of first-order subsumption. Formal Methods Syst. Design (2024)
16. De Moura, L., Bjørner, N.: Z3: An efficient SMT solver. In: TACAS, pp. 337–340 (2008)
17. Desharnais, M., Vukmirović, P., Blanchette, J., Wenzel, M.: Seventeen provers under the hammer. In: ITP, pp. pp. 8:1–8:18 (2022)
18. Eén, N., Sörensson, N.: An extensible SAT-solver. In: SAT, pp. 502–518 (2003)
19. Graf, P.: Substitution tree indexing. In: RTA, pp. 117–131 (1995)
20. Granlund, T.: The GNU Multiple Precision Arithmetic Library (2023). https://gmplib.org/gmp-man-6.3.0.pdf
21. Hajdu, M., Coutelier, R., Kovács, L., Voronkov, A.: Term ordering diagrams. In: CADE (2025), to appear
22. Hajdu, M., Hozzová, P., Kovács, L., Reger, G., Voronkov, A.: Getting Saturated with Induction. In: Principles of Systems Design, pp. 306–322 (2022)
23. Hajdu, M., Hozzová, P., Kovács, L., Schoisswohl, J., Voronkov, A.: Induction with generalization in superposition reasoning. In: CICM, pp. 123–137 (2020)
24. Hajdu, M., Kovacs, L., Rawson, M., Voronkov, A.: The VAMPIRE Approach to Induction. EasyChair Preprint no. 9217 (EasyChair, 2022)

25. Hajdu, M., Kovács, L., Rawson, M.: Rewriting and inductive reasoning. In: LPAR, pp. 278–294 (2024)
26. Hajdu, M., Hozzová, P., Kovács, L., Voronkov, A.: Induction with recursive definitions in superposition. In: FMCAD, pp. 1–10 (2021)
27. Hozzová, P., Amrollahi, D., Hajdu, M., Kovács, L., Voronkov, A., Wagner, E.M.: Synthesis of recursive programs in saturation. In: IJCAR, pp. 154–171 (2024)
28. Hozzová, P., Kovács, L., Norman, C., Voronkov, A.: Program synthesis in saturation. In: CADE, pp. 307–324 (2023)
29. Hozzová, P., Kovács, L., Voronkov, A.: Integer induction in saturation. In: CADE, pp. 361–377 (2021)
30. ISO: ISO/IEC 14882:2017: Programming languages — C++. International Organization for Standardization, Geneva, Switzerland (Dec 2017)
31. Järvisalo, M., Biere, A., Heule, M.: Blocked clause elimination. In: TACAS, pp. 129–144 (2010)
32. Jeanteur, S., Kovács, L., Maffei, M., Rawson, M.: CryptoVampire: automated reasoning for the complete symbolic attacker cryptographic model. In: SP, pp. 3165–3183 (2024)
33. Kaufmann, M., Manolios, P., Moore, J.S.: Computer-Aided Reasoning: An Approach, vol. 3. Springer (June 2000). https://doi.org/10.1007/978-1-4615-4449-4
34. Kiesl, B., Suda, M., Seidl, M., Tompits, H., Biere, A.: Blocked clauses in first-order logic. In: LPAR, pp. 31–48 (2017)
35. Kitware, I.: CMake (2025). https://cmake.org/
36. Korovin, K.: iProver — an instantiation-based theorem prover for first-order logic (system description). In: IJCAR, pp. 292–298 (2008)
37. Korovin, K., Kovács, L., Reger, G., Schoisswohl, J., Voronkov, A.: ALASCA: reasoning in quantified linear arithmetic. In: TACAS, pp. 647–665 (2023)
38. Kotelnikov, E., Kovács, L., Reger, G., Voronkov, A.: The VAMPIRE and the FOOL. In: CPP, pp. 37–48 (2016)
39. Kotelnikov, E., Kovács, L., Voronkov, A.: A FOOLish encoding of the next state relations of imperative programs. In: IJCAR, pp. 405–421 (2018)
40. Kovács, L., Hozzová, P., Hajdu, M., Voronkov, A.: Induction in saturation. In: IJCAR, pp. 21–29 (2024)
41. Kovács, L., Voronkov, A.: First-order theorem proving and VAMPIRE. In: CAV, pp. 1–35 (2013)
42. Lifschitz, V., Lühne, P., Schaub, T.: Towards Verifying logic programs in the input language of clingo. In: Fields of Logic and Computation III, pp. 190–209 (2020)
43. Microsoft: Windows Subsystem for Linux (WSL). https://ubuntu.com/desktop/wsl
44. Milner, R.: The Definition of Standard ML: Revised. MIT press (1997)
45. Racine, J.: The Cygwin Tools: a GNU Toolkit for Windows (2000)
46. Ramakrishnan, I.V., Sekar, R., Voronkov, A.: Term Indexing. In: Handbook of Automated Reasoning, pp. 1853–1964. Elsevier and MIT Press (2001)
47. Reger, G., Bjørner, N.S., Suda, M., Voronkov, A.: AVATAR Modulo Theories. In: GCAI, pp. 39–52 (2016)
48. Reger, G., Bjørner, N.S., Suda, M., Voronkov, A.: Making Theory Reasoning Simpler. . In: TACAS, pp. 164-21 (2016)
49. Reger, G., Suda, M., Voronkov, A.: Finding finite models in multi-sorted first-order logic. In: SAT, pp. 323–341 (2016)
50. Reger, G., Suda, M., Voronkov, A.: New techniques in clausal form generation. In: GCAI, pp. 11–23 (2016)

51. Reger, G., Suda, M., Voronkov, A.: Unification with abstraction and theory instantiation in saturation-based reasoning. In: TACAS, pp. 3–22 (2018)
52. Reger, G., Voronkov, A.: Induction in saturation-based proof search. In: CADE, pp. 477–494 (2019)
53. Riazanov, A., Voronkov, A.: Partially adaptive code trees. In: JELIA, pp. 209–223 (2000)
54. Rungta, N.: A billion SMT queries a day (invited paper). In: CAV, pp. 3–18 (2022)
55. Schoisswohl, J., Kovács, L., Korovin, K.: VIRAS: conflict-driven quantifier elimination for integer-real arithmetic. In: LPAR, pp. 147–164 (2024)
56. Schulz, S., Cruanes, S., Vukmirović, P.: Faster, higher, stronger: E 2.3. In: CADE, pp. 495–507 (2019)
57. Smallbone, N.: Twee: an equational theorem prover. In: CADE, pp. 602–613 (2021)
58. Sonnex, W., Drossopoulou, S., Eisenbach, S.: Zeno: An automated prover for properties of recursive data structures. In: TACAS, pp. 407–421 (2012)
59. Steen, A., Benzmüller, C.: The higher-order prover Leo-III. In: IJCAR, pp. 108–116 (2018)
60. Suda, M.: VAMPIRE getting noisy: will random bits help conquer chaos? (system description). In: IJCAR, pp. 659–667 (2022)
61. Sutcliffe, G.: The CADE ATP system competition - CASC. AI Mag. **37**(2), 99–101 (2016)
62. Sutcliffe, G.: The logic languages of the TPTP world. Logic J. IGPL (2022). https://doi.org/10.1093/jigpal/jzac068
63. Sutcliffe, G.: The 12th IJCAR automated theorem proving system competition — CASC-J12. Euro. J. Artifi. Intell. **0**(0), 30504554241305110 (0)
64. Sutcliffe, G.: The SZS ontologies for automated reasoning software. In: LPAR Workshops (2008)
65. Sutcliffe, G.: The TPTP World — infrastructure for automated reasoning. In: LPAR, pp. 1–12 (2010)
66. Tunney, J.: Cosmopolitan Libc (2025). https://justine.lol/cosmopolitan/
67. Voronkov, A.: AVATAR: the architecture for first-order theorem provers. In: CAV, pp. 696–710 (2014)
68. Voronkov, A.: Spider: Learning in the Sea of Options (2023). https://easychair.org/smart-program/Vampire23/2023-07-05.html#talk:223833
69. Vukmirovic, P., Bentkamp, A., Blanchette, J., Cruanes, S., Nummelin, V., Tourret, S.: Making higher-order superposition work. J. Autom. Reason. **66**(4), 541–564 (2022)
70. Weber, T., Conchon, S., Déharbe, D., Heizmann, M., Niemetz, A., Reger, G.: The SMT competition 2015-2018. J. Satisf. Boolean Model. Comput. **11**(1), 221–259 (2019). https://doi.org/10.3233/SAT190123
71. Weidenbach, C., Dimova, D., Fietzke, A., Kumar, R., Suda, M., Wischnewski, P.: SPASS version 3.5. In: CADE, pp. 140–145 (2009)

Engineering an Efficient Probabilistic Exact Model Counter

Mate Soos[1] and Kuldeep S. Meel[1,2]

[1] Department of Computer Science, University of Toronto, Toronto, Canada
soos.mate@gmail.com
[2] School of Computer Science, Georgia Institute of Technology,
Atlanta, GA, USA
meel@cs.toronto.edu

Abstract. Given a formula F, the problem of model counting, also known as #SAT, is to compute the number of satisfying assignments of F. While model counting has emerged as a crucial primitive in diverse domains from quantitative information flow analysis to neural network verification, scalability remains a fundamental challenge despite advances in both exact and approximate counting techniques.

We present Ganak2, a novel framework that achieves substantial performance improvements through three key technical innovations: (1) refined residual formula processing incorporating SAT-specific techniques while maintaining seamless state transitions, (2) dual independent set framework maintaining distinct SAT-eligibility and decision sets, and (3) chronological backtracking specifically adapted to model counting.

Our empirical evaluation on 1600 previous model counting competition instances demonstrates that Ganak2 successfully computes counts for 1121 instances within the one hour time limit, compared to 1032 instances by the prior state of the art approach, representing an 8.7% improvement. This progress is especially remarkable considering the extensive development and refinement of model counting tools over the years, driven by yearly competitive evaluation in the field.

1 Introduction

Given a Boolean formula F, the problem of model counting, also known as #SAT, is to compute $|\text{Sol}(F)|$, i.e., the number of satisfying assignments of F. Model counting is #P-complete [37], a complexity class that characterizes counting problems associated with NP decision problems. Despite its computational intractability, the practical significance of model counting has driven sustained research into developing effective algorithmic techniques, particularly in response to applications across diverse domains, including quantitative information flow analysis [8], network reliability [6], neural network verification [1], and probabilistic inference. For example, given a neural network $\mathcal{N}$ and an input domain $\mathcal{X}$, verifying robustness properties involves encoding the network's behavior as a Boolean formula F such that each satisfying assignment of F corresponds to an input-output pair (x, y) where $x \in \mathcal{X}$ and $y = \mathcal{N}(x)$ violates the desired

© The Author(s) 2025
R. Piskac and Z. Rakamarić (Eds.): CAV 2025, LNCS 15933, pp. 72–91, 2025.
https://doi.org/10.1007/978-3-031-98682-6_5

property. The verification question then reduces to determining if $|\mathsf{Sol}(F)| = 0$, while quantitative guarantees about the network's behavior can be obtained by computing $|\mathsf{Sol}(F)|/|\mathcal{X}|$, representing the fraction of inputs leading to property violations. The practical impact of model counting in these domains has led to sustained interest in developing scalable counters, as evidenced by yearly model counting competitions [9].

The development of model counting techniques has followed two primary trajectories. The first trajectory focuses on exact counting techniques, which integrate core technical advances from SAT solving: component caching to exploit problem decomposition, conflict-driven clause learning (CDCL) to prune the search space, and decision heuristics informed by structural properties of the formula. The second trajectory pursues approximate model counting through universal hashing techniques, exemplified by ApproxMC, which provides theoretical guarantees of (ε, δ) while achieving improved scalability. Recent efforts have focused on the development of specialized preprocessing techniques and advanced component caching schemes to handle industrial-scale instances. Although significant progress has been made in both exact and approximate counting techniques, the fundamental challenge of scalability remains a crucial bottleneck for practical deployment.

This work focuses on advancing exact model counting through careful algorithmic improvements to Ganak, a well-performing probabilistic exact model counter. We call the resulting counter Ganak2, which achieves significant performance improvements through the following technical contributions:

1. **Enhanced Residual Formula Processing:** Development of an optimized SAT solver architecture for residual formula processing that incorporates VSIDS scoring, restarts, and polarity caching.
2. **Dual Independent Set Framework:** Development of a novel algorithmic framework that maintains distinct SAT-eligibility (S) and decision (D) sets, where the S-set determines SAT solver transitions while the D-set guides branching decisions. This separation enables more efficient search space exploration, especially combined with enhanced residual formula processing.
3. **Chronological Backtracking:** Adaptation of chronological backtracking to model counting, with the aim to mitigate challenges associated with learnt clause retention, and a specific emphasis on addressing the complications that arise in the context of weighted model counting.

Our extensive empirical evaluation demonstrates significant performance improvements across different configurations of Ganak2. The optimal configuration of Ganak2 solves 1121 instances within the timeout period of 3600 seconds, compared to the baseline configuration that solves only 784 instances. This represents a substantial improvement of over 40% in the number of solved instances. In comparison to prior state of the art, Ganak shows significant runtime performance improvement: prior state of the art counter finishes only on 1032 instances within the same one hour time limit, a loss of 89 instances. Furthermore, the time-to-solution curves show that Ganak2 maintains better performance throughout the solving process, with particularly strong gains in the 500-1000 second range. These results demonstrate that careful algorithmic engineering can substantially improve the practical efficiency of exact model counting while maintaining theoretical guarantees.

The rest of the paper is organized as follows: Section 2 provides essential preliminaries and background on model counting and top-down counters. Section 3 surveys related work in model counting. Section 4 presents our key technical contributions: chronological backtracking integration, SAT solver optimizations for residual formula processing, and our dual independent set framework. Section 5 provides a comprehensive experimental evaluation of Ganak2, analyzing the impact of each algorithmic improvement on counter performance. Finally, Section 6 provides a summary of the key contributions and findings of this work.

2 Preliminaries

Let $X = \{x_1, x_2, \ldots x_n\}$ be a set of Boolean variables. A literal is either a variable (x) or its negation $(\neg x)$. A clause is a disjunction of literals, and a Boolean formula F is in conjunctive normal form (CNF) if it is a conjunction of clauses. An assignment $\sigma : X \mapsto \{0, 1\}$ is called a *satisfying assignment* or *solution* of F if it makes F evaluate to true. We denote the set of all solutions of F by $\mathsf{Sol}(F)$.

In weighted model counting, each literal l is assigned a weight $W(l) \in [0, 1]$. The weight of an assignment σ, denoted $w(\sigma)$, is the product of weights of all literals that are satisfied by σ: $W(\sigma) = \prod_{l : \sigma \text{ satisfies } l} w(l)$. Given a formula F and weight function W, the weighted model count of F, denoted $W(F)$, is the sum of weights of all satisfying assignments: $W(F) = \sum_{\sigma \in \mathsf{Sol}(F)} w(\sigma)$

A probabilistic exact counter takes in a formula F, a weight function W, and δ, and returns c such that $\Pr[c = W(F)] \geq 1 - \delta$. The unweighted model counting problem is a special case where all literal weights are 1, in which case $W(F) = |\mathsf{Sol}(F)|$. Often, we are interested in counting over a subset of variables. Given a subset of variables $P \subseteq X$, we denote by $\mathsf{Sol}(F)_{\downarrow P}$ the projection of $\mathsf{Sol}(F)$ onto variables in P. Formally, two assignments σ_1 and σ_2 belong to the same equivalence class if they agree on their assignments to P. For weighted model counting, the weight of a projected solution is the sum of weights of all solutions in its equivalence class.

Components and Residual Formulas Modern model counters employ component decomposition and caching [30] to achieve scalability. A component is a subformula that can be solved independently of the rest of the formula. Formally, given a formula F and an assignment σ to a subset of variables, a component is a maximal set of clauses $C \subseteq F|_\sigma$ such that for any other component C', we have $\mathsf{Vars}(C) \cap \mathsf{Vars}(C') = \emptyset$, where $F|_\sigma$ denotes the formula obtained by substituting the assignment σ in F. This $F|_\sigma$ is called a *residual formula* when it is being created by the model counter while running: residual formulas are being created at a high pace in model counters, as after each decision and propagation, the remaining formula $F|_\sigma$ is a residual formula that needs to be counted. A residual formula is made up of one or more components, each component being a connected, independent (sub)formula of a residual formula.

Probabilistic Component Caching Component caching is crucial for the performance of model counters. Each component is uniquely identified by its signature, which typically consists of (1) the list of variables appearing in the component (vars), and (2) the list of clause IDs in the component (cls). The efficiency of component caching significantly impacts the overall performance of model counters, as it allows reuse of previously computed results when identical components are encountered during the counting process. Ganak [32] introduced probabilistic component caching, where the vars + cls signature is hashed to reduce the memory footprint. This introduces the possibility of hash collisions, which may lead to incorrect results with arbitrarily small (but nonzero) probability, controlled by the user-specified parameter δ.

Tree Decompositions Treewidth is a graph parameter that measures how closely a graph resembles a tree [4], capturing the complexity of problems [29] by decomposing the graph into a tree-like structure of bounded-size subsets.

Independent Set Instances to be counted always contain a so-called projection set P, which in the case of so-called unprojected instances is the set of all variables. The independent set of an instance is a set of variables I such that if P was replaced with I, the instance would have the same exact model count. Hence, the most trivial independent set is $I = P$. Minimization of the independent set is a key optimization in model counting, as demonstrated by the work of Lagniez et al. [21]. While I is often a subset of P (as is the case in [21,33]), this does not have to be the case. It can be a subset, superset, or entirely different than P. As long as the model count remains the same, the independent set is valid. In our work, we consider independent sets that are either subsets or supersets of P.

3   Related Work

The development of efficient model counting techniques has witnessed sustained research effort over the past two decades, with several distinct algorithmic paradigms emerging. The earliest approaches to practical model counting extended the DPLL framework through systematic enumeration of partial solutions [3]. A significant breakthrough came with Bayardo and Pehoushek's introduction of component caching [18], which exploits the observation that for a formula φ decomposable into components $C_1, C_2, \ldots, C_n$ with disjoint variable sets, $|\mathsf{Sol}(\varphi)| = \prod_i |\mathsf{Sol}(C_i)|$. The key insight was that identical components often recur in different parts of the search, making caching an effective optimization strategy.

Integration of component caching with Conflict Driven Clause Learning (CDCL) marked another pivotal development, first realized in the Cachet model counter [30]. This approach was further refined by Thurley through sharpSAT

[35], which introduced improved component encoding schemes and enhanced decision heuristics. More recently, Ganak [32] advanced this line of research by incorporating probabilistic caching strategies and leveraging independent set information to guide search heuristics. Recent years have seen growing interest in exploiting low-width tree decompositions for model counting. Notable implementations include gpusat [11], NestHDB [15], and DPMC-LG [5], each taking distinct approaches to leveraging tree structure. While gpusat and the tensor implementation of DPMC-LG employ pure dynamic programming approaches with time complexity exponential in treewidth, NestHDB adopts a hybrid strategy, incorporating sharpSAT-style[‡] search for high-treewidth subproblems. SharpSAT-TD [19] represents a significant advancement in this direction by integrating tree decomposition information directly into variable selection heuristics while maintaining the core CDCL architecture.

Recent work has focused on integrating algorithmic techniques from satisfiability solving to improve performance. Enhanced preprocessing techniques, such as those by B+E [21], SharpSAT-TD's preprocessor [20], and Arjun [33] have been developed that preserve model count while reducing formula size. In a similar vein, blocked clause elimination [17] has been adopted [22] to the counter d4 with great success. Despite these advances, substantial challenges remain in scaling to challenging instances and handling diverse formula structures.

4 Technical Overview

This section presents our key technical contributions in enhancing the scalability of exact model counting. Section 4.1 describes our refined SAT solver integration, which incorporates restarts, VSIDS scoring, and polarity caching for residual formula processing. Section 4.2 introduces our dual independent set framework, which maintains distinct sets for SAT-eligibility and decision variables to optimize search space exploration. Finally, Section 4.3 describes our adaptation of chronological backtracking for model counting, with particular attention to the challenges arising in weighted counting scenarios.

4.1   Enhanced Residual Formula Processing

A key optimization in modern model counting is the integration of SAT solving for residual formula processing in gpmc by Suzuki et al. [34]. This approach leverages the observation that once all variables in any given independent set are assigned, the residual formula can be processed using a SAT solver rather than continuing with the more expensive model counting procedure. The intuition behind this approach is that if the SAT solver finds a satisfying assignment, the count of the residual formula is 1; otherwise, it is 0.

The original implementation in gpmc ensures consistency with the model counter through several design choices. It shares core data structures including

---

[‡]Note that the respective authors chose to capitalize sharpSAT and SharpSAT-TD differently.

watchlists, propagation queues, and assignment stacks between the SAT solving and model counting phases. Our implementation builds upon this foundation through several enhancements to the SAT solving phase. We adopt VSIDS scoring [24] in place of VSADS [31]§ for more efficient variable decisions, make use of polarity caching [28] and introduce Luby-based restarts [16] that were previously absent. We also seamlessly integrate it with chronological backtracking [26] as later explained, to allow smooth transition between SAT solving and model counting phases.

These improvements integrate established SAT solving techniques within the model counter's SAT solving engine. Our implementation maintains the same core data structures and algorithms as the model counter, with two key differences: component analysis is disabled, and the component cache is ignored during SAT solving phases, as they hold no relevance to the SAT solver, and would only slow it down. Conflict analysis, clause database management, and propagation proceed as normal. The system handles two critical scenarios elegantly: when a learned clause necessitates backtracking to a level prior to the SAT solver's initialization, the system smoothly reverts to model counting. Conversely, upon finding a satisfying assignment, the solver computes the appropriate count, 1 for unweighted, or the product of weights for weighted counting, and returns control to the model counting procedure. In case of weighted model counting and a satisfying assignment, the count may be different than 1, because we allow projected (and hence often weighted) variables to be part of the SAT solver's assignment, as explained below.

4.2 Dual Independent Set Framework

Model counting techniques have traditionally sought to minimize the given projection set, which is an independent set, driven by two key objectives: (1) enabling Bounded Variable Elimination (BVE) [7] for non-independent set variables, and (2) facilitating early transition to SAT solving through a small independent set. However, this unified approach imposes unnecessary constraints on model counting performance. We propose a novel framework that explicitly maintains two distinct independent set sets optimized for different purposes.

Definition 1 (Dual Independent Set). *Given a Boolean formula F defined over variables V and a projection set $\mathcal{P}$, a dual independent set consists of:*

S-set *A SAT-eligibility set $S \subseteq \mathcal{P}$ that determines when SAT solver mode transition is permissible.*

D-set *A decision set $D \subseteq V$ that guides branching variable selection, where $D \supseteq \mathcal{P}$.*

---

§VSADS is a variant of VSIDS that uses additional literal frequency information called DLCS, to make better decisions. However, DLCS is expensive to compute, and hence no high-performance SAT solver uses it. We follow suit, using VSIDS in SAT solving mode, improving performance.

This formulation generalizes traditional approaches where $D = S \subseteq P$, instead aiming for $S \subseteq P \subseteq D$.

The key insight underlying our framework is that the D and S-sets serve fundamentally different purposes in the model counting process. Consider a variable y that is functionally determined by a set of variables X, where $y \in P, X \subset P, y \notin X$. While y can be excluded from S since its value is fully determined once all variables in P are assigned (as established by Padoa's Theorem [27]), including y in D may still enable more efficient search space exploration as it allows more flexible branching. Note that this works even if y is weighted, as its value (and hence contribution to the weight) is always fixed given the values of X[¶].

The aim of maintaining a larger decision set (D-set) than SAT-eligibility set (S-set) is to reduce the treewidth of the residual formula after the decision has been made and propagated. Treewidth has been established to be a key factor in model counting performance [19]: lower treewidth is known to lead to significantly better performance. A larger D-set provides more flexibility in variable ordering, which can reduce the residual formulas' treewidth and minimize the formula's interconnectedness. This means the counter can choose variables that create more independent subproblems, effectively breaking the original complex formula into smaller, more manageable components. Hence, fewer components can cover the same search space. This behavior is demonstrated in our experimental results in Section 5, where the number of components encountered *decreases* as we enable (and extend) dual independent set—and count significantly more instances.

Example 1. Consider the following formula F over variables $X = \{x_1, x_2, x_3, y, z\}$ and projection set $\mathcal{P} = \{x_1, x_2, x_3\}$

$$F = (x_1 \vee x_2) \wedge (x_2 \vee x_3) \wedge$$
$$(y \leftrightarrow (x_1 \wedge x_2)) \wedge (x_3 \leftrightarrow (x_1 \oplus x_2)) \wedge (z \leftrightarrow (x_1 \vee y))$$

Observe that x_3 is functionally determined by $\{x_1, x_2\}$, y is determined by $\{x_1, x_2\}$, and z is determined by $\{x_1, y\}$. With these dependencies in mind, here is one possible S and D-set: $S = \{x_1, x_2\} \subset \mathcal{P}$, and $D = \{x_1, x_2, x_3, y, z\} \supset \mathcal{P}$ This dual set configuration reduces the S-set by one variable while allowing a set one larger than $\mathcal{P}$ for decisions. This allows the SAT solver to be invoked earlier, while maintaining flexible branching choices during the model counting phase.

Given an initial projection set $\mathcal{P}$, we are interested in computing approximations of $D_{\max}$ and $S_{\min}$ such that $D_{\max} = \text{maximize}_{D \supseteq \mathcal{P}}\{|D|\}$ and $S_{\min} =$

[¶]In our framework if a variable x_w is weighted, it can be removed from D but cannot be removed from S and hence cannot be eliminated. The elimination of x_w would require the function $x_w = f(X)$ to be computed, a technique from functional synthesis [13], which is beyond the scope of this work.

minimize$_{S \subseteq \mathcal{P}}\{|S|\}$. We aim for approximations only, since computing these can be computationally expensive, as they both rely on definability, which is known to be hard [21,33,12].

S-Set Minimization We now turn our attention to the computation of minimal S-sets, which happens to coincide with the well-studied problem of independent set minimization. We demonstrate the non-confluence property using a formula F defined over the variable set $X = \{x_1, x_2, x_3\}$ with projection set $\mathcal{P} = X$:

$$F = (x_3 \leftrightarrow (x_1 \vee x_2)) \wedge (x_2 \leftrightarrow (x_1 \vee x_3))$$

Starting with $S = X$, let us examine variable removal sequences. Variable x_3 can be removed from S since it is functionally determined by assignments to x_1 and x_2. Similarly, x_2 can be removed since it is functionally determined by assignments to x_1 and x_3. However, attempting to remove both x_2 and x_3 simultaneously yields an invalid S-set $\{x_1\}$.

Thus, the minimal S-set obtained depends critically on the order of variable removal operations, as previously noted by Lagniez et al. [21]. We employ Arjun [33], a state of the art independent set minimization tool to efficiently compute our SAT-eligibility sets.

D-Set Maximization A trivial D-set that is often (much) larger than the S-set is the projection set given by the instance, $\mathcal{P}$. In fact, for unprojected instances, this encompasses all variables. For projected instances however, it maybe possible to enlarge $\mathcal{P}$, as we explain below.

Algorithm 1 formalizes our approach to D-set maximization. The first phase performs syntactic expansion through gate-based analysis (identifying gates as per [33]), systematically identifying variables that could be part of the decision set (D-set) due to structural properties of the formula. This phase exploits the observation that if all inputs to a logical gate (OR[||], ITE, XOR) are in the D-set, its output variable can be added without requiring expensive semantic analysis. The algorithm iteratively applies this rule until reaching a fixed point, ensuring complete coverage of syntactically derivable additions.

The second phase deals with variables whose inclusion cannot be determined through purely syntactic means. Here, we employ semantic analysis through the VALIDATEDECISIONVAR routine, which verifies whether adding a variable to the D-set preserves model counting correctness. This is exactly the algorithm as presented in [21] except when it is definable, we include the variable, rather than exclude it, thus making the algorithm confluent. While computationally more expensive than syntactic analysis, this phase is necessary to identify more valid decision variables that may elude syntactic detection.

The separation into syntactic and semantic phases offers significant practical benefits. By exhaustively applying lightweight syntactic analysis before moving

---

[||]Note that AND gates are OR gates, with all inputs and the output negated. See De Morgan's laws [23]. Since we deal with literals, OR gates are sufficient to extract.

Algorithm 1 Computing maximal decision set $D_{\max}$. SEMANTICEXPANSION is step-limited, aborting if it takes too many computing steps

---

Require: Formula F, projection set $\mathcal{P}$
Ensure: Maximal decision set $D_{\max}$ where $\mathcal{P} \subseteq D_{\max}$
1: $D \leftarrow \mathcal{P}$ ▷ Initialize with projection variables
2: $G \leftarrow \text{EXTRACTGATES}(F)$ ▷ Extract OR, ITE, XOR gates
3: **procedure** SYNTACTICEXPANSION(V)
4:      changed $\leftarrow V$
5:      **while** changed is not empty **do**
6:         $v \leftarrow$ changed.$pop()$
7:         **for** gate $g \in G$ where v is input **do**
8:             **if** INPUTS(g) $\subseteq D \wedge$ OUTPUT(g) $\notin D$ **then**
9:                $D \leftarrow D \cup \{\text{OUTPUT}(g)\}$
10:              changed.$append(\text{OUTPUT}(g))$
11:      **return** D
12: **end procedure**
13: **procedure** SEMANTICEXPANSION
14:      **for** $v \notin D$ **do**
15:         **if** VALIDATEDECISIONVAR($D \cup \{v\}, F$) **then**
16:            $D \leftarrow D \cup \{v\}$
17:            $D \leftarrow$ SYNTACTICEXPANSION($\{v\}$) ▷ Quick check with syntactic analysis
18:      **return** D
19: **end procedure**
20: $D \leftarrow$ SYNTACTICEXPANSION(P)   ▷ Phase 1: Syntactic analysis
21: $D \leftarrow$ SEMANTICEXPANSION   ▷ Phase 2: Semantic analysis
22: **return** D

---

to costly semantic checks, the algorithm often achieves substantial decision set expansion while minimizing computational overhead.

4.3 Chronological Backtracking

Chronological backtracking [26] (i.e. ChronoBT) is a technique in SAT solving invented to mitigate the issue that SAT solvers would backtrack to decision level 0 whenever a unit clause is learnt. The requirement to backtrack to level 0 in case of a learned unit clause is due to the strict invariants imposed by classical, non-chronological CDCL architecture. In case of very large industrial instances, such as those that the inventors of ChronoBT were working on [25], this lead to a lot of wasted work: solver would go back to level 0, re-decide and re-propagate much of the current trail, soon find another unit clause, go back to level 0, etc.

Within the context of model counting, the idea of chronological backtracking serves a different purpose. Whenever a clause is learnt that would necessitate backtracking to a level lower than the one below, all current top-down model counters discard the learned clause and backtrack only one level, considering the branch to have zero solutions. While this avoids counting a branch that contains no solutions, it also means that the same fact is either re-learnt again, or never

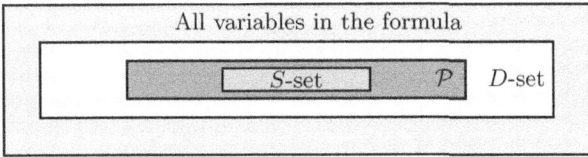

Fig. 1: Illustration of the relationship between the projection set $\mathcal{P}$, the decision set D-set, and the SAT-eligibility set S-set. Previous model counters have $D = S$. In our framework we first set $D = \mathcal{P}$, and then extend D to include more variables, if possible, using Algorithm 1.

Algorithm 2 Deciding when to perform chronological backtracking

---

1: **Input:** backtrack level b, current decision level d, threshold t
2: **Output:** New decision level b
3: $h \leftarrow$ highest decision level in learnt clause except d
4: **if** only one literal from highest level in conflict clause **then**
5:     **return** $h - 1$ ▷ Chronological backtrack
6: **if** $d - b > t$ **then return** $h - 1$ ▷ Chronological backtrack
7: **else return** b ▷ Non-Chronological backtrack

---

learnt. Hence, the counter may find itself attempting to repeatedly count parts of the space that contain no solutions—solutions that would already have been banned by the discarded learned clause. As shown in Table 2, our experiments demonstrate that the number of conflicts is significantly reduced when using ChronoBT: to count *more* formulas, we need to conflict on average *2.5x less*.

The algorithm that decides whether chronological backtracking is performed in [26] is shown in Algorithm 2. The key insight of this algorithm is that it only performs non-chronological backtracking when it is beneficial to do so. This is the case when the analyzer suggests backtracking more than a certain threshold of levels, which can lead to much wasted work. In in our framework, ChronoBT is used to avoid re-learning the same clause or re-counting already counted components, and is always on.

The adaptation of chronological backtracking to model counting introduces additional complexities related to component caching and solution counting that are not present in SAT solving. In weighted model counting, when a solver performs non-chronological backtracking, it must not only maintain the logical consistency of the search, but also ensure the correctness of weight computations. In particular, each partial assignment contributes to the final weight multiplicatively. When chronological backtracking is employed, the solver must carefully track which weights need to be preserved and which should be discarded.

In our implementation, we took the approach that all components start with a weight of one, and only when a literal is unset, and the literal is part of the currently counted component, the literal's weight is multiplied into the current component's weight. In order to know if a variable is part of the current component, during decision analysis, we set $incomp[lev][var] = mark$ for all

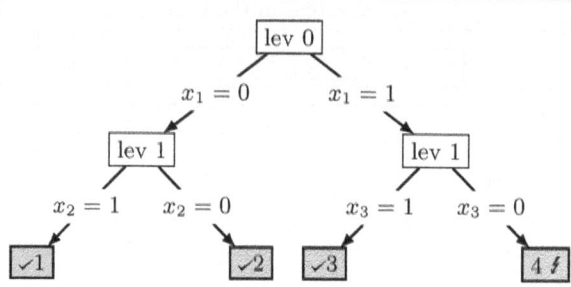

Fig. 2: In this example, we illustrate what happens when the system explores the left side of a graph, nodes 1 and 2. Then backtracks to level 0 and explores the right side, nodes 3 and 4. At node 4, the system learns the unit clause x_3. This unit clause's level is 0, but due to ChronoBT, we only backtrack to level 1. However, the system has already multiplied in the weight of x_3 into nodes 1, 2, and 3. These nodes' weights, which are all on the left side of an already explored branch (branches "lev 0" and "lev 1"), need to be compensated

variables considered for decision (i.e. part of the D-set of the component), where $mark$ is a 64-bit number starting at 0 and incremented at each decision. This $mark$ is saved for each level at $marks[lev] = mark$. Hence, while unsetting the literal (i.e. while backtracking), it is a cheap check of $incomp[lev][var] == marks[lev]$ to decide if at decision level lev variable var was in the component. If it was, its weight is multiplied in. This approach is cheap and works well, counting all components' weights correctly as long as there is no chronological backtracking.

Weight Management During Counting. Chronological backtracking introduces significant complexities to the weight management system in model counting. Consider the scenario illustrated in Figure 2. The counter first explores left, and then the right branches. The complications arise during right branch exploration, where a weighted literal previously set&unset during left branch exploration may be unset again at a higher decision level, if the variable is assigned at a lower decision level due to ChronoBT. When backtracking, the literal will be unset again, multiplying its weight twice into the left components. To maintain correct weight calculations, the system must compensate by dividing he left branches' current counts by the literal's weight, in order to avoid double-counting.

A second, more subtle complexity emerges from the interaction between learned clauses and component decomposition, illustrated in Figure 3. Component separation in state of the art model counters examine only the original formula clauses, not learned clauses. Consider variables x and y where y is not in the current component under examination. A learned clause of the form $\neg x \lor y$ may enable propagation of y, despite y not being part of the component. This creates an interesting scenario: had $\neg x \lor y$ been an original clause, x and y would necessarily belong in the same component. As demonstrated in Figure

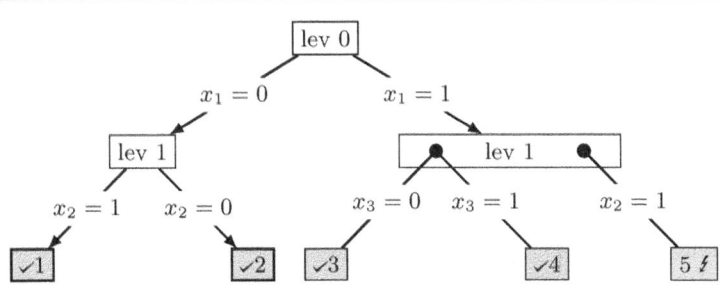

Fig. 3: In this example, x_4, which is part of components 1,2,3, and 4, but not part of component 5 is learned to be false at level 0. This sounds impossible, as x_4 is clearly not part of component 5 (since it is part of 3 and 4), so it should never be part of a learned clause while examining component 5. However, components are decided *purely* based on irredundant clauses. It is possible that learned clauses connect components. These can lead to contradictions over variables *not* part of the component currently examine, and hence a learned clause that implies a literal that's *not* in the component we are examining.

3, this interaction allows learned clauses within the current component to force assignments to variables outside the component's scope. This can lead to learned clauses asserting literals outside the scope of the current component, attached at a higher level than the current component. When backtracking, this literal will be unset, and its weight multiplied in. However, since it is not part of the currently examined component, it may have *already* been multiplied in, when examining previous components. To account for this case, we need to check sibling components if the asserted, lower level literal is in them, and compensate accordingly, as in Algorithm 3.

5 Experimental Evaluation

We implemented Ganak2 in C++**, building upon the codebase of the original Ganak probabilistic exact model counter. Our implementation integrates Arjun [33] for preprocessing with Ganak's core architecture for exact model counting, with the improvements described in Section 4: enhanced SAT solving for residual formula processing, dual independent set framework with SAT-eligibility set (S-set) minimization and decision set (D-set) maximization, and chronological backtracking adapted to model counting.

The experimental evaluation was conducted on a cluster consisting of AMD EPYC 7713 CPUs, with each particular benchmark running on a single core with a memory limit of 9 GB and a time limit of one hour. For all other counters,

---

**The tool is available open-source at https://github.com/meelgroup/ganak

---

Algorithm 3 Weight fixing for chronological backtracking. We use the remaining components to figure out if the variable has been counted by the already processed components. This is because sharpSAT, on which Ganak2 is based, only keeps detailed track of remaining components.

1: **Executed:** every time a literal is set
2: **Inputs:** literal to set: lit decision level to set: lit_lev current decision level: lev
3: **Invariants:** $lit\_lev \leq lev$
4: **for** $i \leftarrow lit\_lev$ **to** lev **do**
5: $inside \leftarrow incomp[i][var] == marks[i]$
6: **if** $\neg inside$ **then break**   ▷ Cannot be in greater decision levels
7: **if** $i > lit\_lev$ AND on right side of branch at decision level i **then**
8:   divide left side of branch at level i by $weight(lit)$
9:   $already\_counted \leftarrow true$
10:   $d \leftarrow$ decision node at level i
11:   **for** all remaining components $comp$ of d **do**
12:    **for all** variable v in $comp$ **do**
13:     **if** $v == lit.var$ **then** $\{already\_counted \leftarrow false;$ **break**$\}$
14:   **if** $already\_counted$ **then** divide active branch at level i by $weight(lit)$

---

we used a memory limit of 45 GB[††]. Both Arjun and Ganak2 uses the GNU MP infinite precision arithmetic library[‡‡] for weighted computations. While this is known to be often slower and more memory-hungry than high-precision floating-point arithmetic, it is exact. All other tools used high-precision floating-point arithmetic for weighted model counting, as default. To establish the correctness of Ganak2, it was extensively fuzzed via SharpVelvet[§§], a tool that generates random (un)projected and (un)weighted benchmarks in the Model Counting Competition format, and compares the count across different model counters.

Our benchmark suite comprised of the Model Counting Competition [10] benchmark suite from 2023 and 2024, for all standard standard tracks: un/weighted and un/projected in all combinations. This makes up 2x4x200=1600 publicly accessible benchmarks[¶¶] ranging from small to large benchmarks with diverse structural characteristics, sourced from a broad range of application domains.

To rigorously evaluate Ganak2's performance, we conduct comprehensive comparisons against three leading state of the art model counters: SharpSAT-TD, gpmc, and d4. The selection of these tools is motivated by their distinct technical approaches and established performance profiles. SharpSAT-TD represents the current performance frontier in preprocessing [20] and introduced treewidth

---

[††]Counters are optimized for the large amount of memory available during the Model Counting Competition (32GB). While Ganak2 can deal with smaller memory footprint, partially due to its probabilistic component caching scheme, we did not want to unfairly penalize other counters

[‡‡]https://gmplib.org/

[§§]https://github.com/meelgroup/SharpVelvet

[¶¶]MCComp 2023 benchmarks at: https://zenodo.org/records/10012864
MCComp 2024 benchmarks at: https://zenodo.org/records/14249068

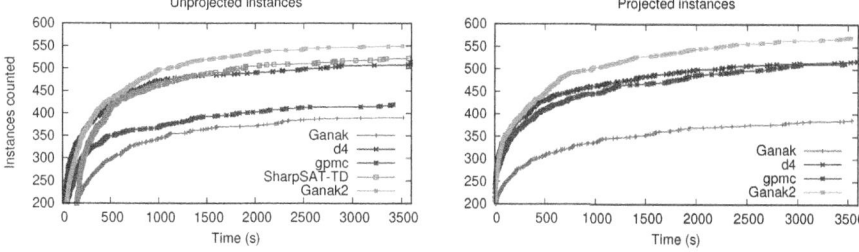

Fig. 4: Cumulative distribution function of Ganak2 against prior state of the art counters

decomposition techniques to exact model counting [19]. The d4 counter has long been at the forefront of d-DNNF compilation-based model counting, and recently introduced a novel approach based on dynamic blocked clause elimination [22]. The inclusion of gpmc is motivated by its original idea of using a SAT solver to compute a solution to the residual formula [34], and its strong performance in previous competitions. All tools were obtained from the 2024 Model Counting Competition Zenodo repository***. and were run with their configurations as per their respective competition scripts. All tools have preprocessing systems similar to Arjun, integrated. Note that SharpSAT-TD only supports unprojected benchmarks, hence it has been left out of comparisons where projected benchmarks are considered. It is worth remarking that Ganak2, Ganak, and SharpSAT-TD rely on probabilistic component caching, and therefore are probabilistic exact counters. The value of δ is determined by the bit-width of the hash functions, which is set to 64, leading to a δ of 0.001.

The primary objectives of our experimental evaluation were twofold: (1) To systematically evaluate Ganak2's performance relative to other state of the art model counters, and (2) to quantitatively assess the runtime performance improvements achieved by Ganak2 compared to the baseline Ganak.

5.1 Comparison with Prior State of the Art

We conducted an extensive empirical evaluation to compare Ganak2 against state of the art model counters: Ganak, gpmc, d4, and SharpSAT-TD.

Figure 4 presents the cumulative distribution function (CDF) plots showing the number of instances solved within different time limits. For unprojected benchmarks (left plot), Ganak2 exhibits consistently superior performance, solving 550 instances compared to 523 instances by SharpSAT-TD, the next best performer. For projected benchmarks (right plot), where SharpSAT-TD is not applicable, the improvement is even more substantial, with Ganak2 solving 571 instances compared to 518 by d4, representing a 10% improvement over the closest competitor.

*** https://zenodo.org/records/14249109

(a) Unprojected benchmarks

Tool	Counted	PAR2	Avg Mem(MB)
Ganak	391	2030	1176
gpmc	420	1881	1506
d4	514	1496	1314
SharpSAT-TD	523	1530	1129
Ganak2	550	1362	869

(b) Projected benchmarks

Tool	Counted	PAR2	Avg Mem(MB)
Ganak	387	2027	1383
gpmc	513	1519	1588
d4	518	1461	1867
Ganak2	571	1283	925

Combined Results

Tool	Counted	PAR2	Avg Mem(MB)
Ganak	784	2022	1279
gpmc	933	1700	1151
d4	1032	1478	1591
Ganak2	1121	1322	898

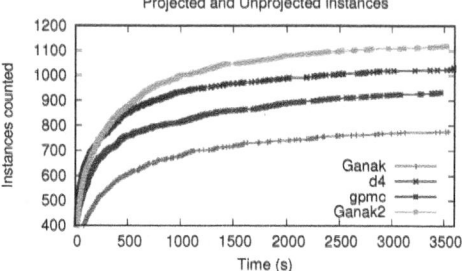

Table 1: Performance analysis of Ganak2 vis-a-vis other state of the art counters across different benchmark categories

Table 1 provides a detailed quantitative analysis of the performance metrics. We begin with results on all the instances. We see that Ganak2 is able to return counts for 1121 instances while d4 finishes only on 1032 instances, an increase of 89 instances. As model counting tools have matured over the years, such an increase in the number of instances counted would be considered significant. Furthermore, observe that the PAR2[†††] score for d4 is 1478 while Ganak2 achieves a PAR2 score of 1322. For unprojected benchmarks, Ganak2 achieves a PAR2 score of 1362, representing an 11% improvement over d4's score of 1496. The results are similarly impressive for projected benchmarks, where Ganak2 achieves a PAR2 score of 1283, significantly better than d4's 1461 and gpmc's 1519. The memory consumption pattern is consistent across both benchmark sets, with Ganak2 maintaining an approximately 25-50% lower memory footprint compared to other counters.

5.2   Analysis of Algorithmic Improvements

To understand the relative contribution of different algorithmic innovations in Ganak2, we conducted a comprehensive evaluation across multiple configurations.

[†††]The PAR2 score is a performance metric, the Penalized Average Runtime for each benchmark: if the benchmark is counted, the score is the runtime, and if a timeout occurs, a value of double the time limit (7200 in our case) is used.

Table 2: Ablation study of Ganak2 with improvements added incrementally, on all benchmarks. First row is baseline Ganak, last row is equivalent to Ganak2

Configuration	Counted	PAR2	Avg Mem(MB)	Avg Confls(M)	Avg Comps(M)
Ganak baseline	778	2029	1279	1.04	64.05
+ ChronoBT + SAT solver	906	1766	1059	0.42	56.94
+ SAT solver Enhancements	924	1738	1048	0.36	55.56
+ $D = \mathcal{P}$	1071	1418	900	0.28	45.72
+ D-set Max (=Ganak2)	1121	1322	898	0.28	45.41

Table 3: Benchmark 149.cnf from the Model Counting Competition 2023 Track 3 (projected model counting) with different configurations of Ganak2

Configuration	Time (s)	Mem (MB)	Confls (K)	Decs (M)	Comps (K)	S-set	D-set
Ganak baseline	timeout	962	N/A	N/A	N/A	39	–
+ ChronoBT + SAT solver	1049.25	554	2063	112.21	5464	39	–
+ SAT solver Enhancements	821.05	550	1319	20.65	5315	39	–
+ $D = \mathcal{P}$	815.54	547	1214	20.53	5307	39	41
+ D-set Max (=Ganak2)	738.32	549	1230	20.90	5292	39	47

Table 2 presents a comprehensive analysis of Ganak2's performance across different configurations, where each row represents an incremental enhancement to the system's capabilities. The columns show the most relevant metrics for model counting performance: the number of benchmarks counted, the PAR2 score, average memory usage (Mem), the average number of components processed (Comps), and the average number of conflicts encountered (Confls).

Let's turn our attention to the dual independent set framework and its improvement, the decision set extension algorithm. The 1600 benchmarks had 2297 median number of variables, of which a median of 208 were projection variables. After simplification algorithms such as backbone detection [2], equivalent literal substitution [14], and bounded variable elimination [7], the median number of variables was reduced to 410 by Arjun [33]. Further, Arjun computed a median S-set 89 for these CNFs. By allowing the now reduced projection set to be the D-set, this number could be increased to a median of 182. Once our maximal decision set algorithm (Algorithm 1) is enabled, this climbs to 208. This extension took an average of 0.26s for the SYNTACTICEXPANSION and 44.7s for the SEMANTICEXPANSION functions. They extended the projection set, whenever they could, by a median of 9 and 87 variables, respectively.

In Table 3, we present the performance of Ganak2 on a single benchmark, 149.cnf from the Model Counting Competition 2023 Track 3 (projected model counting), with different configurations. The benchmark originally had 6629 variables and 19329 clauses, with a projection set size of 68. Arjun reduced this to 638 variables and 4110 clauses, meanwhile reducing the projection set size to 41. It then computed an SAT-eligibility (S-set) of size 39. Using our maximal decision set algorithm, we extended the decision set (D-set) size from 41 to 47. As we turn on our enhancements, the instance is solved significantly faster, with less memory usage, fewer components, and fewer conflicts.

The results demonstrate several key insights. First, using Chronological Backtracking and a SAT solver significantly improves performance while decreasing memory usage, decreasing the number of conflicts, and visited components. Furthermore, the dual independent set framework significantly enhances performance, leading to measurable reductions across all key metrics. Finally, extending the D-set yields additional performance improvements, though these gains are comparatively modest relative to the other enhancements. Comparing Ganak2 vis-a-vis the baseline, particularly interesting is the reduction in the number of components processed, dropping from an average of 64.05M in the baseline configuration to 45.41M for Ganak2. This substantial decrease suggests that enhancements in Ganak2 effectively guide the counter toward more efficient benchmark decomposition strategies.

6   Conclusion

In this paper, we presented Ganak2, a novel framework for model counting that achieves significant performance improvements thanks to three key algorithmic contributions. First, our dual independent set framework demonstrates that maintaining distinct SAT-eligibility and decision sets enables more efficient space exploration while preserving counting correctness. Second, our enhanced chronological backtracking mechanism, specifically adapted for model counting, addresses the computational challenges in both projected and unprojected scenarios through careful management of component caching and learned clauses. Finally, our refined SAT solver integration achieves seamless state transitions while incorporating advanced features from modern SAT solvers. Our comprehensive empirical evaluation demonstrates that these technical innovations translate into substantial practical improvements.

Acknowledgements We acknowledge the support of the Natural Sciences and Engineering Research Council of Canada (NSERC), funding reference number RGPIN-2024-05956. The computational work for this article was performed on resources of the National Supercomputing Centre, Singapore (https://www.nscc.sg) and on the Niagara supercomputer at the SciNet HPC Consortium. SciNet is funded by Innovation, Science and Economic Development Canada; the Digital Research Alliance of Canada; the Ontario Research Fund: Research Excellence; and the University of Toronto.

Disclosure of Interests. The authors declare that they have no competing interests.

References

1. Baluta, T., Shen, S., Shinde, S., Meel, K.S., Saxena, P.: Quantitative verification of neural networks and its security applications. In: Proc. of CCS. pp. 1249–1264 (2019)
2. Biere, A., Froleyks, N., Wang, W.: Cadiback: Extracting backbones with cadical. In: Mahajan, M., Slivovsky, F. (eds.) SAT. LIPIcs, vol. 271, pp. 3:1–3:12. Schloss Dagstuhl - Leibniz-Zentrum für Informatik (2023). https://doi.org/10.4230/LIPICS.SAT.2023.3, https://doi.org/10.4230/LIPIcs.SAT.2023.3
3. Birnbaum, E., Lozinskii, E.L.: The good old Davis-Putnam procedure helps counting models. J. Artif. Intell. Res. **10**, 457–477 (1999). https://doi.org/10.1613/JAIR.601
4. Bodlaender, H.L.: Discovering treewidth. In: Vojtás, P., Bieliková, M., Charron-Bost, B., Sýkora, O. (eds.) SOFSEM 2005. LNCS, vol. 3381, pp. 1–16. Springer (2005)
5. Dudek, J.M., Phan, V.H.N., Vardi, M.Y.: DPMC: Weighted model counting by dynamic programming on project-join trees. In: Simonis, H. (ed.) CP. LNCS, vol. 12333, pp. 211–230. Springer (2020)
6. Duenas-Osorio, L., Meel, K.S., Paredes, R., Vardi, M.Y.: Counting-based reliability estimation for power-transmission grids. In: Proc. of AAAI (2017)
7. Eén, N., Biere, A.: Effective preprocessing in SAT through variable and clause elimination. In: Proc. of SAT. vol. 3569, pp. 61–75 (2005)
8. Eiers, W., Saha, S., Brennan, T., Bultan, T.: Subformula caching for model counting and quantitative program analysis. In: Proc. of ASE. pp. 453–464 (2019)
9. Fichte, J.K., Hecher, M., Hamiti, F.: The model counting competition 2020. Journal of Experimental Algorithmics (JEA) **26**, 1–26 (2021)
10. Fichte, J.K., Hecher, M., Hamiti, F.: The model counting competition 2020. ACM J. Exp. Algorithmics **26** (oct 2021). https://doi.org/10.1145/3459080
11. Fichte, J.K., Hecher, M., Zisser, M.: An improved GPU-based SAT model counter. In: Schiex, T., de Givry, S. (eds.) CP. pp. 491–509. Springer International Publishing, Cham (2019)
12. Fleury, M., Biere, A.: Mining definitions in kissat with kittens. Formal Methods Syst. Des. **60**(3), 381–404 (2022). https://doi.org/10.1007/S10703-023-00421-2, https://doi.org/10.1007/s10703-023-00421-2
13. Fried, D., Tabajara, L.M., Vardi, M.Y.: BDD-based boolean functional synthesis. In: Chaudhuri, S., Farzan, A. (eds.) CAV 2016. LNCS, vol. 9780, pp. 402–421. Springer (2016). https://doi.org/10.1007/978-3-319-41540-6_22
14. Gelder, A.V.: Toward leaner binary-clause reasoning in a satisfiability solver. Ann. Math. Artif. Intell. **43**(1), 239–253 (2005). https://doi.org/10.1007/S10472-005-0433-5, https://doi.org/10.1007/s10472-005-0433-5
15. Hecher, M., Thier, P., Woltran, S.: Taming high treewidth with abstraction, nested dynamic programming, and database technology. In: Pulina, L., Seidl, M. (eds.) SAT. LNCS, vol. 12178, pp. 343–360. Springer (2020). https://doi.org/10.1007/978-3-030-51825-7_25
16. Huang, J.: The effect of restarts on the efficiency of clause learning. In: Veloso, M.M. (ed.) IJCAI 2007. pp. 2318–2323 (2007)
17. Järvisalo, M., Biere, A., Heule, M.: Blocked clause elimination. In: Proc. of TACAS. LNCS, vol. 6015, pp. 129–144. Springer (2010)
18. Jr., R.J.B., Pehoushek, J.D.: Counting models using connected components. In: Kautz, H.A., Porter, B.W. (eds.) AAAI/IAAI. pp. 157–162. AAAI Press / The MIT Press (2000)

19. Korhonen, T., Järvisalo, M.: Integrating tree decompositions into decision heuristics of propositional model counters. In: CP (2021)
20. Korhonen, T., Järvisalo, M.: SharpSAT-TD in model counting competitions 2021-2023 (2023), https://arxiv.org/abs/2308.15819
21. Lagniez, J., Lonca, E., Marquis, P.: Improving model counting by leveraging definability. In: Proc. of IJCAI. pp. 751–757 (2016)
22. Lagniez, J., Marquis, P., Biere, A.: Dynamic blocked clause elimination for projected model counting. In: Chakraborty, S., Jiang, J.R. (eds.) SAT. LIPIcs, vol. 305, pp. 21:1–21:17. Schloss Dagstuhl - Leibniz-Zentrum für Informatik (2024). https://doi.org/10.4230/LIPICS.SAT.2024.21
23. Morgan, A.D.: Formal Logic. Taylor and Walton, London (1847)
24. Moskewicz, M.W., Madigan, C.F., Zhao, Y., Zhang, L., Malik, S.: Chaff: Engineering an efficient SAT solver. In: DAC 2001. pp. 530–535. ACM (2001). https://doi.org/10.1145/378239.379017
25. Nadel, A.: Introducing Intel(R) SAT solver. In: Proc. of SAT. pp. 8:1–8:23 (2022)
26. Nadel, A., Ryvchin, V.: Chronological backtracking. In: Proc. of SAT. pp. 111–121 (2018)
27. Padoa, A.: Essai d'une théorie algébrique des nombres entiers, précédé d'une introduction logique à une theorie déductive quelconque. In: Bibliothèque du Congrès international de philosophie. vol. 3, pp. 309–365 (1901)
28. Pipatsrisawat, K., Darwiche, A.: A lightweight component caching scheme for satisfiability solvers. In: Marques-Silva, J., Sakallah, K.A. (eds.) SAT 2007. LNCS, vol. 4501, pp. 294–299. Springer (2007). https://doi.org/10.1007/978-3-540-72788-0_28
29. Robertson, N., Seymour, P.D.: Graph minors. II. Algorithmic aspects of tree-width. Journal of Algorithms 7(3), 309–322 (1986)
30. Sang, T., Bacchus, F., Beame, P., Kautz, H.A., Pitassi, T.: Combining component caching and clause learning for effective model counting. In: Proc. of SAT (2004)
31. Sang, T., Beame, P., Kautz, H.A.: Heuristics for fast exact model counting. In: Bacchus, F., Walsh, T. (eds.) SAT. LNCS, vol. 3569, pp. 226–240. Springer (2005). https://doi.org/10.1007/11499107_17
32. Sharma, S., Roy, S., Soos, M., Meel, K.S.: GANAK: A scalable probabilistic exact model counter. In: Proc. of IJCAI. pp. 1169–1176 (2019)
33. Soos, M., Meel, K.S.: Arjun: an efficient independent support computation technique and its applications to counting and sampling. In: ICCAD. pp. 1–9 (2022)
34. Suzuki, R., Hashimoto, K., Sakai, M.: Improvement of projected model-counting solver with component decomposition using SAT solving in components. Tech. Rep. SIG-FPAI-103-B506, JSAI Technical Report (Mar 2017)
35. Thurley, M.: sharpSAT – counting models with advanced component caching and implicit BCP. In: Biere, A., Gomes, C.P. (eds.) SAT. LNCS, vol. 4121, pp. 424–429. Springer (2006). https://doi.org/10.1007/11814948_38
36. Toda, S.: PP is as hard as the polynomial-time hierarchy. SIAM J. Comput. 20(5), 865–877 (1991). https://doi.org/10.1137/0220053
37. Valiant, L.G.: The complexity of enumeration and reliability problems. SIAM Journal on Computing 8(3), 410–421 (1979)

Panini: An Efficient and Flexible Knowledge Compiler*

Yong Lai[1]✉ ⓘ, Kuldeep S. Meel[2,3] ⓘ, and Roland H. C. Yap[4] ⓘ

[1] Jilin University, Changchun, China
laiy@jlu.edu.cn
[2] Georgia Institute of Technology, Atlanta, USA
[3] University of Toronto, Toronto, Canada
[4] National University of Singapore, Singapore, Singapore

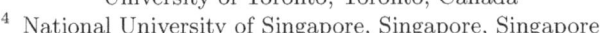

Abstract. Knowledge compilation (KC) involves compiling propositional constraints into tractable target languages which in turn efficiently support multiple analyses or queries of the constraints. Solving these queries plays a crucial role in the synthesis and verification of hardware and software systems. Recently, we proposed the target language, Constrained Conjunction & Decision Diagrams (CCDD), experimentally shown to be promising for individual model counting queries. Here, we present the compiler, Panini, which compiles CNF into CCDD.

Panini supports a range of queries. We present an empirical evaluation focusing on two fundamental queries, uniform sampling and (multiple) model counting, with a wide range of applications. While counting and sampling have witnessed significant performance improvements over the years, scalability still remains the primary challenge. Our evaluation over 600 instances from model counting competitions 2022–2024 show that Panini achieves state of art compilation by solving 322 instances, which is 183, 148, and 38 more than Dsharp, miniC2D, and D4 respectively. Secondly, on repetitive tasks, Panini solves 53 and 50 more instances than ExactMC and SharpSAT-TD for model counting, and 175 and 132 more instances than SPUR and KUS for uniform sampling, respectively.

1 Introduction

Propositional reasoning, which involves the analysis of constraints within propositional logic, plays a central role in a diverse range of fields such as hardware verification, probabilistic inference, software testing, and system reliability analysis [4]. A key challenge in these domains is the need to perform repeated analyses over the same set of constraints, necessitating efficient strategies to amortize computational costs across multiple queries. The choice of system architecture for handling multiple queries critically depends on the nature of these queries and the underlying constraints.

Two dominant architectural paradigms have emerged to address this challenge. The assumptions-based framework [13], pioneered in SAT solving, enables incremental computation by preserving and reusing partial results across queries. While efficient for certain query types, this approach faces scalability

---

* The author list has been sorted alphabetically by last name.

ⓒ The Author(s) 2025
R. Piskac and Z. Rakamarić (Eds.): CAV 2025, LNCS 15933, pp. 92–105, 2025.
https://doi.org/10.1007/978-3-031-98682-6_6

limitations for more complex analyses. The alternative knowledge compilation paradigm transforms constraints into specialized representations that support tractable querying, where tractability refers to polynomial time computation guarantees [11]. Despite its overhead in initial compilation, this approach has proven particularly effective for applications requiring diverse types of analyses.

The efficacy of knowledge compilation hinges on three key elements: the input language for specifying constraints, the target compilation language, and the supported query types [11]. Given that any Boolean formula can be converted to Conjunctive Normal Form (CNF) with only linear overhead, CNF has emerged as the de facto input language. The choice of target language depends on the complexity requirements of desired queries, with various restrictions on Negation Normal Form (NNF) yielding different tractability guarantees. Decision-DNNF is the dominant target language due to the availability of efficient compilation tools such as c2d [9], Dsharp [20], and D4 [17], supporting both model counting and uniform sampling capabilities [26], two fundamental queries with a wide range of applications ranging from hardware and software testing, system reliability, quantified information flow, and like [21,14,27,3,29,12,5,25,24].

However, despite significant advances in compilation techniques, scalability remains a critical challenge, particularly for complex real-world instances. While recent theoretical work has introduced CCDD, a generalization of Decision-DNNF that enables more compact representations [19], there remains a need for practical, efficient compilers that can leverage such advances while maintaining tractability guarantees. This raises a fundamental question: *Can we develop an efficient compiler that leverages these theoretical advances to enhance the scalability of important queries such as counting and sampling?*

This paper introduces Panini, an open-source knowledge compiler that addresses this challenge through several key innovations:

1. Efficient compilation algorithms that target both CCDD and traditional representations like Decision-DNNF, providing flexibility while maintaining performance guarantees;
2. The first tool with support for multiple target languages including CCDD, Decision-DNNF, OBDD[∧], smooth OBDD[∧], and OBDD, allowing users to select the most appropriate representation for their specific needs;
3. Efficient implementation of core operations including conditioning, model counting, and uniform sampling, designed for practical performance;
4. Comprehensive query support encompassing consistency check, validity check, clausal entailment, implicant check, equivalance check, and sentential entailment.

Our experimental evaluation demonstrates that Panini achieves state-of-art compilation performance in both running time and size of the compiled form. For repetitive querying tasks such as conditioned model counting and sampling, Panini significantly improves over prior state of the art.

The remainder of the paper is organized as follows. We introduce necessary notations in Section 2. Section 3 introduces the Panini tool architecture and usage. Section 4 details key implementation aspects and and supported queries. Section 5 presents experimental results and analysis. We conclude in Section 6.

2   Background

Our work builds upon well-established concepts in knowledge compilation. This section introduces key concepts essential for understanding Panini's functionality.

A propositional formula in Negation Normal Form (NNF) is represented as a directed acyclic graph (DAG) where internal nodes are labeled with conjunction ($\land$) or disjunction ($\lor$), and leaf nodes are labeled with $\bot$ (*false*), $\top$ (*true*), or literals. For a node v, $Vars(v)$ denotes the variables labeling its descendants. A formula in Conjunctive Normal Form (CNF) has a conjunctive root with disjunctive children and leaf grandchildren.

A conjunction node v is called *decomposable* if its children do not share variables, i.e., for each pair of children w and w' of v, $Vars(w) \cap Vars(w') = \emptyset$. An NNF is called Decomposable NNF (DNNF) if each conjunction node is decomposable [7]. A disjunction node is *deterministic* if its children are pairwise logically contradictory. If each disjunction node of a DNNF formula is deterministic, we say the formula is in deterministic DNNF (d-DNNF) [8].

Decision-DNNF, a subset of d-DNNF where disjunctions are restricted to decision nodes, has emerged as a practical target for compilation [22]. OBDD[$\land$] is a subset of Decision-DNNF with ordered decision [18]. Smooth OBDD[$\land$] requires that each subgraph of a decision node contains the same variables [11]. OBDD is a subset of OBDD[$\land$] without conjunctive nodes beyond decision [6]. The recently introduced Constrained Conjunction & Decision Diagrams (CCDD) [19] augments Decision-DNNF with specialized nodes called kernelized conjunctions. A kernelized conjunction node consists of a distinguished core child and a set of literal equivalences of the form $x \leftrightarrow l$ where x is a variable and l is a literal, with the key constraint that variables appearing in the literals l do not occur in the core. This structure enables capturing equivalence relations between variables while preserving tractability.

Key polytime queries supported by these languages include consistency (CO), validity (VA), clausal entailment (CE), implicant check (IM), equivalence check (EQ), sentential entailment (SE), model counting (CT), and uniform sampling (US). Some languages also support conditioning operations, enabling queries under partial assignments, as well as weighted variants of counting (wCT) and sampling (wUS). For a detailed theoretical treatment of these concepts, we refer readers to [11,19]. Figure 1 illustrates the relationship between different target languages and their supported queries in Panini. The following sections focus on Panini's practical implementation and capabilities.

3   The Panini Compiler

Panini is a knowledge compiler that transforms CNF formulas into CCDD or its subsets while maintaining tractability guarantees for key queries. The choice

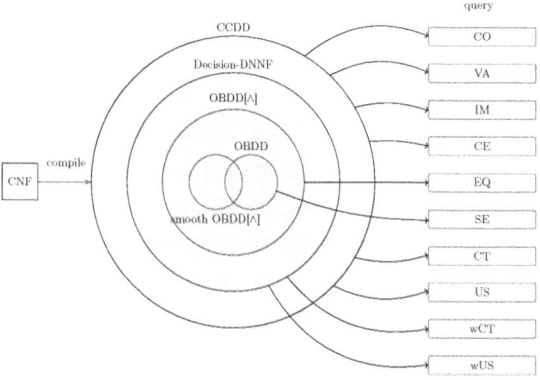

Fig. 1: Language hierarchy and supported queries in Panini.

of CNF as input enables linear-time conversion of arbitrary Boolean formulas. CCDD serves as the primary target language due to its compact representation through kernelized conjunctions while preserving tractability of model counting and uniform sampling queries. The compilation framework of Panini is given in Algorithm 1. As it is similar to the counting framework of ExactMC, please refer to the details in [19]. The main differences lie in the asterixed line numbers in Algorithm 1, which generate the compiled representation. The Panini compiler constructs a kernelized conjunction node in lines 9–10, a decomposed conjunction node in line 12, and a decision node in line 17. The compiled representation allows more efficient multiple (different) queries while ExactMC only implements individual model counting for CNF formulas.

System Architecture The system architecture consists of four integrated components: pre-processing engine, compilation core, query engine, and cache management system. The pre-processing engine applies simplification techniques including backbone detection, occurrence reduction, and literal equivalence processing. The compilation core executes the primary CNF-to-target transformation algorithms. The query engine implements polynomial-time algorithms for analyzing compiled representations. The cache management system optimizes memory utilization through component caching and redundancy elimination.

Multi-Language Support Panini implements compilation algorithms for multiple target languages to address varying application requirements. Beyond CCDD, Panini supports compilation to Decision-DNNF, which enables polynomial-time weighted model counting and sampling through decomposability and determinism properties. For applications requiring canonical representations, such as equivalence verification, Panini supports OBDD[∧] and OBDD targets. Panini also support smooth OBDD[∧], which can be used to accelerate a family of similar weighted model counting queries that often occur in probabilistic inference. This multi-language approach enables selection of representations based on specific query requirements.

Algorithm 1: COMPILE (φ)

---

1 **if** $\varphi = \textit{false}$ **then return** $\langle \bot \rangle$
2 **if** $\varphi = \textit{true}$ **then return** $\langle \top \rangle$
3 **if** $Cache(\varphi) \neq nil$ **then return** $Cache(\varphi)$
4 **if** SHOULDKERNELIZE(φ) **then**
5       $E \leftarrow$ DETECTLITEQU(φ)
6   **if** $\|\lfloor E \rfloor\| > 0$ **then**
7           $\hat{\varphi} \leftarrow$ CONSTRUCTCORE$(\varphi, \lfloor E \rfloor)$
8           $v \leftarrow$ COMPILE$(\hat{\varphi})$
9* $V \leftarrow \{\langle x \leftrightarrow l \rangle \mid x \leftrightarrow l \in \lfloor E \rfloor\}$
10*   **return** $Cache(\varphi) \leftarrow \langle \wedge_k, \{v\} \cup V \rangle$

11 $\Psi \leftarrow$ DECOMPOSE(φ)
12* **if** $|\Psi| > 1$ **then return** $Cache(\varphi) \leftarrow \langle \wedge_d, \{\text{COMPILE}(\psi) \mid \psi \in \Psi\} \rangle$
13 **else**
14       $x \leftarrow$ PICKGOODVAR(φ)
15       $w_0 \leftarrow$ COMPILE$(\varphi[x \mapsto \textit{false}])$
16       $w_1 \leftarrow$ COMPILE$(\varphi[x \mapsto \textit{true}])$
17*   **return** $Cache(\varphi) \leftarrow \langle x, w_0, w_1 \rangle$

Query Support The query interface implements polynomial-time algorithms for standard knowledge compilation operations. The consistency check (CO) determines formula satisfiability. Validity verification (VA) identifies tautologies. Clausal entailment testing (CE) verifies logical implications. The model counting algorithm (CT) computes exact solution counts with support for conditioning constraints. The uniform sampling implementation (US) generates random solutions with provable uniformity guarantees. The combination of counting and sampling capabilities with conditioning support enables complex analysis scenarios in verification and probabilistic inference applications. All query algorithms maintain polynomial-time complexity in the size of the compiled representation, as guaranteed by the structural properties of the target languages.

Usage Interface The command-line interface provides access to compilation and query functionality:

```
Panini [options] <input_file>
Options:
--lang          Target language selection
--query         Query specification
--condition     Conditioning constraints
```

The interface supports both direct compilation and query execution modes. Compilation options control target language selection and ordering heuristics. Query options specify analysis operations and conditioning constraints. This separation enables optimization of either one-time compilation followed by multiple queries, or integrated compilation and querying for single-query scenarios. The application programming interface will be described at https://kcbox-project. github.io/API/.

4   Implementation Details

Panini is implemented in C++. It is open-sourced in a set of tools called KCBox available at https://github.com/meelgroup/KCBox.

4.1   Implementation Optimizations

Memory Management We use a hash table to manage all nodes to avoid duplication. When a DAG is returned by a recursive call, we try to simplify it to save space which improves the efficiency of queries that depend on the compilation size. We apply some DAG flattening and sharing transformations. Like [19], for a decision node, we try to extract shared decomposed factors between low and high children to generate a decomposed conjunction node. In a similar vein, we try to extract shared literal equivalences between low and high children to generate a kernelized conjunction node. For a decomposed conjunction node u, if it has a decomposed conjunction child v, we flatten it by removing v and promoting its children up to u. For a kernelized conjunction node u, if its core v is another kernelized conjunction node, we can merge the literal equivalences of u and v to generate a new kernelized conjunction node. These transformations may lead to redundant nodes in the hash table, thus, we periodically try to remove redundant nodes.

Adaptive Variable Ordering The default branching heuristic, *auto*, is a combination of the widely used heuristics minfill [10] and DLCP [19]. Let $\#NonUnitVars$ be the number of variables appearing in the non-unit clauses of φ. If the minfill treewidth is greater than a crossover constant $\min(128, \#NonUnitVars/5)$, we use DLCP, otherwise, minfill. We observed from the experiments that the auto heuristic performs best for CCDD and Decision-DNNF while minfill performs best for OBDD[$\wedge$].[5] Our *auto* heuristic dynamically switches between minfill (for low-treewidth problems) and DLCP (for dense instances) using adaptive thresholding. The transition condition $\theta = \min(128, \#NonUnitVars/5)$ was empirically derived.

Formula Simplification Pipeline A key difference between Panini and other compilers is our use of in-processing where we try to simplify sub-formulas to accelerate compilation. We first use the backbone technique [16] to simplify the sub-formula. Then we iteratively use the techniques of occurrence reduction [16], vivification [16] and literal equivalence for simplification. We detect literal equivalence by using implicit boolean constraint propagation [28]. For each pair x and $\neg x$, we use boolean constraint propagation to compute the sets L and L' of implied literals, and then detect a literal equivalence $x \leftrightarrow l$ if $l \in L$ and $\neg l \in L'$.

---

[5] Panini also includes other heuristics, e.g., FlowCutter and dynamic_minfill.

Algorithm 2: PROPAGATELITEQU (E, ω)

---

1 **if** $\exists x \leftrightarrow l, x \leftrightarrow l' \in E.\omega \models l \land \omega \models \neg l'$ **then return** $\{\bot\}$
2 $\omega' \leftarrow \emptyset$
3 **foreach** $x \leftrightarrow l \in E$ *such that* x *does not appear in* ω *but* $var(l)$ *does* **do**
4   **if** $\omega \models l$ **then** $\omega' \leftarrow \omega' \cup \{x = true\}$
5   **else** $\omega' \leftarrow \omega' \cup \{x = false\}$
6 **foreach** $x \leftrightarrow l \in E$ *such that* x *appears in* $\omega \cup \omega'$ *and* $var(l)$ *does not* **do**
7   **if** $l = var(l)$ **then** $\omega' \leftarrow \omega' \cup \{var(l) = \omega(x)\}$
8   **else** $\omega' \leftarrow \omega' \cup \{var(l) = \neg\omega(x)\}$
9 **return** ω'

We have also implemented other detection schemes, but observed from the experiments that this strategy works better.

4.2 Query Algorithms

Panini implements polynomial-time algorithms for standard queries such as consistency check, validity check, clausal entailment, implicant check, and model counting, as presented in [19] (the query algorithms for supported subsets of CCDD can be refered to [6,7,8,18]). In this section, we focus on two fundamental operation algorithms not covered in prior work: conditioning and uniform sampling. These operations are crucial building blocks for applications in probabilistic inference, verification, and testing, enabling analysis under varying constraints and generation of unbiased samples from the solution space.

Conditioning Conditioning operations enable analysis under varying constraints, a crucial capability for applications such as hardware validation and probabilistic inference. Given a formula φ and assignment ω, conditioning $(\varphi|_\omega)$ replaces variables in φ according to ω. While conditioning algorithms exist for simpler representations like BDDs, handling CCDD requires careful treatment of kernelized nodes. Algorithm 3 presents our conditioning approach. The key innovation lies in handling kernelized conjunction nodes (lines 7–13). For such nodes, we first propagate the conditioning assignment through literal equivalences using Algorithm 2. This generates additional implied assignments that must be considered. The algorithm manages the original conditioning assignment ω, implied assignments ω' from literal equivalence propagation, and core-specific assignments ω'' that affect the kernelized node's core.

The final step combines these assignments with the remaining unconstrained literal equivalences to construct the conditioned node. Our implementation integrates conditioning with subsequent queries, applying them incrementally to avoid materializing unnecessary intermediate nodes.

Uniform Sampling Algorithm 4 implements uniform sampling on CCDDs. The algorithm leverages the fact that we can efficiently compute model counts

---

Algorithm 3: CONDITION (u, ω)

---

1 **if** $sym(u) = \bot$ **then return** $\langle \bot \rangle$
2 **if** $sym(u) = \top$ **then return** $\langle \top \rangle$
3 **else if** $Cache(u, \omega) \neq nil$ **then return** $Cache(u, \omega)$
4 **else if** $sym(u) = \wedge_d$ **then**
5 $\quad | \quad Cache(u, \omega) \leftarrow \langle \wedge_d, \{\text{CONDITION}(v, \omega) \mid v \in Ch(u)\} \rangle$
6 **else if** $sym(u) = \wedge_k$ **then**
7 $\quad | \quad \omega' \leftarrow \text{PROPAGATELITEQU}(E_u, \omega)$
8 $\quad | \quad$ **if** $\omega' = \{\bot\}$ **then return** $\langle \bot \rangle$
9 $\quad | \quad$ eqLits $\leftarrow \{x \leftrightarrow l \in E_u \mid x \notin Vars(\omega \cup \omega')\}$
10 $\quad | \quad \omega'' \leftarrow \{(x = b) \in \omega' \mid x \leftrightarrow l \in E_u\}$
11 $\quad | \quad w \leftarrow \text{CONDITION}(u, \omega \cup \omega'')$
12 $\quad | \quad v \leftarrow \langle \wedge_k, \{w\} \cup \{\langle x \leftrightarrow l \rangle \mid x \leftrightarrow l \in \text{eqLits}\} \rangle$
13 $\quad | \quad Cache(u, \omega \cup \omega'') \leftarrow \langle \wedge_d, \{v\} \cup \{\langle l \rangle \mid \omega' \models l\} \rangle$
14 **else**
15 $\quad | \quad$ **if** $\omega \models \neg sym(u)$ **then** $Cache(u, \omega) \leftarrow \text{CONDITION}(lo(u), \omega)$
16 $\quad | \quad$ **else if** $\omega \models sym(u)$ **then** $Cache(u, \omega) \leftarrow \text{CONDITION}(hi(u), \omega)$
17 $\quad | \quad$ **else** $Cache(u, \omega) \leftarrow \langle sym(v), \text{CONDITION}(lo(u), \omega'), \text{CONDITION}(hi(u), \omega) \rangle$
18 **return** $Cache(u)$

---

for each node v ($CT(v, X)$ denotes its model count over variable set X), allowing sampling probabilities to be calculated precisely. The sampling process follows a top-down traversal, with decomposable nodes sampled independently from each child component, maintaining uniformity through component independence. For kernelized nodes, we first sample an assignment for the core, then extend it by sampling the remaining literal equivalences while respecting the core assignment's constraints.

The key technical innovation lies in handling decision nodes (lines 9–14). Here, we compute the exact sampling probability by taking the ratio of model counts between branches. This ensures perfect uniformity in the generated samples, contrasting with approximate techniques used in other tools.

The sampling algorithm maintains polynomial time complexity in the CCDD size while guaranteeing uniformity - a crucial property for applications like probabilistic inference and constrained random testing. Our empirical evaluation demonstrates that this theoretical guarantee translates to practical efficiency gains over state-of-the-art sampling tools. The implementation optimizes memory usage by avoiding explicit storage of intermediate assignments where possible and reuses model count computations across multiple sampling operations.

5 Experimental Evaluation

Our experimental evaluation seeks to answer two key research questions:

1. How does Panini's compilation performance compare with state-of-the-art knowledge compilers in terms of both runtime and representation size?

Algorithm 4: SAMPLE (u, X)

---

1 **if** $sym(u) = \top$ **then return** $\emptyset$
2 **else if** $sym(u) = \wedge_d$ **then return** $\bigcup_{v \in Ch(u)}$ SAMPLE(v, X)
3 **else if** $sym(u) = \wedge_k$ **then**
4       $\omega \leftarrow$ SAMPLE$(ch_{core}(u), X)$
5   **for** *each equivalence* $v \in Ch(u)$ **do**
6   **if** $(sym(v) = false) \in \omega$ **then** $\omega \leftarrow \omega \cup \omega(lo(v))$
7   **else if** $(sym(v) = true) \in \omega$ **then** $\omega \leftarrow \omega \cup \omega(hi(v))$
8   **else** $\omega \leftarrow \omega \cup$ SAMPLE(v, X)
9 **else**
10      $p = \frac{CT(hi(u),X)}{CT(lo(u),X)+CT(hi(u),X)}$
11      $b \sim Bernoulli(p)$
12   **if** $b = false$ **then**
13   **return** $\{sym(u) = false\} \cup$ SAMPLE$(lo(u), X)$
14   **else return** $\{sym(u) = true\} \cup$ SAMPLE$(hi(u), X)$

---

2. To what extent does the compilation-based approach provide advantages for repetitive analyses, specifically in counting and sampling tasks?

We evaluated Panini on 600 instances from the Model Counting Competitions 2022–2024 [1]. The experiments were run on a large cluster of Lenovo SD530 servers. Each instance was run on a single core with 3600 seconds timeout and 4GB memory.

Our empirical evaluation shows that Panini produces more compact representations while maintaining faster compilation times and exhibits performance improvements on model counting and sampling queries.

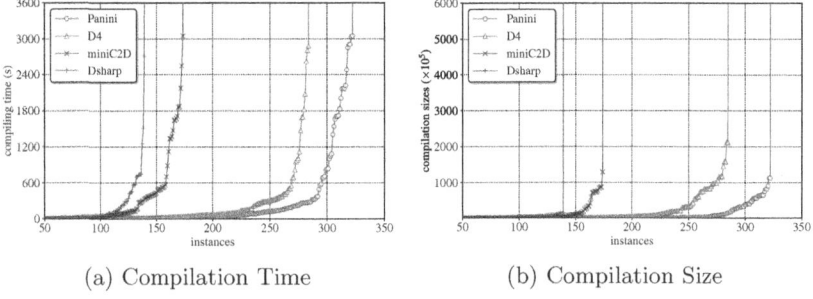

(a) Compilation Time   (b) Compilation Size

Fig. 2: Comparing the performance of different compilers. (Best viewed in color)

5.1   Compilation

We compared Panini with state-of-the-art compilers for the following target languages: miniC2D for SDD [23], and D4 [17] and Dsharp [20] for Decision-DNNF. (The computing platform is 64-bit and does not support 32-bit binary of c2d. However, the results of model counting competitions have demonstrated that D4 is more efficient than c2d.) We employed the minfill heuristic for variable ordering in miniC2D, which has been shown to significantly improve runtime and space performance [20,18]. Dsharp and D4 employ their own (recommended) custom heuristics [20,17]. Panini uses our default heuristics.

Figure 2 shows the total performance of the four compilers compiling from CNF to their target language. Overall, Panini compiled a total of 322 instances, which was 148, 183, and 38 more than miniC2D, Dsharp, and D4, respectively. Figures 2a and 2b show the cactus plots for runtime and compilation sizes (in terms of edges in the DAG) for all compilers. The x-axis gives the number of benchmarks; and the y-axis is compiling time (resp. compilation sizes), i.e., a point (x, y) in Figure 2a (resp. 2b) shows that x benchmarks took less than or equal to y seconds (resp. edges) to compile. The results show that Panini can give start-of-the-art compilation both in runtime and compiled size. Table 1 presents the performance of each tool on compiling six selected instances. The results show that for compilation, Panini obviously outperformed D4, Dsharp, and miniC2D in terms of both compiling time and compilation size.

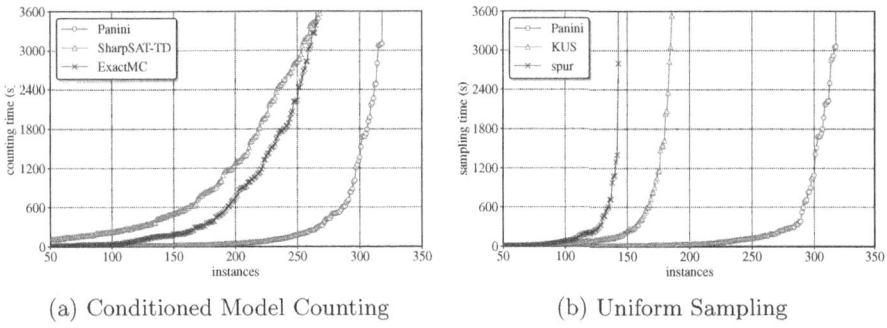

(a) Conditioned Model Counting   (b) Uniform Sampling

Fig. 3: Query performance of Panini. (Best viewed in color)

5.2   Query Performance

A key advantage of knowledge compilation lies in its ability to amortize the initial compilation cost across multiple queries. We evaluate this capability through two fundamental query types: conditioned model counting and uniform sampling. These operations form the backbone of many probabilistic inference and

Table 1: Compilation statistics on selected instances, where "–" denotes timeout or out of memory, times are in seconds, and sizes are the numbers of edges in compiled forms

instance		Panini	D4	Dsharp	miniC2D
mc2022_track1_050	time	2.33	419.38	–	–
	size	6.90×10^4	3.47×10^7	–	–
mc2022_track1_123	time	130.47	421.78	–	–
	size	6.33×10^7	1.59×10^8	–	–
mc2023_track1_047	time	9.15	317.59	43.24	–
	size	3.63×10^5	3.11×10^7	2.49×10^5	–
mc2023_track1_064	time	5.34	138.47	–	–
	size	5.90×10^5	9.27×10^6	–	–
mc2024_track1_134	time	31.26	287.06	–	1477.38
	size	4.37×10^5	3.13×10^7	–	7.06×10^6
mc2024_track1_197	time	12.94	29.50	–	93.96
	size	1.48×10^5	1.47×10^6	–	2.31×10^5

verification tasks, where practitioners often need to perform repeated analyses under varying conditions. While dedicated tools exist for each query type, Panini's compilation-based approach enables efficient handling of multiple queries through a single compiled representation.

Conditioned Model Counting We compare Panini with ExactMC and SharpSAT-TD on the task of performing multiple counting on each instance. The experiment is similar to Koriche et al. [15] for their tool cnf2eadt. For each instance φ, we generated 100 queries with a random 3-literal partial assignment γ where we answer the model count of φ conditioned on γ. For the model counters, ExactMC and SharpSAT-TD which generate the count directly, they need to answer all queries on each instance φ individually.

For Panini, we first compile φ and then answer the queries using the compiled result. The solving time for Panini is the compiling time plus the time to answer all queries. Figure 3a shows the performance of ExactMC, SharpSAT-TD and Panini. Panini solves 318 instances, 53 and 50 more than ExactMC and SharpSAT-TD, respectively. Moreover, the number of instances Panini solves is 34 greater than that of instances D4 only performs compilation. We remark that the cnf2eadt tool only solves 112 instances. Table 2 presents the performance of each tool on conditioned counting on the six selected instances. The results show that for conditioned counting, Panini obviously outperformed ExactMC and SharpSAT-TD.

Uniform Sampling We compare uniform sampling of Panini with the samplers spur [2] and KUS [26]. To the best of our knowledge, spur and KUS are the only tools that can perform sampling on CNF formulas with theoretical guarantees of uniformity. Consistent with the previous studies, each tool generated 1000

Table 2: Conditioned counting statistics on selected instances (times in seconds)

instance	Panini	ExactMC	SharpSAT-TD
mc2022_track1_050	3.15	136.99	270.33
mc2022_track1_123	430.37	1848.81	2606.27
mc2023_track1_047	16.21	162.65	896.17
mc2023_track1_064	21.01	203.02	3424.01
mc2024_track1_134	41.07	1065.72	–
mc2024_track1_197	13.23	299.86	2544.77

Table 3: Uniform sampling statistics on selected instances (times in seconds)

instance	Panini	spur	KUS
mc2022_track1_050	2.68	–	–
mc2022_track1_123	141.6	–	–
mc2023_track1_047	18.85	2802.1	–
mc2023_track1_064	7.23	–	–
mc2024_track1_134	34.17	–	–
mc2024_track1_197	13.52	128.66	135.93

samples for each instance. Figure 3b shows the performance of spur, KUS, and Panini. Overall, Panini solves 132 and 175 more instances than SPUR and KUS, respectively. Table 3 presents the performance of each tool on uniform sampling on the six selected instances. The results show that uniform sampling, Panini obviously outperformed spur and KUS in terms of solving time.

6   Conclusion

In this tool paper, we presented, Panini, a compiler that transforms a given CNF formula into CCDD. Panini is able to support a wide array of queries; for our evaluation, we focused on uniform sampling and model counting. We demonstrated that Panini gives state-of-art results for compilation time and sizes. In uniform sampling and model counting use cases, Panini significantly improves on prior state of the art counters and samplers.

Acknowledgments. We are grateful to the anonymous reviewers for their constructive feedback. We thank Junjie Li and Lambang Akbar Wiyajadi for testing the artifact. The first author was supported by Jilin Provincial Natural Science Foundation [20240101378JC] and Jilin Provincial Education Department Research Project [JJKH20241286KJ]; the second author was supported by the Natural Sciences and Engineering Research Council of Canada (NSERC), funding reference number RGPIN-2024-05956; and the third author was supported by grant T1 251RES2302.

Disclosure of Interests. The authors declare that they have no competing interests.

References

1. Model counting competition, https://mccompetition.org
2. Achlioptas, D., Hammoudeh, Z.S., Theodoropoulos, P.: Fast sampling of perfectly uniform satisfying assignments. In: Theory and Applications of Satisfiability Testing - SAT 2018 - 21st International Conference. pp. 135–147 (2018)
3. Baluta, T., Shen, S., Shinde, S., Meel, K.S., Saxena, P.: Quantitative verification of neural networks and its security applications. In: Proceedings of the 2019 ACM SIGSAC Conference on Computer and Communications Security. pp. 1249–1264 (2019)
4. Biere, A., Heule, M., van Maaren, H., Walsh, T. (eds.): Handbook of Satisfiability - Second Edition. IOS Press (2021)
5. Biondi, F., Enescu, M.A., Heuser, A., Legay, A., Meel, K.S., Quilbeuf, J.: Scalable approximation of quantitative information flow in programs. In: VMCAI (2018)
6. Bryant, R.E.: Graph-based algorithms for boolean function manipulation. IEEE Transactions on Computers **35**(8), 677–691 (1986)
7. Darwiche, A.: Decomposable negation normal form. Journal of the ACM **48**(4), 608–647 (2001)
8. Darwiche, A.: On the tractability of counting theory models and its application to truth maintenance and belief revision. Journal of Applied Non-Classical Logics **11**(1–2), 11–34 (2001)
9. Darwiche, A.: New advances in compiling CNF into decomposable negation normal form. In: Proceedings of the 16th Eureopean Conference on Artificial Intelligence (ECAI-04). pp. 328–332 (2004)
10. Darwiche, A.: Modeling and Reasoning with Bayesian Networks. Cambridge University Press (2009)
11. Darwiche, A., Marquis, P.: A knowledge compilation map. Journal of Artificial Intelligence Research **17**, 229–264 (2002)
12. Dueñas-Osorio, L., Meel, K.S., Paredes, R., Vardi, M.Y.: Counting-based reliability estimation for power-transmission grids. In: Proceedings of the Thirty-First AAAI Conference on Artificial Intelligence. pp. 4488–4494 (2017)
13. Eén, N., Sörensson, N.: Temporal induction by incremental SAT solving. In: First International Workshop on Bounded Model Checking, BMC@CAV 2003. pp. 543–560 (2003)
14. Geldenhuys, J., Dwyer, M.B., , Visser, W.: Probabilistic symbolic execution. In: ISSTA (2012)
15. Koriche, F., Lagniez, J., Marquis, P., Thomas, S.: Knowledge compilation for model counting: Affine decision trees. In: Proc. of IJCAI. pp. 947–953 (2013)
16. Lagniez, J., Marquis, P.: Preprocessing for propositional model counting. In: Proc. of AAAI. pp. 2688–2694 (2014)
17. Lagniez, J.M., Marquis, P.: An improved Decision-DNNF compiler. In: Proc. of IJCAI. pp. 667–673 (2017)
18. Lai, Y., Liu, D., Yin, M.: New canonical representations by augmenting OBDDs with conjunctive decomposition. Journal of Artificial Intelligence Research **58**, 453–521 (2017)
19. Lai, Y., Meel, K.S., Yap, R.H.C.: The power of literal equivalence in model counting. In: Proceedings of Thirty-Fifth AAAI Conference on Artificial Intelligence (AAAI-21). pp. 3851–3859. AAAI Press (2021)
20. Muise, C.J., McIlraith, S.A., Beck, J.C., Hsu, E.I.: Dsharp: Fast d-DNNF compilation with sharpSAT. In: Proceedings of the 25th Canadian Conference on Artificial Intelligence. pp. 356–361 (2012)

21. Naveh, Y., Emek, R.: Random stimuli generation for functional hardware verification as a CP application. In: CP (2005)
22. Oztok, U., Darwiche, A.: On compiling CNF into Decision-DNNF. In: Proc. of CP. pp. 42–57 (2014)
23. Oztok, U., Darwiche, A.: A top-down compiler for sentential decision diagrams. In: Proc. of AAAI. pp. 3141–3148 (2015)
24. Palacios, H., Darwiche, A., Bonet, B., Geffner, H.: Pruning conformant plans by counting models on compiled d-DNNF representations. In: Proc. of ICAPS. pp. 141–150 (2005)
25. Saad, F.A., Rinard, M.C., Mansinghka, V.K.: SPPL: probabilistic programming with fast exact symbolic inference. In: PLDI '21: 42nd ACM SIGPLAN International Conference on Programming Language Design and Implementation. pp. 804–819 (2021)
26. Sharma, S., Gupta, R., Roy, S., Meel, K.S.: Knowledge compilation meets uniform sampling. In: LPAR-22. 22nd International Conference on Logic for Programming, Artificial Intelligence and Reasoning. pp. 620–636 (2018)
27. Sundermann, C., Kuiter, E., Heß, T., Raab, H., Raab, H., Thüm, T.: On the benefits of knowledge compilation for feature-model analyses. Annals of Mathematics and Artificial Intelligence (2023)
28. Thurley, M.: sharpSAT — counting models with advanced component caching and implicit BCP. In: Proceedings of the 9th International Conference on Theory and Applications of Satisfiability Testing. pp. 424–429 (2006)
29. Zhou, Z., Qian, Z., Reiter, M.K., Zhang, Y.: Static evaluation of noninterference using approximate model counting. In: IEEE Symp. on Security and Privacy. pp. 514–528 (2018)

Regex Decision Procedures in Extended RE#

Ian Erik Varatalu[1], Margus Veanes[2]([✉]), Ekaterina Zhuchko[1], and Juhan Ernits[1]

[1] Tallinn University of Technology, Tallinn, Estonia
{ian.varatalu,ekzhuc,juhan.ernits}@taltech.ee
[2] Microsoft Research, Redmond, USA
margus@microsoft.com

Abstract. We develop decision procedures for *extended regular expressions* in the new **ERE#** framework that uses *span semantics*, utilizing the power of *symbolic derivatives*. We prove a normal form theorem in Lean for **ERE#** that is closed under all Boolean operations and provides the basis for the given decision procedures. The tool is evaluated on existing SMT benchmarks for regexes that shows it to be the fastest solver to date – *often orders of magnitude faster than state-of-the-art* – albeit specialized for the *single-variable fragment* of string theory.

1 Introduction

The new and currently *fastest nonbacktracking* regex matcher **RE#** [46] supports match search with regexes extended with *intersection* (&), *complement* (~), and restricted *lookarounds*. Extended operators in **RE#** provide a *separation of concerns* making it possible to express typical search patterns more naturally and compactly, as discussed at length in [46]. In this work, we develop decision procedures for the *Boolean closure* **ERE#** of **RE#** that enables various practical applications for *debugging, compiler optimizations*, and *verification* tasks.

Support for & and ~ implies a need to decide *nonemptiness* of regexes as a basic *debugging* feature. For example, the regex .*\d.*&~(.*\w.*) must match at least one digit but may not contain any word-letters – thus, it *matches nothing* because all digits are word-letters. Character classes can also be easily misunderstood due to subtle semantic differences between platforms or feature interactions in combination with common regex options, such as *case insensitivity* (typically inlined with (?i:...)) where *equivalence* checking is essential for ensuring correctness and consistency of the intended behavior. It is possible that $R_1 \equiv R_2$ but (?i:R_1) $\not\equiv$ (?i:R_2), e.g., for $R_1 =$ [^D] and $R_2 =$ [\u0000-CE-\uFFFF].

During derivative based compilation of regexes into DFAs, it is common to encounter unions of the form $R_1 | R_2$ as target states of transitions. In order to reduce memory footprint, it is crucial to decide if R_i *subsumes* R_j, and if so, to reuse R_i as the sole target state, instead of introducing a new state for the union.

© The Author(s) 2025
R. Piskac and Z. Rakamarić (Eds.): CAV 2025, LNCS 15933, pp. 106–129, 2025.
https://doi.org/10.1007/978-3-031-98682-6_7

Several basic rewrites necessary were already pointed out in [40], but *bounded loops* in particular are highly problematic [44]. E.g., the derivative of a regex $R = .*a?\{k\}$ for a is $R\,|\,a?\{k-1\}$ that can be simplified to R because R subsumes $a?\{k-1\}$, where a? abbreviates $a\,|\,\varepsilon$. Omitting such rewrites can quickly lead to a state space explosion up to size 2^k – *observe that $k = O(2^{|R|})$ here*! For DFA generation, such subsumption checking must be fast in practice.

Dealing with differences between PCRE and POSIX semantics for a regex is a common problem.[1] In PCRE, also known as *backtracking* or *leftmost-eager* semantics, the union operator $|$ is *noncommutative* where in a regex $R_1\,|\,R_2$, a match for R_2 is only sought when R_1 fails to match. Note that this difference is relevant for *span* semantics that has recently been formalized in Lean [50], but irrelevant for *language* semantics (IsMatch) that is identical under both PCRE and POSIX. A technique to decide if a union $R_1\,|\,R_2$ in PCRE has the same span semantics under POSIX, where union is *commutative*, is to decide match equivalence between $R_1\,|\,R_2$ and $R_1\,|\,R_2 \&\sim(R_1 \cdot \_*)$.

If the span semantics of a regex *differs* between PCRE and POSIX then the regex may contain unreachable cases under PCRE. E.g., the BurntSushi/rebar benchmarking tool [24] – *widely used for industrial PCRE matchers* – uses a dictionary benchmark containing unions such as may|mayo. The regex may|mayo will never match "mayo" for any input under PCRE semantics and has the exact same behavior as the regex may. Most industrial regex matchers use PCRE semantics, resulting in different behavior to what is intuitively assumed, as $|$ is not union of languages in PCRE. It is a common programming error to define a regex with unintended behavior this way. For example, by using the above technique, may|mayo&$\sim$(may_*) effectively deletes the alternative mayo from may|mayo while mayo|may would remain intact because may&$\sim$(mayo_*) $\equiv$ may.

The logic **ERE#**, that is introduced in Sect. 4, is a novel contribution and fundamental for many decision problems. In particular, it lifts **RE#** to the status of an *Effective Boolean Algebra* over spans. **RE#** is closed only under *intersection* and each regex admits a *linear* translation to a core regex of the form $(?<=R_1)R_2(?=R_3)$ where no R_i contains lookarounds. The *span semantics* $(u_1, u_2, u_3) \models (?<=R_1)R_2(?=R_3)$ intuitively means that $u_1u_2u_3$ is a word such that $u_i \in \mathcal{L}(R_i)$ where u_2 is the main match with u_1 and u_3 as the surrounding context. For many decision problems, like subsumption, it became necessary to support regexes like $(?<=R_1)R_2(?=R_3)\&\sim((?<=R_1')R_2'(?=R_3'))$ that fall outside the fragment for matching in **RE#**.

Currently, **ERE#** semantics is not directly expressible in SMT-LIB as it would require support for lookarounds and span semantics. Section 7 proposes an *SMT-LIB format* for extending RegLan with *lookarounds* and *span semantics*.

Contributions. We introduce an extension **ERE#** of the **RE#** class that is Boolean closed and formalize a normal form theorem (Theorem 2) for it in *Lean* allowing us to develop decision procedures for **ERE#**, including *emptiness*, *subsumption*, and *equivalence*, that are of primary interest in the **ERE#** framework,

---

[1] See for example https://stackoverflow.com/questions/4733416.

as discussed above. It is also possible to use **ERE#** for pre-processing in SMT solvers. One can invoke **ERE#** from the simplifier in Z3 [39], to pre-process RegLan constraints, which can moreover be supported incrementally [12]. The main decision procedures for **ERE#** reduce, via the normal form theorem and the nonemptiness algorithm (Theorem 1), to nonemptiness in **ERE**.

We have conducted extensive evaluation on existing SMT benchmarks for the fragment of **ERE#** without lookarounds. The evaluation focuses on available SMT benchmarks that include all we could find on RegLan and benchmarks that reduce to the single string variable fragment of string constraints. The experiments demonstrate that **ERE#** consistently outperforms all state-of-the-art solvers, often by orders of magnitude, see Fig. 1. The main reasons are: 1) *specialization to regex decision problems* combined with alphabet compression to bit-vectors; 2) aggressive rewrite rules that rely on symbolic derivatives and transition regex rewrites [43] – in particular lazy propagation rules for *intersection* and *complement*; 3) use of reversal theorem for $\mathbf{ERE}_{\leq}$ [50] – to decide nonemptiness of the *reverse* of a regex; 4) use of XOR as a Boolean operator directly supported by derivatives, for deciding equivalence in some cases.

Artifact. The paper is accompanied by an *artifact* [47] for Lean formalization of Theorem 2, and evaluation confirming the results in Fig. 1 and Table 1.

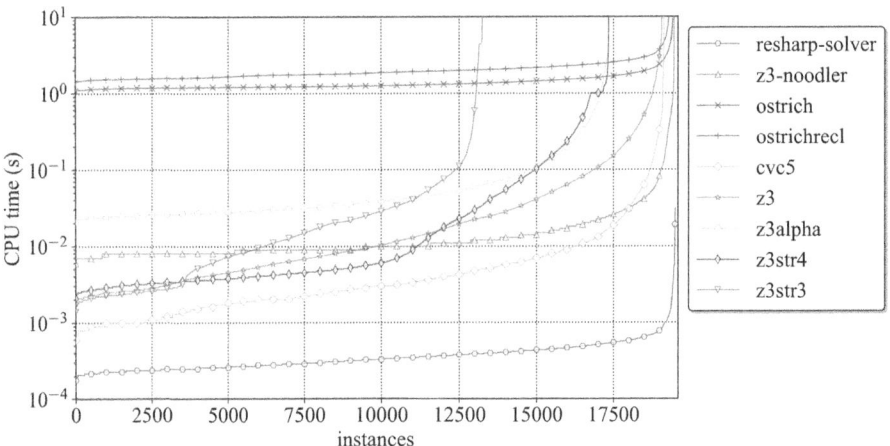

Fig. 1. Cactus plot of CPU time for 9 solvers and 19 509 SMT benchmarks. The y-axis is in **log-scale**. For **ERE#**-solver (resharp-solver) no benchmark needed >0.1 s and less than 100 benchmarks needed >0.01 s.

2 Related Work

The development of string constraint solvers has a long-standing history, with prominent general-purpose SMT solvers such as Z3 [39] and CVC5 [5], alongside specialized solvers [10,11,19,36]. String constraint solving approaches vary widely, with methods based on a mixture of automata, word equations, and other techniques. Many existing tools handle a broader range of constraints, including those beyond regular languages, such as context-free constraints. However, our work is not intended to compete with these general-purpose solvers; instead, we focus on a specialized fragment relevant to our setting. For a comprehensive overview of existing techniques and tools, we refer to the recent surveys [3,26]. Below we outline the key differences between the existing tools and our approach.

The solvers which support derivative-based lazy exploration of regular expressions are the sequence solver [43] in Z3 and CVC5 [5]. The former was the first to use transition regexes as part of the solver. However, our method leverages systematic simplifications and rewrites, enabling us to solve many SMT-LIB benchmarks in a fraction of a second, whereas the sequence solver fails to do so even after hours. Additionally, our solution is specialized for regexes, avoiding the overhead of supporting other theories. CVC5 [5] also uses a derivatives based approach [32] to solve regular expression constraints in its string solver [31,41], similarly relying on aggressive simplifications.

Kepler$_{22}$, introduced in [30], employs a two-phase approach for solving string constraints. In the first phase, it constructs a cyclic reduction tree that represents all solutions to a conjunction of word equations and regular membership predicates. The second phase uses specialized procedures to infer length constraints from the set of all solutions, constituting a decision procedure for the straight line and quadratic fragments of string equations. While the authors report promising experimental results, we were not able to find an implementation to include in our evaluation. The tool NFA2SAT, presented in [33], performs an eager reduction of string operations and regular expression constraints into SAT, enabling incremental SAT solving. However, we were not able to find an artifact to include in our evaluation.

Several extensions to Z3 incorporate support for string constraints. The analysis in [9] focuses on fragments without string equality (i.e., without word equations), which aligns with the scope of our solver. Z3-Noodler [19] utilizes the MATA library [20] that implements basic algorithms for automata and also fast simulation reduction and antichain-based language inclusion checking. It uses novel techniques such as a stabilization-based procedure [14,18] for string-constraint solving. Z3str4 [36] builds on Z3str3 [10] and extends it with a string-to-bit-vector reduction. Z3alpha [34] is built on top of Z3 and the novelty lies in untilizing Monte Carlo Tree Search based SMT strategy synthesis. It ranked second in the 24-second performance category at SMT-COMP 2024, solving more tasks than all other solvers except Z3-Noodler.

Another notable tool is Ostrich [17], a solver that supports advanced regular expression features such as capture groups, lazy quantifiers, and anchors. Several extensions of Ostrich have been developed. For instance, [16] introduces a model based on prioritized streaming string transducers, while [27,28] builds on cost-enriched finite-state automata. Another recent extension to Ostrich is the tool SECO [29] based on parametric symbolic automata which extends symbolic automata to allow free variables on the transition guards. Ostrich has also been extended using Parikh images [23] to reason about word lengths. While these Parikh image-based approaches have also been applied to accelerate string constraint solving [25], they fall outside the scope of this paper.

Equivalence algorithms for classical regular expressions have been studied in [1,2] based on *partial derivatives* [4]. The main algorithm was also implemented in [37] using Coq, and it operates incrementally by avoiding the construction of the full automaton during the process. The additional challenge in the case of **ERE#** is twofold: to support intersection and complement incrementally, and to work modulo large (or infinite) alphabets $\mathcal{A}$ (given as an EBA), which we are currently investigating. Moreover, in the case of **ERE#**, equivalence should ideally also support lookarounds and therefore be based on span semantics.

3   Preliminaries

This section includes the main background notations and definitions used in the rest of the paper. To support large alphabets such as Unicode, we use *effective Boolean algebras* [22] (EBAs) to represent *character classes* symbolically via predicates, typical examples include: *digits* \d, *word-letters* \w, and *white-space characters* \s. Extended regular expressions or regexes support *intersection* and *complement* as well as *lookarounds* in the full class **ERE$_\leq$** [46,50]. The latter requires their semantics to be based on *locations* and *spans* due to context conditions imposed by lookarounds. Regexes use nested if-then-else terms called *transition regexes* [43,50] to represent their *symbolic derivatives*. The main intuition is that the symbolic derivative $\delta(R)$ of a regex R is a transition regex representing a *partial evaluation* for R of the Brzozowski derivative [15] $D_a(R)$ for $a \in \Sigma$. The *evaluation* of $\delta(R)$ for $a \in \Sigma$, $\delta(R)[a]$, equals $D_a(R)$. The class **ERE#**, defined in Sect. 4, forms a *proper* subclass of **ERE$_\leq$** but its match semantics is also based on spans and coincides with the match semantics of the whole **ERE$_\leq$**. The rest of this section defines these notions formally.

Before the formal definitions below, we illustrate the notions using the regex $R = \_*\backslash d\_*\&\_*\backslash w\_*\&\_*\backslash s\_*$ that matches any string containing a digit, a word-letter, and a white-space character, where _ matches *all* characters and & is regex *intersection*. The symbolic derivative $\delta(R)$ of R is the transition regex:

$$\delta(R) = \mathrm{ite}(\backslash d, \_*\backslash s\_*, \mathrm{ite}(\backslash w, \_*\backslash d\_*\&\_*\backslash s\_*, \mathrm{ite}(\backslash s, \_*\backslash d\_*\&\_*\backslash w\_*, R)))$$

The transition regex is illustrated as a binary decision tree in Fig. 2 whose *conditions* are the highlighted predicates \d, \w, and \s. The *else-case* branches of $\delta(R)$ are *dashed* and the *leaves* of $\delta(R)$ are regexes (including R itself). E.g., $\delta(R)[\text{'a'}] = \_*\backslash d\_*\&\_*\backslash s\_*$ and $\delta(R)[\text{'#'}] = R$. When computing $\delta(R)$ the alphabet EBA was used to to eliminate unreachable subterms in $\delta(R)$ through *cleaning* [43]. Therefore, $\delta(R)$ was simplified by using the facts that \d implies \w (since all digits are word-letters), while \s is disjoint from both \w and \d.

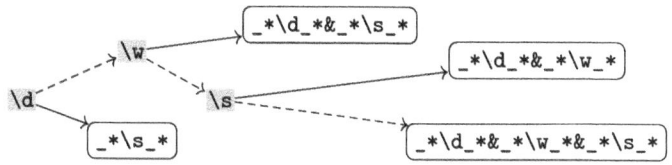

Fig. 2. Clean symbolic derivative of the regex _*\d_*&_*\w_*&_*\s_*.

Effective Boolean Algebras. An *Effective Boolean Algebra (EBA)* over an element universe Σ is a tuple $(\Sigma, \mathcal{A}, \vDash, \bot, \_, \sqcup, \sqcap, {}^c)$ where $\mathcal{A}$ is a set of *predicates* that is closed under the Boolean connectives and contains $\bot$ and $\_$. For $a \in \Sigma$ and $\alpha \in \mathcal{A}$ the *models* relation $a \vDash \alpha$ with $[\![\alpha]\!] \overset{\mathrm{DEF}}{=} \{a \in \Sigma \mid a \vDash \alpha\}$ obeys classical Tarski laws such that $[\![\bot]\!] = \emptyset$ and $[\![\_]\!] = \Sigma$. For $\alpha, \beta \in \mathcal{A}$ let $\alpha \equiv \beta \overset{\mathrm{DEF}}{=}$ $[\![\alpha]\!] = [\![\beta]\!]$. If $\alpha \not\equiv \bot$ then α is *satisfiable* (**SAT**(α)). All the connectives must be *computable* and $\vDash$ must be *decidable*.

We write $\mathcal{A}$ also for the EBA itself and say that $\mathcal{A}$ is *decidable* if **SAT**(α) is decidable. We use $(\Sigma, \mathcal{A}, \vDash, \bot, \_, \sqcup, \sqcap, {}^c)$ as a given *core alphabet* EBA. When working with regexes, it is a standard assumption that $\bullet$ is a predicate denoting all characters *except* the newline character (predicate) \n, i.e., $\_ \equiv \bullet \sqcup \text{\textbackslash}n$.

Locations and Spans. A *location* is a pair of words in $\Sigma^* \times \Sigma^*$. Let $w \in \Sigma^*$. A *location in w* is a location (u, v) such that $w = uv$. The intuition is that a location in w specifies a border inside w. A location (ϵ, w) is *initial* and a location (w, ϵ) is *final*. For any location x let the *kind* of x be $(IsInitial(x), IsFinal(x)) \in \mathbb{B} \times \mathbb{B}$ where $\mathbb{B} = \{\mathbf{true}, \mathbf{false}\}$.

A *span* is a triple of words in $\mathbf{Span} \overset{\mathrm{DEF}}{=} \Sigma^* \times \Sigma^* \times \Sigma^*$. A span $\theta = (u, v, s)$ has two locations the *beginning* location $beg(\theta) \overset{\mathrm{DEF}}{=} (u, vs)$ and the *end* location $end(\theta) \overset{\mathrm{DEF}}{=} (uv, s)$; $prefix(\theta) \overset{\mathrm{DEF}}{=} u$ is the *prefix* of the span, $suffix(\theta) \overset{\mathrm{DEF}}{=} s$ is the *suffix* of the span, and $match(\theta) \overset{\mathrm{DEF}}{=} v$ is the *match* of the span. The *word* of the span is $word(\theta) \overset{\mathrm{DEF}}{=} uvs$. We lift all the definitions to *sets* of spans as usual.

A *span in w* is a span (u, v, s) such that $w = uvs$. Intuitively, a span (u, v, s) represents a regex match in a word w with v as the primary matched substring of w where the prefix and the suffix are some sufficient lookaround context words. The *width* of a span (u, v, s) is the length $|v|$ of its match v.

Full Class ERE with Lookarounds. The class $\mathbf{ERE}_{\le}$ is defined as follows. Members of $\mathbf{ERE}_{\le}$ are denoted here by R. *Concatenation* $(\cdot)$ is often implicit by juxtaposition. All operators appear in order of precedence where *union* $(\mid)$ binds weakest and *complement* $(\tilde{\ })$ binds strongest. Let $\psi \in \mathcal{A}$ and let $m > 0$.

$$R ::= \psi \mid \varepsilon \mid R_1 \mid R_2 \mid R_1 \& R_2 \mid R_1 \cdot R_2 \mid R\{m\} \mid R* \mid \tilde{\ }R \mid$$
$$(?<=R) \mid (?<!R) \mid (?=R) \mid (?!R)$$

The regex denoting *nothing* is the predicate $\bot$. Let $R\{0\} \overset{\mathrm{DEF}}{=} \varepsilon$. We write $R+$ for $R \cdot R*$. Union is also called *alternation* or *disjunction*. The regexes $(?=R)$, $(?!R)$,

(?<=R), and (?<!R) are *lookarounds*; (?=R) is *(positive) lookahead*, (?!R) is *negative lookahead*, (?<=R) is *(positive) lookbehind*, and (?<!R) is *negative lookbehind*. Let \A $\stackrel{\text{DEF}}{=}$ (?<!_) and \z $\stackrel{\text{DEF}}{=}$ (?!_).

ERE is the subclass of **ERE**$_\le$ without lookarounds and **ERE**$_{\text{⊥}}$ extends **ERE** by allowing also the *start anchor* \A and the *end anchor* \z as primitive regexes. **RE**$_\le$ (resp. **RE**) is the subclass of **ERE**$_\le$ (resp. **ERE**) without & and ~.

Match Semantics of ERE with Lookarounds. The match semantics of regexes in **ERE**$_\le$ uses spans [46, 50]. Equivalent formulations of the semantics of **RE** with lookarounds appear originally in [38, Section 3.7] via derivation relations, and in [7, 35] using a variant of spans. Let $\theta = (u, v, s)$ be a span in a word w. Then θ *models* R or R *matches* θ is denoted by $\theta \models R$. We say that R *matches* w iff R matches some span in w. Recall that $R\{0\} \stackrel{\text{DEF}}{=} \varepsilon$ and let $m > 0$.

$$
\begin{aligned}
\theta &\models L \mid R & \stackrel{\text{DEF}}{=}\ & \theta \models L \vee \theta \models R \\
\theta &\models L \,\&\, R & \stackrel{\text{DEF}}{=}\ & \theta \models L \wedge \theta \models R \\
\theta &\models {\sim}R & \stackrel{\text{DEF}}{=}\ & \theta \not\models R \\
\theta &\models R* & \stackrel{\text{DEF}}{=}\ & \exists n \ge 0 : \theta \models R\{n\} \\
(u, v, s) &\models \varepsilon & \stackrel{\text{DEF}}{=}\ & v = \epsilon \\
(u, v, s) &\models \psi & \stackrel{\text{DEF}}{=}\ & |v| = 1 \wedge v \vDash \psi \\
(u, v, s) &\models L{\cdot}R & \stackrel{\text{DEF}}{=}\ & \exists x, y : v = xy \wedge (u, x, ys) \models L \wedge (ux, y, s) \models R \\
(u, v, s) &\models R\{m\} & \stackrel{\text{DEF}}{=}\ & \exists x, y : v = xy \wedge (u, x, ys) \models R \wedge (ux, y, s) \models R\{m{-}1\} \\
(u, v, s) &\models (?{<}{=}R) & \stackrel{\text{DEF}}{=}\ & v = \epsilon \wedge (\epsilon, u, s) \models {\_}*{\cdot}R \\
(u, v, s) &\models (?{<}!R) & \stackrel{\text{DEF}}{=}\ & v = \epsilon \wedge (\epsilon, u, s) \not\models {\_}*{\cdot}R \\
(u, v, s) &\models (?{=}R) & \stackrel{\text{DEF}}{=}\ & v = \epsilon \wedge (u, s, \epsilon) \models R{\cdot}{\_}* \\
(u, v, s) &\models (?!R) & \stackrel{\text{DEF}}{=}\ & v = \epsilon \wedge (u, s, \epsilon) \not\models R{\cdot}{\_}* \\
\mathcal{M}(R) & & \stackrel{\text{DEF}}{=}\ & \{\theta \in \textbf{Span} \mid \theta \models R\} \\
L &\equiv R & \stackrel{\text{DEF}}{=}\ & \mathcal{M}(L) = \mathcal{M}(R)
\end{aligned}
$$

Intuitively, $(u, \epsilon, s) \models (?{=}R)$ means that there exists a match of R *starting* from the location (u, s), and $(u, \epsilon, s) \models (?{<}{=}R)$ means that there exists a match of R *ending* in the location (u, s). For all lookarounds, the matched span has always 0 width, i.e., lookarounds are a generalized form of anchors.

Observe that $\mathcal{M}({\_}*) = \textbf{Span}$, $\mathcal{M}(\bot) = \emptyset$, and all the Boolean connectives satisfy the EBA conditions of **ERE**$_\le$. Thus, (**Span**, **ERE**$_\le$, $\models$, $\bot$, ${\_}*$, $\mid$, &, ~) is an EBA, since $sp \models R$ is decidable for all $sp \in \textbf{Span}$ and $R \in \textbf{ERE}_\le$ because $\vDash$ is decidable in $\mathcal{A}$.

Transition Regexes. A *transition regex* is either a *leaf* $R \in \textbf{ERE}_{\text{⊥}}$, or an ITE expression $\textbf{ite}(\psi, f, g)$ with *condition* $\psi \in \mathcal{A}$, *then-case* f and an *else-case* g that are transition regexes. The *evaluation* of f for $a \in \Sigma$, denoted by $f[a]$, is the leaf regex reached by a.

$$
R[a] \stackrel{\text{DEF}}{=} R \qquad \textbf{ite}(\psi, f, g)[a] \stackrel{\text{DEF}}{=} \begin{cases} f[a], \text{ if } a \vDash \psi; \\ g[a], \text{ otherwise.} \end{cases}
$$

All binary operators ◇ over regexes are lifted to transition regexes by propagating the operations into the leaves. Unary operators such as ˜ and (?=) are propagated analogously. Here $R \in \mathbf{ERE_{\mathcal{J}}}$.

$$R \diamond \mathbf{ite}(\psi, f, g) \stackrel{\mathrm{DEF}}{=} \mathbf{ite}(\psi, R \diamond f, R \diamond g) \quad \mathbf{ite}(\psi, f, g) \diamond h \stackrel{\mathrm{DEF}}{=} \mathbf{ite}(\psi, f \diamond h, g \diamond h)$$

The set of leaves of a transition regex f, denoted by $Lvs(f)$, are the *reachable* leaves of f. In practice, transition regexes are kept *clean* [43] by construction, but here we filter out unreachable leaves explicitly. So $\mathcal{A}$ is assumed *decidable*.

$$Lvs(f) \stackrel{\mathrm{DEF}}{=} Lvs(\_, f) \qquad Lvs(\psi, R) \stackrel{\mathrm{DEF}}{=} \begin{cases} \{R\}, & \text{if } \mathbf{SAT}(\psi); \\ \emptyset, & \text{otherwise.} \end{cases}$$

$$Lvs(\psi, \mathbf{ite}(\alpha, f, g)) \stackrel{\mathrm{DEF}}{=} Lvs(\psi \sqcap \alpha, f) \cup Lvs(\psi \sqcap \alpha^c, g)$$

Symbolic Derivatives in ERE with Anchors. Here we define *nullability* and *symbolic derivatives* for regexes $R \in \mathbf{ERE_{\mathcal{J}}}$. A (symbolic) derivative of R is either taken with respect to an *initial* (and nonfinal) location or a *noninitial* (and nonfinal) location, *final* locations are not used for computing derivatives. Nullability is defined for all locations.

We let the *kind* κ of a location x be $(IsInitial(x), IsFinal(x)) \in \mathbb{B} \times \mathbb{B}$. The three main kinds are INI = $(\mathbf{true}, \mathbf{false})$, MID = $(\mathbf{false}, \mathbf{false})$, and FIN = $(\mathbf{false}, \mathbf{true})$. Using the definitions below we let $Null(R) \stackrel{\mathrm{DEF}}{=} Null_{\mathrm{MID}}(R)$ and $\delta(R) \stackrel{\mathrm{DEF}}{=} \delta_{\mathrm{MID}}(R)$.

Nullability. We define nullability $Null_{\kappa}(R)$ of a regex $R \in \mathbf{ERE_{\mathcal{J}}}$ relative to a *location kind* $\kappa \in \mathbb{B} \times \mathbb{B}$. Let $m > 0$ and recall that $R\{0\} \stackrel{\mathrm{DEF}}{=} \varepsilon$.

$$Null_{(initial, final)}(\backslash \mathsf{A}) \stackrel{\mathrm{DEF}}{=} initial \qquad Null_{\kappa}(R \mid S) \stackrel{\mathrm{DEF}}{=} Null_{\kappa}(R) \vee Null_{\kappa}(S)$$

$$Null_{(initial, final)}(\backslash \mathsf{z}) \stackrel{\mathrm{DEF}}{=} final \qquad Null_{\kappa}(R \,\&\, S) \stackrel{\mathrm{DEF}}{=} Null_{\kappa}(R) \wedge Null_{\kappa}(S)$$

$$Null_{\kappa}(\varepsilon) \stackrel{\mathrm{DEF}}{=} \mathbf{true} \qquad Null_{\kappa}(R{\cdot}S) \stackrel{\mathrm{DEF}}{=} Null_{\kappa}(R) \wedge Null_{\kappa}(S)$$

$$Null_{\kappa}(R*) \stackrel{\mathrm{DEF}}{=} \mathbf{true} \qquad Null_{\kappa}(R\{m\}) \stackrel{\mathrm{DEF}}{=} Null_{\kappa}(R)$$

$$Null_{\kappa}(\psi) \stackrel{\mathrm{DEF}}{=} \mathbf{false} \qquad Null_{\kappa}(\tilde{\ }R) \stackrel{\mathrm{DEF}}{=} \neg \, Null_{\kappa}(R)$$

So $Null_{\mathrm{INI}}(R)$ is applied in locations of kind INI and $Null_{\mathrm{FIN}}(R)$ is applied in locations of kind FIN. The trivial special case of the single empty location (ϵ, ϵ) in an empty word ϵ that is both initial and final is omitted from discussions.

Symbolic Derivatives. Symbolic derivatives, represented by transition regexes, are only evaluated for *nonfinal* locations, i.e., $\kappa \in \{\mathrm{INI}, \mathrm{MID}\}$ below. We apply the definition of derivatives from [48] and simultaneously lift the definition to transition regexes, similar to [43]. Let $\psi \in \mathcal{A}$, $m > 0$, and $\mathcal{J} \in \{\backslash \mathsf{A}, \backslash \mathsf{z}\}$.

$$\delta_{\kappa}(\mathcal{J}) \stackrel{\mathrm{DEF}}{=} \bot \qquad \delta_{\kappa}(R*) \stackrel{\mathrm{DEF}}{=} \delta_{\kappa}(R){\cdot}R*$$

$$\delta_{\kappa}(\varepsilon) \stackrel{\mathrm{DEF}}{=} \bot \qquad \delta_{\kappa}(R\{m\}) \stackrel{\mathrm{DEF}}{=} \delta_{\kappa}(R){\cdot}R\{m-1\}$$

$$\delta_{\kappa}(R \,\&\, S) \stackrel{\mathrm{DEF}}{=} \delta_{\kappa}(R) \,\&\, \delta_{\kappa}(S) \qquad \delta_{\kappa}(\psi) \stackrel{\mathrm{DEF}}{=} \mathbf{ite}(\psi, \varepsilon, \bot)$$

$$\delta_{\kappa}(R \mid S) \stackrel{\mathrm{DEF}}{=} \delta_{\kappa}(R) \mid \delta_{\kappa}(S) \qquad \delta_{\kappa}(R{\cdot}S) \stackrel{\mathrm{DEF}}{=} \begin{cases} \delta_{\kappa}(R){\cdot}S \mid \delta_{\kappa}(S), & \text{if } Null_{\kappa}(R); \\ \delta_{\kappa}(R){\cdot}S, & \text{otherwise.} \end{cases}$$

$$\delta_{\kappa}(\tilde{\ }R) \stackrel{\mathrm{DEF}}{=} \tilde{\ }\delta_{\kappa}(R)$$

Observe that, by definition, all regex operators are lifted to transition regexes.

4   Decision Procedures for ERE#

The focus of the paper in on the subclass **ERE#** of **ERE$_\leq$** that contains **ERE$_{\downarrow}$** combined with a restricted fragment of lookarounds. In the formal definition below L defines **ERE$_{\downarrow}$**, and R defines **ERE#**. Let $\psi \in \mathcal{A}$ and $m > 0$.

$$L ::= \psi \mid \varepsilon \mid \backslash\mathtt{A} \mid \backslash\mathtt{z} \mid L_1 \mid L_2 \mid L_1 \& L_2 \mid L_1 \cdot L_2 \mid L\{m\} \mid L* \mid \mathtt{\sim}L$$

$$R ::= L \mid (\mathtt{?<=}L)\cdot R \mid (\mathtt{?<!}L)\cdot R \mid R\cdot(\mathtt{?=}L) \mid R\cdot(\mathtt{?!}L) \mid R_1 \mid R_2 \mid R_1 \& R_2 \mid \mathtt{\sim}R$$

We show below that all regexes in **ERE#** have a normal form that is a union of *core regexes* that are regexes of the form $(\mathtt{?<=}L_1)\cdot L_2\cdot(\mathtt{?=}L_3)$ where $L_i \in$ **ERE$_{\downarrow}$**, with L_2, $(\mathtt{?<=}L_1)\cdot L_2$, $L_2\cdot(\mathtt{?=}L_3)$ as special cases because $(\mathtt{?<=}\varepsilon) \equiv (\mathtt{?=}\varepsilon) \equiv \varepsilon$. The definition of **ERE#** properly subsumes the definition of **RE#** in [46] where **RE#** contains all core regexes and is only closed under &.

The match semantics of **ERE#** is based on **ERE$_\leq$**. In particular, it follows that $(\mathbf{Span}, \mathbf{ERE\#}, \models, \bot, \_*, \mid, \&, \mathtt{\sim})$ is an EBA. The main decision procedures we are focusing on for **ERE#** are *emptiness*, *subsumption*, and *equivalence*.

4.1   Deciding Nonemptiness of Core Regexes in ERE#

Here we consider nonemptiness of *core regexes* in **ERE#**. We later show how the general case of nonemptiness of all regexes in **ERE#** reduces to nonemptiness of core regexes by showing that **ERE#** is a *decidable* EBA. The nonemptiness algorithm builds on symbolic derivatives and transition terms and can be abstractly formulated as a fixpoint procedure that relies on the associativity, commutativity, and idempotence (ACI) of regex union, which guarantees finiteness of the state space and thus termination.

For a union regex let $Set(R_1 \mid R_2) \stackrel{\mathrm{DEF}}{=} Set(R_1) \cup Set(R_2)$. Let $Set(\bot) \stackrel{\mathrm{DEF}}{=} \emptyset$ and for all other regexes R let $Set(R) \stackrel{\mathrm{DEF}}{=} \{R\}$. Let f be a transition regex. The set of all *states* of f is the set of all $q \in Set(\ell)$ for $\ell \in Lvs(f)$, i.e.,

$$States(f) \stackrel{\mathrm{DEF}}{=} \bigcup_{\ell \in Lvs(f)} Set(\ell)$$

For all $R = (\mathtt{?<=}L_1)\cdot L_2\cdot(\mathtt{?=}L_3) \in$ **ERE#**, where $L_i \in$ **ERE$_{\downarrow}$**, we decide nonemptiness of R by reducing it to nonemptiness in **ERE$_{\downarrow}$** as follows.

$$IsNonempty((\mathtt{?<=}L_1)\cdot L_2\cdot(\mathtt{?=}L_3)) \stackrel{\mathrm{DEF}}{=} IsNonempty(\_*\cdot L_1\cdot L_2\cdot L_3\cdot\_*)$$

Let $L \in$ **ERE$_{\downarrow}$**. The function $IsNonempty(L)$, unless L is trivially nullable, computes reachable states from L and returns **true** upon reaching a nullable state.

$IsNonempty(L) \stackrel{\mathrm{DEF}}{=}$ **if** $Null_{(\mathrm{true,true})}(L) \vee Null_{\mathrm{INI}}(L)$ **return true**

$\quad\quad \rho(L) \leftarrow \delta_{\mathrm{INI}}(L);\ Q \leftarrow \{L\} \cup States(\rho(L))$

$\quad\quad$ **while** $\nexists q \in Q : (Null(q) \vee Null_{\mathrm{FIN}}(q)) \wedge \exists q \in Q \setminus Dom(\rho)$ **do**

$\quad\quad\quad \rho(q) \leftarrow \delta(q);\ Q \leftarrow Q \cup States(\rho(q))$

$\quad\quad$ **return** $\exists q \in Q : Null(q) \vee Null_{\mathrm{FIN}}(q)$

$$\text{NOT-ELIM} \frac{\sim((?<=X)Y(?=Z))}{(?<!X)\_* \mid \sim Y \mid \_*(?!Z)} \qquad \text{L-DISTR} \frac{(Y\mid Z)X}{YX\mid ZX} \qquad \text{R-DISTR} \frac{X(Y\mid Z)}{XY\mid XZ}$$

$$\text{NLA-ELIM} \frac{(?!X)}{(?=\sim(X\_*)\backslash z)} \qquad \text{LA-JOIN} \frac{(?=X)(?=Y)}{(?=X\_*\&Y\_*)} \qquad \text{LB-JOIN} \frac{(?<=X)(?<=Y)}{(?<=\_*X\&\_*Y)}$$

$$\text{NLB-ELIM} \frac{(?<!X)}{(?<=\backslash A\sim(\_*X))} \qquad \text{AND-ELIM} \frac{(?<=X)Y(?=Z)\&(?<=X')Y'(?=Z')}{(?<=X)(?<=X')(Y\&Y')(?=Z)(?=Z')}$$

Fig. 3. Main inference rules in $\textbf{ERE}_\le$ used in Theorem 2. Let NOT-ELIM#= NOT-ELIM∘NLB-ELIM∘NLA-ELIM, and AND-ELIM#= AND-ELIM∘LB-JOIN∘LA-JOIN.

Example 1. Let $R := (?<=\backslash A)\varepsilon(?=\sim\backslash z)$. Then $Null_{\text{INI}}(\_*\backslash A\sim\backslash z\_*) = \textbf{true}$. Here R only matches spans of 0 width whose start location is initial and end location in nonfinal, i.e., $\mathcal{M}(R) = \{(\epsilon, \epsilon, v) \mid v \in \Sigma^+\}$.

Let $R := (?<=\backslash A)\_(?=\backslash z)$. Then $L = \_*\backslash A\_\backslash z\_*$ and $\rho(L) = L\mid \backslash z\_*$. So initially $Q = \{L, \backslash z\_*\}$ because $States(L\mid \backslash z\_*) = \{L, \backslash z\_*\}$ and we have that $Null_{\text{FIN}}(\backslash z\_*) = \textbf{true}$. Note that $\mathcal{M}(R) = \{(\varepsilon, a, \varepsilon) \mid a \in \Sigma\}$.

Theorem 1 (NonEmptiness). $\mathcal{M}(R) \ne \emptyset \Leftrightarrow IsNonempty(R)$ *holds for all core regexes R in* $\textbf{ERE\#}$.

$IsNonempty(R)$ can be extended to produce a *witness* when **true**. In most precise form, the produced witness can be in form of a *symbolic span* $(\alpha_1, \alpha_2, \alpha_3) \in \mathcal{A}^* \times \mathcal{A}^* \times \mathcal{A}^*$ such that, for all spans (u_1, u_2, u_3), such that $u_i \vDash \alpha_i$, it holds that $(u_1, u_2, u_3) \models R$, where $(a_i)_{i<n} \vDash (\psi_i)_{i<m}$ stands for $n = m$ and $\bigwedge_{i<n}(a_i \vDash \psi_i)$.

4.2 Lookaround Normal Form of ERE#

We start by providing a collection of equivalence preserving inference rules in $\textbf{ERE}_\le$, see Fig. 3, that are used to rewrite regexes in $\textbf{ERE\#}$ into the desired normal form. All rules have been formalized and proved correct in Lean. Observe that all rules preserve $\textbf{ERE\#}$, i.e., lookaround bodies remain in $\textbf{ERE}_\ddagger$.

The key new rule is NOT-ELIM. The other rules involving lookarounds are derived from similar rewrites in [46] where the normal form is *linear* in the size of the original $\textbf{RE\#}$ formula. In the case of $\textbf{ERE\#}$ the lookaround normal form can be *exponential* in the size of the original formula.

Let R be a Boolean combination of *core regexes*. We define the *negation normal form* $NNF(R)$ of R where regex complement $\sim$ has been propagated via de Morgan extended with the rule NOT-ELIM#. It follows that no subregex of $NNF(R)$ outside $\textbf{ERE}_\ddagger$ is negated and all lookarounds are positive.

Many further simplification laws are used as rewrites. The basic ones are treating $(\_*, \bot)$ as the units of $(\&, \mid)$ and as the zeros of $(\mid, \&)$, and $\bot$ is also the zero of $\cdot$ and ε is the unit of $\cdot$. Further rules include $(?<!\varepsilon) \equiv \bot$ and $(?!\varepsilon) \equiv \bot$, as well as $(?=\bot) \equiv \bot$ and $(?<=\bot) \equiv \bot$. Also, $\_*\backslash A \equiv \backslash A$ and $\backslash z\_* \equiv \backslash z$.

Further practical rewrites for negative lookarounds with body $\psi \in \mathcal{A}$ are $(?<!\psi) \equiv (?<=\psi^c\mid\backslash A)$ and $(?!\psi) \equiv (?=\psi^c\mid\backslash z)$ as equivalent but simplified variants of NLB-ELIM and NLA-ELIM, respectively.

Example 2. The regex (?!abc\z) is intuitive, it states that the suffix of a match must not be abc. So (?=~(abc\z)\z) is equivalent but less intuitive.

To illustrate some rules, consider ~((?<=a)_*b_*|_*c_*) in **ERE#**. Here we also make use of ~(_*b_*) ≡ [^b]* and ~(_*c_*) ≡ [^c]*, as well as [^b]*&[^c]* ≡ [^bc]* (using standard negated character class notation).

$$\text{~((?<=a)\_*b\_*|\_*c\_*)} \overset{\text{DeMorgan}}{\equiv} \text{~((?<=a)\_*b\_*)\&~(\_*c\_*)}$$

$$\overset{\text{NOT-ELIM}}{\equiv} \text{((?<!a)\_*|~(\_*b\_*))\&~(\_*c\_*)}$$

$$\overset{\text{NLB-ELIM}}{\equiv} \text{((?<=[^a]|\textbackslash A)\_*|~(\_*b\_*))\&~(\_*c\_*)}$$

$$\equiv \text{((?<=[^a]|\textbackslash A)\_*|[^b]*)\&[^c]*}$$

$$\equiv \text{(?<!a)[^c]*|[^bc]*}$$

For example, $(\varepsilon, \mathrm{b}, \varepsilon) \models$ (?<!a)[^c]* but $(\varepsilon, \mathrm{b}, \varepsilon) \not\models$ (?<=a)_*b_*|_*c_*.

4.3   Formalization in Lean

We now present the key result that establishes the correctness of the Lookaround Normal Form (LNF). Our approach follows the formalization presented in [50], which defines the match semantics for the entire class of regular expressions **ERE$_\leq$**. In this work, we explicitly handle three distinct types of match semantics, each corresponding to different subclasses of regular expressions: **ERE$_\pm$**, **ERE#**, and **ERE$_\leq$**, and establish their relationships to ensure correct correspondence between their semantics. Additionally, we introduce an internal conversion between the RESharp type and its positive fragment, PosRESharp, which excludes complements and negative lookarounds.

First, we present some auxiliary definitions. The central definition in our formalization is the lnf function, which converts a regex in **ERE#** into a list of core regexes. The normalization function LNF in Theorem 2 is defined in terms of lnf. The lnf function is defined inductively and implements the inference rules presented in Fig. 3. Components such as la_join, lb_join, and intersection closely follow the corresponding rules.

The lnf function definition, returning a list of core regexes, is as follows.[2]

```
def lnf (r : RESharp 𝒜) : List (CoreRegex 𝒜) :=
match r with
| Ere r            => [EREa_to_CoreRegex r]
| Lookahead r la   => map (la_join la) (lnf r)
| Lookbehind lb r  => map (lb_join lb) (lnf r)
| NLookahead r la  => map (la_join (nLookahead la)) (lnf r)
| NLookbehind lb r => map (lb_join (nLookbehind lb)) (lnf r)
| Alt l r          => lnf l ++ lnf r
| Inter l r        => productWith intersection (lnf l) (lnf r)
| Compl r          => takeNegations (lnf r)
```

---

[2] The full Lean formalization is available in the supplemental material.

The most intricate case involves the complement operation. To handle this case more easily and to simplify the proof structure, we introduce an auxiliary function, `takeNegations`, that specifically deals with negated expressions.

```
def takeNegations (rs : List (CoreRegex 𝒜)) : List (CoreRegex 𝒜) :=
match rs with
| []      => [EREa_to_CoreRegex _*]
| c :: cs => let cs' := takeNegations cs
  map (.lb_join (nLookbehind c.left)) cs' ++
  map (.la_join (nLookahead c.right)) cs' ++
  map (intersection (EREa_to_CoreRegex (~c.regex))) cs'
```

Intuitively, the three lists correspond to the inference rule NOT-ELIM where any of the three components of the union can be satisfied in order to satisfy the negation of the whole expression.

Let us give the remaining definition, LNF, in the Theorem 2.

```
def LNF (r : RESharp 𝒜) : RESharp 𝒜 := re_sum_pos (map sem (lnf r))
```

It first transforms the input regex into its Lookaround Normal Form (LNF) using the `lnf` function. Then, it applies the `sem` function to each core regex in the LNF list, converting them into their corresponding **ERE#** representation e.g., the core regex (L_1, L_2, L_3) is converted into $(?<=L_1)\cdot L_2\cdot(?=L_3)$. Finally, `re_sum_pos` combines the resulting list of **ERE#** expressions with the union operator.

Finally, we are ready to state the main theorem where RESharp denotes **ERE#**.

Theorem 2 (LNF)

```
theorem lnf_correct {R : RESharp 𝒜} {sp : Span Σ} : sp ⊨ R ↔ sp ⊨ LNF R
```

Theorem 2 states that the match semantics of a regex R remains unchanged when it is transformed into its equivalent Lookaround Normal Form (LNF). In other words, converting a regex into LNF preserves its matching behavior. The proof proceeds by induction on R, where we demonstrate that the normalization function behaves as expected for each case.

Theorem 3 (Decidability). *If $\mathcal{A}$ is decidable then so is* **ERE#** *modulo $\mathcal{A}$.*

Proof. Let $R \in$ **ERE#**. Then $\mathcal{M}(R) \neq \emptyset \Leftrightarrow \exists S \in LNF(R) : \mathcal{M}(S) \neq \emptyset$ holds by Theorem 2 and $\mathcal{M}(S) \neq \emptyset \Leftrightarrow IsNonempty(S)$ holds by Theorem 1, where *IsNonempty(S)* uses *cleaning* which requires $\mathcal{A}$ to be decidable.   ☒

Decidability of **RE** extended with arbitrary lookaheads has been shown in [8]. Note that **ERE#** supports a restricted form of lookaheads, e.g., nested lookaheads are not supported and **ERE#** is not closed under concatenation. On the other hand, **ERE#** supports also restricted lookbehinds and is closed under reversal. Although we have provided a decision procedure for **ERE#**, an efficient symbolic decision procedure for the full class **ERE**$_{\leq}$ remains an open problem.

4.4   Subsumption and Equivalence in ERE#

Let $R, S \in$ **ERE#**. Then S *subsumes* R or R *is subsumed by* S, denoted by $R \sqsubseteq S$ means that $M(R) \subseteq M(S)$. Subsumption is equivalent to *emptiness* of R & $\~S$, since $M(R \ \& \ \~S) = \emptyset \Leftrightarrow M(R) \setminus M(S) = \emptyset \Leftrightarrow M(R) \subseteq M(S)$.

One can also consider various *language semantics* of R such as $word(M(R))$ and $match(M(R))$ and related equivalence relations. In general, those are weaker than $\equiv$. E.g., $M((?<=\backslash Aa\backslash z)) = \{(a, \varepsilon, \varepsilon)\}$ and $M((?=\backslash Aa\backslash z)) = \{(\varepsilon, \varepsilon, a)\}$ while the *word* language is $\{a\}$ and the *match* language is $\{\varepsilon\}$ in both cases. The important special case is for regexes $\backslash AR\backslash z$ whose language $match(M(\backslash AR\backslash z))$ corresponds exactly to $M(\backslash AR\backslash z)$.

One method to decide equivalence $R \equiv S$ is to decide that both $R \sqsubseteq S$ and $S \sqsubseteq R$ hold, that is emptiness of $R \ \& \ \~S \ | \ S \ \& \ \~R$. A different method is to use an additional Boolean operator for *symmetric difference* (XOR) $\oplus$ whose derivative rule in **ERE$_\pm$** would remain the same as for all the other binary operators:

$$\delta_\kappa(R \oplus S) = \delta_\kappa(R) \oplus \delta_\kappa(S) \qquad Null_\kappa(R \oplus S) \overset{\text{DEF}}{=} (Null_\kappa(R) \neq Null_\kappa(S))$$

Thus, $IsNonempty(R \oplus S) \Leftrightarrow R \not\equiv S$. While this works for $R, S \in$ **ERE$_\pm$**, it is unclear if this method generalizes to the whole **ERE#** in a "useful" manner, since $LNF(R \oplus S)$ would have to break the problem into separate disjuncts. The $\oplus$ operator also has a dual $XNOR$ operator $\odot$ so that $\~(R \oplus S) \equiv \~R \odot \~S$:

$$\delta_\kappa(R \odot S) = \delta_\kappa(R) \odot \delta_\kappa(S) \qquad Null_\kappa(R \odot S) \overset{\text{DEF}}{=} (Null_\kappa(R) = Null_\kappa(S))$$

So $\oplus$ and $\odot$ can be used like any other binary operator in any regex.

Example 3. Given the regex $q_0 = \backslash A([ab]+\&\~(\_*aa\_*))\backslash z$ and the regex $r_0 = \backslash A(a(b+a?)*|b(a?(\backslash z|b+))*)\backslash z$, we consider their equivalence. Both regexes match all strings in [ab]+ without aa as a substring. While q_0 is quite transparent in this regard, r_0 is less clear but avoids & and $\~$. We prove their equivalence below, by using $\oplus$. We first describe their symbolic derivatives and resulting (symbolic) DFAs separately, as illustrated in Fig. 4. For example, for the regex q_0 we get that $\delta_{\text{INI}}(q_0) = \mathbf{ite}(a, q_2, \mathbf{ite}(b, q_1, \bot)) = \delta(q_1)$, and for the regex r_0 we get that $\delta_{\text{INI}}(r_0) = \mathbf{ite}(a, r_1, \mathbf{ite}(b, r_2, \bot))$ and $\delta(r_1) = \mathbf{ite}(b, r_3, \bot)$, etc., where the leaf regexes are shown as states in Figs. 4a and 4b. Now, returning to equivalence, the DFA for $r_0 \oplus q_0$ looks similar to Fig. 4b, e.g.,

$$\delta_{\text{INI}}(r_0 \oplus q_0) = \mathbf{ite}(a, q_2, \mathbf{ite}(b, q_1, \bot)) \oplus \mathbf{ite}(a, r_1, \mathbf{ite}(b, r_2, \bot))$$
$$\equiv \mathbf{ite}(a, q_2 \oplus r_1, \mathbf{ite}(b, q_1 \oplus r_2, \bot))$$

except that the DFA has no accepting states. E.g., $Null_{\text{FIN}}(q_2 \oplus r_1) = \mathbf{false}$ because both q_2 and r_1 are nullable, similarly for all the other states. Thus $r_0 \equiv q_0$.

An algorithm for regex equivalence based on $\oplus$ would not need to construct a complete DFA for $\oplus$, in particular when a witness of inequivalence is not needed. Such an algorithm is ongoing work that falls outside the scope of this paper.

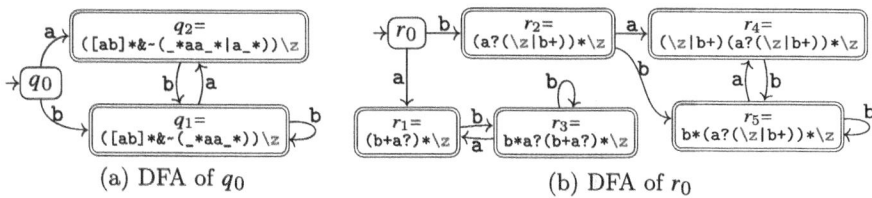

(a) DFA of q_0 (b) DFA of r_0

Fig. 4. $q_0=$\A([ab]+&~(_*aa_*))\z and $r_0=$\A(a(b+a?)*|b(a?(\z|b+))*)\z. The *sink* state $\bot$ is implicit – from each state s there is a symbolic transition to the sink state for all the other characters, e.g., $\delta(q_1)[c] = \bot$ and $\delta(r_1)[a] = \bot$.

5 Implementation

Our implementation of the decision procedures is done in the Rust programming language. The implementation is available on GitHub [45]. It supports a subset of the Unicode Strings theory in SMT-LIB [13], with a parser that converts smt2 format into our internal representation of regexes.

All the supported operations are implemented as operations on **ERE#**, and we support all the RegLan operations in the SMT-LIB standard. Operations that can not be represented as regexes in a straightforward manner such as str.replace are considered out of scope, as well as operations on a higher level of abstraction, such as the loop R$\{n\}$, where n is not a constant. In the formal semantics, the regex $R\{m,n\}$, where $0 < m \leq n$, stands for $R\{m\}\cdot(R|\varepsilon)\{n-m\}$.

The operations supported in the implementation include the following.

- All operations starting with re. on constants or other regexes, such as re.++, re.union, re.*, etc.
- **ERE** membership str.in_re on variables and constants
- String assertions that translate intuitively into **ERE**, such as:
  $$\frac{\texttt{str.len } x < 5}{\_\{0,4\}} \quad \frac{\texttt{str.prefixof"abc" } x}{\texttt{abc\_*}} \quad \frac{\texttt{str.contains "abc" } x}{\texttt{\_*abc\_*}}$$
- Boolean operations such as and, or, not on any of the above, e.g.,
  $$\frac{(\texttt{str.len } x > 3) \texttt{ and } (\texttt{str.len } x < 9)}{\_\{4,\}\&\_\{0,8\} \ (\equiv \_\{4,8\})}$$
- Standard conversions and utilities such as str.to_int, str.to_re, str.++

5.1 Representation of Regexes

In the implementation, each regex is represented as a tree structure of nodes, where each node has:

1. a unique identifier (unsigned 32-bit integer)
2. a kind specifier (e.g., predicate, union, concatenation, etc.)
3. the unique identifiers of the left and right child (or 0 if missing)
4. various additional information (e.g., bit-flags, and relevant character set)

Data stored as additional information includes a compact integer encoding of a predicate φ_r for each node r that approximates the relevant characters in r, as defined in [46, Section 5.3] with related rewrites. Additionally, r maintains several bit-flags that can be inferred during construction, such as whether the language contains the empty string (i.e., r is nullable), the presence of anchors in r, or whether r contains extended operations such as & or ~.

When working with UTF8 representation, the character EBA $\mathcal{A}$ is over *bytes* as Σ. The representation of valid UTF8 strings is the regex R_{UTF8}:

$$([\text{\x00-\x7F}] \mid [\text{\xC0-\xDF}]\beta \mid [\text{\xE0-\xEF}]\beta\{2\} \mid [\text{\xF0-\xF7}]\beta\{3\})*$$

where $\beta = [\text{\x80-\xBF}]$ is the *continuation byte* predicate. When working with any regex $R \in \textbf{ERE}_{\pm}$, the intersection $R\ \&\ \backslash A R_{\text{UTF8}} \backslash z$ restricts the accepted word language to $\mathcal{L}(R_{\text{UTF8}})$ that is a proper subset of Σ^*.

The predicates ψ in $\mathcal{A}$ are represented as 256-bit bit-vectors, allowing for efficient constant-time Boolean operations. Each $i \in \Sigma$ corresponds to the i'th bit of ψ. $\mathcal{A}$ has trivial checks for $\psi \equiv \bot$ and for $\psi \equiv \_$ since $\bot = 0$ and $\_ = 2^{256}-1$.

To accelerate the bit-vector operations further, we perform the operations in parallel over the 64-bit integers using Single Instruction Multiple Data (SIMD) instructions available in modern CPUs, e.g., AVX2 or SSE4.2.

We assign a unique identifier to each predicate, allowing us to represent the predicate of a node as a 32-bit integer instead of a 256-bit bit-vector. This reduces the maximum number of unique predicates in a given regex to 2^{32}, but in practice this is a reasonable trade-off, as it is very unlikely that a regex would contain more than a thousand unique character sets, let alone 2^{32}.

The identifier of the node represents the syntactic structure of the regex, and is used to memoize the results of the operations on the regexes. The integers are assigned sequentially during construction, for example, the regex (a|b) would be assigned the integer 3, and point to the corresponding leaf nodes 1 and 2, representing the characters a and b respectively. To prevent duplicate identifiers, we use a hash map to store the regexes that have been constructed so far.

While not strictly relevant to the theory, we also have several rules for normalization, such as always having the left child of a union or intersection operation be the smaller identifier. Thus, the regexes (a|b) and (b|a) would be normalized to the same regex, which ever is constructed first. We also enforce that concatenations can only contain inner concatenations on the right to prevent ambiguous nesting. Together, these rules ensure that the syntactic construction of the regex is unique up to commutativity and associativity, but this does not prevent the construction of equivalent regexes in terms of the language they represent. For example, $(\varepsilon|b)\{50\}$ and $(b\{0,25\})\{2\}$ represent the same language, but are constructed as different regexes – to detect equivalence between such examples, we would need to use the equivalence decision procedure.

5.2   Rewrite Rules and Simplifications

An important part of the implementation is the simplification and memoization of regexes during construction. The simplifications are applied bottom-up, i.e., when a regex is constructed, the children of the regex are already simplified. The simplifications are based on the rules in [46], but in a more general way, as, in addition to the algebraic rules, we can perform language-level operations on the regexes directly.

For example, the regex _*a_*b_*|_*b_* would be simplified to _*b_* during construction, as the left branch of the union is subsumed by the right branch. In other words, the language of _*a_*b_* is a subset of the language of _*b_*. Subsumption plays a crucial role in the construction of intersections and unions, as it allows us to prevent construction of redundant definitions, often considerably reducing the size of the regex. We can also check satisfiability of a regex during construction, which allows us to rewrite unsatisfiable regexes to ⊥, which represents the empty language.

For the key rewrite rules on the *match semantics* level, which are used in the implementation, see Fig. 5.

$$\frac{R}{\perp}(\mathcal{M}(R)=\emptyset) \qquad \frac{R}{\_*}(\mathcal{M}(R)=\mathbf{Span}) \qquad \frac{R_1\,|\,R_2}{R_2}(\mathcal{M}(R_1){\subseteq}\mathcal{M}(R_2)) \qquad \frac{R_1\,\&\,R_2}{R_1}(\mathcal{M}(R_1){\subseteq}\mathcal{M}(R_2))$$

Fig. 5. Main rewrite rules at the level of *match semantics*.

Performing these operations during construction gives us a very important property for optimization, which is that any remaining regex after construction is either ⊥ or satisfiable. This allows us to skip many unnecessary satisfiability checks during the decision procedure.

This satisfiability check (leftmost rule in Fig. 5) only needs to be performed when constructing a concatenation with an anchor, an intersection, or complement, as these operations can result in an unsatisfiable regex, given that the children of the operation are satisfiable. The other operations will always result in a satisfiable regex, which we propagate as bit-flags in the implementation.

While the construction of a concatenation node with a satisfiable node and an anchor may result in an unsatisfiable regex, this satisfiability check takes constant time, as it only requires to check whether the language of the other child of the concatenation contains the empty string, which is already known as a bit-flag during construction. For example, the regex b\A is trivially unsatisfiable, and rewritten to ⊥, as the language of b does not contain the empty string, therefore the anchor \A cannot be at the beginning. Similarly, the regex \zb is rewritten to ⊥, as the language of b does not contain the empty string, therefore the anchor \z cannot be at the end.

The second rule in Fig. 5 provides a more efficient way to check for satisfiability of the complement operation, as the only unsatisfiable complement is ~(_*). This means that we can check that a complement is satisfiable by ensuring that the complement body is not equivalent to _*, effectively searching for the existence of a non-accepting state in the body of the complement. While it is not more efficient asymptotically, it is slightly more efficient memory-wise, as we do not need to construct derivatives of the (outer) complement node itself. Often, in practice, such non-accepting state is the very state we start from, skipping the check entirely.

In the solver implementation, we do not perform the satisfiability check for the intersection operation eagerly, as the tasks often consist of many intersections, and proving nonemptiness of a subset of intersections does not necessarily help us in proving nonemptiness of all the intersections combined. Instead, we label each regex with a bit-flag, that indicates whether the regex contains an intersection, and only perform the satisfiability check when requested. If the flag is missing, we can be sure that the regex is already known to be satisfiable.

The solver also includes several variants of rewrite rules that are applied to *bounded loops*. In particular, it uses the LOOP rule and the predicate subsumption rule from [46, Figure 6]. To summarize, the majority of time spent in the solver is proving nonemptiness of intersection, which is done lazily, while the rest of the operations are performed eagerly during construction.

6   Evaluation

The evaluation is based on existing SMT benchmarks. All regular expressions supported in SMT belong to the class **ERE** and therefore do not support anchors, i.e., in terms of $\mathbf{ERE_{\updownarrow}}$ R can be treated as \A$R$\z. For language semantics in $\mathbf{ERE_{\updownarrow}}$, anchors can also be systematically eliminated through preprocessing. We did not use such preprocessing here, because our evaluation did not require it.

We have collected a set of SMT benchmarks for regexes. The benchmarks consist of approximately 20 000 SMT-LIB files, which are a mix of satisfiability problems for regexes, such as equivalence, subsumption, and membership queries. The benchmarks include AutomatArk [21], Denghang and Sygus-qgen benchmark sets from the QF_S and QF_SLIA categories of the SMT-LIB [6] repository, as well as additional benchmarks from the repository [42] designed specifically around difficult regular expression problems.

We compared our implementation (**ERE#**-solver) with the following state-of-the-art tools: cvc5 [5], Z3 [49], Z3str3 [10] , Z3str4 [36] , Z3alpha [34] , OSTRICH [17], OSTRICH^{RECL} [27,28] and Z3-Noodler [19]. The benchmark results (when solved) are identical between **ERE#**-solver, cvc5, Z3 and Z3-Noodler. There are discrepancies in the results of some solvers that we have not yet investigated. Table 1 shows the number of unsolved problems for each benchmark category.

Our solver is a specialized tool for regex constraint solving and analysis, rather than a general purpose SMT solver. As a result, it only supports a subset of the SMT operations that the other tools support. Nevertheless, for the regex benchmarks, our solver consistently outperforms the other tools, see Fig. 1 in the introduction for the cactus plot of the time taken to solve the benchmarks, and Table 1 for the number of unsolved benchmarks.

For our solver, under 100 of the benchmarks took more than 0.01 s to solve, and none of the benchmarks took more than 0.1 s to solve. Many individual

Table 1. Unsolved problems by solver in the various benchmark categories, where **min** and **max** are highlighted in color. Timeout for each problem is **6 s**.

	Syg	Denghang	Aut	Ark	Bool	Date	Blowup	Passwd	Mem	Int	Sub	State	Σ
Included	343	999	15995	21	19	14		34	1907	55	100	22	19509
ERE#-solver	**0**	**0**	**0**	**0**	**0**	**0**		**0**	**0**	**0**	**0**	**0**	**0**
Z3-Noodler	0	1	41	0	0	0		0	0	0	0	0	42
OSTRICH	0	0	75	0	0	0		1	1	2	3	0	82
OSTR^{RECL}	0	26	76	0	0	0		0	1	1	3	1	108
cvc5	1	26	152	2	3	1		7	3	27	28	0	250
Z3	0	124	322	1	0	2		16	2	20	9	8	504
Z3alpha	0	126	210	1	0	3		18	1537	**55**	99	8	2057
Z3str4	0	3	58	1	5	1		17	**1907**	**55**	**100**	6	2153
Z3str3	**37**	**773**	**5353**	1	**14**	0		20	129	21	26	7	**6381**

benchmarks take very little time to solve for other solvers as well, e.g., cvc5 solves thousands of the benchmarks in less than 0.01s, and is generally closest to the time of our solver in Fig. 1. The high lower-bound of the time taken for OSTRICH is likely due to a cold start of the process, as it is a Java-based tool, but in terms of the number of benchmarks solved, it is the third best tool after our solver and Z3-Noodler. The key factors contributing to our solver's significant performance improvement are discussed in the following section.

Performance Analysis. The key differences between our solver and others are in the way in which we represent and solve the problem:

- Our solver contains the problem fully within the regex theory, and does not need to convert any part of the problem to a different theory, such as linear arithmetic. Several other solvers solve regex problems with a combination of regex and linear arithmetic, e.g., encoding length constraints [19].
- Our solver never constructs an automaton for the regex, neither as a DFA nor as an NFA. Instead, it performs the operations symbolically, and the nonemptiness check is done through lazy unfolding of the problem encoded in our regex theory. This is in contrast to many other solvers, which construct an automaton for the regex and perform operations on the automaton.
- Our solver explores *language complement* lazily through derivatives, which is not done in other derivative-based string solvers such as cvc5. Complement is often the bottleneck in equivalence and subsumption checks.

The time required for checking nonemptiness of a regex is *proportional to the number of derivatives constructed*, where each derivative is a deterministic memoized operation that is cached upon the first computation. This reduces the amount of work done to the number of *unique* derivatives reached.

SMT benchmarks for regexes typically fall into two categories: they are either solved within a few milliseconds or remain unsolved due to excessive memory consumption, often caused by an exponential blowup in automaton size. However, our tool avoids the explicit automaton construction, which mitigates the memory usage and allows us to solve many of the benchmarks that other tools fail to solve.

It is important to note that even the lazy graphs constructed by unwinding the problem can grow exponentially in size, and we have to perform simplifications whenever possible to reduce the effect of such blowup. It is done by rewriting the regexes, both algebraically and on the language level, as described in Sect. 4.1.

Many benchmarks are specifically designed to expose the exponential blowup. However, they can be solved almost immediately by performing certain simplifications and short-circuiting. In the following we explain the simplifications and their effect on the benchmarks in more detail.

State Space Considerations. Although the graphs can grow exponentially in size, our solver has several optimizations to mitigate blowup. In many practical cases where other solvers run out of memory, our heuristics enable us to solve the problems much more efficiently. Here we highlight some key optimizations and heuristics demonstrated on problems from the set of collected benchmarks.

Many benchmarks where solvers run out of memory involve the use of large quantifiers, such as `str.len x > 1000` or `re.loop 100 100`. These come with an enormous growth of state space, but as we *do not construct an automaton*, and are not looking for the shortest solution, a depth-first traversal of the state graph is sufficient. Table 2 shows the impact of the approach on satisfiable benchmarks with large quantifiers. The benchmarks are measured by the number of derivatives constructed to reach a solution, with depth-first search significantly outperforming breadth-first search. E.g., depth-first search solves the last benchmark in Table 2 with 495 derivatives in less than 0.002 s, including parsing and pre-processing the problem itself, while breadth-first search takes about 0.725 s.

Table 2. Effect of lazy depth-first search on satisfiable problems

Satisfiability Problem	DFS derivatives	BFS derivatives
`(_*a_*){25}&(_*b_*){25}&_{0,50}`	120	6749
`(_*a_*){50}&(_*b_*){50}&_{0,100}`	245	47874
`(_*a_*){100}&(_*b_*){100}&_{0,200}`	495	358249

While it has an impressive effect on satisfiable problems with a large number of possible solutions, it brings limited advantage for unsatisfiable benchmarks, as search has to exhaust all possibilities before concluding that the regex is unsatisfiable. For unsatisfiable problems, early elimination of trivially unsatisfiable regexes is crucial, as it can reduce search time by several orders of magnitude.

A key simplification for unsatisfiable problems is to prioritize checking length constraints of intersections, as this can be done without taking derivatives and will often eliminate the need for further search.

For example, the regex _{4000,5000}&_{8000,9000} can be rewritten to ⊥ in constant time, as there is no overlap between the minimum and maximum lengths of the two. If there is an overlap, the regex can be rewritten to the intersection of the two length constraints, as was shown in Sect. 5.

Another important heuristic is checking the emptiness of a regex in reverse. It is particularly useful for addressing a common pathological case where large state space is combined with an unsatisfiable suffix. For example, the satisfiability of the regex _*b_{100}& _*a_{100} can be checked for emptiness by reversing the regex to _{100}b_* & _{100}a_* and checking it for emptiness. The reversed approach simplifies the problem significantly, as illustrated in Table 3.

Table 3. Effect of solving unsat suffix problems in reverse

Satisfiability Problem	Rev. derivatives	Fwd. derivatives
_*b_{10}&_*a_{10}& _{10,}abc_{10,}	9	279
_*b_{20}&_*a_{20}& _{20,}abc_{20,}	19	11 833
_*b_{30}&_*a_{30}& _{30,}abc_{30,}	29	539 145
_*b_{40}&_*a_{40}& _{40,}abc_{40,}	39	5 000 000+

7 Proposal for SMT-LIB

We believe that a conservative extension of SMT-LIB to support RegLan = $\mathbf{ERE}_{\leq}$ would be noncontroversial. For positive and negative lookaheads, positive and negative lookbehinds, and *span membership* or *matching* the minimal extension could be as follows where the start anchor re.A and the end anchor re.z could be included as regex constants for convenience:

$(\text{re.lb } r) \overset{\text{DEF}}{=} (?<=r)$ $(\text{re.nlb } r) \overset{\text{DEF}}{=} (?<!r)$ $\text{re.A} \overset{\text{DEF}}{=} (\text{re.nlb re.allchar})$

$(\text{re.la } r) \overset{\text{DEF}}{=} (?=r)$ $(\text{re.nla } r) \overset{\text{DEF}}{=} (?!r)$ $\text{re.z} \overset{\text{DEF}}{=} (\text{re.nla re.allchar})$

$(\text{str.matches } u \ v \ s \ r) \overset{\text{DEF}}{=} (u, v, s) \models r$

Regarding compatibility with **ERE**, $(\text{str.in\_re } \ v \ r)$ fully retains its original interpretation for $r \in \mathbf{ERE}$. It follows by easy induction over $r \in \mathbf{ERE}$ that $\forall u, v, s : (u, v, s) \models r \Leftrightarrow v \in \mathcal{L}(r)$, i.e., $v \in match(\mathcal{M}(r)) \Leftrightarrow v \in \mathcal{L}(r)$. Thus,

$\forall u, v, s \in \text{String}, r \in \mathbf{ERE} : (\text{str.matches } u \ v \ s \ r) \Leftrightarrow (\text{str.in\_rev } r)$

Using lookarounds, one can support other standard anchors such as the *line* anchors ^ and \$ and the *wordborder* anchor \b as (?<!\w)(?=\w) | (?<=\w)(?!\w). One can also express different match semantics like *POSIX match* semantics of $w = uvs \wedge (u, v, s) \models r$, where $|u|$ is minimal and $|v|$ maximal for $|u|$ – the *leftmost longest* match in w – as an SMT optimization problem.

It is also practical to support $\oplus$, say `re.xor`, and $\odot$, say `re.xnor`, natively, in order to avoid their indirect encodings in various algorithms, such as equivalence checking, since $r_1 \equiv r_2 \Leftrightarrow r_1 \oplus r_2 \equiv \bot$. Moreover, *reversal* of sequences and regexes is beneficial, as illustrated above. In particular, $(u, v, s) \models r \Leftrightarrow (s^{\mathrm{r}}, v^{\mathrm{r}}, u^{\mathrm{r}}) \models r^{\mathrm{r}}$.

Acknowledgement. E. Zhuchko is supported by the Estonian Research Council grant *Automata in Learning, Interaction and Concurrency* (PRG1210).

Disclosure of Interests. The authors have no competing interests to declare that are relevant to the content of this article.

References

1. Almeida, M., Moreira, N., Reis, R.: Antimirov and Mosses's rewrite system revisited. Int. J. Found. Comput. Sci. **20**(4), 669–684 (2009). https://doi.org/10.1142/S0129054109006802
2. Almeida, M., Moreira, N., Reis, R.: Testing the equivalence of regular languages. J. Autom. Lang. Comb. **15**(1/2), 7–25 (2010). https://doi.org/10.25596/jalc-2010-007
3. Amadini, R.: A survey on string constraint solving. ACM Comput. Surv. **55**(2), 16:1–16:38 (2023). https://doi.org/10.1145/3484198
4. Antimirov, V.M.: Partial derivatives of regular expressions and finite automaton constructions. Theor. Comput. Sci. **155**(2), 291–319 (1996). https://doi.org/10.1016/0304-3975(95)00182-4
5. Barbosa, H., et al.: cvc5: a versatile and industrial-strength SMT solver. In: Fisman, D., Rosu, G. (eds.) TACAS. LNCS, vol. 13243, pp. 415–442. Springer (2022). https://doi.org/10.1007/978-3-030-99524-9_24
6. Barrett, C., Fontaine, P., Tinelli, C.: The Satisfiability Modulo Theories Library (SMT-LIB) (2016). https://www.SMT-LIB.org
7. Barrière, A., Pit-Claudel, C.: Linear matching of javascript regular expressions. Proc. ACM Program. Lang. **8** (2024). https://doi.org/10.1145/3656431
8. Berglund, M., van der Merwe, B., van Litsenborgh, S.: Regular expressions with lookahead. J. Univ. Comput. Sci. **27**(4), 324–340 (2021). https://doi.org/10.3897/jucs.66330
9. Berzish, M., et al.: Towards more efficient methods for solving regular-expression heavy string constraints. Theor. Comput. Sci. **943**, 50–72 (2023). https://doi.org/10.1016/j.tcs.2022.12.009
10. Berzish, M., Ganesh, V., Zheng, Y.: Z3str3: a string solver with theory-aware heuristics. In: Stewart, D., Weissenbacher, G. (eds.) FMCAD, pp. 55–59. IEEE (2017). https://doi.org/10.23919/FMCAD.2017.8102241
11. Berzish, M., et al.: An SMT solver for regular expressions and linear arithmetic over string length. In: Silva, A., Leino, K.R.M. (eds.) CAV. LNCS, vol. 12760, pp. 289–312. Springer (2021). https://doi.org/10.1007/978-3-030-81688-9_14
12. Bjørner, N., Fazekas, K.: On incremental pre-processing for SMT. In: Pientka, B., Tinelli, C. (eds.) Automated Deduction – CADE 29, pp. 41–60. Springer, Cham (2023). https://doi.org/10.1007/978-3-031-38499-8_3

13. Bjørner, N., Ganesh, V., Michel, R., Veanes, M.: An SMT-LIB format for sequences and regular expressions. In: Fontaine, P., Goel, A. (eds.) SMT, pp. 76–86 (2012). https://doi.org/10.29007/w5m5
14. Blahoudek, F., et al.: Word equations in synergy with regular constraints. In: Chechik, M., Katoen, J., Leucker, M. (eds.) Formal Methods. LNCS, vol. 14000, pp. 403–423. Springer (2023). https://doi.org/10.1007/978-3-031-27481-7_23
15. Brzozowski, J.A.: Derivatives of regular expressions. JACM **11**, 481–494 (1964). https://doi.org/10.1145/321239.321249
16. Chen, T., et al.: Solving string constraints with regex-dependent functions through transducers with priorities and variables. Proc. ACM Program. Lang. **6**(POPL) (2022). https://doi.org/10.1145/3498707
17. Chen, T., Hague, M., Lin, A.W., Rümmer, P., Wu, Z.: Decision procedures for path feasibility of string-manipulating programs with complex operations. Proc. ACM Program. Lang. **3**(POPL), 49:1–49:30 (2019). https://doi.org/10.1145/3290362
18. Chen, Y., Chocholatý, D., Havlena, V., Holík, L., Lengál, O., Síc, J.: Solving string constraints with lengths by stabilization. Proc. ACM Program. Lang. **7**(OOPSLA2), 2112–2141 (2023). https://doi.org/10.1145/3622872
19. Chen, Y., Chocholatý, D., Havlena, V., Holík, L., Lengál, O., Síc, J.: Z3-noodler: an automata-based string solver. In: Finkbeiner, B., Kovács, L. (eds.) TACAS. LNCS, vol. 14570, pp. 24–33. Springer (2024). https://doi.org/10.1007/978-3-031-57246-3_2
20. Chocholatý, D., et al.: Mata: a fast and simple finite automata library. In: Finkbeiner, B., Kovács, L. (eds.) TACAS. LNCS, vol. 14571, pp. 130–151. Springer (2024). https://doi.org/10.1007/978-3-031-57249-4_7
21. D'Antoni, L.: AutomatArk (2018). https://github.com/lorisdanto/automatark
22. D'Antoni, L., Veanes, M.: Automata modulo theories. Commun. ACM **64**(5), 86–95 (2021). https://doi.org/10.1145/3419404
23. Eriksson, B., Stjerna, A., Masellis, R.D., Rümmer, P., Sabelfeld, A.: Black ostrich: web application scanning with string solvers. In: Meng, W., Jensen, C.D., Cremers, C., Kirda, E. (eds.) CCS, pp. 549–563. ACM (2023). https://doi.org/10.1145/3576915.3616582
24. Gallant, A.: BurntSushi: rebar (2024). https://github.com/BurntSushi/rebar
25. Hague, M., Jez, A., Lin, A.W.: Parikh's theorem made symbolic. Proc. ACM Program. Lang. **8**(POPL), 1945–1977 (2024). https://doi.org/10.1145/3632907
26. Hojjat, H., Rümmer, P., Shamakhi, A.: On strings in software model checking. In: Lin, A.W. (ed.) APLAS. LNCS, vol. 11893, pp. 19–30. Springer (2019). https://doi.org/10.1007/978-3-030-34175-6_2
27. Hu, D., Wu, Z.: String constraints with regex-counting and string-length solved more efficiently. In: Hermanns, H., Sun, J., Bu, L. (eds.) SETTA. LNCS, vol. 14464, pp. 1–20. Springer (2023). https://doi.org/10.1007/978-981-99-8664-4_1
28. Hu, D., Wu, Z.: An efficient string solver for string constraints with regex-counting and string-length. J. Syst. Archit., 1–38 (2025). https://doi.org/10.1016/j.sysarc.2025.103340
29. Jez, A., Lin, A.W., Markgraf, O., Rümmer, P.: Decision procedures for sequence theories. In: Enea, C., Lal, A. (eds.) CAV. LNCS, vol. 13965, pp. 18–40. Springer (2023). https://doi.org/10.1007/978-3-031-37703-7_2
30. Le, Q.L., He, M.: A decision procedure for string logic with quadratic equations, regular expressions and length constraints. In: Ryu, S. (ed.) APLAS. LNCS, vol. 11275, pp. 350–372. Springer (2018). https://doi.org/10.1007/978-3-030-02768-1_19

31. Liang, T., Reynolds, A., Tsiskaridze, N., Tinelli, C., Barrett, C., Deters, M.: An efficient SMT solver for string constraints. Formal Methods Syst. Des. **48**(3), 206–234 (2016). https://doi.org/10.1007/s10703-016-0247-6
32. Liang, T., Tsiskaridze, N., Reynolds, A., Tinelli, C., Barrett, C.W.: A decision procedure for regular membership and length constraints over unbounded strings. In: Lutz, C., Ranise, S. (eds.) FroCoS. LNCS, vol. 9322, pp. 135–150. Springer (2015). https://doi.org/10.1007/978-3-319-24246-0_9
33. Lotz, K., et al.: Solving string constraints using SAT. In: Enea, C., Lal, A. (eds.) CAV. LNCS, vol. 13965, pp. 187–208. Springer (2023). https://doi.org/10.1007/978-3-031-37703-7_9
34. Lu, Z., Siemer, S., Jha, P., Day, J.D., Manea, F., Ganesh, V.: Layered and staged Monte Carlo tree search for SMT strategy synthesis. In: IJCAI, pp. 1907–1915. ijcai.org (2024). https://doi.org/10.24963/ijcai.2024/211
35. Mamouras, K., Chattopadhyay, A.: Efficient matching of regular expressions with lookaround assertions. Proc. ACM Program. Lang. **8**(POPL), 2761–2791 (2024). https://doi.org/10.1145/3632934
36. Mora, F., Berzish, M., Kulczynski, M., Nowotka, D., Ganesh, V.: Z3str4: a multi-armed string solver. In: FM, pp. 389–406. Springer, Heidelberg (2021). https://doi.org/10.1007/978-3-030-90870-6_21
37. Moreira, N., Pereira, D., de Sousa, S.M.: Deciding regular expressions (in-)equivalence in CoQ. In: Kahl, W., Griffin, T.G. (eds.) RAMiCS. LNCS, vol. 7560, pp. 98–113. Springer, Heidelberg (2012). https://doi.org/10.1007/978-3-642-33314-9_7
38. Moseley, D., et al.: Derivative based nonbacktracking real-world regex matching with backtracking semantics. Proc. ACM Program. Lang. **7**(PLDI), 148:1–148:24 (2023). https://doi.org/10.1145/3591262
39. de Moura, L., Bjørner, N.: Z3: an efficient SMT solver. In: TACAS. LNCS, vol. 4963, pp. 337–340. Springer, Heidelberg (2008). https://doi.org/10.1007/978-3-540-78800-3_24
40. Owens, S., Reppy, J.H., Turon, A.: Regular-expression derivatives re-examined. J. Funct. Program. **19**(2), 173–190 (2009). https://doi.org/10.1017/S0956796808007090
41. Reynolds, A., Woo, M., Barrett, C.W., Brumley, D., Liang, T., Tinelli, C.: Scaling up DPLL(T) string solvers using context-dependent simplification. In: Majumdar, R., Kuncak, V. (eds.) CAV. LNCS, vol. 10427, pp. 453–474. Springer (2017). https://doi.org/10.1007/978-3-319-63390-9_24
42. Stanford, C.: Boolean Regular Expression SMT Benchmarks (2021). https://github.com/cdstanford/regex-smt-benchmarks
43. Stanford, C., Veanes, M., Bjørner, N.S.: Symbolic boolean derivatives for efficiently solving extended regular expression constraints. In: Freund, S.N., Yahav, E. (eds.) PLDI, pp. 620–635. ACM (2021). https://doi.org/10.1145/3453483.3454066
44. Turoňová, L., Holík, L., Homoliak, I., Lengál, O., Veanes, M., Vojnar, T.: Counting in regexes considered harmful: exposing ReDoS vulnerability of nonbacktracking matchers. In: 31st USENIX Security Symposium (USENIX Security 2022), pp. 4165–4182. USENIX Association, Boston (2022). https://www.usenix.org/conference/usenixsecurity22/presentation/turonova
45. Varatalu, I.E.: Implementation of RE#-solver (2025). https://github.com/ieviev/cav25-resharp-smt
46. Varatalu, I.E., Veanes, M., Ernits, J.: RE#: high performance derivative-based regex matching with intersection, complement, and restricted lookarounds. Proc. ACM Program. Lang. **9**(POPL), 1:1–1:32 (2025). https://doi.org/10.1145/3704837

47. Varatalu, I.E., Zhuchko, E., Ernits, J.: Artifact for regex decision procedures in extended RE# (2025). https://doi.org/10.5281/zenodo.15210805
48. Veanes, M., Ball, T., Ebner, G., Zhuchko, E.: Symbolic automata: Omega-regularity modulo theories. Proc. ACM Program. Lang. **9**(POPL), 2:1–2:34 (2025). https://doi.org/10.1145/3704838
49. Z3 Prover. https://github.com/Z3Prover/z3/wiki
50. Zhuchko, E., Veanes, M., Ebner, G.: Lean formalization of extended regular expression matching with lookarounds. In: Timany, A., Traytel, D., Pientka, B., Blazy, S. (eds.) CPP, pp. 118–131. ACM (2024). https://doi.org/10.1145/3636501.3636959

Verified and Optimized Implementation of Orthologic Proof Search

Simon Guilloud$^{(\boxtimes)}$ and Clément Pit-Claudel

School of Computer and Communication Sciences, EPFL,
Station 14, 1015 Lausanne, Switzerland
{simon.guilloud,clement.pit-claudel}@epfl.ch

Abstract. We report on the development of an optimized and verified decision procedure for orthologic equalities and inequalities. This decision procedure is quadratic-time and is used as a sound, efficient and predictable approximation to classical propositional logic in automated reasoning tools. We formalize, in the Coq proof assistant, a proof system in sequent-calculus style for orthologic. We then prove its soundness and completeness with respect to the algebraic variety of ortholattices, and we formalize a cut-elimination theorem. In doing so, we discover and fix a missing case in a previously published proof.

We then implement and verify a complete proof search procedure for orthologic. A naive implementation is exponential; to obtain an optimal quadratic run time, we optimize the implementation by memoizing its results and simulating reference equality testing. We leverage the resulting correctness theorem to implement a reflective Coq tactic. We present benchmarks showing that the procedure, under various optimizations, matches its theoretical complexity.

Finally, we develop a collection of tactics, including normalization with respect to orthologic and a boolean solver, which we also benchmark. We make tactics available as a standalone Coq plugin.

1 Introduction

Specialized, reliable and efficient building blocks are indispensable in scaling automated reasoning software. Program verifiers, SMT solvers, proof assistants and automated theorem provers use them to tackle the various theories and subproblems that comprise a logical statement. As they build up, so does the possibility of an implementation error. To ensure that they can be used as trusted components in program verification pipelines, these verification algorithms should themselves be verified.

One fragment of particular interest is propositional logic. Despite significant progress in SAT solvers, solving satisfiability or validity of propositional formulas remains a major challenge to scalability of decision procedures. An alternative and complementary approach to heuristics is orthologic-based reasoning. Orthologic (OL) is a non-distributive generalization of classical propositional

© The Author(s) 2025
R. Piskac and Z. Rakamarić (Eds.): CAV 2025, LNCS 15933, pp. 130–152, 2025.
https://doi.org/10.1007/978-3-031-98682-6_8

logic which admits polynomial-time $(\mathcal{O}(n^2))$ validity checking and normalization algorithms [4,9,12]. Orthologic offers a trade-off: it sacrifices completeness (with respect to classical semantics) in exchange for guaranteed efficiency and predictability. It also admits a quadratic-time normalization algorithm, allowing to compute a unique normal form (with respect to the laws of orthologic) of guaranteed minimal size.

In the Lisa proof assistant [10], orthologic is key in making proofs shorter and easier to write: while the proof system supports classical sequent calculus, any formula transformation that holds true in (a first order extension of) orthologic can be deduced implicitly in a single step. This in particular takes into account a variety of intuitive transformations, such as negation normal form, absorption and reordering conjuncts and disjuncts, and keeps proof checking efficient.

In [9], orthologic normal form is used to improve the cache hit ratio of verification conditions, and to simplify them before sending them to an SMT solver.

The foundations of an extension to Datalog with negation and disjunction based on orthologic has been suggested in [12]. Indeed, by generalizing orthologic to *predicate orthologic*, and restricting the presence of function symbols, we obtain the orthologic equivalent of effectively propositional logic, but with exponentially faster decision procedure. Moreover, the resulting theory has the same semantics as Datalog on the Datalog subset of all problems, yielding a proper extension.

The fact that orthologic admits the interpolation property [11,18], suggests possible use in model checking, and additional applications have been proposed in [12], including in type systems with subtyping or refinement/liquid types. Table 1 presents the laws of orthologic.

Table 1. Laws of ortholattices, algebraic varieties with signature $(S, \wedge, \vee, 0, 1, \neg)$.

V1: $x \vee y = y \vee x$	V1': $x \wedge y = y \wedge x$
V2: $x \vee (y \vee z) = (x \vee y) \vee z$	V2': $x \wedge (y \wedge z) = (x \wedge y) \wedge z$
V3: $x \vee x = x$	V3': $x \wedge x = x$
V4: $x \vee 1 = 1$	V4': $x \wedge 0 = 0$
V5: $x \vee 0 = x$	V5': $x \wedge 1 = x$
V6: $\neg\neg x = x$	
V7: $x \vee \neg x = 1$	V7': $x \wedge \neg x = 0$
V8: $\neg(x \vee y) = \neg x \wedge \neg y$	V8': $\neg(x \wedge y) = \neg x \vee \neg y$
V9: $x \vee (x \wedge y) = x$	V9': $x \wedge (x \vee y) = x$

In this work, we present the first formalization and verification, using the Coq proof assistant, of an efficient decision procedure for the validity and equivalence problems for propositional formulas in orthologic. This algorithm [12] is based on proof search in a proof system for orthologic that is a restriction of the classical sequent calculus where a sequent can never contain more than two distinct

formulas at a time. Despite this restriction, the proof system admits cut elimination, which we formalize. The cut elimination property implies a subformula
property, which is key to the completeness of the proof search procedure.

A naive implementation of the decision procedure has exponential complexity.
To obtain a polynomial version, we leverage memoization, i.e. storing in a table
the intermediate results of the recursive calls. Moreover, using structural equality
to check if a key is in the memoization map costs an additional linear runtime
factor. To obtain an optimal quadratic version, we modify the algorithm to use
a form of reference equality. As our algorithm is purely functional, this means
we have to extend our formulas' abstract syntax trees to assign to each node a
unique identifier (or pointer) that can then be used in the memoization map.
We formally prove the correctness of these constructions.

We implement and verify multiple versions of the algorithm: without opti-
mization $(\widetilde{\mathcal{O}}(2^n))$, with memoization using lists $(\widetilde{\mathcal{O}}(n^5))$, using AVL maps
$(\widetilde{\mathcal{O}}(n^3))$, and using AVL maps and simulated reference equality $(\widetilde{\mathcal{O}}(n^2))$. Memoization and reference equality are generic, and important in many tools and algo-
rithms. Our approach to verifying these optimizations is not specific to ortho-logic
proof search and we expect it to extend to any recursive algorithm over algebraic
datatypes (ADT).

Using the technique of proofs by reflection, we then obtain a set of executable
proof tactics, each deciding equality modulo orthologic rule and, applicable to
any ortholattice and in particular the type `bool` of boolean values. This tactic is
able to solve automatically, for example,

```
true = (a && b) || (negb a) || (negb b)
```

We present benchmarks attesting that each version of the proof search procedure (with memoization using a list-based map, with memoization using AVL
trees, and with both memoization and reference equality) meets the theoretical
complexity.

Many formulas are not completely provable in the fragment of orthologic,
in which case the decision procedure alone cannot do anything, even if most
of the structure of the formula reduces under orthologic rules. The orthologic
simplification algorithm [9] on the other hand is widely applicable, and can make
substantial progress on a problem even if the formula is not equivalent to true.
This is also very useful if the propositional formulas are built on some theories,
such as arithmetic, in which case even classical boolean decision procedures
would not work. We implement this simplifier in OCaml as a Coq plugin, using
the above tactic to efficiently prove equivalence with the original expression.
This yields a generic simplification tactic for terms of type `bool`.

We finally leverage this normalization tactic to implement a boolean solver
which alternates between branching on a variable and normalizing the formulas,
as in [10]. We present benchmarks comparing this procedure to the built-in `btauto`
tactic.

We expect that our approach and results, such as the proof of soundness and
completeness and the cut elimination theorem, can be replicated to other similar

logics, although they may not satisfy the key subformula property that yields an algorithm that is both complete and polynomial. Moreover, our verification of optimization techniques for proof search using memoization and reference equality are very general by nature and we expect our approach to generalize well to other logics. All our tactics are available as a Coq plugin alongside with benchmarks at

github.com/SimonGuilloud/orthologic-coq.

A permanent record is also available at

doi.org/10.5281/zenodo.15215613.

1.1   Contributions

In Sect. 2, we first formalize in the Coq proof assistant a proof system for ortho-logic (in the style of sequent calculus) and its soundness and completeness with respect to truth in every ortholattice. In Sect. 3, we then formalize the cut elim-ination theorem (without non-logical axioms) of orthologic, and in the process discover a missing edge case in the proof of [12].

In Sect. 4, we implement the proof-search-based decision procedure for ortho-logic from [12]. We prove soundness and completeness of the algorithm. We then use reflection to obtain a Coq proof tactic which can solve any equality or inequality valid in orthologic, for any ortholattice, in particular the type `bool` of truth values. In Sect. 5, we describe our implementation and verification of the memoized version of the algorithm. In Sect. 6, we discuss reference equal-ity. This optimization is significantly more complex. It requires redefining trees representing orthologic terms to include pointers and proving that the trans-formation from pointer-free terms to terms with pointers is correct, which was surprisingly difficult.

In Sect. 7, we present an alternative tactic that directly produces proof terms instead of using reflection, which is faster in practice but less space efficient. We also implement tactics for OL-normalization and an orthologic-based boolean solver.

In Sect. 8, we present a series of benchmarks which are supposed to hit the asymptotic worst case of every implementation of the proof search procedure, using different reduction strategies, and find that the resulting curves match the theoretical complexity. We then present benchmarks comparing our OL-based boolean validity tactic to the built-in `btauto` tactic of Coq on random formulas generated according to [19].

1.2   Related Work

The word problem for ortholattices (deciding if given two terms, one is always $\leq$ than the other) was first solved by [4], extended in [9] to obtain normal forms of terms. A similar proof system for orthologic, with the property that sequents never contain more than one formula, was already described by [20]. Different proof systems have also been considered [15–17].

The authors of [5] formalize cut elimination for intuitionistic logic and those of [7] formalze cut elimination for the logic of bunched implications in Coq, but their approach is semantic rather than syntactic. [23], still using Coq, shows cut elimination for a class of coalgebraic logics, including a variety of modal logics. They propose both a syntactic and a semantic proof. In Isabelle, [25] formalizes a particular, strongly normalizing version of cut elimination for classical first order logic.

Whitman's algorithm, a decision procedure for inequalities holding in every lattice (without negation), has been formalized in Coq by [14], also using reflection. Reflection has also been used to verify and import proofs from SMT solvers [2].

Ortholattices have been defined in Mizar [24], but little about them proven. In Coq, [16] formalized results about a different proof system for orthologic.

Verified memoization has been studied in [26]. The authors propose a framework for automatic verified memoization of programs in Isabelle/HOL. In Coq, [3] studies the related topic of hash-consing, which can be seen as memoization of constructors. In their approach, they entirely replace nodes of an ADT by identifiers, so that the recursive structure only exist in the hash-consing map, while we add identifiers to the tree.

```
Class Ortholattice := {
  A : Set;
  equiv: relation A where "x == y" := (equiv x y);
  leq : relation A where "x ≤ y" := (leq x y);
  meet : A → A → A where "x ∩ y" := (meet x y);
  join : A → A → A where "x ∪ y" := (join x y);
  neg : A → A where "¬ x" := (neg x);
  zero : A; one : A;
  ...
}.
```

Listing 1.1. Definition of an Ortholattice

2   Formalizing Ortholattices and Orthologic

We first formalize the algebraic class of ortholattices as a typeclass (Listing 1.1). Ortholattices are of course *lattices*, and in particular a partial order with $\leq$ given by

$$x \leq y \iff x \wedge y = x$$

or equivalently

$$x \leq y \iff x \vee y = y.$$

Ortholattices can be axiomatized equivalently as an algebraic variety, such as in Table 1, or as a partial order.

We then implement using Ltac *Whitman's algorithm* [6], a simple decision procedure for lattices. This helps us to quickly show a number of useful lemmas about ortholattices. This simple tactic is subsumed by the tactic for ortholattices we will obtain with reflection. We then show that $=$, under the axiom $x = y \leftrightarrow x <0 y \land y \leqslant x$, is a congruence relation for $\leqslant$, $\cap$, $\cup$ and $\neg$. This makes ortholattices *setoids*, and enables the use of *generalized rewriting* [22].

Orthologic

We define in the standard way the type of ortholattice terms, and the evaluation of a term in an arbitrary ortholattice:

```
Inductive Term : Set :=
  | Var : positive → Term
  | Meet : Term → Term → Term
  | Join : Term → Term → Term
  | Not : Term → Term.

Fixpoint eval {OL: Ortholattice}
  (t: Term) (f: positive → A) : A := ...
```

and then implement the OL proof system of [12] (without axioms), formulated as a sequent calculus. One can think of this proof system as Gentzen's sequent calculus for classical logic [8] restricted to ensure that at any given point in a proof, a sequent never has more than two formulas on both sides combined.

We represent sequents as (ordered) pairs of annotated formulas as in [12]:

```
Inductive AnTerm : Set :=
  | N : AnTerm
  | L : Term → AnTerm
  | R : Term → AnTerm.
Definition Sequent (l r : AnTerm) := (l, r).
```

where N represents no formula, L a formula on the left and R a formula on the right. For example, $(L\,\phi, R\,\psi)$ stands for $\phi \vdash \psi$ in more conventional notation.

We implement the proof system using dependent inductive types, so that the correctness of a proof is guaranteed by construction, and no additional proof-checking function is required. For example, the RightAnd rule from [12], is

$$\frac{\Gamma, \phi^R \qquad \Gamma, \psi^R}{\Gamma, (\phi \land \psi)^R} \; \text{RightAnd}$$

and is encoded as

```
Inductive OLProof : AnTerm*AnTerm → Set :=
  ...
  | RightAnd: forall {a} {b} {g},
      OLProof (g, R a) → OLProof (g, R b) → OLProof (g, R (Meet a b))
  ...
```

In [12], sequents are formally considered as sets. We have defined them in Coq using ordered pairs and hence need to define two additional rules, simulating the set-like nature of sequents: the Swap and Contract rules.

$$\frac{\Gamma, \Delta}{\Delta, \Gamma} \text{ Swap} \qquad \frac{\Gamma, \Gamma}{\Gamma, N} \text{ Contract}$$

Soundness of the proof systems states that if a sequent is provable, then the corresponding inequality must be true in every ortholattice (semantic truth), and completeness is the converse. Both are straightforward to prove.

3   Cut Elimination for Ortholuogic

The key property of the orthologic proof system is that it admits cut elimination: any provable sequent can be proved without using the cut rule. Cut elimination has important theoretical and practical consequences. Since the |Cut| step is the only one in which a term can appear in the premise but not the conclusion, cut elimination implies the subformula property: if a sequent has a proof, then it has a proof where only subterms of the conclusion appear. This is key to the orthologic proof search procedure.

```
Theorem cut_elimination  s (proof : OLProof s):
    {p: OLProof s | is_cut_free  p}.
```

This theorem is not straightforward to formalize. The paper proof starts with "Consider the topmost instance of the cut rule in the proof". This deceptively short step requires a double induction, first on the number of instances of the cut rule appearing in a proof (fuelCut), then on the size of the proof (fuelSize)[1]. The corresponding lemma takes as arguments proofs that the given fuel is larger than the metric it represents, and every induction step needs to justify that the measures are decreasing. This step allows to reduce the problem to the case where the proof ends with a single Cut step whose premises are cut-free.

Graphically, we have the following situation:

$$\frac{\dfrac{\mathcal{A}}{\Gamma, b^R} \quad \dfrac{\mathcal{B}}{b^L, \Delta}}{\Gamma, \Delta} \text{ Cut}$$

and need to obtain the conclusion Γ, Δ with a cut-free proof. The proof again works by double induction: first on the size of the cut formula b (fuelB), then on the total size of $\mathcal{A}$ and $\mathcal{B}$ (fuelSize), as expressed in the lemma's statement:

---

[1] Two nested inductions on natural numbers is equivalent to transfinite induction on ω^2.

```
Lemma inner_cut_elim : forall
  (fuelB: nat)
  (b: Term) (good_fuelB: fuelB ≥ termSize b)
  (fuelSize: nat)
  (gamma: AnTerm) (delta: AnTerm)
  (A: OLProof (gamma, R b)) (p1: isCutFree A)
  (B: OLProof (L b, delta)) (p2: isCutFree B)
  (good_fuelSize: fuelSize ≥ (Size A + Size B)),
  {p: OLProof (gamma, delta) | isCutFree p}.
```

The proof proceeds by case analysis on $\mathcal{A}$ and $\mathcal{B}$, and gives in each case a specific transformation resulting in a cut-free proof of Γ, Δ. We provide two examples to illustrate the process.

Example 1.
$$\cfrac{\cfrac{\cfrac{\cfrac{\mathcal{A}'}{\alpha^L, b^L}}{\neg\alpha^R, b^L}\ \text{RightNot} \qquad \cfrac{\mathcal{B}'}{b^R, \Delta}}{\neg\alpha^R, \Delta}\ \text{Cut}}{} \quad \hookrightarrow \quad \cfrac{\cfrac{\cfrac{\mathcal{A}'}{\alpha^L, b^L} \qquad \cfrac{\mathcal{B}'}{b^R, \Delta}}{\alpha^L, \Delta}\ \text{Cut}}{\neg\alpha^R, \Delta}\ \text{RightNot}$$

Example 2.
$$\cfrac{\cfrac{\cfrac{\mathcal{A}'}{\Gamma, \alpha^R}}{\Gamma, (\alpha \vee \beta)^R}\ \text{RightOr} \qquad \cfrac{\cfrac{\mathcal{B}'}{\alpha^L, \Delta} \qquad \cfrac{\mathcal{B}''}{\beta^L, \Delta}}{(\alpha \vee \beta)^L, \Delta}\ \text{LeftOr}}{\Gamma, \Delta}\ \text{Cut}$$

$$\hookrightarrow$$

$$\cfrac{\cfrac{\mathcal{A}'}{\Gamma, \alpha^R} \qquad \cfrac{\mathcal{B}'}{\alpha^L, \Delta}}{\Gamma, \Delta}\ \text{Cut}$$

Note that in both examples, the transformed proof contains instances of the Cut rule. But since they have a smaller cut formula, by induction their conclusion have cut-free proofs. Every single recursive use of the induction hypothesis has to provide the required proof of decreasing measures corresponding to the fuel properties.

The main challenge of the proof comes from the sheer size of the case analysis: the Swap step essentially duplicates every other proof step by allowing them to act on the first or second formula, which implies we have to analyse each of $\mathcal{A}$ and $\mathcal{B}$ on 23 cases each, for a total of more than 500 cases. In practice, we can first do the analysis on $\mathcal{A}$, and for some cases the proof is independent of the structure of $\mathcal{B}$, as in Example 1. However, there is no way to undo the case analysis on $\mathcal{A}$ when conversely the cases of pattern matching on $\mathcal{B}$ have a proof independent of the structure of $\mathcal{A}$.

Then, some combinations of cases are impossible. For example, it is not possible for $\mathcal{A}$ to conclude with a RightAnd and $\mathcal{B}$ with LeftOr1, as the cut formula

b would then need to be both a conjunction and a disjunction. Thanks to the use of dependent types to define the proof system, those cases are automatically eliminated. The paper proof can also afford a lot of reasoning by symmetry. There are particular combined symmetries between left and right rules, meet and join, swapped and non-swapped cases, $\mathcal{A}$ and $\mathcal{B}$, etc., which can easily be informally treated in a paper proof but not in Coq. In the end, the formal proof contains around 200 cases.

Among these cases, we caught one in particular that was not properly considered in the paper proof of [12]. Indeed, the example reduction in Example 2 would fail in the presence of an implicit contraction due to set semantics. Written with an explicit contraction, this is:

$$
\cfrac{
  \cfrac{\mathcal{A}'}{
    \cfrac{\Gamma, \alpha^R}{\Gamma, (\alpha \vee \beta)^R} \text{ RightOr}
  }
  \qquad
  \cfrac{
    \cfrac{
      \cfrac{\mathcal{B}'}{\alpha^L, (\alpha \vee \beta)^L} \quad \cfrac{\mathcal{B}''}{\beta^L, (\alpha \vee \beta)^L}
    }{(\alpha \vee \beta)^L, (\alpha \vee \beta)^L} \text{ LeftOr}
  }{(\alpha \vee \beta)^L, N} \text{ Contract}
}{\Gamma, N} \text{ Cut}
$$

And the transformation above would yield $\Gamma, (\alpha \vee \beta)^L$ instead of Γ, N, and hence is not correct. In this case, a correct transformation is:

$$
\cfrac{
  \cfrac{\mathcal{A}'}{\Gamma, \alpha^R}
  \qquad
  \cfrac{
    \cfrac{\cfrac{\mathcal{A}'}{\Gamma, \alpha^R}}{\Gamma, (\alpha \vee \beta)^R} \text{ RightOr} \qquad \cfrac{\mathcal{B}'}{(\alpha \vee \beta)^L, \alpha^L}
  }{\alpha^L, \Gamma} \text{ Cut}
}{\cfrac{\Gamma, \Gamma}{\Gamma, N} \text{ Contract}} \text{ Cut}
$$

The topmost cut is justified by induction because its proof is smaller. The second, however, is not: after recursive elimination from the cut above, we cannot guarantee that the new proof is smaller. Instead, this cut needs to be justified by outer induction on the size of the cut formula.

4   Decision Procedure for Orthologic

The *word problem* for ortholattices consists in deciding, for arbitrary terms s and t over $(\wedge, \vee, \neg)$, if $s = t$ in all ortholattices. Cases of particular interest involve deciding if $s = 1$ (validity) or $s = 0$ (unsatisfiability). Since $s = t \iff s \le t$ & $t \le s$, and vice-versa $s \le t \iff s = s \wedge t$, we can equivalently see the word problem as deciding inequality between arbitrary words. By soundness and completeness of the orthologic proof system, this is in turn equivalent to deciding if the sequent s^L, t^R has a proof.

This is decidable with a recursive backward proof search procedure, as in [12]: given a sequent Γ, Δ, try to apply all the rules which can conclude with Γ, Δ, and recursively solve the premise. Since orthologic admits cut elimination, we never need to consider the Cut step. Moreover, because the orthologic proof system admits the subformula property, we also know that the depth of a proof of a sequent of size n will never exceed $4n^2$. We implement this proof search procedure as a Coq function in Listing 1.2, and show soundness and completeness of the proof system with respect to validity in all ortholattices.

The soundness of this algorithm, which is required for obtaining a reflection tactic, is expressed as

```
Theorem decideOL_base_correct :
    forall n g d,
    (decideOL_base n g d) = true →
    exists _: (OLProof (g, d)).
```

```
Fixpoint decideOL_base (fuel: nat) (g d: AnTerm) : bool :=
  match fuel with
  | 0 ⇒ false
  | S n ⇒
    match (g, d) with
    | (L (Var a), R (Var b) ) ⇒ (Pos.eqb a b) | _ ⇒ false (* Hyp *)
    end || (
    decideOL_base n g N || ( (* Weaken *)
    match d with
    | N ⇒ decideOL_base n g g | _ ⇒ false (* Contract *)
    end || (
    match g with
    | L (Meet a b) ⇒ decideOL_base n (L a) d | _ ⇒ false (* LeftAnd1 *)
    end || (
    match g with
    | L (Meet a b) ⇒ decideOL_base n (L b) d | _ ⇒ false (* LeftAnd2 *)
    end || (
    match g with
    | L (Join a b) ⇒ decideOL_base n (L a) d && decideOL_base n (L b) d |
    _ ⇒ false (* LeftJoin *)
    end || (
    match g with
    | L (Not a) ⇒ decideOL_base n (R a) d | _ ⇒ false (* LeftNot*)
    end || (
    ... (* Symmetric right cases *)
    || (
    decideOL_base n d g (* Swap *)
    ))))))))))
  end.
```

Listing 1.2. Decision procedure for the *word problem for ortholattices*.

Reflection

Suppose we have a goal $s \leq t$ or $s = t$, where s and t are expressions in an arbitrary ortholattice, for example:

```
Lemma example a b: a && negb a = negb b && (a && b).
```

We want to solve this problem by executing the above algorithm, which we proved correct. First, we split $s = t$ in two independent inequalities. Then, reflection consists in two separate steps: *reification* and *evaluation* (or type checking).

Reification consists in finding two terms `s'` and `t'` as well as a function `f: positive → bool`[22] such that `eval s' f` is convertible to `s` and `eval t' f` is convertible to `t`. Here, convertible means that the two expressions are equivalent up to $\beta\alpha$ conversion, unfolding of definitions, and additional relations defined by Coq[3]. In particular, any expression can always be freely replaced by one it is convertible to, without additional proof. Hence, the inequality in the goal is convertible to (and can be changed to):

```
eval ((Var 0) ∩ ¬ (Var 0)) f       ⩽
eval ¬( (Var 1) ∩ ((Var 0) ∩ (Var 1))) f.
```

We can then apply a lemma derived from the soundness of the decision procedure with respect to the proof system, and of the proof system with respect to the class of ortholattices to reduce the problem to:

```
decideOL (L ((Var 0) ∩ ¬ (Var 0)))
         (R ¬( (Var 1) ∩ ((Var 0) ∩ (Var 1))))
    = true.
```

Now, we can complete this proof using the term `eq_refl bool true : (true = true)`, which is by definition a proof of `true = true`. For this to typecheck, the left-hand side of the equality needs to be convertible to `true`. Hence to typecheck the proof, Coq *evaluates* the algorithm. Effectively, we have offloaded the burden of proof to the evaluator inside Coq's kernel. Note also that the proof has constant size.

We now describe how to find a suitable `f` in our reification process, which is implemented in its own tactic. First, put all the leaves of s and t in a list named `env`. A leaf is a subexpression that is neither a meet, a join or a negation. These leaves will correspond to variables in `s'` and `t'`. f is then the function that maps n to the element in the list at place n. The reification tactic then uses this list to compute the terms `s'` and `t'`. We mechanize the entire process as the tactic `solveOL`, solving, for example:

```
Lemma example a b:
    a && negb a = negb b && (a && b).
Proof. solveOL BoolOL. Qed.
```

Note on Soundness and Completeness. An error of implementation in a decision procedure can take two forms: soundness (incorrectly accepting a wrong equality) and completeness (incorrectly rejecting a correct equality). However, Coq's logical kernel guarantees the soundness of every tactic. In the process above, the decision algorithm is proven sound. However, the reification process is not

---

[2] In general, `f: positive → OL`, where `OL` is the ortholattice in which the terms live.

[3] See https://rocq-prover.org/doc/v8.18/refman/language/core/conversion.html.

(and it cannot be), so it may contain errors and produce incorrect terms. In that case however, Coq's kernel will refuse to replace the goal and produce an error message.

5   Verified Memoization

The naively implemented proof search procedure has superexponential runtime complexity, making it unusable in practice. We need to optimize it. First, observe that some proof steps, when applied backward, are not merely sufficient conditions but also necessary. For example, consider a sequent of the form $\Gamma, (\phi_1 \wedge \phi_2)^L$. It is a theorem of lattices that $s \leq t_1 \wedge t_2 \iff s \leq t_1 \ \& \ s \leq t_2$, corresponding to the RightAnd step. Hence, for $\Gamma, (s \wedge t)^R$ to have a proof, it is not only sufficient but also necessary that both Γ, s^R and Γ, t^R have a proof. It follows that if RightAnd is applicable, we do not need to try other steps, and similarly with LeftOr, Hyp, RightNot and LeftNot. Moreover, note that the algorithm will naively try to apply the Swap rule over and over. This makes the algorithm structurally non-terminating, and only fuel prevents infinite loops. This can be prevented by "unfolding" the swap step, and ensuring that a meaningful rule is always applied, but loops also are possible using the Contract and Weaken rules. To handle this situation, we add two boolean variables to the input of the algorithm, each one denoting respectively weather g N and N d have already been tried. We implement a second version of the algorithm, named decideOL_opti implementing these optimizations:

```
Fixpoint decideOL_opti (fuel: nat)(g d: AnTerm)(cg cd: bool): bool:=
  match fuel with
  | 0 ⇒ false
  | S n ⇒ match (g, d) with
    ...
  end.
```

We prove its soundness and implement a corresponding reflection tactic solve_OL_opti.

The algorithm still has an exponential runtime of $\mathcal{O}(2^{n^2})$. To obtain a polynomial time procedure, we need to implement *memoization*. Observe that since orthologic admits cut elimination, it also admits the subformula property:

Theorem 1. (Subformula Property, [12]). *If an orthologic sequent Γ, Δ has a proof, then it has a proof where only subformulas of Γ and Δ appear.*

Let n be the size of the input sequent, i.e. the number of subformulas. The number of subformulas of the initial input sequent is $\mathcal{O}(n)$, and there can only exist at most $\mathcal{O}(n^2)$ different sequents built from these subformulas. Hence, in a full run of decideOL_bool, there can only be at most $\mathcal{O}(n^2)$ unique recursive calls. Using memoization, we can ensure that the body of the program is never executed more than $\mathcal{O}(n^2)$ times. Note that we also need to memoize the two boolean flags cg and cd, but this only multiplies the number of input by 4.

We implement this version of the algorithm using the *state monad* paradigm. Let MemoMap be some type of maps with keys in (AnTerm * AnTerm) and values in bool. The function decideOL_memo then returns an object of type MemoMap → (bool, MemoMap). Boolean conjunctions and disjunctions are modified to compute the results in series, as in:

```
Definition mor (left : MemoMap → (bool * MemoMap))
               (right : MemoMap → (bool * MemoMap))   :=
  fun (memo : MemoMap) ⇒
    match left memo with
    | (true, m) ⇒ (true, m)
    | (false, m) ⇒ right m
    end.
```

and the decision algorithm is modified as follows:

```
Fixpoint decideOL_memo (fuel: nat) (g d: AnTerm) (cg cd: bool) (memo:
    MemoMap) : (bool * MemoMap) :=
  match find (g, d, cg, cd) memo with
  | Some (_, b) ⇒ (b, memo)
  | None ⇒ (match fuel with
    | 0 ⇒ (false, memo)
    | S n ⇒ let (b, m) := ... in
        (b, ((g, d, cg, cd), b) :: m) end)
  end.
```

The correctness of the algorithm is expressed as equivalence with the non-memoized version of the algorithm, and relative to the correctness of the map given as input. A map is correct if and only if for every key k with a value of true, the non-memoized version of the algorithm returns true on k.

```
Definition memomap_correct (l: MemoMap) := forall g d cg cd,
  match find (g, d, cg, cd) l with
  | Some (_, true) ⇒ exists n, (decideOL_opti n g d cg cd = true)
  | _ ⇒ True
  end.
```

In particular, the empty map is correct. Note that the two versions of the algorithm are not necessarily equivalent for an arbitrary allowance of fuel: the memoized version might require less. We prove the soundness of the memoized algorithm[4]:

```
Theorem decideOL_memo_correct :
  forall n g d cg cd l,
  (memomap_correct l) →
  (memomap_correct (snd (decideOL_memo n g d cg cd l))) ∧
  ( ((fst (decideOL_memo n g d cg cd l)) = true) →
    exists n0, (decideOL_opti n0 g d cg cd) = true ).
Proof.
```

---

[4] Note that completeness is not required to define a reflection-based tactic.

The induction has to be performed jointly on the statement that the returned map is correct, and that the returned truth value is the same as that of the original algorithm. The proof again proceeds with a large case analysis, which required significant custom automation and side lemmas about the monadic structure of the memoization, but was carried completely independently of the orthologic proof system and would work similarly with any other recursive algorithm on algebraic datatypes.

We first implement the algorithm using a list of pairs as a base for the memoization map. However, lookup inside a list takes time linear in its size. As explained above, the number of stored values is quadratic in the size of the input. Moreover, checking equality between the input and the elements of the list costs an additional linear factor. Overall, the complexity of lookup is cubic, for a total runtime of $\mathcal{O}(n^5)$.

We then implement a second version, using AVL maps from the Coq standard library. This requires to define a total order on anTerm, which we do following the usual total order on labelled ordered trees. Sorted maps such as AVL maps only require a logarithmic number of comparisons, down from quadratic with a list-based implementation. However, comparison still takes linear time, for a total time complexity of $\mathcal{O}(n^3 \log n)$.

We hence obtain two more versions of the algorithm, decideOL_memo and decideOL_fmap, and two corresponding tactics solveOL_memo and solveOL_fmap.

6 Reference Equality

Lookup in a map requires deciding either equality or ordering between two terms, which takes linear time in the size of the terms and even in a Hashmap, equality checking is necessary to avoid collisions. In the previous two algorithms, either based on lists or on AVL maps, equality is structural: two terms are equal if they have the same constructor and recursively their arguments are equal. However, this is *too strong* for memoization.

First, observe that if we replace this notion of equality by a strictly weaker relation, the algorithm is still sound, and we only risk losing some of the benefits of memoization.

Then recall that by the subformula property, the algorithm only ever sees the $\mathcal{O}(n^2)$ different subnodes of the original input. Assigning a different binary identifier to each of these nodes requires only $\mathcal{O}(\log n)$ bits for each identifier. Then, if two terms have the same identifier, they must be structurally equal. However, the converse does not hold in general: if the original input contains multiple copies of the same subtree, they will be assigned different identifiers.

This corresponds, in imperative programming, to *pointer equality*. Checking if two objects have the same location in memory is a sound approximation to deciding if they are structurally equal. Formally, we defined an extended version of the datatype of terms:

```
Inductive TermPointer : Set :=
  | VarP : positive → Pointer → TermPointer
  | MeetP : TermPointer → TermPointer → Pointer → TermPointer
  | JoinP : TermPointer → TermPointer → Pointer → TermPointer
  | NotP : TermPointer → Pointer → TermPointer.
```

where `Pointer := positive` is the type of binary positive numbers. We define the projection onto regular terms `ForgetPointer : TermPointer → Term` and a getter `GetPointer : TermPointer → Pointer` as expected. We extend pointers to annotated pointers:

```
Inductive AnPointer : Set :=
  | NP : AnPointer
  | LP : Pointer → AnPointer
  | RP : Pointer → AnPointer.
```

and `TermPointer` to `AnTermPointer` similarly. For `g` an `AnTermPointer` (that is, a term with a pointer and a left or right annotation), we denote `[[g]]` its corresponding `AnPointer`. We again use AVL maps, but this time with keys being pairs of `AnPointer`. The algorithm is modified accordingly:

```
Fixpoint decideOL_pointers
    (fuel: nat) (g d: AnTermPointer)
    (cg cd: bool) (memo: MemoMap)
    : (bool * MemoMap) :=
  match M.find ([[g]], [[d]], cg, cd) memo with
  | Some b ⇒ (b, memo)
  | None ⇒ (match fuel with
    | 0 ⇒ (false, memo)
    | S n ⇒ let (b, m) := ... in
      (b, AnPointerPairAVLMap.add ([[g]], [[d]], cg, cd) b m)
    end)
  end.
```

As a reminder, `fuel` is an accessory argument ensuring termination, `g` and `d` are the actual input formulas augmented with pointers, `cg` and `cd` are flags used to prevent loops and `memo` is the memoization map. In practice, we define a separate function `decideOL_pointers_simp g d`, setting initial `fuel` to $(|g| + |d|)^2$, `cg` and `cd` to false, `memo` to the empty map and computing the pointers for `g` and `d`.

The correctness of the algorithm of course depends on how pointers are assigned. If two different terms are assigned the same pointer, the algorithm will not be correct. Formally, `GetPointer` must be injective on the domain of all subterms of the input. In the correctness theorem, it is convenient to express this condition as the existence of a function `f: Pointer → TermPointer`, corresponding to address lookup, which is left and right inverse to `GetPointer` on all subterms of the input.

Proving the correctness of the algorithm extends with moderate effort from the previous algorithm with some additional side lemmas and boilerplate. However, showing that the pointer assignment is correct is significantly more challenging. We define a function `add_pointer` assigning pointers with depth-first, preorder traversal of the syntactic tree, such as in Example 3.

Example 3. The following trees represent the formula $\neg(x \wedge \neg y)$ as respectively a `Term` and the corresponding `TermPointer`.

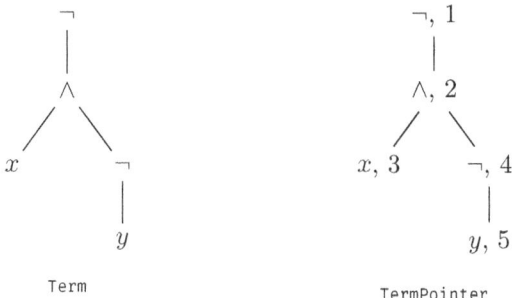

To construct the required inverse function, we first compute the list of subterms of a term, and map a pointer to the first term of the list with this pointer. It seems very obvious from the definition of our pointer assignment function `add_pointer` that there exists only one such term and hence that the two functions are inverse of each other, yet this was surprisingly difficult to prove, and required a lot of intermediate lemmas about the structure of subterms, the monotonicity of `add_pointer` along subterms, correspondence between the pointer and non-pointer version of terms, etc. The development is however independent of the orthologic proof system, and only depends upon the number and arity of constructors of orthologic terms. Hence, the theorems can straightforwardly be transfered to any other algebraic datatypes.

7   Proof-Producing Tactics and Validity Solvers

An alternative to verified decision procedures is *proof-producing decision procedures*, which also allows to implement tactics for proof assistants. Instead of relying on a soundness theorem, a proof-producing tactic will compute a proof (in Coq, a proof term) that is then checked by the logical kernel.

We implement a proof-producing version of the proof search algorithm of [12] in OCaml, and make it available as a Coq tactic, which we refer to as `olcert_goal`. In theory, this should be less efficient, as producing a proof takes additional time, but in practice an OCaml implementation (leveraging, in particular, mutability) is a faster computation method than reducing lambda-terms. Compared to `solveOL_pointer`, it has the additional practical advantage of persistence of its memoization across calls, as the pointers are assigned once and memoization is maintained globaly. Moreover, when possible, we memoize results as fields of the term nodes rather than in a map, making retrieval more efficient.

On the other hand, the proof term produced has size up to $\mathcal{O}(n^2)$, while the proof term of solveOL_pointer has constant size. Moreover, the proof-producing tactic is not verified, so it is not guaranteed that it does not contain a bug and outputs an incorrect proof. In fact, because Coq's logic is rather complex and its inner workings hard to work with (and sparsely documented), it is quite unlikely that our implementation does not have issues with edge cases, for example involving universes or unification variables. This is less likely with reflection-based tactic, where only the reification step is sensible to such issues.

We then develop a tactic olnormalize, a tactic to normalize OL terms according to [9]. An OCaml algorithm computes the normal form f' of a formula f, and we then use either solveOL_pointer or olcert_goal to prove $f = f'$. We believe this tactic has the most impact for automation, as [9] demonstrated it can significantly reduce the size of formulas in practical contexts. For example in the first benchmark of next section, the goal is not an OL tautology, but olnormalize significantly simplifies it.

```
Theorem test_tauto02_0 (x0 x1: bool) :
  ! ((( ! x0 && ! x0) || (x0 && x1) || (x0 && ! x1) || (! x0 && ! x0)) &&
    ((x1 && x0) || (! x0 && x1) || (! x0 && ! x1) || (! x0 && x1)))
    =
    true
. Proof.
  olnormalize.
  (* (! x1 || ! x0) && (x0 || x1) && (x0 || ! x1)   = true*)
```

Finally, we use the olnormalize tactic as basis for a complete tactic for Boolean equality (i.e. validity). This tactic is similar to the DPLL algorithm: it recursively branches on a literal and simplifies the result. The simplification is performed using olnormalize. We implement two versions of this tactic, one named oltauto which uses the reflexive orthologic tactic and one named oltauto_cert, which uses the proof-producing orthologic tactic. Figure 1 presents an overview of the different components and their relations to each other.

8 Evaluation of Resulting Tactics

Evaluation of the OL Proof Search Tactics. The implementations of the previous section yield six algorithms and corresponding proof tactics for deciding equality in orthologic, each with different time complexity[5]:

- solveOL $\left(\text{"OL"}, \mathcal{O}(2^n)\right)$
- solve_OL_opti $\left(\text{"OL+o"}, \mathcal{O}(2^n)\right)$
- solve_OL_memo $\left(\text{"OL+o+l"}, \widetilde{\mathcal{O}}(n^5)\right)$

---

[5] Exact complexity of algorithms up to logarithmic factors depends on the precise model of computation; for simplicity, the algorithmic complexity below assume the usual Word RAM model, where checking equality of words takes constant time, even though this does not precisely match Coq's evaluation of terms.

- `solve_OL_fmap` ("OL+o+m", $\widetilde{\mathcal{O}}(n^3)$)
- `solve_OL_pointers` ("OL+o+m+ϕ", $\widetilde{\mathcal{O}}(n^2)$)
- `olcert_goal` ("OCaml", $\mathcal{O}(n^2)$)

The difference of complexity is not only theoretical, but also highly observable in practice. Consider the family of propositions

$$(x_1||x_2)\&\&(x_3||x_4)\&\&...\&\&(x_{n-1}||x_n)$$

$$= (x_2||x_1)\&\&(x_4||x_3)\&\&...\&\&(x_n||x_{n-1})$$

These equalities are solvable by the laws of ortholattices. Table 2 shows the time taken by each implementation for $n = 30$. For comparison, we also include the runtime of btauto, the solver for boolean equalities included in Coq's standard distribution.

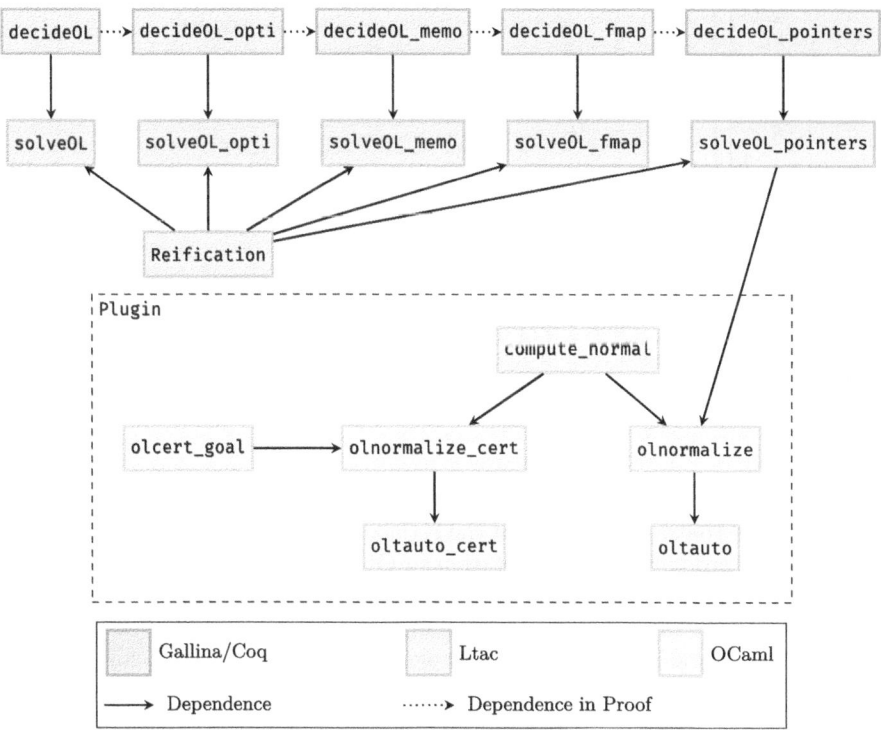

Fig. 1. Diagram illustrating the interaction between each algorithm and tactic. Elements in bold have been benchmarked.

To confirm the scaling characteristics of our implementation variants, we solved the family of equalities above for sizes ranging from 2 to 100 variables.

Table 2. Wall clock time required to prove an equality involving 30 variables.

solver	mean	std
btauto	35.96	13.30
OL+o+l	19.89	0.26
OL+o+m	0.36	0.01
OL+o+m+ϕ	0.25	0.01
OCaml	0.12	0.00

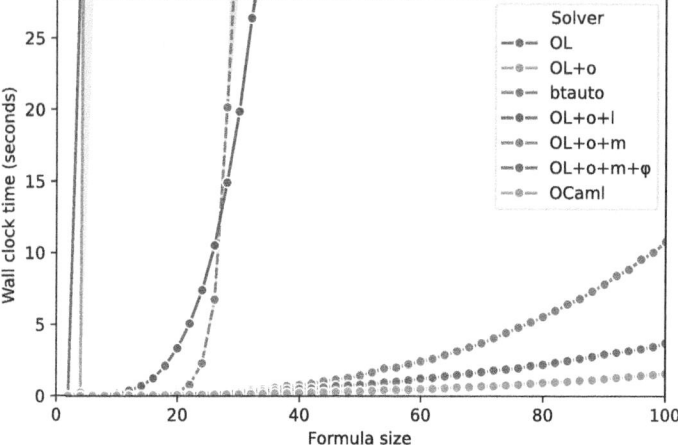

Fig. 2. Wall clock time required to prove a family of equalities with sizes ranging from 2 to 100 variables. Shaded regions indicate 95% confidence intervals. Colours indicate which implementation was used. Benchmarks were run on an Intel Core i7-1365U CPU with 32 GB RAM.

Figure 2 shows our results. We confirm the theoretical complexity by verifying for each tactic that a polynomial of the right degree fits the measurements.

The proof-producing implementation in OCaml outperforms the implementation as a Coq function (i.e. in Gallina), but it produces longer proof terms, and since its soundness is not proven it may contain bugs. But it also demonstrates the inadequacy of algorithms implemented directly in Coq for practical purposes, as reduction of lambda-terms is not an efficient computational strategy. This suggests that in an ideal world, it should be possible to verify functions implemented in a general-purpose programming language and then trust their output, so that they can run as fast as possible. This was done in some flavour with the Candle proof assistant (a verified implementation of HOL Light) in [1].

Evaluating Propositional Solvers. To judge the tactics oltauto and oltauto_cert compared to the standard btauto solver, we generate a series of formulas according to the techniques of [19]. These formulas have a fixed structure and are believed to be typically hard for SAT solvers. Some of the formulas we generated are valid and some are not, but this does not affect the runtime meaningfully as all three algorithms do not stop early if a dissatisfying assignment is found and still explore the entire search space. We generate a total of 80 random formulas, with up to 20 different variables and 192 literals, and a timeout of 30 s. The results appear in Fig. 3 and show that oltauto_cert (OCaml+n) consistently outperforms oltauto (OLT), which in turn consistently outperforms btauto, which scales very poorly with respect to formula size even with a low number of variables (<6).

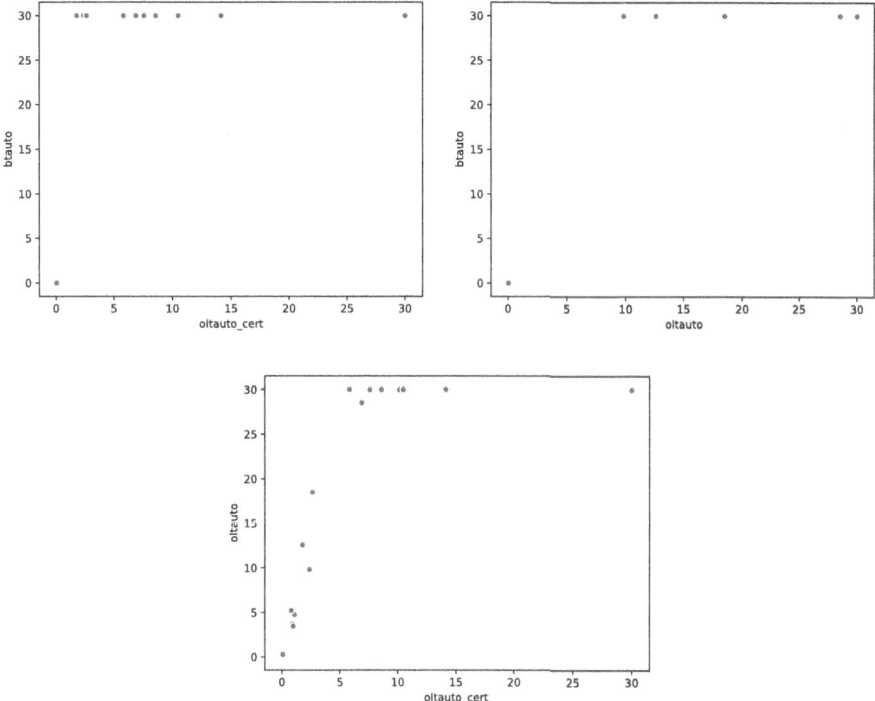

Fig. 3. Wall clock time required to prove random hard non-clausal formulas. Each point is an experiment and indicates the running time for two of the three solvers.

9   Conclusion

We formalized orthologic in the Coq proof assistant, including soundness and completeness of orthologic sequent calculus with respect to the class of all ortho-lattices and the cut elimination theorem for orthologic. Doing so, we discovered a missing edge case in the proof from [12].

We implemented and verified a proof search procedure for orthologic, and used reflection to obtain a proof tactic that decides equalities and inequalities in ortholattices. We improved the algorithm with important but typically imperative programming features: memoization and pointer equality, improving the algorithm from exponential to quadratic. We implemented additional specialized tactics enabling orthol021ic-based reasoning for Coq users, all of which are available in a Coq plugin.

Orthol021ic is used as a core component of reasoning tools, and the formalization of its key properties increases the trust we can have in existing and future such systems. Our work also opens for further mechanization of orthol021ic-based reasoning, such as orthol021ic with axioms and effectively propositional orthol021ic [12], interpolation in orthol021ic [11, 18], and more [4, 13, 21].

Finally, verification of memoization and reference equality-based optimizations, which represents a significant part of the formalization effort, is in no way specific to orthol021ic proof search. These techniques are also of great practical relevance, and necessary to obtain optimal complexity of a wide range of algorithms. We expect that our formalization can be a useful source to anyone verifying efficient algorithms relying on memoization or reference equality in the future.

Acknowledgements. We thank the anonymous reviewers for their useful suggestions and feedback.

The authors have no competing interests to declare that are relevant to the content of this article.

References

1. Abrahamsson, O., Myreen, M.O.: Fast, verified computation for candle. In: Naumowicz, A., Thiemann, R. (eds.) 14th International Conference on Interactive Theorem Proving (ITP 2023). Leibniz International Proceedings in Informatics (LIPIcs), vol. 268, pp. 4:1–4:17. Schloss Dagstuhl – Leibniz-Zentrum für Informatik, Dagstuhl, Germany (2023). https://doi.org/10.4230/LIPIcs.ITP.2023.4
2. Besson, F., Cornilleau, P.-E., Pichardie, D.: Modular SMT proofs for fast reflexive checking inside Coq. In: First International Conference on Certified Programs and Proofs, Kenting, Taiwan (2011)
3. Braibant, T., Jourdan, J.-H., Monniaux, D.: Implementing and reasoning about Hash-consed data structures in Coq. J. Autom. Reason. **53**(3), 271–304 (2014). https://doi.org/10.1007/s10817-014-9306-0
4. Bruns, G.: Free ortholattices. Can. J. Math. **28**(5), 977–985 (1976). https://doi.org/10.4153/CJM-1976-095-6
5. Forster, Y., Kirst, D., Wehr, D.: Completeness theorems for first-order logic analysed in constructive type theory: extended version. J. Log. Comput. **31**(1), 112–151 (2021). https://doi.org/10.1093/logcom/exaa073
6. Freese, R., Jezek, J., Nation, J.: Free Lattices. Mathematical Surveys and Monographs, vol. 42. American Mathematical Society, Providence, Rhode Island, March 1995. https://doi.org/10.1090/surv/042

7. Frumin, D.: Semantic cut elimination for the logic of bunched implications, formalized in Coq, December 2021. arXiv:2112.05515. https://doi.org/10.48550/arXiv.2112.05515

8. Gentzen, G.: Untersuchungen über das logische Schließen I. Math. Z. **39**, 176–210 (1935)

9. Guilloud, S., Bucev, M., Milovancevic, D., Kuncak, V.: Formula normalizations in verification. In: 35th International Conference on Computer Aided Verification, Paris, LNCS, pp. 398–422. Springer, Cham (2023)

10. Guilloud, S., Gambhir, S., Kuncak, V.: LISA – a modern proof system. In: 14th Conference on Interactive Theorem Proving, Leibniz International Proceedings in Informatics, pp. 17:1–17:19. Daghstuhl, Bialystok (2023)

11. Guilloud, S., Gambhir, S., Kunčak, V.: Interpolation and quantifiers in ortholattices. In: Verification, Model Checking, and Abstract Interpretation: 25th International Conference, VMCAI 2024, London, United Kingdom, 15–16 January 2024, Proceedings, Part I, pp. 235–257. Springer, Heidelberg (2024). https://doi.org/10.1007/978-3-031-50524-9_11

12. Guilloud, S., Kunčak, V.: Orthologic with axioms. Proc. ACM Programm. Lang. **8**(POPL), 39:1150–39:1178 (2024). https://doi.org/10.1145/3632881

13. Herrmann, C., Roddy, M.S.: On varieties of modular ortholattices which are generated by their finite-dimensional members, p. 9 (2014)

14. James, D.W.H., Hinze, R.: A reflection-based proof tactic for lattices in Coq. In: Symposium on Trends in Functional Programming (2009)

15. Kawano, T.: Labeled sequent calculus for orthologic. Bull. Sect. Logic **47**(4), 217–232 (2018). https://doi.org/10.18778/0138-0680.47.4.01

16. Laurent, O.: Focusing in orthologic. In: Kesner, D., Pientka, B. (eds.) 1st International Conference on Formal Structures for Computation and Deduction, FSCD 2016, 22–26 June 2016, Porto, Portugal. LIPIcs, vol. 52, pp. 25:1–25:17. Schloss Dagstuhl - Leibniz-Zentrum für Informatik, Porto, Portugal (2016). https://doi.org/10.4230/LIPIcs.FSCD.2016.25

17. Meinander, A.: A solution of the uniform word problem for ortholattices. Math. Struct. Comput. Sci. **20**(4), 625–638 (2010). https://doi.org/10.1017/S0960129510000125

18. Miyazaki, Y.: Some properties of orthologics. Studia Logica Int. J. Symbolic Logic **80**(1), 75–93 (2005). arXiv:2001.6705

19. Navarro, J.A., Voronkov, A.: Generation of hard non-clausal random satisfiability problems. In: Proceedings of the 20th National Conference on Artificial Intelligence - Volume 1, AAAI 2005, pp. 436–442. AAAI Press, Pittsburgh, Pennsylvania, July 2005

20. Mönting, J.S.: Cut elimination and word problems for varieties of lattices. Algebra Universalis **12**(1), 290–321 (1981). https://doi.org/10.1007/BF02483891

21. Sherif, M.: Decision problem for orthomodular lattices. Algebra Universalis **37**(1), 70–76 (1997). https://doi.org/10.1007/PL00000328

22. Sozeau, M.: A new look at generalized rewriting in type theory. J. Formalized Reasoning **2**(1), 41–62 (2009). https://doi.org/10.6092/issn.1972-5787/1574

23. Tews, H.: Formalizing cut elimination of coalgebraic logics in Coq. In: Galmiche, D., Larchey-Wendling, D. (eds.) TABLEAUX 2013. LNCS (LNAI), vol. 8123, pp. 257–272. Springer, Heidelberg (2013). https://doi.org/10.1007/978-3-642-40537-2_22

24. Truszkowska, W., Grabowski, A.: On the two short axiomatizations of ortholattices (2003)

25. Urban, C., Zhu, B.: Revisiting cut-elimination: one difficult proof is really a proof. In: Voronkov, A. (ed.) RTA 2008. LNCS, vol. 5117, pp. 409–424. Springer, Heidelberg (2008). https://doi.org/10.1007/978-3-540-70590-1_28
26. Wimmer, S., Hu, S., Nipkow, T.: Verified memoization and dynamic programming. In: Avigad, J., Mahboubi, A. (eds.) ITP 2018. LNCS, vol. 10895, pp. 579–596. Springer, Cham (2018). https://doi.org/10.1007/978-3-319-94821-8_34

Accelerating Automated Program Verifiers by Automatic Proof Localization

Kiran Gopinathan[1], Dionysios Spiliopoulos[2(✉)], Vikram Goyal[3], Peter Müller[2], Markus Püschel[2], and Ilya Sergey[3]

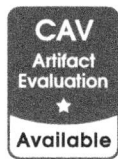

[1] University of Illinois Urbana-Champaign, Champaign, USA
[2] Department of Computer Science, ETH Zurich, Zürich, Switzerland
`dionysios.spiliopoulos@inf.ethz.ch`
[3] National University of Singapore, Singapore, Singapore

Abstract. Automated program verifiers such as Dafny, F*, Verus, and Viper are now routinely used to verify real-world software. Unfortunately, the performance of the SMT solvers employed by these tools is not always able to keep up with the increasing size and complexity of verification problems, resulting in long verification times and verification failures due to time-outs. This performance degradation occurs because large SMT queries increase the search space for the SMT solver, in particular, the number of possible quantifier instantiations. Most existing attempts to mitigate this problem require substantial manual effort to reduce the size of the search space, for instance, by decomposing proofs.

In this paper, we present an automatic technique to significantly improve the performance of SMT-based program proofs by drastically reducing the proof search space for each assertion, in particular, the performed quantifier instantiations. Starting from a successful verification, we automatically extract for each assertion the quantified axioms used by the SMT solver to show that the assertion is valid. Crucially, these include *lurking axioms*, which are logically irrelevant, but needed to trigger the instantiation of other, relevant axioms. We describe a novel *proof localization* algorithm that implements a semantics-preserving source-to-source translation of a program such that re-verifying an assertion in the optimized program uses only the axioms in its proof essence. This rewriting greatly reduces the possible quantifier instantiations and, thereby, the search space for the SMT solver, such that all future runs of the verifier, for instance as part of continuous integration, are substantially faster. We implemented our algorithm for the Boogie verifier and demonstrated its effectiveness on examples from Dafny and Viper. Specifically, for files with verification times over a minute, we show significant speedups of up to 100–1000 times and no slowdowns. We also provide some evidence that these improvements persist as projects evolve.

K. Gopinathan—Work done while at National University of Singapore.

R. Piskac and Z. Rakamarić (Eds.): CAV 2025, LNCS 15933, pp. 153–174, 2025.
https://doi.org/10.1007/978-3-031-98682-6_9

1   Introduction

Automated program verification has become an increasingly popular approach to certifying real world systems, with the most recent developments tackling larger and more ambitious targets such as distributed systems [18], cryptographic libraries [1,28], file systems [7], and access protocols [9]. By delegating proof obligations to Satisfiability Modulo Theories (SMT) solvers, such as Z3 [11] or cvc5 [2], automated verification tools such as Dafny [21], F* [30], Verus [20], and verifiers built on top of Viper [25] or Why3 [15] substantially reduce the proof burden for users and provide a lighter alternative to interactive proof assistants.

However, with the growing ambition of verification projects, automated verifiers increasingly face performance-related maintenance problems. Complex proof obligations substantially increase the proof search space, which may lead to long verification times and failures due to time-outs [18,27]. This performance degradation is primarily caused by an explosion of the number of quantifier instantiations performed by the SMT solver. Most program verifiers use the SMT solver's e-matching algorithm [12], which associates each universal quantifier with a syntactic matching pattern (often called *trigger*) and instantiates the quantifier when a ground term in the proof context matches the pattern. Large queries contain thousands of quantifiers and many ground terms that trigger instantiations, introducing additional ground terms and, thus, even more instantiations.

The prevalent solution to date is to address maintenance concerns by manually refactoring verified programs in order to reduce the number of quantifiers as well as the general size of the proof context. For instance, Dafny and Verus allow programmers to control which function definitions (encoded as quantified axioms) are available in a proof. Dafny and Gobra [31] also allow programmers to break up proofs into smaller pieces, which reduces the size of the proof context for each piece. Both approaches are helpful, but require substantial manual effort and insight to decide when to refactor. Moreover, they are difficult to apply, even for expert users, because the effect of a code refactoring on verification time is rather unpredictable due to the SMT solver's complex heuristics. Bordis and Leino use a syntactic analysis to automatically pre-instantiate some quantified axioms [5], which improves verification times, but may lead to spurious errors if the analysis cannot determine all necessary instantiations.

This Work. We present *proof localization*, an automatic procedure to systematically minimize the proof search space for the SMT solver and, thereby, improve verification time. Given an initial successful verification of an assertion, we extract from the SMT solver the *essence of the proof*, which includes the information needed for the solver to efficiently re-prove the assertion on all future runs of the verifier. The proof essence contains the ∀-quantified axioms used by the SMT solver to prove that the assertion is valid. Moreover, it includes additional axioms that are logically irrelevant for the proof, but needed by the SMT solver to trigger the instantiation of other, relevant axioms—we refer to them as *lurking axioms*.

Once we have identified all axioms needed to prove an assertion, we automatically rewrite the input program in a semantics-preserving way, such that computing standard verification conditions over the rewritten program includes, for each assertion, only those axioms strictly needed by the SMT solver (rather than all available in the context). The result is a drastically reduced search space.

Since proof localization requires the existence of a proof, it does not improve performance of the initial verification of each assertion. Nevertheless, speeding up future runs of the verifier is of great practical value. In an active project, each assertion is typically verified a countless number of times. For example, when the code evolves, when iteratively verifying increasingly-strong properties, when code is reused in different contexts, when upgrading the program verifier or the underlying SMT solver, or when verification is integrated into continuous integration pipelines. Caching of verification results is helpful in only a few of these cases, when a proof obligation remains entirely unchanged compared to the cached result; however, even a small, irrelevant change requires re-verification.

Our implementation performs a source-to-source transformation on programs in the Boogie intermediate verification language [3]. It could easily be integrated into any Boogie-based source verifier by performing a corresponding transformation on the source program, such that the unmodified translation into Boogie produce the optimized program. Alternatively, the proof essence could be stored separately from the source program and used by an adapted Boogie translation.

We have implemented our technique in a tool called Axolocl and evaluated it on Boogie programs generated by Dafny and Viper, including various benchmarks from industrial verification projects. Our evaluation shows significant speedups for files with verification times over a minute. Using semantics-preserving mutations of SMT queries, we also provide some evidence that the positive effects of our transformations persist as verification projects evolve.

Contributions. We make the following specific technical contributions:

-   We present a systematic approach to extracting the proof essence for a proof obligation, that is, the axioms needed for the proof. We identify the phenomenon of *lurking axioms*, which must be included in the essence to ensure that an SMT solver can reconstruct the proof from the essence.
-   We introduce *proof localization*, a simple semantics-preserving translation that embeds the proof essence for each assertion *directly into the verified program*, such that verification conditions over the resulting program include, for each assertion, only the axioms strictly needed by the SMT solver. Our technique is applicable with all SMT-based verifiers.
-   We have implemented our technique in a tool called Axolocl [16] for the Boogie intermediate language, which enables the optimization of all verifiers built on top of Boogie, including Dafny and Viper.
-   We present an extensive evaluation of Axolocl on a diverse set of benchmarks from eight verification projects. Specifically, for long-running files, we show significant speedups of up to 100–1000 times and no slowdowns.

2   Overview

The positive effect of proof localization is best observed at scale, *i.e.*, on large programs with complex specifications. For the sake of clarity, in this section, we provide the intuition for the most likely sources of long proof runtimes and the ways we mitigate them via proof localization, by means of a simple example.

2.1   A Primer on SMT-Based Verification

Our approach for proof localization works by performing a source-to-source transformation on verified programs written in the Boogie intermediate verification language [3]. Figure 1 presents an example program written in Boogie. Let us ignore the highlighted parts, which will be explained later. A Boogie program can be broadly considered as being composed of three main components: firstly, a declaration context, consisting of a series of uninterpreted types (line 1), constants (line 2), and functions (lines 3–5); secondly, a series of axioms (lines 7–12) that provide an interpretation for the prior declarations; and finally a series of verified procedures (lines 14–19) each specified in terms of the previous definitions using a pre- (line 15) and postcondition (line 16), and whose body (lines 17–18) is written in imperative style. Our example procedure concatenates the input sequences x and y and returns the result. Its specification expresses that, provided that the input sequences are non-empty (as required by the precondition), the result will also be non-empty. The latter property is expressed as a postcondition and, for illustration purposes, also as an assertion in line 18. The postcondition follows from the precondition and the axiom in line 7. When run on this program, Boogie checks its correctness by computing a verification condition (VC) using weakest preconditions calculus and proves its validity using an SMT solver.

Let us delve a little into the internals of how Boogie's SMT-based verification works. In this discussion, we ignore the postcondition in line 16 because the same check is already expressed by the assertion in line 18. Ignoring various optimizations, Boogie computes a VC expressing that the assertion on line 18 holds for the result of the program, given the assumptions in the precondition:

$$BG \; \land \; NonEmpty(x) \; \land \; NonEmpty(y) \; \Rightarrow \; NonEmpty(Append(x,y))$$

In this VC, BG is the so-called background theory, which includes the axioms declared in our program and various built-in axioms, *e.g.*, about lists. To prove that this VC is valid, Boogie uses an SMT solver to show that its negation is unsatisfiable, that is, that there are no counterexamples to the VC's validity. To achieve this, the underlying SMT solver must instantiate the axiom in line 7. Boogie, like most program verifiers, rely on e-matching [12] to instantiate quantifiers. Each quantifier is associated with a *matching pattern* (often called *trigger*), a term using variables bound by the quantifier. When the SMT solver encounters a term that matches the trigger, it uses unification to instantiate the quantifier.

```
1  type Seq;
2  const Emp: Seq;
3  function Length(Seq): int;
4  function Append(Seq, Seq): Seq;
5  function NonEmpty(Seq): bool;
6
7  axiom (∀ 1: Seq, r: Seq •  {NonEmpty(Append(1, r))}
8     {Length(1), Length(r)}
9     NonEmpty(Append(1, r)) = (NonEmpty(1) ∨ NonEmpty(r)));
10
11 axiom (∀ s: Seq •  {NonEmpty(s)}  NonEmpty(s)=(1≤Length(s)));
12
13 procedure test(x: Seq, y: Seq)
14    returns (res: Seq)
15    requires NonEmpty(x) ∧ NonEmpty(y);
16    ensures NonEmpty(res); {
17    res := Append(x,y);
18    assert NonEmpty(res);
19 }
```

Fig. 1. An example Boogie program. The final assert statement is redundant and used for illustration purposes. The color-highlighted lines specify different matching patterns (triggers) for the ∀-quantifiers.

In our running example, Fig. 1, the blue areas highlight possible triggers for the two axioms. These are used by the SMT solver to guide instantiation based on the terms available in the context. In particular, the conclusion of the implication NonEmpty(Append(x,y)) in the VC matches the trigger of the first axiom. This enables the SMT solver to instantiate the axiom with x for 1 and y for r, after which the proof can be completed using the obtained equality. The terms NonEmpty(x), NonEmpty(y), and NonEmpty(Append(x,y)) in the VC all also match the trigger of the second axiom in line 11. However, *none* of these three instantiations are useful for the proof and correspond to redundant instantiations.

Triggers give program verifiers such as Boogie fine-grained control over the heuristics used by the underlying SMT solver to instantiate quantifiers. However, even with carefully-chosen triggers, the SMT solver will still often consider several redundant instantiations, and the search space remains vast. Verifying realistic VCs often involves hundreds or thousands of quantifier instantiations. Whether such SMT queries are solved efficiently, in particular, before a time-out occurs, largely depends on how effectively the SMT solver's heuristics navigate the search space of possible instantiations. Therefore, *reducing the search space of quantifier instantiations is key to improving the efficiency of SMT-based verification*. In the rest of this section, we will present the key ideas for achieving this goal.

2.2   Capturing the Essence of a Proof

To improve the efficiency of the prover, our main objective is to reduce the space of possible quantifier instantiations it has to make. We achieve this in two steps. First, we extract from the SMT solver which axioms it used to prove the validity of an assertion. Second, we rewrite the input program such that the VC for this assertion contains *exactly* the relevant axioms rather than the entire background theory. In the following, we explain these steps in the context of Boogie and its underlying SMT solver Z3, but our approach can be implemented in any verifier whose SMT solver supports triggers and UNSAT cores.

Extracting Relevant Axioms. To determine which axioms were used to verify an assertion, we instruct Boogie to compute a separate VC for each assertion (rather than a single VC for the entire procedure). Moreover, we assign a unique label to each axiom in the background theory. Recall that an SMT solver proves validity of a formula by showing that its negation is unsatisfiable. Consequently, when verification of an assertion succeeds, we can obtain the UNSAT core from the SMT solver, which includes the facts used to prove validity, and, in particular, the (labels of) the axioms that were used in the proof. In our example from Fig. 1, the UNSAT core contains the first axiom. The second one might have been instantiated during the proof search. However, since these instantiations were not helpful for the proof, the axiom does not show up in the UNSAT core.

Axiom Guarding. Once we have obtained the relevant axioms for each assertion, we transform the input program to ensure that future attempts to re-prove the assertion consider only the relevant axioms and, thus, have to explore a drastically reduced search space. We call this transformation *axiom guarding*.

As explained in Sect. 2.1, the VC for each assertion contains a background theory with all axioms. Conceptually, we would like to customize the background theory for each assertion to include only the relevant axiom. However, different background theories per assertion lead to a substantial overhead for the SMT solver (for instance, for parsing the different background theories). Therefore, instead, we use the same background theory for all assertions, but *guard* each axiom in a way that lets us enable and disable individual axioms for a proof.

In order to *guard* an axiom, we add another trigger to the axiom such that the axiom is instantiated *only* if a VC includes a term that matches this dedicated trigger. Figure 2 shows the guarded version of the

```
1  // dedicated guard for axiom 1
2  function ax1(bool): bool;
3  axiom (∀ b • {ax1(b)}
4    (∀ l,r • {NonEmpty(Append(l,r))}
5     NonEmpty(Append(l, r)) =
6     (NonEmpty(l) ∨ NonEmpty(r))));
```

Fig. 2. Example guarded axiom.

first axiom from Fig. 1. To obtain a trigger that is specific to this axiom, we first define a unique uninterpreted *guard function*, ax1 (line 2) and then wrap the axiom in a second ∀-quantifier with the guard function as trigger (line 3). Now we can selectively enable the axiom by including the term ax1(true) in a VC. This will allow the SMT solver to instantiate the outer quantifier and get access to the original axiom. If no such term is present, the axiom is disabled.

To enable axioms selectively per assertion, we rewrite each assertion into a nondeterministic if-statement, where one branch proves the assertion and then stops verification, and the other branch simply assumes the asserted property and then

```
1  if (*) {
2    assume ax1(true);
3    assert NonEmpty(res);
4    assume false;
5  }
6  assume NonEmpty(res)
```

Fig. 3. A transformed assertion.

proceeds to the subsequent statement. This allows us to enable axioms selectively in the first branch without polluting the proof of the subsequent code with unnecessary facts. Since a verifier considers both branches of an if-statement, this encoding both proves the assertion and verifies the subsequent code; verifying the first branch justifies the assumption in the second one.

Figure 3 illustrates this translation for the assertion from the line 18 of Fig. 1. The first branch of the non-deterministic if-statement enables the axiom relevant for the assertion (that is, our first axiom), by mentioning the dedicated trigger ax1 in an assume statement (line 2). After proving the original assertion (line 3), we kill off this branch by assuming false (line 4), which ensures that the subsequent code verifies trivially. In the second branch, we assume that the property holds (line 6) without introducing any axioms into the context and continue with the rest of the verification.

```
1  function ax1(bool): bool;
2  function ax2(bool): bool;
3
4  axiom (∀ b: bool • {ax1(b)}
5   (∀ l: Seq, r: Seq
6      • {NonEmpty(Append(l,r))}
7      NonEmpty(Append(l, r)) =
8      (NonEmpty(l)∨NonEmpty(r))));
9
10 axiom (∀ b: bool • {ax2(b)}
11  (∀ s: Seq • {NonEmpty(s)}
12    NonEmpty(s) = (1≤Length(s))));
13
14 procedure test(x: Seq, y: Seq)
15 returns (res: Seq)
16 requires NonEmpty(x) ∧
17          NonEmpty(y);
18 ensures NonEmpty(res); {
19  res := Append(x,y);
20  if (*) {
21    assume ax1(true);
22    assert NonEmpty(res);
23    assume false;
24  }
25  assume NonEmpty(res);
26 }
```

(a) An initial transformed version.

```
1  function ax1(bool): bool;
2  function ax2(bool): bool;
3
4  axiom (∀ b: bool • {ax1(b)}
5   (∀ l: Seq, r: Seq
6      • {Length(l), Length(r)}
7      NonEmpty(Append(l, r)) =
8      (NonEmpty(l)∨NonEmpty(r))));
9
10 axiom (∀ b: bool • {ax2(b)}
11  (∀ s: Seq • {NonEmpty(s)}
12    NonEmpty(s) = (1≤Length(s))));
13
14 procedure test(x: Seq, y: Seq)
15 returns (res: Seq)
16 requires NonEmpty(x) ∧
17          NonEmpty(y);
18 ensures NonEmpty(res); {
19  res := Append(x,y);
20  if (*) {
21    assume ax1(true)∧ax2(true);
22    assert NonEmpty(res);
23    assume false;
24  }
25  assume NonEmpty(res);
26 }
```

(b) The final version.

Fig. 4. Proof-localized example of the Boogie program from Fig. 1; the left version enables UNSAT core axioms only, the right one also includes lurking axioms.

Proof Localization. We apply the procedure described above to each proof obligation in a Boogie program. These include assert statements, procedure preconditions (at call sites), procedure postconditions (at the end of the procedure body), and loop invariants (before the loop and at the end of the loop body). Boogie internally makes all of these proof obligations explicit as assert statements (just like our assertion in line 18 makes the proof obligation for the postcondition explicit), which we then transform. Figure 4a presents a transformed version of the example from Fig. 1 (with the blue triggers) using the localization procedure described so far. Our transformation effectively removes the second axiom from the search space for the assertion. Note that our proof-localizing transformation is able to remove this axiom even though it syntactically seems relevant since both the trigger and the quantified assertion share terms with the assertion. This *fine-grained* pruning of the search space is important for realistic examples, where many axioms are syntactically related.

2.3   The Missing Piece: Lurking Axioms

Unfortunately, the story does not yet end here. To see why, consider the variation of the example from Fig. 1, but this time with the orange trigger for the first axiom instead of the blue (and still the blue trigger for the second axiom). The orange trigger is contrived in this example, but illustrates a problem that occurs frequently, as we demonstrate in our evaluation.

The program with the orange trigger from Fig. 1 verifies successfully. However, when we apply the localization procedure described so far, the resulting program fails to verify! As it turns out, successful verification requires an entire class of additional axioms that are not included in the UNSAT core and, thus, are not enabled in our transformation from Sect. 2.2. Next, we explain how such hidden dependencies can arise, and present a systematic solution for identifying them.

The transformed program enables the first axiom, which is *logically* sufficient to prove the assertion. However, with the orange trigger, the SMT solver will not instantiate this axiom during the proof search because it does not encounter any term that matches the orange trigger (Length does not occur in the proof obligation). Consequently, the proof fails. In contrast, the non-transformed program verifies because the SMT solver will instantiate the second axiom with both x and y, which produces the Length terms to instantiate the first axiom. This shows that even though the second axiom is logically irrelevant and, thus, not included in the UNSAT core, it is *essential* for the SMT solver to find the proof. We call such axioms *lurking axioms*. Therefore, we must extend our proof essence to include not only the axioms from the UNSAT core, but also these lurking axioms. We identify them by extracting from the debug output of Z3 an *instantiation graph* that reflects the dependencies between quantifier instantiations [4].

Figure 5 shows the instantiation graph for our example. The white boxes are terms from the solver's context, such as NonEmpty(x) or NonEmpty(y). The rounded colored boxes depict axiom instantiations, *e.g.*, ax2 @ x is the instantiation of the second axiom with the expression x. We use blue for axioms in the UNSAT core and red for all other axioms. Arrows between the nodes capture dependencies between terms and

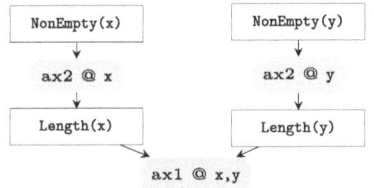

Fig. 5. Instantiation graph for Fig. 1 (with the orange trigger for axiom 1).

axioms: the line between `NonEmpty(x)` and `ax2 @ x` means that during the proof search, the solver used the term `NonEmpty(x)` to match the trigger for `ax2` and instantiate it. By examining this graph, we can see that for the solver to instantiate the necessary axiom (`ax1` with `x` and `y`) in the actual proof search, it first instantiated `ax2` with both `x` and `y` to obtain the terms `Length(x)` and `Length(y)`, thereby triggering `ax1`.

We identify lurking axioms by inspecting each path from a root of the instantiation graph to an axiom in the UNSAT core. All axioms on this path that are not in the UNSAT core are considered lurking axioms. The *proof essence* for an assertion consists of all axioms in the UNSAT core plus all lurking axioms, and we use all of them in our proof localization. In our example, the proof essence contains both axioms, the first one because it is in the UNSAT core and the second because it is a lurking axiom. Consequently, the proof-localized program, shown in Fig. 4b, enables both axioms and thus verifies successfully. So for the orange trigger, proof localization does not actually reduce the search space for the SMT solver. However, as we discussed above, this trigger is contrived; in a realistic example, the transformation effectively reduces the search space and, thereby, proof search runtime, as we will show in our evaluation.

2.4 Putting It All Together

Figure 6 presents the high-level overview of our approach, which integrates the proof localization process presented throughout this section behind a push-button interface. Our tool, Axolocl, takes as input any standard Boogie file, and produces as output a proof-localized version where all the axioms and assertions have been guarded in order to improve its stability. Axolocl does so in four steps: (1) It copies the declaration context, consisting of the types, constants, and functions, over to the new file. (2) It performs a straightforward syntactic

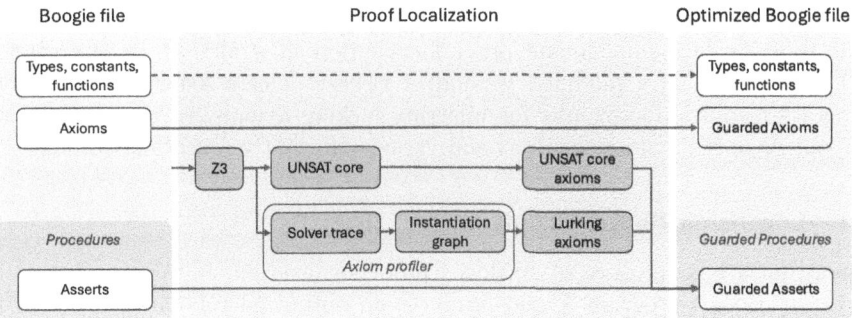

Fig. 6. Overview of the approach. Boxes with white background are user-provided components; the gray background indicates Boogie source files; boxes with green backgrounds are generated components; blue boxes depict intermediate artifacts; the red box indicates the external executable Z3. The dashed arrow indicates that the components are copied verbatim from the old to the new program.

ALGORITHM 3.1: Proof Localization

Procedure `Localize-Proofs`(P)

　　Input: Original Boogie program P

　　Output: Transformed Boogie program with localized proofs

　　$C \leftarrow \texttt{ExtractDeclContext}(P)$

　　$A \leftarrow \texttt{BuildGuardedAxioms}(P)$

　　$I \leftarrow [\,]$

　　for *proc* **in** P **do**

　　　　essence $\leftarrow [\,]$

　　　　for a **in** `SplitVCByAsserts`(*proc*) **do**

　　　　　　$q \leftarrow \texttt{ConstructSMTQuery}(a)$

　　　　　　$c, t \leftarrow \texttt{VerifyWithZ3}(q)$

　　　　　　$g \leftarrow \texttt{ExtractInstGraph}(t)$

　　　　　　$c' \leftarrow \texttt{ComputeEssence}(c,\ g)$

　　　　　　essence[a] $\leftarrow c'$

　　　　proc' $\leftarrow \texttt{BuildGuardedProc}(proc,\ essence)$

　　　　$I \leftarrow I + [proc']$

　　$P' \leftarrow \texttt{BuildBoogieProgram}(C,\ A,\ I)$

　　return P'

---

translation to wrap each axiom into a quantifier with a unique trigger. (3) It verifies each assertion in the original program, and obtains from the Z3 SMT solver both the UNSAT core and a solver trace, from which it extracts the instantiation graph for the proof search. Combining these two components, for each assertion, provides the proof essence. (4) It rewrites each of the assertions in the original program to enable exactly the axioms in its proof essence. The resulting proof-localized program is semantically equivalent to the input program, contains all information to verify successfully, and its proof is typically substantially faster.

3　Algorithms and Encoding

Our tool, Axolocl, implements proof localization in a fork of Boogie version 3.0.12.0, vendoring a modified version of Becker *et al.*'s Axiom Profiler [4] to generate instantiation graphs for inferring lurking axioms. In this section, we present Axolocl's main algorithms and various alternative encoding schemes.

3.1　Localizing Boogie Proofs

Algorithm 3.1 is the core of Axolocl's proof localization. It takes as input an arbitrary Boogie program P and produces an optimized version as depicted in Fig. 6. The algorithm operates in three steps: (1) it retrieves the declaration context (`ExtractDeclContext`) composed of all the types, constants, and functions shared between the original and optimized program; (2) it then constructs guarded forms of each axiom in P (`BuildGuardedAxioms`), generating a unique guard function and rewriting the axiom body to wrap it with a trigger-based guard; (3) it performs proof localization on each of the procedures in P.

ALGORITHM 3.2: Compute Proof Essence

Procedure ComputeEssence(C, G)

    Input: UNSAT Core C and Instantiation Graph G

    Output: Set of Required Axioms

    $C' \leftarrow [\,]$

    for a **in** C **do**

        $deps \leftarrow \{a\}$

        $s \leftarrow [a]$

        while $s \neq [\,]$ **do**

            $n, s \leftarrow$ TakeFirst(s)

            $deps \leftarrow deps \cup \{n\}$

            for $n' \leftarrow$ GetAxiomDependencies(G, n) **do**

                if $n' \notin deps$ **then**

                    $s \leftarrow$ Append(s, n')

        $C' \leftarrow C' + deps$

    return C'

For the latter, the algorithm partitions each procedure into the verification conditions for each assertion in the code (SplitVCByAsserts). For each of these verification conditions, the algorithm constructs an SMT query (ConstructSMTQuery) including appropriate annotations to allow extracting the axiom dependencies. It is submitted to the Z3 SMT solver (VerifyWithZ3), to obtain both an UNSAT core c and a solver debug trace t, which contains a log of each of the axiom instantiations that the solver performed during the proof search. This solver trace is then used to construct an instantiation graph g (ExtractInstGraph), capturing the dependencies between each of the axioms in the query. The algorithm uses the UNSAT core c and the instantiation graph g to infer any missing lurking axioms and constructs the minimal set of required axioms c' to complete the proof (ComputeEssence). Once this proof essence has been constructed for all verification conditions, the algorithm optimizes the original Boogie procedure (BuildGuardedProc), replacing each assertion with a guarded version that explicitly enables the axioms in the proof essence. The last step of the algorithm concatenates the declaration context C, the guarded axioms A, and the optimized procedures I to produce the final optimized Boogie program.

3.2   Identifying Lurking Axioms

Algorithm 3.2 determines the necessary set of axioms for a verification query. It takes as input an UNSAT core C and the instantiation graph G generated by the solver for a given SMT query. It then iterates through each of the axioms in the UNSAT core, and, for each axiom a, performs a basic breadth first search over the instantiation graph rooted at a to retrieve the set of dependencies of a. We allocate a list of nodes s to visit, initially populated by a, and a set $deps$ to track the set of lurking axioms required for a. While s is non-empty, the algorithm repeatedly takes the first element n, adds it to the list of dependencies and uses the instantiation graph to retrieve the list n' of axioms that were required for n to be instantiated. If any of these dependencies are not present in *deps* then they are added to s to be visited. Finally, the algorithm takes the union of all the axiom dependencies for each axiom in the UNSAT core (including the core axiom itself) to produce the final proof essence.

3.3   Encoding Schemes

After extracting the proof essence for each assertion, Axolocl rewrites the program into a guarded form to improve verification times. One subtle aspect of our design is in the particular trigger-based encoding that we use to localize proofs. Given a proof essence, there are several possible encodings that we considered in order to enable these axioms in the source program. As we will show in the evaluation (Sect. 3.3), the choice of encoding has a major effect on verification times.

```
function                  function
   ax(bool): bool;           ax(bool): bool;
axiom                     axiom
(∀ b: bool • {ax(b)} A);  (∀ b: bool • {ax(b)} A);

procedure foo(x) {        procedure foo(x) {        procedure foo(x) {
 if(*) {                    assume ax;               if(*) {
  assume ax(true);          ...                       axiom A;
  assert P;                assert P;                  assert P;
  assume false;            ...                        assume false;
 }                                                  }
 assume P;                                          assume P;
 ...                                                 . ..
}                         }                         }
```

(a) Trigger-based (fine)   (b) Trigger-based (coarse)   (c) Inlining-based

Fig. 7. Comparison of different guarded proof encoding schemes.

Figure 7 presents three different encoding schemes that we considered for guarding axioms and restricting the proof context at the source level. Figure 7a presents the trigger-based encoding used by our implementation that constrains the proof context at a fine-grained per-assertion level. We introduce a unique guard function ax for each axiom A, and move the axiom under a universal quantifier over a Boolean variable b with a trigger using that guard {ax(b)}. At each assertion, we introduce branching; one branch selectively enables the relevant axioms by assuming their guards ax(true) and then verifies the assertion. The other branch continues with the rest of the verification assuming the assertion. This encoding allows rewriting programs with minimal changes and achieves the largest performance improvements in our evaluation.

Figure 7b presents an alternative, coarse-grained trigger-based encoding. It performs the same transformation on each of the axioms, but instead of rewriting each assertion individually, it triggers all axioms needed for the entire procedure at the beginning of the procedure body. In other words, this encoding localizes proofs at the procedure (rather than assertion) level. Compared to the previous fine-grained encoding, the coarse-grained encoding leads to simpler verification conditions because it does not complicate the control-flow of the programs. It also restricts the proof search space in comparison to the original program, but not as effectively as the fine-grained encoding. As we will see in the evaluation, the benefit of fine-grained proof localization outweighs the increased complexity of the verification conditions.

Figure 7c presents an alternative encoding based on inlining axioms rather than disabling them via triggers. With this encoding, we remove all axioms from the global context, and then instead, at each assertion, we selectively *assume* the (quantified) body of each axiom in the proof essence. This encoding is as precise as our first encoding. It avoids the overhead of guarding each axiom, but duplicates axiom bodies at each assertion. For most real-world **Boogie** programs that we tried it on, it produced results that are too large to even fit into memory.

For our trigger-based encodings, we also considered adding the guard as an additional pattern to the triggers of the existing axioms, rather than wrapping them in an additional universal quantifier:

```
axiom (∀ s: Seq, b: bool • {Length(s), ax(b)}  1 ≤ Length(s) );
```

This encoding reduces the total number of universal quantifiers, but, as it turns out, does not improve verification times.

4   Evaluation

We evaluate Axolocl on a broad range of benchmarks. Most important is its effectiveness in reducing verification time, but we also assess whether the achieved runtime improvements can be expected to be maintained across changes as the verification project. Measuring the latter on real projects would require detailed information about revisions, manual performance optimizations, and updates of the verifier and SMT solver. Since we do not have access to this information, we use robustness against semantics-preserving mutations as proxy; prior work has shown that such mutations can already perturb verification times substantially [13]. Finally, we also compare the different proof localization strategies from Sect. 3.3. Specifically, we answer the following research questions:

- **RQ1**: Is Axolocl effective at reducing verification times?
- **RQ2**: Are these improvements robust to mutations of the input?
- **RQ3**: Is Axolocl's encoding for localizing axioms effective?

4.1 Evaluation Setup

We explain the benchmark set used and the evaluation methodology.

Benchmarks. To answer the above research questions, we apply Axolocl to a suite of Boogie programs, all extracted from existing verification projects. Specifically, we consider eight benchmark sets, seven of which are publicly-available open-source Dafny projects. The last one is based on the Viper test suite. We chose these benchmarks for their size and to assess the effectiveness of Axolocl on a diverse set of verified systems. The resulting benchmark suite consists of:

- **Cedar**: The Dafny formalization of the Cedar authorization language [9]
- **AWS**: The AWS Cryptographic Material providers library [1]
- **Daisy-NFSD**: The Daisy-NFSD verified crash-safe file system [7]
- **EVM**: An EVM disassembler in Dafny [6]
- **Dafny-VMC**: A verified library for Monte Carlo algorithms [32]
- **Komodo**: An implementation of an SGX-like enclave protection model in a formally verified privileged software stack for ARMv7 TrustZone [17]
- **VeriBetrKV**: A formally verified key-value store based on a B^eTree [14]
- **Viper**: Various test cases from the Viper program verifier's test suite

Methodology. We use Axolocl to optimize each Boogie file from the benchmark suite and compare the verification times before and after proof localization. All experiments are conducted on a 2-vCPU Intel Xeon Platinum 8000 series processor (up to 3.6 GHz) running Ubuntu 22.04. We use Z3 version 4.8.7.

Since verification times are dominated by SMT solving, we measure the runtime at the SMT level rather than at the Boogie level. For each Boogie file, we measure the wall-clock time spent in the SMT solver, averaged over 50 runs, in which we alter the Z3 random seed to account for different Z3-heuristic behaviors. The timeout for each verification run is set to ten minutes.

Axolocl is designed to accelerate verification on slow inputs. Therefore, we discard Boogie files for which the mean verification time is at most two seconds. These are fast already, such that further optimization is not justified. This leaves us with 365 Boogie files across our eight projects; see Table 1 for more details.

4.2 Runtime Improvement (RQ1)

Our first research question investigates whether our tool is effective at reducing verification times. Figure 8 plots the speedup (verification time before divided by verification time after) achieved by Axolocl versus the original verification time for each file. A speedup of less than one is thus a slowdown. We first observe that Axolocl achieves a speedup in the majority of cases. Importantly, slowdown occur only for files whose verification is very fast to begin with, with one exception that takes around 35 s and suffers a 4× slowdown. Conversely, for slow files beyond that, Axolocl yields very significant speedup of up to a 1000× and, equally important, never incurs a slowdown.

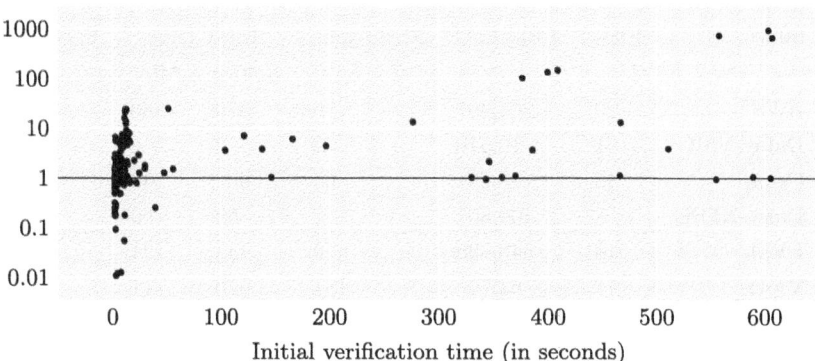

Speedup by Axolocl

Fig. 8. Average speedup per Axolocl-optimized file as a function of the initial verification time over our 365 benchmark files. The y axis is logarithmic.

Table 1 presents the aggregate effect of Axolocl on the verification times across the eight projects in our benchmark suite. It shows the number of Boogie files for each project, the total number of lines of code in the Boogie files, the mean verification time for the original files, as well as the total verification time for all files in the project, before and after using Axolocl. The speedup obtained for this total time is shown in the last column and reflects what would be experienced by a developer working on the project or in CI. Except for AWS, Axolocl reduces the overall verification time by up to 4.3 times for the Viper test suite. Among the considered projects, the AWS codebase is the only one that is actively maintained and has verification integrated as part of its CI pipeline; therefore, we hypothesize that it already underwent considerable manual optimization.

Table 2 shows the impact of Axolocl on the number of quantifier instantiations (QIs) across the same set of projects. For each test case, we measured the number of QIs over multiple runs and computed the average to mitigate the effects of proof instability. The table reports the mean number of QIs across the entire test suite before applying proof localization. Unlike earlier experiments, we include all files in this analysis, regardless of whether their verification time was below two seconds. The table also reports the total number of QIs before and after proof localization, as well as the reduction factor for each project. Proof localization significantly reduces the number of QIs, providing evidence that the observed performance improvements indeed stem from a decrease in quantifier instantiations.

We conclude that Axolocl is a viable solution to improve verification runtimes for slow files and for entire large-scale projects.

4.3   Robustness to Mutation (RQ2)

Improving verification times alone does not tell the complete picture: if a program (as well as the employed verifier and SMT solver) remained entirely unchanged,

Table 1. Effect of Axolocl on verification times. All times in seconds.

Suite	Files	Total LoC	Mean time	Total Time		Speedup
				Before	After	
AWS	23	1,264,497	16	370	380	1.0
Dafny-VMC	1	10,916	2	2	2	1.0
Cedar	15	1,198,291	64	967	349	2.8
Daisy-NFSD	8	109,801	7	69	50	1.4
EVM	16	548,790	9	141	131	1.1
Viper	17	63,790	181	3,070	711	4.3
Komodo	5	26,371	9	45	15	3.0
VeriBetrKV	280	6,718,495	23	6,569	5,757	1.1

Table 2. Effect of Axolocl on quantifier instantiations (QIs).

Suite	Mean QIs	Total QIs		Reduction factor
		Before	After	
AWS	41,930	2,138,465	664,442	3.2
Dafny-VMC	4,796	47,960	21,623	2.2
Cedar	812,507	26,000,237	3,792,461	6.9
Daisy-NFSD	36,956	628,261	203,276	3.1
EVM	45,121	1,308,522	185,303	7.1
Viper	540,591	6,487,097	3,243,952	2.0
Komodo	677	74,567	13,406	5.6
VeriBetrKV	6,716	4,996,978	1,272,005	3.9

then a developer could improve verification times by simple caching. Our second research question investigates whether the performance improvements achieved by Axolocl are likely to persist across changes in the project. We focus on the simplest kind of such changes, semantic-preserving re-orderings and renamings of variables and declarations, and investigate how the generated files' verification times behave with respect to them. Such simple mutations can have a substantial effect on verification times; therefore, they are a good proxy for other changes.

Concretely, we measure the verification times of each Boogie file before and after proof localization, averaged across several runs with random mutations applied at the SMT level. We consider two kinds of mutations: renaming user-defined symbols (*e.g.*, functions, types) and reordering assertions. We then calculate the mean verification time over 50 measurements while considering both mutations and variations in the random seed. The results of this evaluation are presented in Fig. 9, which plots the speedups against the initial mean verification time over 50 mutations.

We can see from this diagram that mutations have a significantly greater impact on verification time than changes in the verification seed as considered in Sect. 4.2. For reference, mutations increase the mean verification time of 16 out of the 20 files in the Viper test suite. On average, each Viper file takes 42.59 s longer to verify under mutation.

Due to the increased average verification time, more files *excluded* in Sect. 4.2 for being verified in less than 2 s are *included* in this experiment. Since proof-localization is generally less effective for fast queries with few quantifier instantiations, the inclusion of these queries leads to a lower average speedup across all files.

Despite the additional variability introduced by mutation, the general trends from Fig. 8 still persist, especially among the slowest files.

We conclude that Axolocl achieves substantial performance improvements for files with long verification times, even under mutation.

Speedup by Axolocl

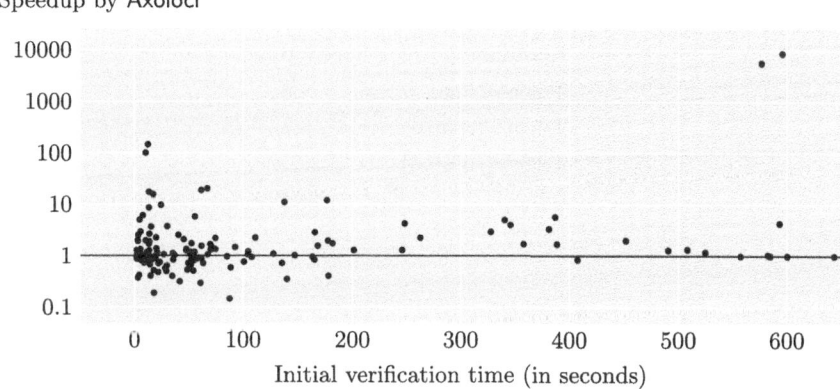

Fig. 9. Average speedup of Axolocl-optimized files under mutations as a function of the initial verification time, over 365 benchmark files. The y axis is logarithmic.

4.4 Encoding Effectiveness (RQ3)

In the final experiment, we assess the benefit of the chosen fine-grained trigger-based encoding in Axolocl, compared to the alternatives explained in Sect. 3.3:

- **Trigger (fine)**: Axolocl's default encoding strategy (see Fig. 7a).
- **Trigger (coarse)**: Enabling all axioms at a procedure level (see Fig. 7b).
- **Trigger (embedded)**: Embedding the axiom guard within existing triggers for the axiom.
- **Inline**: Inlining axiom bodies at each assertion (see Fig. 7c).

For this research question, we focus on the Viper suite of benchmarks specifically as it contains the files with the largest verification times, and on which Axolocl exhibits the greatest speedups (see Table 1).

We run Axolocl to generate optimized versions of each of the Viper files in the benchmark suite for each encoding scheme, and then measure the verification times averaged over 25 runs. Table 3 presents total speedups achieved for each different encoding scheme as before. It shows that our chosen fine-grained encoding outperforms all other encodings by far, and is the only scheme which produces improvements in verification times. The slowdown caused by the coarse-grained trigger-based encoding demonstrates the importance of constraining axioms at a per-assertion level. The speedup achieved for Viper is slightly different from the speedup reported in Table 1 primarily because one of the files couldn't be transformed for the inlining encoding. As a result, the speedups were calculated only for the remaining files.

Table 3. Comparison of different encoding strategies.

Encoding	Speedup
Trigger (fine)	4.8
Trigger (coarse)	0.6
Trigger (nested)	0.4
Inline	0.4

5   Related Work

Performance problems in SMT-based deductive verifiers are typically addressed by manual code refactorings using three different strategies. (1) Modularization by breaking up the verification of a method into several smaller proofs reduces the number of terms in the proof context and, thereby, quantifier instantiations, leading to better performance. Some verifiers offer language support for this strategy, for instance, Dafny's `opaque` blocks, Gobra's `outline` statement [31] allow one to specify code blocks with pre- and postconditions and verify them separately from the enclosing code, as if they had been extracted into separate methods. Similarly, Ivy's [26] `isolate`s achieve the same goal in the context of automatically verifying safety properties of state-transition systems, providing a scoping mechanism to confine a logical fragment or theory that a prover can handle reliably and efficiently.[1] (2) Carefully controlling the availability of quantified assertions also reduces the number of instantiations. For instance, Dafny and Verus allow for hiding the quantified axiom by defining a specification function and revealing it selectively. (3) Several verifiers allow the addition of

---

[1] *Cf.* https://microsoft.github.io/ivy/proving.html.

proof hints to assertions, for instance to invoke lemmas or reveal definitions. Both Dafny and Verus offer assert-by statements, whose encoding ensures that the provided proof hints do not pollute the proof context of other assertions. All three approaches require substantial manual effort. Moreover, they are difficult to apply, even for expert users, because the effect of a code refactoring on verification times is unpredictable due to the SMT solver's complex heuristics and thus its inherent black-box character. In contrast, our proof localization technique is completely automatic and requires no expertise in SMT solving.

Bordis and Leino [5] aim at reducing the number of quantified axioms and, thereby, the number of quantifier instantiations by automatically pre-instantiating some quantified axioms based on syntactic clues. However, their syntactic analysis cannot reliably identify all instantiations needed for a proof. In contrast, our technique starts from an existing proof, from which we can extract all necessary axioms, including lurking axioms.

The Axiom Profiler [4] supports developers and users of automated verifiers in understanding and debugging performance and completeness issues. It offers visualizations and analyses of SMT traces to identify issues with quantifier instantiations such as matching loops. This tool is useful to improve the matching patterns of quantifiers, but does not address the general problem of improving verification performance. We use it in our technique to identify lurking axioms.

Qed [8] simplifies verification conditions before handing them to the SMT solver, which reduces the proof context and, therefore, might have a positive effect on verification time, but this is not assessed in their evaluation.

A lot of work on the performance of SMT-based verifiers targets proof instability (also called *brittleness*) [13], which occurs when small changes in the SMT query have large effects on the verification time or even verification success. Most research into a systematic solution focuses on techniques to characterize particular instances of instability [24,34] or develops strategies for mitigating the instability in specific cases [10,19,22,23,29]. The recent Shake tool [33] offers an approach to mitigating proof instability. For an already verified project, it intercepts SMT queries emitted by verification tools and dynamically rewrites them to simplify and constrain the verification context, omitting irrelevant axioms and assumptions that are not required for the solver to prove correctness. Similarly to our algorithm, Shake aims at reducing the size of the proof context. Unlike our algorithm, it does not identify lurking axioms and instead relies on a *syntactic* dependency analysis to determine which axioms *might* be relevant. This coarse analysis may include axioms that are not actually needed, making the context (and, thus, the search space for the SMT solver) larger than necessary. On the other hand, it may also miss lurking axioms; as a result, the SMT solver may fail to prove the rewritten queries, leading to spurious verification errors requiring expensive post-hoc repair. Zhou *et al.* demonstrate Shake's effectiveness in reducing proof instability, but do not demonstrate performance improvements. Moreover, Shake does not offer a way to *persist* the rewritten queries, so that the tool needs to be rerun even at the slightest change in the file being verified. By contrast, our proof localization determines precisely which axioms are needed to rerun a proof and can record this information for future runs.

6   Conclusion

In this work we have presented Axolocl, a tool for the systematic performance optimizations of SMT-based program verifiers. Given an initial successful verification, it computes for each assertion the proof essence and encodes it into the input program, such that the assertion can be proved more efficiently in the future, for instance, during code maintenance or as part of continuous integration.

As future work, we plan to integrate proof localization in source verifiers, for instance, using Dafny's or Verus' assert-by statements. We also plan to explore whether proof localization can be applied also to address proof instability.

Acknowledgements. We thank CAV'25 reviewers for their detailed and insightful comments. This work has been supported by a Singapore Ministry of Education (MoE) Tier 1 grant T1 251RES2108 "Automated Proof Evolution for Verified Software Systems" and Singapore MoE Tier 3 grant "Automated Program Repair" MOE-MOET32021-0001.

Disclosure of Interests. The authors have no further competing interests to declare that are relevant to the content of this article.

References

1. AWS: AWS Cryptographic Material Providers Library (2024). https://github.com/aws/aws-cryptographic-material-providers-library. Accessed 8 Sept 2024
2. Barbosa, H., et al.: cvc5: a versatile and industrial-strength SMT solver. In: Fisman, D., Rosu, G. (eds.) TACAS 2022. LNCS, vol. 13243, pp. 415–442. Springer, Cham (2022). https://doi.org/10.1007/978-3-030-99524-9_24
3. Barnett, M., Chang, B.-Y.E., DeLine, R., Jacobs, B., Leino, K.: Boogie: a modular reusable verifier for object-oriented programs. In: de Boer, F.S., Bonsangue, M.M., Graf, S., de Roever, W.-P. (eds.) FMCO 2005. LNCS, vol. 4111, pp. 364–387. Springer, Heidelberg (2006). https://doi.org/10.1007/11804192_17
4. Becker, N., Müller, P., Summers, A.J.: The axiom profiler: understanding and debugging SMT quantifier instantiations. In: Vojnar, T., Zhang, L. (eds.) TACAS 2019. LNCS, vol. 11427, pp. 99–116. Springer, Cham (2019). https://doi.org/10.1007/978-3-030-17462-0_6
5. Bordis, T., Leino, K.R.M.: Free facts: an alternative to inefficient axioms in dafny. In: FM. LNCS, vol. 14933, pp. 151–169. Springer (2024). https://doi.org/10.1007/978-3-031-71162-6_8
6. Cassez, F.: EVM-dis: an EVM bytecode disassembler/assembler (2024). https://github.com/franck44/evm-dis. Accessed 1 Nov 2024
7. Chajed, T., Tassarotti, J., Kaashoek, M.F., Zeldovich, N.: Verifying concurrent, crash-safe systems with Perennial. In: SOSP, pp. 243–258. ACM (2019). https://doi.org/10.1145/3341301.3359632

8. Correnson, L.: Qed. Computing what remains to be proved. In: Badger, J.M., Rozier, K.Y. (eds.) NFM 2014. LNCS, vol. 8430, pp. 215–229. Springer, Cham (2014). https://doi.org/10.1007/978-3-319-06200-6_17

9. Cutler, J.W., et al.: Cedar: a new language for expressive, fast, safe, and analyzable authorization. Proc. ACM Program. Lang. **8**(OOPSLA), 670–697 (2024). https://doi.org/10.1145/3649835

10. Cutler, J.W., Torlak, E., Hicks, M.: Improving the stability of type soundness proofs in Dafny. In: Proceedings of the First Workshop on Dafny (2024)

11. de Moura, L., Bjørner, N.: Z3: an efficient SMT solver. In: Ramakrishnan, C.R., Rehof, J. (eds.) TACAS 2008. LNCS, vol. 4963, pp. 337–340. Springer, Heidelberg (2008). https://doi.org/10.1007/978-3-540-78800-3_24

12. Detlefs, D., Nelson, G., Saxe, J.B.: Simplify: a theorem prover for program checking. J. ACM **52**(3), 365–473 (2005). https://doi.org/10.1145/1066100.1066102

13. Dodds, M.: Formally verifying industry cryptography. IEEE Secur. Priv. **20**(3), 65–70 (2022). https://doi.org/10.1109/MSEC.2022.3153035

14. Ferraiuolo, A., Baumann, A., Hawblitzel, C., Parno, B.: Komodo: using verification to disentangle secure-enclave hardware from software. In: SOSP, pp. 287–305. ACM (2017). https://doi.org/10.1145/3132747.3132782

15. Filliâtre, J.-C., Paskevich, A.: Why3 — where programs meet provers. In: Felleisen, M., Gardner, P. (eds.) ESOP 2013. LNCS, vol. 7792, pp. 125–128. Springer, Heidelberg (2013). https://doi.org/10.1007/978-3-642-37036-6_8

16. Gopinathan, K., Spiliopoulos, D., Goyal, V., Müller, P., Püschel, M., Sergey, I.: Axolocl: accelerating automated program verifiers by automatic proof localization. Software Artifact (2025). https://doi.org/10.5281/zenodo.15201479

17. Hance, T., Lattuada, A., Hawblitzel, C., Howell, J., Johnson, R., Parno, B.: Storage systems are distributed systems (so verify them that way!). In: OSDI, pp. 99–115. USENIX Association (2020). https://www.usenix.org/conference/osdi20/presentation/hance

18. Hawblitzel, C., et al.: IronFleet: proving practical distributed systems correct. In: SOSP, pp. 1–17. ACM (2015). https://doi.org/10.1145/2815400.2815428

19. Ho, S., Pit-Claudel, C.: Incremental Proof Development in Dafny with Module-Based Induction. In: Proceedings of the First Workshop on Dafny (2024)

20. Lattuada, A., et al.: Verus: a practical foundation for systems verification. In: SOSP, pp. 438–454. ACM (2024). https://doi.org/10.1145/3694715.3695952

21. Leino, K.: Dafny: an automatic program verifier for functional correctness. In: Clarke, E.M., Voronkov, A. (eds.) LPAR 2010. LNCS (LNAI), vol. 6355, pp. 348–370. Springer, Heidelberg (2010). https://doi.org/10.1007/978-3-642-17511-4_20

22. Leino, K., Pit-Claudel, C.: Trigger selection strategies to stabilize program verifiers. In: Chaudhuri, S., Farzan, A. (eds.) CAV 2016. LNCS, vol. 9779, pp. 361–381. Springer, Cham (2016). https://doi.org/10.1007/978-3-319-41528-4_20

23. McLaughlin, S., Jaloyan, G.A., Xiang, T., Rabe, F.: Enhancing proof stability. In: Proceedings of the First Workshop on Dafny (2024)

24. Mugnier, E., McLaughlin, S., Tomb, A.: Portfolio solving for dafny. In: Proceedings of the First Workshop on Dafny (2024)

25. Müller, P., Schwerhoff, M., Summers, A.J.: Viper: a verification infrastructure for permission-based reasoning. In: Jobstmann, B., Leino, K. (eds.) VMCAI 2016. LNCS, vol. 9583, pp. 41–62. Springer, Heidelberg (2016). https://doi.org/10.1007/978-3-662-49122-5_2

26. Padon, O., McMillan, K.L., Panda, A., Sagiv, M., Shoham, S.: Ivy: safety verification by interactive generalization. In: PLDI, pp. 614–630. ACM (2016). https://doi.org/10.1145/2908080.2908118

27. Pereira, J.C., et al.: Protocols to code: formal verification of a next-generation internet router (2024). https://arxiv.org/abs/2405.06074
28. Protzenko, J., et al.: EverCrypt: a fast, verified, cross-platform cryptographic provider. In: S&P, pp. 983–1002. IEEE (2020). https://doi.org/10.1109/SP40000.2020.00114
29. Srinivasan, P., Padon, O., Howell, J., Lattuada, A.: Domesticating automation. In: Proceedings of the First Workshop on Dafny (2024)
30. Swamy, N., et al.: Dependent types and multi-monadic effects in F*. In: POPL, pp. 256–270. ACM (2016). https://doi.org/10.1145/2837614.2837655
31. Wolf, F.A., Arquint, L., Clochard, M., Oortwijn, W., Pereira, J.C., Müller, P.: Gobra: modular specification and verification of go programs. In: Silva, A., Leino, K. (eds.) CAV 2021. LNCS, vol. 12759, pp. 367–379. Springer, Cham (2021). https://doi.org/10.1007/978-3-030-81685-8_17
32. Zaiser, F., Zetzsche, S., Tristan, J.B.: VMC: a dafny library for verified Monte Carlo algorithms. In: Proceedings of the First Workshop on Dafny (2024)
33. Zhou, Y., Bosamiya, J., Li, J., Heule, M.J., Parno, B.: Context pruning for more robust SMT-based program verification. In: FMCAD, pp. 59–69. TU Wien Academic Press, IEEE (2024)
34. Zhou, Y., Bosamiya, J., Takashima, Y., Li, J., Heule, M., Parno, B.: Mariposa: measuring SMT instability in automated program verification. In: FMCAD 2023, pp. 178–188. IEEE (2023). https://doi.org/10.34727/2023/ISBN.978-3-85448-060-0_26

Lean-Auto: An Interface Between Lean 4 and Automated Theorem Provers

Yicheng Qian[1]([⊠])[iD], Joshua Clune[2][iD], Clark Barrett[1][iD], and Jeremy Avigad[2][iD]

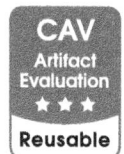

[1] Stanford University, Stanford, USA
pratherc@stanford.edu
[2] Carnegie Mellon University, Pittsburgh, USA

Abstract. Proof automation is crucial to large-scale formal mathematics and software/hardware verification projects in ITPs. Sophisticated tools called hammers have been developed to provide general-purpose proof automation in ITPs such as Coq and Isabelle, leveraging the power of ATPs. An important component of a hammer is the translation algorithm from the ITP's logical system to the ATP's logical system. In this paper, we propose a novel translation algorithm for ITPs based on dependent type theory. The algorithm is implemented in Lean 4 under the name Lean-auto. When combined with ATPs, Lean-auto provides general-purpose, ATP-based proof automation in Lean 4 for the first time. Soundness of the main translation procedure is guaranteed, and experimental results suggest that our algorithm is sufficiently complete to automate the proof of many problems that arise in practical uses of Lean 4. We also find that Lean-auto solves more problems than existing tools on Lean 4's math library Mathlib4.

Keywords: Proof Automation · Lean 4 · Dependent Type Theory

1 Introduction

Interactive Theorem Provers (ITPs) [16] are widely used in formal mathematics and software/hardware verification. When using ITPs, straightforward but tedious proof tasks often arise during the proof development process. Due to the limited built-in automation in ITPs, discharging these proof tasks can require significant manual effort. Hammers [6,13] are proof automation tools for ITPs which utilize Automated Theorem Provers (ATPs, including Satisfiability Modulo Theories (SMT) solvers). Hammers have proved useful because they can solve many proof tasks automatically [26].

A hammer has three main components: premise selection, translation from ITP to ATP, and proof reconstruction from ATP to ITP. Premise selection collects the necessary premises (usually a list of theorems) needed to solve a proof task, translation exports the collected information from the ITP to the ATP, and proof reconstruction generates a proof in the ITP based on the output of the

© The Author(s) 2025
R. Piskac and Z. Rakamarić (Eds.): CAV 2025, LNCS 15933, pp. 175–196, 2025.
https://doi.org/10.1007/978-3-031-98682-6_10

ATP. Our project Lean-auto primarily focuses on the translation from Lean 4 to ATPs. We note that Lean-auto does have a proof reconstruction procedure which fully supports one of the three types of ATPs we use to evaluate Lean-auto. For ATPs with proof reconstruction support, if the ATP successfully finds a proof, Lean-auto will generate proof terms and check them using the Lean 4 kernel. For other ATPs, if the ATP successfully finds a proof, Lean-auto will mark the problem as solved in Lean 4, but will generate a warning to indicate that Lean-auto trusts the ATPs' output. Ongoing projects are expected to implement premise selection and more proof reconstruction support. See Sect. 8 for more discussion.

The discrepancies between logical systems of ATPs and ITPs pose significant challenges to translation procedures between them. Several popular ITPs are based on highly expressive logical systems. For example, Isabelle [35] is based on polymorphic higher-order logic, while Coq [4] and Lean 4 [24][1] are based on an even more expressive logical system called dependent type theory (also known as λC in the lambda cube) [3,11].[2] Moreover, features such as typeclasses [14], universe polymorphism [31], and inductive types [12] are commonly used as extensions to the base logical system to enhance usability of the ITPs. On the other hand, ATPs are usually based on less expressive logical systems such as first-order logic (FOL) [2,20,23,30] and (in recent years) higher-order logic (HOL) [5,33,34]. An overview of the various logical systems relevant to our work is given in Sect. 2.2 (Fig. 1).

There are two existing approaches for translation from more expressive logical systems to less expressive ones: encoding-based translation and monomorphization. Encoding-based translation is used in CoqHammer [13] to translate Coq into untyped FOL. Monomorphization is used to eliminate polymorphism in Isabelle Sledgehammer [6,7,26]. Our small-scale experiment[3] on Mathlib4 suggests that encoding-based translation tends to produce much larger outputs than monomorphization, which could negatively affect the performance of ATPs. Therefore, we use monomorphization in Lean-auto. An overview of these two translation methods and related discussions are given in Sect. 3.

Since ATPs have started supporting HOL in recent years [5,33,34], Lean-auto translates Lean 4 to HOL. The overall translation has two stages: preprocessing and monomorphization. Monomorphization itself has three stages: quantifier instantiation, $\lambda^*_{\to}$ abstraction, and universe lifting. Roughly speaking, preprocessing translates Lean 4 into dependent type theory,[4] and monomorphization translates dependent type theory into HOL. The monomorphization procedure of Lean-auto is inspired by Isabelle Sledgehammer. However, since dependent type theory is considerably different from Isabelle's HOL, the monomorphization procedure is thoroughly redesigned, and presented in a different way in

---

[1] Agda [8] is also dependently typed, but is based on Martin-Löf type theory.

[2] Or *calculus of inductive constructions (CIC)*, depending on whether inductive types are considered as an extension.

[3] See Appendix I of [28].

[4] As mentioned before, Lean 4 is different from dependent type theory because it includes various additional language features.

our paper. Challenges related to dependent type theory and Lean 4 are discussed in Sect. 4.3.

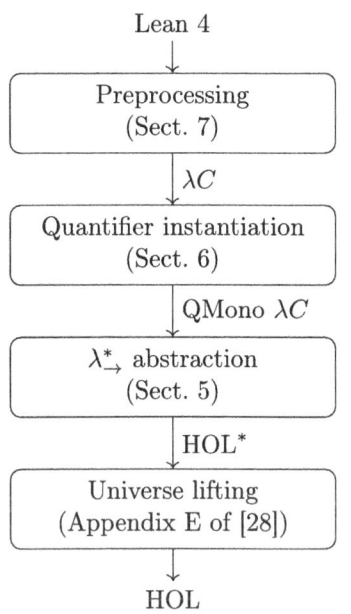

Lean 4

↓

Preprocessing
(Sect. 7)

↓ λC

Quantifier instantiation
(Sect. 6)

↓ QMono λC

$\lambda^*_\rightarrow$ abstraction
(Sect. 5)

↓ HOL*

Universe lifting
(Appendix E of [28])

↓

HOL

Fig. 1. Translation workflow of Lean-auto.

In our paper, we work backwards in Lean-auto's translation workflow. We start from $\lambda^*_\rightarrow$ abstraction (Sect. 5), then quantifier instantiation (Sect. 6), and end with preprocessing (Sect. 7). This is because it is easier to begin with the simpler logical system and progressively take into account more features of the highly expressive Lean 4 language. We leave universe lifting to Appendix E of [28] since it is relatively straightforward compared to the other steps.

1.1 Related Work

Hammers are not restricted to ITPs with expressive logical systems. Several ITPs based on FOL or HOL also have their hammers, for example, the hammer of Mizar [19], the hammer of MetaMath [9], and HOL(y)Hammer [18]. Apart from hammers, there are various other ITP proof automation tools. For example, Coq and Lean both come with a *tactics* language, and built-in tactics provide users with low-level proof automation, such as Coq's `apply`, `rewrite`, and `destruct` tactics [4], and Lean's `apply`, `rw`, and `cases` tactics [1]. Domain-specific automation tools are also common, such as the intuitionistic propositional logic solver `tauto` of Coq, congruence closure algorithm `congruence` of Coq, and integer linear arithmetic solver `omega` of Lean 4, all implemented as tactics. Lightweight proof search procedures in ITPs include Coq's `auto` and Lean 4's Aesop [21]. There are also lightweight ATPs implemented in ITPs, such as Isabelle's Metis [17] and `blast_tac` [25], HOL Light's Meson [15], and Lean 4's Duper [10]. Finally, machine learning algorithms have also been used to automate proof in ITPs, for example, MagnusHammer [22] of Isabelle, LeanDojo [37] of Lean, GPT-f [27] of Metamath, and ASTactic [36] of Coq.

2 Preliminaries

2.1 Dependent Type Theory

Dependent type theory, or λC in the λ-cube, or the *calculus of constructions* (CoC) [3], is a highly expressive type system and logical system. It is the logical foundation of Coq, Lean 4, and Agda. To align with Lean 4, we use the variant of λC which contains a countable number of non-cumulative universe levels. The syntax of λC terms is defined inductively as follows:

$$\mathcal{T}_C ::= V \mid \mathsf{U}_\ell \mid \mathcal{T}_C \, \mathcal{T}_C \mid \lambda(V : \mathcal{T}_C).\mathcal{T}_C \mid \forall(V : \mathcal{T}_C).\mathcal{T}_C,$$

where V is the set of variables, U_ℓ ($\ell \in \mathbb{N}$) are the sorts (i.e., the types of types), $\mathcal{T}_C \, \mathcal{T}_C$ is function application, $\lambda(V : \mathcal{T}_C).\mathcal{T}_C$ is λ abstraction, and $\forall(V : \mathcal{T}_C).\mathcal{T}_C$ is the product type. ℓ is called the universe level of U_ℓ. We use $\forall$ instead of Π to align with the syntax of Lean, Coq, and Agda. Syntactical equality of terms will be denoted as $=$, and $\beta\eta$-equivalence of terms will be denoted as $\cong$.

We adopt the following commonly-used notational conventions: function application binds stronger than λ and $\forall$, and is left-associative; consecutive λs and $\forall$s can be merged, and λs and $\forall$s with the same binder type can be further merged into the same parenthesis; when the product type is non-dependent, $\rightarrow$ can be used instead of $\forall$. Importantly, $\rightarrow$ binds stronger than $\forall$, i.e., $\forall(x : \alpha).\beta \rightarrow \gamma$ is interpreted as $\forall(x : \alpha).(\beta \rightarrow \gamma)$ instead of $(\forall(x : \alpha).\beta) \rightarrow \gamma$, the latter being the convention in FOL and HOL. The abbreviations $\bot, \neg, \wedge, \vee, \leftrightarrow, =_\ell$, and $\exists_\ell$ are defined in the usual way.[5]

A context Γ is a list of variable declarations $x_1 : \alpha_1, \ldots, x_n : \alpha_n$. Type judgements will be written as $\Gamma \vdash t : \alpha$, which stands for "λC term t has type α under context Γ."[6] If $\Gamma \vdash t : \alpha$, then t is called a *well-formed term*, and α is called a (well-formed) *type*.[7] Under context Γ, a type α is called *inhabited* iff there exists t such that $\Gamma \vdash t : \alpha$, in which case t is called an *inhabitant* of α. Propositions are types of type U_0. A *proof* of a proposition $p : \mathsf{U}_0$ is an inhabitant of p. A proposition $p : \mathsf{U}_0$ is *provable* iff it is inhabited. Given a context Γ and a proposition p, we use $\Gamma \vdash ?p$ to represent the *problem* of finding a proof of p under context Γ.

For a function $f : \forall(x_1 : \alpha_1) \ldots (x_n : \alpha_n).\beta$ (here β may begin with $\forall$), the nth argument of f is called a *static dependent argument* iff x_n occurs in β. In many cases, static dependent arguments are also type arguments; for example, the first and second arguments of List.map : $\forall(\alpha \, \beta : \mathsf{U}_1).(\alpha \rightarrow \beta) \rightarrow$ List $\alpha \rightarrow$ List β are both static dependent arguments. Another important concept is *dependent argument*.[8] In practical scenarios, "dependent argument" and "static dependent argument" usually have the same meaning. Their intricate difference is explained in Sect. 4.3.

We use λC notation for all logical systems that can be embedded in λC. When presenting Lean 4 examples, we use additional Lean 4 notational conventions. These are explained in Sect. 2.4.

2.2   Logical Systems of ITPs and ATPs

In this section, we give an overview of the various logical systems that are relevant to our work. In the following list, the logical systems are ordered from

---

[5] See Appendix A of [28].

[6] Derivation rules for type judgements of λC are given in Appendix B of [28].

[7] In λC, all well-formed types are also well-formed terms.

[8] See Appendix G of [28] for its formal definition.

the least expressive to the most expressive. Note that, except for λC and more expressive systems, all other logical systems have two components: term calculus (which specifies the construction and computation rules of terms), and logical axioms/rules.

1. Untyped FOL, or predicate logic.
2. Many-sorted FOL.
3. Many-sorted HOL (monomorphic HOL, or just HOL), where functions are allowed to take functions as arguments, and quantifiers can quantify over functions. Its term calculus is simply typed lambda calculus $\lambda_\rightarrow$ [3].
4. Many-sorted HOL with a countable number of universe levels, denoted as HOL*, which is discussed in Sect. 2.3. This is an intermediate logical system used in Lean-auto's monomorphization. It is essentially equivalent to HOL[9].
5. HOL with rank-1 polymorphism, or polymorphic HOL. Its term calculus is $\lambda 2$ in the λ-cube [3]. In polymorphic HOL, functions are allowed to take type arguments, and quantifiers can quantify over types. However, type constructors, or types dependent on types, are not allowed.
6. Isabelle's logical system. Based on polymorphic HOL. Supports (co)inductive datatypes and recursive functions.
7. Dependent type theory, or λC. Compared to polymorphic HOL, types can depend on terms and types in λC.
8. Coq, Lean 4, and Agda's logical systems. Based on λC. Extensions to λC that are present in (at least one of) these ITPs include (co)inductive types, universe levels, universe polymorphism, typeclasses, and many others.

All previously mentioned hammers translate between these logical systems. Isabelle Sledgehammer translates between Isabelle and HOL/FOL.[10] CoqHammer translates between Coq and untyped FOL. Lean-auto translates between Lean 4 and monomorphic HOL. As mentioned before, Lean-auto's preprocessing translates Lean 4 into λC, and monomorphization translates λC into HOL. More specifically, quantifier instantiation and $\lambda_\rightarrow^*$ abstraction translates λC into HOL*, and universe lifting translates HOL* into HOL.

2.3   Pure Type Systems $\lambda C, \lambda_\rightarrow, \lambda_\rightarrow^*$ and Related Logical Systems

The Pure Type System (PTS) [3] formalism enables concise specification of a class of type systems. We use PTS to formally specify the underlying type systems of the logical systems used in Lean-auto's translation.

The specification of a PTS consists of a triple $(\mathcal{S}, \mathcal{A}, \mathcal{R})$, where $\mathcal{S}$ is the set of *sorts*, $\mathcal{A} \subseteq \mathcal{S} \times \mathcal{S}$ is the set of *axioms*, and $\mathcal{R} \subseteq \mathcal{S} \times \mathcal{S} \times \mathcal{S}$ is the set of *rules*. An axiom $(s_1, s_2) \in \mathcal{A}$ is intended to represent the typing axiom $s_1 : s_2$. The syntax of PTS terms is given by

$$\mathcal{T} ::= V \mid \mathcal{S} \mid \mathcal{T}\ \mathcal{T} \mid \lambda(V : \mathcal{T}).\mathcal{T} \mid \forall(V : \mathcal{T}).\mathcal{T}$$

---

[9] In Appendix E of [28], we show that HOL* is essentially equivalent to HOL.
[10] The exact logical system depends on the mode being used.

Three type systems, λC, $\lambda_\rightarrow$, and $\lambda^*_\rightarrow$, will be formulated using PTS.[11] As mentioned above, $\lambda_\rightarrow$ is the term calculus of HOL, and $\lambda^*_\rightarrow$ is the term calculus of HOL*. Note that U_0 is not present in $\lambda_\rightarrow$ and $\lambda^*_\rightarrow$ because it is a special sort for propositions in λC. The type of propositions in HOL and HOL* will be represented by a special symbol $\mathsf{Bool} : \mathsf{U}_1$.

$\lambda^*_\rightarrow$ and $\lambda_\rightarrow$ are similar, except that $\lambda^*_\rightarrow$ allows a countable number of universe levels $\ell \in \mathbb{N}^*$, where $\mathbb{N}^*$ is the set of positive integers. For example, in the type $(\alpha \rightarrow \beta) \rightarrow \gamma$, the subterms α, β, and γ must be of type U_1 in the system $\lambda_\rightarrow$; however, in $\lambda^*_\rightarrow$, it is possible that $\alpha : \mathsf{U}_{\ell_1}, \beta : \mathsf{U}_{\ell_2}, \gamma : \mathsf{U}_{\ell_3}$ where ℓ_1, ℓ_2, ℓ_3 may be different. A technicality related to PTS requires the presence of the sorts U'_ℓ in $\lambda^*_\rightarrow$, with axioms $\mathsf{U}_\ell : \mathsf{U}'_\ell$.

The logical systems HOL and HOL* are $\lambda_\rightarrow$ and $\lambda^*_\rightarrow$ augmented with the symbols $\mathsf{Bool}, \perp', \rightarrow', \forall'_s$ (for each type s), their corresponding typing rules, and logical rules. The abbreviations $\wedge', \vee', \neg', \leftrightarrow, ='_s, \exists'_s$ are defined in a way consistent with their λC counterparts. The set of HOL and HOL* terms are denoted as $\mathcal{T}_\rightarrow$ and $\mathcal{T}^*_\rightarrow$, respectively.[12]

2.4 Lean and Mathlib

Lean is an ITP based on dependent type theory. Lean-auto is implemented in Lean 4, the latest version of Lean. At present, the most prominent project in Lean is Mathlib [32], which was renamed to Mathlib4[13] when it was moved to Lean 4. Notably, Mathlib is the foundation of the Liquid Tensor Experiment [29], which successfully formalizes cutting-edge results in mathematics.

We will follow Lean 4 conventions when presenting Lean 4 examples. $\mathsf{Sort}\ \ell$ represents U_ℓ, and $\mathsf{Type}\ \ell$ represents $\mathsf{U}_{\ell+1}$. $\mathsf{Sort}\ 1$ (or $\mathsf{Type}\ 0$) can be abbreviated as Type, and $\mathsf{Sort}\ 0$ can be abbreviated as Prop. All user-declared symbols, including functions, are called *constants* in Lean 4. Constants can have universe level parameters, but for simplicity, they are not shown in many of our Lean 4 examples. Functions are allowed to have implicit arguments, which are represented by $\{x : \alpha\}$ instead of $(x : \alpha)$ in the type of the function. Prepending @ to the name of a function causes implicit arguments to become explicit. For example, given the polymorphic list map function with the first and second argument being implicit:

$$\mathsf{List.map} : \forall\ \{\alpha\ \beta : \mathsf{Type}\},\ (\alpha \rightarrow \beta) \rightarrow \mathsf{List}\ \alpha \rightarrow \mathsf{List}\ \beta,$$

the expression $\mathtt{@List.map}\ \alpha\ \beta\ \mathtt{f}$ is the same as $\mathtt{List.map}\ \mathtt{f}$, where $\mathtt{f} : \alpha \rightarrow \beta$.

Typeclasses are extensively used by Lean 4's built-in library and Mathlib4 to overload arithmetic operators and represent mathematical structures. For example, consider the HAdd typeclass and the $\mathsf{HAdd.hAdd}$ function used to represent the addition operator in Lean 4.

$$\mathsf{HAdd} : \forall\ (\alpha\ \beta\ \gamma : \mathsf{Type}),\ \mathsf{Type}$$

---

[11] The derivation rules of PTS are given in Appendix B of [28].

[12] The specifications of $\lambda C, \lambda_\rightarrow$, and $\lambda^*_\rightarrow$ using PTS are given in Appendix C of [28]. The formal definitions of HOL and HOL* are given in Appendix D of [28].

[13] GitHub link: https://github.com/leanprover-community/mathlib4.

`HAdd.hAdd` : $\forall$ {α β γ : `Type`} [`self` : `HAdd` α β γ], $\alpha \rightarrow \beta \rightarrow \gamma$
An inhabitant of `HAdd` α β γ, called a typeclass instance, is a wrapper of a "heterogeneous" addition operator, with α and β as its input types and γ as its output type. The square bracket in the type of `HAdd.hAdd` indicates that the enclosed argument is an instance argument, which is a special type of implicit argument intended to be filled by Lean 4's typeclass inference algorithm. Given the syntax `x + y` where `x` : α and `y` : β, the typeclass inference algorithm will attempt to find a type γ and an instance `inst` : `HAdd` α β γ, and elaborate the syntax `x + y` into the expression `@HAdd.hAdd` α β γ `inst x y`. In `@HAdd.hAdd` α β γ `inst`, the `HAdd.hAdd` function unwraps `inst` and returns the addition operator. This provides a mechanism for overloading operators. The same mechanism is used to represent mathematical structures in Mathlib4.

Lean 4 supports definitional equality. Two terms are definitionally equal iff they can be converted to each other via Lean 4's built-in conversion rules. To test definitional equality of two terms s and t, we can either reduce s and t to their normal forms and check syntactical equality, or use the optimized built-in function `isDefEq`[14] which checks definitional equality of a pair of terms.

Inductive type is another important Lean 4 feature relevant to Lean-auto. It is handled by Lean-auto's preprocessing stage and is discussed in Sect. 7.

Lean 4 supports classical axioms such as function extensionality, excluded middle, and axiom of choice. Plain CoC does not include classical axioms. In contrast, classical axioms are built-in[15] in Lean 4. Lean-auto uses them during proof reconstruction.

3   Encoding-Based Translation and Monomorphization

Encoding-based translation and monomorphization are two approaches to translating from more expressive logical systems to less expressive logical systems.

The idea behind encoding-based translations is to encode constructions in the more expressive system using function symbols in the less expressive system and to define the translation as a recursive function on the terms and formulas of the more expressive system. For example, in the dependent type theory of Coq, we have the type judgement relation $\Gamma \vdash x : w$, which means "x is of type w under context Γ." There is no direct equivalent of this typing relation in untyped FOL. To express Coq type judgements in untyped FOL, CoqHammer first introduces the uninterpreted FOL predicate $T(u^*, a^*)$, where u^* and a^* are FOL terms translated from Coq term u and *atomic* Coq type a (here *atomic* roughly means that a cannot be further decomposed by the translation procedure of CoqHammer). Then, a recursive function $\mathcal{G}_\Gamma(u, w)$ is defined on the Coq context Γ and the Coq terms u, w. The function $\mathcal{G}_\Gamma(u, w)$ translates the typing relation $\Gamma \vdash u : w$ into an untyped FOL formula, in which the T predicate is used to express type judgements involving atomic types.

---

[14] Its full Lean 4 name is `Lean.Meta.isDefEq`.

[15] They are either declared as axioms or derived from previously declared axioms, and they are imported during initialization.

Encoding-based translation has the advantage of being (almost) complete and straightforward to compute. However, certain features of the more expressive logical system must be omitted to produce translation results of reasonable size, which sacrifices soundness [13]. Moreover, even with this tradeoff, the translated expression is usually much larger than the original expression.

The idea behind monomorphization is the fact that the proof of many propositions in the more expressive system can *essentially* be conducted in the less expressive system. For example, in polymorphic HOL, given

1. the list map function $\mathsf{List.map} : \forall(\alpha\ \beta : \mathsf{U}_1).(\alpha \to \beta) \to \mathsf{List}\ \alpha \to \mathsf{List}\ \beta$
2. two lists of natural numbers $xs\ ys : \mathsf{List}\ \mathbb{N}$ and two functions $f\ g : \mathbb{N} \to \mathbb{N}$
3. the premise $xs = ys \wedge f = g$

The equality

$$\mathsf{List.map}\ \mathbb{N}\ \mathbb{N}\ f\ xs = \mathsf{List.map}\ \mathbb{N}\ \mathbb{N}\ g\ ys \tag{1}$$

is provable using two rewrites $xs \Rightarrow ys, f \Rightarrow g$. The crucial observation is that, although $\mathsf{List.map}$ is polymorphic, the term $\mathsf{List.map}\ \mathbb{N}\ \mathbb{N}$ as a whole behaves just like a monomorphic function, and therefore the rewrites can essentially be performed in monomorphic HOL. More formally, the formula (1) is the image of the monomorphic HOL formula $h\ f^*\ xs^* = h\ g^*\ ys^*$ under the inter-logical-system "substitution"

$$\sigma := \{h \mapsto \mathsf{List.map}\ \mathbb{N}\ \mathbb{N}, f^* \mapsto f, g^* \mapsto g, xs^* \mapsto xs, ys^* \mapsto ys\},$$

and the rewrites $xs \Rightarrow ys, f \Rightarrow g$ in polymorphic HOL are just manifestations of the rewrites $xs^* \Rightarrow ys^*, f^* \Rightarrow g^*$ in monomorphic HOL.

Monomorphization is sound, produces small translation results, and preserves term structures during translation. However, monomorphization is incomplete, since it is not always possible to find an appropriate formula in the less expressive logical system that reflects the original formula in the more expressive logical system.

The difference in output size between encoding-based translation and monomorphization is particularly pronounced in Lean 4 (see Appendix I of [28] for experimental results). As mentioned in Sect. 2.4, a user-facing Lean 4 syntax as simple as $x+y$ corresponds to the complicated expression $\mathsf{HAdd.hAdd}\ \alpha\ \beta\ \gamma$ `inst` `x y`, where `inst` itself is a potentially large expression synthesized by typeclass inference. The result of encoding-based translation on the above expression is larger than the expression itself. On the other hand, our monomorphization procedure will translate the above expression into a much smaller one: $h\ x^*\ y^*$, where $\mathsf{HAdd.hAdd}\ \alpha\ \beta\ \gamma$ `inst` is "absorbed" into h via the inter-logical-system "substitution."

4   An Overview of Lean-Auto

As mentioned before, the translation workflow of Lean-auto consists of four stages: preprocessing, and the three stages of monomorphization: quantifier instantiation, $\lambda^*_{\to}$ abstraction, and universe lifting.

Roughly speaking, the preprocessing stage translates Lean 4 into dependent type theory (λC), which involves handling definitional equality and inductive types. It also performs minimal transformation on the translated λC problem. This includes introducing all leading $\forall$ quantifiers into the context and applying proof by contradiction.[16] Then, everything in the context with type Prop is collected by Lean-auto and added to the list of premises. Section 7 contains a more detailed discussion of preprocessing.

Universe lifting translates HOL* into HOL. Conceptually, it erases all the universe level information in the input expression. However, implementing it as a sound translation procedure in Lean 4 requires a decent amount of work. Details about universe lifting are given in Appendix E of [28].

In Sect. 4.1 and 4.2, we provide intuition for the $\lambda_\rightarrow$ abstraction and quantifier instantiation stages by giving a simplified explanation of their execution on an example. Section 4.3 gives a high-level discussion of some of the challenges posed by dependent type theory and Lean 4.

4.1 $\lambda_\rightarrow^*$ Abstraction

```
map : ∀ {α β : Type}, (α → β) → List α → List β
reverse : ∀ {α : Type}, List α → List α
map_reverse : ∀ {α β : Type} (f : α → β) (l : List α),
  map f (reverse l) = reverse (map f l)
reverse_reverse : ∀ {α : Type} (as : List α),
  reverse (reverse as) = as
⊢ ∀ (A B : Type) (f : A → B) (xs : List A),
    reverse (map f (reverse xs)) = map f xs
```

Fig. 2. Lean 4 proof state of a problem involving **List**.

The Lean 4 proof state of the problem we will consider is shown in Fig. 2. The hypotheses (premises) and variable declarations are displayed before ⊢, while the goal comes after ⊢. map_reverse states that map commutes with reverse, and reverse_reverse states that reverse is the inverse function of itself.

Since the problem is already in the λC fragment of Lean, the only preprocessing step required is to introduce the universal quantifiers appearing in the goal into the context and then apply proof by contradiction. The resulting proof state is shown in Fig. 3. For clarity, we have displayed the implicit arguments of all the functions.

First, we focus on translating neg_goal into HOL*. Following the discussion in Sect. 3, we would like to find a HOL* formula φ and a "substitution" σ such

---

[16] Proof by contradiction introduces the negation of the goal into the context and replaces the goal with ⊥.

```
map : ∀ {α β : Type}, (α → β) → List α → List β
reverse : ∀ {α : Type}, List α → List α
map_reverse : ∀ {α β : Type} (f : α → β) (l : List α),
    @Eq (List β) (@map α β f (@reverse α l)) (@reverse β (@map α β f l))
reverse_reverse : ∀ {α : Type} (as : List α),
    @Eq (List α) (@reverse α (@reverse α as)) as
A B : Type
f : A → B
xs : List A
neg_goal : Not (@Eq (List B)
    (@reverse B (@map A B f (@reverse A xs))) (@map A B f xs))
⊢ False
```

Fig. 3. Lean 4 proof state after variable introduction and application of proof by contradiction, with implicit arguments displayed. Note that the equality sign in Fig. 2 is syntactic sugar for the polymorphic function Eq shown here.

that the image of φ under σ is neg_goal. We also want the problem to be provable after the translation, so φ should preserve as much information in neg_goal as possible.

Three polymorphic functions: Eq, map and reverse, occur in neg_goal. Although these functions are polymorphic, instances of these functions with their dependent arguments instantiated behave like HOL* variables (we will refer to such instances as *HOL* instances*). The type constructor List is also not allowed in HOL*, but List A and List B behave just like HOL* type variables (we will refer to expressions such as List A and List B as *HOL* type instances*). Therefore, we can choose

$$\varphi := \neg(\mathsf{EqLB}\ (\mathsf{rB}\ (\mathsf{mAB}\ f^*\ (\mathsf{rA}\ xs^*)))\ (\mathsf{mAB}\ f^*\ xs^*))$$

$$\sigma := \{\mathsf{EqLB} \mapsto @\mathsf{Eq}\ (\mathsf{List}\ \mathsf{B}),\ \mathsf{mAB} \mapsto @\mathsf{map}\ \mathsf{A}\ \mathsf{B},$$

$$\mathsf{rA} \mapsto @\mathsf{reverse}\ \mathsf{A},\ \mathsf{rB} \mapsto @\mathsf{reverse}\ \mathsf{B},\ f^* \mapsto f,\ xs^* \mapsto \mathsf{xs}$$

$$\mathsf{LA} \to \mathsf{List}\ \mathsf{A},\ \mathsf{LB} \to \mathsf{List}\ \mathsf{B},\ \mathsf{A} \to \mathsf{A},\ \mathsf{B} \to \mathsf{B}\},$$

where $\mathsf{EqLB} : \mathsf{LB} \to \mathsf{LB} \to \mathsf{Bool}$, $\mathsf{rA} : \mathsf{LA} \to \mathsf{LA}$, $\mathsf{rB} : \mathsf{LB} \to \mathsf{LB}$, $\mathsf{mAB} : (\mathsf{A} \to \mathsf{B}) \to \mathsf{LA} \to \mathsf{LB}$, $f^* : \mathsf{A} \to \mathsf{B}$, $xs^* : \mathsf{LA}$.

In a sense, the HOL* (type) instances are "abstracted" to HOL* (type) variables. Note that the logical rules of HOL* are not relevant to this abstraction procedure—only the term calculus $\lambda^*_\rightarrow$ is involved. Therefore, we name this procedure $\lambda^*_\rightarrow$ *abstraction*.

However, $\lambda^*_\rightarrow$ abstraction is not directly applicable to map_reverse and reverse_reverse, because dependent arguments of polymorphic functions occurring in them contain universally quantified variables. Naturally, we would like to instantiate the quantifiers to make $\lambda^*_\rightarrow$ abstraction applicable.

4.2   Quantifier Instantiation

To understand how quantifiers should be instantiated, we investigate how they would be instantiated if we were to prove the goal manually. There are at least two ways we can proceed. We can either first use @map_reverse A B to swap the outer reverse with map, then use @reverse_reverse A to eliminate reverse; or, first use @map_reverse A B to swap the inner reverse with map, then use @reverse_reverse B to eliminate reverse. Notice how the dependent arguments of a function f[17] in the instantiated hypotheses match the dependent arguments of f in the HOL* instances of f in the goal.

Quantifier instantiation in Lean-auto's monomorphization procedure is based on a matching procedure that reflects the above observation. Given a set of formulas S, the matching procedure first computes the set M of HOL* instances occurring in S and then matches expressions in S with elements of M. For example, given $S = \{$@map_reverse, @reverse_reverse, neg_goal$\}$, the set M is $\{$@reverse A, @reverse B, @map A B, @Eq (List B)$\}$, all of whose elements are collected from neg_goal. The matching procedure will preform the following matchings:

1. @Eq (List β) in map_reverse with @Eq (List B), which produces fun α => @map_reverse α B
2. @map α β in map_reverse with @map A B, which produces @map_reverse A B
3. @reverse α in map_reverse with @reverse A and @reverse B, which produces @map_reverse A and @map_reverse B
4. @reverse β in map_reverse with @reverse A and @reverse B, which produces fun α => @map_reverse α A and fun α => @map_reverse α B
5. @Eq (List α) in reverse_reverse with @Eq (List B), which produces @reverse_reverse B
6. @reverse α in reverse_reverse with @reverse A and @reverse B, which produces @reverse_reverse A and @reverse_reverse B

Since @reverse_reverse A, @reverse_reverse B and @map_reverse A B are present, the instances produced are already sufficient for proving the goal. But generally speaking, newly generated hypothesis instances and HOL* instances[18] can still be matched with each other (and existing ones) to produce new useful results. Hence, Lean-auto's monomorphization uses a saturation loop which repeats the matching procedure until either no new instances can be produced or a prescribed threshold is reached.

4.3   Challenges Related to Dependent Type Theory and Lean 4

---

[17] In the context of this problem, f could be reverse or map.
[18] New HOL* instances are collected from newly generated hypothesis instances.

```
@DFunLike.coe : {F : Type (max u_1 u_5)}
    → {α : outParam (Type u_1)} → {β : outParam (α → Type u_5)}
    → [self : DFunLike F α β] → F → (a : α) → β a
```

$$@DFunLike.coe\ (A_0 \to^+ B_0)\ A_0\ (fun\ x => B_0)\ AddMonoidHom.instFunLike\ f_0\ a$$

Fig. 4. The function `DFunLike.coe` from MathLib4 and an expression containing it.

Dependent Arguments are Dynamic: In λC, whether an argument is dependent depends on how previous arguments are instantiated. Consider the example shown in Fig. 4. Here `DFunLike.coe` is a low-level utility which turns a function-like object into its corresponding function. In the signature of `DFunLike.coe`, the return type β `a` depends on the last argument `a` : α. However, when β is instantiated with `fun x => B`$_0$, as in the expression at the bottom of Fig. 4, the return type β `a` reduces to B$_0$, which no longer depends on the last argument. Our monomorphization procedure takes preceding arguments into consideration when determining whether an argument is dependent.

HOL* Instances are Dynamic: In λC, whether an expression is a HOL* instance is also context-dependent. Consider the simple expression `@reverse = @reverse`, where `reverse` is the same as in Fig. 3. Although `@reverse` is polymorphic, it *behaves like* a HOL* variable in `@reverse = @reverse`. More formally, let

$$\varphi := (f = f)$$
$$\sigma := \{f \mapsto @reverse, \quad \gamma \mapsto (\forall \{\alpha\ \beta\ : \ Type\}, List\ \alpha \to List\ \beta)\}$$

where $f : \gamma$. Then, `@reverse = @reverse` is the image of the HOL* formula φ under σ. Intuitively, the dependent arguments in the type of `reverse` can be "absorbed" into the HOL* type variable γ because neither of the dependent arguments of `reverse` are present. Our monomorphization procedure is able to detect such context-dependent HOL* instances.

Definitional Equality: As mentioned before, two syntactically different expressions can be definitionally equal in Lean 4. Somehow, we need to account for this in Lean-auto's translation. Theoretically speaking, reducing all expressions to normal forms would solve the problem to a large extent. However, full reduction is prohibitively expensive on complex expressions in real-life Lean 4 projects, and the reduced expressions could be much larger than the original expressions.[19] Moreover, the reduced expressions might contain complex dependent types that Lean-auto cannot handle. Therefore, we devise several other methods to address definitional equality.

In Lean-auto, there are three separate occasions where definitional equality has to be addressed.

First, when a symbol is defined in Lean 4, (potentially multiple) *equational theorems* that reflect the definitional equalities related to the symbol are automatically generated. Lean-auto can be configured to collect these equational theorems and to use them to perform reduction and unfold constants (see Sect. 7).

---

[19] Appendix J of [28] presents a set of experiments that demonstrate these issues.

Second, during $\lambda_{\rightarrow}^{*}$ abstraction, we would like HOL* instances that are syntactically different but definitionally equal to be abstracted to the same HOL* variable. Our $\lambda_{\rightarrow}^{*}$ abstraction algorithm keeps a set H of mutually definitionally unequal HOL* instances. Whenever a new HOL* instance t is found, we test definitional equality of t with elements of H using `isDefEq`. Since `isDefEq` is expensive, a *fingerprint*[20] is computed for each HOL* instance, and fingerprint equality is tested before calling `isDefEq`.

Finally, even if two HOL* instances are definitionally unequal, there could still be nontrivial relations between them. For example, if $f : \mathbb{N} \rightarrow \mathbb{N}$ is defined as $f := \lambda(x : \mathbb{N}).g\ x\ x$, the equation $\forall(x : \mathbb{N}).f\ x = g\ x\ x$ would be a nontrivial relationship between f and g. Lean-auto will attempt to generate such equational theorems during quantifier instantiation. For each pair of HOL* instances c_1, c_2, Lean-auto attempts to find terms $t_1, \dots, t_n$ such that $\lambda x_1 \dots x_m.\ c_1\ y_1\ \dots\ y_l = c_2\ t_1\ \dots\ t_n$, where $x_1, \dots, x_m$ are variables occurring in $t_1, \dots, t_n$, and $\{y_1, \dots, y_l\}$ is a subset of $\{x_1, \dots, x_m\}$.

Absorbing Typeclass Instance Arguments: In Lean 4, many functions have instance arguments that are not dependent arguments. An example is the fourth argument of `HAdd.hAdd` mentioned in Sect. 2.4. Since instance arguments are usually large expressions synthesized by Lean 4's typeclass inference algorithm, translating them can result in large HOL* terms. Lean-auto's implementation attempts to absorb typeclass arguments into HOL* variables by instantiating typeclass instance quantifiers and requiring HOL* instances to take typeclass arguments with them.[21]

5 $\lambda_{\rightarrow}^{*}$ Abstraction

In this section, we discuss the $\lambda_{\rightarrow}^{*}$ abstraction procedure, the second step of Lean-auto's monomorphization. Note that universe lifting, the first step, is presented in Appendix E of [28]. As mentioned before, we use $\Gamma \vdash ?p$ to represent the *problem* of finding a proof of p under context Γ.

The goal of $\lambda_{\rightarrow}^{*}$ abstraction is to translate essentially higher-order problems (EHOPs) into HOL*. Intuitively, a λC problem $\Gamma \vdash ?p$ is EHOP iff there exists a provable HOL* problem $\Gamma' \vdash ?p'$ and a "substitution" σ such that $\Gamma \vdash ?p$ is the image of $\Gamma' \vdash ?p'$ under σ. Given $\Gamma \vdash ?p$, $\lambda_{\rightarrow}^{*}$ abstraction attempts to find such a triple (Γ', p', σ). The formal definition of EHOP relies on the concept of HOL*-to-λC substitution and canonical embedding (see Appendix F of [28]).

Definition 1. *A λC problem $\Gamma \vdash ?p$ is essentially higher-order provable (EHOP) iff there exists a provable HOL* problem $\Gamma' \vdash ?p'$ and a substitution $(\pi^{*}(\Gamma'), \Gamma, \sigma)$ such that $p \cong \bar{\sigma}(\pi^{*}(p'))$.*

---

[20] Roughly speaking, a *fingerprint* of an expression is a summary of the expression's syntax.

[21] For simplicity, this detail is not discussed in Appendix G of [28] and H.

As a practical algorithm, Lean-auto's $\lambda^*_\to$ abstraction only works on input problems $\Gamma \vdash ?p$ where p is a λC term structurally similar to HOL* terms. We call such λC terms *quasi-monomorphic terms*. They serve as the intermediate representation between quantifier instantiation and $\lambda^*_\to$ abstraction. We use QMono($\Gamma; B, t$) to represent "t is quasi-monomorphic under context Γ, with variables in B being bound variables."[22] QMono has the following properties:

1. Canonically embedded HOL* terms are QMono.
2. In QMono terms, proofs cannot be bound by λ or dependent $\forall$ binders.
3. A dependently typed free variable does not break the QMono property iff its dependent arguments do not contain bound variables.
4. A dependently typed bound variable does not break the QMono property iff its dependent arguments are not instantiated.
5. Except for within type declarations of bound variables, bodies of $\forall$ abstractions must be propositions.

The $\lambda^*_\to$ abstraction algorithm itself is conceptually simple, but it involves many technical details because it must handle all possible features of QMono terms.[23] Given a λC problem $\Gamma \vdash ?p$, the $\lambda^*_\to$ abstraction algorithm traverses p and turns HOL* instances it finds into HOL* variables. The "substitution" it returns is the map from HOL* variables to their corresponding HOL* instances.

6   Quantifier Instantiation

In this section, we discuss the first step of Lean-auto's monomorphization : quantifier instantiation. Given a context Γ and a list of hypotheses $h_1 : t_1, \ldots, h_n : t_n$, the quantifier instantiation procedure of Lean-auto attempts to instantiate quantifiers in $t_1, \ldots, t_n$ to obtain terms suitable for $\lambda^*_\to$ abstraction (i.e., to obtain terms that satisfy the QMono predicate).

As mentioned in Sect. 4.2, quantifier instantiation is based on a saturation loop which matches HOL* instances of functions with subterms of hypothesis instances. There are two main algorithms in quantifier instantiation: matchInst and saturate. The matchInst algorithm is responsible for matching HOL* instances with subterms of hypothesis instances to generate new hypothesis instances, and the saturate algorithm is the main saturation loop. The saturate algorithm is given in Algorithm 1.[24]

The saturate algorithm maintains a queue of active HOL* instances and hypothesis instances, denoted as *active*. In each loop, an element is popped from *active*. If it is a HOL* instance, it is matched with all existing hypothesis instances; if it is a hypothesis instance, it is matched with all existing HOL* instances. For each newly generated hypothesis instance h, both h and all the HOL* instances occurring in h are added to *active*.

---

[22] See Appendix G of [28] for the formal definition of QMono.

[23] See Appendix G of [28] for details of the algorithm.

[24] See Appendix H of [28] for the matchInst algorithm and details of the saturate algorithm.

Function saturate(Γ; H, $maxInsts$)

   In : λC context Γ, list of λC terms H, and threshold $maxInsts$

   Out : A list of λC terms

   $hi := H$ /* A list of hypothesis instances */

   $ci :=$ List.empty() /* A list of constant instances */

   /* A queue of active constant and hypothesis instances */

   $active :=$ Queue.empty()

   for $h : H$ **do**

      hi.push($(0, h)$)

      for c : holInsts(Γ; $\emptyset$, h) **do**

         ci.push(c); $active$.push($(1, c)$)

   while ! $active$.empty() **do**

      if hi.size() $+ ci$.size() $> maxInsts$ **then break**

      $(type, front) := active$.front()

      $active$.popFront()

      if $type = 0$ **then**

         $prevci := ci$.copy()

         for $c : prevci$ **do**

            matchOnePair($c, front, ci, hi, active$)

      else

         $prevhi := hi$.copy()

         for $h : prevhi$ **do**

            matchOnePair($front, h, ci, hi, active$)

      end

   end

   $monohi :=$ List.empty()

   for $h : hi$ **do**

      if QMono(Γ; $\emptyset$, h) **then** $monohi$.push(h)

   return $monohi$

end

Function matchOnePair($c, h, ci, hi, active$)

   $newhi :=$ matchInst(Γ; c, h)

   for $nh : newhi$ **do**

      if $nh \in hi$ **then continue**

      hi.push(nh); $active$.push($(0, nh)$)

      $newci :=$ holInsts(Γ; $\emptyset$, nh)

      for $nc : newci$ **do**

         if $nc \in ci$ **then continue**

         ci.push(nc); $active$.push($(1, nc)$)

end

Algorithm 1: Main saturation loop of quantifier instantiation

The saturate algorithm also handles equational theorem generation of HOL* instances.[25] For each new HOL* instance c, we generate equational theorems between c and existing HOL* instances. The newly generated equational the-

---

[25] For simplicity, equational theorem generation is not shown in Algorithm 1.

orems are added to the set of existing hypothesis instances so that they can participate in later matchings.

7   Preprocessing

Preprocessing translates Lean 4 into dependent type theory, with the exception that part of definitional equality handling happens during monomorphization. In this section, we list the major steps of Lean-auto's preprocessing.

Definitional Equality: To handle definitional equality in Lean 4, Lean-auto partially reduces the input expressions, using Lean 4's built-in `Meta.transform` and `Meta.whnf`. This includes $\beta\zeta\eta\iota$ reduction and part of δ reduction. In Lean 4, δ reduction is controlled by a reducibility setting, and Lean-auto allows users to specify the reducibility setting used by the preprocessor. For finer-grained control over which constants should be unfolded, Lean-auto allows users to supply a *definitional equality instruction* $d[g_1, \ldots, g_n]$ and an *unfolding instruction* $u[f_1, \ldots, f_n]$, where f_i, g_i are constants.

For the definitional equality instruction, Lean-auto automatically collects all the definitional equalities associated with $g_1, \ldots, g_n$ and combines them with the premises supplied by the user. For the unfolding instruction, Lean-auto recursively unfolds $f_1, \ldots, f_n$. To ensure termination, Lean-auto performs a topological sort on $f_1, \ldots, f_n$, where f_i is sorted before f_j if f_j occurs in the definition of f_i. Lean-auto will fail if there is a cyclic dependency between $f_1, \ldots, f_n$.

The preprocessing stage also performs equational theorem generation. It collects all maximal subexpressions of the input that do not contain logical symbols, and generates equational theorems between them. These equational theorems are also added to the list of premises.

Inductive Types: Currently, Lean-auto supports polymorphic, nested, and mutual inductive types when SMT solvers are used as the backend ATP. For other ATPs or unsupported inductive types, users can always manually supply the properties related to the inductive types as a workaround.

The translation procedure for inductive types resembles monomorphization. For a polymorphic inductive type $T : \forall(\alpha_1 : \mathsf{U}_{\ell_1}) \ \ldots \ (\alpha_n : \mathsf{U}_{\ell_n}).\mathsf{U}_\ell$, the translation attempts to find all relevant instances $T \ \alpha_1 \ \ldots \ \alpha_n$, and translates each instance to a monomorphic inductive type in the SMT solver. For mutual and nested inductive types, the type of their constructors might contain other inductive types not occurring in the input premises. These inductive types will be recursively collected and monomorphized by the translation procedure.

Quantifier Introduction and Proof by Contradiction: To prepare for monomorphization, Lean-auto performs quantifier introduction on the goal and applies proof by contradiction. Suppose the goal is $\forall(x_1 : \alpha_1) \ \ldots \ (x_n : \alpha_n).\beta$. Quantifier introduction will introduce $x_1 : \alpha_1, \ldots, x_n : \alpha_n$ into the context and replace the goal with β. Then, proof by contradiction will introduce the negation of the the goal $h : \neg\beta$ into the context and replace the goal with $\bot$.

8 Experiments

We evaluate Lean-auto and existing tools on user-declared theorems in Mathlib4,[26] using version `leanprover/lean4:v4.15.0` of Lean 4. A Lean 4 constant is considered a user-declared theorem if it is marked as a theorem, is declared somewhere in a `.lean` file,[27] and is not a projection function. Due to technical reasons,[28] 27762 of the 176904 user-declared theorems are excluded in our evaluation. Therefore, our benchmark set consists of 149142 theorems (problems). Evaluation is conducted on an Amazon EC2 `c5ad.16xlarge` instance with 64 CPU cores and 128GB memory. Each theorem is given a time limit of 10 s. Technical details of our experimental setup are discussed in Appendix L of [28].

Since our primary goal is to evaluate Lean-auto's translation procedure, we do not use premise selection in our evaluation. Instead, for each theorem T used in the evaluation, we collect all the theorems used in T's human proof, and send them to Lean-auto and existing tools as premises. This simple procedure emulates an ideal premise selection algorithm.

Three types of ATPs are used together with Lean-auto:

1. Native provers, or ATPs implemented in Lean 4 itself. Currently, the only general-purpose native prover supported by Lean-auto is Duper [10]. Although Duper can accept Lean 4 problems directly, it has difficulty handling Lean 4 features such as typeclasses and definitional equality. Our small-scale experiment shows that Duper only works well when used as a backend of Lean-auto.[29] Considering that we also encountered technical issues when we attempted full-scale evaluation using Duper without Lean-auto, we decided to not include "Duper without Lean-auto" in our evaluation.
2. TPTP solvers. We chose Zipperposition, a higher-order superposition prover. Lean-auto sends problems to Zipperposition in TPTP TH0 format.
3. SMT solvers. For this category, we chose Z3 and CVC5. Since SMT solvers still don't fully support HOL, we implemented a slightly modified version of the monomorphization procedure which generates FOL output. The modification introduces some extra incompleteness to the translation, which might have given Z3 and CVC5 a slight disadvantage.

Currently, Lean-auto only supports proof reconstruction for native provers, utilizing a verified checker implemented in Lean-auto. The independent ongoing project Lean-smt[30] aims to support SMT proof reconstruction in the future.

We compare Lean-auto with the following existing tools:

---

[26] Commit 29f9a66d622d9bab7f419120e22bb0d2598676ab.

[27] We use `Lean.findDeclarationRanges?` to test whether a theorem is declared in a `.lean` file.

[28] Refer to Appendix L of [28].

[29] Refer to Appendix K of [28].

[30] GitHub link: https://github.com/ufmg-smite/lean-smt.

1. Lean 4's built-in tactic `rfl`. The `rfl` tactic proves theorems of the form `lhs` = `rhs` where `lhs` is definitionally equal to `rhs`. Note that `rfl` does not accept premises.
2. Lean 4's built-in tactic `simp_all`. Similar to Lean-auto, `simp_all` accepts a list of user-provided premises. In Lean 4, users can tag theorems with the "simp" attribute. The `simp_all` tactic succeeds on a decent portion of Math-lib4 even if we do not supply it with premises, because it has access to the theorems tagged with the "simp" attribute, and will use these theorems to simplify the input expressions. Therefore, we evaluate `simp_all` in two different ways: with premises ("simp_all" in Fig. 5) and without premises ("simp_all - p" in Fig. 5).
3. The rule-based proof search procedure Aesop [21]. Since Aesop invokes the `simp_all` tactic during its execution, it also benefits from theorems tagged with "simp." We evaluate Aesop in two different ways: with premises[31] ("Aesop" in Fig. 5) and without premises ("Aesop - p" in Fig. 5).

Due to limited time and resources, this work does not compare Lean-auto with hammers implemented in other ITPs. Differences in logical systems make it very difficult to translate datasets between ITPs. For example, even though Lean 4 and Coq are both based on dependent type theory, they extend dependent type theory in different ways.[32] Translation procedures between Lean 4 and Coq would need to modify expressions in nontrivial ways, which would cause typechecking and definitional equality issues.

	Solved	Unique Solves	Avg Time(ms)
rfl	19896	35	5.7
simp_all - p	9833		19.8
simp_all	28096		52.0
simp_all VBS	28204	3035	44.4
Aesop - p	33762		61.3
Aesop	47060		93.5
Aesop VBS	48413	6512	92.2
Lean-auto + Duper	54570		1092.5
Lean-auto + Z3	54210		863.5
Lean-auto + CVC5	54316		808.0
Lean-auto + Zipper.	54817		774.9
Lean-auto VBS	61906	22020	756.8
Overall VBS	79396		314.7

Fig. 5. Comparison with existing tools. Our benchmark set contains 149135 problems.

---

[31] Specifically, for each premise p, we add (`add unsafe p`) to the `aesop` invocation.
[32] For example, Cumulative Universe Levels in Coq and Quotient Types in Lean 4.

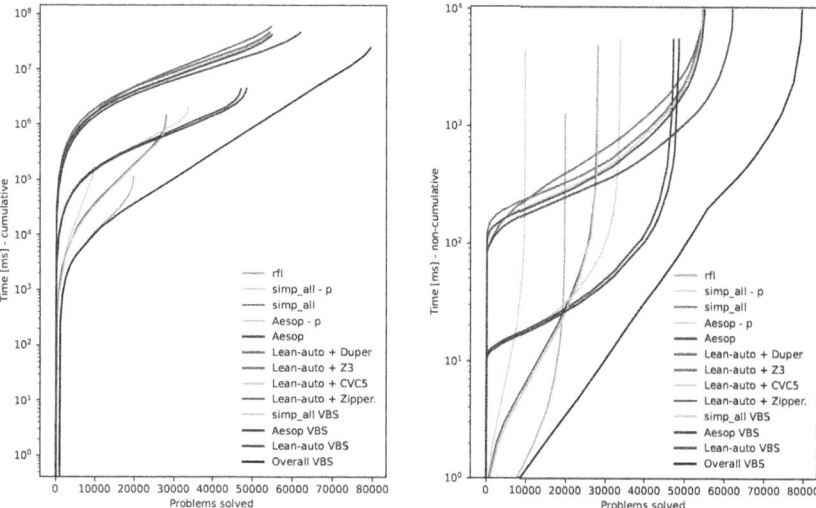

Fig. 6. #Solved - Cumulative Time plot (left) and #Solved - Time plot (right)

Results are shown in Fig. 5. For "simp_all", "aesop," and "Lean-auto," we show the results of their virtual best solvers (VBSes).[33] We compute unique solves among "rfl" and these three VBSes.

We find that Lean-auto solves more problems than all existing tools. Specifically, "Lean-auto + Duper", which supports proof reconstruction, solves 36.6% problems in our benchmark set, which is 5.0% better than the best previous tool "Aesop". The fact that "Lean-auto VBS" achieves 14.8% unique solves shows that Lean-auto is complementary to existing tools. The overall VBS, which combines Lean-auto and all existing tools, solves more than half (53.2%) of the problems in our benchmark set. On the other hand, Lean-auto is significantly slower than existing tools on solved problems. This is potentially caused by Lean-auto's verified checker and the frequent definitional equality testing in Lean-auto's monomorphization.

To better compare the performance of the various tools, we plot, for each tool, the number of solved problems vs. solving time and cumulative solving time. The results are shown in Fig. 6. We see that Lean-auto is slower than existing tools on simple problems, but eventually solves more problems than all existing tools.

9   Conclusion

In this paper, we presented the ITP to ATP translation implemented in Lean-auto. Our contributions are three-fold. First, we addressed challenges posed by

---

[33] The virtual best solver of a given category is equivalent to running all the tools in the given category in parallel and taking the first success produced.

Lean 4's dependent type theory and its various language features. Second, we designed a novel monomorphization procedure for dependent type theory. Finally, we implemented the translation procedure in Lean-auto and evaluated it on Mathlib4.

A possible direction for future work is to design a complete $\lambda^*_\to$ abstraction algorithm. Another direction is to investigate potential ways of handling existential type quantifiers and non-leading universal type quantifiers. We would also like to further investigate causes of Lean-auto's inefficiencies and improve Lean-auto's performance.

Acknowledgments. The authors thank: Prof. Jasmin Blanchette (Ludwig Maximilian University of Munich) for insightful discussions on the monomorphization procedure in Isabelle Sledgehammer; Mario Carneiro (Chalmers University of Technology) for helping us understanding implementation details of Lean 4; and Leonardo de Moura (Amazon Web Services) for his advice on the translation from Lean 4 to SMT solvers. We also greatly appreciate the help of the Lean Zulip users who answered our questions related to Lean 4 and Mathlib4. This work was supported in part by the Stanford Graduate Fellowship, the Stanford Center for Automated Reasoning, and AFRL and DARPA under Agreement FA8750-24-9-1000.

Disclosure of Interests. Clark Barrett is an Amazon Scholar.

References

1. Avigad, J., de Moura, L., Kong, S., Ullrich, S.: Theorem Proving in Lean4 (2025). https://leanprover.github.io/theorem_proving_in_lean4
2. Barbosa, H., et al.: cvc5: a versatile and industrial-strength SMT solver. In: TACAS 2022. LNCS, vol. 13243, pp. 415–442. Springer, Cham (2022). https://doi.org/10.1007/978-3-030-99524-9_24
3. Barendregt, H.P.: Lambda calculi with types, pp. 117–309. Oxford University Press, Inc., USA (1993). https://dl.acm.org/doi/10.5555/162552.162561
4. Barras, B., et al.: The Coq proof assistant: reference manual, version 6.1 (1997). https://api.semanticscholar.org/CorpusID:54117279
5. Bhayat, A., Suda, M.: A higher-order Vampire (short paper). In: Benzmüller, C., Heule, M.J., Schmidt, R.A. (eds.) Automated Reasoning, pp. 75–85. Springer, Cham (2024). https://doi.org/10.1007/978-3-031-63498-7_5
6. Blanchette, J.C., Kaliszyk, C., Paulson, L.C., Urban, J.: Hammering towards QED. J. Formaliz. Reason. **9**, 101–148 (2016). https://api.semanticscholar.org/CorpusID:218028818
7. Böhme, S.: Proving Theorems of Higher-Order Logic with SMT Solvers. Ph.D. thesis, Technical University Munich (2012). https://nbn-resolving.org/urn:nbn:de:bvb:91-diss-20120511-1084525-1-4
8. Bove, A., Dybjer, P., Norell, U.: A brief overview of Agda – a functional language with dependent types. In: Berghofer, S., Nipkow, T., Urban, C., Wenzel, M. (eds.) TPHOLs 2009. LNCS, vol. 5674, pp. 73–78. Springer, Heidelberg (2009). https://doi.org/10.1007/978-3-642-03359-9_6

9. Carneiro, M., Brown, C.E., Urban, J.: Automated theorem proving for Metamath. In: Naumowicz, A., Thiemann, R. (eds.) 14th International Conference on Interactive Theorem Proving (ITP 2023). Leibniz International Proceedings in Informatics (LIPIcs), vol. 268, pp. 9:1–9:19. Schloss Dagstuhl – Leibniz-Zentrum für Informatik, Dagstuhl, Germany (2023). https://doi.org/10.4230/LIPIcs.ITP.2023.9

10. Clune, J., Qian, Y., Bentkamp, A., Avigad, J.: Duper: a proof-producing superposition theorem prover for dependent type theory. In: International Conference on Interactive Theorem Proving (2024). https://api.semanticscholar.org/CorpusID:272330518

11. Coquand, T., Huet, G.: The calculus of constructions. Inf. Comput. **76**(2), 95–120 (1988). https://doi.org/10.1016/0890-5401(88)90005-3

12. Coquand, T., Paulin, C.: Inductively defined types. In: Martin-Löf, P., Mints, G. (eds.) COLOG 1988. LNCS, vol. 417, pp. 50–66. Springer, Heidelberg (1990). https://doi.org/10.1007/3-540-52335-9_47

13. Czajka, Ł., Kaliszyk, C.: Hammer for Coq: automation for dependent type theory. J. Autom. Reason. **61**, 423 – 453 (2018). https://api.semanticscholar.org/CorpusID:11060917

14. Hall, C.V., Hammond, K., Jones, S.L.P., Wadler, P.: Type classes in Haskell. In: TOPL (1994). https://api.semanticscholar.org/CorpusID:9227770

15. Harrison, J.: Optimizing proof search in model elimination. In: McRobbie, M.A., Slaney, J.K. (eds.) CADE 1996. LNCS, vol. 1104, pp. 313–327. Springer, Heidelberg (1996). https://doi.org/10.1007/3-540-61511-3_97

16. Harrison, J., Urban, J., Wiedijk, F.: History of interactive theorem proving. In: Computational Logic (2014). https://api.semanticscholar.org/CorpusID:30345151

17. Hurd, J.: First-order proof tactics in higher-order logic theorem provers. Design and Application of Strategies/Tactics in Higher Order Logics, number NASA/CP-2003-212448 in NASA Technical Reports, pp. 56–68 (2003). https://api.semanticscholar.org/CorpusID:11201048

18. Kaliszyk, C., Urban, J.: HOL(y)Hammer: online ATP service for HOL Light. Math. Comput. Sci. **9**(1), 5–22 (2014). https://doi.org/10.1007/s11786-014-0182-0

19. Kaliszyk, C., Urban, J.: MizAR 40 for Mizar 40. J. Autom. Reason. **55**(3), 245–256 (2015). https://doi.org/10.1007/s10817-015-9330-8

20. Kovács, L., Voronkov, A.: First-order theorem proving and VAMPIRE. In: Sharygina, N., Veith, H. (eds.) CAV 2013. LNCS, vol. 8044, pp. 1–35. Springer, Heidelberg (2013). https://doi.org/10.1007/978-3-642-39799-8_1

21. Limperg, J., From, A.H.: Aesop: white-box best-first proof search for Lean. In: Proceedings of the 12th ACM SIGPLAN International Conference on Certified Programs and Proofs, CPP 2023, pp. 253–266. Association for Computing Machinery, New York (2023). https://doi.org/10.1145/3573105.3575671

22. Mikuła, M., et al.: Magnushammer: a transformer-based approach to premise selection. arXiv (2024). https://arxiv.org/abs/2303.04488

23. de Moura, L., Bjørner, N.: Z3: an efficient SMT solver. In: Ramakrishnan, C.R., Rehof, J. (eds.) TACAS 2008. LNCS, vol. 4963, pp. 337–340. Springer, Heidelberg (2008). https://doi.org/10.1007/978-3-540-78800-3_24

24. de Moura, L.M., Ullrich, S.: The Lean 4 theorem prover and programming language. In: CADE (2021). https://api.semanticscholar.org/CorpusID:235800962

25. Paulson, L.C.: A generic tableau prover and its integration with Isabelle. J. Univers. Comput. Sci. **5**, 73–87 (1999). https://api.semanticscholar.org/CorpusID:2551237

26. Paulson, L.C., Blanchette, J.C.: Three years of experience with Sledgehammer, a practical link between automatic and interactive theorem provers. In: IWIL@LPAR (2012). https://api.semanticscholar.org/CorpusID:598752
27. Polu, S., Sutskever, I.: Generative language modeling for automated theorem proving. arXiv abs/2009.03393 (2020). https://api.semanticscholar.org/CorpusID: 221535103
28. Qian, Y., Clune, J., Barrett, C., Avigad, J.: Lean-auto: an interface between lean 4 and automated theorem provers (2025). https://arxiv.org/abs/2505.14929
29. Scholze, P.: Liquid tensor experiment. Exp. Math. **31**(2), 349–354 (2022). https://doi.org/10.1080/10586458.2021.1926016
30. Schulz, S.: E - a brainiac theorem prover. AI Commun. **15**, 111–126 (2002). https://api.semanticscholar.org/CorpusID:884116
31. Sozeau, M., Tabareau, N.: Universe polymorphism in CoQ. In: Klein, G., Gamboa, R. (eds.) ITP 2014. LNCS, vol. 8558, pp. 499–514. Springer, Cham (2014). https://doi.org/10.1007/978-3-319-08970-6_32
32. The Mathlib Community: The Lean mathematical library. In: Proceedings of the 9th ACM SIGPLAN International Conference on Certified Programs and Proofs, CPP 2020, pp. 367–381. Association for Computing Machinery, New York (2020). https://doi.org/10.1145/3372885.3373824
33. Vukmirović, P., Bentkamp, A., Blanchette, J., Cruanes, S., Nummelin, V., Tourret, S.: Making higher-order superposition work. J. Autom. Reason. **66**(4), 541–564 (2022). https://doi.org/10.1007/s10817-021-09613-z
34. Vukmirović, P., Blanchette, J.C., Schulz, S.: Extending a high-performance prover to higher-order logic. In: International Conference on Tools and Algorithms for Construction and Analysis of Systems (2023). https://api.semanticscholar.org/CorpusID:249226027
35. Wenzel, M., Paulson, L.C., Nipkow, T.: The Isabelle framework. In: International Conference on Theorem Proving in Higher Order Logics (2008). https://api.semanticscholar.org/CorpusID:13752195
36. Yang, K., Deng, J.: Learning to prove theorems via interacting with proof assistants. arXiv abs/1905.09381 (2019). https://api.semanticscholar.org/CorpusID: 162184110
37. Yang, K., et al.: Leandojo: Theorem proving with retrieval-augmented language models. arXiv abs/2306.15626 (2023). https://api.semanticscholar.org/CorpusID: 259262077

LEAN-SMT: An SMT Tactic for Discharging Proof Goals in Lean

Abdalrhman Mohamed[1] , Tomaz Mascarenhas[4] , Harun Khan[1] ,
Haniel Barbosa[4] , Andrew Reynolds[2,3] , Yicheng Qian[1] ,
Cesare Tinelli[2] , and Clark Barrett[1(✉)]

[1] Stanford University, Stanford, USA
barrett@cs.stanford.edu
[2] The University of Iowa, Iowa City, USA
[3] Amazon Web Services, Seattle, WA, USA
[4] Universidade Federal de Minas Gerais,
Belo Horizonte, Brazil

Abstract. Lean is an increasingly popular proof assistant based on
dependent type theory. Despite its success, it still lacks important
automation features present in more seasoned proof assistants, such as
the Sledgehammer tactic in Isabelle/HOL. A key aspect of Sledgehammer is the use of proof-producing SMT solvers to prove a translated
proof goal and the reconstruction of the resulting proof into valid justifi-
cations for the original goal. We present LEAN-SMT, a tactic providing this
functionality in Lean. We detail how the tactic converts Lean goals into
SMT problems and, more importantly, how it reconstructs SMT proofs
into native Lean proofs. We evaluate the tactic on established benchmarks used to evaluate Sledgehammer's SMT integration, with promising results. We also evaluate LEAN-SMT as a standalone proof checker for
proofs of SMT-LIB problems. We show that LEAN-SMT offers a smaller
trusted core without sacrificing too much performance.

1 Introduction

Proof assistants, also known as interactive theorem provers (ITPs), allow users to
write mechanized proofs of statements written in a formal language, whose validity can be verified by a small, trusted kernel. They help users construct trustworthy, formal, machine-checkable proofs of theorems, and have been increasingly
used to mechanize proofs of various mathematical results [18,19]. This process
has significantly accelerated in recent years with the adoption of the Lean 4 proof
assistant [28] by leading members of the mathematical community [12,14,37].
Proof assistants are also commonly used in certain areas of computer science to
model and formally verify systems, thanks to the high expressiveness of their
underlying language and logic [23,29].

The trustworthiness of proof assistants relies on the kernel correctly verifying
every proof step. For this reason, ITP kernels are designed to be simple and small,
implementing just straightforward logical operations from the logical framework

© The Author(s) 2025
R. Piskac and Z. Rakamarić (Eds.): CAV 2025, LNCS 15933, pp. 197–212, 2025.
https://doi.org/10.1007/978-3-031-98682-6_11

underlying the proof assistant. This means that, in principle, each proof step must be explicitly formulated by the user, with the consequence that a naive use of ITPs may require a prodigious amount of expertise and effort. A major challenge, then, is the extension of the kernel with trustworthy facilities for automating the writing of mechanized proofs as much as possible, thereby reducing the burden on users.[1] Automation is generally achieved via *tactics*, proof-producing algorithms, traditionally written in a special-purpose language, that discharge proof obligations for certain classes of subgoals, often by simulating common proof techniques, such as case analysis or induction.

An alternative is to use external automatic theorem provers (ATPs) to solve subgoals when possible. Tools such as HOLYHammer [22], MizAR [21], Sledgehammer [26], and Why3 [10], provide a one-click connection from proof assistants to first-order provers and have led to considerable improvements in proof-assistant automation [9]. Sledgehammer, a particularly successful tactic in Isabelle/HOL [30], includes an integration with proof-producing SMT solvers [8,36]. Sledgehammer translates certain proof goals into SMT-LIB [6], a standard format for SMT problems, and sends them to a supported SMT solver. The proof returned by the solver is reconstructed by essentially reproducing each step within the proof assistant. The integration of SMT solvers in Sledgehammer has been especially useful for proof goals arising from formal verification efforts carried out in Isabelle/HOL [8]. We conjecture that any tactic in Lean with the same ambition and expected impact as Sledgehammer will require a similar level of SMT solver integration.

In this paper, we present LEAN-SMT,[2] which provides an initial implementation of a similar integration in Lean and can be seen as a stepping stone towards a full Sledgehammer-like tactic for Lean. LEAN-SMT operates by translating Lean proof goals expressible in the first-order logic fragment of dependent type theory (Section 3.2) into SMT problems, leveraging SMT theories to model corresponding elements from Lean, such as uninterpreted functions, propositional equality, first-order quantifiers, and arithmetic operators. To bridge the gap between this restricted fragment and the goals that arise in practice in Lean formalizations, we rely on LEAN-AUTO, a tactic developed by Qian et al. [34], to reduce Lean proof goals to first-order logic, together with dedicated preprocessing in LEAN-SMT itself to express them in the language of selected SMT theories (Section 3.1). LEAN-SMT currently supports the state-of-the-art proof-producing SMT solver CVC5 [3]. CVC5's extensive proof production capabilities [4] and strong performance on the fragment of interest make it well suited for such an integration. CVC5's proofs are reconstructed into native Lean proofs (Section 3.3) by using either a Lean theorem, a Lean tactic, or a formally verified Lean program.

We evaluate LEAN-SMT (Section 4) on proof goals from a standard benchmark set used to evaluate Sledgehammer, showing that LEAN-SMT performs compara-

---

[1] In mathematics, the cost of mechanizing a proof is currently estimated to be ~ 20x the original cost of writing the proof [37]. Using ITPs to formally verify large systems is well known to be very costly, in the range of multiple person-years [23].

[2] LEAN-SMT is available online at https://github.com/ufmg-smite/lean-smt.

bly with Sledgehammer's SMT integration. We also evaluate it as a verified proof checker for SMT proofs. Although, as expected, LEAN-SMT is less performant than standalone, unverified SMT proof checkers, its performance is generally within an order of magnitude of theirs. Additionally, it offers comparable performance to SMTCoq [16], a similarly verified checker for Rocq, while supporting a larger logical fragment.

2   Related Work

While our main inspiration for LEAN-SMT has been the SMT integration in Sledgehammer, there are other ways in which Sledgehammer leverages the power of automatic theorem provers. Sledgehammer includes a premise selection module, which filters lemmas from Isabelle's libraries that are potentially useful for proving the goal. These lemmas are added to the problem to be sent to the solver. An alternative strategy to directly reconstructing a proof returned by the SMT solver is to simply identify the input lemmas actually used in the proof and pass them, together with the original goal, to *metis* [20], a proof-producing superposition-based theorem prover written as an Isabelle tactic. While there is no equivalent for Sledgehammer in Lean, there is a growing ecosystem of tools that eventually can be combined into a comparable tool. Recently Aesop [25], a tableaux-based prover, and Duper [13] which is, like *metis*, a superposition-based prover, were introduced as proof-producing Lean tactics. No equivalent for the premise selection mechanism is readily available in Lean yet, although there has been initial work in this direction [32].

Another integration between a proof assistant and SMT solvers is offered by SMTCoq [16], a plug-in for the Rocq proof assistant [7]. It supports proof reconstruction for the SMT solvers veriT [11] and CVC4 [5], but rather than replaying each individual proof step within Rocq, as Sledgehammer and LEAN-SMT do, it applies a formally verified checker that, if successful, confirms the original proof goal as a theorem. This approach relies heavily on the efficiency of the proof assistant itself, since the proof checker runs within the proof assistant and may have to analyze and simplify huge proof terms. The Rocq proof assistant is designed to be very fast at this; on the other hand, Lean is not [2]. Moreover, the verified checker approach can be rather rigid, since any modification to the supported proof format requires the checker's correctness theorem to be proven again. This can require a significant effort, even for tools with a highly modular architecture like SMT-Coq. In contrast, in the *proof replay* approach, one needs to change the reconstruction tactic by modifying the step corresponding to the changed element of the format. These observations motivated our decision to use proof replay in LEAN-SMT. The decision has been crucial for its development so far since CVC5's proof calculus and infrastructure are still evolving [4,24,31].

3   System Overview

Figure 1 depicts the LEAN-SMT architecture, which takes as input a Lean goal, whose type is represented as the formula F, and generates a proof for it by solving

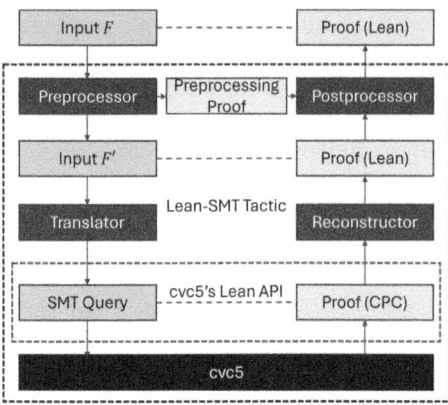

Fig. 1. Architecture of the LEAN-SMT tactic.

a corresponding unsatisfiability problem in SMT and reconstructing its proof into a Lean proof for F. The arrows illustrate the tactic's pipeline, through which the input formula is simplified, translated into an SMT query, and sent to CVC5. The solver's proof is then reconstructed as a proof in Lean for the input formula. The light green boxes represent the proofs used during the reconstruction stage, which correspond directly to the formulas (light blue) processed during the translation stage. The dashed lines emphasize this correspondence.

The *preprocessor* module converts the initial input F into an intermediate form F', simplifying or restructuring the input to make it more suitable for translation into an SMT query. During this phase, a preprocessing proof is generated, capturing the transformations applied. The *translator* module generates a formula in SMT-LIB format whose unsatisfiability corresponds to the validity of F'. The formula is passed to the CVC5 solver which produces a proof for it if it determines it to be unsatisfiable. The proof is expressed in the Cooperating Proof Calculus (CPC).[3] The tactic interfaces with CVC5 through Lean's Foreign Function Interface (FFI) and the solver's Lean API, which we added to the solver to facilitate the integration. The *reconstructor* module translates the CPC proof into a Lean proof of F', mapping the CPC proof structure to corresponding Lean constructs and ensuring logical equivalence. The *postprocessor* combines the preprocessing proof and the reconstruction proof into a single Lean proof for the original formula F, which is then checked by Lean's kernel.

---

[3] See https://cvc5.github.io/docs/cvc5-1.2.1/proofs/output_cpc.html. A complete list of the proof rules in CPC can be found at https://cvc5.github.io/docs/cvc5-1.2.1/api/cpp/enums/proofrule.html. The semantics of the rules is also defined in the Eunoia logical framework, described in the user manual of the Ethos proof checker: https://github.com/cvc5/ethos/blob/main/user_manual.md.

3.1 Preprocessing Original Lean Goal

Lean's type system, rooted in dependent type theory (DTT) [1], is far more expressive than the many-sorted first-order logic (FOL) [17] used by SMT solvers. To bridge this gap, we employ proof-producing preprocessing steps that simplify Lean goals into a form more amenable to translation into SMT-LIB.

We first use LEAN-AUTO[4] to reduce the goal to FOL. LEAN-AUTO normalizes universe levels, monomorphizes definitions, adds lemmas related to inductive types, and replaces type class instances by their corresponding values. All of these transformations are implemented in Lean and are proof producing, so their soundness is guaranteed by Lean's kernel. However, they are inherently incomplete, given the expressivity gap between DTT and FOL.

The preprocessing applied by LEAN-AUTO is not specific to SMT solvers, so while the resulting goal is in FOL, it is not aligned with the SMT-LIB standard. We apply a further preprocessing step so that certain Lean types and constructs (e.g., Prop, Nat, Rat, and Iff) that don't have direct counterparts in SMT-LIB can be transformed into types and constructs that do.

Example 1. Consider the following Lean goal, which asserts the uniqueness of the identity element in a group:

⊢ ∀ (G : Type u) [Group G] (e : G), (∀ (a : G), e * a = a) ↔ e = 1

This goal cannot be directly translated into SMT-LIB due to the presence of the type class Group and the logical operator ↔. During preprocessing, the goal is transformed and expanded to:

```
G: Type u
inst: Group G
e e': G
op: G → G → G
inv: G → G
one_mul: ∀ (a : G), op e a = a
inv_mul_cancel: ∀ (a : G), op (inv a) a = e
mul_assoc: ∀ (a b c : G),
op (op a b) c = op a (op b c)
⊢ (∀ (a : G), (op e' a = a)) = (e' = e)
```

Here, LEAN-AUTO replaces the type class Group with explicit assumptions about the group operations (e.g., associativity, identity, and inverse axioms), and LEAN-SMT's preprocessing transforms the bidirectional logical operator ↔ into a suitable equality comparison. These transformations make the goal compatible with SMT-LIB's logic while preserving its original meaning.

3.2 Translation to SMT-LIB

After preprocessing, translating Lean goals into SMT-LIB is relatively straightforward, as the fragments mostly overlap. However, one key challenge stems

---

[4] https://github.com/leanprover-community/lean-auto.

from differing assumptions about sorts: SMT-LIB assumes sorts are non-empty, while Lean allows types to be empty. This discrepancy can make the translation unsound. The reconstruction stage ensures soundness by failing if a proof step depends on a type being non-empty and Lean cannot establish that the type is an instance of the type class of non-empty types. As long as the instances are found, this discrepancy between the logic systems is successfully addressed.

Example 2. Continuing from our previous example, the preprocessed goal is translated into SMT-LIB as follows:

```
(declare-sort G 0)
(declare-const e G)
(declare-const |e'| G)
(declare-fun op (G G) G)
(declare-fun inv (G) G)
(assert (forall ((a G)) (= (op e a) a)))
(assert (forall ((a G)) (= (op (inv a) a) e)))
(assert (forall ((a G) (b G) (c G)) (= (op (op a b) c) (op a (op b c)))))
(assert (distinct (forall ((a G)) (= (op |e'| a) a) (= |e'| e))))
(check-sat)
```

Note that the translation is sound in this example because any group G is guaranteed to be non-empty due to the existence of the identity element e.

3.3 cvc5's Proof Format and Reconstruction

When cvc5 establishes that an SMT query is unsatisfiable, it can optionally generate a proof in the CPC format that accurately mirrors its internal reasoning. In CPC, each proof rule can be represented as follows:

$$\frac{\varphi_1 \ \cdots \ \varphi_m \ \mid \ t_1 \ \cdots \ t_n}{\psi} \text{ if } C$$

where $\varphi_1, \ldots, \varphi_m$ are the premises, $t_1, \ldots, t_n$ are the arguments provided to the proof rule, and C (which is optional) denotes a decidable side-condition. The proof format currently specifies over 662 proof rules in various domains, including arithmetic, strings, quantifiers, and higher-order logic. LEAN-SMT supports around 200 of these proof rules, which currently amounts to approximately 30% of cvc5's proof rules. We prioritized this subset because it suffices to support the most common proof goals in Lean.[5] The remaining rules are required for less common reasoning steps used by specific theory solvers. To reconstruct the cvc5 proofs in Lean, LEAN-SMT processes the CPC proof step by step, translating each proof step into an equivalent one in Lean. After LEAN-SMT completes proof reconstruction, the entire proof is submitted to the Lean kernel for verification. In cases where a proof step cannot be reconstructed, it is presented to the user as a subgoal to be proved manually, ensuring that the reconstruction

---

[5] For comparison, it corresponds to the same logical fragment supported initially by Sledgehammer and SMTCoq.

process remains sound. Note that since the logic of SMT-LIB is classical, certain parts of the proof rely heavily on the axiom of choice. Below we detail each of the reconstruction techniques we apply.

Reconstruction Via Theorems. Proof rules without side conditions generally correspond directly to theorems in Lean. We proved an extensive library of such theorems, which cover 163 proof rules, to use for proof reconstruction.

Example 3. Consider the `ARITH_MULT_TANGENT` proof rule from CPC.

$$\frac{-\mid x, y, a, b, \sigma}{(xy \leq tplane) = ((x \leq a \wedge y \geq b) \vee (x \geq a \wedge y \leq b))} \text{ if } \sigma = \top$$

$$\frac{-\mid x, y, a, b, \sigma}{(xy \leq tplane) = ((x \leq a \wedge y \leq b) \vee (x \geq a \wedge y \geq b))} \text{ if } \sigma = \bot$$

where x, y are real terms, a, b are real constants, $\sigma \in \{\top, \bot\}$ and $tplane :=$ $b \cdot x + a \cdot y - a \cdot b$ is the tangent plane of $x \cdot y$ at (a, b). Formalizing this proof rule into a Lean theorem is straightforward:

```
theorem arithMulTangentLowerEq :
(x * y ≤ b * x + a * y - a * b) = ((x ≤ a ∧ y ≥ b) ∨ (x ≥ a ∧ y ≤ b))
theorem arithMulTangentUpperEq :
(x * y ≤ b * x + a * y - a * b) = ((x ≤ a ∧ y ≤ b) ∨ (x ≥ a ∧ y ≥ b))
```

There are several CPC rules, however, which are more complex and require careful consideration in order to correctly capture their semantics when stating the corresponding Lean theorems.

Example 4. Consider for example the `RESOLUTION` proof rule:

$$\frac{C_1 \quad C_2 \mid pol, L}{C},$$

where C_1, C_2 are disjunctions, L is a disjunct occurring positively (respectively, negatively) in C_1 and negatively (resp., positively) in C_2 if pol is the Boolean constant *true* (resp., *false*). The result C is a disjunction consisting of the disjuncts from C_1 minus L (resp., $\neg L$) and the disjuncts from C_2 minus $\neg L$ (resp., L) if pol is *true* (resp., *false*). Moreover, C is a *flat* disjunction of disjuncts from C_1 and C_2 as opposed to a nested disjunction, reflecting CVC5's treatment of logical disjunction as a variadic operator. To capture the semantics of this rule precisely in Lean, where logical disjunction is expressed by a binary operator, one needs to carefully reason about the associativity and commutativity of that operator. We encapsulate the semantics in a Lean theorem as follows:

```
theorem orN_resolution (hps : orN ps) (hqs : orN qs)
      (hi : i < ps.length) (hj : j < qs.length)
      (hij : ps[i] = ¬qs[j]) :
      orN (ps.eraseIdx i ++ qs.eraseIdx j)
```

The premises, hps : orN ps and hqs : orN qs, are disjunctions but are built with the orN function, which takes a List of literals, each represented as a Prop. This formulation avoids representing ps and qs as, for example, inductively defined instances of Prop instead of List or encoding the literals as Bool instead of Prop. Using List also permits leveraging general theorems about List that we proved for eliminating tedious corner cases that would otherwise arise in a Prop implementation. Additionally, the choice to encode Boolean literals as Prop is a deliberate choice due to the type-theoretic foundations of Lean.

Reconstruction Via Tactics. Some proof rules without side conditions require the application of multiple lemmas or more complex reasoning. We implement specialized tactics to encapsulate these steps. This streamlines the reconstruction process by automating repetitive or intricate reasoning steps. We cover 37 proof rules this way, which required implementing a library with around 400 theorems.

Example 5. A proof rule that is very general, making it hard to state and prove as a theorem, is the ARITH_SUM_UB proof rule:

$$\frac{\bigwedge_{i=1}^{n} a_i \bowtie_i b_i \mid a_i, b_i}{\sum_{i=1}^{n} a_i \bowtie^* \sum_{i=1}^{n} b_i}$$

where $\bowtie_i$ can be either $<$, $\leq$ or $=$, and $\bowtie^*$ is either $<$, if at least one of the $\bowtie_i$ is $<$, or $\leq$, otherwise. Moreover, while each pair of variables a_i and b_i always have the same type, it is possible that different pairs have different types, some being integers and some being reals. It is possible to encode this proof rule as a single theorem in Lean, but the statement of the theorem would be quite intricate, due to the necessity of lifting the integer variables to reals and of combining the inequalities statically. Also, it is likely that this would make it very hard to prove. In this case, it is easier to write a tactic that considers the different cases of the rule and applies an appropriate, simpler theorem for each case. The implementation of this tactic requires 9 variations of the following general theorem:

```
sumBoundsThm {α : Type} [LinearOrderedRing α] {a b c d : α} :
  a < b → c < d → a + c < b + d
```

Each variation corresponds to one possible combination of the inequality symbols in the hypothesis. The relation symbol in the conclusion is adapted accordingly in each theorem. Since the proof rule accepts mixing of integer and real variables, we need a variation of each one of those 9 theorems for each combination of the types of the variables. Instead of stating all the combinations explicitly, which would result in a total of 36 theorems and a long branch in the implementation of the tactic, we state only one polymorphic version of each, as indicated by the type parameter α in theorem sumBoundsThm. Obviously, the theorem does not hold for just any type α. In fact, it cannot even be stated if there are no comparison or addition operators defined over α. We solve this issue by adding a restriction, stating that α satisfies the axioms of a *Linear Ordered Ring* (a class of types that contains both Int and Real defined in Lean's mathlib library). With this restriction, we can prove each of the 36 theorems. The full tactic can be seen in the appendix of a longer version of this paper [27].

Reconstruction Via Reflection. For proof rules involving complex side conditions or computations such as arithmetic simplifications, we encode the side condition into a reflective decision procedure, which we have formally verified in Lean. The proof rule is then translated into a theorem with the side condition as an additional premise. Applications of such rules are verified by the Lean kernel using definitional equality. We cover 5 proof rules this way. We reused one program from Lean's library, `ac_rfl`, which applies associative and commutative properties of addition and multiplication to normalize arithmetic expressions; and we implemented a new program, `poly_norm`, which normalizes polynomials up to associativity, commutativity, and distributivity by expanding polynomials.

Example 6. Consider the example:

```
example (x y : Int) (z : Real) :
  1 * ↑(x + y) * z / 4 = 1 / (2 * 2) * (z * ↑ y + ↑ x * z) := by
    poly_norm
```

Proving the correctness of `poly_norm` required proving around 70 theorems, amounting to 620 lines of Lean code. We define a monomial as an ordered list of natural numbers representing variable indices, so that equality of two monomials is immediate. Polynomials are defined as lists of monomials, and theorems about monomials generalize to polynomials using induction. We define `denote`, which essentially evaluates polynomial expressions. Using lemmas we proved about lists and the objects we defined, we prove a theorem pushing `denote` into each operator.

```
theorem denote_mul {p q : Polynomial} :
  (p.mul q).denote ctx = p.denote ctx * q.denote ctx
```

Proving similar theorems for each operator (addition, multiplication, division by a constant, and negation) yields a correctness theorem.

```
theorem denote_eq_from_toPoly_eq {e₁ e₂ : RealExpr}
  e₁.toPoly = e₂.toPoly → e₁.denote ictx rctx = e₂.denote ictx rctx
```

Since variables are represented as natural numbers, the premise of the theorem does not contain actual variables. Therefore, Lean can establish the premise through definitional equality. Moreover, the premise is decidable, allowing us to compile it into machine code for enhanced performance. In our experiments, this approach achieved speedups of up to 25x on very large arithmetic expressions compared to using definitional equality.

4   Evaluation and Results

The LEAN-SMT tactic is mainly designed to prove Lean goals provided by users, but can also act as a proof checker for CPC proofs in supported fragments. We evaluate it[6] in these scenarios with two sets of benchmarks: a set of 5000 SMT-LIB benchmarks generated by Sledgehammer from Isabelle/HOL, taken from *Seventeen Provers Under the Hammer* [15]; and a set of 24,817 unsatisfiable SMT-LIB benchmarks used in SMT-COMP 2024[7] that fit the supported fragments of LEAN-SMT: UF, IDL, RDL, LIA, LRA, LIRA, and their quantifier-free subfragments. The Sledgehammer benchmarks allow us to assess LEAN-SMT's performance in both mathematics and formal verification domains and include lemmas selected by Sledgehammer with its premise selection mechanism. The problems in SMT-COMP are used together with proof-producing SMT solvers to generate proofs that are passed on to a set of proof checkers, including LEAN-SMT.

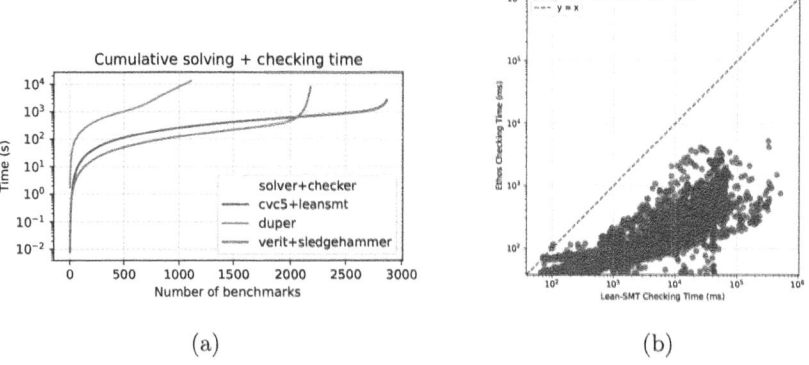

(a)   (b)

Fig. 2. (a) shows the performance of LEAN-SMT on Sledgehammer benchmarks, while (b) compares proof checking performance of LEAN-SMT with Ethos.

4.1   Isabelle Sledgehammer Benchmarks

We chose these benchmarks over other options (e.g., Lean's MathLib) due to Lean's lack of a premise selection mechanism, which is crucial for reducing false positives (i.e., goals found to be invalid by the SMT solver due to missing premises). These benchmarks also stress test solvers, as they contain many (up to 512) lemmas. We compare the performance of LEAN-SMT against Sledgehammer with the veriT back end, which supports similar proof reconstruction techniques, and Duper. We do not include CVC4 as a back end for Sledgehammer because

---

[6] All benchmarks were executed on a cluster with nodes equipped with 48 AMD Ryzen 9 7950X processors running at 4.50GHz and 128GB of RAM each.

[7] https://smt-comp.github.io/2024/.

its proof production is unstable and does not provide sufficient detail for reliable reconstruction. The results in Figure 2a show that LEAN-SMT effectively solves a large variety of Sledgehammer benchmarks, underscoring its potential for integration into general-purpose proof environments. LEAN-SMT outperforms veriT+Sledgehammer mainly because CVC5 outperforms veriT on this set of benchmarks. LEAN-SMT takes less than a second to replay proofs for 98% of the benchmarks, with the remaining 2% taking less than 5 seconds. Sledgehammer, by comparison, is faster at reconstructing shorter proofs, but does not scale as well for larger proofs.

4.2 SMT-COMP Benchmarks

We evaluate LEAN-SMT on the selected SMT-COMP benchmarks against the proof checkers Ethos[8] v0.1.0 and SMTCoq v2.2. Ethos is a proof checker implemented in C++ for the Eunoia logical framework, in which CPC has been formalized. SMTCoq is a proof checker in OCaml extracted from a formally verified Rocq program, and supports proofs in a subset of the Alethe proof format [35]. It can check proofs produced by versions of the veriT SMT solver up to 2016. Since the different approaches use different SMT solvers, our evaluation includes both proof-checking and SMT solving times. All benchmarks were run with a standard 20-minute timeout.

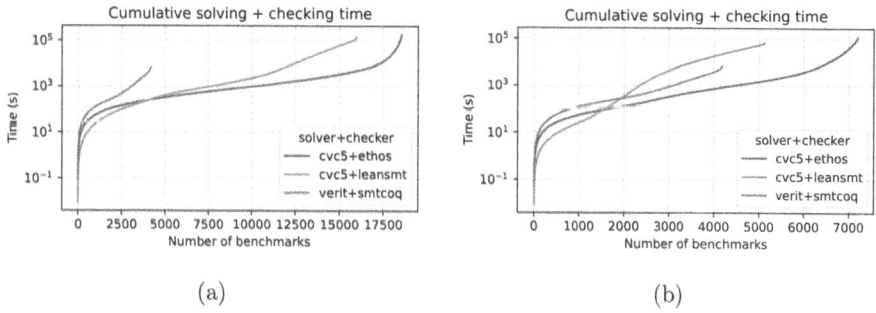

Fig. 3. Figure (a) shows the performance of LEAN-SMT on supported SMT-LIB fragments, while Figure (b) shows the performance on the quantifier-free subset.

Note that both LEAN-SMT and SMTCoq are highly trustworthy, since they both rely on small kernels. However, SMTCoq's code extraction mechanism, which extracts OCaml code from verified Rocq code, has to be trusted as well. The trusted base for Ethos, besides its kernel, also includes the Eunoia signature formalizing CPC. Moreover, its kernel includes native support for arithmetic (via GMP) and arrays for efficiency, while Lean's kernel only natively supports arithmetic.

---

[8] https://github.com/cvc5/ethos/.

Supported SMT-LIB Benchmarks. Figure 3a compares the cumulative solving and checking times for all SMT-LIB benchmarks. Out of the $21,595^9$ benchmarks for which proofs can be generated[10] by CVC5, LEAN-SMT successfully verified 15,271 proofs (71%), despite relying solely on the Lean kernel for soundness. Ethos verifies 98% of the proofs. Figure 2b compares the performance of LEAN-SMT to Ethos on proof checking times. LEAN-SMT stays within an order of magnitude of Ethos for most benchmarks. One reason for Ethos' superior performance is the lack of specialized support for arrays in Lean's kernel. This difference could be mitigated by switching to a more efficient array representation in Lean.

Quantifier-Free Fragment. Figure 3b focuses on the quantifier-free subset of SMT-LIB benchmarks, where SMTCoq's verified approach shines in terms of speed. However, SMTCoq falls short in the total number of proofs verified, primarily because, due to its fully verified architecture, it has not kept pace with the rapidly evolving features of modern SMT solvers. In contrast, LEAN-SMT benefits from the flexibility of proof replay, which has allowed us to adapt it more easily to updates in CVC5's proof production capabilities, resulting in broader coverage with respect to SMTCoq.

Overall, LEAN-SMT balances flexibility and performance, achieving promising results for a proof checker deeply integrated into Lean. While it trails Ethos in raw speed, its ability to verify a wide range of benchmarks with a small trusted base makes it an attractive option for checking SMT proofs in critical domains.

5   Conclusion

LEAN-SMT, a trustworthy integration of the CVC5 SMT solver into the Lean 4 proof assistant, is a significant step toward building a Lean hammer that enhances automation and verifies proofs generated by CVC5. LEAN-SMT shows promising results when compared to the state-of-the-art proof checker Ethos, both in terms of performance and effectiveness. It is already being used by other Lean-based projects [33] and is capable of verifying a diverse range of SMT-LIB benchmarks. Future work includes creating a dedicated Lean benchmark set for more targeted evaluation and expanding LEAN-SMT to support additional SMT-LIB theories, such as bit-vectors, floats, datatypes, and strings. We also plan to extend its proof coverage beyond the current 200 rules and incorporate more preprocessing steps to boost performance. Finally, we plan to improve integration with LEAN-AUTO to support higher-order logic and extend support for common Lean datatypes (e.g., tuples, structures, and modular arithmetic). Our ultimate objective is to develop a Lean hammer that brings unprecedented automation and verification capabilities to Lean.

---

[9] This number is for CVC5 +LEAN-SMT; for CVC5 +Ethos, 21,541 proofs are produced. The difference is due to the overhead of proof printing and piping for the latter combo, while in the former, the proof is passed directly via the API to LEAN-SMT.

[10] On occasion, CVC5 will produce proofs containing holes. Both Ethos and LEAN-SMT verify every non-hole proof step.

Acknowledgments. This work was partially supported by a gift from Amazon Web Services, the Stanford Center for Automated Reasoning, the Coordenação de Aperfeiçoamento de Pessoal de Nível Superior - Brasil (CAPES) - Finance Code 001, and the Defense Advanced Research Projects Agency (DARPA) under contract FA8750-24-2-1001. Any opinions, findings, and conclusions or recommendations expressed here are those of the authors and do not necessarily reflect the views of DARPA.

Disclosure of Interest. Clark Barrett is an Amazon Scholar.

References

1. Avigad, J., de Moura, L., Kong, S., Ullrich, S.: Theorem proving in Lean 4. https://leanprover.github.io/theorem_proving_in_lean4/
2. Baanen, A.: Formalizing Fundamental Algebraic Number Theory. Phd-thesis - research and graduation internal, Vrije Universiteit Amsterdam (2024). https://doi.org/10.5463/thesis.541
3. Barbosa, H., et al.: cvc5: A Versatile and Industrial-Strength SMT Solver (2022). https://doi.org/10.1007/978-3-030-99524-9_24
4. Barbosa, H., et al.: Flexible proof production in an industrial-strength SMT solver. In: Blanchette, J., Kovács, L., Pattinson, D. (eds.) International Joint Conference on Automated Reasoning (IJCAR). Lecture Notes in Computer Science, vol. 13385, pp. 15–35. Springer (2022). https://doi.org/10.1007/978-3-031-10769-6_3
5. Barrett, C., Conway, C.L., Deters, M., Hadarean, L., Jovanović, D., King, T., Reynolds, A., Tinelli, C.: CVC4. In: Gopalakrishnan, G., Qadeer, S. (eds.) Computer Aided Verification (CAV), pp. 171–177. Springer (2011). https://doi.org/10.1007/978-3-642-22110-1_14
6. Barrett, C., Fontaine, P., Tinelli, C.: The SMT-LIB Standard: Version 2.6 Tech. rep., Department of Computer Science, The University of Iowa (2017). www.SMT-LIB.org
7. Bertot, Y., Castéran, P.: Interactive Theorem Proving and Program Development - Coq'Art: The Calculus of Inductive Constructions. Texts in Theoretical Computer Science. An EATCS Series, Springer (2004). https://doi.org/10.1007/978-3-662-07964-5
8. Blanchette, J.C., Böhme, S., Paulson, L.C.: Extending sledgehammer with SMT solvers. In: Bjørner, N.S., Sofronie-Stokkermans, V. (eds.) Automated Deduction - CADE-23 - 23rd International Conference on Automated Deduction, Wroclaw, Poland, July 31–August 5, 2011. Proceedings. Lecture Notes in Computer Science, vol. 6803, pp. 116–130. Springer (2011). https://doi.org/10.1007/978-3-642-22438-6_11
9. Blanchette, J.C., Kaliszyk, C., Paulson, L.C., Urban, J.: Hammering towards QED. J. Formalized Reasoning **9**(1), 101–148 (2016)
10. Bobot, F., Filliâtre, J.C., Marché, C., Paskevich, A.: Why3: shepherd your herd of provers. In: Boogie 2011: First International Workshop on Intermediate Verification Languages, pp. 53–64 (2011)
11. Bouton, T., Caminha B. de Oliveira, D., Déharbe, D., Fontaine, P.: veriT: an open, trustable and efficient SMT-Solver. In: Schmidt, R.A. (ed.) CADE 2009. LNCS (LNAI), vol. 5663, pp. 151–156. Springer, Heidelberg (2009). https://doi.org/10.1007/978-3-642-02959-2_12

12. Castelvecchi, D.: Mathematicians welcome computer-assisted proof in "grand unification" theory. Nature **595** (2021). https://doi.org/10.1038/d41586-021-01627-2

13. Clune, J., Qian, Y., Bentkamp, A., Avigad, J.: Duper: a proof-producing superposition theorem prover for dependent type theory. In: Bertot, Y., Kutsia, T., Norrish, M. (eds.) 15th International Conference on Interactive Theorem Proving (ITP 2024). Leibniz International Proceedings in Informatics (LIPIcs), vol. 309, pp. 10:1–10:20. Schloss Dagstuhl – Leibniz-Zentrum für Informatik, Dagstuhl, Germany (2024). https://doi.org/10.4230/LIPIcs.ITP.2024.10, https://drops.dagstuhl.de/entities/document/10.4230/LIPIcs.ITP.2024.10

14. mathlib Community, T.: The Lean mathematical library. In: Proceedings of the 9th ACM SIGPLAN International Conference on Certified Programs and Proofs. pp. 367–381. CPP 2020. Association for Computing Machinery, New York (2020). https://doi.org/10.1145/3372885.3373824

15. Desharnais, M., Vukmirovic, P., Blanchette, J., Wenzel, M.: Seventeen provers under the hammer. In: Andronick, J., de Moura, L. (eds.) 13th International Conference on Interactive Theorem Proving, ITP 2022, August 7–10, 2022, Haifa, Israel. LIPIcs, vol. 237, pp. 8:1–8:18. Schloss Dagstuhl - Leibniz-Zentrum für Informatik (2022). https://doi.org/10.4230/LIPICS.ITP.2022.8

16. Ekici, B., Mebsout, A., Tinelli, C., Keller, C., Katz, G., Reynolds, A., Barrett, C.: SMTCoq: a plug-in for integrating SMT solvers into Coq. In: Majumdar, R., Kunčak, V. (eds.) Computer Aided Verification, pp. 126–133. Springer International Publishing, Cham (2017)

17. Enderton, H.B.: A mathematical Introduction to Logic, 2 edn. Academic Press (2001)

18. Gonthier, G.: The four colour theorem: engineering of a formal proof. In: Kapur, D. (ed.) Computer Mathematics, 8th Asian Symposium, ASCM 2007, Singapore, December 15–17, 2007. Revised and Invited Papers. Lecture Notes in Computer Science, vol. 5081, p. 333. Springer (2007). https://doi.org/10.1007/978-3-540-87827-8_28

19. Hales, T., et al.: A formal proof of the kepler conjecture (2015)

20. Hurd, J.: First-order proof tactics in higher-order logic theorem provers in proc (2003). https://api.semanticscholar.org/CorpusID:11201048

21. Jakubuv, J., et al.: Mizar 60 for mizar 50. In: Naumowicz, A., Thiemann, R. (eds.) Interactive Theorem Proving (ITP). LIPIcs, vol. 268, pp. 19:1–19:22. Schloss Dagstuhl - Leibniz-Zentrum für Informatik (2023). https://doi.org/10.4230/LIPICS.ITP.2023.19

22. Kaliszyk, C., Urban, J.: Hol(y)hammer: online ATP service for HOL light. Math. Comput. Sci. **9**(1), 5–22 (2015). https://doi.org/10.1007/s11786-014-0182-0

23. Klein, G., et al.: seL4: formal verification of an operating-system kernel. Commun. ACM **53**(6), 107–115 (2010). https://doi.org/10.1145/1743546.1743574

24. Lachnitt, H., et al.: Isarare: automatic verification of SMT rewrites in isabelle/hol. In: Finkbeiner, B., Kovács, L. (eds.) Tools and Algorithms for Construction and Analysis of Systems (TACAS), Part I. Lecture Notes in Computer Science, vol. 14570, pp. 311–330. Springer (2024). https://doi.org/10.1007/978-3-031-57246-3_17

25. Limperg, J., From, A.H.: Aesop: white-box best-first proof search for lean. In: Proceedings of the 12th ACM SIGPLAN International Conference on Certified Programs and Proofs. pp. 253–266. CPP 2023. Association for Computing Machinery, New York (2023). https://doi.org/10.1145/3573105.3575671

26. Meng, J., Quigley, C., Paulson, L.C.: Automation for interactive proof: First proto-type. Inf. Comput. **204**(10), 1575–1596 (2006). https://doi.org/10.1016/j.ic.2005.05.010
27. Mohamed, A., et al.: Lean-SMT: an SMT tactic for discharging proof goals in Lean (2025). https://arxiv.org/abs/2505.15796
28. Moura, L., Ullrich, S.: The lean 4 theorem prover and programming language. In: Platzer, A., Sutcliffe, G. (eds.) CADE 2021. LNCS (LNAI), vol. 12699, pp. 625–635. Springer, Cham (2021). https://doi.org/10.1007/978-3-030-79876-5_37
29. Nelson, L., Geffen, J.V., Torlak, E., Wang, X.: Specification and verification in the field: Applying formal methods to BPF just-in-time compilers in the Linux kernel. In: 14th USENIX Symposium on Operating Systems Design and Implementation, OSDI 2020, Virtual Event, November 4–6, 2020, pp. 41–61. USENIX Association (2020). https://www.usenix.org/conference/osdi20/presentation/nelson
30. Nipkow, T., Wenzel, M., Paulson, L.C. (eds.): Isabelle/HOL. LNCS, vol. 2283. Springer, Heidelberg (2002). https://doi.org/10.1007/3-540-45949-9
31. Nötzli, A., et al.: Reconstructing fine-grained proofs of rewrites using a domain-specific language. In: Griggio, A., Rungta, N. (eds.) Formal Methods In Computer-Aided Design (FMCAD), pp. 65–74. IEEE (2022). https://doi.org/10.34727/2022/isbn.978-3-85448-053-2_12
32. Piotrowski, B., Mir, R.F., Ayers, E.: Machine-learned premise selection for Lean (2023). https://arxiv.org/abs/2304.00994
33. Pîrlea, G., Gladshtein, V., Kinsbruner, E., Zhao, Q., Sergey, I.: Veil: a framework for automated and interactive verification of transition systems. In: Piskac, R., Rakamaric, Z. (eds.) Computer Aided Verification - 37th International Confer-ence, CAV 2025, Zagreb, Croatia, July 21–25, 2025, Proceedings. Lecture Notes in Computer Science, Springer (2025)
34. Qian, Y., Clune, J., Barrett, C., Avigad, J.: Lean-auto: an interface between lean 4 and automated theorem provers. In: Piskac, R., Rakamaric, Z. (eds.) Com-puter Aided Verification - 37th International Conference, CAV 2025, Zagreb, Croa-tia, July 21–25, 2025, Proceedings. Lecture Notes in Computer Science. Springer (2025), to appear
35. Schurr, H., Fleury, M., Barbosa, H., Fontaine, P.: Alethe: towards a generic SMT proof format (extended abstract). CoRR **abs/2107.02354** (2021). https://arxiv.org/abs/2107.02354
36. Schurr, H., Fleury, M., Desharnais, M.: Reliable reconstruction of fine-grained proofs in a proof assistant. In: Platzer, A., Sutcliffe, G. (eds.) Automated Deduc-tion - CADE 28 - 28th International Conference on Automated Deduction, Virtual Event, July 12-15, 2021, Proceedings. Lecture Notes in Computer Science, vol. 12699, pp. 450–467. Springer (2021). https://doi.org/10.1007/978-3-030-79876-5_26
37. Tao, T.: Machine assisted proof. AMS Notices **72**(1), 86–95 (2025). https://doi.org/10.1090/noti3041

Networks and Protocols

Automatic Verification of Floating-Point Accumulation Networks

David K. Zhang$^{(\boxtimes)}$ and Alex Aiken

Stanford University, Stanford, USA
dkzhang@stanford.edu

Abstract. Floating-point accumulation networks (FPANs) are key building blocks used in many floating-point algorithms, including compensated summation and double-double arithmetic. FPANs are notoriously difficult to analyze, and algorithms using FPANs are often published without rigorous correctness proofs. In fact, on at least one occasion, a published error bound for a widely used FPAN was later found to be incorrect. In this paper, we present an automatic procedure that produces computer-verified proofs of several FPAN correctness properties, including error bounds that are tight to the nearest bit. Our approach is underpinned by a novel floating-point abstraction that models the sign, exponent, and number of leading and trailing zeros and ones in the mantissa of each number flowing through an FPAN. We also present a new FPAN for double-double addition that is faster and more accurate than the previous best known algorithm.

Keywords: Automatic theorem proving · Floating-point arithmetic · Error-free transformations · TwoSum algorithm · Double-double arithmetic · Quad-double arithmetic · Rounding error

1 Introduction

Many scientific and mathematical problems demand calculations that exceed the native precision limits of floating-point hardware (typically IEEE 64-bit or Intel x87 80-bit). To address this need, numerical programmers turn to *compensated algorithms*, such as Kahan–Babuška–Neumaier summation [5,37,48], and *floating-point expansions* [52], such as double-double and quad-double arithmetic [21,33]. These techniques enable a processor to execute floating-point operations with double, quadruple, or even higher multiples of its native precision. They are widely adopted in dense [42] and sparse [26] numerical linear algebra, high-precision quadrature [8], robust computational geometry [57], fluid dynamics [6,32], quantum chemistry [29,30], correctly rounded transcendental functions [19,58], and the discovery of new mathematical identities [9].

All of these techniques are based on common building blocks known as *error-free transformations* [51], which are floating-point algorithms that exactly compute their own rounding errors. For example, the Møller–Knuth TwoSum algorithm [39,47] takes a pair of floating-point numbers (x, y) and computes both

© The Author(s) 2025
R. Piskac and Z. Rakamarić (Eds.): CAV 2025, LNCS 15933, pp. 215–237, 2025.
https://doi.org/10.1007/978-3-031-98682-6_12

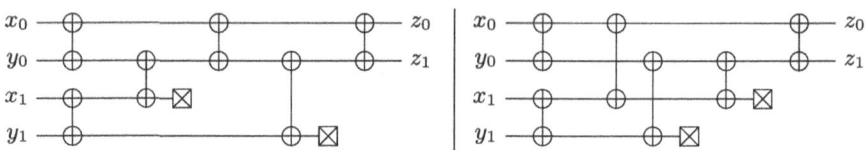

Fig. 1. Network diagram of the ddadd algorithm due to Li et al. (left) and madd, our new double-double addition algorithm (right). This graphical FPAN notation will be explained in detail in Sect. 3.

their rounded sum $s := x \oplus y$ and the exact rounding error $e := (x + y) - (x \oplus y)$ incurred in that sum. Here, $\oplus$ denotes rounded floating-point addition, while $+$ denotes true mathematical addition.

Although the TwoSum algorithm has been extensively studied, proven correct by both pen-and-paper [11,39] and formal methods [12,46], issues arise when multiple TwoSum operations are combined to accumulate three or more floating-point values. Multiple rounding error terms can interact in subtle and unexpected ways, significantly affecting the precision of the overall result when terms that are incorrectly assumed to be negligible are discarded.

In 2017, Joldes, Muller, and Popescu [35] discovered an error of this type in the ddadd algorithm designed by Li et al. for the XBLAS extended-precision linear algebra library [42]. Li et al. originally claimed that ddadd computes sums with relative error bounded by $2 \cdot 2^{-106} = 2\mathbf{u}^2$ when executed in IEEE binary64 (double precision) arithmetic, where $\mathbf{u} = 2^{-53}$ denotes the unit roundoff. Joldes, Muller, and Popescu refuted this claim by identifying a class of inputs in which two discarded error terms interfere constructively, producing a relative error of $2.25 \cdot 2^{-106} = 2.25\mathbf{u}^2$ in the final sum. While this weakened bound does not invalidate the usefulness of XBLAS, it demonstrates that even expert numerical analysts can make subtle mistakes in the analysis of rounding errors.

The ddadd algorithm is a prototypical example of a *floating-point accumulation network (FPAN)*—a term we introduce to describe a branch-free linear sequence of floating-point sum and TwoSum operations. Although this class of algorithms, to our knowledge, has never been explicitly named in the floating-point literature, FPANs pervade floating-point algorithms and occur in every single paper referenced in this introduction, along with dozens of software packages [7,19,25,27,33,36,43,53,56,58,62]. In addition to their obvious uses for high-precision addition and subtraction, FPANs also occur as subroutines in multiplication, division, and square root algorithms [33,38], which in turn are used to implement transcendental functions, including the exponential, logarithm, and trigonometric functions, in many standard libraries [19,53,58].

In this paper, we present an automatic procedure for proving several FPAN correctness properties, including error bounds and nonoverlapping invariants. Our key technical insight is a one-sided reduction from a correctness property P of an FPAN F to a satisfiability problem $S_{P,F}$ in quantifier-free Presburger arithmetic (QF_LIA). Here, one-sidedness means that if $S_{P,F}$ is unsatisfiable, then

$P(F)$ provably holds, but if $S_{P,F}$ is satisfiable, then $P(F)$ may or may not hold. In all cases we have tested, we find that the satisfiability of $S_{P,F}$ is far easier for SMT solvers to determine than direct verification of $P(F)$ in a floating-point theory (QF_FP). Our reduced problems $S_{P,F}$ can be solved in less than one second, while direct $P(F)$ verifiers fail to terminate after multiple days of runtime.

Using our procedure, we discover and prove the correctness of a new algorithm for double-double addition—the same problem that ddadd solves—with strictly smaller relative error and lower circuit depth. Thus, our algorithm, named madd (for "More Accurate Double-Double addition," shown in Fig. 1) is both faster and more accurate than the previous best known algorithm for this task. We expect our automatic decision procedure to enable additional novel algorithms to be found by computer search in future work.

Our reduction strategy uses a novel abstraction of floating-point arithmetic that does not consider the full bitwise representation of a floating-point number x, but tracks only its sign s_x, exponent e_x, and the number of leading and trailing zeros and ones in its mantissa ($\mathsf{nlz}_x, \mathsf{nlo}_x, \mathsf{ntz}_x, \mathsf{nto}_x$). Using this reduced representation, we construct abstract overapproximations of the floating-point sum and TwoSum operations, expressed as linear inequalities in the variables ($s_x, e_x, \mathsf{nlz}_x, \mathsf{nlo}_x, \mathsf{ntz}_x, \mathsf{nto}_x$). Although we lose completeness by passing to an overapproximation, we show that our abstraction is nonetheless precise enough to prove best-possible error bounds, tight to the nearest bit, for several FPANs of practical interest, including ddadd and madd. Moreover, we use floating-point SMT solvers to directly verify the soundness of our abstraction.

In summary, this paper makes the following contributions:

1. We define *floating-point accumulation networks* (*FPANs*) and show that FPANs occur in many widely used floating-point algorithms.
2. We give a procedure for reducing correctness properties P of an FPAN F to satisfiability problems $S_{P,F}$ in quantifier-free Presburger arithmetic. Our strategy uses a novel formally verified abstraction of floating-point arithmetic that may be of independent interest.
3. We empirically demonstrate that $S_{P,F}$ is far easier for modern SMT solvers to reason about than $P(F)$, solving otherwise intractable verification problems in under one second.
4. We state a new double-double addition algorithm, madd, with lower circuit depth and strictly smaller relative error than the previous best known algorithm, as rigorously proven by our reduction procedure.

2   Background

2.1   Floating-Point Numbers

A *floating-point number* in base $b \in \mathbb{N}$ with precision $p \in \mathbb{N}$ is an ordered triple (s, e, m) consisting of a *sign bit* $s \in \{0, 1\}$, an *exponent* $e \in \mathbb{Z}$, and a *mantissa* $m = (m_0, m_1, \ldots, m_{p-1})$, which is an sequence of p *digits* $m_k \in \{0, 1, \ldots, b-1\}$.

The value represented by (s, e, m) is defined as the following real number:

$$(-1)^s \times (m_0.m_1m_2 \ldots m_{p-1}) \times b^e = (-1)^s \sum_{k=0}^{p-1} m_k b^{e-k} \tag{1}$$

Floating-point hardware is almost always designed for base $b = 2$, and we assume $b = 2$ throughout this paper.

The IEEE 754 standard [2–4] defines a family of encodings of floating-point numbers (s, e, m) into fixed-width bit-vectors with a specified base b, precision p, and exponent range $e_{\min} \leq e \leq e_{\max}$. These standard encodings, listed in Table 1, have several additional features that are relevant to our analysis.

– A floating-point number with $m_0 = 1$ is said to be *normalized*. A nonzero floating-point number can be normalized without changing its represented real value by shifting its first nonzero bit m_k to position m_0 and adjusting its exponent e to $e - k$. IEEE 754 requires floating-point numbers to be normalized whenever possible so that the *implicit leading bit* $m_0 = 1$ does not need to be explicitly stored.
– The only floating-point numbers that cannot be normalized are zero and very small numbers whose adjusted exponent would fall below the minimum threshold $e_{\min}$. These small nonzero numbers are called *subnormal* and use a special alternative representation with no implicit leading bit.
– Zero has two distinct IEEE 754 encodings with opposite sign bits, denoted by +0.0 (*positive zero*) and –0.0 (*negative zero*). These two values are considered to be equal, i.e., +0.0 == –0.0 evaluates to **true** in any IEEE 754-compliant programming environment.
– IEEE 754 defines three non-numeric floating-point values, called *positive infinity* $(+\infty)$, *negative infinity* $(-\infty)$, and *not-a-number* (NaN). These special values are returned from operations that would otherwise yield an unrepresentably large or indeterminate result. All floating-point values other than $\pm\infty$ and NaN are called *finite*.

We assume throughout this paper that all floating-point numbers are normalized or zero, ignoring subnormal numbers, $\pm\infty$, and NaN. We also identify +0.0 with –0.0, writing $\pm$0.0 to denote zero with either sign. These assumptions serve only to simplify exposition and do not affect the generality of our results. Indeed, we prove in Sect. 5 that our automated proof technique handles all finite floating-point values, including subnormal numbers. Non-finite inputs require no consideration because the algorithms discussed in this paper simply return NaN when given $\pm\infty$ or NaN inputs.

2.2 Rounding and Error-Free Transformations

In general, the sum or difference of two precision-p floating-point numbers may not be exactly representable as another precision-p floating-point number. To perform calculations at a fixed precision p, the result of every operation must be *rounded* by the following procedure:

Table 1. Parameters of the floating-point formats defined by the IEEE 754 standard and the nonstandard bfloat16 format commonly used in deep learning accelerators.

Format	Base b	Precision p	Exponent range $\{e_{\min}, \ldots, e_{\max}\}$
binary16	$b = 2$	$p = 11$	$e \in \{-14, \ldots, +15\}$
bfloat16	$b = 2$	$p = 8$	$e \in \{-126, \ldots, +127\}$
binary32	$b = 2$	$p = 24$	$e \in \{-126, \ldots, +127\}$
binary64	$b = 2$	$p = 53$	$e \in \{-1022, \ldots, +1023\}$
binary128	$b = 2$	$p = 113$	$e \in \{-16382, \ldots, +16383\}$

1. Compute the exact sum or difference of the real values represented by the floating-point inputs, as if to infinite precision.
2. Find and return the closest precision-p floating-point number to the exact result. A *tie-breaking* rule must be used whenever the exact result is equidistant to two neighboring floating-point values.

As is standard in studies of extended-precision floating-point arithmetic [11, 12], we assume throughout this paper that all floating-point operations are rounded to nearest with ties broken to even, denoted by RNE. This is the default rounding mode defined by IEEE 754 and is supported on virtually all general-purpose computing hardware. In fact, RNE is the only rounding mode available in many programming environments, including Python, JavaScript, and WebAssembly [1, 24]. Following Knuth's convention [39], we distinguish between rounded and exact arithmetic operations using circled operators.

$$x \oplus y := \mathsf{RNE}(x + y) \tag{2}$$
$$x \ominus y := \mathsf{RNE}(x - y) \tag{3}$$

Rounding errors in precision-p floating-point arithmetic are characterized by the *unit roundoff*[1] constant $\mathbf{u} := 2^{-p}$, which bounds the relative error of any individual rounded operation [55]. For example, for all floating-point numbers a and b such that $|a + b| < (2 - \mathbf{u})2^{e_{\max}}$, there exists $\delta \in \mathbb{R}$ satisfying

$$a \oplus b = (a + b)(1 + \delta) \quad \text{where} \quad |\delta| \leq \mathbf{u}. \tag{4}$$

Analogous results also hold for subtraction and other floating-point operations.

An *error-free transformation* is a floating-point algorithm that computes a rounded arithmetic operation together with the exact rounding error incurred by that operation. The oldest and most important example of an error-free transformation is the Møller–Knuth TwoSum algorithm, first discovered by Møller [47] and proven correct by Knuth [39], which computes the rounding error of a floating-point sum $s := x \oplus y$ or difference $d := x \ominus y$.

---

[1] The definition $\mathbf{u} := 2^{-p}$ is appropriate when floating-point operations are rounded to nearest. For other rounding modes, the larger value $\mathbf{u} := 2^{-(p-1)}$ is used instead.

Algorithm: TwoSum(x, y)
Input: Two floating-point numbers (x, y).   **Output:** Two floating-point numbers (s, e) such that $\quad\quad\quad s = x \oplus y$ and $e = (x + y) - (x \oplus y)$ exactly.
1 $s := x \oplus y$ 2 $x_{\text{eff}} := s \ominus y$ 3 $y_{\text{eff}} := s \ominus x_{\text{eff}}$ 4 $\delta_x := x \ominus x_{\text{eff}}$ 5 $\delta_y := y \ominus y_{\text{eff}}$ 6 $e := \delta_x \oplus \delta_y$ 7 **return** (s, e)

Fig. 2. Pseudocode for the Møller–Knuth TwoSum algorithm. This algorithm can also be applied to subtraction by flipping the sign of y throughout.

Although the algorithm itself is straightforward, the existence of TwoSum is a highly nontrivial result. It is not obvious *a priori* that the rounding error $e := (x + y) - (x \oplus y)$ is always exactly representable as a floating-point number, let alone that it can be recovered using rounded floating-point operations. Despite the apparent simplicity of the pseudocode in Fig. 2, proving the correctness of TwoSum requires lengthy case analysis [39, Sec. 4.2.2]. Analogous error-free transformations also exist for floating-point multiplication [21,59,60] and the fused multiply-add operation [14].

2.3   Floating-Point Expansions

Floating-point expansion is a technique for representing high-precision numbers as sequences of machine-precision numbers. The basic idea is to represent a high-precision constant $C \in \mathbb{R}$ as a sequence of successive approximations:

$$
\begin{aligned}
x_0 &:= \mathsf{RNE}(C) \\
x_1 &:= \mathsf{RNE}(C - x_0) \\
x_2 &:= \mathsf{RNE}(C - x_0 - x_1) \\
&\;\;\vdots \\
x_{n-1} &:= \mathsf{RNE}(C - x_0 - x_1 - \cdots - x_{n-2})
\end{aligned}
\tag{5}
$$

Provided that no overflow or underflow occurs in this process, the final n-term expansion $(x_0, x_1, \ldots, x_{n-1})$ approximates C with precision $np + n - 1$, i.e.,

$$
|C - (x_0 + x_1 + \cdots + x_{n-1})| \le 2^{-(np+n-1)}|C|
\tag{6}
$$

where p denotes the underlying machine precision. To achieve the full precision of $np + n - 1$ bits, a floating-point expansion must be *nonoverlapping*, i.e.,

$$
x_i = \mathsf{RNE}(x_i + x_{i+1})
\tag{7}
$$

high-precision constant $C = 1\,0\,1\,.\,0\,1\,1\,1\,0\,1\,1\,0\,1\,0\,1\,1\,\ldots$

$$|x_1| > \mathsf{ulp}(x_0) \left\{ \begin{array}{l} x_0 = 1\,0\,1\,.\,0\,0\,0 \\ x_1 = \quad 0\,.\,0\,1\,1\,1\,0\,1\,1 \end{array} \right\} \text{10-bit precision}$$

$$|x_1| \le \mathsf{ulp}(x_0) \left\{ \begin{array}{l} x_0 = 1\,0\,1\,.\,0\,1\,1 \\ x_1 = \quad 0\,.\,0\,0\,0\,1\,0\,1\,1\,0\,1 \end{array} \right\} \text{12-bit precision}$$

$$x_0 = \mathsf{RNE}(x_0 + x_1) \left\{ \begin{array}{l} x_0 = 1\,0\,1\,.\,1\,0\,0 \\ x_1 = -0\,.\,0\,0\,0\,0\,1\,0\,0\,1\,0\,1 \end{array} \right\} \text{13-bit precision}$$

Fig. 3. Decomposition of a high-precision constant C into overlapping and nonoverlapping floating-point expansions with $p = 6$ mantissa bits per term. Light blue digits represent a shift stored in the exponent and are not part of the mantissa. Note that the final expansion rounds x_0 up instead of down. In this case, x_1 is negative, and the mantissa of x_1 contains the one's complement of the corresponding digits in C.

for each $i = 0, \ldots, n - 2$. This property, illustrated in Fig. 3, ensures that no bit of C is redundantly covered by more than one component of the expansion. Intuitively, if there were such a redundant bit, then at least one bit would flip when adding x_i to x_{i+1}, causing $x_i \oplus x_{i+1}$ to differ from x_i.

Arithmetic with floating-point expansions is a delicate procedure that requires skillful use of error-free transformations to propagate rounding errors between terms. Moreover, the nonoverlapping property is easily broken and must be restored after every few operations to avoid loss of precision. Designing sequences of error-free transformations with correct error propagation and nonoverlapping semantics is a remarkably difficult problem; the literature on this subject is punctuated by refutations, corrections, and corrections to those corrections [35,46]. Some general constructions are known, but these algorithms are far from optimal, particularly when the number of inputs is small [18,45].

In principle, a nonoverlapping floating-point expansion can contain up to $\lceil (e_{\max} - e_{\min} + p)/(p+1) \rceil$ terms before underflow occurs, causing all subsequent terms to round down to zero. However, in practice, it is more common to use fixed-length floating-point expansions consisting of two, three, or four terms [19, 33,41,42,58]. These fixed-length expansions are called *double-word, triple-word, quadruple-word* or *double-double, triple-double, quad-double* representations. The latter names are used when the underlying machine format is IEEE binary64 (double precision), but most algorithms for double-double, triple-double, and quad-double arithmetic also work for other underlying formats.

3   Floating-Point Accumulation Networks

In this section, we formally define floating-point accumulation networks as a class of branch-free floating-point algorithms using a graphical notation inspired by sorting networks [40].

Definition 1. *A **floating-point accumulation network** (**FPAN**) is a diagram consisting of horizontal **wires** and vertical* TwoSum ***gates** that connect*

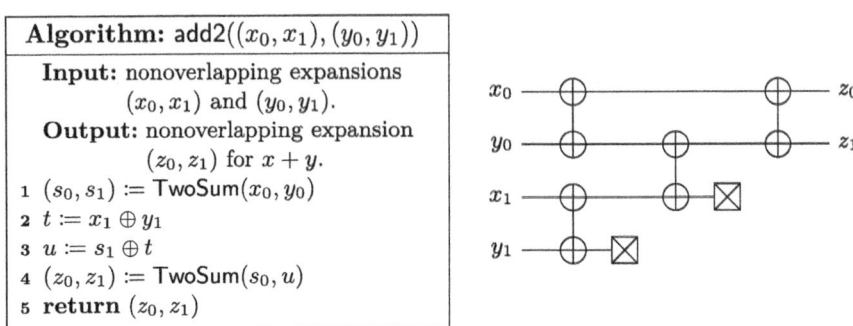

Fig. 4. Gate representations of the floating-point sum and TwoSum operations. In our notation, $x \oplus y$ is treated as a special case of $\mathsf{TwoSum}(x,y)$ with the error term discarded. Note that the inputs are unordered (i.e., $\mathsf{TwoSum}(x,y) = \mathsf{TwoSum}(y,x)$) but the order of the outputs is significant, with larger-magnitude outputs on top.

Algorithm: add2$((x_0, x_1), (y_0, y_1))$

Input: nonoverlapping expansions (x_0, x_1) and (y_0, y_1).
Output: nonoverlapping expansion (z_0, z_1) for $x + y$.
1 $(s_0, s_1) := \mathsf{TwoSum}(x_0, y_0)$
2 $t := x_1 \oplus y_1$
3 $u := s_1 \oplus t$
4 $(z_0, z_1) := \mathsf{TwoSum}(s_0, u)$
5 **return** (z_0, z_1)

Fig. 5. Pseudocode and network diagram representations of Dekker's add2 algorithm. Note that the intermediate variables s_0, s_1, t, u are unnamed in the network diagram representation, implicitly represented by the wire segments in between TwoSum gates.

exactly two wires. Each wire may optionally be terminated by the symbol ⊠, *indicating that it is **discarded**.*

An FPAN with n wires, of which k are discarded, represents the following algorithm with n floating-point inputs and $n - k$ floating-point outputs. Each input value $(x_1, x_2, \ldots, x_n)$ enters on the left-hand side of each wire, ordered top-to-bottom unless otherwise specified by explicit labels. The values flow left-to-right along the wires, and whenever two values (x_i, x_j) encounter a TwoSum gate, they are updated by $(x_i, x_j) \leftarrow \mathsf{TwoSum}(x_i, x_j)$ as specified in Fig. 4. After all TwoSum gates have been executed, all values on wires that are not discarded are returned in top-to-bottom order. To illustrate this definition, Fig. 5 presents equivalent pseudocode and network diagram representations of Dekker's add2 algorithm, the first algorithm ever proposed for double-double addition [21].

The purpose of an FPAN is to compute a nonoverlapping floating-point expansion of the exact value of the sum of its inputs. By the defining property of the TwoSum algorithm, this value is invariant to the application of a TwoSum gate to any two wires; it is only ever changed by discarding a wire. Therefore, to prove the correctness of an FPAN, it suffices to show the following:

1. The non-discarded outputs, denoted by $(a_0, a_1, \ldots, a_{n-k-1})$, must satisfy the nonoverlapping invariant $a_i = \mathsf{RNE}(a_i + a_{i+1})$ for all $i = 0, \ldots, n - k - 2$.

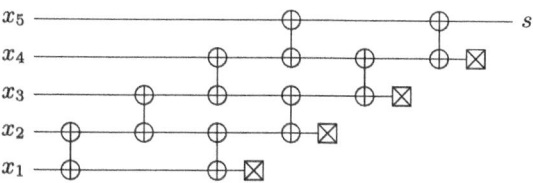

Fig. 6. Network diagram for Kahan–Babuška–Neumaier summation applied to five inputs. This double staircase accumulation pattern generalizes to any number of inputs.

2. The discarded outputs, denoted by $(b_0, b_1, \ldots, b_{k-1})$, must satisfy an *error bound* of the form $|b_i| \leq C_i \mathbf{u}^{n-k} |a_0|$ for some small constant C_i for each $i = 0, \ldots, k - 1$.

Dekker's add2 algorithm is notable for violating these correctness properties. Assuming nonoverlapping inputs (x_0, x_1) and (y_0, y_1), Dekker proved [21] that the relative difference between the sum (z_0, z_1) computed by add2 and the true sum $x_0 + x_1 + y_0 + x_1$ is bounded above by:

$$\frac{|(z_0 + z_1) - (x_0 + x_1 + y_0 + y_1)|}{|x_0 + x_1 + y_0 + y_1|} \leq 4\mathbf{u}^2 \frac{|x_0 + x_1| + |y_0 + y_1|}{|x_0 + x_1 + y_0 + y_1|} \tag{8}$$

Although this relative error bound is reasonably tight when (x_0, x_1) and (y_0, y_1) have the same sign, it can be extremely loose when (x_0, x_1) and (y_0, y_1) have different signs, in which case $|x_0 + x_1| + |y_0 + y_1|$ can be orders of magnitude larger than $|x_0 + x_1 + y_0 + y_1|$. Joldes, Muller, and Popescu [35] identified example inputs for which add2 computes sums with 100% relative error, i.e., zero accurate bits compared to the true value of $x_0 + x_1 + y_0 + y_1$.

This observation highlights the surprising difficulty of computing accurate floating-point sums, even for as few as four inputs. At first glance, the network diagram shown in Fig. 5 may not appear to have any obvious deficiencies. Indeed, when interpreted as a sorting network, this diagram gives a correct algorithm for partially sorting four inputs satisfying the preconditions $x_0 > x_1$ and $y_0 > y_1$. However, there are two key differences that make floating-point accumulation harder than sorting. First, the outputs of an FPAN not only need to be sorted by magnitude; they also require a degree of mutual separation to satisfy nonoverlapping invariants and error bounds. Second, unlike a comparator which merely reorders its inputs, a TwoSum gate actually modifies its inputs, potentially introducing new overlap and ordering issues with every operation.

Example: KBN Summation. Kahan–Babuška–Neumaier (KBN) summation is an algorithm that uses TwoSum to compute floating-point sums with a running compensation term to improve the accuracy of the final result [5,37,48]. This technique is frequently used in floating-point programs and is implemented in both the Python and Julia standard libraries. In particular, Python's built-in sum() function uses KBN summation when given floating-point inputs [27].

In our graphical notation, the KBN algorithm is written as an FPAN with a double staircase structure illustrated in Fig. 6. The first staircase computes the naïve floating-point sum of the inputs, while the second staircase computes the running compensation term used to correct the naïve sum.

4   Abstraction

Existing methods for floating-point verification are ill-suited for FPANs. On one hand, techniques based on interval analysis or projection from real arithmetic are too imprecise to reason about error-free transformations. On the other hand, bit-blasting produces enormous satisfiability problems that are only tractable for tiny mantissa widths. Verifying FPANs requires a technique that can precisely specify the magnitude and shape of a floating-point sum without reasoning through the value of every bit. To this end, we introduce a new abstract domain for floating-point reasoning, which we call the SELTZO abstraction.

Definition 2. *Let x be a floating-point number. The **sign-exponent leading-trailing zeros-ones (SELTZO) abstraction** of x is the ordered 6-tuple $(s_x, e_x, \mathsf{nlz}_x, \mathsf{nlo}_x, \mathsf{ntz}_x, \mathsf{nto}_x)$ consisting of:*

1. *the sign bit s_x and exponent e_x of x;*
2. *the counts $(\mathsf{nlz}_x, \mathsf{nlo}_x)$ of leading zeros and ones, respectively, in the mantissa of x, ignoring the implicit leading bit; and*
3. *the counts $(\mathsf{ntz}_x, \mathsf{nto}_x)$ of trailing zeros and ones, respectively, in the mantissa of x, ignoring the implicit leading bit.*

For example, the SELTZO abstraction of $-1.0010011111_2 \times 2^7$ is $(1, 7, 2, 0, 0, 5)$, and the SELTZO abstraction of $+1.1111111111_2 \times 2^{-2}$ is $(0, -2, 0, 10, 0, 10)$. (Recall that the implicit leading bit is ignored when computing nlz_x and nlo_x.) When $x = \pm 0.0$, we set $e_x := e_{\min} - 1$ for consistency with IEEE 754 representation. Because we assume all floating-point numbers to be normalized or zero, $x = \pm 0.0$ is the only value we consider to have the property $e_x < e_{\min}$.

Our definition of the SELTZO abstraction is motivated by several design considerations that we will explore in the remainder of this section.

- The SELTZO abstraction precisely captures all of the FPAN correctness properties defined in Sect. 3 using linear inequalities in the precision p and the variables $(s_x, e_x, \mathsf{nlz}_x, \mathsf{nlo}_x, \mathsf{ntz}_x, \mathsf{nto}_x)$.
- The variables of the SELTZO abstraction are particularly well-behaved under the floating-point sum and TwoSum operations, which interact in a highly predictable fashion with long stretches of leading or trailing zeros and ones.
- As shown by the worst-case inputs found by Joldes, Muller, and Popescu [35], FPANs tend to exhibit pathological behavior near powers of two, which mark the boundaries between different exponent values.

Note that distinct SELTZO abstract values correspond to disjoint sets of concrete floating-point values. In particular, the bit counts $(\mathsf{nlz}_x, \mathsf{nlo}_x, \mathsf{ntz}_x, \mathsf{nto}_x)$ are *not* cumulative; $\mathsf{ntz}_x = 3$ specifies concrete values with *exactly* three trailing zeros, no more. As these bit counts increase, the number of concrete values that correspond to a particular abstract value drops exponentially, making the SELTZO abstraction more precise for floating-point numbers with many leading mantissa zeros or ones. These are precisely the floating-point numbers that lie near the boundaries between different exponent values.

4.1   SELTZO Correctness Properties

To verify FPANs, the SELTZO abstraction must be able to express necessary and sufficient conditions for the FPAN correctness properties defined in Sect. 3, i.e., nonoverlapping invariants of the form $x = \mathsf{RNE}(x + y)$ and relative error bounds of the form $|y| \le C\mathbf{u}^k|x|$. The following propositions express these properties as linear inequalities in the SELTZO variables $(s_x, e_x, \mathsf{nlz}_x, \mathsf{nlo}_x, \mathsf{ntz}_x, \mathsf{nto}_x)$ and the precision p of the underlying floating-point format.

Proposition 1. *Let x and y be finite precision-p floating-point numbers in the binary16, bfloat16, binary32, binary64, or binary128 formats (defined in Table 1). Using the notation of Definition 2, x and y satisfy the nonoverlapping property $x = \mathsf{RNE}(x + y)$ if and only if at least one of the following conditions holds:*

1. $y = \pm 0.0$.
2. $e_x - e_y > p + 1$.
3. $e_x - e_y = p + 1$ and one or more of the following sub-conditions holds:
   (a) $s_x = s_y$.
   (b) $\mathsf{ntz}_x < p - 1$ *(i.e., x is not a power of 2).*
   (c) $\mathsf{ntz}_y = p - 1$ *(i.e., y is a power of 2).*
4. $e_x - e_y = p$, $\mathsf{ntz}_y = p - 1$, $\mathsf{ntz}_x \ge 1$, and one or more of the following sub-conditions holds:
   (a) $s_x = s_y$.
   (b) $\mathsf{ntz}_x < p - 1$.

We prove Proposition 1 by direct verification with a floating-point SMT solver for each of the formats listed in Table 1. All such solvers we are aware of, namely, Z3 [20], CVC5 [10], MathSAT [17], and Bitwuzla [49], report that the existence of a counterexample to Proposition 1 is unsatisfiable in all listed formats.

Because the SELTZO abstraction works directly with the bitwise representation of a floating-point number, it most naturally expresses relative error bounds $|y| \le C\mathbf{u}^k|x|$ where $C = 2^j$ is a power of two. We will restrict attention to error bounds in this form in the remainder of this paper.

Proposition 2. *Let x and y be finite precision-p floating-point numbers in any format. If $e_x - e_y > kp - j$ or $e_y = e_{\min} - 1$, then $|y| \le 2^j \mathbf{u}^k |x|$.*

Proof. If $e_y = e_{\min} - 1$, then $y = \pm 0.0$ and the desired conclusion holds trivially. Otherwise, we have $|x| \in [2^{e_x}, (2 - 2\mathbf{u})2^{e_x}]$ and $|y| \in [2^{e_y}, (2 - 2\mathbf{u})2^{e_y}]$. From the lower bound on x and the upper bound on $|y|$, it follows that:

$$\frac{|y|}{|x|} \leq \frac{(2 - 2\mathbf{u})2^{e_y}}{2^{e_x}} = (1 - \mathbf{u})2^{-(e_x - e_y - 1)} \leq (1 - \mathbf{u})2^{j - kp} < 2^j \mathbf{u}^k \qquad (9)$$

This proves $|y| < 2^j \mathbf{u}^k |x|$, as required. □

4.2   SELTZO Abstraction of TwoSum

In addition to expressing correctness properties, the SELTZO abstraction must also precisely capture the behavior of the TwoSum operation. In particular, it must be able to state relations between abstract inputs and outputs that rule out impossible input-output pairs. Relations of this type allow us to verify FPANs by ruling out the possibility of an output that violates a correctness property. The following proposition shows that the set of possible outputs of the TwoSum operation is highly constrained.

Proposition 3. *Let x and y be finite precision-p floating-point numbers in the binary16, bfloat16, binary32, binary64, or binary128 formats (defined in Table 1). The pair (x, y) is a possible output of TwoSum if and only if x and y satisfy at least one of the conditions listed in Proposition 1.*

Proof. First, observe that TwoSum is an idempotent operation, i.e., every output of TwoSum is a fixed point. To see this, let (x, y) be an arbitrary pair of finite precision-p floating-point numbers and set $(s_1, e_1) := \mathsf{TwoSum}(x, y)$ and $(s_2, e_2) := \mathsf{TwoSum}(s_1, e_1)$. By the defining property of TwoSum, we have $x + y = s_1 + e_1 = s_2 + e_2$, from which we deduce $s_2 = \mathsf{RNE}(s_1 + e_1) = \mathsf{RNE}(x + y) = s_1$ and $e_2 = x + y - s_2 = x + y - s_1 = e_1$.

Next, observe that $x = \mathsf{RNE}(x, y)$ if and only if $(x, y) = \mathsf{TwoSum}(x, y)$. Indeed, if $x = x \oplus y$, then $\mathsf{TwoSum}(x, y) = (x \oplus y, (x + y) - (x \oplus y)) = (x, y)$. Combining these two observations, we see that (x, y) is a possible output of TwoSum if and only if $x = \mathsf{RNE}(x + y)$, which is the desired result. □

Propositions 1 and 3 give a sharp characterization of the set of all possible outputs of TwoSum ranging over all possible inputs. However the inputs to a TwoSum gate inside an FPAN are typically constrained, either by assumed hypotheses (e.g., inputs y_0 and y_1 are assumed to be nonoverlapping) or as a consequence of previous TwoSum gates producing its inputs. Thus, the analysis of FPANs requires characterizing the set of possible TwoSum outputs not only over the full domain of all possible inputs, but also on restricted subdomains created by these input constraints.

In an associated technical report [61], we state a collection of several dozen lemmas that precisely characterize possible TwoSum outputs on various input subdomains. We have formally verified the correctness of all of these lemmas for the binary16, bfloat16, binary32, binary64, and binary128 formats using a portfolio of floating-point SMT solvers, including Z3 [20], CVC5 [10], MathSAT [17], and Bitwuzla [49]. In many cases, we have also proven that these lemmas are the strongest possible in the sense that every abstract output not explicitly ruled out by the lemma is witnessed by some concrete input. We provide a full listing of these lemmas in mechanized form using the Z3 Python API in our implementation, available at https://github.com/dzhang314/FPANVerifier.

5   Verification

With the SELTZO abstraction defined, we can now state our automatic FPAN verification procedure. Suppose we are given an FPAN F and a property P that is expressible as a logical combination of linear inequalities in the SELTZO variables $(s_x, e_x, \mathsf{nlz}_x, \mathsf{nlo}_x, \mathsf{ntz}_x, \mathsf{nto}_x)$. We construct a statement $S_{P,F}$ in quantifier-free Presburger arithmetic that expresses the existence of an abstract counterexample to $P(F)$. If this statement is unsatisfiable, then $P(F)$ has no abstract counterexamples. Hence, no concrete counterexample exists, and $P(F)$ is proven.

The first step of this procedure is to assign a unique label v_i to every wire segment in F. Every TwoSum gate delineates a new segment of the wires it connects. Thus, an FPAN with n wires and g gates has $n + 2g$ distinct wire segments. We then introduce SELTZO variables $(s_{v_i}, e_{v_i}, \mathsf{nlz}_{v_i}, \mathsf{nlo}_{v_i}, \mathsf{ntz}_{v_i}, \mathsf{nto}_{v_i})$ indexed by the labels v_i, creating a total of $6n + 12g$ variables.

We construct the statement $S_{P,F}$ as a logical conjunction of three types of conditions: (1) *consistency conditions* that enforce the validity of the abstract values $(s_v, e_v, \mathsf{nlz}_v, \mathsf{nlo}_v, \mathsf{ntz}_v, \mathsf{nto}_v)$; (2) *execution conditions* that constrain the possible outputs of each TwoSum gate; and (3) *counterexample conditions* that encode the negation of the property $P(F)$ that we wish to prove.

We first state the consistency conditions in Eqs. (10)–(17), which give a necessary and sufficient characterization of all valid SELTZO abstract values. One copy of these consistency conditions is instantiated for each label v_i.

1. The sign bit must be zero or one, and the exponent must be bounded below.

$$(s_v = 0) \lor (s_v = 1) \qquad\qquad e_v \geq e_{\min} - 1 \qquad (10)$$

We use $e = e_{\min} - 1$ to encode zero. Note that we do *not* impose an upper bound on e to ease handing of subnormal values, as explained in Sect. 5.1.

2. If a floating-point variable is zero (i.e., $e_v = e_{\min} - 1$), then its mantissa must consist entirely of zeros.

$$(e_v = e_{\min} - 1) \to [(\mathsf{nlz}_v = \mathsf{ntz}_v = p - 1) \land (\mathsf{nlo}_v = \mathsf{nto}_v = 0)] \qquad (11)$$

3. The leading and trailing bits of the mantissa are either 0 or 1.

$$[(\mathsf{nlz}_v > 0) \land (\mathsf{nlo}_v = 0)] \lor [(\mathsf{nlz}_v = 0) \land (\mathsf{nlo}_v > 0)] \qquad (12)$$

$$[(\mathsf{ntz}_v > 0) \land (\mathsf{nto}_v = 0)] \lor [(\mathsf{ntz}_v = 0) \land (\mathsf{nto}_v > 0)] \qquad (13)$$

4. The number of leading and trailing bits must be bounded by $p-1$, the width of the mantissa.

$$(\mathsf{nlz}_v = \mathsf{ntz}_v = p - 1) \vee (\mathsf{nlz}_v + \mathsf{ntz}_v < p - 1) \tag{14}$$

$$(\mathsf{nlo}_v = \mathsf{nto}_v = p - 1) \vee (\mathsf{nlo}_v + \mathsf{nto}_v < p - 1) \tag{15}$$

$$(\mathsf{nlz}_v + \mathsf{nto}_v = p - 1) \vee (\mathsf{nlz}_v + \mathsf{nto}_v < p - 2) \tag{16}$$

$$(\mathsf{ntz}_v + \mathsf{nlo}_v = p - 1) \vee (\mathsf{ntz}_v + \mathsf{nlo}_v < p - 2) \tag{17}$$

The upper bound of $p-2$ in the last two conditions expresses the constraint that, in a bit string of the form $00\cdots0b11\cdots1$, the middle bit b either belongs to the group of leading zeros or trailing ones. Thus, $\mathsf{nlz}_v + \mathsf{nto}_v \neq p - 2$.

We then adjoin a set of execution conditions to $S_{P,F}$ to constrain the possible outputs of each TwoSum gate conditioned on its inputs. Each of these sets comprises hundreds of inequalities collectively stated in Propositions 1 and 3, along with the lemmas given in the associated technical report [61]. A separate copy of the execution conditions must be instantiated on each TwoSum gate in F.

Finally, we add counterexample conditions to encode the *negation* of the property $P(F)$ that we wish to prove. These conditions must be formulated such that any concrete counterexample to the desired property $P(F)$ would have SELTZO abstract values that violate the counterexample conditions. Any property that is expressible in as a logical combination of linear inequalities in the SELTZO variables can be used to construct these conditions. By Propositions 1 and 2, this class includes both nonoverlapping invariants of the form $x = \mathsf{RNE}(x + y)$ and relative error bounds of the form $|y| \leq 2^j \mathbf{u}^k |x|$.

By combining our procedure with an SMT solver for the theory QF_LIA of quantifier-free Presburger arithmetic, we now have all necessary technical tools to automatically verify correctness properties of FPANs. Note that our procedure is sound but not complete; successful verification proves that no counterexamples exist, but failure to verify does not prove that a concrete counterexample exists. However, an abstract counterexample serves as an excellent starting point from which to either construct a concrete counterexample or to prove none exists by adding additional lemmas on new input subdomains to the execution conditions.

5.1 Handling Subnormal Values

Note that our consistency conditions do not impose an upper bound on the exponent e_x of any abstract value. This means that the unsatisfiability of $S_{P,F}$ actually proves a stronger result: there are no counterexamples to $P(F)$ even in a hypothetical floating-point format with infinite exponent range. This key observation enables all of the analysis we have presented so far to generalize to subnormal inputs, as long as the property P depends only on differences between exponents $e_x - e_y$ and not absolute exponent values. In particular, all of the properties stated in Propositions 1 and 2 satisfy this requirement.

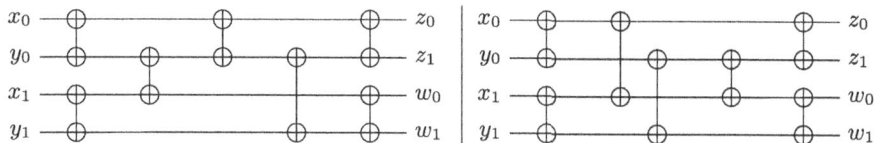

Fig. 7. Augmented network diagrams for ddadd (left) and madd (right), our new double-double addition algorithm, with error terms explicitly computed and named. The extra TwoSum gate used to compute these error terms serves only to facilitate our analysis and should not be included in an actual implementation of either algorithm.

Proposition 4. *If $S_{P,F}$ is unsatisfiable and the property P is expressible using only $(s_v, \mathsf{nlz}_v, \mathsf{nlo}_v, \mathsf{ntz}_v, \mathsf{nto}_v)$ and exponent differences of the form $e_v - e_w$, then $P(F)$ holds for all finite inputs.*

Proof. We prove the contrapositive. Suppose there exists a concrete counterexample to $P(F)$ consisting of finite (possibly subnormal) floating-point input values $(x_1, x_2, \ldots, x_n)$. Any property P expressible in this form is invariant under a global shift of all exponents. Hence, for any sufficiently large k, the SELTZO abstraction of $(2^k x_1, 2^k x_2, \ldots, 2^k x_n)$ yields an abstract counterexample to $P(F)$ consisting only of normalized abstract values. We may ignore the possibility of overflow in this construction because our abstraction uses an unbounded exponent range. This proves that $S_{P,F}$ is satisfiable.   □

6   Results

We apply the machinery developed in this paper to prove tight error bounds for both the current state-of-the-art double-double addition algorithm (ddadd), used in many software libraries [19,42,58], and a novel algorithm that is simultaneously faster and more accurate than ddadd. Our new algorithm, named madd (for "More Accurate Double-Double addition"), reduces the relative error of double-double addition from $3\mathbf{u}^2$ to $2\mathbf{u}^2$ while lowering its circuit depth from 5 to 4. FPANs for both algorithms are shown in Fig. 1.

Theorem 1. *Let (x_0, x_1) and (y_0, y_1) be floating-point expansions in the binary16, bfloat16, binary32, binary64, or binary128 format with $x_0 = \mathsf{RNE}(x_0 + x_1)$ and $y_0 = \mathsf{RNE}(y_0 + y_1)$. The ddadd algorithm, depicted in Fig. 1 (left), computes a floating-point expansion (z_0, z_1) that approximates the exact sum $x_0 + x_1 + y_0 + y_1$ with relative error bounded above by $(1 + 2\mathbf{u})2^{-(2p-2)} \approx 4\mathbf{u}^2$.*

Theorem 2. *Let (x_0, x_1) and (y_0, y_1) be floating-point expansions in the binary16, bfloat16, binary32, binary64, or binary128 format with $x_0 = \mathsf{RNE}(x_0 + x_1)$ and $y_0 = \mathsf{RNE}(y_0 + y_1)$. The madd algorithm, depicted in Fig. 1 (right), computes a floating-point expansion (z_0, z_1) that approximates the exact sum $x_0 + x_1 + y_0 + y_1$ with relative error bounded above by $(1 + 2\mathbf{u})2^{-(2p-1)} \approx 2\mathbf{u}^2$.*

We prove Theorems 1 and 2 by using the SELTZO abstraction to establish $P(F)$ for a suitably chosen property P given below. Some subsequent algebraic manipulation is then necessary to transform P into a true relative error bound that considers all discarded outputs.

Proof. Consider the augmented FPANs depicted in Fig. 7, which include an extra TwoSum gate to compute the error terms (w_0, w_1). Using the SELTZO encodings stated in Propositions 1 and 2, we use an SMT solver to prove

$$P := (x_0 = \mathsf{RNE}(x_0 + x_1)) \wedge (y_0 = \mathsf{RNE}(y_0 + y_1)) \rightarrow (|w_0| \leq 2^j \mathbf{u}^2 |z_0|) \quad (18)$$

where $j = 2$ for ddadd and $j = 1$ for madd. Moreover, by Proposition 3, we have $z_0 = \mathsf{RNE}(z_0, z_1)$ and $w_0 = \mathsf{RNE}(w_0, w_1)$ because (z_0, z_1) and (w_0, w_1) are TwoSum outputs. It follows that $w_0 + w_1 = (1 + \delta_w)w_0$ and $z_0 + z_1 = (1 + \delta_z)z_0$ for some $|\delta_w|, |\delta_z| \leq \mathbf{u}$. Hence, the relative error of the sums computed by ddadd and madd is bounded above by:

$$\frac{|(z_0 + z_1) - (x_0 + x_1 + y_0 + y_1)|}{|x_0 + x_1 + y_0 + y_1|} = \frac{|(1 + \delta_w)w_0|}{|(1 + \delta_z)z_0 + (1 + \delta_w)w_0|}$$

$$\leq \frac{(1 + \mathbf{u})|w_0|}{(1 - \mathbf{u})(|z_0| - |w_0|)} \leq \frac{(1 + \mathbf{u})2^j\mathbf{u}^2}{1 - (1 - \mathbf{u})2^j\mathbf{u}^2} \leq (1 + 2\mathbf{u})2^j\mathbf{u}^2 \quad (19)$$

This expression is asymptotically equivalent to $4\mathbf{u}^2 + O(\mathbf{u}^3)$ for ddadd and $2\mathbf{u}^2 + O(\mathbf{u}^3)$ for madd. □

In Table 2, we compare the speed of directly verifying the property P defined above using a variety of floating-point theory solvers (QF_FP) to resolving the satisfiability problems $S_{P,F}$ constructed by the SELTZO abstraction with a Presburger arithmetic solver (QF_LIA). We benchmark a portfolio of state-of-the-art SMT solvers using the latest software versions available at the time of writing, with the SELTZO abstraction implemented using the Z3 Python API. Our implementation is freely available at https://github.com/dzhang314/FPANVerifier. In all cases, the SELTZO abstraction produces problems that are many orders of magnitude faster to solve. We also note that our SELTZO solve times remain constant with respect to the precision p of the floating-point format, enabling scalability to wide formats that are intractable for bit-blasting.

Note that our bound of $4\mathbf{u}^2$ for ddadd is slightly looser than the $3\mathbf{u}^2$ bound proven by Joldes, Muller, and Popescu [35]. Our use of the SELTZO abstraction restricts us to proving bounds of the form $2^j\mathbf{u}^k + O(\mathbf{u}^{k+1})$, which we say are *tight to the nearest bit* if the leading constant factor is the smallest possible power of two (i.e., j is as small as possible). The following example due to Muller and Rideau [46] shows that our ddadd bound ($j = 2$) is tight to the nearest bit:

$$x_0 := 1 \qquad x_1 := \mathbf{u} - \mathbf{u}^2 \qquad y_0 := -\frac{1}{2} + \frac{\mathbf{u}}{2} \qquad y_1 := -\frac{\mathbf{u}^2}{2} + \mathbf{u}^3 \quad (20)$$

It is straightforward to verify that the result returned by ddadd has relative error $\approx 3\mathbf{u}^2$ on these inputs. Moreover, the following example shows that our madd

Table 2. Execution time for various SMT solvers to directly verify property P in a floating-point theory (QF_FP) compared to deciding the satisfiability of $S_{P,F}$ in quantifier-free Presburger arithmetic (QF_LIA). A "DNF" entry indicates that a solver did not terminate within three days, while an "N/A" entry indicates that a solver rejected the problem as unsolvable. These benchmarks were performed on an AMD Ryzen 9 9950X processor using Z3 4.13.4, CVC5 1.2.0, MathSAT 5.6.11, Bitwuzla 0.7.0, and Colibri2 0.4. SELTZO satisfiability problems were solved using Z3 4.13.4.

FPAN	Format	Z3	CVC5	MathSAT	Bitwuzla	Colibri2	SELTZO
ddadd	binary16	DNF	153 min	DNF	72 min	N/A	0.927 s
madd	binary16	DNF	120 min	3898 min	72 min	N/A	0.713 s
ddadd	bfloat16	DNF	704 min	DNF	71 min	N/A	0.838 s
madd	bfloat16	DNF	946 min	DNF	99 min	N/A	0.689 s
ddadd	binary32	DNF	1088 min	DNF	640 min	N/A	0.774 s
madd	binary32	DNF	1019 min	DNF	518 min	N/A	0.722 s
ddadd	binary64	DNF	DNF	DNF	DNF	N/A	0.623 s
madd	binary64	DNF	DNF	DNF	DNF	N/A	0.923 s
ddadd	binary128	DNF	DNF	DNF	DNF	N/A	0.880 s
madd	binary128	DNF	DNF	DNF	DNF	N/A	0.991 s

bound ($j = 1$) is also tight to the nearest bit:

$$x_0 := 1 + 2\mathbf{u} \qquad x_1 := -\frac{\mathbf{u}}{2} - 2\mathbf{u}^2 \qquad y_0 := -\mathbf{u} \qquad y_1 := -\frac{\mathbf{u}^2}{2} - \mathbf{u}^3 \qquad (21)$$

The result returned by madd has relative error $\approx 1.5\mathbf{u}^2$ on these inputs.

6.1   Ablated Abstractions

It is natural to ask whether simpler abstractions than SELTZO can prove Theorems 1 and 2. To investigate this question, we consider two ablated abstractions that use subsets of the SELTZO variables $(s_x, e_x, \mathsf{nlz}_x, \mathsf{nlo}_x, \mathsf{ntz}_x, \mathsf{nto}_x)$.

Definition 3. *Let x be a floating-point number. Using the notation of Definition 2, the **SE abstraction** of x is the 2-tuple (s_x, e_x), and the **SETZ abstraction** of x is the 3-tuple $(s_x, e_x, \mathsf{ntz}_x)$.*

The SE and SETZ abstractions are natural simplifications of SELTZO that omit some or all information about mantissa bit patterns. Notably, the SETZ abstraction is still expressive enough to capture all of the conditions of Proposition 1, none of which refer to leading bits or trailing ones.

To perform FPAN verification with these simpler abstractions, we construct SE and SETZ satisfiability problems $S_{P,F}$ using special sets of reduced lemmas [61] that make no reference to the omitted variables nlz_x, nlo_x, nto_x, and (for the SE abstraction) ntz_x. We then find the minimum value of j for which the

Table 3. Strongest relative error bounds for ddadd and madd that are provable in the SE, SETZ, and SELTZO abstractions.

FPAN	SE	SETZ	SELTZO
ddadd	$2^{-(2p-7)} = 128\mathbf{u}^2$	$2^{-(2p-4)} = 16\mathbf{u}^2$	$2^{-(2p-2)} = 4\mathbf{u}^2$
madd	$2^{-(2p-6)} = 64\mathbf{u}^2$	$2^{-(2p-3)} = 8\mathbf{u}^2$	$2^{-(2p-1)} = 2\mathbf{u}^2$

property P defined above holds in each abstraction. These values are reported in Table 3. While SE and SETZ are unable to match the tight error bounds provable in the SELTZO abstraction, they still establish nontrivial bounds that are difficult to prove by hand. However, these results show that modeling leading mantissa bits is necessary to prove tight FPAN error bounds.

7   Related Work

Automatic Floating-Point Verification. Most existing techniques for automatic verification of floating-point algorithms rely on abstractions derived from rational or real arithmetic, such as interval enclosures, polyhedra, and relational domains [15,16,44,54]. These abstractions are fundamentally inapplicable to FPANs. The notion of an error-free transformation like TwoSum only exists in finite-precision rounded arithmetic and has no semantically equivalent analogue in exact real arithmetic. Indeed, in real arithmetic, $\mathsf{TwoSum}(x, y) = (x + y, 0)$ is a trivial operation. As our results show, precise reasoning about FPANs requires explicitly modeling the interaction between the sum and error terms, taking into account the shape of the mantissa, which these abstractions cannot express.

Interactive Floating-Point Verification. To the best of our knowledge, the only existing methods that can reason about error-free transformations and FPANs use interactive, as opposed to automatic, theorem provers. Tools such as Flocq [13] and Gappa [22] have been used to verify algorithms involving FPANs [19,58], but they require a high degree of user expertise to construct sophisticated proof scripts. The SELTZO abstraction provides a complementary approach that could be integrated with these tools to provide a greater degree of automation.

Other Approaches to High-Precision Arithmetic. Libraries for arbitrary-precision arithmetic, including GMP, MPFR, and Arb, make no internal use of floating-point operations [28,31,34]. Instead, they implement arithmetic purely in terms of digit-by-digit integer operations. This approach allows for truly arbitrary precision, unconstrained by floating-point overflow and underflow limits, and avoids the complexity of propagating rounding errors that accompanies the use of error-free transformations. However, at moderate precision levels (2–8 machine words), these algorithms are many times slower than FPANs, requiring complex branching logic and more operations per bit on average. While FPANs are hard to discover and prove correct, they enable high-performance branch-free arithmetic that massively accelerates high-precision scientific applications.

Scalable Abstraction in Other Domains. Recent work on the Bitwuzla SMT solver [50] has used lemmas for integer multiplication and division to accelerate bit-vector verification, enabling scalability to previously intractable bit-widths. The SELTZO abstraction can be thought of as a floating-point analogue of this approach, characterizing the TwoSum operation in a precision-independent fashion to avoid full-width bit-blasting. One notable difference is that our approach does not require abstraction refinement tailored to a specific mantissa width or FPAN.

Sorting Networks. FPANs are close analogues of sorting networks. Although they compute different operations, both are branch-free algorithms that accelerate sorting or accumulation of a fixed number of inputs in a data-parallel fashion. Because they both occupy a similar large combinatorial space, techniques for discovering and optimizing sorting networks, such as evolutionary algorithms [23], can also be applied to FPANs. Our work on the SELTZO abstraction provides an efficient correctness check that can be used to perform such a search.

8   Conclusion

In this paper, we defined *floating-point accumulation networks* (FPANs) and showed that FPANs are key building blocks used to construct extended-precision floating-point algorithms. To address the difficulty of analyzing floating-point rounding errors, which critically affects the correctness of FPANs, we introduced the SELTZO abstraction to enable efficient and precise automatic reasoning about FPANs using SMT solvers. Using the SELTZO abstraction, we developed computer-verified proofs of a number of FPAN correctness properties. In particular, we automatically and rigorously proved that madd, a novel FPAN for double-double addition, is simultaneously faster and more accurate than ddadd, the previous best known algorithm.

Acknowledgments. The authors thank Matthew Sotoudeh, Michael Paperr, Alexander J. Root, and the anonymous CAV reviewers for insightful comments on early drafts of this paper. We also thank Alan H. Karp and David H. Bailey for helpful discussions, references, and advice.

Disclosure of Interests. The authors have no conflicts of interest to declare that are relevant to the content of this article.

References

1. WebAssembly Core Specification. https://www.w3.org/TR/wasm-core-2/
2. IEEE standard for binary floating-point arithmetic: ANSI/IEEE Std 754-1985, pp. 1–20 (1985). https://doi.org/10.1109/IEEESTD.1985.82928

3. IEEE standard for floating-point arithmetic: IEEE Std 754-2008, pp. 1–70 (2008). https://doi.org/10.1109/IEEESTD.2008.4610935
4. IEEE standard for floating-point arithmetic. IEEE Std 754-2019 (Revision of IEEE 754-2008), pp. 1–84 (2019). https://doi.org/10.1109/IEEESTD.2019.8766229
5. Babuška, I.: Numerical stability in problems of linear algebra. SIAM J. Numer. Anal. **9**(1), 53–77 (1972). https://doi.org/10.1137/0709008
6. Bailey, D.H., Krasny, R., Pelz, R.: Multiple precision, multiple processor vortex sheet roll-up computation. Society for Industrial and Applied Mathematics (SIAM), Philadelphia (1993). https://www.osti.gov/biblio/54379
7. Bailey, D.H.: High-precision software directory (2024). https://www.davidhbailey.com/dhbsoftware/
8. Bailey, D.H., Borwein, J.M.: Hand-to-hand combat with thousand-digit integrals. J. Comput. Sci. **3**(3), 77–86 (2012). https://doi.org/10.1016/j.jocs.2010.12.004. https://www.sciencedirect.com/science/article/pii/S1877750310000773. Scientific Computation Methods and Applications
9. Bailey, D.: High-precision floating-point arithmetic in scientific computation. Comput. Sci. Eng. **7**(3), 54–61 (2005). https://doi.org/10.1109/MCSE.2005.52
10. Barbosa, H., et al.: cvc5: a versatile and industrial-strength SMT solver. In: TACAS 2022. LNCS, vol. 13243, pp. 415–442. Springer, Cham (2022). https://doi.org/10.1007/978-3-030-99524-9_24
11. Boldo, S., Graillat, S., Muller, J.M.: On the robustness of the 2Sum and Fast2Sum algorithms. ACM Trans. Math. Softw. **44**(1) (2017). https://doi.org/10.1145/3054947
12. Boldo, S., Joldes, M., Muller, J.-M., Popescu, V.: Formal verification of a floating-point expansion renormalization algorithm. In: Ayala-Rincón, M., Muñoz, C.A. (eds.) ITP 2017. LNCS, vol. 10499, pp. 98–113. Springer, Cham (2017). https://doi.org/10.1007/978-3-319-66107-0_7
13. Boldo, S., Melquiond, G.: Flocq: a unified library for proving floating-point algorithms in Coq. In: 2011 IEEE 20th Symposium on Computer Arithmetic, pp. 243–252 (2011). https://doi.org/10.1109/ARITH.2011.40
14. Boldo, S., Muller, J.M.: Exact and approximated error of the FMA. IEEE Trans. Comput. **60**(2), 157–164 (2011). https://doi.org/10.1109/TC.2010.139
15. Chapoutot, A.: Interval slopes as a numerical abstract domain for floating-point variables. In: Cousot, R., Martel, M. (eds.) SAS 2010. LNCS, vol. 6337, pp. 184–200. Springer, Heidelberg (2010). https://doi.org/10.1007/978-3-642-15769-1_12
16. Chen, L., Miné, A., Cousot, P.: A sound floating-point polyhedra abstract domain. In: Ramalingam, G. (ed.) APLAS 2008. LNCS, vol. 5356, pp. 3–18. Springer, Heidelberg (2008). https://doi.org/10.1007/978-3-540-89330-1_2
17. Cimatti, A., Griggio, A., Schaafsma, B.J., Sebastiani, R.: The MathSAT5 SMT solver. In: Piterman, N., Smolka, S.A. (eds.) TACAS 2013. LNCS, vol. 7795, pp. 93–107. Springer, Heidelberg (2013). https://doi.org/10.1007/978-3-642-36742-7_7
18. Collange, C., Joldes, M., Muller, J.M., Popescu, V.: Parallel floating-point expansions for extended-precision GPU computations. In: 2016 IEEE 27th International Conference on Application-specific Systems, Architectures and Processors (ASAP), pp. 139–146 (2016). https://doi.org/10.1109/ASAP.2016.7760783
19. Daramy-Loirat, C., et al.: CR-LIBM A library of correctly rounded elementary functions in double-precision. Research report, LIP (2006). https://ens-lyon.hal.science/ensl-01529804
20. de Moura, L., Bjørner, N.: Z3: an efficient SMT solver. In: Ramakrishnan, C.R., Rehof, J. (eds.) TACAS 2008. LNCS, vol. 4963, pp. 337–340. Springer, Heidelberg (2008). https://doi.org/10.1007/978-3-540-78800-3_24

21. Dekker, T.J.: A floating-point technique for extending the available precision. Numer. Math. **18**(3), 224–242 (1971). https://doi.org/10.1007/BF01397083
22. de Dinechin, F., Lauter, C., Melquiond, G.: Certifying floating-point implementations using Gappa (2007). https://ens-lyon.hal.science/ensl-00200830. Working paper or preprint
23. Dobbelaere, B.: SorterHunter (2024). https://github.com/bertdobbelaere/SorterHunter
24. ECMA International: Standard ECMA-262 - ECMAScript Language Specification, 15 edn. (2024). https://ecma-international.org/publications-and-standards/standards/ecma-262/
25. Elrod, C., Févotte, F.: Accurate and Efficiently Vectorized Sums and Dot Products in Julia (2019). https://hal.science/hal-02265534. Version submitted to the Correctness2019 workshop
26. Evstigneev, N., Ryabkov, O., Bocharov, A., Petrovskiy, V., Teplyakov, I.: Compensated summation and dot product algorithms for floating-point vectors on parallel architectures: error bounds, implementation and application in the krylov subspace methods. J. Comput. Appl. Math. **414**, 114434 (2022). https://doi.org/10.1016/j.cam.2022.114434. https://www.sciencedirect.com/science/article/pii/S0377042722002047
27. Python Software Foundation: The Python standard library: Built-in functions (2001–2025). https://docs.python.org/3/library/functions.html
28. Fousse, L., Hanrot, G., Lefèvre, V., Pélissier, P., Zimmermann, P.: MPFR: a multiple-precision binary floating-point library with correct rounding. ACM Trans. Math. Softw. **33**(2), 13-es (2007). https://doi.org/10.1145/1236463.1236468
29. Frolov, A.M.: High-precision, variational, bound-state calculations in coulomb three-body systems. Phys. Rev. E **62**, 8740–8745 (2000). https://doi.org/10.1103/PhysRevE.62.8740
30. Frolov, A.M., Bailey, D.H.: Highly accurate evaluation of the few-body auxiliary functions and four-body integrals. J. Phys. B At. Mol. Opti. Phys. **36**(9), 1857 (2003). https://doi.org/10.1088/0953-4075/36/9/315
31. Granlund, T., Team, G.D.: GNU MP 6.0 Multiple Precision Arithmetic Library. Samurai Media Limited, London, GBR (2015)
32. He, Y., Ding, C.: Using accurate arithmetics to improve numerical reproducibility and stability in parallel applications. J. Supercomput. **18**(3), 259–277 (2001). https://doi.org/10.1023/A:1008153532043
33. Hida, Y., Li, X., Bailey, D.: Algorithms for quad-double precision floating point arithmetic. In: Proceedings 15th IEEE Symposium on Computer Arithmetic. ARITH-15 2001, pp. 155–162 (2001). https://doi.org/10.1109/ARITH.2001.930115. https://ieeexplore.ieee.org/document/930115. ISSN: 1063-6889
34. Johansson, F.: Arb: efficient arbitrary-precision midpoint-radius interval arithmetic. IEEE Trans. Comput. **66**, 1281–1292 (2017). https://doi.org/10.1109/TC.2017.2690633
35. Joldes, M., Muller, J.M., Popescu, V.: Tight and rigorous error bounds for basic building blocks of double-word arithmetic. ACM Trans. Math. Softw. **44**(2) (2017). https://doi.org/10.1145/3121432
36. Joldes, M., Muller, J.M., Popescu, V., Tucker, W.: CAMPARY: cuda multiple precision arithmetic library and applications. In: 5th International Congress on Mathematical Software (ICMS), Berlin, Germany (2016). https://hal.science/hal-01312858
37. Kahan, W.: Pracniques: further remarks on reducing truncation errors. Commun. ACM **8**(1), 40 (1965). https://doi.org/10.1145/363707.363723

38. Karp, A.H., Markstein, P.: High-precision division and square root. ACM Trans. Math. Softw. **23**(4), 561–589 (1997). https://doi.org/10.1145/279232.279237
39. Knuth, D.E.: The Art of Computer Programming, Volume II: Seminumerical Algorithms. Addison-Wesley (1969). https://www.worldcat.org/oclc/310551264
40. Knuth, D.E.: The Art of Computer Programming, Volume III: Sorting and Searching. Addison-Wesley (1973)
41. Lauter, C.Q.: Basic building blocks for a triple-double intermediate format. Research Report RR-5702, LIP RR-2005-38, INRIA, LIP (2005). https://inria.hal.science/inria-00070314
42. Li, X.S., et al.: Design, implementation and testing of extended and mixed precision BLAS. ACM Trans. Math. Softw. **28**(2), 152–205 (2002). https://doi.org/10.1145/567806.567808
43. Lu, M., He, B., Luo, Q.: Supporting extended precision on graphics processors. In: Proceedings of the Sixth International Workshop on Data Management on New Hardware, DaMoN 2010, pp. 19–26. ACM, New York (2010). https://doi.org/10.1145/1869389.1869392
44. Monniaux, D.: The pitfalls of verifying floating-point computations. ACM Trans. Program. Lang. Syst. **30**(3) (2008). https://doi.org/10.1145/1353445.1353446
45. Muller, J.M., et al.: Handbook of Floating-Point Arithmetic. Springer, Cham (2018). https://doi.org/10.1007/978-3-319-76526-6
46. Muller, J.M., Rideau, L.: Formalization of double-word arithmetic, and comments on "tight and rigorous error bounds for basic building blocks of double-word arithmetic". ACM Trans. Math. Softw. **48**(1) (2022). https://doi.org/10.1145/3484514
47. Møller, O.: Quasi double-precision in floating point addition. BIT Numer. Math. **5**(1), 37–50 (1965). https://doi.org/10.1007/BF01975722
48. Neumaier, A.: Rundungsfehleranalyse einiger verfahren zur summation endlicher summen. ZAMM J. Appl. Math. Mech./Zeitschrift für Angewandte Mathematik und Mechanik **54**(1), 39–51 (1974). https://doi.org/10.1002/zamm.19740540106
49. Niemetz, A., Preiner, M.: Bitwuzla. In: Enea, C., Lal, A. (eds.) Computer Aided Verification - 35th International Conference, CAV 2023, Paris, France, 17–22 July 2023, Proceedings, Part II. Lecture Notes in Computer Science, vol. 13965, pp. 3–17. Springer (2023). https://doi.org/10.1007/978-3-031-37703-7_1
50. Niemetz, A., Preiner, M., Zohar, Y.: Scalable bit-blasting with abstractions. In: Gurfinkel, A., Ganesh, V. (eds.) Computer Aided Verification, pp. 178–200. Springer, Cham (2024)
51. Ogita, T., Rump, S.M., Oishi, S.: Accurate sum and dot product. SIAM J. Sci. Comput. **26**(6), 1955–1988 (2005). https://doi.org/10.1137/030601818
52. Priest, D.: Algorithms for arbitrary precision floating point arithmetic. In: [1991] Proceedings 10th IEEE Symposium on Computer Arithmetic, pp. 132–143 (1991). https://doi.org/10.1109/ARITH.1991.145549
53. The Julia Project: Julia standard library: Arrays (2017). https://docs.julialang.org/en/v0.6/stdlib/arrays
54. Rivera, J., Franchetti, F., Püschel, M.: Floating-point TVPI abstract domain. Proc. ACM Program. Lang. **8**(PLDI) (2024). https://doi.org/10.1145/3656395
55. Rump, S.M., Lange, M.: On the definition of unit roundoff. BIT Numer. Math. **56**(1), 309–317 (2016). https://doi.org/10.1007/s10543-015-0554-0
56. Sarnoff, J.: DoubleFloats.jl (2024). https://github.com/JuliaMath/DoubleFloats.jl
57. Shewchuk, J.R.: Adaptive precision floating-point arithmetic and fast robust geometric predicates. Discrete Comput. Geom. **18**(3), 305–363 (1997). https://doi.org/10.1007/PL00009321

58. Sibidanov, A., Zimmermann, P., Glondu, S.: The CORE-MATH Project. In: 2022 IEEE 29th Symposium on Computer Arithmetic (ARITH), virtual, France, pp. 26–34. IEEE (2022). https://doi.org/10.1109/ARITH54963.2022.00014. https://inria.hal.science/hal-03721525

59. Veltkamp, G.W.: ALGOL procedures voor het berekenen van een inwendig product in dubbele precisie. Technical Report 22, Technische Hogeschool Eindhoven (1968)

60. Veltkamp, G.W.: ALGOL procedures voor het rekenen in dubbele lengte. Technical Report 21, Technische Hogeschool Eindhoven (1969)

61. Zhang, D.K., Aiken, A.: Automatic verification of floating-point accumulation networks (2025)

62. Zhang, D.K.: MultiFloats.jl (2024). https://github.com/dzhang314/MultiFloats.jl

Counting Abstraction and Decidability for the Verification of Structured Parameterized Networks

Marius Bozga[1] , Radu Iosif[1] , Arnaud Sangnier[2] , and Neven Villani[1(✉)]

[1] Univ. Grenoble Alpes, CNRS, Grenoble INP,
VERIMAG, 38401 Saint Martin d'Hères, France
{marius.bozga,radu.iosif,
neven.villani}@univ-grenoble-alpes.fr
[2] DIBRIS, University of Genova, Genoa, Italy
arnaud.sangnier@unige.it

Abstract. We consider the verification of parameterized networks of replicated processes whose architecture is described by hyperedge-replacement graph grammars in the style of Courcelle. Due to the undecidability of verification problems such as reachability or coverability of a given configuration, in which we count the number of replicas in each local state, we develop two orthogonal verification techniques. We present a counting abstraction able to produce, from a graph grammar describing a parameterized system, a finite set of Petri nets that over-approximate the behaviors of the original system. The counting abstraction is implemented in a prototype tool, evaluated on a non-trivial set of test cases. Moreover, we identify a decidable fragment, for which the coverability problem is in 2EXPTIME and PSPACE-hard.

1 Introduction

The architecture is a crucial design aspect for the functionality of a computer network. For instance, the code of a consensus protocol changes depending on whether it is used in a ring or a clique-shaped network. The architecture also influences the traffic balance and overall efficiency of communication. Formal modelling of network architectures is a key enabler for the use of verification algorithms that prove absence of error scenarios in a distributed environment (*e.g.* deadlocks, races or mutual exclusion violations), or convergence towards a desired goal (*e.g.* building a spanning-tree or electing a leader).

The impressive size of present day networks requires *parameterized models*, that describe infinite families of networks having an unbounded number of nodes. The problem of *parameterized verification* (*i.e.* proving correctness for any number of processes) often amounts to model-checking a small cut-off of the system (see [8] for a survey). In cases where a cut-off does not exist or is too large, symbolic representations of invariants (*i.e.* sets of configurations closed under local and communication actions) using *e.g.* boolean constraints [19], well-structured transitions systems [1], monadic second-order logic [11] or finite-state

R. Piskac and Z. Rakamarić (Eds.): CAV 2025, LNCS 15933, pp. 238–262, 2025.
https://doi.org/10.1007/978-3-031-98682-6_13

automata [28] can be used to decide a parameterized safety problem in a matter of seconds. This is because, in particular, parameterized verification methods do not suffer from the state explosion problem of classical model-checking techniques, that scale poorly in the number of concurrent processes.

However, a current limitation is that most techniques rely on hard-coded network topologies, typically cliques [22], rings [14] or combinations thereof [5]. Many architecture description languages have been developed by the software engineering community (see, e.g. [13,15] for surveys) to support network design but, in general, these languages lack support for verification. Only few recent parameterized verification techniques take architectures as input of the problem, described using, e.g. first-order [9] or separation logic [12]. Such descriptive (logic-based) languages are typically hard to use, because of the generality of their semantics, that requires complex frame conditions to specify what is actually *not* part of the architecture.

Contributions. We consider the parametric verification problem for process networks specified by *graph grammars* that use operations of the standard *hyperedge-replacement* (HR) algebra of graphs [17] to describe how graphs are inductively build from smaller subgraphs. This constructive aspect of graph grammars makes them appealing for network design, because recursive specification of types and datastructures are widespread among programmers. Graph grammars are, moreover, at the core of a solid theory (see [17] for a comprehensive survey). In principle, HR graph grammars can specify families of graphs having bounded tree-width, such as chains, rings, stars, trees (of unbounded rank) and beyond, e.g. overlaid structures such as trees or stars with certain nodes linked in a list. Since cliques and grids are families of unbounded tree-width, neither can be specified using HR graph grammars.

Because the parameterized verification problem is undecidable, even for chain-like networks, we consider two orthogonal lines of work. First, following the seminal work of German and Sistla [22], where identities of processes communicating through rendezvous in a clique is ignored to keep only the number of processes in each state, we define a *counting abstraction* that folds the infinite set of networks specified using a HR grammar into a finite set of Petri nets, which subsumes the behaviors of the original set of networks. As a consequence, if a set of places is not covered by an execution of some of the resulting Petri nets, then it is not covered by the original set of behaviors. These coverability problems can be used to express mutual exclusion, and can encode other properties (e.g. finite-valued consensus). Even though, computing the counting abstraction for clique networks is fairly simple [22], it is less trivial for families of networks specified by a grammar. We circumvent these technical challenges by defining appropriate HR algebras, in which the abstraction can be computed by a finite Kleene iteration of the grammar. This line of work is motivated by several recent advances on the theory [20] and tool support [31] for the reachability and coverability problem for Petri nets. The abstraction has been implemented in a prototype tool and a number of experiments showing the effectiveness of the method have been carried out.

Second, we define a decidable fragment of the original problem, by restricting the local behavior of the nodes to *pebble-passing systems*, where a finite (but unbounded) number of identical pebbles can be moved from one node to another. We inspire ourselves from token-passing systems [4,6] for which a restriction on the behavior of each process allows to get decidability results of some verification problems. Note that in our case, the processes definition are simple, but we allow an unbounded number of tokens/pebbles. Interestingly, our decidable restriction applies only to the local behavior and does not restrict the family of networks considered, other than that they must be the language of a given HR grammar. Examples of problems from this decidable fragment include token-rings, tree-traversal used, in general, for notification and binary consensus among the participants of general (HR-specified) architectures. We have studied the complexity of the decidable fragment and found it to be doubly-exponential in the unary size of the coverability property and in the maximal tree-width the set of networks generated by the grammar. At the same time, we found the problem to be PSPACE-hard.

Related Work. Traditionally, verification of unbounded networks of parallel processes considers known architectural patterns, typically cliques or rings [14,22]. Because the price for decidability is drastic restriction on architecture styles [8], more recent works propose practical semi-algorithms, *e.g. regular model checking* [24] or *automata learning* [16]. Here the architecture is implicitly determined by the class of language recognizers: word automata encode pipelines or rings, whereas tree automata describe trees.

Specifying parameterized concurrent systems inductively is reminiscent of *network grammars* [23,26,29], that use inductive rules to describe systems with linear (pipeline, token-ring) architectures obtained by composition of an unbounded number of processes. In contrast, our language is based on the HRgraph algebra. Verification of network grammars against safety properties (reachability of error configurations) requires the synthesis of *network invariants* [33], computed by costly fixpoint iterations [27] or by abstracting (forgetting the particular values of indices in) the composition of a small number of instances [25]. A more recent line of work considers a lightweight invariant synthesis method based on the inference of *structural invariants*[1] of an infinite family of Petri nets, for parameterized systems whose network architectures are specified using logic [9,12]. This method is geared towards deadlock-freedom and mutual exclusion, whereas our counting abstraction method works for coverability properties, in general.

Other methods to verify safety properties of parameterized networks consist in changing the semantics of behaviors to obtain an over-approximation having a decidable safety verification problem. In [2], the authors have implemented such a scheme using a *monotonic abstraction*, where the resulting abstraction is a *well-structured transition systems* [1]. They first consider pipeline architectures,

---

[1] Invariants that depend on the structure of a Petri net, which hold for any of its executions.

where communication is done by checking existentially or universally the state of the other process. In [3], a similar technique is applied to networks with clique architectures, where processes can manipulate shared boolean and natural variables. In contrast, both our methods target network architectures defined by unrestricted HR graph grammars.

2 Preliminaries

We denote by $\mathbb{N}$ the set of positive integers, including zero. For $i, j \in \mathbb{N}$, we denote by $[i, j]$ the set $\{i, \ldots, j\}$, considered empty if $i > j$. The cardinality of a finite set A is denoted $\|A\|$. A singleton $\{a\}$ will be denoted a. By $A \subseteq_{fin} B$, we mean that A is a finite subset of B. The union of two disjoint sets A and B is denoted as $A \uplus B$. The Cartesian product of two sets A and B is denoted $A \times B$. As usual, we denote by A^* the set of (possibly empty) sequences of elements from A.

For a function $f : A \rightarrow B$ and $C \subseteq A$, we write $f(C) \stackrel{\text{def}}{=} \{f(c) \mid c \in C\}$ and $f \downharpoonright_C \stackrel{\text{def}}{=} \{(c, f(c)) \mid c \in C\}$. The inverse of a function $f : A \rightarrow B$ is the relation $f^{-1} \stackrel{\text{def}}{=} \{(f(a), a) \mid a \in A\}$. To alleviate notation, we write $f(x, y)$ instead of $f((x, y))$, when no confusion arises. For two functions $f : A \rightarrow B$ and $g : C \rightarrow D$, the function $f \times g : A \times B \rightarrow C \times D$ maps each pair $(a, c) \in A \times C$ into the pair $(f(a), g(c)) \in B \times D$. A bijective function $f : A \rightarrow A$ is a *finite permutation* if the set $\{a \in A \mid f(a) \neq a\}$ is finite. In particular, $a \leftrightarrow b$ denotes the finite permutation that switches a with b and leaves the other elements of the domain unchanged. A finite partial function is denoted as $f : A \rightharpoonup_{fin} B$ and $\text{dom}(f)$, $\text{img}(f)$ denote its domain and range, respectively. When $f : A \rightarrow C$ and $g : B \rightarrow C$ coincide on their shared domain $A \cap B$, we write $f \cup g : A \cup B \rightarrow C$ the function such that $(f \cup g) \downharpoonright_A = f$ and $(f \cup g) \downharpoonright_B = g$. The full version of the paper contains proofs of technical results [10].

2.1 Petri Nets

A *net* is a tuple $N = (Q, T, W)$, where Q is a finite set of *places*, T is a finite set of *transitions* such that $Q \cap T = \emptyset$ and $W : (Q \times T) \cup (T \times Q) \rightarrow \mathbb{N}$ is a *weighted incidence relation* between places and transitions. We denote by Q_N, T_N and W_N the places, transitions and incidence relation of N, respectively. For all $x, y \in Q \cup T$ such that $W(x, y) > 0$, we say that there is an *edge of weight* $W(x, y)$ between x and y. For an element $x \in Q \cup T$, we define the set of *predecessors* ${}^\bullet x \stackrel{\text{def}}{=} \{y \in Q \cup T \mid W(y, x) > 0\}$, *successors* $x^\bullet \stackrel{\text{def}}{=} \{y \in Q \cup T \mid W(x, y) > 0\}$ and predecessor-successor pair ${}^\bullet x^\bullet \stackrel{\text{def}}{=} ({}^\bullet x, x^\bullet)$.

A *marking* of $N = (Q, T, W)$ is a function $m : Q \rightarrow \mathbb{N}$. A transition t is *enabled* in m if $m(q) \geq W(q, t)$, for each place $q \in Q$. For all markings m, m' and transitions $t \in T$, we write $m \stackrel{t}{\leadsto} m'$ when t is enabled in m and $m'(q) = m(q) - W(q, t) + W(t, q)$, for all $q \in Q$. Given two markings m and m', a finite sequence of transitions $\mathbf{t} = (t_1, \ldots, t_n)$ is a *firing sequence*, written $m \stackrel{\mathbf{t}}{\leadsto} m'$, if and only if either (i) $n = 0$ and $m = m'$, or (ii) $n \geq 1$ and there exist markings $m_1, \ldots, m_{n-1}$ such that $m \overset{t_1}{\leadsto} m_1 \overset{t_2}{\leadsto} \ldots \overset{t_{n-1}}{\leadsto} m_{n-1} \overset{t_n}{\leadsto} m'$. A sequence t is *fireable* from m whenever there exists a marking m' such that $m \overset{t}{\leadsto} m'$.

A *Petri net* (PN) is a pair $\mathcal{N} = (N, m_0)$, where N is a net and m_0 is the *initial marking* of N. For simplicity, we write $Q_{\mathcal{N}} \overset{\text{def}}{=} Q_N$, $T_{\mathcal{N}} \overset{\text{def}}{=} T_N$, $W_{\mathcal{N}} \overset{\text{def}}{=} W_N$ and $\text{init}_{\mathcal{N}} \overset{\text{def}}{=} m_0$ for the elements of $\mathcal{N}$. A marking m is *reachable* in $\mathcal{N}$ iff there exists a firing sequence t such that $m_0 \overset{t}{\leadsto} m$. We denote by $\text{reach}(\mathcal{N})$ the set of reachable markings of $\mathcal{N}$. The *reachability problem* asks, given a PN $\mathcal{N}$ and a marking m, does $m \in \text{reach}(\mathcal{N})$? The *coverability problem* asks, for a given PN $\mathcal{N}$ and marking m, does there exists a marking $m' \in \text{reach}(\mathcal{N})$ such that $m \leq m'$? Here the order of markings is the pointwise order on $\mathbb{N}$, *i.e.* $m \leq m'$ iff $m(q) \leq m'(q)$ for all $q \in Q_{\mathcal{N}}$. The coverability problem is more concisely stated using the set of covered markings $\text{cover}(\mathcal{N}) \overset{\text{def}}{=} \{m \mid \exists m' \in \text{reach}(\mathcal{N}) \,.\, m \leq m'\}$, *i.e.* given $\mathcal{N}$ and m, does $m \in \text{cover}(\mathcal{N})$?

2.2   Parameterized Systems

We begin by defining parameterized communicating systems, *i.e.* graphs whose vertices model network nodes that run identical copies of one or more process types. Neighbouring processes synchronize their transitions according to the observable edge labels of the network graph. In most of the literature (see, *e.g.* [7] for a survey) process types are represented by finite labeled transition systems (LTS), *e.g.* with disjoint observable and internal alphabets of transition labels. For simplicity, here we use PNs whose transitions mimick closely the transitions of a LTS, thus avoiding the formal definition of the latter.

Let Λ and Δ be finite disjoint alphabets of vertex and edge labels, respectively. A (binary labeled) *graph* is a tuple $G = (V, E, \lambda)$, where V is a finite set of vertices, $E \subseteq V \times \Delta \times V$ is a set of labeled binary edges and $\lambda : V \to \Lambda$ maps each vertex to a vertex label. Edges (v_1, a, v_2) are written $v_1 \overset{a}{\to} v_2$. We denote by V_G, E_G and λ_G the vertices, edges and vertex labeling of G, respectively. We do not distinguish isomorphic graphs, *i.e.* graphs that differ only in the identities of their vertices.

Definition 1. *A process type* p *is a PN having weights at most 1 and exactly one marked place initially, whose transitions are partitioned into observable* T_p^{obs} *and internal* T_p^{int}, *i.e.* $T_p = T_p^{obs} \uplus T_p^{int}$, *and each transition has exactly one predecessor and one successor. Let* $\mathcal{P} = \{p_1, \ldots, p_k\}$ *be a finite fixed set of process types such that* $Q_{p_i} \neq \emptyset$, *for all* $i \in [1, k]$ *and* $Q_{p_i} \cap Q_{p_j} = \emptyset$, *for all* $1 \leq i < j \leq k$.

Because a process type has exactly one initial token and all transitions have one predecessor and one successor, both with weight exactly 1, every reachable marking of a process type has exactly one initial token. A PN having this property is said to be *automata-like*. We denote by $Q_{\mathcal{P}}$ and $T_{\mathcal{P}}^{obs}$ the sets of places and observable transitions from some $p \in \mathcal{P}$, respectively.

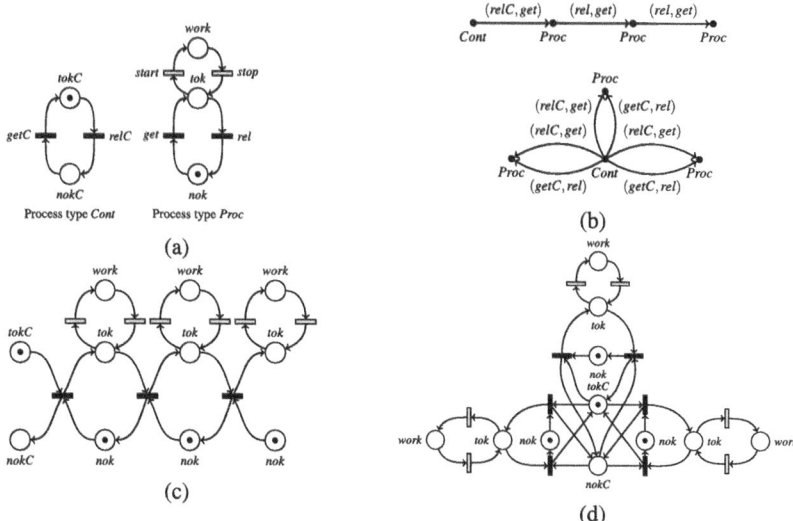

Fig. 1. Two process types (a), A system with chain-shape network S_1 (top) and a system with star-shape network S_2 (bottom) (b). Behavior of S_1 (c). Behavior of S_2 (d) (Color figure online)

Example 1. Figure 1(a) shows two process types *Cont* and *Proc*. They both represent entities that can hold a token and they can either grab a token, if they do not have it, or release the token, otherwise. The first one, which we identify as a controller, has only observable transitions, whereas the second one, which represents a worker process, has two internal transitions *start* and *stop* depicted in yellow. These transitions are used to simulate the fact that when the worker has the token, it can move to a working state, from which he cannot release the token and when it stops working, it can move back to a state from which the token can be released.

Definition 2. *A system* $S = (V, E, \lambda)$ *is a graph whose vertices are labeled with process types from* $\mathcal{P}$ *($\Lambda = \mathcal{P}$) and edges with pairs of observable transitions from* $T_{\mathcal{P}}^{obs}$ *(i.e.* $\Delta = T_{\mathcal{P}}^{obs} \times T_{\mathcal{P}}^{obs}$*), such that* $t_i \in T_{\lambda(v_i)}^{obs}$*, for both* $i = 1, 2$*, for each edge* $v_1 \xrightarrow{(t_1, t_2)} v_2 \in E_S$*.*

Example 2. Figure 1(b) shows two systems labeled with the process types given by Fig. 1(a). They both represent a network with four entities, one controller of type *Cont* and three working processes of type *Proc*. In S_1, the controller can pass a token to the first working process, which can pass the token to the second one which can pass the token to the third one. In S_2, the controller is at the center and it communicate with all the working processes that get and release the token.

The communication (*i.e.* synchronization between processes) in a system is formally captured by the following notion of behavior:

Definition 3. *A* behavior *is a PN* $\mathcal{N}$ *such that* $1 \leq \|{}^\bullet t\| = \|t^\bullet\| \leq 2$, *for each* $t \in T_{\mathcal{N}}$. *The* behavior *of a system* $S = (V, E, \lambda)$ *is* $\beta(S) \overset{\text{def}}{=} (N, m_0)$, *where:*

- $Q_N \overset{\text{def}}{=} \{(q, v) \mid q \in Q_{\lambda(v)}, v \in V\}$, *a place* (q, v) *corresponds to the place* q *of the process type* $\lambda(v)$ *that labels the vertex* v;
- $T_N \overset{\text{def}}{=} E \cup \{(t, v) \mid t \in T^{int}_{\lambda(v)}, v \in V\}$, *the transitions are either edges of the system (i.e. modeling the synchronizations of two processes) or pairs* (t, v) *corresponding to an internal transition* t *of the process type* $\lambda(v)$ *that labels the vertex* v;
- *the weight function* W_N *is defined below:*

$$W_N((q, v), v_1 \xrightarrow{(t_1, t_2)} v_2) \overset{\text{def}}{=} \begin{cases} W_{\lambda(v)}(q, t_i), & \text{if } v = v_i, \text{ for } i = 1, 2 \\ 0, & \text{otherwise} \end{cases}$$

$$W_N(v_1 \xrightarrow{(t_1, t_2)} v_2, (q, v)) \overset{\text{def}}{=} \begin{cases} W_{\lambda(v)}(t_i, q), & \text{if } v = v_i, \text{ for } i = 1, 2 \\ 0, & \text{otherwise} \end{cases}$$

$$W_N((q, v), (t, v')) \overset{\text{def}}{=} \begin{cases} W_{\lambda(v)}(q, t), & \text{if } v = v' \\ 0, & \text{otherwise} \end{cases} \quad W_N((t, v'), (q, v)) \overset{\text{def}}{=} \begin{cases} W_{\lambda(v)}(t, q), & \text{if } v = v' \\ 0, & \text{otherwise} \end{cases}$$

- $m_0(q, v) \overset{\text{def}}{=} \text{init}_{\lambda(v)}(q)$, *for all* $v \in V$ *and* $q \in Q_{\lambda(v)}$.

For example, Fig. 1(c) and (d) show the behaviors of the systems from Fig. 1(b). By construction, among places $\{(q, v) \mid q \in Q_{\lambda(v)}\}$ for any v, there is exactly one token in all reachable markings because $\lambda(v)$ is automata-like. By extension we say that such behaviors are automata-like.

A *parameterized system* $\mathbf{S} = \{S_1, S_2, \ldots\}$ is a possibly infinite set of systems, called *instances*. A parameterized system has an infinite set of behaviors, denoted as $\beta(\mathbf{S})$, *i.e.* one for each instance. The verification problems considered in this paper are, given a parameterized system $\mathbf{S}$ and a marking m for a subset Q of the places in $\mathcal{P}$, does there exist an instance of $\mathbf{S}$ whose behavior reaches (covers) a marking that agrees with m over Q? We shall define these problems formally, once we have introduced the language for the specification of parameterized systems.

2.3   Algebras

We recall a few notions on algebras needed in the following. A *signature* is a set of function symbols $F = \{op_1, op_2, \ldots\}$. An F-*term* is a term built with function symbols from F and variables of arity zero. An F-term is *ground* if it has no variables. An F-*algebra* $\mathcal{A} = (\mathbb{A}, op_1^{\mathcal{A}}, op_2^{\mathcal{A}}, \ldots)$ interprets the function symbols from F as functions over the *domain* $\mathbb{A}$. Given F-algebras $\mathcal{A}$ and $\mathcal{B}$ having domains $\mathbb{A}$ and $\mathbb{B}$, respectively, a *homomorphism* is a function $h : \mathbb{A} \to \mathbb{B}$ such that $h(op^{\mathcal{A}}(a_1, \ldots, a_n)) = op^{\mathcal{B}}(h(a_1), \ldots, h(a_n))$, for each function symbol $op \in F$ of arity n and $a_1, \ldots, a_n \in \mathbb{A}$. The *kernel* of a function $f : \mathbb{A} \to \mathbb{B}$ is the equivalence relation $\sim_{\ker(f)} \subseteq \mathbb{A} \times \mathbb{A}$ defined as $a_1 \sim_{\ker(f)} a_2 \iff f(a_1) = f(a_2)$. An equivalence relation $\sim\,\subseteq\,\mathbb{A}\times\mathbb{A}$ is an F-*congruence* if and only if, for each function symbol op $\in$ F of arity n and $a_1, a_1', \ldots, a_n, a_n' \in \mathbb{A}$ such that $a_i \sim a_i'$, for all $i \in [1, n]$, we have $\mathsf{op}^{\mathcal{A}}(a_1, \ldots, a_n) \sim \mathsf{op}^{\mathcal{A}}(a_1', \ldots, a_n')$.

Proposition 1. *Let $\mathcal{A}$ be an F-algebra having domain $\mathbb{A}$, and $f : \mathbb{A} \to \mathbb{B}$ be a function such that $\sim_{\ker(f)}$ is an F-congruence. Then f is a homomorphism between $\mathcal{A}$ and $\mathcal{B} \stackrel{\text{def}}{=} (f(\mathbb{A}), \{\mathsf{op}^{\mathcal{B}}\}_{\mathsf{op}\in\mathsf{F}})$, where $\mathsf{op}^{\mathcal{B}}(b_1, \ldots, b_n) \stackrel{\text{def}}{=} f(\mathsf{op}^{\mathcal{A}}(f^{-1}(b_1), \ldots, f^{-1}(b_n)))^2$, for each function symbol* op $\in$ F *of arity n and all $b_1, \ldots, b_n \in f(\mathbb{A})$. Consequently, $f(\theta^{\mathcal{A}}) = \theta^{\mathcal{B}}$, for each ground F-term θ.*

We introduce a standard signature of operations on graphs and define two algebras, of open systems and behaviors. Let Σ be a countably infinite set of *source labels*, fixed in the rest of the paper. With no loss of generality, we assume that Σ is partitioned into disjoint sets indexed by the process types $\mathcal{P} = \{\mathsf{p}_1, \ldots, \mathsf{p}_k\}$, *i.e.* $\Sigma = \Sigma_{\mathsf{p}_1} \uplus \ldots \uplus \Sigma_{\mathsf{p}_k}$. A source label $\sigma \in \Sigma$ uniquely identifies a process type $\mathrm{ptype}(\sigma) \in \mathcal{P}$ such that $\sigma \in \Sigma_{\mathrm{ptype}(\sigma)}$. A function $\alpha : \Sigma \to \Sigma$ is $\mathcal{P}$-*preserving* if $\mathrm{ptype}(\alpha(\sigma)) = \mathrm{ptype}(\sigma)$, for all $\sigma \in \Sigma$.

The signature of the *hyperedge-replacement* graph algebra (HR) [17] consists of the constants a_{σ_1, σ_2}, for all edge labels $a \in \Delta$ and source labels $\sigma_1, \sigma_2 \in \Sigma$, the unary symbols $\mathsf{restrict}_\tau$, for all $\tau \subseteq_{fin} \Sigma$, rename_α, for all $\mathcal{P}$-preserving finite permutations $\alpha : \Sigma \to \Sigma$ and the binary symbol $\oplus$. By HR congruence we mean an equivalence relation that is a congruence for the HR signature.

An *open system* is a pair $\check{\mathsf{S}} \stackrel{\text{def}}{=} (\mathsf{S}, \xi)$, where $\mathsf{S} = (\mathsf{V}, \mathsf{E}, \lambda)$ is a system and $\xi : \Sigma \to_{fin} \mathsf{V}_\mathsf{S}$ is an injective partial function that assigns source labels to vertices of S such that $\mathrm{ptype}(\sigma) = \lambda(\xi(\sigma))$, for each $\sigma \in \mathrm{dom}(\xi)$, *i.e.* the source label of a vertex has the process type of that vertex. We say that a vertex $v \in \mathsf{V}_\mathsf{S}$ is the σ-source of $\check{\mathsf{S}}$ if $\xi(\sigma) = v$. The *type* of $\check{\mathsf{S}}$ is $\mathrm{type}(\check{\mathsf{S}}) \stackrel{\text{def}}{=} \mathrm{dom}(\xi)$, *i.e.* the set of source labels that occurs in S. Since systems (Definition 2) are in fact open systems of empty type, we blur the distinction and refer to open systems as systems from now on.

The algebra $\mathcal{S}$ (Fig. 2) interprets the HR signature over the set $\mathbb{S}$ of systems:

- $a^{\mathcal{S}}_{\sigma_1, \sigma_2}$ is the system having a single a-labeled edge between its two vertices labeled with process types $\mathrm{ptype}(\sigma_1)$ and $\mathrm{ptype}(\sigma_2)$, that are the σ_1- and σ_2-sources, respectively, for each edge label $a \in \Delta$ and source labels $\sigma_1, \sigma_2 \in \Sigma$.
- $\mathsf{restrict}^{\mathcal{S}}_\tau(\mathsf{S}, \xi) \stackrel{\text{def}}{=} (\mathsf{S}, \xi\!\mid_\tau)$ removes the source labels that are not in $\tau \subseteq_{fin} \Sigma$,
- $\mathsf{rename}^{\mathcal{S}}_\alpha(\mathsf{S}, \xi) \stackrel{\text{def}}{=} (\mathsf{S}, \xi \circ \alpha^{-1})$ relabels the sources according to α; note that $\xi \circ \alpha^{-1}$ is an injective partial mapping, since α is a finite permutation of Σ,
- $(\mathsf{S}_1, \xi_1) \oplus^{\mathcal{S}} (\mathsf{S}_2, \xi_2)$ is the disjoint union of (S_1, ξ_1) and (S_2, ξ_2), followed by:
  * fusion of each pair of common σ-sources $v_i \in \mathsf{V}_{\mathsf{S}_i}$, for $\sigma \in \mathrm{type}(\mathsf{S}_1) \cap \mathrm{type}(\mathsf{S}_2)$ and $i = 1, 2$, into a σ-source labeled with $\mathrm{ptype}(\sigma)$,
  * fusion of all identical edges into a single edge with the same label and endpoints.

---

2 The right-hand side of this definition is a singleton that we identify with its element.

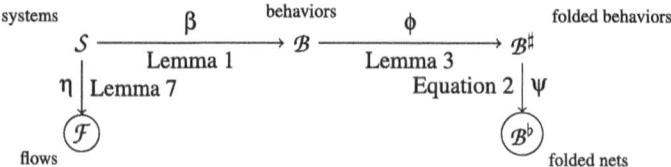

Fig. 2. Homomorphisms between the HR algebras used in this paper. The circled algebras are the finite and effectively computable ones.

Every other HR algebra considered in the rest of this paper will be defined from S via an homomorphism. Figure 2 shows the diagram of these algebras and homomorphisms. Each such homomorphism h (except for Ψ, which has a trivial definition) has a reference to a lemma proving that $\sim_{\mathrm{ker}(h)}$ is an HR congruence.

An *open behavior* is a pair $\tilde{\mathcal{N}} \overset{\text{def}}{=} (\mathcal{N}, \xi)$, where $\mathcal{N}$ is a behavior and $\xi : \Sigma \times Q_{\mathcal{P}} \overset{\rightharpoonup}{\to}_{fin} Q_{\mathcal{N}}$ is an injective partial function assigning pairs (σ, q) to places of $\mathcal{N}$, where σ is a source label and q is a place from some process type in $\mathcal{P}$. A place $r \in Q_{\mathcal{N}}$ is a (σ, q)-source of $\tilde{\mathcal{N}}$ if $\xi(\sigma, q) = r$ and type$(\tilde{\mathcal{N}}) \overset{\text{def}}{=} \mathrm{dom}(\xi)$ denotes the type of $\tilde{\mathcal{N}}$. Since behaviors (Definition 3) are actually open behaviors of empty type, we blur the distinction and refer to open behaviors as behaviors, when no confusion arises.

To define the algebra of behaviors, we extend the β function introduced by Definition 3 to (open) systems, as follows. The behavior of the system $\check{S} = (S, \xi)$ is $\beta(\check{S}) \overset{\text{def}}{=} (\beta(S), \overline{\xi})$, where $\beta(S)$ is given in Definition 3 and the source labeling $\overline{\xi}$ is $\overline{\xi}(\sigma, q) \overset{\text{def}}{=} (q, \xi(\sigma))$ if $\xi(\sigma)$ is defined and $(q, \xi(\sigma)) \in Q_{\mathcal{N}}$, and undefined otherwise, for all $\sigma \in \Sigma$ and $q \in Q_{\mathcal{P}}$.

Lemma 1. $\sim_{\mathrm{ker}(\beta)}$ *is a HR congruence.*

We introduce an algebra $\mathcal{B}$ of behaviors (Fig. 2), whose domain and interpretation of HR function symbols are defined as in Proposition 1. Since $\sim_{\mathrm{ker}(\beta)}$ is a HR congruence (Lemma 1), it follows that β is a homomorphism between S and $\mathcal{B}$. As we discuss next, a grammar that describes a parameterized system $\mathbf{S} = \{S_1, S_2, \ldots\}$ can be reused to describe its set of behaviors $\beta(\mathbf{S})$.

2.4 Grammars

A *grammar* over a signature F is a pair $\Gamma = (\Xi, \Pi)$ consisting of a finite set Ξ of *nonterminals* and a finite set Π of *rules* of the form, either (1) $X \to \rho[X_1, \ldots, X_n]$, where $X, X_1, \ldots, X_n \in \Xi$ are nonterminals and ρ is an F-term whose only variables are $X_1, \ldots, X_n$, or (2) $\to X$, where $X \in \Xi$; the rules of this form are called *axioms*. Given terms θ and η, a *step* $\theta \Rightarrow_\Gamma \eta$ obtains η from θ by replacing an occurrence of a nonterminal X with the term ρ, for some rule $X \to \rho$ of Γ. An X-*derivation* is a sequence of steps starting with a nonterminal X. The derivation is *complete* if it ends in a ground term. Let

$L^{\mathit{a}}_X(\Gamma) \overset{\text{def}}{=} \{\theta^{\mathit{a}} \mid X \Rightarrow^*_\Gamma \theta \text{ is a complete derivation}\}$ and $L^{\mathit{a}}(\Gamma) \overset{\text{def}}{=} \bigcup_{\to X \in \Pi} L^{\mathit{a}}_X(\Gamma)$ be the *language* of Γ in the algebra $\mathcal{A}$.

The following result, also known as the *Filtering Theorem*, allows to build a grammar for the intersection between the language of a grammar and a *recognizable set*, *i.e.* the image of a finite set via an inverse homomorphism [17, Theorem 3.88]:

Theorem 1. *Let* $\mathsf{F} = \{op_1, op_2, \ldots\}$ *be a signature,* $\mathcal{A} = (\mathbb{A}, op_1^{\mathcal{A}}, op_2^{\mathcal{A}}, \ldots)$ *and* $\mathcal{B} = (\mathbb{B}, op_1^{\mathcal{B}}, op_2^{\mathcal{B}}, \ldots)$ *be* F-*algebras, such that* $\mathbb{B}$ *is finite, and* h *be a homomorphism between* $\mathcal{A}$ *and* $\mathcal{B}$. *For each* F-*grammar* Γ *and set* $C \subseteq \mathbb{B}$, *one can build a grammar* $\Gamma_{h,C}$ *such that* $L^{\mathit{a}}(\Gamma_{h,C}) = L^{\mathit{a}}(\Gamma) \cap h^{-1}(C)$.

The construction of the filtered grammar $\Gamma_{h,C}$ is effective: for each rule $X \to \rho[X_1, \ldots, X_n]$ of Γ and each sequence of elements $b, b_1, \ldots, b_n \in \mathbb{B}$ such that $b = \rho^{\mathcal{B}}(b_1, \ldots, b_n)$, the grammar $\Gamma_{h,C}$ has a rule $X^b \to \rho[X_1^{b_1}, \ldots, X_n^{b_n}]$; the axioms of $\Gamma_{h,C}$ are $\to X^c$, for each axiom $\to X$ of Γ and each element $c \in C$.

The grammars from the rest of the paper use the HR signature to describe parameterized systems. The following example shows two grammars that specify parameterized systems with chain-like and star-like network topologies, as in Fig. 1(b):

Example 3. The grammar Γ_{Chain} below defines systems with chain-like network topologies and at least three processes including the controller (Fig. 1(b) top):

$\to C$

$C \to \mathsf{restrict}_{\{\sigma_1\}}((relC, get)_{(\sigma_3, \sigma_2)} \oplus (rel, get)_{(\sigma_2, \sigma_1)})$

$C \to \mathsf{restrict}_{\{\sigma_1\}}\mathsf{rename}_{\sigma_1 \leftrightarrow \sigma_2}(C \oplus (rel, get)_{(\sigma_1, \sigma_2)})$

The right-hand sides of the last two rules correspond to the graphs on the right. Similarly, the Γ_{Star} grammar below defines systems with star-shaped network topology and at least two processes including the controller (Fig. 1(b) bottom):

$\to Z$

$Z \to \mathsf{restrict}_{\{\sigma_1\}}((relC, get)_{(\sigma_1, \sigma_2)} \oplus^s (getC, rel)_{(\sigma_1, \sigma_2)})$

$Z \to \mathsf{restrict}_{\{\sigma_1\}}(Z \oplus (relC, get)_{(\sigma_1, \sigma_2)} \oplus^s (getC, rel)_{(\sigma_1, \sigma_2)})$

The following argument will be repeated several times: if $\mathcal{A}$ is some HR algebra related to $\mathcal{S}$ by a homomorphism h, then $h(L^s(\Gamma)) = L^{\mathit{a}}(\Gamma)$, for each grammar Γ written using the HR signature. Moreover, if the domain of $\mathcal{A}$ is finite, the language $L^{\mathit{a}}(\Gamma)$ is finite and effectively computable by a finite Kleene iteration, provided that the interpretation of each function symbol from the HR signature in $\mathcal{A}$ is effectively computable. The finite and effectively computable algebras in question are circled in Fig. 2.

As a consequence of Lemma 1, a grammar that specifies a parameterized system defines also its set of behaviors:

Lemma 2. *For each HR grammar* Γ, *we have* $\beta(\mathcal{L}^s(\Gamma)) = \mathcal{L}^\mathcal{B}(\Gamma)$.

We consider the problems of reachability and coverability for parameterized systems specified by grammars and give the formal definitions of the decision problems:

Definition 4. *The* Reach(Γ, Q, m) *(resp.* Cover(Γ, Q, m)*) problem takes in input a grammar* Γ, *a set of places* $Q \subseteq Q_\mathcal{P}$, *a mapping* $\mathsf{m} : Q \to \mathbb{N}$ *and asks for the existence of a system* $\mathsf{S} \in \mathcal{L}^s(\Gamma)$ *and marking* $\overline{m} \in$ reach$(\beta(\mathsf{S}))$ *(resp.* $\overline{m} \in$ cover$(\beta(\mathsf{S}))$*) where* $\sum_{v \in V_\mathsf{S}: q \in Q_{\lambda_\mathsf{S}(v)}} \overline{m}(q, v) = \mathsf{m}(q)$, *for all* $q \in Q$.

Unsurprisingly, both problems are undecidable, even for simple grammars defining parameterized systems with chain-like topologies (see Example 3), when the structure of the process types is unrestricted.

Theorem 2. *The* Reach *and* Cover *problems are undecidable.*

Proof Sketch. With 3 process types one can write a grammar whose language consists of nets that simulate executions of two-counter Minsky machines, and the halting problem thus reduces to coverability.   □

3   Counting Abstraction

We define the *counting abstraction* of a set of behaviors as a set of PNs having finitely many underlying nets with possibly infinitely many initial markings each. The basic idea is to fold (i) the copies of the same place from some process type into a single place and (ii) the transitions having the same sets of predecessors and successors into a single transition. We show that the counting abstraction of the set of behaviors of a parameterized system described by an HR grammar can be computed by evaluating the same grammar in a finite HR algebra. Moreover, the infinite set of initial markings of a folded PN can be finitely described by another PN derived from the initial grammar describing the system. While the counting abstraction itself is not inherently tied to HR, and may abstract any family, the generation of initial markings on the other hand is strongly based on the HR-grammar (Sect. 3.2).

3.1   Folding

We define a folding function on the domain $\mathbb{B}$ of system behaviors. Let $\check{\mathsf{S}} = (\mathsf{S}, \xi)$ be a system and $(\mathcal{N}, \overline{\xi}) = \beta(\check{\mathsf{S}})$ be its behavior (Definition 3). The folding is defined as quotienting a behavior $\mathcal{N}$ via an equivalence relation $\equiv$ on the places of $\mathcal{N}$. Note that quotienting is a standard operation, meaning that equivalent places and transitions having the same sets of predecessor and successor equivalence classes $[q]_\equiv$, for $q \in Q_\mathcal{N}$, are joined together, the result being denoted as $\mathcal{N}_{/\equiv}$.

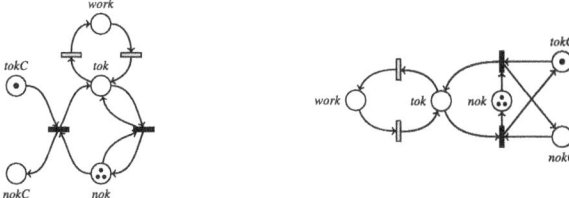

Fig. 3. Foldings of the behaviors given in Fig. 1(c) and (d), respectively.

We recall that the places of $\mathcal{N}$ are pairs (q, v), where $q \in Q_P$, $v \in V_S$ and the sources of the behavior are labeled by the function $\overline{\xi}$. A function $\eta : \Sigma \to V_S$, having $dom(\eta) \supseteq dom(\xi)$, defines the following equivalence relation $\equiv_{[\eta]} \subseteq Q_\mathcal{N} \times Q_\mathcal{N}$:

$$(q_1, v_1) \equiv_{[\eta]} (q_2, v_2) \iff q_1 = q_2 \text{ and } \{v_1, v_2\} \cap img(\eta) \neq \emptyset \Rightarrow v_1 = v_2 \quad (1)$$

i.e. two places of $\mathcal{N}$ corresponding to the same place of a process type (within two distinct instances thereof) are considered equivalent, except for the sources with labels η, that are equivalent only with themselves. The equivalence class of a place $(q, v) \in Q_\mathcal{N}$ is denoted $[(q, v)]_{\equiv_{[\eta]}}$. Because we have assumed that the set of places corresponding to different process types are disjoint, $(q_1, v_1) \equiv_{[\xi]} (q_2, v_2)$ implies that $\lambda_S(v_1) = \lambda_S(v_2)$, *i.e.* the two vertices are instances of the same process type.

The *folding* of $(\mathcal{N}, \overline{\xi})$ is defined as $\phi(\mathcal{N}, \overline{\xi}) \overset{def}{=} (\mathcal{N}_{/\equiv_{[\xi]}}, \overline{\xi}_{/\equiv_{[\xi]}})$, where, for each mapping $\eta : \Sigma \to V_S$ having $dom(\eta) \supseteq dom(\xi)$, we define $\overline{\xi}_{/\equiv_{[\eta]}} (\sigma, [q]_{\equiv_{[\eta]}}) \overset{def}{=} [\overline{\xi}(\sigma, q)]_{\equiv_{[\eta]}}$ if $\sigma \in dom(\eta)$, else undefined, for each $\sigma \in \Sigma$. We refer to Fig. 3 for examples.

The following lemma allows to define an algebra of abstract behaviors $\mathcal{B}^\sharp$ (Fig. 2) from the algebra $\mathcal{B}$ of behaviors, using Proposition 1. The domain of $\mathcal{B}^\sharp$ is the set $\mathbb{B}^\sharp$ of folded behaviors, *i.e.* quotients of behaviors $(\mathcal{N}, \overline{\xi})$ w.r.t. the $\equiv_{[\xi]}$ relation.

Lemma 3. $\sim_{\ker(\phi)}$ *is an HR congruence.*

As an immediate consequence of Lemma 3, we obtain that ϕ is a homomorphism between $\mathcal{B}$ and $\mathcal{B}^\sharp$, hence the same HR grammar can be used to both specify an infinite set of behaviors and compute its folded abstraction:

Corollary 1. *For each HR grammar Γ, we have $\phi(\mathcal{L}^{\mathcal{B}}(\Gamma)) = \mathcal{L}^{\mathcal{B}^\sharp}(\Gamma)$.*

Because $\mathcal{P}$ is a finite set of process types, each having finitely many places, the folded language $\mathcal{L}^{\mathcal{B}^\sharp}(\Gamma)$ has a finite set of underlying nets. This is because each transition t in a behavior $\mathcal{N} \in \mathcal{L}^{\mathcal{B}}(\Gamma)$ has at most two incoming/outgoing edges. Since the same holds for each transition of its quotient, *i.e.* $\mathcal{N}_{/\equiv_{[\xi]}}$, there are finitely many places and transitions in each underlying net of some $\mathcal{N} \in \mathcal{L}^{\mathcal{B}^\sharp}(\Gamma)$.

Nevertheless, the language $\mathcal{L}^{\mathcal{B}^{\sharp}}(\Gamma)$ is unbounded, because the set of initial markings is unbounded. In order to represent this set in a finite way, we shall proceed in two steps:

1. Isolate the initial markings that correspond to a given net from $\mathcal{L}^{\mathcal{B}^{\sharp}}(\Gamma)$; we address this problem using the Filtering Theorem (Theorem 1).
2. Give a finite representation to the set of initial markings of each net; we tackle this problem using Esparza's idea [18] of building PNs that simulate the derivations of the "filtered" grammars obtained in the previous step.

To formally define the finite set of underlying nets from a language $\mathcal{L}^{\mathcal{B}^{\sharp}}(\Gamma)$, we consider the function Ψ on the domain $\mathbb{B}^{\sharp}$, that drops the initial marking:

$$\Psi((\mathsf{N}, \mathsf{m}_0), \xi) \stackrel{\text{def}}{=} (\mathsf{N}, \xi) \tag{2}$$

Then, $\Psi(\mathcal{L}^{\mathcal{B}^{\sharp}}(\Gamma))$ is finite, because the numbers of places and transitions in each net from this set are bounded by $\|Q_{\mathcal{P}}\|$ and $\|Q_{\mathcal{P}}\|^4$ (*i.e.* each transition has at most 2 incoming and 2 outgoing edges of weight 1), respectively.

Since none of the operations from $\mathcal{B}^{\sharp}$ modify the initial markings, it is straightforward that $\sim_{\ker(\Psi)}$ is a HR congruence. We define the algebra $\mathcal{B}^{\flat}$ (Fig. 2) having the finite domain $\mathbb{B}^{\flat} \stackrel{\text{def}}{=} \Psi(\mathbb{B}^{\sharp})$ and the usual interpretations of the HR function symbols given by Proposition 1. By standard arguments (similar to Lemma 2 and Corollary 1), we obtain that Ψ is a homomorphism between $\mathcal{B}^{\sharp}$ and $\mathcal{B}^{\flat}$, *i.e.* $\Psi(\mathcal{L}^{\mathcal{B}^{\sharp}}(\Gamma)) = \mathcal{L}^{\mathcal{B}^{\flat}}(\Gamma)$.

As previously discussed, $\mathcal{L}^{\mathcal{B}^{\flat}}(\Gamma)$ is a finite set. However, to ensure that this set can be effectively computed, the computation of the interpretation of the HR signature in $\mathcal{B}^{\flat}$ needs to be effective:

Proposition 2. *For each function symbol* op *from the HR signature, the function* $\mathsf{op}^{\mathcal{B}^{\flat}}$ *is effectively computable.*

By the previous arguments, the language $\mathcal{L}^{\mathcal{B}^{\flat}}(\Gamma)$ is finite and effectively computable, hence it can be produced by a finite Kleene iteration of the monotonic function that maps a tuple of sets indexed by the nonterminals of Γ into their $\mathcal{B}^{\flat}$ interpretations, given by the rules of Γ. Let $\{(\mathsf{N}_1, \overline{\xi_1}), \ldots, (\mathsf{N}_n, \overline{\xi_n})\} \stackrel{\text{def}}{=} \mathcal{L}^{\mathcal{B}^{\flat}}(\Gamma)$ be this set. Using the Filtering Theorem (Theorem 1) one can effectively build grammars $\Gamma_1, \ldots, \Gamma_n$ such that:

$$\Psi(\mathcal{L}^{\mathcal{B}^{\sharp}}(\Gamma_i)) = \mathcal{L}^{\mathcal{B}^{\flat}}(\Gamma_i) = \{(\mathsf{N}_i, \overline{\xi_i})\}, \text{ for each } i \in [1, n] \tag{3}$$

More precisely, the Filtering Theorem gives, for each $i \in [1, n]$, a grammar Γ_i such that $\mathcal{L}^{\mathcal{B}^{\sharp}}(\Gamma_i) = \mathcal{L}^{\mathcal{B}^{\sharp}}(\Gamma) \cap \Psi^{-1}(\{(\mathsf{N}_i, \overline{\xi_i})\})$. By applying Ψ to both sides of the equality, we obtain (Eq. 3), thus taking care of the first step of the construction (1).

3.2   Initial Markings

Let $\Gamma = (\Xi, \Pi)$ be any of the grammars $\Gamma_1, \ldots, \Gamma_n$ (Eq. 3). To simplify matters at hand, we assume w.l.o.g that the right-hand side of each rule in Γ has exactly one occurrence of an HR function symbol, *i.e.* a constant a_{σ_1, σ_2}, a unary function symbol restrict$_\tau$ or rename$_\alpha$, or the binary function symbol $\oplus$, applied to 0, 1 or 2 variables, respectively. Note that each grammar can be put in this form, at the cost of adding polynomially many extra nonterminals.

First, we annotate each nonterminal $X \in \Xi$ with sets of sources τ that are *visible* (*i.e.* have been introduced by a constant a_{σ_1, σ_2} and have not been removed by some application of restrict$_{\tau'}$) in each complete derivation starting in X^τ, where X^τ is a shorthand for the pair (X, τ). The annotated grammar $\widehat{\Gamma} = (\widehat{\Xi}, \widehat{\Pi})$ can be built from Γ by a standard worklist iteration[3] The language of the annotated grammar $\widehat{\Gamma}$ is the same as the original grammar Γ. Next, we use the annotated grammar $\widehat{\Gamma} = (\widehat{\Xi}, \widehat{\Pi})$, to build a PN $\mathfrak{J}(\widehat{\Gamma})$ that generates the initial markings of Γ in the set of folded PNs (Corollary 1).

This construction is quite intuitive: by reinterpreting each rule of $\widehat{\Gamma}$ as a transition of $\mathfrak{J}(\widehat{\Gamma})$, we get a PN whose firing sequences mimick derivations of $\widehat{\Gamma}$ in which the rules/transitions of $\widehat{\Gamma}$ and $\mathfrak{J}(\widehat{\Gamma})$ are applied in the same order. More precisely, we create a Petri net with one place representing each nonterminal $X \in \widehat{\Xi}$, in which each rule of the form $X \to \rho[X_1, \ldots, X_n]$ is translated to some transition t such that $^\bullet t = (X, \{X_1, \ldots, X_n\})$, and each rule of the form $\to X$ is translated to some transition t such that $^\bullet t = (O, X)$ (here $O \notin \widehat{\Xi}$ is a newly created place that receives the initial token, as in Fig. 4). This construction is such that a partial derivation having k occurrences of the nonterminal variable X, when reinterpreted as a firing sequence, leads to a marking with k tokens in the place corresponding to X. Assume that $X^\tau \Rightarrow^*_{\widehat{\Gamma}} \theta$ is a complete derivation, *i.e.* θ is a ground HR term. Then, every instance of some process type p that occurs in the system $(\mathsf{S}, \xi) \stackrel{\text{def}}{=} \theta^{\mathcal{S}}$ starts in a vertex labeled by a source label $\sigma \in \Sigma$ such that, either:

(a) σ is removed by an application of restrict$_{\tau'}$ such that $\sigma \notin \tau'$, then σ occurs in the subtree of θ rooted at the particular occurrence of restrict$_{\tau'}$ that removed it, or

(b) σ is visible at the root of θ, *i.e.* $\sigma \in \tau$.

When processing the rules of the form $X^\tau \to$ restrict$_{\tau'}(X_1^{\tau_1})$ and $\to X^\tau$ in the construction of $\mathfrak{J}(\widehat{\Gamma})$, we add an outgoing edge to each place q that is initially marked in ptype(σ), for some $\sigma \in \tau_1 \setminus \tau'$ or $\sigma \in \tau$. Then, for every instance of the process type that occurs in the system, its initial marking will be added to q by a firing sequence of $\mathfrak{J}(\widehat{\Gamma})$. We refer to Fig. 4 for examples of initialization PNs obtained by this construction applied to $\widehat{\Gamma}_{Chain}$ and $\widehat{\Gamma}_{Star}$, *i.e.* the annotated versions of the two grammars from Example 3. For a PN $\mathcal{N}$ and a set of places

---

[3] The annotation algorithm is given in the full version of the paper. [10].

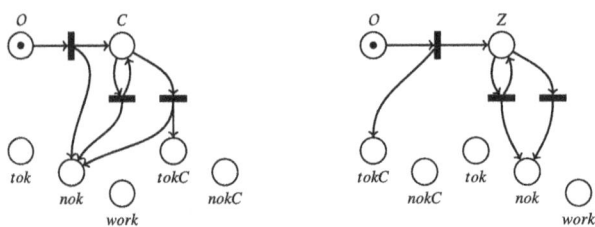

Fig. 4. $\mathfrak{J}(\widehat{\Gamma}_{Chain})$ (left) and $\mathfrak{J}(\widehat{\Gamma}_{Star})$ (right), showing how to initialize the marking of stars and chains generated by the grammars presented in Example 3.

$Q \subseteq Q_{\mathcal{N}}$, we denote by:

$$\text{reach}_Q^0(\mathcal{N}) \overset{def}{=} \{m \in \text{reach}(\mathcal{N}) \mid m(q) = 0, \text{ for all } q \in Q\} \tag{4}$$

the set of reachable markings having zero tokens in a place from Q. For a set $\mathcal{M}$ of markings and a set Q of places, we denote by $\mathcal{M} \downarrow_Q$ the set of restrictions of each $m \in \mathcal{M}$ to the places in Q. The relation between the set of folded PNs described by an annotated grammar $\widehat{\Gamma}$ and the PN $\mathfrak{J}(\widehat{\Gamma})$ is formally captured below:

Lemma 4. *Let $\widehat{\Gamma} = (\widehat{\Xi}, \widehat{\Pi})$ be an annotated grammar. Then, we have:*

$$\{\text{init}_{\mathcal{N}} \mid (\mathcal{N}, \xi) \in \mathcal{L}^{\mathcal{B}^\sharp}(\widehat{\Gamma})\} = \text{reach}_{\{o\} \uplus \widehat{\Xi}}^0(\mathfrak{J}(\widehat{\Gamma})) \downarrow_{Q_p}$$

3.3   Soundness

We now have all the elements to describe our counting abstraction method and prove its soundness, *i.e.* if the reachability (resp. coverability) problem has a negative answer for the abstraction, then the concrete reachability (resp. coverability) problem has a negative answer.

For each grammar $\Gamma_i = (\Xi_i, \Pi_i)$ defined at (Eq. 3), that corresponds to the (open) net (N_i, ξ_i), for $i \in [1, n]$, we define the PN $\mathfrak{N}(\Gamma_i) \overset{def}{=} (\mathcal{N}_i, \xi_i)$, where:

$$Q_{\mathcal{N}_i} \overset{def}{=} Q_{\mathfrak{J}(\widehat{\Gamma}_i)} \cup Q_{N_i} \quad T_{\mathcal{N}_i} \overset{def}{=} T_{\mathfrak{J}(\widehat{\Gamma}_i)} \uplus T_{N_i} \quad W_{\mathcal{N}_i} \overset{def}{=} W_{\mathfrak{J}(\widehat{\Gamma}_i)} \cup W_{N_i} \quad \text{init}_{\mathcal{N}_i} \overset{def}{=} \text{init}_{\mathfrak{J}(\widehat{\Gamma}_i)}$$

Note that $\text{reach}_{Q_{\mathfrak{J}(\widehat{\Gamma}_i)} \setminus Q_{N_i}}^0(\mathfrak{N}(\Gamma_i))$ is the set of markings of $\mathfrak{N}(\Gamma_i)$ that can be reached *after* the full generation of its initial marking, *i.e.* from those markings that have no more tokens in any of the places of $\mathfrak{J}(\widehat{\Gamma}_i)$, excepted the initially marked places of Q_p.

Our verification method for the grammar-based parameterized reachability and coverability problems (Definition 4) relies on the construction of a finite number of PNs $\mathfrak{N}(\Gamma_1), \dots, \mathfrak{N}(\Gamma_n)$ from a given grammar Γ that describes a set of systems.

The soundness of the method is formally captured below:

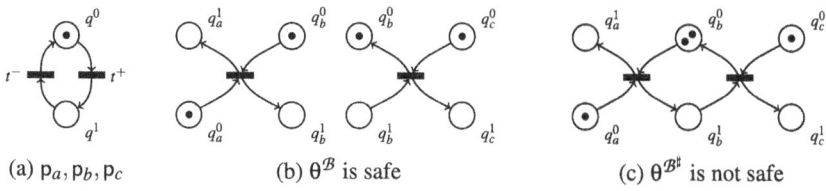

(a) p_a, p_b, p_c (b) $\theta^{\mathcal{B}}$ is safe   (c) $\theta^{\mathcal{B}^{\sharp}}$ is not safe

Fig. 5. 3 process types with the same net, and a way of connecting them that produces a false positive when folded. $\theta \stackrel{\text{def}}{=} (t^+, t^+)_{\sigma_a, \sigma_b} \oplus (t^-, t^+)_{\sigma'_b, \sigma_c}$ with $\text{ptype}(\sigma_a) = p_a$, $\text{ptype}(\sigma_b) = \text{ptype}(\sigma'_b) = p_b$, $\text{ptype}(\sigma_c) = p_c$. The safety property is $m_{\text{tgt}}(q_c^1) \geq 1$.

Theorem 3. *Let* Γ *be an* HR *grammar such that* $\mathcal{L}^{\mathcal{B}^b}(\Gamma) = \{(N_1, \xi_1), \ldots, (N_n, \xi_n)\}$, $Q \subseteq Q_P$ *a set of places,* $m : Q \to \mathbb{N}$ *a mapping. Then, one can effectively build grammars* $\Gamma_1, \ldots, \Gamma_n$ *such that* $\mathcal{L}^{\mathcal{B}^b}(\Gamma_i) = \{(N_i, \xi_i)\}$, *for all* $i \in [1, n]$ *and:*

1. $\text{Reach}(\Gamma, Q, m)$ *has a negative answer if* $m \notin \bigcup_{i=1}^{n} \text{reach}^0_{Q_{\mathfrak{N}(\Gamma_i)} \backslash Q_P}(\mathfrak{N}(\Gamma_i)) \downarrow_Q$.
2. $\text{Cover}(\Gamma, Q, m)$ *has a negative answer if* $m \notin \bigcup_{i=1}^{n} \text{cover}(\mathfrak{N}(\Gamma_i)) \downarrow_Q$.

Note that, if $\text{Reach}(\Gamma, Q, m)$ (*resp.* $\text{Cover}(\Gamma, Q, m)$) has a negative answer, then each instance the parameterized system described by Γ (*i.e.* the set of systems $\mathcal{L}^s(\Gamma)$) is safe with respect to the property encoded by the marking m, *i.e.* does not reach (*resp.* cover) the marking m over the set of places Q. For instance, mutual exclusion (only one process of a certain type in a certain state) is naturally encoded as a coverability problem.

3.4 False Positives

As we have announced, our abstraction is sound but not complete. Before we explore a decidable fragment, we show here a simple example of a net on which false positives appear (*i.e.* the abstraction exhibits a violation of safety, but the original net is safe).

Figure 5 illustrates one phenomenon that is a possible cause of false positives. Here, the folding changes the connectivity of the network: two instances of p_b are folded together and make a path from p_a to p_c appear that was absent from the original system. The coverability query $m_{\text{tgt}}(q_c^1) \geq 1$ is unsatisfiable in $\theta^{\mathcal{B}}$, but satisfiable in $\theta^{\mathcal{B}^{\sharp}}$.

To enable the verification of infinite systems that exhibit a similar issue, here is one possible approach. We give ourselves a new process type p'_b, identical copy of p_b, and we alter the grammar and/or the assignment $\text{ptype}(\cdot)$ to distinguish between the instances we do not want folded together. Here we could change $\text{ptype}(\sigma'_b) = p_{b'}$ (instead of p_b). The same abstraction applied to the new system will not fold together instances of p_b with instances of p'_b, making the false positive disappear. In general on infinite families, we may modify the grammar to select a subset of instances of a process type to instead use a copy of the process type that is folded separately. Repeating this process finitely many times keeps the abstraction finite. This refinement technique constitute what we call a *partial unfolding*, because we select a few instances to not be folded with the rest. Automated detection of when this technique is applicable, and more advanced transformations of the grammar constitute a research avenue orthogonal to the abstraction technique we explore here, and may be the topic of future work.

4   A Decidable Fragment

We have shown that the parameterized coverability problem is undecidable, for systems with fairly simple network topologies (chains) and unrestricted process types (Theorem 2). We refine this result by proving that only restricting the process types, but not the topology of the network, suffices to recover decidability. This approach is inspired by [5], in which *token-passing systems* (TPS) are found to admit cutoffs, and thus decidable model-checking, provided that the architecture is definable in monadic second order logic and of bounded tree-width, like ours. TPS and PPS are similar, with the tradeoff that TPS may have internal transitions, but only one token in the system.

Albeit based on a simple communication pattern (*i.e.* passing a pebble from one node to a neighbour having no pebble), our decidable fragment is non-trivial: we found it to be in 2EXPTIME, with a PSPACE-hard lower bound.

4.1   Pebble-Passing Systems

The class of pebble-passing systems (PPS) is defined by restricting the process types and interactions of a system, as in Fig. 6. The example from Fig. 5 also happens to be of this form. We give the formal definition below:

Definition 5. *Let* $\mathcal{P}_{\mathsf{pps}}$ *be a set of process types, where* $Q_{\mathsf{p}} = \{q_{\perp}^{\mathsf{p}}, q_{\top}^{\mathsf{p}}\}$ *and* $T_{\mathsf{p}} = T_{\mathsf{p}}^{obs} = \{\mathsf{send}, \mathsf{recv}\}$, *such that* $\bullet\mathsf{send}\bullet = (q_{\top}^{\mathsf{p}}, q_{\perp}^{\mathsf{p}})$ *and* $\bullet\mathsf{recv}\bullet = (q_{\perp}^{\mathsf{p}}, q_{\top}^{\mathsf{p}})$, *for each* $\mathsf{p} \in \mathcal{P}_{\mathsf{pps}}$. *Let* $\Delta_{\mathsf{pps}} \overset{\text{def}}{=} \{(\mathsf{send}, \mathsf{recv}), (\mathsf{recv}, \mathsf{send})\}$ *be a set of edge labels. A system* $S = (V, E, \lambda)$ *over* $\mathcal{P}_{\mathsf{pps}}$ *and* Δ_{pps} *is said to be* pebble-passing.

Intuitively, a token in $q_{\top}^{\mathsf{p}}$ (*i.e.* $\mathsf{m}(q_{\top}^{\mathsf{p}}) = 1$) represents the ownership of a resource, called *pebble*, and a token in $q_{\perp}^{\mathsf{p}}$ is the absence of a pebble, called *hole*. Since each process type is automata-like (*i.e.* has a token in exactly one place), each node of the system can have either a pebble or a hole, in all the reachable markings of its behavior (Definition 3). An edge $(v, (\mathsf{send}, \mathsf{recv}), v')$ (*resp.* $(v, (\mathsf{recv}, \mathsf{send}), v')$) will be denoted $v \rightarrow v'$ (*resp.* $v' \rightarrow v$). Intuitively, firing an interaction $v \rightarrow v'$ moves a pebble from v to v' and simultaneously moves a hole from v' to v. Thus each transition preserves the total numbers of pebbles and holes in the system, respectively.

Pebble-passing systems have very strict constraints on their process types and interactions, but no constraints on the set of network topologies, other than that it is definable by an HR grammar written with constants of the form

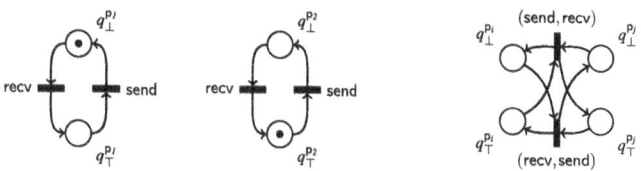

Fig. 6. Two process types (left), and two kinds of interactions (right), which all other process types and interactions in our restriction have the same shape as.

$(\mathsf{send}, \mathsf{recv})_{\sigma_1, \sigma_2}$ or $(\mathsf{recv}, \mathsf{send})_{\sigma_1, \sigma_2}$, for some source labels $\sigma_1, \sigma_2 \in \Sigma$, where Σ is the set of source labels that may occur in a grammar. We denote by $\mathsf{HR_{pps}}$ the signature of these grammars. The rest of this section is concerned with the proof of the following theorem:

Theorem 4. *The* Cover *problem for grammars written using the* $\mathsf{HR_{pps}}$ *signature is in* 2EXPTIME *and* PSPACE-*hard.*

The proof of Theorem 4 is organized as follows. The double exponential upper bound relies on a result showing that, in order to cover a target marking $\mathsf{m_{tgt}}$ it is sufficient to consider only firing sequences that cross (*i.e.* move a pebble to and from) each place at most K times, where K is the size of the unary encoding of $\mathsf{m_{tgt}}$. Based on this result (Lemma 6), we define an effectively computable algebra $\mathcal{F}$ (Fig. 2), having the property that the coverability problem reduces to a membership test on the language of the input grammar in $\mathcal{F}$. Here the use of HR guarantees that $\mathcal{F}$ is finite. The upper bound follows from the fact that $L^{\mathcal{F}}(\Gamma)$ is computable in double exponential time (see Proposition 3 for a precise estimation). The lower bound uses a polynomial reduction from the emptiness problem for 2-way nondeterministic automata [21] (2NFA). This construction works because (1) 2NFAs run on words which have a chain-like and thus HR-expressible structure, and (2) 2NFAs have only finite memory, which we are able to encode within the constraints of PPS.

4.2   Firing Sequences

For the rest of this section, let $\check{\mathsf{S}} = (\mathsf{S}, \xi)$ be a fixed open pebble-passing system, having an underlying system $\mathsf{S} = (\mathsf{V}, \mathsf{E}, \lambda)$ whose behavior is $\beta(\mathsf{S}) \stackrel{\text{def}}{=} (\mathsf{N}, \mathsf{m_0})$. Below, we introduce an equivalent characterization of the firing sequences of $\beta(\mathsf{S})$.

The *footprint* of a marking m is a mapping $\mathsf{fp_m} : \mathsf{V} \to \{0, 1\}$ defined as $\mathsf{fp_m}(v) \stackrel{\text{def}}{=} \mathsf{m}(q_\top^{\lambda(v)}, v)$, for each vertex $v \in \mathsf{V}$. Note that $\mathsf{fp_m}$ evaluates to 1 on pebble and to 0 on hole vertices. We say that a marking footprint π is *valid over* $\mathcal{V} \subseteq \mathsf{V}$ iff $0 \le \pi(v) \le 1$ for each vertex $v \in \mathcal{V}$, resp. *valid*, when $\mathcal{V} = \mathsf{V}$ follows from the context.

Given a subset of states $Q \subseteq Q_{\mathcal{P}}$ and a marking to cover $\mathsf{m_{tgt}} : Q \to \mathbb{N}$, the coverability problem asks for the existence of a reachable marking $\mathsf{m} : Q_\mathbb{N} \to$

$\{0, 1\}$ such that, for each process type $\mathsf{p} \in \mathcal{P}$ and each place $q \in Q$:

$$\|\{v \in \lambda^{-1}(\mathsf{p}) \mid \mathsf{fp_m}(v) = 0\}\| \geq \mathsf{m_{tgt}}(q_\perp^\mathsf{p}) \tag{5}$$

$$\|\{v \in \lambda^{-1}(\mathsf{p}) \mid \mathsf{fp_m}(v) = 1\}\| \geq \mathsf{m_{tgt}}(q_\top^\mathsf{p}) \tag{6}$$

The footprint $\mathsf{fp}_{v \to v'} : V \to \mathbb{Z}$ of an edge $v \to v' \in E$ is defined as $\mathsf{fp}_{v \to v'}(u) \stackrel{\text{def}}{=} 1$ if $u = v$, -1 if $u = v'$ and 0, otherwise. We extend footprints to sequences of edges $\mathbf{e} \in E^*$ as in $\mathsf{fp_e} \stackrel{\text{def}}{=} \sum_{e \in \mathbf{e}} \tau_e$. Because each edge $v \to v' \in E$ corresponds to the transition that moves a token from $(q_\top^{\lambda(v)}, v)$ to $(q_\perp^{\lambda(v)}, v)$ (resp. from $(q_\perp^{\lambda(v')}, v')$ to $(q_\top^{\lambda(v')}, v'))$ in the PN $\beta(\mathsf{S})$, we shall abuse notation and write $\beta(v \to v')$ for the transition corresponding to $v \to v'$ in $\beta(\mathsf{S})$ and $\beta(\mathbf{e})$ for the sequence of transitions corresponding to $\mathbf{e} \in E^*$.

We remark that, for each firing sequence $\mathsf{m} \stackrel{\beta(\mathbf{e})}{\leadsto} \mathsf{m}'$, we have $\mathsf{fp_{m'}} - \mathsf{fp_m} = \mathsf{fp_e}$. Intuitively, $\mathsf{fp_e}$ is a witness of the fact that the effect of firing the transitions $\beta(\mathbf{e})$ is to move pebbles from $\{v \mid \mathsf{fp_e}(v) = -1\}$ to $\{v \mid \mathsf{fp_e}(v) = 1\}$; the vertices from $\{v \mid \mathsf{fp_e}(v) = 0\}$ may store pebbles in between, but are ultimately restored to their initial state.

We denote by $\#_e(\mathbf{e})$ the number of times the edge e occurs in the sequence $\mathbf{e}$. We use the shorthands $\#_{u \to}(\mathbf{e}) \stackrel{\text{def}}{=} \sum_{u' \in V} \#_{u \to u'}(\mathbf{e})$ and $\#_{\to u}(\mathbf{e}) \stackrel{\text{def}}{=} \sum_{u' \in V} \#_{u' \to u}(\mathbf{e})$. We define the following partial orders between sequences of edges: $\mathbf{e}' \preceq \mathbf{e} \stackrel{\text{def}}{\Longleftrightarrow} \#_e(\mathbf{e}') \leq \#_e(\mathbf{e})$, for each $e \in E$, and $\mathbf{e}' \sqsubseteq \mathbf{e} \stackrel{\text{def}}{\Longleftrightarrow} \mathbf{e}' \preceq \mathbf{e}$ and $\mathsf{fp_{e'}} = \mathsf{fp_e}$. The following lemma characterizes the existence of fireable sub-sequences:

Lemma 5. *For each marking* m *and sequence of edges* $\mathbf{e}$, *the following are equivalent:*

(i) $\mathsf{fp_m} + \mathsf{fp_e}$ *is a valid marking footprint,*
(ii) there exists a sequence of edges $\mathbf{e}' \sqsubseteq \mathbf{e}$ *such that* $\beta(\mathbf{e}')$ *is fireable from* m.

Using the previous lemma, we prove that, in order to cover a given marking $\mathsf{m_{tgt}}$, it suffices to consider only those firing sequences that cross each vertex a bounded number of times, where the bound is the size of the unary encoding of $\mathsf{m_{tgt}}$. To that end, we define the *degree* of a sequence $\mathbf{e} \in E^*$ as the maximum number of occurrences of one vertex in the sequence, *i.e.* $\deg(\mathbf{e}) \stackrel{\text{def}}{=} \max\{\#_{u \to}(\mathbf{e}), \#_{\to u}(\mathbf{e}) \mid u \in V\}$. From now on, the domain of $\mathsf{m_{tgt}}$ will implicitly be the set $Q \subseteq Q_\mathcal{P}$. To simplify the following statement, we say that $\mathsf{m} : Q_\mathbb{N} \to \mathbb{N}$ covers $\mathsf{m_{tgt}}$ iff $\sum_{(q,v) \in Q_\mathbb{N}} \mathsf{m}(q, v) \geq \mathsf{m_{tgt}}(q)$, for each $q \in Q$ and that $\mathsf{m_{tgt}}$ is *coverable* by S iff there exists $\mathsf{m} \in \mathrm{reach}(\beta(\mathsf{S}))$ that covers $\mathsf{m_{tgt}}$. Since, in a pebble-passing system, markings can be equated to their footprints, we say that $\mathsf{fp_m}$ covers $\mathsf{m_{tgt}}$ whenever m and $\mathsf{m_{tgt}}$ satisfy the conditions (5) and (6) above.

Lemma 6. *A marking* $\mathsf{m_{tgt}}$ *is coverable by* S *iff there exists* $\mathbf{e} \in E^{* \leq K}$ *such that* $\mathsf{fp_{m_0}} + \mathsf{fp_e}$ *covers* $\mathsf{m_{tgt}}$, *where* $K \stackrel{\text{def}}{=} \sum_{q \in Q} \mathsf{m_{tgt}}(q)$, *and* $E^{* \leq K} \stackrel{\text{def}}{=} \{\mathbf{e} \in E^* \mid \deg(\mathbf{e}) \leq K\}$.

4.3   Flows

To check coverability, we consider an algebra $\mathcal{F}$ whose elements represent the sequences of edges that cross each vertex at most K times. The domain of $\mathcal{F}$ is $\mathbb{F} \subseteq \text{pow}([0,K]^\Sigma \times [0,K]^\Sigma \times [0,K]^Q)$. The elements $(f^+, f^-, n) \in \mathbb{F}$ represent sequences of edges, such that $f^+(\sigma)$ (*resp.* $f^-(\sigma)$) is the in-degree (*resp.* out-degree) of the σ-source of S and $n(q)$ is the number of tokens that end in $q \in Q$. Intuitively, a tuple (f^+, f^-, n) witnesses the existence of a sequence that covers n, that can later be combined with other sequences which compensate its surplus f^+ and deficit f^- on the sources of S. Since we consider only systems with finitely many sources (guaranteed by HR) and since $Q \subseteq Q$ is finite, $\mathcal{F}$ is a finite algebra. We will later characterize its exact size. Formally, we define the following mappings, where $\mathbb{S}$ denotes the set of open systems, *i.e.* systems with sources:

$$\omega : \mathsf{E}^{* \leq K} \times \mathsf{V}^\Sigma \to [0,K]^\Sigma \times [0,K]^\Sigma \times [0,K]^Q$$

$$\omega(\mathbf{e}, \xi) = (f^+, f^-, n) \overset{\text{def}}{\Longleftrightarrow}$$

$$\begin{cases} f^+(\sigma) = \#_{\xi(\sigma) \to}(\mathbf{e}) \qquad f^-(\sigma) = \#_{\to \xi(\sigma)}(\mathbf{e}) \\ n(q_\perp^\mathsf{p}) = \min(\mathsf{m}_{\text{tgt}}(q_\perp^\mathsf{p}), \|\{v \in \lambda^{-1}(\mathsf{p}) \setminus \text{img}(\xi) \mid (\mathsf{fp}_{\text{init}_\mathsf{p}} + \mathsf{fp}_\mathbf{e})(v) = 0\}\|) \\ n(q_\top^\mathsf{p}) = \min(\mathsf{m}_{\text{tgt}}(q_\top^\mathsf{p}), \|\{v \in \lambda^{-1}(\mathsf{p}) \setminus \text{img}(\xi) \mid (\mathsf{fp}_{\text{init}_\mathsf{p}} + \mathsf{fp}_\mathbf{e})(v) = 1\}\|) \end{cases}$$

$$\eta : \mathbb{S} \to \text{pow}([0,K]^\Sigma \times [0,K]^\Sigma \times [0,K]^Q)$$

$$\eta(\mathsf{S}, \xi) \overset{\text{def}}{=} \{\omega(\mathbf{e}, \xi) \mid \mathbf{e} \in \mathsf{E}_\mathsf{S}^{* \leq K}, \ \mathsf{fp}_{\text{init}_{\beta(\mathsf{S})}} + \mathsf{fp}_\mathbf{e} \text{ is a valid marking footprint over } \mathsf{V}_\mathsf{S} \setminus \text{img}(\xi)\}$$

We define the finite algebra of *flows* $\mathcal{F}$ using Proposition 1, where η is taken to be the homomorphism between $\mathcal{S}$ and $\mathcal{F}$:

Lemma 7. $\sim_{\ker(\eta)}$ *is a HR congruence.*

This implies $\eta(\mathcal{L}^s(\Gamma)) = \mathcal{L}^{\mathcal{F}}(\Gamma)$, so all we need is a way of computing $\mathcal{L}^{\mathcal{F}}(\Gamma)$. The remainder of the proof for the upper bound from Theorem 4 thus relies on the fact that the interpretation of the HR signature in $\mathcal{F}$ is effectively computable, which is the purpose of the proposition below. The size of the grammar Γ is the total number of occurrences of a nonterminal or function symbol in a rule from Γ, denoted as $|\Gamma|$.

Proposition 3. *The size of each element* $f \in \mathbb{F}$ *is* $2^{O((\|\Sigma\| + \|\mathcal{P}\|) \cdot \log K)}$ *and the function* $\text{op}^{\mathcal{F}}(f_1, \ldots, f_n)$ *can be computed in time* $2^{O((\|\Sigma\| + \|\mathcal{P}\|) \cdot \log K)}$, *for each HR-function symbol* op *of arity* $n \geq 0$ *and all elements* $f_1, \ldots, f_n \in \mathbb{F}$. *Moreover, for each grammar* Γ *using source labels from* Σ, *the language* $\mathcal{L}^{\mathcal{F}}(\Gamma)$ *is computable in time* $2^{|\Gamma| \cdot 2^{O((\|\Sigma\| + \|\mathcal{P}\|) \cdot \log K)}}$.

Deciding whether m_{tgt} is coverable by some instance $\mathsf{S} \in \mathcal{L}^s(\Gamma)$, for a given HR grammar Γ, is done by checking $\text{restrict}_\emptyset^{\mathcal{F}}(\mathcal{L}^{\mathcal{F}}(\Gamma)) \cap \{(0, 0, \mathsf{m}_{\text{tgt}})\} \overset{?}{=} \emptyset$. We apply $\text{restrict}_\emptyset$ to $\mathcal{L}^{\mathcal{F}}(\Gamma)$ to ensure that the sequences of edges considered lead to valid marking footprints on every vertex of a system $(\mathsf{S}, \xi) \in \mathcal{L}^s(\Gamma)$, including the sources from img(ξ), that were exempt from satisfying this condition (see the above definition of η). Computing $\mathsf{restrict}_\emptyset^{\mathcal{T}}(\mathcal{L}^{\mathcal{T}}(\Gamma))$ simply adds a linear factor compared to $\mathcal{L}^{\mathcal{T}}(\Gamma)$, and so does checking if it contains $(0, 0, \mathsf{m_{tgt}})$. Thus we have an overall 2EXPTIME upper bound.

The PSPACE lower bound is obtained by a polynomial reduction from the PSPACE-complete emptiness problem for 2-way nondeterministic finite automata (2NFA). The idea of the reduction is to simulate a run of a 2NFA on a given word by a grid-like system. This system encodes each letter of the word horizontally, and each state of the automaton vertically. The possible movements of the pebble are determined by the transition relation of the 2NFA. Since there are finitely many states in the automaton, we have a grid of constant height and unbounded width, which is expressible in HR.

5   Experiments

We have implemented the counting abstraction method in the prototype tool ParCoSys (Parameterized Coverability) [30]. The input of the tool is a grammar describing the system and a safety property to be checked. The output is a finite set of Petri nets that is fed to the LoLA analyzer [32]. Our choice for LoLA was driven by its robustness and performance, but any Petri net analyzer can be used as back-end, in principle.

Name	Architecture	PPS	TPS	Result	Size	Runtime (ms)
fig-1c	chain		✓	2/2	$(\bigcirc 12, \square 13) \times 2$	$(59+9) \pm 6$
fig-1d	star		✓	2/2	$(\bigcirc 11, \square 10) \times 2$	$(59+9) \pm 4$
fig-5	trivial	✓	✓	1/2	$(\bigcirc 13, \square 10) \times 3$	$(49+2) \pm 4$
ring	ring	✓	✓	2/2	$(\bigcirc 9, \square 11) \times 16$	$(80+21) \pm 4$
double-ring	ring	✓		1/1	$(\bigcirc 8, \square 14) \times 34$	$(113+44) \pm 10$
philos	ring			1/1	$(\bigcirc 16, \square 14) \times 8$	$(134+21) \pm 5$
consensus	star			5/5	$(\bigcirc 29, \square 23) \times 6$	$(83+26) \pm 6$
leader-election	ring			1/2	$(\bigcirc 27, \square 32) \times 2$	$(58+35) \pm 5$
tree-dfs	binary tree		✓	2/2	$(\bigcirc 19, \square 16) \times 2$	$(52+5) \pm 4$
tree-down	binary tree	✓	✓	1/1	$(\bigcirc 11, \square 12) \times 20$	$(125+36) \pm 7$
tree-halves	binary tree			4/4	$(\bigcirc 26, \square 23) \times 8$	$(92+190) \pm 7$
tree-nav	chained binary tree	✓	✓	2/2	$(\bigcirc 12, \square 19) \times 12$	$(139+46) \pm 7$
lock	star		✓	1/3	$(\bigcirc 9, \square 11) \times 4$	$(59+8) \pm 5$
star	star	✓	✓	3/3	$(\bigcirc 12, \square 11) \times 4$	$(58+11) \pm 5$
star-ring	chained star		✓	3/3	$(\bigcirc 17, \square 14) \times 2$	$(63+12) \pm 4$
server-loop	ring of stars			2/3	$(\bigcirc 19, \square 19) \times 8$	$(112+4627) \pm 20$
coverapprox	star			1/2	$(\bigcirc 3, \square 8) \times 6$	$(70+62) \pm 8$
simplify-me	star			1/2	$(\bigcirc 7, \square 9) \times 4$	$(64+21) \pm 5$
propagation	ring			1/2	$(\bigcirc 13, \square 13) \times 4$	$(90+278) \pm 10$
open	ring			0/1	$(\bigcirc 13, \square 14) \times 4$	$(74+269) \pm 13$

Fig. 7. Table of experiments. "PPS", these are pebble-passing systems (Sect. 4). "TPS", these are token-passing systems [4]. "Result", S/T means that of T safety properties, we proved S. "Size", $(\bigcirc p, \square t) \times n$ means that LoLA analyzed n nets, consisting of on average p places and t transitions. "Runtime", $(p+l) \pm e$ means that ParCoSys ran for $p + l$ milliseconds with a standard deviation of e milliseconds, including p computing the abstraction and l waiting for LoLA.

We tested[4] our tool on the examples listed in Fig. 7

- `fig-1c` and `fig-1d` are the systems used as examples in Fig. 1(c) and (d) respectively. We easily verify nonduplication of the token ($m_{tgt}(tok) + m_{tgt}(tokC) > 1$) and mutual exclusion of processes in the critical section $work$ ($m_{tgt}(work) > 1$).
- `fig-5` is the example shown in Fig. 5. Here the "Result" 1/2 denotes that $m_{tgt}(q_c^1) > 0$ exhibits a false positive with the default folding, but there is an easy refinement of the grammar that leads to a successful verification on the second attempt.
- `ring` is a standard token ring, on which we verify mutual exclusion ($m_{tgt}(tok) > 1$).
- `double-ring` is a token ring with two tokens instead of one ($m_{tgt}(tok) > 2$). It is mainly interesting as an example of a PPS that is *not* TPS.
- `philos` implements the algorithm of dining philosophers. We prove that adjacent processes p_1 and p_2 do not enter their critical section *eating* simultaneously ($m_{tgt}(eating^{p_1}) > 0 \land m_{tgt}(eating^{p_2}) > 0$).
- `consensus` has a star of processes performing 2-valued consensus. All processes must choose the same value: ($m_{tgt}(choose_0) > 0 \land m_{tgt}(choose_1) > 0$)).
- `leader-election` performs a leader election with predetermined winner (found in [9]). We prove that p_0 is the unique winner ($m_{tgt}(win^{p_0}) > 0 \land m_{tgt}(win) > 0$).

The rest of the tests are more *ad hoc*, designed to showcase a wider range of architectures as well as interesting false positives:

- `tree-dfs`, `tree-down`, `tree-halves`, `tree-nav` are binary trees on which we prove different ways of expressing mutual exclusion with one or two tokens.
- `lock` should satisfy a mutual exclusion ($m_{tgt}(on) > 1$), but a false positive occurs. A partial unfolding (Sect. 3.4) allows proving the desired property.
- `star` and `star-ring` are stars with easy mutual exclusion properties.
- `server-loop` is a ring where each node has itself a star of child processes. One false positive here could theoretically be solved by a partial unfolding, but we have not yet implemented the logic that would allow for this specific pattern.
- `coverapprox`, `simplify-me` and `propagation` each have a false positive that can be solved by a refinement technique consisting of deleting transitions that are found to be unfireable during intermediate stages of the fixed point computation.
- `open` so far evades our ideas for refinements. We can prove that partial unfolding on its own is insufficient, since all finite foldings exhibit false positives.

---

[4] The times were obtained on a Intel Ultra 7 laptop, with 16 GiB RAM, under Ubuntu 24.04. All benchmark specifications and logs are provided as additional material [30].

6 Conclusions

We present two orthogonal verification results for parameterized process networks with topology specified using hyperedge-replacement graph grammars. The first result is a finitary counting abstraction, that consists in collapsing nodes of the same type in the parameterized family of Petri nets that gives the semantics of behaviors. The second result identifies a decidable fragment of the (undecidable) parameterized verification problem and evaluates its complexity bounds.

Acknowledgements. This research is supported by the French National Research Agency project "Parametic Verification of Dynamic Distributed Systems" (PaVeDyS) under grant number ANR-23-CE48-0005.

Disclosure of Interests. The authors have no competing interests to declare that are relevant to the content of this article.

References

1. Abdulla, P.A., Cerans, K., Jonsson, B., Tsay, Y.: General decidability theorems for infinite-state systems. In: Proceedings, 11th Annual IEEE Symposium on Logic in Computer Science, New Brunswick, New Jersey, USA, 27–30 July 1996, pp. 313–321. IEEE Computer Society (1996)
2. Abdulla, P.A., Delzanno, G., Henda, N.B., Rezine, A.: Monotonic abstraction: on efficient verification of parameterized systems. Int. J. Found. Comput. Sci. **20**(5), 779–801 (2009)
3. Abdulla, P.A., Delzanno, G., Rezine, A.: Approximated parameterized verification of infinite-state processes with global conditions. Formal Methods Syst. Des. **34**(2), 126–156 (2009)
4. Aminof, B., Jacobs, S., Khalimov, A., Rubin, S.: Parameterized model checking of tokenpassing systems. In: VMCAI 2014. LNCS, vol. 8318, pp. 262–281. Springer (2014)
5. Aminof, B., Kotek, T., Rubin, S., Spegni, F., Veith, H.: Parameterized model checking of rendezvous systems. Distributed Comput. **31**(3), 187–222 (2018)
6. Aminof, B., Rubin, S.: Model checking parameterised multi-token systems via the composition method. In IJCAR 2016. LNCS, vol. 9706, pp. 499–515. Springer (2016)
7. Bloem, R., Jacobs, S., Khalimov, A.: Decidability of Parameterized Verification. Morgan & Claypool Publishers (2015)
8. Bloem, R., et al.: Decidability of Parameterized Verification. Synthesis Lectures on Distributed Computing Theory. Morgan & Claypool Publishers (2015)
9. Bozga, M., Esparza, J., Iosif, R., Sifakis, J., Welzel, C.: Structural invariants for the verification of systems with parameterized architectures. In: Biere, A., Parker, D. (eds.) Tools and Algorithms for the Construction and Analysis of Systems - 26th International Conference, TACAS 2020, Held as Part of the European Joint Conferences on Theory and Practice of Software, ETAPS 2020, Dublin, Ireland, 25–30 April 2020, Proceedings, Part I. LNCS, vol. 12078, pp. 228–246. Springer (2020)

10. Bozga, M., Iosif, R., Sangnier, A., Villani, N.: Counting abstraction for the verification of structured parameterized networks (full version) (2025). arxiv.org/abs/2502.15391

11. Bozga, M., Iosif, R., Sifakis, J.: Checking deadlock-freedom of parametric component-based systems. J. Log. Algebraic Methods Program. **119**, 100621 (2021)

12. Bozga, M., Iosif, R., Sifakis, J.: Verification of component-based systems with recursive architectures. Theor. Comput. Sci. **940**(Part), 146–175 (2023)

13. Bradbury, J., Cordy, J., Dingel, J., Wermelinger, M.: A survey of self-management in dynamic software architecture specifications. In: Proceedings of the 1st ACM SIGSOFT Workshop on Self-Managed Systems, pp. 28–33. ACM (2004)

14. Browne, M., Clarke, E., Grumberg, O.: Reasoning about networks with many identical finite state processes. Inf. Comput. **81**(1), 13–31 (1989)

15. Butting, A., Heim, R., Kautz, O., Ringert, J.O., Rumpe, B., Wortmann, A.: A classification of dynamic reconfiguration in component and connector architecture description. In: Proceedings of MODELS 2017 Satellite Event: Workshops (ModComp). CEUR Workshop Proceedings, vol. 2019, pp. 10–16. CEUR-WS.org (2017)

16. Chen, Y., Hong, C., Lin, A.W., Rümmer, P.: Learning to prove safety over parameterised concurrent systems. In: Stewart, D., Weissenbacher, G. (eds.) 2017 Formal Methods in Computer Aided Design, FMCAD 2017, pp. 76–83. IEEE (2017)

17. Courcelle, B., Engelfriet, J.: Graph Structure and Monadic Second-Order Logic: A Language-Theoretic Approach. Encyclopedia of Mathematics and its Applications. Cambridge University Press (2012)

18. Esparza, J.: Petri nets, commutative context-free grammars, and basic parallel processes. In: Fundamentals of Computation Theory, pp. 221–232. Springer, Heidelberg (1995)

19. Esparza, J., Raskin, M.A., Welzel, C.: Regular model checking upside-down: an invariant-based approach. In: Klin, B., Lasota, S., Muscholl, A. (eds.) 33rd International Conference on Concurrency Theory, CONCUR 2022, Warsaw, Poland, 12–16 September 2022. LIPIcs, vol. 243, pp. 23:1–23:19. Schloss Dagstuhl - Leibniz-Zentrum für Informatik (2022)

20. Finkel, A., Leroux, J.: Recent and simple algorithms for petri nets. Softw. Syst. Model. **14**(2), 719–725 (2015)

21. Galil, Z.: Hierarchies of complete problems. Acta Informatica **6**(1), 77–88 (1976). https://doi.org/10.1007/BF00263744

22. German, S.M., Sistla, A.P.: Reasoning about systems with many processes. J. ACM **39**(3), 675–735 (1992)

23. Hirsch, D., Inverardi, P., Montanari, U.: Graph grammars and constraint solving for software architecture styles. In: Proceedings of the Third International Workshop on Software Architecture, ISAW 1998, New York, NY, USA, pp. 69–72. Association for Computing Machinery (1998)

24. Kesten, Y., Maler, O., Marcus, M., Pnueli, A., Shahar, E.: Symbolic model checking with rich assertional languages. Theoret. Comput. Sci. **256**(1), 93–112 (2001)

25. Kesten, Y., Pnueli, A., Shahar, E., Zuck, L.D.: Network invariants in action. In: CONCUR 2002 - Concurrency Theory, 13th International Conference. LNCS, vol. 2421, pp. 101–115. Springer (2002)

26. Le Metayer, D.: Describing software architecture styles using graph grammars. IEEE Trans. Software Eng. **24**(7), 521–533 (1998)

27. Lesens, D., Halbwachs, N., Raymond, P.: Automatic verification of parameterized linear networks of processes. In: The 24th ACM SIGPLAN-SIGACT Symposium on Principles of Programming Languages, pp. 346–357. ACM Press (1997)

28. Lin, A.W., Rümmer, P.: Regular model checking revisited. In: Olderog, E., Steffen, B., Yi, W. (eds.) Model Checking, Synthesis, and Learning - Essays Dedicated to Bengt Jonsson on The Occasion of His 60th Birthday. LNCS, vol. 13030, pp. 97–114. Springer (2021)
29. Shtadler, Z., Grumberg, O.: Network grammars, communication behaviors and automatic verification. In: Sifakis, J. (ed.) Automatic Verification Methods for Finite State Systems, International Workshop. LNCS, vol. 407, pp. 151–165. Springer (1989)
30. Villani, N., Iosif, R., Sangnier, A., Bozga, M.: Parcosys: counting abstraction for the verification of structured parameterized networks (2025). Ongoing development version at https://gricad-gitlab.univ-grenoble-alpes.fr/neven/parcosys
31. Wolf, K.: Petri net model checking with LoLA 2. In: Khomenko, V., Roux, O.H. (eds.) Application and Theory of Petri Nets and Concurrency - 39th International Conference, PETRI NETS 2018, Bratislava, Slovakia, 24–29 June 2018, Proceedings. LNCS, vol. 10877, pp. 351–362. Springer (2018)
32. Wolf, K., Lohmann, N.: LoLA: a low level petri net analyzer. https://theo.informatik.uni-rostock.de/theo-forschung/tools/lola/
33. Wolper, P., Lovinfosse, V.: Verifying properties of large sets of processes with network invariants. In: Automatic Verification Methods for Finite State Systems, International Workshop. LNCS, vol. 407, pp. 68–80. Springer (1989)

QSM-Cutoff: Systematic Derivation of Quantified Cutoff Formulas for Distributed Protocols

Yun-Rong Luo[1], Aman Goel[2], and Karem Sakallah[1($\boxtimes$)]

[1] University of Michigan, Ann Arbor, USA
karem@umich.edu
[2] Amazon Web Services, Seattle, USA

Abstract. We introduce `QSM-Cutoff`, a new procedure that employs the quantified symmetric minimization algorithm from [12] to systematically derive quantified formulas that precisely capture the onset of cutoff and saturation in distributed protocols. `QSM-Cutoff` performs symmetry-aware forward reachability to enumerate the reachable states of a finite protocol instance, and applies symmetry-preserving logic minimization to express these states as a minimum-cost finitely-quantified reachability formula. `QSM-Cutoff` repeats this finite analysis process to derive a sequence of reachability formulas $R_1, R_2, R_3, \cdots$ at increasing protocol sizes. This process terminates at size k when R_k is a *unique* solution to symmetric minimization that yields the exact set of reachable states when evaluated at size $k + 1$. We define $c := k$ as the *cutoff size* and $R_c := R_k$ as the *cutoff formula*. Empirically, R_c is shown to be a *reachability invariant* that encodes the reachable states for any protocol size.

`QSM-Cutoff` extends the finite analysis process in [12] by introducing two algorithmic enhancements: a depth-first search algorithm that enumerates the reachable states of a finite protocol by searching only for their symmetric quotient, and an extended quantification pattern inference algorithm that expresses explicit clause orbits of finite instances by logically equivalent quantified formulas. Empirical results demonstrate that, compared to the techniques used in [12], `QSM-Cutoff` is able to analyze a larger corpus of protocols, derive more compact quantified inductive invariants, and converge at smaller cutoffs. In contrast to previous scholarship, `QSM-Cutoff` offers a new angle for understanding the notions of cutoff and saturation of distributed protocols. In particular, it raises intriguing questions about the unexpected role of symmetric logic minimization in this much-researched area and opens new directions for further research.

Keywords: Distributed protocols · cutoff formula · symmetric logic minimization · reachability invariant · saturation · quantification-pattern inference

© The Author(s) 2025
R. Piskac and Z. Rakamarić (Eds.): CAV 2025, LNCS 15933, pp. 263–286, 2025.
https://doi.org/10.1007/978-3-031-98682-6_14

1 Introduction

The availability of powerful Satisfiability Modulo Theories (SMT) solvers [8] has enabled the automated analysis and verification of distributed protocols, particularly the *discovery* of quantified inductive invariants that serve as proof certificates for protocol safety [12,16,19,22–24,26,29,31,32].

In this paper we propose QSM-Cutoff, a new approach for analyzing and understanding the behavior of distributed protocols. The intuition behind this approach is that the inherent regularity of a distributed protocol (aka a parameterized system), namely its structural symmetry, must *necessarily* yield a compact quantified first-order logic (FOL) formula that encodes its reachable states. This may seem surprising since finding compact formulas for the reachable states of non-parameterized irregular finite systems (e.g., hardware) is generally intractable.

Our starting point for deriving such a formula is the oft-cited cutoff phenomenon that many researchers have documented over the past several decades [7,10,11,21,27,30]. Without loss of generality, assume a protocol defined over a single sort whose domain size parameter is k. The key insight is that it should be possible to identify this cutoff by deriving a sequence of "special" finitely-quantified reachability formulas $R_1, R_2, R_3, \cdots$ at increasing domain sizes that eventually converge, i.e., become domain size-independent, at cutoff. Intuitively, at any given size k, the protocol cannot exhibit fewer "behaviors" than at sizes less than k. On the other hand, the protocol's behaviors saturate at the cutoff.

The main innovation in our approach for deriving these reachability formulas is the use of a symmetry-enhanced extension of classical logic minimization whose output is a minimum-cost conjunction of FOL sentences, where cost (denoted as $qCost$) accounts for both the number of quantified variables in the prefix and the number of literals in the matrix. By construction, the reachability formula R_k implicitly captures the explicit set of reachable states denoted by Reach[k]. Cutoff is reached at k if minimization yields a unique formula[1] R_k whose evaluation at the $(k + 1)$-size domain gives the exact set of reachable states Reach[$k + 1$]. We denote this formula as R_c and refer to it as the *cutoff formula* with $c = k$.

We conjecture that R_c is a *reachability invariant*, i.e., a formula that encodes the exact set of reachable states for any protocol size. This conjecture is supported by compelling empirical evidence. We are currently working on formalizing a proof of the conjecture that we hope will demystify the cutoff phenomenon by clarifying its connection to symmetric minimization. In particular, the min-$qCost$ reachability formulas at protocol sizes less than c may not have enough symmetries to capture the full behavior of the protocol. In fact, in some cases,

---

[1] Protocol specifications may contain redundancies, such as having two literals with identical values in all reachable states. This leads to multiple logically equivalent minimum-$qCost$ R_k formulas. In this case, QSM-Cutoff simply picks one of the equivalent literals to express the minimum-$qCost$ solution, and appends an additional invariant to R_k to express the logical equivalence between the two literals.

minimization yields multiple non-unique reachability formulas at sizes below the cutoff. Cutoff can now be viewed as the minimum protocol size that has enough symmetries to capture all possible behaviors and signal the onset of behavior saturation.

In addition to providing this precise definition of cutoff, QSM-Cutoff makes the following additional extensions to QSM [12] that allow it to derive compact FOL formulas for a protocol's reachable states and to scale its application to a larger set of protocols.

- SymDFS, a depth-first search algorithm that produces the set of reachable states of a finite protocol by searching only for their symmetric quotient.
- QPI, a *Quantification-Pattern Inference* algorithm that generalizes the quantifier inference algorithm in [16] for encoding explicit sets of finite clause orbits by logically equivalent quantified formulas. Specifically, QPI introduces two algorithmic improvements that result in expressing R using fewer and more compact invariants:
  - Native handling of protocol relations, such as *message*(src: node, dst: node), that have more than one argument of the same sort.
  - Merging a set of disjoint prime implicate orbits that share similar literals into an *orbit family* that is encoded using a single equivalent lower-cost *logically prime* quantified sentence. Such orbit families consist of prime implicate orbits that are *symmetrically prime* but *logically sub-prime*, allowing them to be logically combined.

The paper is organized as follows. Section 2 gives a high-level overview of QSM-Cutoff using a simple protocol. Section 3 provides preliminaries. Section 4 describes the QSM Cutoff procedure. Section 5 describes the SymDFS algorithm. Section 6 presents the QPI algorithm. Section 7 provides the empirical evaluation of QSM-Cutoff on a set of publicly-available protocols. Section 8 gives a brief review of related work. Section 9 concludes the paper with future research directions. Section A provides the appendix.

2 Motivating Example

Conceptually, QSM-Cutoff reads a protocol specification, models it as a state transition system parameterized by the cardinality of the protocol sorts, and derives a *cutoff formula* R_c that encodes the protocol's reachable states. R_c is expressed as a conjunction of finitely-quantified FOL invariants derived by a symmetric minimization algorithm. We will use the firewall protocol in Fig. 1 to give a high-level overview of how QSM-Cutoff accomplishes this task.

The firewall protocol specification in Fig. 1a refers to a single sort named node and three relations that describe the state of nodes: internal, sent, and allowed_in. Figure 1b shows the *cutoff formula* R_c derived by QSM-Cutoff for this protocol. This formula is derived by analyzing firewall at different domain sizes of the node sort. In the following, we define node[k] as the k-element domain $\{n_1, n_2, \cdots, n_k\}$, where the elements represent indistinguishable "constants." We

```
 1: sort node
 2: relation i(node)
 3: relation s(node, node)
 4: relation a(node)
 5: init ∀S, D, N. ¬s(S, D) ∧ ¬a(N)
 6: action send_from_int(src:node,
        dst:node)
 7:    require i(src) ∧ ¬i(dst)
 8:    s(src, dst) ∧ a(dst)
 9: action send_to_int(src:node, dst:node)
10:    require ¬i(src) ∧ i(dst) ∧ a(src)
11:    s(src, dst)
12: safety ∀S, D. (s(S, D) ∧ i(D) →
                    ∃I. i(I) ∧ s(I, S))
```

a: Protocol Specification

$$R_c := \Phi_1 \wedge \Phi_2 \wedge \Phi_3 \wedge \Phi_4 \wedge \Phi_5$$

$$\Phi_1 := \forall N \in \text{node}. \ \neg s(N, N)$$

$$\Phi_2 := \forall D \in \text{node}, \exists S \in \text{node}.$$
$$a(D) \rightarrow [(S \neq D) \wedge s(S, D)]$$

$$\Phi_3 := \forall N \in \text{node}. \ \neg i(N) \vee \neg a(N)$$

$$\Phi_4 := \forall S, D \in \text{node}.$$
$$S \neq D \rightarrow [s(S, D) \rightarrow i(S) \vee i(D)]$$

$$\Phi_5 := \forall S, D \in \text{node}.$$
$$S \neq D \rightarrow [s(S, D) \rightarrow a(S) \vee a(D)]$$

b: Cutoff Formula

Fig. 1. The `firewall` protocol in IVy [3]. The relations internal, sent, and allowed_in are abbreviated as i, s, and a, respectively. The init, action, and safety constructs specify the initial states, transition relation, and safety property, respectively.

use R_k to denote a closed finitely-quantified FOL formula that represents the reachable states of the finite instance `firewall[k]` with a node[k] domain. For any given value of k, QSM-Cutoff derives R_k by performing the following steps:

- Creating `firewall[k]`, a finite instance of `firewall` based on node[k].
- Using a symmetry-enhanced depth-first search algorithm to produce Reach[k], the finite *explicit* set of the reachable states of `firewall[k]`.
- Using an enhanced SAT-based symmetry-preserving version of classical logic minimization to construct a minimum-*qCost* k-reachability finitely-quantified FOL formula R_k that represents Reach[k]. This formula is expressed as a conjunction of first-order sentences, where each sentence encodes a *prime implicate orbit* (PI orbit) of Reach[k]. For $l \neq k$, we denote the interpretation of R_k on node[l] as $R_k[l]$. For consistency, we will also use $R_k[k]$ to emphasize that R_k is derived from and interpreted on node[k].

Figure 2a shows that Reach[2] for `firewall[2]` consists of 8 reachable states, which are partitioned into 5 symmetric state orbits/equivalence classes. Symmetric logic minimization on Reach[2] yields a set of 13 PI orbits, 5 of which correspond to the unique min-*qCost* formula $R_2[2]$ in the first column of Fig. 2b. Repeating this procedure for Reach[3] yields $R_3[3]$ in the second column of Fig. 2b. Apart from the chosen finite domain, the two formulas $R_2[2]$ and $R_3[3]$ differ in the red highlighted sentences. Their relationship is illustrated visually in Fig. 2c.

For $k = 2, 3$, the construction of the formula $R_k[k]$ ensures that it represents Reach[k], denoted as Models(R_k)[k] = Reach[k]. When interpreting R_2 on node[3], we observe that Models(R_2)[3] $\neq$ Reach[3], indicating that R_2 is not general enough to describe the full behavior of `firewall[3]`. In contrast, R_3 is

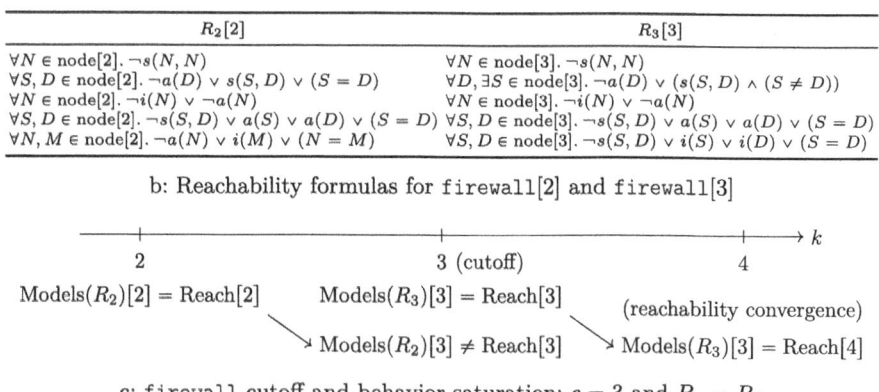

$$\text{State Vars} = [i(n_1), i(n_2), a(n_1), a(n_2), s(n_1, n_1), s(n_1, n_2), s(n_2, n_1), s(n_2, n_2)]$$
$$\text{Reach}[2] = \{\{0x00\}, \{0xC0\}, \{0x80, 0x40\}, \{0x94, 0x62\}, \{0x96, 0x66\}\}$$

a: Reachable states for `firewall[2]` in hexadecimal notation.

$R_2[2]$	$R_3[3]$
$\forall N \in \text{node}[2].\ \neg s(N, N)$	$\forall N \in \text{node}[3].\ \neg s(N, N)$
$\forall S, D \in \text{node}[2].\ \neg a(D) \lor s(S, D) \lor (S = D)$	$\forall D, \exists S \in \text{node}[3].\ \neg a(D) \lor (s(S, D) \land (S \neq D))$
$\forall N \in \text{node}[2].\ \neg i(N) \lor \neg a(N)$	$\forall N \in \text{node}[3].\ \neg i(N) \lor \neg a(N)$
$\forall S, D \in \text{node}[2].\ \neg s(S, D) \lor a(S) \lor a(D) \lor (S = D)$	$\forall S, D \in \text{node}[3].\ \neg s(S, D) \lor a(S) \lor a(D) \lor (S = D)$
$\forall N, M \in \text{node}[2].\ \neg a(N) \lor i(M) \lor (N = M)$	$\forall S, D \in \text{node}[3].\ \neg s(S, D) \lor i(S) \lor i(D) \lor (S = D)$

b: Reachability formulas for `firewall[2]` and `firewall[3]`

c: `firewall` cutoff and behavior saturation: $c = 3$ and $R_c = R_3$

Fig. 2. The QSM-Cutoff procedure on `firewall`.

capable of representing Reach[4] since Models$(R_3)[4]$ = Reach[4]. We can now view R_3 as having reached a fixed point, i.e., *reachability convergence/behavior saturation*, since adding a new node to the protocol does not introduce any new behaviors that R_3 does not already capture. Using c to indicate the cutoff size, we can now set $c = 3$ and refer to R_c as the *cutoff formula*. We conjecture that R_c actually represents Reach[k] of `firewall[k]` for any $k \geq 1$. The empirical evaluation in Sect. 7 provides strong evidence of this conjecture.

This illustration of the QSM-Cutoff procedure on the `firewall` protocol shows that the systematic construction of a sequence of symmetrically-minimized quantified formulas for the reachable states reaches a fixed point and provides an intuitive explanation of the cutoff and saturation phenomenon of parameterized systems. Figure 5 in Sect. A provides a further visual illustration of this phenomenon by showing the *regular expansion* of the five PI orbits of `firewall`'s cutoff formula as a function of $k = 1, 2, 3, 4$. For future work, we plan to explore a deeper formal and theoretical understanding of the connection between symmetric minimization and cutoff.

3 Preliminaries

3.1 Distributed Protocols: Parameterized Transition Systems

In this paper, we focus on protocols without arithmetic operations whose sorts consist of identical and indistinguishable constants. This excludes protocols such as Paxos [25] that contain sorts with totally-ordered constants. For simplicity of presentation, we assume a protocol has a single sort.

Syntax. A protocol specification $\mathcal{P}$ is given by $\mathcal{P} := (\Sigma, I, T, S)$, where $\Sigma := (\sigma, \hat{r})$ is the *signature* of $\mathcal{P}$ with σ being the sort symbol and $\hat{r} := (r_1, \ldots, r_m)$ being the relations describing states, I is a closed first-order formula over Σ representing initial states, T is the actions representing the transition relation, and S is the safety property, specified with a closed first-order formula over Σ representing safe states.

Finite Parameterization. These distributed protocols can be viewed as parameterized systems with the sort interpreted as a domain of indistinguishable and identical constants [6]. The protocol parameter k is a positive integer greater than or equal to 1 that specifies the domain size of the sort σ. The finite instance of protocol $\mathcal{P}$ under parameter k is denoted as $\mathcal{P}[k] := ((\sigma[k], \hat{r}[k]), I[k], T[k], S[k])$, where the sort σ is interpreted as a k-element domain $\sigma[k] := \{n_1, \ldots, n_k\}$ of indistinguishable constants, and $\hat{r}[k], I[k], T[k]$, and $S[k]$ denote that sort symbols in $\hat{r}, I, T$, and S are interpreted using the domain of discourse defined by $\sigma[k]$. In the following, the notation $f[k]$ for a first-order formula f indicates that we fix its domain of discourse to be $\sigma[k]$.

A *state* of $\mathcal{P}[k]$ is an interpretation of $\hat{r}[k]$, i.e., an evaluation for all relations $r_i[k] \in \hat{r}[k]$. State s is an *initial state* if $s \models I[k]$. We write $(s, t) \models T[k]$ or $T[k](s) = t$ if state s can transition to state t. A state s is *reachable* if there is a finite sequence of states $(s_i)_{i=0}^n$ such that $s_0 \models I[k]$, $s = s_n$, and $(s_i, s_{i+1}) \models T[k]$ for all $0 \leqslant i < n$.

Definition 1 (Models). *Given a finite protocol instance $\mathcal{P}[k]$ and a closed first-order formula f over the protocol's signature, we write $\mathrm{Models}(f)[k]$ to denote the states of $\mathcal{P}[k]$ that satisfy f.*

3.2   Structural Symmetry in Distributed Protocols

Our focus in this paper is on protocols whose sorts are interpreted as domains of indistinguishable constants. Consequently, the behavior of such protocols remains invariant under any permutation of their domain constants, allowing the application of symmetry analysis to infer/understand their behavior [9,12,16,21]. Readers who are not familiar with the basic notions of symmetry groups, cycle notation, symmetry orbits, etc., can refer to standard textbooks on Abstract Algebra, e.g. [14].

Given a finite protocol instance $\mathcal{P}[k]$ with domain $\sigma[k] := \{n_1, \ldots, n_k\}$, the symmetry group of $\mathcal{P}[k]$, denoted as $\mathrm{Sym}[k]$, is the *symmetric group* consisting of the $k!$ permutations of the indistinguishable constants in $\sigma[k]$. The behavior of $\mathcal{P}[k]$ behavior remains invariant under these $k!$ permutations. Given a state s of $\mathcal{P}[k]$ and a permutation $\gamma \in \mathrm{Sym}[k]$, the action of γ on s, denoted as s^γ, yields a *symmetrically-equivalent* state of $\mathcal{P}[k]$. The *orbit* of s in $\mathcal{P}[k]$, denoted as $\mathrm{Orbit}(s) := \{s^\gamma : \gamma \in \mathrm{Sym}[k]\}$, is the set of $\mathcal{P}[k]$'s states that are related to s by a permutation in $\mathrm{Sym}[k]$. Similarly, the action of a permutation $\gamma \in \mathrm{Sym}[k]$ on an arbitrary formula $f[k]$ yields a symmetrically-equivalent formula $f^\gamma[k]$ and the orbit of $f[k]$, denoted as, $\mathrm{Orbit}(f)[k] := \{f^\gamma[k] : \gamma \in \mathrm{Sym}[k]\}$ is the set of formulas that are symmetrically-equivalent to $f[k]$.

4   The QSM-Cutoff Procedure

The high-level flow of QSM-Cutoff is shown in Fig. 3 and its pseudocode is presented in Algorithm 1. Starting with protocol $\mathcal{P}[k]$ and an initial domain size $k = 1^2$ QSM-Cutoff analyzes a sequence of finite protocol instances at increasing sizes, synthesizes their respective reachability formulas $R_1, R_2, \ldots$, and outputs the cutoff formula R_c when this sequence converges. The following definitions formalize the central concepts in QSM-Cutoff and are followed by a detailed description of its two main computational steps Synthesize_Rmin and Check_Converge, and how it is used to verify safety properties.

Definition 2 (Quantified Cost: $qCost$ **[12]).** *The quantified cost of a first-order sentence Φ is defined as $qCost(\Phi) := n_Q + n_L$, where n_Q and n_L are, respectively, the number of quantified variables and literals in Φ.*

Definition 3 (Reachable States). *Reach[k] denotes the explicit enumeration of $\mathcal{P}[k]$'s set of reachable states.*

Definition 4 (k-Reachability Formula). *A k-reachability formula R_k is a min-qCost closed finitely-quantified first-order formula that implicitly represents Reach[k], formally: $Models(R_k)[k] = Reach[k]$.*

Definition 5 (Cutoff Formula). *A k-reachability formula R_k is a cutoff formula, denoted as R_c, if it is the first formula in a sequence of reachability formulas $R_1, R_2, R_3, \cdots$ at increasing protocol sizes that a) is a unique solution of symmetric minimization, and b) $Models(R_k)[k+1] = Reach[k+1]$. If these two conditions hold, we set $c = k$ and $R_c = R_k$ where c is the cutoff size and R_c is the cutoff formula. Cutoff indicates that the sequence of reachability formulas has reached a fixed-point, i.e., reachability convergence.*

Definition 6 (Reachability Invariant). *A closed first-order formula R is a reachability invariant for protocol $\mathcal{P}$ if $\forall k \in \mathbb{Z}^+. Models(R)[k] = Reach[k]$.*

Corollary 1. *A reachability invariant R is the strongest inductive invariant for a protocol since, by definition, it includes the initial states and is closed under the transition relation.*

4.1   Synthesizing k-Reachability Formula R_k

The Synthesize_Rmin subroutine in Algorithm 1 takes a finite protocol instance $\mathcal{P}[k]$ as input and uses the *quantified cost* metric in Definition 2 to return a symmetrically-minimized finitely-quantified k-reachability formula R_k as output. The main steps in Synthesize_Rmin are:

- Step 1 (Line 2): Generate Reach[k] using the *symmetric quotient depth-first search* (SymDFS) algorithm described in Sect. 5.

---

^{2} For protocols that include quorum sorts that model node majorities, QSM-Cutoff starts with an initial node domain size $k = 2$ to form a non-trivial majority.

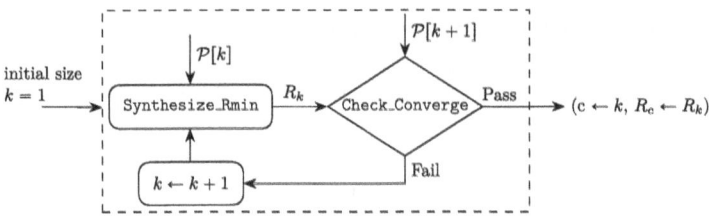

Fig. 3. Computation flow for `QSM-Cutoff`.

- Step 2 (Line 3): Generate the complete set of prime implicant orbits for $\neg\text{Reach}[k]$ using the symmetry-preserving SAT-based logic minimization algorithm in [12]. Negation of these orbits yields the complete set of *explicit prime implicate orbits* for Reach$[k]$ denoted as PIs$[k] := \{\Psi_1[k], \ldots, \Psi_n[k]\}$, such that Reach$[k] \equiv \bigwedge_{i=1}^{n} \Psi_i[k]$.
- Step 3 (Line 4–5): Express each explicit PI orbit $\Psi_i[k] \in$ PIs$[k]$ by a logically-equivalent first-order sentence Φ_i using the quantification-pattern inference (`QPI`) algorithm described in Sect. 6.
- Step 4 (Line 6): Derive a min-$qCost$ cover for Reach$[k]$ as a subset of MinPIs$[k] \subseteq$ PIs$[k]$ using the SAT-based branch-and-bound search algorithm in [12].
- Step 5 (Line 7): Construct the k-reachability formula $R_k :- \bigwedge_{\Psi_i[k]\in\text{MinPIs}[k]} \Phi_i$.

```
 1: procedure Synthesize_Rmin(P[k])        14: procedure QSM-Cutoff(P, k)
 2:    Reach[k] ← SymDFS(P[k])             15:    while true do
 3:    PIs[k] ← PI_Orbit_Gen(Reach[k])     16:       Rk ← Synthesize_Rmin(P[k])
 4:    for all Ψi[k] ∈ PIs[k] do           17:       if Check_Converge(Rk, P[k + 1])
 5:       Φi ← QPI(Ψi[k])                             then
 6:    MinPIs[k] ← PI_Orbit_Min(PIs[k])    18:          return (c ← k, Rc ← Rk)
 7:    Rk ← ⋀Ψi[k]∈MinPIs[k] Φi            19:       else k ← k + 1
 8:    return Rk

 9: procedure Check_Converge(Rk, P[l])
10:    Reach[l] ← SymDFS(P[l])
11:    if Models(Rk)[l] = Reach[l] then
12:       return Pass
13:    else return Fail
```

Algorithm 1: The `QSM-Cutoff` Procedure

Proposition 1 (Correctness of Synthesize_Rmin [12]). *Given a finite protocol instance* $\mathcal{P}[k]$, *the formula* R_k *returned by* **Synthesize_Rmin** *is a k-reachability formula, i.e.,* $Models(R_k)[k] = Reach[k]$.

Proof. The proposition can be proved by the construction of `Synthesize_Rmin`.

$$R_k[k] \overset{\text{By Step 5}}{:=} \bigwedge_{\Psi_i[k]\in\text{MinPIs}[k]} \Phi_i[k] \overset{\text{By Step 3}}{\equiv} \bigwedge_{\Psi_i[k]\in\text{MinPIs}[k]} \Psi_i[k] \overset{\text{By Step 4}}{\equiv} \text{Reach}[k]$$

□

```
1: procedure QSM-Cutoff(𝒫, k)
2:    while true do
3:       R_k^1, ..., R_k^m ← Synthesize_Rmin(𝒫[k])
4:       if m = 1 then
5:          if Check_Converge(R_k, 𝒫[k + 1]) then
6:             return (c ← k, R_c ← R_k)
7:          else k ← k + 1
8:       else
9:          l ← 1
10:         while Check_Converge(R_k^i, 𝒫[k + l]) passes for all i = 1, ..., m do
11:            l ← l + 1
12:         k ← k + l
```

Algorithm 2: Updated QSM-Cutoff Procedure

4.2   Reachability Convergence and Derivation of Cutoff Formula R_c

The QSM-Cutoff procedure described in Fig. 3 and Algorithm 1 assumes that Synthesize_Rmin returns a unique minimum-$qCost$ k-reachability formula R_k. While this is true at and beyond cutoff, at domain sizes k that are less than cutoff Synthesize_Rmin may return multiple non-unique solutions. To correctly identify the cutoff and the cutoff formula R_c as stated in Definition 5, the actual implementation of QSM-Cutoff is based on the updated convergence procedure in Algorithm 2.

When Synthesize_Rmin returns a unique solution R_k, the updated procedure (Lines 5–7) converges if $\text{Models}(R_k)[k + 1] = \text{Reach}[k + 1]$ and indicates that the cutoff has been reached. Otherwise, it sets $k \leftarrow k + 1$ to synthesize and check the convergence of the reachability formula at the next protocol size. However, when Synthesize_Rmin returns multiple min-$qCost$ solutions, the updated procedure (Lines 9–12) recognizes that k cannot be the cutoff size (since it violates the uniqueness requirement) and proceeds to determine the next protocol size $k \leftarrow k + l$ at which the next reachability formula must be synthesized. Let $pass[k + j]$ be a predicate defined as follows,

$$pass[k + j] := (\forall i \in [1, m]. \text{Models}(R_k^i)[k + j] = \text{Reach}[k + j]),$$

which denotes that all m non-unique min-$qCost$ solutions pass the convergence check at protocol size $k + j$. The protocol size for synthesizing the next reachability formula is now set to $k + l$, with l being the smallest integer $l \geqslant 1$ that satisfies

$$\neg pass[k + l] \bigwedge_{j \in [1, l)} pass[k + j]$$

4.3   Verification of Safety Properties with QSM-Cutoff

Our current procedure for verifying that a given safety property S holds for protocol $\mathcal{P} := (\Sigma, I, T, S)$ is to use ivy_check [28] to *prove* that:

- R_c is an inductive invariant, i.e., $I \rightarrow R_c$ and $R_c \wedge T \rightarrow R_c'$
- R_c implies the safety property, i.e., $R_c \rightarrow S$

We also derive strengthening assertions A for S by finding minimal unsatisfiable subsets (MUSes) of the set of invariants comprising R_c from the UNSAT formula $A = MUS[(R_c \wedge S) \wedge T \wedge \neg(R_c' \wedge S')]$.

Our experimental evaluation in Sect. 7 shows that, for all the protocols we tested, the cutoff formula derived by QSM-Cutoff is indeed an inductive invariant. Combined with the empirical observation that $\mathrm{Models}(R_c)[k]) = \mathrm{Reach}[k]$ for various k larger and smaller than c, this lends strong support for stating the following conjecture:

Conjecture. *The cutoff formula R_c returned by QSM-Cutoff is a reachability invariant, i.e., the strongest inductive invariant.*

Formally proving this conjecture is still work-in-progress that requires understanding the role of symmetric logic minimization in explaining the phenomenon of cutoff and behavior saturation.

5   Symmetric Quotient Depth-First-Search

The first step in the QSM-Cutoff flow is the computation of $\mathrm{Reach}[k]$, the set of reachable states for a finite protocol instance $\mathcal{P}[k]$. This step was performed in QSM using a BDD-based symbolic image computation procedure that did not scale in several cases where the reachable state space became very large due to the protocols' structural symmetries [12]. QSM-Cutoff addresses this problem by introducing an explicit *Symmetric Quotient Depth-First-Search* algorithm (SymDFS) that leverages these symmetries directly.

```
 1: procedure SymDFS(P[k])              8: procedure SymDFS_rec(s, Reach)
 2:    Reach ← ∅                         9:    for all t ∈ T[k](s) do
 3:    for all s ⊨ I[k] do              10:       if t ∉ Reach then
 4:       if s ∉ Reach then             11:          Reach ← Reach ∪ Orbit(t)
 5:          Reach ← Reach ∪ Orbit(s)   12:          Reach ← SymDFS_rec(t, Reach)
 6:          Reach ← SymDFS_rec(s, Reach)  13:    return Reach
 7:    return Reach
```

Algorithm 3: Symmetric Quotient Depth-First-Search (SymDFS)

The key idea in SymDFS is to limit the traversal of a protocol's state graph to just the graph's *symmetric quotient* and recording, as it proceeds, the orbits of symmetric states. Specifically, as shown in Algorithm 3, whenever a reachable state s is visited for the first time (Lines 4 and 10), SymDFS labels it as a *representative state*, and automatically adds its entire state orbit, Orbit(s), to the explored set of reachable states (Lines 5 and 11). This prevents future branching from any state in this orbit. Essentially, SymDFS performs a recursive depth-first search from only the representative states (Lines 6 and 12). Upon the termination of SymDFS, the set of explored states produced by SymDFS is the reachable states $\mathrm{Reach}[k]$ (Line 7). Note that SymDFS adds the complete orbit of every newly visited state to the currently explored states (Line 5 and 11) to eventually produce the complete set of reachable states $\mathrm{Reach}[k]$.

6   Quantification-Pattern Inference

A critical step in `QSM-Cutoff` is the encoding of the *explicit* set of clauses in a symmetry orbit by an equivalent first-order sentence that *implicitly* captures this set. Specifically, Quantification-Pattern Inference (`QPI`) refers to the derivation of a first-order sentence Φ_i that represents the exact set of clauses in a PI orbit $\Psi_i[k] \in \mathrm{PIs}[k]$. `QPI` enables the generalization of finite analysis and is key to demonstrating the phenomena of cutoff and saturation.

We should note that quantification is commonly used to implicitly represent sets by capturing the "set builder" constraint that set members must satisfy. For example, the set of odd numbers $\{1, 3, 5, \cdots\}$ can be expressed by the first-order formula $Odd(x) := (\exists y \in \mathbb{N}.\, x = 2y + 1)$ where $\mathbb{N}$ is the set of natural numbers. In this sense, the quantification patterns derived by the `QPI` procedure can be viewed as the set builders that capture the structural symmetry constraints that must be satisfied by a set of clauses to be members of a given symmetry orbit.

In this section, we describe the procedure for deriving the first-order sentences that capture single PI orbits as well as *orbit families* consisting of PI orbits that share similar literals.

6.1   Quantification-Pattern Inference for Prime Implicate Orbits

The basic quantifier inference (QI) procedure for encoding an explicit PI orbit by an equivalent first-order sentence was introduced in [16]. The procedure, which is used in `QSM` [12], is based on an analysis of the structural distribution of sort constants in a representative PI clause to derive an appropriate first-order sentence that correctly captures the representative's explicit PI orbit.

The procedure assumes that constants of a given sort cannot appear in more than one argument in any protocol relation. For example, in the `firewall` protocol, the procedure can handle a relation such as *allowed_in*(node), but not *sent*(node, node). This significantly limits the set of protocols that `QSM` is able to analyze. `QSM-Cutoff` adopts the basic framework of this procedure, but extends it to remove its *"single arity"* limitation, allowing it to handle a much larger corpus of protocols. For details of the QI procedure, we refer the reader to [16] but provide a brief *generic* sketch below to contextualize its extension in `QSM-Cutoff`.

The procedure uses two structural metrics of sort constants in a representative clause to assign the clause to one of three possible quantification patterns. These metrics, defined below, are the count of sort constants in the clause and a partition of these constants into suitable equivalence classes.

Definition 7 (Constant Count). $\#(\psi, \sigma[k])$ *is the number of constants from domain $\sigma[k]$ that appear in clause ψ.*

Definition 8 (Constant Partition). $\pi(\psi, \sigma[k])$ *is a partition of all domain constants $n \in \sigma[k]$ induced by how they are distributed in the clause.*

The three quantification patterns are determined as follows:

- Case 1: $\#(\psi, \sigma[k]) < k$, infer $\forall^+$.
- Case 2: $\#(\psi, \sigma[k]) = k$ and $|\pi(\psi, \sigma[k])| = 1$, infer $\exists^+$.
- Case 3: $\#(\psi, \sigma[k]) = k$ and $|\pi(\psi, \sigma[k])| > 1$, infer $\forall^+\exists^+$.

In cases 2 and 3, $|\pi(\psi, \sigma[k])|$ is the cardinality of the partition, i.e., the number of its equivalence classes. In addition to the above classification of quantification patterns, appropriate inequality constraints for quantified variables are added to ensure correctness.

The main difference between the QI procedure in QSM and the QPI procedure in QSM-Cutoff is the criterion used to partition the constants.

Definition 9 (Identical Occurence). *Given a clause ψ, let n_1 and n_2 be two distinct constants from the $\sigma[k]$ domain. Constants n_1 and n_2 are said to appear identically in the literals of ψ if $\psi^{(n_1\ n_2)} \equiv \psi$. In other words, swapping n_1 and n_2 leaves ψ logically unchanged.*

Definition 10 (Argument Position Signature). *Given a clause ψ and a constant $n \in \sigma[k]$, the argument position signature of n in ψ, denoted as $aps(\psi, n)$, is the set of all tuples (lit, pos, tot), where tot is the total number of n's occurrences at argument position pos of literal lit in ψ.*

QSM partitions sort constants using Definition 9, which limits it to protocols containing single arity relations. On the other hand, QPI partitions sort constants using Definition 10, allowing it to handle relations of arbitrary arity. QPI also adds a check in cases 2 and 3 to determine if existential quantification successfully captures the given PI orbit, and reverts back to universal quantification if the check fails.

Table 1 illustrates QSM-Cutoff's QPI procedure on 4 example PI orbits derived from the firewall protocol.

6.2 Quantification-Pattern Inference for Orbit Families

While the number of PI orbits for most protocols we analyzed was quite manageable, for several protocols, the PI orbit generation step produced a large number of PI orbits that shared the same set of literal symbols but with different distribution patterns of the sort constants in the literals' arguments. Further analysis showed that such PI orbits are *symmetrically, but not logically prime*. We will refer to such PI orbits as *orbit families* and show how to logically merge an orbit family and encode it by a single first-order sentence with a significantly lower *qCost*.

We will illustrate *orbit family quantification pattern inference* using the Simple Decentralized Lock protocol [4]. This protocol maintains a distributed lock among a number of nodes such that only one node has the lock at any given time. The protocol has a single sort node and two relations: *message*(node, node) and *has_lock*(node). Without merging orbit families, QSM-Cutoff converged at a cutoff of 4 nodes, yielding a solution consisting of 16 PI orbits and a total *qCost* of 99. These sixteen PI orbits in the solution consisted of two 1-orbit families,

Table 1. Examples of `QPI` steps.

PI orbit	$\Psi_A[3] := \{a(n_1) \vee i(n_2)\}_{(\psi_A)} \wedge \{a(n_1) \vee i(n_3)\} \wedge \{a(n_2) \vee i(n_1)\}$ $\wedge \{a(n_2) \vee i(n_3)\}$ $\wedge \{a(n_3) \vee i(n_1)\} \wedge \{a(n_3) \vee i(n_2)\}$
Case 1	$\#(\psi_A, \text{node}[3]) = 2 < 3$
QPI result	$\Phi_A[3] := \forall N_1, N_2 \in \text{node}[3]. (N_1 \neq N_2) \rightarrow a(N_1) \vee i(N_2)$
PI orbit	$\Psi_B[3] := \{ s(n_1, n_1) \vee s(n_1, n_2) \vee s(n_1, n_3) \vee s(n_2, n_1) \vee s(n_2, n_2) \vee$ $s(n_2, n_3) \vee s(n_3, n_1) \vee s(n_3, n_2) \vee s(n_3, n_3)\}_{(\psi_B)}$
Signature	$aps(\psi_B, n_1) = aps(\psi_B, n_2) = aps(\psi_B, n_3) = \{(s, 1, 3), (s, 2, 3)\}$
Case 2	$\#(\psi_B, \text{node}[3]) = 3$ $\qquad \pi(\psi_B, \text{node}[3]) = \{\{n_1, n_2, n_3\}\}$
Check-∃ (pass)	$\psi_B \equiv \exists N_1, N_2 \in \{n_1, n_2, n_3\}. s(N_1, N_2)$ PASSES
QPI result	$\Phi_B[3] := \exists N_1, N_2 \in \text{node}[3]. s(N_1, N_2)$
PI orbit	$\Psi_C[3] := \{a(n_1) \vee s(n_2, n_1) \vee s(n_3, n_1)\}_{(\psi_C)} \wedge$ $\{a(n_2) \vee s(n_1, n_2) \vee s(n_3, n_2)\} \wedge \{a(n_3) \vee s(n_1, n_3) \vee s(n_2, n_3)\}$
Signature	$aps(\psi_C, n_1) = \{(a, 1, 1), (s, 2, 2)\}, aps(\psi_C, n_2) = aps(\psi_C, n_3) = \{(s, 1, 1)\}$
Case 3	$\#(\psi_C, \text{node}[3]) = 3$ $\qquad \pi(\psi_C, \text{node}[3]) = \{\{n_1\}, \{n_2, n_3\}\}$
Check-∃ (pass)	$\psi_C \equiv \exists N_1 \in \{n_2, n_3\}. a(n_1) \vee s(N_1, n_1)$ PASSES
QPI result	$\Phi_C[3] := \forall N_2 \in \text{node}[3], \exists N_1 \in \text{node}[3]. a(N_2) \vee (s(N_1, N_2) \wedge (N_1 \neq N_2))$
PI orbit	$\Psi_D[2] := \{s(n_1, n_2) \vee s(n_2, n_1)\}_{(\psi_D)}$
Signature	$aps(\psi_D, n_1) = aps(\psi_D, n_2) = \{(s, 1, 1), (s, 2, 1)\}$
Case 2	$\#(\psi_D, \text{node}[2]) = 2$ $\qquad \pi(\psi_D, \text{node}[2]) = \{\{n_1, n_2\}\}$
Check-∃ (fail)	$\psi_D \not\equiv \exists N_1, N_2 \in \{n_1, n_2\}. s(N_1, N_2)$ FAILS
QPI result	$\Phi_D[2] := \forall N_1, N_2 \in \text{node}[2]. (N_1 \neq N_2) \rightarrow s(N_1, N_2) \vee s(N_2, N_1)$

1. The table shows three crafted PI orbits $\Psi_A[3]$, $\Psi_B[3]$, and $\Psi_C[3]$ for `firewall[3]` and their respective quantified form Φ_A, Φ_B, and Φ_C produced by `QPI`. We also provide an additional crafted PI orbit $\Psi_D[2]$ for `firewall[2]` to illustrate a case where the check for existential quantification fails.

2. The representative clause in each PI orbit Ψ_i is marked with a subscript annotation (ψ_i).

3. In each partition π, a multi-constant class $C \in \pi$ with $|C| > 1$ is highlighted in red.

one 9-orbit family whose clause template is $[\neg message(\cdot, \cdot) \vee \neg message(\cdot, \cdot)]$, and one 5-orbit family with clause template $[\neg has\_lock(\cdot) \vee \neg message(\cdot, \cdot)]$. Merging the orbit families allows `QSM-Cutoff` to converge at a cutoff of 3 nodes with a 4 quantified invariants solution whose total $qCost$ is 22.

To facilitate the description of the QPI procedure for orbit families, it is helpful to use $\lambda, \pi,$ and ϕ to identify the three parts of a first-order sentence Φ as shown by the example in Eq. (1), where:

- λ denotes the quantification prefix consisting of universal quantifier(s), quantified variables, and a domain of quantification,
- π denotes any required constraints on the quantified variables, and
- ϕ denotes the quantifier-free clause.

$$\Phi := \underbrace{\forall X, Y \in \text{node}[2].}_{\lambda} \underbrace{(X \neq Y)}_{\pi} \rightarrow \underbrace{\neg(has\_lock(X) \land has\_lock(Y))}_{\phi} \quad (1)$$

Table 2. Example of QPI for the orbit family $\Psi := \{\Psi_1, \Psi_2, \Psi_3, \Psi_4\}$

PI Orbit	clauses	Φ_i	qCost
$\Psi_1[2]$	$\{\neg msg(n_1, n_1) \lor \neg msg(n_2, n_2)\}$	$\Phi_1 := \forall R, S. (R \neq S) \rightarrow \neg msg(R, R) \lor \neg msg(S, S)$	5
$\Psi_2[2]$	$\{\neg msg(n_1, n_2) \lor \neg msg(n_2, n_1)\}$	$\Phi_2 := \forall R, S. (R \neq S) \rightarrow \neg msg(R, S) \lor \neg msg(S, R)$	5
$\Psi_3[2]$	$\{\neg msg(n_2, n_1) \lor \neg msg(n_2, n_2)\},$ $\{\neg msg(n_1, n_1) \lor \neg msg(n_1, n_2)\}$	$\Phi_3 := \forall R, S. (R \neq S) \rightarrow \neg msg(R, S) \lor \neg msg(R, R)$	5
$\Psi_4[2]$	$\{\neg msg(n_1, n_1) \lor \neg msg(n_2, n_1)\},$ $\{\neg msg(n_1, n_2) \lor \neg msg(n_2, n_2)\}$	$\Phi_4 := \forall R, S. (R \neq S) \rightarrow \neg msg(R, S) \lor \neg msg(S, S)$	5
$\Phi := \forall N_1, N_2, N_3, N_4 . \neg((N_1 = N_3) \land (N_2 = N_4)) \rightarrow \neg msg(N_1, N_2) \lor \neg msg(N_3, N_4)$ $\equiv \Phi_1 \land \Phi_2 \land \Phi_3 \land \Phi_4$			8

1. The table shows a orbit family $\Psi := \{\Psi_1, \Psi_2, \Psi_3, \Psi_3\}$ for simple-decentralized-lock[2]. For each individual PI orbit Ψ_i in this family, we show its respective quantified form Φ_i if QPI infers Ψ_i individually. The final formula Φ is the quantified form for the entire orbit family Ψ if QPI infers the whole family all together.
2. We use msg to abbreviate the literal *message*.

Table 2 shows the results of separate and merged quantification for one of the orbit families in a 2-node instance of this protocol. This orbit family has 6 clauses split into 4 disjoint PI orbits. Separate quantification of these PI orbits, using the QPI procedure in Sect. 6.1, yields 4 first-order sentences for a total qCost of 20. The last row in the table shows the result of merged quantification, which yields a single first-order sentence with a qCost of 8.

The main steps for deriving this merged first-order sentence are:

Normalization This refers to finding a common first-order sentence template to facilitate the logical conjunction of the PI orbits' individual first-order sentences, and introducing additional quantified variables and suitable constraints among them to preserve the PI orbits.

Minimization This refers to applying logic minimization to the disjunction of the constraints on the extended set of quantified variables to obtain an equivalent expression with the least literal cost.

Normalization of the PI Orbits' First-Order Sentences. Normalization of the 4 PI orbits in Table 2 introduces two additional quantified variables to the prefix of all PI orbits as well as an orbit-specific quantification constraint to each PI orbit. The normalized first-order sentences for the 4 PI orbits will now have the form:

$$\Phi_i := \forall N_1, N_2, N_3, N_4. \; \pi_i \rightarrow \neg msg(N_1, N_2) \lor \neg msg(N_3, N_4) \quad (2)$$

where π_i is the required quantification constraint for the first-order sentence of PI orbit Ψ_i. These constraints, shown in Table 3, are inferred as equalities and inequalities between pairs of the extended quantified variables based on how they map to the original quantified variables in Table 2. It is important to note that the normalized sentence for each PI orbit is logically equivalent to its original sentence in Table 2.

The initial merged first-order sentence Φ can now be constructed using the normalized first-order sentence template along with a constraint $\pi := \pi_1 \vee \pi_2 \vee \pi_3 \vee \pi_4$ as shown in Table 3.

Table 3. Normalization of PI Orbits' First-order Sentences

Normalized sentence template: $\Phi \;=\; \underbrace{\forall N_1, N_2, N_3, N_4.}_{\lambda}\; \pi \;\rightarrow\;$

$\underbrace{\neg msg(N_1, N_2) \vee \neg msg(N_3, N_4)}_{\phi}$

Argument Pattern for Φ_i	Constraints on Quantified Variables π_i	Normalized Φ_i
$\Phi_1 : [N_1, N_2 \mapsto R, N_3, N_4 \mapsto S]$	$\pi_1 := (N_1 = N_2) \wedge (N_3 = N_4) \wedge (N_1 \neq N_3)$	$\Phi_1 := \lambda. \; \pi_1 \rightarrow \phi$
$\Phi_2 : [N_1, N_4 \mapsto R, N_2, N_3 \mapsto S]$	$\pi_2 := (N_1 = N_4) \wedge (N_2 = N_3) \wedge (N_1 \neq N_2)$	$\Phi_2 := \lambda. \; \pi_2 \rightarrow \phi$
$\Phi_3 : [N_1, N_3, N_4 \mapsto R, N_2 \mapsto S]$	$\pi_3 := (N_1 = N_3) \wedge (N_1 = N_4) \wedge (N_1 \neq N_2)$	$\Phi_3 := \lambda. \; \pi_3 \rightarrow \phi$
$\Phi_4 : [N_1 \mapsto R, N_2, N_3, N_4 \mapsto S]$	$\pi_4 := (N_2 = N_3) \wedge (N_2 = N_4) \wedge (N_1 \neq N_2)$	$\Phi_4 := \lambda. \; \pi_4 \rightarrow \phi$

Initial Solution: $\Phi := \{\lambda. (\pi_1 \vee \pi_2 \vee \pi_3 \vee \pi_4) \rightarrow \phi\} \equiv \Phi_1 \wedge \Phi_2 \wedge \Phi_3 \wedge \Phi_4$ $qCost$: 18

Minimization of the Merged Quantification Constraints. The second step in the orbit family merging process is to apply two-level logic minimization [2] to find an expression $\pi_{\min}$ that minimizes the literal cost of π. This is achieved by introducing six *equality* Boolean variables $e_{ij} := (N_i = N_j)$ such that $i, j \in \{1, 2, 3, 4\}$, and $i \neq j$, and formulating π as the following 6-variable Boolean function

$$\pi = (e_{12} \cdot e_{34} \cdot \neg e_{13}) \vee (e_{14} \cdot e_{23} \cdot \neg e_{12}) \vee (e_{13} \cdot e_{14} \cdot \neg e_{12}) \vee (e_{23} \cdot e_{24} \cdot \neg e_{12}) \quad (3)$$

This function has 64 minterms representing the 64 possible combinations of the equality variables. Most of these combinations, denoted as minterms m_i for $i \in [0, 63]$, violate the transitivity of equality since a 4-element set (the four quantified variables in the normalized prefix) can only be partitioned in 15 different ways. Figure 4 shows these 15 partitions and their corresponding *valid* minterms. The green partitions correspond to the 4 quantification constraints in Eq. (3). Minimizing Eq. (3) with an onset corresponding to the 4 green partitions, an offset corresponding to the 11 remaining valid partitions, and a don't-care set corresponding to the 49 invalid minterms yields a solution with a literal cost of 7 and a $qCost$ of 13.

A more optimal solution takes advantage of the fact that the 7 red partitions in Fig. 4 have 3 or more equivalence classes. Since the original quantification of the 4 PI orbits required only 2 quantified variables that can only be partitioned in two ways ($\{\{R\}, \{S\}\}$ and $\{R, S\}$), with at most two equivalence classes, the red partitions in Fig. 4 can also be regarded as don't-cares leading to a solution with a literal cost of 4 and a $qCost$ of 10.

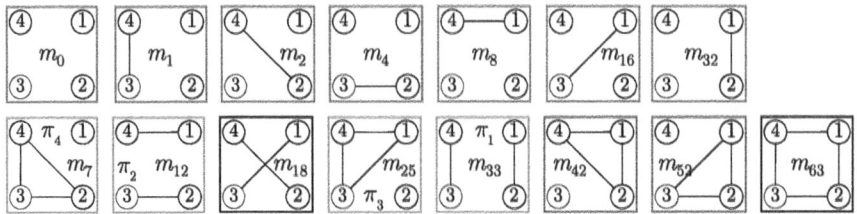

Fig. 4. Partitions on a set of 4 elements. The final minimized first-order sentence in Table 2 is derived with an onset that corresponds to the green and purple partitions, an offset that corresponds to the two black partitions (m_{18} and m_{63}), and a don't-care set that corresponds to the red partitions and the 49 invalid minterms that violate the transitivity of equality. (Color figure online)

Finally, the commutativity of logical OR allows the two msg literals in Eq. (2) to be swapped, yielding the symmetric permutation $(1\ 3)(2\ 4)$ on the normalized quantified variables. This allows us to add the purple partitions m_{42} and m_{52} to the onset since $m_7^{(1\ 3)(2\ 4)} = m_{42}$ and $m_{25}^{(1\ 3)(2\ 4)} = m_{52}$ and drops the literal cost of the minimized solution to 2 and corresponds to the $qCost$ of 8 shown in Table 2.

QSM-Cutoff includes this procedure, with additional optimizations for situations with a larger number of normalized quantified variables, to obtain the final minimized first-order sentence for an orbit family.

7   Experimental Results

We evaluated QSM-Cutoff on 19 protocols, specified in the IVy language [28], from [1,23,26]. This set is a superset of the protocols evaluated in [12], and includes fairly complex models of consensus algorithms as well as protocols such as two-phase commit, sharded key-value store, etc. Several studies [13,20,23,26,28] have indicated the challenges involved in verifying these protocols. The experiments were conducted on a Linux machine with an Intel(R) Xeon(R) Platinum 8358 CPU running at 2.6 GHz. We set a time limit of 6000 s for each run of QSM-Cutoff. Table 4 presents the overall statistics of running QSM-Cutoff on these 19 protocols. Our implementation for QSM-Cutoff is publicly available at [5].

The high-level takeaways from these experiments are:

Table 4. Overall Statistics of `QSM-Cutoff`

Protocol	Cutoff	QSM-Cutoff #A ($\#R_c$, C)	T^d/T^b	QSM-Cutoff-nf ($\#R_c$, C)	T^d/T^b	[12] #Inv
Consensus	v=3	0 (1, 5)	48/22	(1, 5)	49/22	1
naive_consensus ‡	n=3,q=3,v=3	3 (3, 16)	98/45	(3, 16)	95/51	3‡
toy_consensus ‡	n=3,q=3,v=3	2 (4, 20)	106/70	(4, 20)	105/65	4‡
toy_consensus_forall ‡	n=5,q=10,v=3	3 (4, 21)	768/TO	(4, 21)	769/TO	6‡
toy_consensus_epr ‡	n=3,q=3,v=3	3 (5, 24)	107/67	(5, 24)	108/66	6‡
consensus_epr †‡	n=3,q=3,v=2	5 (10, 56)	TO/200	(?, ?)	TO/TO	16‡
lock_server	s=1,c=3	1 (3, 14)	76/31	(3, 14)	78/33	3
lockserv	n=3	8 (**10, 41**)	49/25	(13, 53)	49/23	13
lockserv_automaton	n=3	8 (**10, 41**)	47/26	(13, 53)	51/24	13
simple-decentralized-lock †	n=3	2 (**4, 22**)	56/29	(16, 99)	64/43	18†
client_server_ae	n=1,req=1,res=1	1 (3, 14)	42/15	(3, 14)	43/14	?
Ricart-Agrawala †	n=2	2 (4, 15)	40/15	(4, 15)	39/17	4
sharded_kv	n=3,k=1,v=2	4 (**5, 35**)	122/69	(8, 53)	131/77	8
sharded_kv_no_lost_keys	n=3,k=1,v=2	1 (**6, 40**)	137/77	(9, 58)	136/89	9
firewall †	n=3	2 (5, 22)	54/30	(5, 22)	59/34	5
TCommit	rm=2	1 (**7, 25**)	35/16	(8, 29)	37/16	8
TwoPhase	rm=1	8 (16, 46)	60/64	(16, 46)	61/61	?
simple-election ‡	a=3,q=3,p=3	2 (5, 24)	134/93	(5, 24)	134/88	7‡
quorum-leader-election-wo-maj †‡	n=5,nset=10	2 (**2, 23**)	4376/TO	(5, 37)	4328/TO	?

1. Column Descriptions. **Cutoff**: domain size parameters at cutoff. **#A**: minimum number of R_c invariants needed as strengthening assertions to prove the safety property. (**$\#R_c$,C**): number of quantified invariants in the cutoff formula R_c returned by `QSM-Cutoff` or `QSM-Cutoff-nf`, and total $qCost$ of R_c. $\mathbf{T}^d/\mathbf{T}^b$: total runtime, in seconds, for `QSM-Cutoff` or `QSM-Cutoff-nf` using SymDFS/BDD, respectively; TO stands for time-out after 6000 s. **#Inv**: number of quantified invariants in the reachability formula reported in [12].

2. Abbreviations in the Cutoff column: node $\mapsto$ n, value $\mapsto$ v, resource_manager $\mapsto$ rm, server $\mapsto$ s, client $\mapsto$ c, key $\mapsto$ k, request $\mapsto$ req, response $\mapsto$ res, quorum $\mapsto$ q, acceptor $\mapsto$ a, proposer $\mapsto$ p.

3. Bold numbers in column ($\#R_c$, C) for `QSM-Cutoff` indicate fewer R_c invariants and lower total $qCost$ than `QSM-Cutoff-nf`. Gray shading in column Cutoff indicates smaller cutoffs for `QSM-Cutoff` than `QSM-Cutoff-nf`. Cases where BDD timed out are highlighted in blue. Cases where SymDFS timed out are highlighted in red.

4. The † (resp. ‡) annotations in the Protocol and Inv columns indicate the presence of multi-arity relations on the same sort (resp. member (node, quorum) relations) that were not properly handled in [12] and required manual corrections.

- `QSM-Cutoff` successfully derived the cutoff formula R_c for all 19 protocols. Notably, most cutoffs were in the low single digits.
- Using the verification procedure in Sect. 4.3, R_c successfully proved the safety property of each protocol.

- Spot checks of "Models(R_c)[k] = Reach[k]" at parameter sizes larger and smaller than the cutoff did not produce any counterexamples. This lends strong empirical support for the conjecture that R_c is indeed a reachability invariant, i.e., the strongest inductive invariant.

A detailed comparison between QSM-Cutoff and QSM from [12] was not possible for several reasons. First, QSM uses an ad hoc notion of cutoff and a heuristic method of incrementing domain sizes when searching for the cutoff. Second, QSM's quantifier inference procedure does not properly handle protocols based on relations with multi-arity literals involving the same sort, or protocols with the special "member(node,quorum)" relation used to model set membership in quorums. In both of these cases, QSM's results required manual "fix-ups;" these protocols are annotated in Table 4 with † (for multi-arity literals on the same sort) and ‡ (for protocols with quorums). The updated QPI procedure in QSM-Cutoff eliminates these shortcomings in QSM and provides a fully automatic flow for deriving the cutoff formula.

Instead of such a comparison, the results in Table 4 highlight the effect of QSM-Cutoff's two additional improvements over QSM: replacing BDD symbolic image computation in the derivation of Reach[k] with the SymDFS algorithm in Sect. 5, and replacing the individual first-order sentences that encode the explicit PI orbits in an orbit family with a single lower-cost logically-equivalent first-order sentence using the updated QPI algorithm in Sect. 6.2. In Table 4, we use QSM-Cutoff-nf to denote a variant of QSM-Cutoff that disables QPI for orbit families, and simply performs QPI on individual PI orbits. In addition, we report the runtimes for both QSM-Cutoff and QSM-Cutoff-nf using either SymDFS or BDD symbolic image computation. For completeness, the last column in Table 4 shows the number of invariants in the reachability formulas reported in [12].

Merging Orbit Families. When an orbit family exists, the total *qCost* of the quantified invariants of its separate PI orbits is always higher than the *qCost* of the merged quantified invariant. This should not be surprising since the solutions produced by QSM-Cutoff-nf are not actually minimal because the individual PI orbits of an orbit family are symmetrically but not logically prime. In the 7 protocols marked with bold text in Table 4, orbit family merging yielded fewer quantified invariants in the cutoff formula and a corresponding reduction in its *qCost*. The effect is particularly pronounced for the simple-decentralized-lock protocol where orbit family merging reduced the number of invariants in R_c from 16 to 4 with a corresponding *qCost* reduction from 99 to 22. In the 4 protocols marked with gray shading in Table 4, orbit family merging also enabled QSM-Cutoff to reach smaller cutoff domain sizes than QSM-Cutoff-nf. Finally, QSM-Cutoff-nf failed to converge within the time limit for consensus_epr.

SymDFS*and BDD Comparison.* There is no clear-cut conclusion in this comparison. In the 16 cases solved by both methods, the BDD approach marginally outperformed SymDFS. In two large instances (`toy_consensus_forall`[node=5, quorum=10, value=3] and `quorum-leader-election-wo-maj`[node=5, nset=10]), the BDD approach failed whereas SymDFS successfully derived the reachable states by taking advantage of symmetry. In one case (`consensus_epr`[node=4, quorum=4, value=2]), SymDFS failed to derive Reach[4, 4, 2] due to the large number of orbits in its reachable states whereas the BDD approach succeeded due to its ability to symbolically operate on sets of states. This suggests that further work is needed, perhaps to combine these two approaches or to explore ways of incorporating structural symmetry in the BDD approach.

8   Related Work

The notions of cutoff and saturation of parameterized systems, selectively referenced throughout the paper, have been investigated by many researchers in a variety of contexts that are too numerous to enumerate here. Regardless of how these notions are defined, what they share in common is the intuitive idea that we should be able to infer the behavior of an unbounded system by anlayzing a relatively small finite instance of it[3]. Our work is most closely related to approaches that perform forward reachability on small finite instances, such as [7,27,30], and derive some generalization that can characterize unbounded behavior. This was the major inspiration for our approach. We noticed that, under some restrictions, the search space of a parameterized protocol expanded regularly as its size increased. This suggested that it should be possible to *synthesize* a quantified first-order formula that captures this regularity, specifically the protocol's inherent structural symmetry. The key building blocks for this synthesis were the algorithmic encoding of symmetry orbits by quantified first-order sentences as in [16], and the extension of classical logic minimization to finitely-quantified FOL to yield minimum-*qCost* solutions of the reachability formulas as in [12].

9   Conclusions and Future Work

This paper takes a distinctly different approach from much of the published literature for analyzing a restricted class of distributed protocols. It ties together the well-known notions of structural symmetry, cutoff, and saturation in a single framework that sheds more light on the behavior of these protocols. It also

---

[3] Leslie Lamport recently pointed out in a post to the tlaplus user group that "it's rare for an algorithm to be correct for a set of 3 elements and not for a set of 1000 elements." https://groups.google.com/g/tlaplus/c/mCIrEoSwk-c/m/93m1r0YqAgAJ.

leaves open many questions whose answers may help explain how it is possible to algorithmically derive compact FOL formulas that capture unbounded behavior, despite the well-known undecidability of first-order logic. For example, a formal proof showing that the cutoff formula R_c is, in fact, a reachability invariant, i.e., the strongest inductive invariant, may further our understanding of the role of symmetric minimization in explaining cutoff and saturation. Another curiosity is how the finite prime implicates produced by symmetric minimization morph into *infinite* prime implicates at cutoff, suggesting, perhaps, a connection between finite Boolean functions and a new class of *parameterized* Boolean functions. In addition to establishing a formal foundation for this approach to explore such questions, we also plan to apply it to a larger corpus of protocols to better understand its strengths and limitations, and continue optimizing its implementation.

We also plan to extend this approach to the class of protocol specifications that involve totally-ordered sorts that model behavior evolution "over time." Examples of this include the use of ballots/rounds in consensus protocols such as Paxos, epochs in distributed lock protocols, tickets in bakery protocols, etc. With few exceptions [15,17,18], working with such protocols requires manual effort or the use of interactive theorem provers to derive the necessary inductive invariants for proving safety properties. We conjecture, however, that it should be possible to define notions of *temporal cutoff* and *saturation* that allow for the derivation of compact reachability formulas for these protocols by leveraging another type of regularity, namely *temporal repetitiveness*. The basic intuition here is that despite the fact that the reachable states expand without bound in the temporal dimension, that expansion must necessarily consist of a sequence of repeating *finite transactions* at ever-increasing "times." This repetitiveness implies that the absolute times at which transactions begin and end are not important and can be abstracted as less-than-or-equal constraints between consecutive transactions. Such an abstraction allows for the encoding of the unbounded temporal behavior using compact FOL formulas. At this point, these are still vague notions. Nonetheless, they are compelling enough to warrant further exploration in future work.

Acknowledgments. We would like to thank our shepherd and reviewers for the detailed feedback that helped to significantly improve the readability of the paper.

Conflict of Interest. The authors have no competing interests to declare that are relevant to the content of this article.

A   Appendix

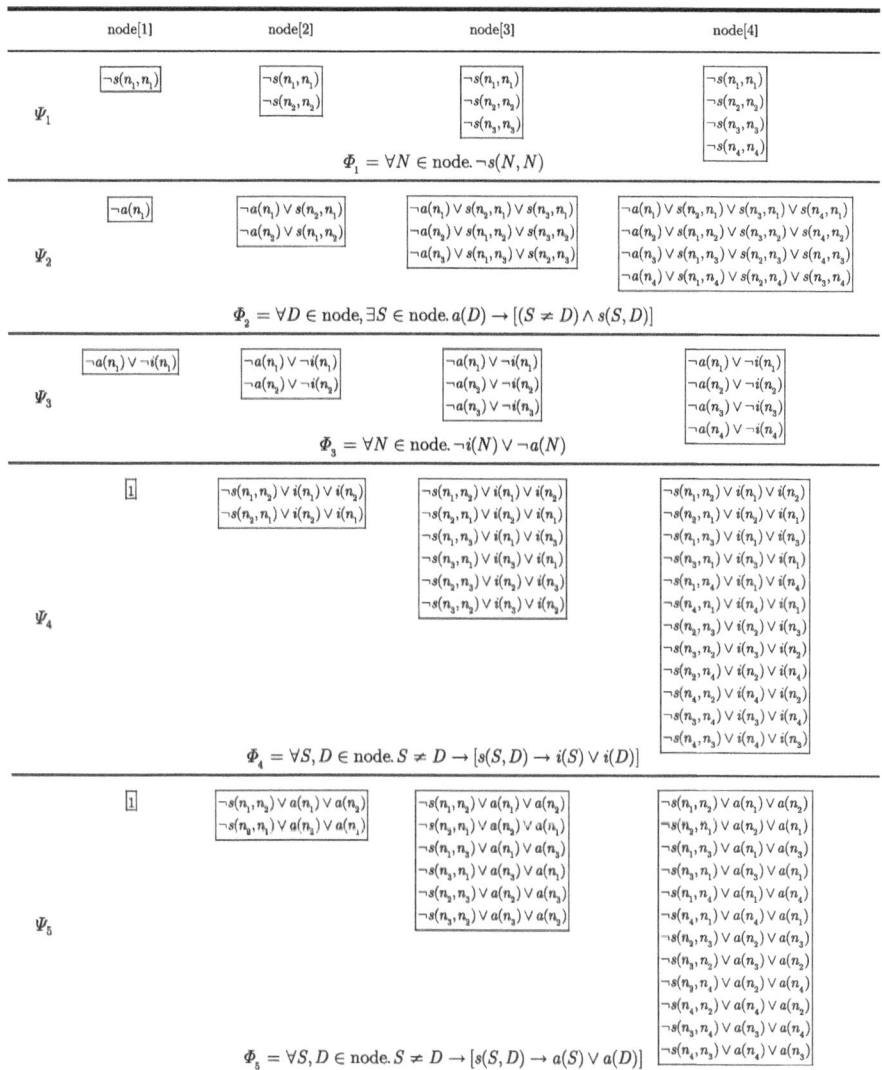

Fig. 5. Explicit Orbits of Firewall's Cutoff Formula Showing Their Regular Expansion Patterns along with their Corresponding FOL Sentences.

References

1. A collection of distributed protocol verification problems. https://github.com/QSM-Cutoff/ivybench
2. Espresso. https://ptolemy.berkeley.edu/projects/embedded/pubs/downloads/espresso

3. firewall.ivy Protocol
4. simple-decentralized-lock.ivy Protocol
5. QSM-Cutoff. https://github.com/QSM-Cutoff/QSM-Cutoff.git
6. Abdulla, P.A., Sistla, A.P., Talupur, M.: Model checking parameterized systems. Presented at the (2018). https://doi.org/10.1007/978-3-319-10575-8_21
7. Arons, T., Pnueli, A., Ruah, S., Xu, Y., Zuck, L.: Parameterized verification with automatically computed inductive assertions. In: Berry, G., Comon, H., Finkel, A. (eds.) Computer Aided Verification, pp. 221–234. Springer, Heidelberg (2001)
8. Barrett, C., Tinelli, C.: Satisfiability modulo theories. In: Handbook of Model Checking, pp. 305–343. Springer (2018)
9. Clarke, E.M., Filkorn, T., Jha, S.: Exploiting symmetry in temporal logic model checking. In: Courcoubetis, C. (ed.) CAV 1993. LNCS, vol. 697, pp. 450–462. Springer, Heidelberg (1993). https://doi.org/10.1007/3-540-56922-7_37
10. Emerson, E.A., Kahlon, V.: Reducing model checking of the many to the few. In: International Conference on Automated Deduction, pp. 236–254. Springer (2000)
11. Emerson, E.A., Namjoshi, K.S.: Reasoning about rings. In: Proceedings of the 22nd ACM SIGPLAN-SIGACT Symposium on Principles of Programming Languages, pp. 85–94 (1995)
12. Fazekas, K., Goel, A., Sakallah, K.A.: SAT-based quantified symmetric minimization of the reachable states of distributed protocols. In: Formal Methods in Computer-Aided Design (FMCAD 2023), pp. 152–161. Ames, Iowa (2023). https://doi.org/10.34727/2023/isbn.978-3-85448-060-0_23
13. Feldman, Y.M., Wilcox, J.R., Shoham, S., Sagiv, M.: Inferring inductive invariants from phase structures. In: International Conference on Computer Aided Verification, pp. 405–425. Springer (2019)
14. Fraleigh, J.B.: A First Course in Abstract Algebra, 6th edn. Addison Wesley Longman, Reading (2000)
15. Goel, A., Merz, S., Sakallah, K.A.: Towards an automatic proof of the bakery algorithm. In: 43nd International Conference on Formal Techniques for Distributed Objects, Components, and Systems (FORTE 2023), Lisbon, Portugal, pp. 21–28 (2023). https://doi.org/10.1007/978-3-031-35355-0_2
16. Goel, A., Sakallah, K.: On symmetry and quantification: a new approach to verify distributed protocols. In: Dutle, A., Moscato, M.M., Titolo, L., Muñoz, C.A., Perez, I. (eds.) NFM 2021. LNCS, vol. 12673, pp. 131–150. Springer, Cham (2021). https://doi.org/10.1007/978-3-030-76384-8_9
17. Goel, A., Sakallah, K.A.: Towards an automatic proof of Lamport's Paxos. In: Piskac, R., Whalen, M.W. (eds.) Formal Methods in Computer-Aided Design (FMCAD 2021), New Haven, Connecticut, pp. 112–122 (2021). https://doi.org/10.34727/2021/isbn.978-3-85448-046-4_20
18. Goel, A., Sakallah, K.A.: Regularity and quantification: a new approach to verify distributed protocols. Innovations Syst. Softw. Eng. 19(4), 359–377 (2023). https://doi.org/10.1007/s11334-022-00460-8
19. Hance, T., Heule, M., Martins, R., Parno, B.: Finding invariants of distributed systems: it's a small (enough) world after all. In: 18th USENIX Symposium on Networked Systems Design and Implementation (NSDI 2021), pp. 115–131. USENIX Association (2021). https://www.usenix.org/conference/nsdi21/presentation/hance
20. Hawblitzel, C., et al.: IronFleet: proving practical distributed systems correct. In: Proceedings of the 25th Symposium on Operating Systems Principles, pp. 1–17. ACM (2015)

21. Ip, C.N., Dill, D.L.: Better verification through symmetry. In: Computer Hardware Description Languages and their Applications, pp. 97–111. Elsevier (1993)
22. Karbyshev, A., Bjørner, N., Itzhaky, S., Rinetzky, N., Shoham, S.: Property-directed inference of universal invariants or proving their absence. J. ACM (JACM) **64**(1), 1–33 (2017)
23. Koenig, J.R., Padon, O., Immerman, N., Aiken, A.: First-order quantified separators. In: Proceedings of the 41st ACM SIGPLAN Conference on Programming Language Design and Implementation, PLDI 2020, pp. 703–717. Association for Computing Machinery, New York (2020). https://doi.org/10.1145/3385412.3386018. https://github.com/wilcoxjay/mypyvy/tree/pldi20-artifact
24. Koenig, J.R., Padon, O., Shoham, S., Aiken, A.: Inferring invariants with quantifier alternations: taming the search space explosion. In: International Conference on Tools and Algorithms for the Construction and Analysis of Systems, pp. 338–356. Springer (2022)
25. Lamport, L.: Paxos made simple, pp. 51–58 (2001). https://www.microsoft.com/en-us/research/publication/paxos-made-simple/
26. Ma, H., Goel, A., Jeannin, J.B., Kapritsos, M., Kasikci, B., Sakallah, K.A.: I4: incremental inference of inductive invariants for verification of distributed protocols. In: The 27th ACM Symposium on Operating Systems Principles (SOSP 2019), Huntsville, Ontario, Canada, pp. 370–384 (2019). https://doi.org/10.1145/3341301.3359651
27. Norris IP, C., Dill, D.L.: Better verification through symmetry. Formal Methods Syst. Des. **9**(1), 41–75 (1996). https://doi.org/10.1007/BF00625968
28. Padon, O., McMillan, K.L., Panda, A., Sagiv, M., Shoham, S.: Ivy: safety verification by interactive generalization. In: Proceedings of the 37th ACM SIGPLAN Conference on Programming Language Design and Implementation, pp. 614–630 (2016)
29. Padon, O., Wilcox, J.R., Koenig, J.R., McMillan, K.L., Aiken, A.: Induction duality: primal-dual search for invariants. Proc. ACM Program. Lang. **6**(POPL), 1–29 (2022)
30. Pnueli, A., Ruah, S., Zuck, L.: Automatic deductive verification with invisible invariants. In: International Conference on Tools and Algorithms for the Construction and Analysis of Systems, pp. 82–97. Springer (2001)
31. Yao, J., Tao, R., Gu, R., Nieh, J.: {DuoAI}: fast, automated inference of inductive invariants for verifying distributed protocols. In: 16th USENIX Symposium on Operating Systems Design and Implementation (OSDI 2022), pp. 485–501 (2022)
32. Yao, J., Tao, R., Gu, R., Nieh, J., Jana, S., Ryan, G.: DistAI: data-driven automated invariant learning for distributed protocols. In: 15th {USENIX} Symposium on Operating Systems Design and Implementation ({OSDI} 2021), pp. 405–421 (2021)

Space Explanations of Neural Network Classification

Faezeh Labbaf[1]([✉]) [iD], Tomáš Kolárik[1] [iD], Martin Blicha[1,4] [iD],
Grigory Fedyukovich[1,3] [iD], Michael Wand[2] [iD], and Natasha Sharygina[1] [iD]

[1] University of Lugano (USI), Lugano, Switzerland
faezeh.labbaf@usi.ch
[2] SUPSI, IDSIA, Lugano, Switzerland
[3] Florida State University, Tallahassee, USA
[4] Ethereum Foundation, Zug, Switzerland

Abstract. We present a novel logic-based concept called *Space Explanations* for classifying neural networks that gives provable guarantees of the behavior of the network in continuous areas of the input feature space. To automatically generate space explanations, we leverage a range of flexible Craig interpolation algorithms and unsatisfiable core generation. Based on real-life case studies, ranging from small to medium to large size, we demonstrate that the generated explanations are more meaningful than those computed by state-of-the-art.

1 Introduction

Explainability of decision-making AI systems (XAI), and specifically neural networks (NNs), is a key requirement for deploying AI in sensitive areas [18]. A recent trend in explaining NNs is based on formal methods and logic, providing explanations for the decisions of machine learning systems [24,30,31,40,41,43] accompanied by provable guarantees regarding their correctness. Yet, rigorous exploration of the *continuous* feature space requires to estimate *decision boundaries* with complex shapes. This, however, remains a challenge because existing explanations [24,30,31,40,41,43] constrain only individual features and hence fail capturing *relationships* among the features that are essential to understand the reasons behind the multi-parametrized classification process.

We address the need to provide interpretations of NN systems that are as meaningful as possible using a novel concept of *Space Explanations*, delivered by a flexible symbolic reasoning framework where Craig interpolation [12] is at the heart of the machinery. When starting from a sample point, the explanation computation is quick, and yields generality and soundness of approximation. Interpolation extracts information from the proof of unsatisfiability which captures a reason why the given input cannot change classification. We showcase explanations for trained neural networks substantially more expressive and meaningful compared to prior work in formal XAI. For example, the classification of the heart attack risk is determined (among others) based on a non-trivial relation

R. Piskac and Z. Rakamarić (Eds.): CAV 2025, LNCS 15933, pp. 287–303, 2025.
https://doi.org/10.1007/978-3-031-98682-6_15

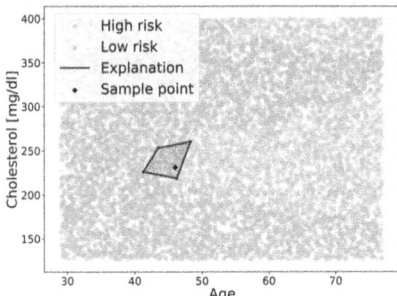

Fig. 1. Example of close approximations of non-trivial decision boundaries using meaningful explanations of the classification: a NN classifier of heart attack risk [25].

of age and cholesterol level of a patient, as illustrated in Fig. 1. Our prototype implementation of the framework, SPEXPLAIN, can automatically compute an explanation that closely approximates the shape of the decision boundary. Furthermore, such non-restricted explanations often cover many sample points at once.

This case study paper is an applied study using existing techniques (mainly Craig interpolation) in a new practical context (XAI). We share our lessons learned after experimenting with various real-life benchmarks, evaluate the quality of explanations generated using different interpolation techniques and further reduced using unsatisfiable cores. We demonstrate the benefits in carefully selected experiments with respect to the state-of-the-art to see how the techniques apply and how different strategies can be combined. For all kinds of benchmarks, no matter the size and the domain, the resulting explanations are more meaningful for the user. Moreover, computing interpolation-based explanations scales better with the size of the input than existing methods.

Related Work. Most of the classic approaches to XAI either perform analysis at the *unit (neuron) level* [17,44], which however fails to capture global properties or interdependencies between units; are *gradient-based* methods [4,42], which describe the network behavior around a particular sample; or *inversion* methods [29], which provide global views, but are still only approximating. There is also a range of *model-agnostic* methods [5,28,38], including SHAP [27] and LIME [37], which can be applied to any classifier (not only NNs), but often yield logically inconsistent explanations [31].

All approaches [4,5,17,27–29,37,38,42,44] rely on approximations or are *sample-based*, that is, the behavior outside the space of the underlying dataset or samples generated from the model remains unknown.

We focus on formal approaches to XAI that offer *strict guarantees*, exploiting computational engines like MARABOU [26] or SMT solvers [6,10,11,16,22,33]. State-of-the-art methods in this area address only special cases of our concept: constraints over individual features, leading to interval-based explanations [24] that cannot reflect feature relationships and hence approximate complex decision boundaries such as in Fig. 1. Section 4 demonstrates generalizations of the existing explanations, resulting in strictly larger spaces. Early methods in this domain aimed at so-called abductive explanations [23,30,31,40,41,43] that are primarily sample-based, resulting in zero-volume spaces. The term *abduction* [1,14,35,36] is misused since unlike abductive explanations, it is not restricted to samples. All the approaches [23,24,30,31,40,41,43] also heavily depend on selecting a specific order of the features in which the constraints are relaxed. Furthermore, they might build an exponential number of verification queries to an off-the-shelf NN verification engine. In contrast, our method directly uses one satisfiability query to an interpolating SMT solver to generate an interpolant.

2 Background

A classification problem [20] is concerned with mapping input data into a pre-defined set of classes $\mathcal{K} = \{c_1, \ldots, c_K\}$. Given a set of *features* $\mathcal{F} = \{1, \ldots, m\}$, each $i \in \mathcal{F}$ takes values from a discrete or continuous *domain* $\mathcal{D}_i$. The *feature space* is defined as $\mathbb{F} = \mathcal{D}_1 \times \mathcal{D}_2 \times \cdots \times \mathcal{D}_m$. By $\mathbf{x} = (x_1, \ldots, x_m)$ we denote a point in $\mathbb{F}$, where each x_i is a *feature variable* (if clear from context, called features) taking values from $\mathcal{D}_i$. A *sample point* $\mathbf{s} = (s_1, \ldots, s_m) \in \mathbb{F}$ contains constants representing concretes value from $\mathcal{D}_i, \ldots, \mathcal{D}_m$. A *classifier* $\mathcal{M} = (\mathcal{F}, \mathcal{D}, \mathbb{F}, \mathcal{K}, \kappa)$ contains a *classification function* $\kappa : \mathbb{F} \rightarrow \mathcal{K}$. An *instance* is a pair $(\mathbf{s}, c)$, where $\mathbf{s} \in \mathbb{F}$ and $c \in \mathcal{K}$ is a prediction $c = \kappa(\mathbf{s})$. Given a classifier $\mathcal{M} = (\mathcal{F}, \mathcal{D}, \mathbb{F}, \mathcal{K}, \kappa)$, the *class space* $\mathbb{F}_c \subseteq \mathbb{F}$ of $c \in \mathcal{K}$ is $\{\mathbf{x} \in \mathbb{F} \mid \kappa(\mathbf{x}) = c\}$. A *classification rule* for c is a formula φ_c such that $\forall \mathbf{x} \in \mathbb{F} . \varphi_c(\mathbf{x}) \iff \kappa(\mathbf{x}) = c$. If κ is defined on the whole feature space $\mathbb{F}$ then it can be partitioned as $\mathbb{F} = \bigcup_{c \in \mathcal{K}} \mathbb{F}_c$, and for all $a, b \in \mathcal{K}$, if $a \neq b$ then $\mathbb{F}_a \cap \mathbb{F}_b = \emptyset$ (because κ must not be ambiguous). A *class boundary* of c is the topological boundary of $\mathbb{F}_c$. The *decision boundary* is the union of class boundaries of all classes $c \in \mathcal{K}$ in a classifier $(\mathcal{F}, \mathcal{D}, \mathbb{F}, \mathcal{K}, \kappa)$.

3 Space Explanations

Explanations produced by existing tools do not capture relations between the input features, and consequently, they cannot approximate the decision boundary. To address it, this paper presents a *logic*-based approach to compute explanations with the flexibility of representing different shapes of the feature space.

Definition 1 (Space Explanation, Impact Space). *Given a classifier* $\mathcal{M}$ *computing a classification function* κ *from feature space* $\mathbb{F}$, *and a class* c, *a space explanation of* c *is a logic formula* φ *such that* $\forall \mathbf{x} \in \mathbb{F} . \varphi(\mathbf{x}) \implies \kappa(\mathbf{x}) = c$. *The* impact space *of* φ, $\mathbb{F}_\varphi \subseteq \mathbb{F}_c$, *is a set* $\{\mathbf{x} \in \mathbb{F} \mid \varphi(\mathbf{x})\}$.

Space explanations represent sufficient conditions of classification to class c. Since $\varphi \implies \varphi_c$, classification rules are also space explanations. Hence, we have a general concept of explanations with the following benefits:

1. The *shape* of the explanations is *not restricted*, hence it is possible to approximate arbitrarily complex class spaces and decision boundaries.
2. It is possible to *capture relationships* among features and truly *explain* the *reasons* behind the classification.
3. Space explanations can be merged or intersected with each other.

In Fig. 1, for example, items 1 and 2 addressed by accurate approximation of the decision boundary using an explanation in the shape of a convex polygon.

We assume that for all classes, at least one sample point is classified into the class, meaning that none of the classes are redundant. Given a formula $\psi := \psi_M \wedge \psi_D \wedge \neg \psi_c$ where: ψ_M encodes the neural network M, ψ_D encodes the domains D of the feature space, i.e. $\mathbf{x} \in \mathbb{F}$, $\neg \psi_c$ encodes the constraint that the outcome of the classification is *not* class c, it is *satisfiable* with no additional restrictions. Now suppose a sample point $\mathbf{s}$ classified as class c. Using the encoding $\varphi_{\mathbf{s}} := \bigwedge_{i \in \mathcal{F}} x_i = s_i$, formula $\varphi_{\mathbf{s}} \wedge \psi$ is in turn *unsatisfiable*.

This principle can be generalized by exploiting the fact that a space explanation φ of class c *guarantees* classification to the class for all points covered by the explanation, so formula $\varphi \wedge \psi$ is also unsatisfiable. Such a formula enables the use of Craig interpolation[1]: interpolant $I = Itp(\varphi, \psi)$ is a space explanation of c and it satisfies $\varphi \implies I$ (and hence $\mathbb{F}_\varphi \subseteq \mathbb{F}_I$).

Hence, we have a universal means of generalization of existing space explanations, still guaranteeing the classification. Although space explanations are not tied to specific data samples, formulas $\varphi_{\mathbf{s}}$ can be used as a starting space explanation, for which the interpolants are computed quickly because all input variables are fixed to concrete values. This offers the following improvements over existing methods:

1. The captured feature relationships stem from a mathematical *proof* of the classification, hence providing *meaningful* information.
2. The concept is *flexible*, offering to use *arbitrary* Craig interpolation algorithms. The resulting explanations exhibit various logical strengths and forms.

3. It is possible to further *generalize* any *existing* space explanation.

Interpolation algorithms can benefit from special cases [19] where a formula can be partitioned. We address just one example when a space explanation can be split into two parts $\varphi_A \wedge \varphi_B$: given a Craig interpolation procedure Itp with $I = Itp(\varphi_A, \varphi_B \wedge \psi)$, then $I \wedge \varphi_B$ is a logically weaker space explanation. We used this technique to identify pair feature relationships in Fig. 1.

Figure 2 gives a high-level representation of a fully functioning and flexible algorithmic *framework* that provides expansion of space explanations using a collection of *strategies* listed below.

---

[1] Given an unsatisfiable formula $A \wedge B$, a *Craig interpolant* [12] is a formula I such that A implies I, $I \wedge B$ is unsatisfiable, and I uses only the common variables of A and B. We denote interpolant I computed by an interpolation procedure Itp from formulas A and B by $I = Itp(A, B)$.

Space Explanation Framework

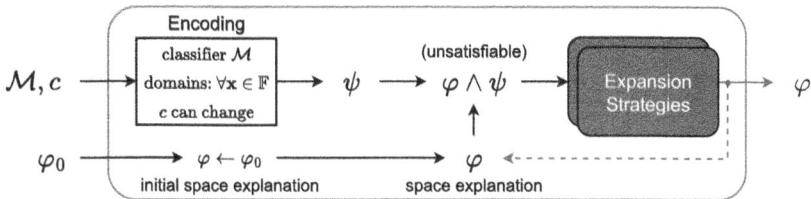

Fig. 2. Algorithmic framework: starting from an initial space explanation φ_0, the impact space is expanded and a logically weaker explanation φ is produced. The user may select from multiple strategies for further optimization (cf. the dashed arrow).

- **Generalize (G).** Compute Craig interpolants on an arbitrary space explanation. We use the algorithms based on Farkas' lemma (Itp_F) or their logically stronger *decomposing* variants [7] (Itp_{DF}), the dual versions of these algorithms (Itp'_F, Itp'_{DF}) to yield weaker interpolants [15], and an algorithm [3] (Itp_f) parametrized by a rational factor $f \in [0, 1]$ with the logical strength in between Itp_F and Itp'_F. These arithmetic interpolation algorithms are combined with McMillan's propositional interpolation algorithm [32].
- **Reduce (R).** Weaken the formula and reduce size by computing an unsatisfiable core. To get irreducible explanations (R_{min}), we use exhaustive minimization which may introduce significant overhead.
- **Capture (C).** Partition an interval-like formula (e.g. a sample) and **Generalize**. Weaken only part φ_A with constraints over at least one of the given features, hence capturing their mutual relationships.

Strategy **Generalize** and **Capture** is often followed by **Reduce** to simplify the formulas from unnecessary constraints.

4 Experimental Evaluation

We showcase[2] the computation of space explanations for selected trained neural networks and demonstrate that they are substantially more expressive and meaningful since our approach captures feature relationships and approximates decision boundaries. We implemented the novel Space Explanation Framework in a prototype tool SPEXPLAIN[3], focusing on QF_LRA logic, on top of the OPENSMT2 solver [8,22] which is an interpolating solver that comes with a set of techniques assembled into the integral framework, combining SMT solving with the computation of the Craig interpolants of various size and strength [2,3,7,9,21,39]. We evaluated the following NN datasets and models:

- Heart attack dataset [25] focuses on predicting the risk of heart attacks based on various medical indicators of patients, it contains 13 input features and 2

---

[2] All table contents are reproducible: https://doi.org/10.5281/zenodo.15490124.
[3] https://github.com/usi-verification-and-security/spexplain.

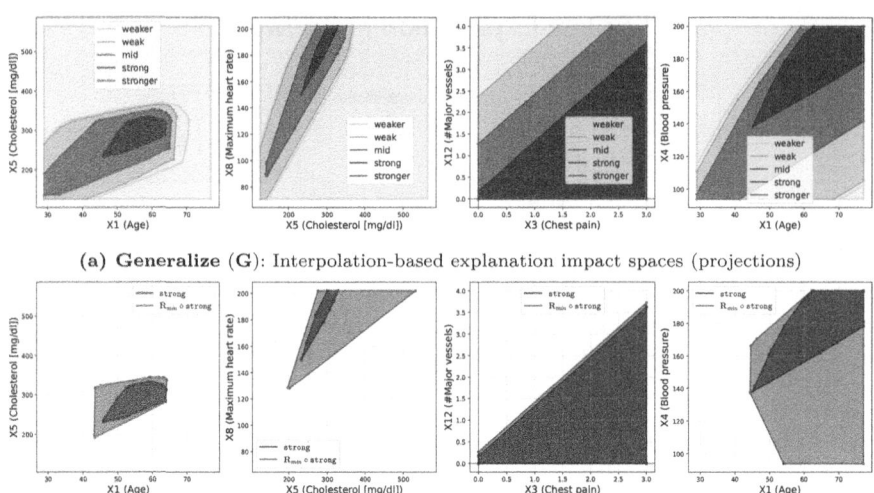

(a) **Generalize (G)**: Interpolation-based explanation impact spaces (projections)

(b) **Reduce ($\mathbf{R}_{min} \circ \mathbf{G}$)**: **G-strong** explanations and their exhaustive simplifications (projections)

Fig. 3. Projections into selected pairs of features of interpolation-based explanations (**G**) of the heart-attack risk model, possibly combined with reduction ($\mathbf{R}_{min}$).

possible classification outcomes: high or low risk. We trained the NN using one hidden layer with 50 neurons and used a dataset with 303 sample points.

- Obesity dataset [34] provides data for estimating obesity levels in individuals based on their eating habits and physical condition, resulting in 15 input features and 7 classes. We trained the model using 3 hidden layers with 10, 20, and 10 neurons, respectively, and used a dataset with 50 sample points.
- MNIST dataset [13] is a collection of grayscale images of handwritten digits (0–9) with 784 inputs, commonly used within image classification tasks as a reference for training, evaluation, and verification of machine learning models. We trained the model using 784 inputs and a hidden layer with 200 neurons, and used a dataset with 50 sample points.

Instances of interpolation algorithms use the notation $Itp_{DF} \mapsto$ stronger, $Itp_F \mapsto$ strong, $Itp'_F \mapsto$ weak, $Itp'_{DF} \mapsto$ weaker, and $Itp_f \mapsto$ mid with $f := 0.5$. The evaluation uses 2 h *time-out* to compute all explanations for a dataset and an explanation setup. It was performed on a Linux 5.4 machine with 256 GB physical memory and AMD® EPYC 7452 32-core CPU.

Evaluation of Strategies. Instantiations of strategy **Generalize (G)** provide flexibility of covering spaces with various size, illustrated in Fig. 3a on selected sample points from the dataset. We resolve the issue of visualizing high-dimensional spaces by selecting candidate pairs of features from the heart attack

Table 1. Average performance of strategy **G** using different *Itp* algorithms.

Itp algorithm	Heart attack			Obesity			MNIST		
	relaxed	#terms	time[s]	relaxed	#terms	time[s]	relaxed	#terms	time[s]
stronger	0%	20.1	0.03	0%	29.0	0.30	0%	927.3	9.17
strong	97%	51.0	0.04	72%	45.8	0.30	100%	209.0	10.12
mid	100%	51.0	0.04	100%	45.8	0.34	100%	209.0	10.25
weak	100%	51.0	0.04	100%	46.1	0.30	100%	209.0	10.42
weaker	100%	198.2	0.04	100%	64.1	0.42	100%	67330.6	10.55

dataset and plotting the projection[4] of the impact spaces into two dimensions. The examples reveal the similarity of feature relations despite aiming at different logical strengths. However, we spot that weaker here always covers the whole projection[5], while stronger in turn results just in the original sample point. This is no exception: Table 1 reports that stronger relaxes no features at all (i.e. each feature is still fixed to the original value), producing way too strong interpolants. Algorithm strong sometimes does not relax all features. Next, the table reports the average size of the resulting formulas term-wise (the number of in/equalities). The average runtimes per sample point are rather small and do not vary among the approaches, but are sensitive to more complex models.

Strategy **Reduce** (**R**, $\mathbf{R}_{min}$) introduces a trade-off between formula simplification and runtime overhead when applied on top of **Generalize** (e.g., $\mathbf{R} \circ \mathbf{G}$), using an unsatisfiable core (**R**) or an irreducible one ($\mathbf{R}_{min}$). Figure 3a demonstrates side by side with Fig. 3b that the projection of strong is further expanded by $\mathbf{R}_{min}$ (**R** expands none of the four presented strong projections), but in different directions compared to weaker algorithms. We confirmed this phenomenon by running extensive subset-comparisons which in cases such as (strong, $\mathbf{R}_{min}$) vs. (weak, −) often yielded not comparable (**NC**) results: the spaces intersect but none of them subsumes the other. Table 2 shows that $\mathbf{R}_{min}$ significantly reduces the formula but with a high cost, while **R** offers a convenient balance. The reduction times-out (**X**) with more complex models.

Figure 4a follows with a comparison of projections between strategy **G** (cf. Fig. 3a), specifically selecting weak algorithm that produces large yet convex impact spaces, and an approach that is based on intervals, denoted as **I**, that computes the explanations on top of an irreducible abductive explanation, denoted by **A**, resulting in **I** ∘ **A**. Since the state-of-the-art-approach [24] is implemented for decision trees and not for NNs, we implemented the specialized

---

[4] Projections offer a visual intuitive understanding of the geometrical differences between impact spaces. While not capturing the complete information contained in higher-dimensional spaces, they are still more informative than simple slices.

[5] Notably, the explanation does not cover the whole feature space. However, high-dimensional projections (e.g., from 13D to 2D) collapse information from other dimensions, making explanations appear larger.

Table 2. Time overhead and impact of **Reduce** on top of **Generalize** ($\mathbf{R} \circ \mathbf{G}$).

	G	#terms			time [s]		
	Itp algorithm	–	**R**	$\mathbf{R}_{min}$	–	**R**	$\mathbf{R}_{min}$
Heart attack	stronger	20.1	20.1	9.5	0.03	0.03	3.14
	strong	51.0	44.6	3.8	0.04	0.83	16.77
	mid	51.0	39.4	4.6	0.04	0.66	11.80
	weak	51.0	38.8	6.4	0.04	0.56	7.95
	weaker	198.2	197.9	25.9	0.04	0.08	7.14
Obesity	stronger	29.0	29.0	X	0.30	0.38	X
	strong	45.8	41.7	X	0.30	7.94	X
	mid	45.8	42.7	X	0.34	20.62	X
	weak	46.1	41.7	X	0.30	35.37	X
	weaker	64.1	58.0	X	0.42	23.44	X
MNIST	stronger	927.3	927.3	X	9.17	10.45	X
	strong	209.0	X	X	10.12	X	X
	mid	209.0	X	X	10.25	X	X
	weak	209.0	X	X	10.42	X	X
	weaker	67330.6	X	X	10.55	X	X

computation of interval explanations using the MARABOU verifier and a strict limit on the number of attempts of particular relaxations.

We concentrate on comparison using the heart attack model. The projections of interval-based explanations form rectangles, lines, or even single points due to the lack of their expressivity. In contrast, **G** explanations cover larger areas with less limited shapes, yet do not entirely subsume interval explanations: Even if a projection is subsumed, it does not mean that the space is subsumed in the other dimensions as well. While the intervals are being relaxed in a certain order, hence strictly preferring certain directions over others, the interpolation aims at more general expansions. Furthermore, the expansion of the interval explanations is limited by decision boundaries in the other dimensions. This observation is confirmed by pairwise subset-comparisons, consistently arriving at **NC** results.

Table 3 gives comparison of the average performance of the approaches (similarly as in Table 1), including irreducible abductive explanations (**A**). **G** explanations (row #3) are computed even faster than **A** explanations, requiring just one call to the logical solver. Interval explanations did not always succeed in relaxing all features. Nevertheless, the formulas are simpler when based on intervals or samples. Formulas from **G** could be reduced but would exceed the computation time of intervals. The observations remain similar when using other algorithms than weak. Figure 4b further illustrates the potentials of strategy **G** when running on top of arbitrary existing explanations, such as interval explanations (i.e., $\mathbf{G} \circ \mathbf{I} \circ \mathbf{A}$), yielding strictly larger spaces (confirmed by subset-comparison

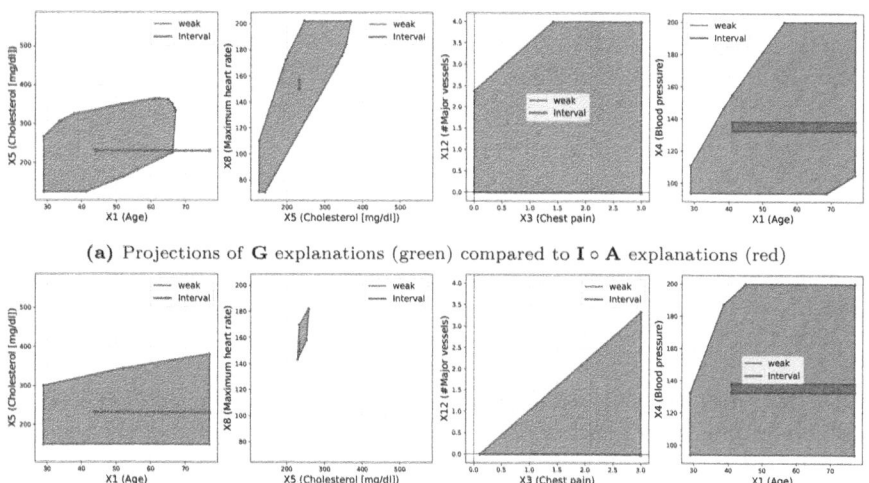

(a) Projections of **G** explanations (green) compared to **I** ∘ **A** explanations (red)

(b) Projections of **G** explanations (green) on top of **I** ∘ **A** explanations (red), resulting in **G** ∘ **I** ∘ **A**

Fig. 4. Comparing projections of interpolation-based (**Generalize, G**) and interval explanations (**I** ∘ **A**) into selected pairs of features of the heart-attack risk model.

Table 3. Average performance of **G** vs. **A** and **I** strategies in heart-attack model.

	relaxed	#terms	#solver calls	time [s]
A	38%	8.1	13	0.08
I ∘ **A**	79%	9.3	40.4	0.53
G	100%	51.0	1	0.04
G ∘ **A**	100%	45.3	1	0.39
G ∘ **I** ∘ **A**	100%	63.5	1	2.53

checks). Nonetheless, the projections of the interpolants in Fig. 4a vs. Fig. 4b (i.e., **G** vs. **G** ∘ **I** ∘ **A**) sometimes differ due to more guided constraints induced by the intervals. Next, we revisit Table 3 on rows #4–5, including **G** ∘ **A** as well. The observations remain similar except that when generalizing on top of a more general starting point, the runtime increases. Still, our generalization of **A** explanations runs faster than if using intervals (i.e., **I** ∘ **A** vs. **G** ∘ **A**).

Strategy **Capture** (**C**) directly aims at identifying relationships among selected features and consequently at approximating decision boundaries. The generalization is guided because it focuses on selected dimensions and picks a slice of the feature space, leaving all other features fixed to the original values. Although such limited exploration does not reveal anything about other dimensions, it extracts partial information helpful to understand the classification. Moreover, it is easy to sample two or three-dimensional slices and compare the explanations with estimated class spaces and decision boundaries. Figure 5 shows the explanations of the sample points and feature pairs as in Fig. 3 and

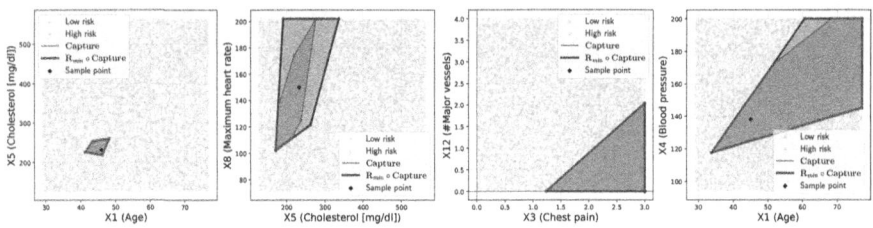

Fig. 5. Approximation of decision boundaries and feature relations using strategies **C** and $\mathbf{R}_{min} \circ \mathbf{C}$ within selected pairs of features of the heart-attack risk model.

Fig. 4, this time using **C** instead of **G**, sticking to algorithm `weak`. The interpolation captures even non-trivial decision boundaries and some of the relations intuitively resemble real-world phenomena. For example, the plot on the right identifies a high risk of heart attack according to increasing age and decreasing blood pressure.

Using **Reduce** (**R**, $\mathbf{R}_{min}$) is especially useful for explanations produced by strategy **C** to enhance their interpretability. Furthermore, the reduction is often more efficient than when applied to **G**. Table 4 shows the quantitative subset-comparison, that is, how many explanations in percentage exhibited the relation superset ($\supset$), equivalent ($=$), subset ($\subset$), or not comparable (**NC**), between **C** and **G** explanations that have been reduced and while focusing just on the slice of selected pairs of features (cf. Fig. 3, Fig. 4, and 5). With no reduction, the slices are equivalent. Yet, the formulas differ, because strategy **C** separates the fixed features from the focused ones[6]. Consequently, the opportunities for reductions offered by the structure of the formulas are different. While strategy **R** usually expands the explanations better when applied to **G** (i.e. $\mathbf{R} \circ \mathbf{G}$), $\mathbf{R}_{min} \circ \mathbf{C}$ always produced a larger space within the slice than $\mathbf{R}_{min} \circ \mathbf{G}$, if excluding **NC** cases. The results for x_5, x_8 are almost the same as for x_1, x_5. Finally, Table 5 shows that the simplification is more efficient in terms of runtime and #terms when using the focused strategy **C** than if interpolating the whole formula with **G**.

Scalability. We conducted two experiments to evaluate how our prototype tool SPEXPLAIN scales with increasing input size and depth of the NN using MNIST. We compare our method with VERIX [43], a state-of-the-art abductive explanation algorithm[7]. While the approaches generate different types of explanations and are not directly comparable, their relative scalability can still be compared.

The first experiment shows how the runtime grows with input size. For that, we used a fixed NN architecture with two hidden layers of size 50^8, and resized MNIST images to input dimensions 10×10, 20×20, 30×30, 40×40, and 50×50. Figure 6a shows how the runtime grows with the input size for computing

---

[6] Example: **G** sliced to x_1, x_2 yields $\left(2x_1 + x_3 \geq 7 \wedge x_1 - x_2 + x_3 \geq 2\right) \wedge x_3 = 1$ which is equivalent to $\left(x_1 \geq 3 \wedge x_1 - x_2 \geq 1\right) \wedge x_3 = 1$ produced by **C** of x_1, x_2.

[7] https://github.com/NeuralNetworkVerification/VeriX, commit b6b2cc0.

[8] A smaller network was used to reduce the number of time-outs.

Table 4. Quantitative subset-comparison of **C** vs. **G** explanations, combined with **R** or $\mathbf{R}_{min}$, ranging over selected features where the others are fixed to the original values.

Features	C		G (sliced)	⊃	=	⊂	NC
x_1, x_5	$\mathbf{R} \circ \mathbf{C}$	vs.	$\mathbf{R} \circ \mathbf{G}$	8%	43%	41%	7%
	$\mathbf{R}_{min} \circ \mathbf{C}$ vs.		$\mathbf{R}_{min} \circ \mathbf{G}$	65%	0%	0%	35%
x_3, x_{12}	$\mathbf{R} \circ \mathbf{C}$	vs.	$\mathbf{R} \circ \mathbf{G}$	2%	92%	5%	1%
	$\mathbf{R}_{min} \circ \mathbf{C}$ vs.		$\mathbf{R}_{min} \circ \mathbf{G}$	89%	5%	0%	6%
$*x_1, x_4$	$\mathbf{R} \circ \mathbf{C}$	vs.	$\mathbf{R} \circ \mathbf{G}$	9%	54%	31%	6%
	$\mathbf{R}_{min} \circ \mathbf{C}$ vs.		$\mathbf{R}_{min} \circ \mathbf{G}$	84%	0%	0%	16%

Table 5. Average performance of strategies **C** and **G** from Table 4 possibly in combination with **Reduce** (**R** or $\mathbf{R}_{min}$).

Reduce	Heart attack				Obesity				MNIST			
	C		G (sliced)		C		G (sliced)		C		G (sliced)	
	#terms	time[s]	#terms	time[s]	#terms	time[s]	#terms	time[s]	#terms	time[s]	#terms	time[s]
–	61.2	0.04	62.0	0.04	59.1	0.33	59.1	0.31	938.9	9.65	991.0	10.54
R	47.0	0.09	49.8	0.56	41.9	1.15	54.7	35.3	834.7	47.1	X	X
$\mathbf{R}_{min}$	9.4	2.52	17.4	7.94	X	X	X	X	X	X	X	X

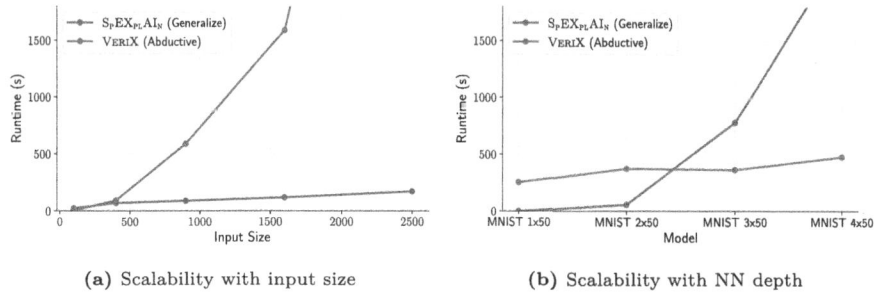

(a) Scalability with input size   (b) Scalability with NN depth

Fig. 6. Scalability comparison of SₚEXₚLAIN and VERIX on MNIST.

G explanations and abductive explanations: the runtime of VERIX increases steeply, while **Generalize** remains relatively stable. The difference is caused by the fact that VERIX performs one verification query per feature, while our method requires only a single query to generate an explanation.

The next experiment examines scalability with respect to model depth. We trained NNs with 1 to 4 hidden layers, each having 50 neurons. Figure 6b shows that the runtime of VERIX grows moderately with the number of layers, while the runtime of **Generalize** increases more significantly with deeper networks. This is likely because, unlike VERIX, our prototype tool does not apply any NN-specific optimizations within its underlying constraint solver. Addressing this limitation is left for future work.

Lessons Learned. The following table summarizes our observations regarding the computation, interpretation, simplification, and comparison of explanations.

Observations	Solution
Problem: Explanations produced by **Generalize** are too complicated to read.	
1. `simplify` command of Z3 or cvc5 SMT solvers is insufficient. 2. **Reduce** simplifies conjunctive formulas, often surprisingly well. 3. McMillan interpolation algorithm extends formulas into conjunctions and its dual into disjunctions.	Use the non-dual algorithm and simplify the explanations using **Reduce** if needed.
Problem: Information regarding just a few features is difficult to extract, even if we use **Reduce**.	
1. Partitioning interval-like formulas separates selected features.	Use **Capture** and **Reduce**.
Problem: It is not clear which interpolation algorithm to choose.	
1. The yielded formulas differ in logical strength and length. 2. The weaker the formula, the larger the space covered, offering the best opportunity to e.g. approximate decision boundaries. 3. Smaller or more focused formulas might be easier to interpret.	Use multiple algorithms depending on the current application and flexibly pick suitable outcomes.
Problem: It is not clear how to visualize explanations with high-dimensional impact spaces.	
1. Projections (cf. Fig. 3) may yield too large area since the information from the other dimensions is collapsed. 2. Slices fix all other dimensions (cf. Fig. 5), but conclusions on those dimensions are very limited. However, they allow direct comparison with decision boundaries or their sampling.	Use slices to show local information and to compare with decision boundaries. Use projections to compare the robustness of explanations.
Problem: Sometimes, quantitative and more rigorous comparisons than visualization are needed.	
1. Computing the volume of high-dimensional spaces is non-trivial. 2. It is easy to check if a space explanation is subsumed by another using the implication of the formulas (in conjunction with $\psi_\mathcal{D}$). 3. Spaces often intersect but are not entirely subsumed by another.	Estimate the quality using multiple metrics. If needed, include a visual comparison.
Idea: What if we compared only selected features?	
1. Computing the volume of 2D or 3D spaces is feasible. 2. Quantifier elimination yields exact projections but is expensive. 3. Projections can be approximated via linear programming. 4. Whole explanations can be compared by exhaustively comparing their projections into all particular pairs (or triplets) of features.	Comparing only selected features is a simpler problem and may also enable more thorough comparisons.

5 Conclusion and Future Work

This paper presented a novel concept of provably correct, logic-based space explanations of the classification process of neural networks. The explanations are associated with complex-shaped spaces and capture relations among the features that stem from mathematical proofs, substantially improving the approximation of decision boundaries over existing methods. The Space Explanations concept is supported by a flexible framework of algorithms including efficient Craig interpolation-based techniques and unsatisfiable core extraction to compute an extensive range of different yet meaningful explanations. On real-world neural networks trained on practical datasets, we performed a series of experiments and computed explanations of different quality. The evaluation of our case studies confirms that our algorithms yield explanations that are more general than existing explanations. We shared lessons learned during the extensive experimentation with the new kind of explanations.

In future work, we will develop an algorithm to approximate decision boundaries and to identify reasons for misclassifications across clusters of the feature space. We will improve the scalability of our tool SPEXPLAIN by using optimizations tailored to NNs, and aim to handle other NN structures, such as convolutional NNs. Finally, we will apply our method to analyze how decisions evolve across the hidden layers of the network.

Acknowledgements. This work was conducted as part of the "Formal Reasoning on Neural Networks" project funded by the Hasler Foundation, Switzerland.

References

1. Albarghouthi, A., Dillig, I., Gurfinkel, A.: Maximal specification synthesis. In: Bodík, R., Majumdar, R. (eds.) Proceedings of the 43rd Annual ACM SIGPLAN-SIGACT Symposium on Principles of Programming Languages, POPL 2016, St. Petersburg, FL, USA, 20–22 January 2016, pp. 789–801. ACM (2016). https://doi.org/10.1145/2837614.2837628
2. Alt, L., Fedyukovich, G., Hyvärinen, A., Sharygina, N.: A proof-sensitive approach for small propositional interpolants. In: Gurfinkel, A., Seshia, S.A. (eds.) VSTTE 2015. LNCS, vol. 9593, pp. 1–18. Springer, Cham (2016). https://doi.org/10.1007/978-3-319-29613-5_1
3. Alt, L., Hyvärinen, A., Sharygina, N.: LRA interpolants from no man's land. In: HVC 2017. LNCS, vol. 10629, pp. 195–210. Springer, Cham (2017). https://doi.org/10.1007/978-3-319-70389-3_13
4. Bach, S., Binder, A., Montavon, G., Klauschen, F., Müller, K.R., Samek, W.: On pixel-wise explanations for non-linear classifier decisions by layer-wise relevance propagation. PLOS One **10**(7) (2015)
5. Baehrens, D., Schroeter, T., Harmeling, S., Kawanabe, M., Hansen, K., Müller, K.: How to explain individual classification decisions. J. Mach. Learn. Res. **11**, 1803–1831 (2010). https://doi.org/10.5555/1756006.1859912https://dl.acm.org/doi/10.5555/1756006.1859912
6. Barbosa, H., et al.: cvc5: A versatile and industrial-strength SMT solver. In: Fisman, D., Rosu, G. (eds.) TACAS 2022, Part I. LNCS, vol. 13243, pp. 415–442. Springer, Cham (2022). https://doi.org/10.1007/978-3-030-99524-9_24
7. Blicha, M., Hyvärinen, A., Kofroň, J., Sharygina, N.: Decomposing Farkas interpolants. In: Vojnar, T., Zhang, L. (eds.) TACAS 2019, Part I. LNCS, vol. 11427, pp. 3–20. Springer, Cham (2019). https://doi.org/10.1007/978-3-030-17462-0_1
8. Bruttomesso, R., Pek, E., Sharygina, N., Tsitovich, A.: The OpenSMT solver. In: Esparza, J., Majumdar, R. (eds.) TACAS 2010. LNCS, vol. 6015, pp. 150–153. Springer, Heidelberg (2010). https://doi.org/10.1007/978-3-642-12002-2_12

9. Bruttomesso, R., Rollini, S., Sharygina, N., Tsitovich, A.: Flexible interpolation with local proof transformations. In: Scheffer, L., Phillips, J.R., Hu, A.J. (eds.) 2010 International Conference on Computer-Aided Design, ICCAD 2010, San Jose, CA, USA, 7–11 November 2010, pp. 770–777. IEEE (2010). https://doi.org/10.1109/ICCAD.2010.5654297

10. Christ, J., Hoenicke, J., Nutz, A.: SMTInterpol: an interpolating SMT solver. In: Donaldson, A., Parker, D. (eds.) SPIN 2012. LNCS, vol. 7385, pp. 248–254. Springer, Heidelberg (2012). https://doi.org/10.1007/978-3-642-31759-0_19

11. Cimatti, A., Griggio, A., Schaafsma, B.J., Sebastiani, R.: The MathSAT5 SMT solver. In: Piterman, N., Smolka, S.A. (eds.) TACAS 2013. LNCS, vol. 7795, pp. 93–107. Springer, Heidelberg (2013). https://doi.org/10.1007/978-3-642-36742-7_7

12. Craig, W.: three uses of the Herbrand-Gentzen theorem in relating model theory and proof theory. J. Symbol. Logic **22**, 269–285 (1957). https://doi.org/10.2307/2963594

13. Deng, L.: The MNIST database of handwritten digit images for machine learning research [best of the web]. IEEE Sig. Process. Mag. **29**(6), 141–142 (2012). https://doi.org/10.1109/MSP.2012.2211477

14. Dillig, I., Dillig, T., Li, B., McMillan, K.L.: Inductive invariant generation via abductive inference. In: Hosking, A.L., Eugster, P.T., Lopes, C.V. (eds.) Proceedings of the 2013 ACM SIGPLAN International Conference on Object Oriented Programming Systems Languages and Applications, OOPSLA 2013, part of SPLASH 2013, Indianapolis, IN, USA, 26–31 October 2013, pp. 443–456. ACM (2013).https://doi.org/10.1145/2509136.2509511

15. D'Silva, V., Kroening, D., Purandare, M., Weissenbacher, G.: Interpolant strength. In: Barthe, G., Hermenegildo, M. (eds.) VMCAI 2010. LNCS, vol. 5944, pp. 129–145. Springer, Heidelberg (2010). https://doi.org/10.1007/978-3-642-11319-2_12

16. Dutertre, B.: Yices 2.2. In: Biere, A., Bloem, R. (eds.) CAV 2014. LNCS, vol. 8559, pp. 737–744. Springer, Cham (2014). https://doi.org/10.1007/978-3-319-08867-9_49

17. Erhan, D., Bengio, Y., Courville, A., Vincent, P.: Visualizing higher-layer features of a deep network. Technical report, University of Montreal (2009)

18. Group, E.E.: Ethics Guidelines for Trustworthy AI. https://ec.europa.eu/newsroom/dae/document.cfm?doc_id=60419

19. Gurfinkel, A., Rollini, S.F., Sharygina, N.: Interpolation properties and SAT-based model checking. In: Van Hung, D., Ogawa, M. (eds.) ATVA 2013. LNCS, vol. 8172, pp. 255–271. Springer, Cham (2013). https://doi.org/10.1007/978-3-319-02444-8_19

20. Heaton, J., Goodfellow, I., Bengio, Y., Courville, A.: Deep learning - the MIT Press, 2016, 800 pp, ISBN: 0262035618. Genet. Program. Evol. Mach. **19**(1–2), 305–307 (2018).https://doi.org/10.1007/S10710-017-9314-Z

21. Hyvärinen, A., Alt, L., Sharygina, N.: Flexible interpolation for efficient model checking. In: Kofroň, J., Vojnar, T. (eds.) MEMICS 2015. LNCS, vol. 9548, pp. 11–22. Springer, Cham (2016). https://doi.org/10.1007/978-3-319-29817-7_2

22. Hyvärinen, A., Marescotti, M., Alt, L., Sharygina, N.: OpenSMT2: an SMT solver for multi-core and cloud computing. In: Creignou, N., Le Berre, D. (eds.) SAT 2016. LNCS, vol. 9710, pp. 547–553. Springer, Cham (2016). https://doi.org/10.1007/978-3-319-40970-2_35

23. Ignatiev, A., Narodytska, N., Marques-Silva, J.: Abduction-based explanations for machine learning models. In: The Thirty-Third AAAI Conference on Artificial Intelligence, AAAI 2019, The Thirty-First Innovative Applications of Artifi-

cial Intelligence Conference, IAAI 2019, The Ninth AAAI Symposium on Educational Advances in Artificial Intelligence, EAAI 2019, Honolulu, Hawaii, USA, 27 January–1 February 2019, pp. 1511–1519. AAAI Press (2019). https://doi.org/10.1609/AAAI.V33I01.33011511

24. Izza, Y., Ignatiev, A., Stuckey, P.J., Marques-Silva, J.: Delivering inflated explanations. In: Wooldridge, M.J., Dy, J.G., Natarajan, S. (eds.) Thirty-Eighth AAAI Conference on Artificial Intelligence, AAAI 2024, Thirty-Sixth Conference on Innovative Applications of Artificial Intelligence, IAAI 2024, Fourteenth Symposium on Educational Advances in Artificial Intelligence, EAAI 2014, 20–27 February 2024, Vancouver, Canada, pp. 12744–12753. AAAI Press (2024). https://doi.org/10.1609/AAAI.V38I11.29170

25. Janosi, A., Steinbrunn, W., Pfisterer, M., Detrano, R.: Heart disease. UCI Machine Learning Repository (1989). https://doi.org/10.24432/C5P338, https://doi.org/10.24432/C52P4X

26. Katz, G., et al.: The Marabou framework for verification and analysis of deep neural networks. In: Dillig, I., Tasiran, S. (eds.) CAV 2019. LNCS, vol. 11561, pp. 443–452. Springer, Cham (2019). https://doi.org/10.1007/978-3-030-25540-4_26

27. König, M., Bosman, A.W., Hoos, H.H., van Rijn, J.N.: Critically assessing the state of the art in neural network verification. J. Mach. Learn. Res. **25**, 12:1–12:53 (2024). https://jmlr.org/papers/v25/23-0119.html

28. Lundberg, S.M., Lee, S.: A unified approach to interpreting model predictions. In: Guyon, I., et al. (eds.) Advances in Neural Information Processing Systems 30: Annual Conference on Neural Information Processing Systems 2017, 4–9 December 2017, Long Beach, CA, USA, pp. 4765–4774 (2017). https://proceedings.neurips.cc/paper/2017/hash/8a20a8621978632d76c43dfd28b67767-Abstract.html

29. Mahendran, A., Vedaldi, A.: Understanding deep image representations by inverting them. In: IEEE Conference on Computer Vision and Pattern Recognition, CVPR 2015, Boston, MA, USA, 7–12 June 2015, pp. 5188–5196. IEEE Computer Society (2015). https://doi.org/10.1109/CVPR.2015.7299155

30. Malfa, E.L., Michelmore, R., Zbrzezny, A.M., Paoletti, N., Kwiatkowska, M.: On guaranteed optimal robust explanations for NLP models. In: Zhou, Z. (ed.) Proceedings of the Thirtieth International Joint Conference on Artificial Intelligence, IJCAI 2021, Virtual Event / Montreal, Canada, 19–27 August 2021, pp. 2658–2665. ijcai.org (2021). https://doi.org/10.24963/IJCAI.2021/366

31. Marques-Silva, J.: Logic-based explainability in machine learning. In: Bertossi, L.E., Xiao, G. (eds.) Reasoning Web. Causality, Explanations and Declarative Knowledge. LNCS, vol. 13759, pp. 24–104. Springer, Cham (2022). https://doi.org/10.1007/978-3-031-31414-8_2

32. McMillan, K.L.: Interpolation and SAT-based model checking. In: Hunt, W.A., Somenzi, F. (eds.) CAV 2003. LNCS, vol. 2725, pp. 1–13. Springer, Heidelberg (2003). https://doi.org/10.1007/978-3-540-45069-6_1

33. de Moura, L., Bjørner, N.: Z3: an efficient SMT solver. In: Ramakrishnan, C.R., Rehof, J. (eds.) TACAS 2008. LNCS, vol. 4963, pp. 337–340. Springer, Heidelberg (2008). https://doi.org/10.1007/978-3-540-78800-3_24

34. Palechor, F.M., Manotas, A.D.l.h.: Estimation of obesity levels based on eating habits and physical condition. UCI Machine Learning Repository (2019). https://doi.org/10.24432/C5H31Z

35. Prabhu, S., D'Souza, D., Chakraborty, S., Venkatesh, R., Fedyukovich, G.: Weakest precondition inference for non-deterministic linear array programs. In: Finkbeiner, B., Kovács, L. (eds.) TACAS 2024, Part II. LNCS, vol. 14571, pp. 175–195. Springer, Cham (2024). https://doi.org/10.1007/978-3-031-57249-4_9

36. Prabhu, S., Fedyukovich, G., D'Souza, D.: Maximal quantified precondition synthesis for linear array loops. In: Weirich, S. (ed.) ESOP 2024, Part II. LNCS, vol. 14577, pp. 245–274. Springer, Cham (2024). https://doi.org/10.1007/978-3-031-57267-8_10

37. Ribeiro, M.T., Singh, S., Guestrin, C.: "Why should I trust you?": explaining the predictions of any classifier. In: Krishnapuram, B., Shah, M., Smola, A.J., Aggarwal, C.C., Shen, D., Rastogi, R. (eds.) Proceedings of the 22nd ACM SIGKDD International Conference on Knowledge Discovery and Data Mining, San Francisco, CA, USA, 13–17 August 2016, pp. 1135–1144. ACM (2016). https://doi.org/10.1145/2939672.2939778

38. Ribeiro, M.T., Singh, S., Guestrin, C.: Anchors: high-precision model-agnostic explanations. In: McIlraith, S.A., Weinberger, K.Q. (eds.) Proceedings of the Thirty-Second AAAI Conference on Artificial Intelligence, (AAAI-18), the 30th innovative Applications of Artificial Intelligence (IAAI-18), and the 8th AAAI Symposium on Educational Advances in Artificial Intelligence (EAAI-18), New Orleans, Louisiana, USA, 2–7 February 2018, pp. 1527–1535. AAAI Press (2018). https://doi.org/10.1609/AAAI.V32I1.11491

39. Rollini, S.F., Alt, L., Fedyukovich, G., Hyvärinen, A., Sharygina, N.: PeRIPLO: a framework for producing effective interpolants in SAT-based software verification. In: McMillan, K., Middeldorp, A., Voronkov, A. (eds.) LPAR 2013. LNCS, vol. 8312, pp. 683–693. Springer, Heidelberg (2013). https://doi.org/10.1007/978-3-642-45221-5_45

40. Seshia, S.A., Sadigh, D.: Towards verified artificial intelligence. CoRR abs/1606.08514 (2016). http://arxiv.org/abs/1606.08514

41. Shih, A., Choi, A., Darwiche, A.: A symbolic approach to explaining Bayesian network classifiers. In: Lang, J. (ed.) Proceedings of the Twenty-Seventh International Joint Conference on Artificial Intelligence, IJCAI 2018, 13–19 July 2018, Stockholm, Sweden. pp. 5103–5111. ijcai.org (2018). https://doi.org/10.24963/IJCAI.2018/708

42. Simonyan, K., Vedaldi, A., Zisserman, A.: Deep inside convolutional networks: visualising image classification models and saliency maps. In: Bengio, Y., LeCun, Y. (eds.) 2nd International Conference on Learning Representations, ICLR 2014, Banff, AB, Canada, 14–16 April 2014, Workshop Track Proceedings (2014). http://arxiv.org/abs/1312.6034

43. Wu, M., Wu, H., Barrett, C.W.: VeriX: towards verified explainability of deep neural networks. In: Oh, A., Naumann, T., Globerson, A., Saenko, K., Hardt, M., Levine, S. (eds.) Advances in Neural Information Processing Systems 36: Annual Conference on Neural Information Processing Systems 2023, NeurIPS 2023, New Orleans, LA, USA, 10–16 December 2023 (2023). http://papers.nips.cc/paper_files/paper/2023/hash/46907c2ff9fafd618095161d76461842-Abstract-Conference.html

44. Zeiler, M.D., Fergus, R.: Visualizing and understanding convolutional networks. In: Fleet, D., Pajdla, T., Schiele, B., Tuytelaars, T. (eds.) ECCV 2014, Part I. LNCS, vol. 8689, pp. 818–833. Springer, Cham (2014). https://doi.org/10.1007/978-3-319-10590-1_53

Sprout: A Verifier for Symbolic Multiparty Protocols

Elaine Li[1]✉ , Felix Stutz[2] , Thomas Wies[1] , and Damien Zufferey[3]*

[1] New York University, New York, USA
ef19013@nyu.edu, wies@cs.nyu.edu
[2] University of Luxembourg, Esch-sur-Alzette, Luxembourg
felix.stutz@uni.lu
[3] NVIDIA, Zürich, Switzerland
rilaak@gmail.com

Abstract. We present Sprout, the first sound and complete implementability checker for symbolic multiparty protocols. Sprout supports protocols with dependent refinements on message values, loop memory, and multiparty communication with generalized, sender-driven choice. Sprout checks implementability via an optimized, sound and complete reduction to the fixpoint logic μCLP, and uses MuVal as a backend solver for μCLP instances. We evaluate Sprout on an extended benchmark suite of implementable and non-implementable examples, and show that Sprout outperforms its competititors in terms of expressivity and precision, and provides competitive runtime performance. Sprout additionally provides support for verifying custom functional correctness properties beyond implementability.

1 Introduction

Implementability is the decision problem at the heart of top-down approaches to protocol verification, including choreographic programming [6,12,13] , high-level message sequence charts [1,2,7–10,18–22] and session types [3,4,14,16,23,26]. Implementability asks whether a global protocol, specifying message exchanges between all participants from a bird's-eye view, admits an asynchronous distributed implementation, namely one that is deadlock-free and exhibits the same behavior as the global specification.

In [17], we identify a sound and complete characterization of implementability for *global communicating labeled transition systems (GCLTSs)*. GCLTS is an expressive semantic model of protocols that subsumes many existing fragments of multiparty session types [3,4,23,25,26] and choreography automata [11]. The characterization of GCLTS implementability consists of three *Coherence Conditions*: Send Coherence, Receive Coherence, and No Mixed Choice, which reduce implementability to reachability and co-reachability in the GCLTS. In a nutshell, these are 2-hyperproperties stating that from two locally indistinguishable global protocol states, a participant can either perform a send action that is enabled

---

*Damien Zufferey was working at SonarSource in Switzerland when this work began.

© The Author(s) 2025
R. Piskac and Z. Rakamarić (Eds.): CAV 2025, LNCS 15933, pp. 304–317, 2025.
https://doi.org/10.1007/978-3-031-98682-6_16

in both states, or perform a receive action that uniquely distinguishes the two states, but cannot choose between performing a send or receive action. *Symbolic protocols* finitely represent infinite-state protocols using dependent refinements and mutable register variables. [17] derives sound and complete Symbolic Coherence Conditions for GCLTS-eligible symbolic protocols, expressed as μCLP instances. μCLP [24] is a fixpoint logic featuring recursive predicates with least and greatest fixpoint semantics, where the predicate body is constrained by a first-order logic formula over a background theory.

In this paper, we present SPROUT[§], the first sound and complete implementability checker for symbolic, multiparty protocols. SPROUT takes as input a symbolic protocol, and first checks whether the protocol is GCLTS-eligible. If so, it proceeds to generate μCLP instances corresponding to the Symbolic Coherence Conditions from [17], which it then discharges to the μCLP solver MUVAL [24]. If all instances return invalid, SPROUT reports that the protocol is implementable; if one instance returns valid, SPROUT reports non-implementable along with the specific states and transitions that violate implementability; otherwise SPROUT returns inconclusive. SPROUT is sound and complete relative to the completeness and soundness of MUVAL.

SPROUT extends [17] with explicit GCLTS checking, optimized μCLP encodings of the Symbolic Coherence Conditions, and support for verification of functional correctness properties beyond implementability. We evaluate SPROUT's expressivity, precision and efficiency against comparable tools [25, 26] on an expanded benchmark suite containing both implementable and non-implementable examples. SPROUT is able to correctly classify protocols that are out of reach of its competitors, outperforming them in terms of expressivity and precision. In terms of efficiency, SPROUT's performance is competitive. On multiparty protocols, its verification times vary with the size of the protocol and are largely bottlenecked by the efficiency of MUVAL, although remaining in the order of seconds in most cases. We envision SPROUT as a complementary intermediate step in existing top-down code generation toolchains for multiparty protocols whose implementability checks are incomplete.

2   Overview

2.1   Running Example

We introduce SPROUT using the running example of the two-bidder protocol [17]. The two-bidder protocol specifies the message-passing behaviors of a seller S and two bidders B_1 and B_2, who negotiate to split the cost of a book. Bidder B_1 initiates the protocol by announcing a book title, identified by its ISBN number. Seller S informs B_1 of the book's price c, which is undisclosed to B_2. Then, B_1 and B_2 enter a bidding loop to determine their respective contributions b_1 and b_2. After B_1 proposes its contribution b_1, B_2 can either respond with a bid, or stop bidding by sending a quit message to S, who forwards it to B_1. The bidding continues until either B_2 chooses to stop, or the sum of the two bids exceeds c, in

---

[§]https://github.com/nyu-acsys/sprout

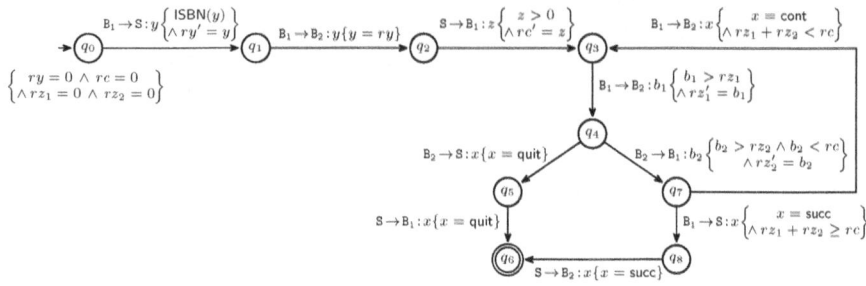

Fig. 1: Candidate specification for the two-bidder protocol.

which case B_1 informs S that the negotiation was successful. Refinements enforce that y is a valid ISBN number, and that B_1 and B_2's bids are increasing from one round to the next, thus guaranteeing termination. A candidate specification for the two-bidder protocol is depicted in Fig. 1.

SPROUT's input format closely follows the definition of *symbolic protocols*, formally defined over a set of participants $\mathcal{P}$ as follows:

Definition 2.1 (Symbolic protocol [17]). *A symbolic protocol is a tuple* $\mathbb{S} = (S, R, \Delta, s_0, \rho_0, F)$ *where*

- *S is a finite set of control states,*
- *R is a finite set of register variables,*
- *$\Delta \subseteq S \times \mathcal{P} \times X \times \mathcal{P} \times \mathcal{F} \times S$ is a finite set that consists of symbolic transitions of the form $s \xrightarrow{p \to q : x\{\varphi\}} s'$, where the formula φ with free variables $R \uplus R' \uplus \{x\}$ expresses a transition constraint over the old and new register values (R and R') and the sent value x,*
- *$s_0 \in S$ is the initial control state,*
- *$\rho_0 : R \to \mathcal{V}$ is the initial register assignment, and*
- *$F \subseteq S$ is a set of final states.*

The definition assumes a fixed but unspecified first-order background theory of message values (e.g. linear integer arithmetic). We denote by $\mathcal{F}$ the set of first-order formulas with free variables drawn from some set X that are interpreted over the set of message values $\mathcal{V}$. We assume standard syntax and semantics for first-order formulas. For a valuation $\rho \in X \to \mathcal{V}$ and $\varphi \in \mathcal{F}(X)$, we write $\rho \models \phi$ to indicate that φ evaluates to true under ρ in the underlying theory. Transition constraints simultaneously describe the current value being communicated and internal register updates. For $q_3 \xrightarrow{B_1 \to B_2 : b_1 \{b_1 > rz_1 \wedge rz_1' = b_1\}} q_4$, the transition constraint both enforces that the bid b_1 sent from B_1 to B_2 is greater than B_1's previous bid, and describes a register assignment $z_1 := b_1$. For readability, we assume implicit equality constraints over unmentioned post-state registers that are not updated. The input file for our candidate specification is given in Fig. 2.

2.2 Implementability

Before checking implementability, SPROUT first determines GCLTS eligibility. GCLTSs satisfy four assumptions: sink-finality, sender-driven choice, determin-

```
Initial state: (0)
Initial register assignments: ry=0, rc=0, rz1=0, rz2=0
(0) B1->S:y{(y>987000000000/\y<9880000000000)/\ry'=y} (1)
(1) B1->B2:y{y=ry} (2)
(2) S->B1:z{z>0/\rc'=z} (3)
(3) B1->B2:b1{b1>rz1/\rz1'=b1} (4)
(4) B2->S:quit{quit=0} (5)
(5) S->B1:quit{quit=0} (6)
(4) B2->B1:b2{b2>rz2/\b2<rc/\rz2'=b2} (7)
(7) B1->S:succ{succ=1/\rz1+rz2>=rc} (8)
(8) S->B2:succ{succ=1} (6)
(7) B1->B2:cont{cont=2/\rz1+rz2<rc} (3)
Final states: (6)
```

Fig. 2: Sprout input file for protocol specification in Fig. 1.

ism, and deadlock freedom. Sink-finality states that only non-final states have outgoing transitions, sender-driven choice states that all outgoing transitions from the same state have a unique sender, determinism states that no transition can lead to two distinct post-states, and deadlock freedom states that every protocol run can be extended to a maximal run.

After confirming that our protocol is GCLTS-eligible, Sprout proceeds to generate μCLP instances corresponding to the implementability characterization from [17], which consists of three Symbolic Coherence Conditions: Symbolic Send Coherence, Symbolic Receive Coherence and Symbolic No Mixed Choice. Sprout generates the queries in negation form, and discharges them to the μCLP solver MuVal [24]. Sprout reports implementable if and only if all instances return invalid, indicating that all conditions are satisfied.

Unfortunately, Sprout reports a violation to Symbolic Send Coherence for B_2 and the transition: (4) B2->B1:b2{b2>rz2/\b2<rc/\rz2'=b2} (7). The violation indicates the existence of two global protocol states both with control state q_4 that are indistinguishable from B_2's point of view, and a message value, such that sending the value to B_1 follows the protocol in one case but violates the protocol in the other. Closer inspection of this transition's constraint reveals that B_2 is required to send a bid that is strictly less than the price of the book c. However, c is not disclosed to B_2 during the protocol: B_2 is bidding in the dark. Thus, depending on the initial exchanges between B_1 and S, which are not observable to B_2, a bid could either satisfy or violate the middle conjunct, subsequently following or violating the entire protocol.

We can repair our candidate protocol by either omitting b2<rc from the aforementioned transition constraint, or by including a transition informing B_2 of the book's price before the bidding loop begins. Upon incorporating either fix, we find that all instances now return invalid as expected, and Sprout reports that the repaired two-bidder protocol is implementable in $\sim$19s.

Sprout also provides support for the verification of functional correctness properties beyond implementability. For example, we can verify that the sum of B_1 and B_2's bids never decreases once they enter the bidding loop. This verification problem can be expressed in negation form as a μCLP instance as follows, where `stcon` is a least fixpoint predicate describing st-connectivity between two states in the global protocol:

```
exists (s1: int) (ry1: int) (rc1: int) (rza1: int) (rzb1: int)
(s2: int) (ry2: int) (rc2: int) (rza2: int) (rzb2: int).
s1 > 3 /\
s2 > 3 /\
stcon s1 ry1 rc1 rza1 rzb1 s2 ry2 rc2 rza2 rzb2 /\
rza2 + rzb2 < rza1 + rzb1
s.t.
stcon (s1: int) ... : bool =mu
...
```

SPROUT provides a suite of least and greatest fixpoint predicate definitions for defining custom verification queries that are then discharged to MUVAL. MUVAL confirms that this instance is indeed invalid in ~9s.

3   Implementation

SPROUT is implemented in ~3500 lines of OCaml code. The tool and benchmarks used in the evaluation are available as part of the artifact accompanying this paper [15]. In this section, we describe aspects of its implementation, focusing on differences from the theory.

3.1   GCLTS Eligibility

The Coherence Conditions from [17] are precise for the GCLTS fragment of symbolic protocols, namely protocols that satisfy sink-finality, sender-driven choice, determinism and deadlock-freedom. Sink-finality and sender-driven choice are syntactic conditions that can be checked on the input protocol straightforwardly, without invoking MUVAL. Determinism and deadlock freedom are undecidable in general. SPROUT encodes the latter two as μCLP instances and discharges them to MUVAL. We present the formal definition and μCLP encoding of each property below, assuming a symbolic protocol $\mathbb{S} = (S, R, \Delta, s_0, \rho_0, F)$ in the remainder of the section.

Determinism states that from a reachable protocol state, no transition can simultaneously satisfy two transition constraints that lead to two distinct post-states. Reachability is expressed as a least fixpoint in μCLP as follows:

Definition 3.1 (Reachability in symbolic protocol). *Let* $s \in S$. *Then,*

$$\mathsf{reach}(s', r') :=_\mu \ (s' = s_0 \wedge r' = \rho_0) \vee \left(\bigvee_{(s, \, p \to q : x\{\varphi\}, \, s') \in \Delta} \exists x \ r. \, \mathsf{reach}(s, r) \wedge \varphi \right) .$$

The reach predicate takes as its arguments a control state s' and a set of registers r', which together constitute a symbolic protocol state. The first disjunct covers the base case in which s' is the initial state, and r' satisfy the initial register assignments. The second disjunct ranges over all transitions with s' as the post-state, and represents following a transition to reach s', which requires the transition predicate φ to hold in addition to *reach* on the pre-state s.

Equipped with the predicate reach, determinism is defined as follows.

Definition 3.2 (Determinism of symbolic protocol). $\mathbb{S}$ *is deterministic when for each pair of transitions* $s \xrightarrow{p \to q : x_1 \{\varphi_1\}} s_1, s \xrightarrow{p \to q : x_2 \{\varphi_2\}} s_2 \in \Delta$, *the following is valid:*

$$\forall x \ r \ r'_1 \ r'_2. \ \text{reach}(s, r) \wedge \varphi_1[x/x_1, r'_1/r'] \wedge \varphi_2[x/x_2, r'_2/r'] \implies s_1 = s_2 \wedge r'_1 = r'_2 \ .$$

Deadlock freedom states that every run in the protocol can be extended to a maximal run, meaning that it is either infinite or ends in a final state. Equivalently, we require that every reachable protocol state has an enabled outgoing transition, stated as follows.

Definition 3.3 (Deadlock freedom of symbolic protocol). $\mathbb{S}$ *is deadlock-free when for each non-final state* $s \in S \setminus F$, *the following is valid:*

$$\forall r. \ \text{reach}(s, r) \implies \bigvee_{(s, p \to q : x \{\varphi\}, s') \in \Delta} \exists x. \ \varphi \ .$$

For determinism, SPROUT generates one μCLP query per state; for deadlock freedom, SPROUT generates one μCLP query per pair of transitions sharing a pre-state. If the input protocol is not GCLTS-eligible, SPROUT reports specifically which assumption is violated by which state or transitions.

The GCLTS checking step of SPROUT is sound and relatively complete with respect to the completeness of MUVAL, and SPROUT only checks implementability of GCLTS-eligible protocols.

3.2 Optimizations

The first SPROUT optimization elides implementability checking for binary protocols, which by [17, Lemma 5.10] are implementable by construction if they satisfy the GCLTS assumptions. Between checking GCLTS eligibility and generating implementability μCLP instances, SPROUT checks whether the input protocol is binary, and if so, returns implementable immediately. Given that a large subset of benchmarks in the multiparty protocol literature are binary protocols, this optimization allows us to achieve performance within the same order of magnitude as existing tools for binary protocols, as we detail in §4.

The second and primary SPROUT optimization concerns the encoding of Symbolic Coherence Conditions into μCLP instances. The conditions universally quantify over participants in the protocol, and then universally quantify over pairs of simultaneously reachable protocol states from the perspective of that participant. Together, the conditions rely on three recursive predicates: $\text{prodreach}_p(s_1, r_1, s_2, r_2)$, which expresses that symbolic protocol states (s_1, r_1) and (s_2, r_2) are simultaneously reachable for p, $\text{unreach}^\varepsilon_{p,q}(s_2, r_2, x_1)$, which expresses that p cannot follow ε transitions from (s_2, r_2) to a state where it can send x_1 to q, and $\text{avail}_{p,q,\mathcal{B}}(x_1, s_2, r_2)$, which expresses that message x_1 from p can be received by q from state (s_2, r_2) without participants from $\mathcal{B}$ sending or receiving messages.

The Symbolic Coherence Conditions are defined as follows:

Definition 3.4 (Symbolic Coherence Conditions [17]). *Let* $\mathbb{S}$ *be a symbolic protocol. Then,*

- $\mathbb{S}$ *satisfies Symbolic Send Coherence when for each participant* $\mathbf{p}$, *transition* $s_1 \xrightarrow{\mathbf{p} \to \mathbf{q}: x_1 \{\varphi_1\}} s_1' \in \Delta_1$ *and state* $s_2 \in S$:

$$\mathsf{prodreach}_{\mathbf{p}}(s_1, \mathbf{r_1}, s_2, \mathbf{r_2}) \ \wedge \ \varphi_1 \wedge \mathsf{unreach}^{\varepsilon}_{\mathbf{p},\mathbf{q}}(s_2, \mathbf{r_2}, x_1) \implies \bot \ .$$

- $\mathbb{S}$ *satisfies Symbolic Receive Coherence when for every pair of transitions* $s_1 \xrightarrow{\mathbf{p} \to \mathbf{q}: x_1 \{\varphi_1\}} s_1' \in \Delta_1$ *and* $s_2 \xrightarrow{\mathbf{r} \to \mathbf{q}: x_2 \{\varphi_2\}} s_2' \in \Delta_2$ *with* $\mathbf{p} \neq \mathbf{r}$:

$$\mathsf{prodreach}_{\mathbf{q}}(s_1, \mathbf{r_1}, s_2, \mathbf{r_2}) \ \wedge \ \varphi_1 \ \wedge \ \varphi_2 \ \wedge \ \mathsf{avail}_{\mathbf{p},\mathbf{q},\{\mathbf{q}\}}(x_1, s_2', \mathbf{r_2'}) \implies \bot \ .$$

- $\mathbb{S}$ *satisfies Symbolic No Mixed Choice when for every pair of transitions* $s_1 \xrightarrow{\mathbf{p} \to \mathbf{q}: x_1 \{\varphi_1\}} s_1' \in \Delta_1$ *and* $s_2 \xrightarrow{\mathbf{r} \to \mathbf{p}: x_2 \{\varphi_2\}} s_2' \in \Delta_2$:

$$\mathsf{prodreach}_{\mathbf{p}}(s_1, \mathbf{r_1}, s_2, \mathbf{r_2}) \ \wedge \ \varphi_1 \ \wedge \ \varphi_2 \implies \bot \ .$$

A μCLP instance is a pair $(\phi, \mathcal{R})$ of a *query* ϕ, which is a first order formula over a background theory, and a *body* $\mathcal{R}$, which is a sequence of inductive predicates with least or greatest fixpoint semantics. Symbolic Send Coherence in negation form thus naturally corresponds to one μCLP instance per participant. Each instance's query existentially quantifies over control states and registers, and is a series of $|Q| * |Q|$ disjuncts that perform case analysis over pairs of control states, i.e. each disjunct is of the form

$$s_1 = q_1 \wedge s_2 = q_2 \wedge \mathsf{prodreach}_{\mathbf{p}}(s_1, \mathbf{r_1}, s_2, \mathbf{r_2}) \ \wedge \ \varphi_1 \wedge \mathsf{unreach}^{\varepsilon}_{\mathbf{p},\mathbf{q}}(s_2, \mathbf{r_2}, x_1)$$

where $q_1 \xrightarrow{\mathbf{p} \to \mathbf{q}: x_1 \{\varphi_1\}} q_2 \in \Delta$. Each instance's body comprises the inductive predicates prodreach and unreach, defined as least and greatest fixpoints respectively:

$$\mathsf{prodreach}_{\mathbf{p}}(s_1, \mathbf{r_1}, s_2, \mathbf{r_2}) =_{\mu} \ldots ; \qquad \mathsf{unreach}^{\varepsilon}_{\mathbf{p},\mathbf{q}}(s_2, \mathbf{r_2}, x_1) =_{\nu} \ldots ;$$

This naive encoding of [17]'s three conditions amounts to $3 * |\mathcal{P}|$ μCLP instances per protocol, where each instance is orders of magnitude larger than the average benchmark in MuVal's benchmark suite[¶], and the verification time for e.g. our running example exceeds 10 minutes. Thus, Sprout takes a different approach to structuring the Symbolic Coherence Conditions as μCLP instances. First, Sprout distributes each disjunct into a separate instance, yielding $|\mathcal{P}| * |Q| * |Q|$ instances for each condition. Next, Sprout decomposes the prodreach and unreach predicates by "currying" state arguments, generating one prodreach predicate per participant per pair of states, amounting to $|\mathcal{P}| * |Q| * |Q|$ predicate definitions, and one unreach predicate per pair of participants per state, amounting to $|\mathcal{P}| * |\mathcal{P}| * |Q|$ predicate definitions. We show in §4 that decomposing large instances into multiple instances with smaller queries and more inductive predicates improves the running time of MuVal by over two orders of magnitude for most protocols.

Thirdly, Sprout implements an overapproximation of simultaneous reachability that pre-filters pairs of control states before generating μCLP instances.

[¶] https://github.com/hiroshi-unno/coar/tree/main/benchmarks/muCLP/popl2023mod

Approximate simultaneous reachability disregards message values, only considering the sender and receiver of each event in a trace, e.g. p!q:4 · r?p:7 · s!q:5 is abstracted to p!q:- · r?p:- · s!q:-. This optimization preserves soundness and completeness of the tool: if two states are not approximately simultaneously reachable, then the Coherence Conditions say nothing about them; if two states are approximately simultaneously reachable, then the corresponding instances will be generated and checked, and in the case that they are not actually simultaneously reachable, will simply return invalid due to the prodreach conjunct being false.

Finally, for Send Coherence instances concerning simultaneously reachable states that share a control state, we add a conjunct to the μCLP query requiring that not all register values in the two simultaneously reachable states are equal. This eliminates quantifier instantiations that simplify to the trivially false formula: $\mathsf{prodreach}_{\mathsf{p}}(s, r, s, r) \wedge \varphi \wedge \mathsf{unreach}^{\varepsilon}_{\mathsf{p},\mathsf{q}}(s, r, x)$.

Bugs found in MuVal. While implementing Sprout, we discovered a soundness bug in MuVal's `parallel` and `parallel_exc` modes that led its output to depend on the order of least and greatest fixpoint predicates in μCLP instances containing only one kind of fixpoint. We also discovered a minor bug in MuVal's constraint simplifier when optimizing queries containing negation or implication. Both bugs were reported to and subsequently fixed by MuVal's developers.

4   Evaluation

All experiments in this section are run on a 2024 MacBook Air with an Apple M3 chip and 16GB of RAM. Verification times reported are the sum of GCLTS checking time and implementability checking time, with timeouts for individual μCLP instances specified separately.

4.1   Optimization Efficacy

We first evaluate the efficacy of Sprout's optimizations, detailed in §3. We compare the verification times of Sprout's pre-filtered, optimized μCLP instances against the naive encoding of definitions in [17]. We benchmark on examples of various sizes, measured by the number of transitions in the protocol specification. All examples are non-binary so as to reflect a difference in implementability checking time. The results in Table 1 show that naively encoding [17]'s conditions renders verification intractable for protocols with more than 2 transitions, and that Sprout's optimizations yield a speedup by over two orders of magnitude.

4.2   Evaluation and Comparison Against Session*

Next, we evaluate Sprout in terms of expressivity, precision and efficiency.

Example	$\|\mathcal{P}\|$	$\|\Delta\|$	Sprout	time	Naive [17]	time
figure12-yes	3	2	impl.	2.0s	impl.	2.4s
figure12-no	3	2	non-impl.	3.0s	non-impl.	2.3s
TwoBuyer	3	9	impl.	3.8s	timeout (300s)	311.2s
higher-lower-ultimate	3	9	impl.	11.1s	out of memory	610.4s
higher-lower-no	3	9	non-impl.	16.1s	non-impl.	349.8s
symbolic-two-bidder-yes	3	10	impl.	27.4s	timeout (300s)	648.4s
symbolic-two-bidder-no1	3	11	non-impl.	30.0s	out of memory	891.5s

Table 1: Comparison of verification times with and without optimizations.

Expressivity. To evaluate expressivity, we took the union of two benchmark suites from tools most closely related to Sprout: Session* [26] and Rumpsteak with refinements [25]. Both works target multiparty protocols with refinements, and in addition to checking implementability, generate type signatures against which user-provided local implementations can be statically type-checked. Session*'s benchmark suite contains 11 examples, all of which utilize refinements. Despite the title of [25], Rumpsteak's suite of 10 examples contains only 5 with refinements, and 4 that are multiparty, for a total of 2/10 multiparty examples with refinements. We omitted finite, binary protocols that can be handled by existing sound and complete tools for finite multiparty session types, such as [16], leaving us with 6 examples from Rumpsteak. Sprout was able to express all 17 examples from the literature. We then attempted to translate Session*'s examples into Rumpsteak's syntax, and vice versa, in an attempt to compare all three tools. Although both Session* and Rumpsteak adopt a Scribble-like syntax, we found that Session* could express all 6 of Rumpsteak's examples, whereas Rumpsteak could only express 3/11 of Session*'s examples, even after accommodating minor discrepancies that were immaterial to the high-level protocol intent. The key expressivity gap lay in the fact that Sprout and Session* both support loop recursion variables, e.g. in the two-bidder protocol, z_1 and z_2 that track B_1 and B_2's respective last bids, whereas Rumpsteak does not.

Precision. The benchmark suites of both Session* and Rumpsteak exclusively contain implementable examples. In evaluating precision, we are interested in both the *soundness* and *completeness* of the tool: does it correctly accept implementable protocols, and correctly reject non-implementable ones? Thus, we expand our benchmark suite with a new set of examples based on protocols from prior works [5, 16, 17], where for each protocol we include *both* an implementable and non-implementable version. We also introduce implementable and non-implementable variations of common protocols in the literature (e.g. two-bidder, higher lower guessing game). Some of the non-implementable examples were inspired by bugs inadvertently introduced in the process of translating examples into Sprout, and most non-implementable examples have a small edit distance to their implementable counterpart. A short description of each new example and any bugs contained can be found at https://github.com/nyu-acsys/sprout/tree/main/examples. In translating our new examples to Session* and Rumpsteak, we found a similar pattern as before: Session* could express 20/21 examples, whereas Rumpsteak could only express 10/21.

`Calculator` was not expressible in SESSION* due to lack of support for multiplication, whereas `higher-lower-no`'s implementability bug was ruled out by SESSION*'s type checker.

The result of evaluating SESSION* and SPROUT on the overall set of 37 examples is given in Table 2. We omitted evaluation results from Rumpsteak due to the tool's lack of formal guarantees and limited expressivity. To achieve a faithful comparison, verification times reported for SESSION* are only for checking projectability of global types and computing local types for each role.

Source	Example	$|\mathcal{P}|$	Impl.	SPROUT	Time	SESSION*	Time
[26]	Calculator	2	✓	✓	0.6s	N/A	2.0s
	Fibonacci	2	✓	✓	0.5s	✓	1.8s
	HigherLower	3	✓	✓	15.2s	✓	3.9s
	HTTP	2	✓	✓	0.4s	✓	1.9s
	Negotiation	2	✓	✓	1.0s	✓	1.9s
	OnlineWallet	3	✓	✓	9.4s	✓	3.3s
	SH	3	✓	✓	237.1s	✓	5.6s
	Ticket	2	✓	✓	0.6s	✓	1.9s
	TravelAgency	2	✓	✓	9.2s	✓	3.1s
	TwoBuyer	3	✓	✓	3.8s	✓	2.8s
[25]	DoubleBuffering	3	✓	✓	1.5s	✓	2.3s
	OAuth	3	✓	✓	6.2s	✓	2.3s
	PlusMinus	3	✓	✓	5.2s	×	2.1s
	RingMax	7	✓	✓	3.7s	✓	4.7s
	SimpleAuth	2	✓	✓	0.5s	✓	2.0s
	TravelAgency2	2	✓	✓	1.7s	✓	1.8s
[16]	send-validity-yes	4	✓	✓	1.9s	×	2.1s
	send-validity-no	4	×	×	1.9s	×	2.1s
	receive-validity-yes	3	✓	✓	5.1s	×	2.3s
	receive-validity-no	3	×	×	3.6s	×	2.0s
[17]	symbolic-two-bidder-yes	3	✓	✓	27.4s	×	2.0s
	symbolic-two-bidder-no1	3	×	×	30.0s	×	2.1s
	figure12-yes	3	✓	✓	2.0s	✓	2.0s
	figure12-no	3	×	×	3.0s	✓	3.0s
	symbolic-send-validity-yes	4	✓	✓	6.5s	×	2.5s
	symbolic-send-validity-no	4	×	×	5.3s	×	2.6s
	symbolic-receive-validity-yes	3	✓	✓	6.6s	×	2.8s
	symbolic-receive-validity-no	3	×	×	7.6s	×	2.8s
[5]	fwd-auth-yes	3	✓	✓	10.3s	×	2.3s
	fwd-auth-no	3	×	?	T/O	×	2.2s
new	symbolic-two-bidder-no2	3	×	×	23.9s	×	2.8s
	higher-lower-ultimate	3	✓	✓	11.1s	×	2.4s
	higher-lower-winning	3	✓	?	T/O	✓	229.8s
	higher-lower-no	3	×	×	16.1s	N/A	2.2s
	higher-lower-encrypt-yes	4	✓	✓	9.3s	×	2.3s
	higher-lower-encrypt-no	4	×	×	177.3s	×	2.4s
	higher-lower-mixed	3	×	×	19.3s	×	2.3s

Table 2: Comparison of verification times with [26]. For each example, we report the number of participants ($|\mathcal{P}|$), ground truth implementability (✓ or ×), verification times for SESSION* [26] and SPROUT with a 30s timeout per μCLP instance (T/O), and the result: ✓ for implementable/projectable, × for non-implementable/non-projectable, and ? for inconclusive due to timeout. Examples not expressible in SESSION* are marked with N/A.

The incompleteness of SESSION* is made apparent by our evaluation: of the 20 new examples expressible in SESSION*, containing an even mix of implementable and non-implementable protocols, SESSION* rejected all but 3/20. The source of incompleteness is twofold. For one, SESSION*'s notion of implementability is relative to *local types*, whose syntax a priori rules out communication patterns such as receiver choice from different senders. In contrast, [17] and SPROUT's notion of implementability is relative to a more expressive semantic model, called communicating labeled transition systems [17, Definition 3.3]. For two, SESSION* implements the merge-based projection operator from [14]. This projection operator is inherently incomplete even for global types without refinements (see [16] for a detailed discussion), and thus the refinement type system presented in [26] inherits all sources of incompleteness. ‖

Efficiency. In terms of efficiency, SESSION*'s verification times were mostly below 5s**, whereas SPROUT's verification times varied widely depending on the number of transitions in the protocol, and whether the protocol is binary. For binary protocols, the verification times of SPROUT are competitive with those of SESSION*. For multiparty protocols, most examples returned in less than 10s, with the exception of 3 timeouts, whose timeout limits were set to 30s per μCLP instance. †† As mentioned in §3, the verification bottleneck of SPROUT lies in the efficiency of MUVAL– instance generation introduces negligible overhead. The modularity of [17]'s Coherence Conditions means SPROUT's efficiency could be improved by running all generated μCLP instances in parallel.

Acknowledgements. The authors thank Hiroshi Unno for his correspondences regarding MUVAL. This work is supported in parts by the National Science Foundation under the grant agreement 2304758 and by the Luxembourg National Research Fund (FNR) under the grant agreement C22/IS/17238244/AVVA.

Disclosure of Interests. The authors have no competing interests to declare that are relevant to the content of this article.

References

1. Alur, R., Etessami, K., Yannakakis, M.: Inference of message sequence charts. IEEE Trans. Software Eng. **29**(7), 623–633 (2003). https://doi.org/10.1109/TSE.2003.1214326, https://doi.org/10.1109/TSE.2003.1214326
2. Alur, R., Yannakakis, M.: Model checking of message sequence charts. In: Baeten, J.C.M., Mauw, S. (eds.) CONCUR '99: Concurrency Theory, 10th International Conference, Eindhoven, The Netherlands, August 24-27, 1999, Proceedings. Lecture Notes in Computer Science, vol. 1664, pp. 114–129. Springer (1999). https://doi.org/10.1007/3-540-48320-9_10, https://doi.org/10.1007/3-540-48320-9_10

‖Note that SESSION*'s false positive result for `figure12-no` does not indicate the tool is unsound; rather, the user will fail to produce an implementation that typechecks against the generated local types because no implementation exists.

**SESSION* was run as a Docker container, and thus its verification times include emulation overhead.

††Note that when SPROUT returns non-implementable for protocols containing instances that timeout, the verification time may increase directly with the timeout limit.

3. Bocchi, L., Demangeon, R., Yoshida, N.: A multiparty multi-session logic. In: Palamidessi, C., Ryan, M.D. (eds.) Trustworthy Global Computing - 7th International Symposium, TGC 2012, Newcastle upon Tyne, UK, September 7-8, 2012, Revised Selected Papers. Lecture Notes in Computer Science, vol. 8191, pp. 97–111. Springer (2012). https://doi.org/10.1007/978-3-642-41157-1_7, https://doi.org/10.1007/978-3-642-41157-1_7

4. Bocchi, L., Honda, K., Tuosto, E., Yoshida, N.: A theory of design-by-contract for distributed multiparty interactions. In: Gastin, P., Laroussinie, F. (eds.) CONCUR 2010 - Concurrency Theory, 21th International Conference, CONCUR 2010, Paris, France, August 31-September 3, 2010. Proceedings. Lecture Notes in Computer Science, vol. 6269, pp. 162–176. Springer (2010). https://doi.org/10.1007/978-3-642-15375-4_12, https://doi.org/10.1007/978-3-642-15375-4_12

5. Cruz-Filipe, L., Graversen, E., Lugovic, L., Montesi, F., Peressotti, M.: Functional choreographic programming. In: Seidl, H., Liu, Z., Pasareanu, C.S. (eds.) Theoretical Aspects of Computing - ICTAC 2022 - 19th International Colloquium, Tbilisi, Georgia, September 27-29, 2022, Proceedings. Lecture Notes in Computer Science, vol. 13572, pp. 212–237. Springer (2022). https://doi.org/10.1007/978-3-031-17715-6_15, https://doi.org/10.1007/978-3-031-17715-6_15

6. Cruz-Filipe, L., Montesi, F.: A core model for choreographic programming. Theor. Comput. Sci. **802**, 38–66 (2020). https://doi.org/10.1016/j.tcs.2019.07.005, https://doi.org/10.1016/j.tcs.2019.07.005

7. Gazagnaire, T., Genest, B., Hélouët, L., Thiagarajan, P.S., Yang, S.: Causal message sequence charts. In: Caires, L., Vasconcelos, V.T. (eds.) CONCUR 2007 - Concurrency Theory, 18th International Conference, CONCUR 2007, Lisbon, Portugal, September 3-8, 2007, Proceedings. Lecture Notes in Computer Science, vol. 4703, pp. 166–180. Springer (2007). https://doi.org/10.1007/978-3-540-74407-8_12, https://doi.org/10.1007/978-3-540-74407-8_12

8. Genest, B., Muscholl, A.: Message sequence charts: A survey. In: Fifth International Conference on Application of Concurrency to System Design (ACSD 2005), 6-9 June 2005, St. Malo, France. pp. 2–4. IEEE Computer Society (2005). https://doi.org/10.1109/ACSD.2005.25, https://doi.org/10.1109/ACSD.2005.25

9. Genest, B., Muscholl, A., Peled, D.A.: Message sequence charts. In: Desel, J., Reisig, W., Rozenberg, G. (eds.) Lectures on Concurrency and Petri Nets, Advances in Petri Nets [This tutorial volume originates from the 4th Advanced Course on Petri Nets, ACPN 2003, held in Eichstätt, Germany in September 2003. In addition to lectures given at ACPN 2003, additional chapters have been commissioned]. Lecture Notes in Computer Science, vol. 3098, pp. 537–558. Springer (2003). https://doi.org/10.1007/978-3-540-27755-2_15, https://doi.org/10.1007/978-3-540-27755-2_15

10. Genest, B., Muscholl, A., Seidl, H., Zeitoun, M.: Infinite-state high-level MSCs: Model-checking and realizability. J. Comput. Syst. Sci. **72**(4), 617–647 (2006). https://doi.org/10.1016/j.jcss.2005.09.007, https://doi.org/10.1016/j.jcss.2005.09.007

11. Gheri, L., Lanese, I., Sayers, N., Tuosto, E., Yoshida, N.: Design-by-contract for flexible multiparty session protocols. In: Ali, K., Vitek, J. (eds.) 36th European Conference on Object-Oriented Programming, ECOOP 2022, June 6-10, 2022, Berlin, Germany. LIPIcs, vol. 222, pp. 8:1–8:28. Schloss Dagstuhl - Leibniz-Zentrum für Informatik (2022). https://doi.org/10.4230/LIPICS.ECOOP.2022.8, https://doi.org/10.4230/LIPIcs.ECOOP.2022.8

12. Giallorenzo, S., Montesi, F., Peressotti, M., Richter, D., Salvaneschi, G., Weisenburger, P.: Multiparty languages: The choreographic and multitier cases (pearl). In: Møller, A., Sridharan, M. (eds.) 35th European Conference on Object-Oriented Programming, ECOOP 2021, July 11-17, 2021, Aarhus, Denmark (Virtual Conference). LIPIcs, vol. 194, pp. 22:1–22:27. Schloss Dagstuhl - Leibniz-Zentrum für Informatik (2021). https://doi.org/10.4230/LIPIcs.ECOOP.2021.22, https://doi.org/10.4230/LIPIcs.ECOOP.2021.22

13. Hirsch, A.K., Garg, D.: Pirouette: higher-order typed functional choreographies. Proc. ACM Program. Lang. 6(POPL), 1–27 (2022). https://doi.org/10.1145/3498684, https://doi.org/10.1145/3498684

14. Honda, K., Yoshida, N., Carbone, M.: Multiparty asynchronous session types. In: Necula, G.C., Wadler, P. (eds.) Proceedings of the 35th ACM SIGPLAN-SIGACT Symposium on Principles of Programming Languages, POPL 2008, San Francisco, California, USA, January 7-12, 2008. pp. 273–284. ACM (2008). https://doi.org/10.1145/1328438.1328472, https://doi.org/10.1145/1328438.1328472

15. Li, E.: Sprout: A verifier for symbolic multiparty protocols (CAV'25 AE) (Apr 2025). https://doi.org/10.5281/zenodo.15313597, https://doi.org/10.5281/zenodo.15313597

16. Li, E., Stutz, F., Wies, T., Zufferey, D.: Complete multiparty session type projection with automata. In: Enea, C., Lal, A. (eds.) Computer Aided Verification - 35th International Conference, CAV 2023, Paris, France, July 17-22, 2023, Proceedings, Part III. Lecture Notes in Computer Science, vol. 13966, pp. 350–373. Springer (2023). https://doi.org/10.1007/978-3-031-37709-9_17, https://doi.org/10.1007/978-3-031-37709-9_17

17. Li, E., Stutz, F., Wies, T., Zufferey, D.: Characterizing implementability of global protocols with infinite states and data. Proc. ACM Program. Lang. 9(OOPSLA1), 1434–1463 (2025). https://doi.org/10.1145/3720493, https://doi.org/10.1145/3720493

18. Lohrey, M.: Realizability of high-level message sequence charts: closing the gaps. Theor. Comput. Sci. 309(1-3), 529–554 (2003). https://doi.org/10.1016/J.TCS.2003.08.002, https://doi.org/10.1016/j.tcs.2003.08.002

19. Mauw, S., Reniers, M.A.: High-level message sequence charts. In: Cavalli, A.R., Sarma, A. (eds.) SDL '97 Time for Testing, SDL, MSC and Trends - 8th International SDL Forum, Evry, France, 23-29 September 1997, Proceedings. pp. 291–306. Elsevier (1997)

20. Morin, R.: Recognizable sets of message sequence charts. In: Alt, H., Ferreira, A. (eds.) STACS 2002, 19th Annual Symposium on Theoretical Aspects of Computer Science, Antibes - Juan les Pins, France, March 14-16, 2002, Proceedings. Lecture Notes in Computer Science, vol. 2285, pp. 523–534. Springer (2002). https://doi.org/10.1007/3-540-45841-7_43, https://doi.org/10.1007/3-540-45841-7_43

21. Muscholl, A., Peled, D.A.: Message sequence graphs and decision problems on Mazurkiewicz traces. In: Kutylowski, M., Pacholski, L., Wierzbicki, T. (eds.) Mathematical Foundations of Computer Science 1999, 24th International Symposium, MFCS'99, Szklarska Poreba, Poland, September 6-10, 1999, Proceedings. Lecture Notes in Computer Science, vol. 1672, pp. 81–91. Springer (1999). https://doi.org/10.1007/3-540-48340-3_8, https://doi.org/10.1007/3-540-48340-3_8

22. Roychoudhury, A., Goel, A., Sengupta, B.: Symbolic message sequence charts. ACM Trans. Softw. Eng. Methodol. 21(2), 12:1–12:44 (2012). https://doi.org/10.1145/2089116.2089122, https://doi.org/10.1145/2089116.2089122

23. Toninho, B., Yoshida, N.: Certifying data in multiparty session types. J. Log. Algebraic Methods Program. **90**, 61–83 (2017). https://doi.org/10.1016/J.JLAMP.2016.11.005, https://doi.org/10.1016/j.jlamp.2016.11.005
24. Unno, H., Terauchi, T., Gu, Y., Koskinen, E.: Modular primal-dual fixpoint logic solving for temporal verification. Proc. ACM Program. Lang. **7**(POPL), 2111–2140 (2023). https://doi.org/10.1145/3571265, https://doi.org/10.1145/3571265
25. Vassor, M., Yoshida, N.: Refinements for multiparty message-passing protocols: Specification-agnostic theory and implementation. In: Aldrich, J., Salvaneschi, G. (eds.) 38th European Conference on Object-Oriented Programming, ECOOP 2024, September 16-20, 2024, Vienna, Austria. LIPIcs, vol. 313, pp. 41:1–41:29. Schloss Dagstuhl - Leibniz-Zentrum für Informatik (2024). https://doi.org/10.4230/LIPICS.ECOOP.2024.41, https://doi.org/10.4230/LIPIcs.ECOOP.2024.41
26. Zhou, F., Ferreira, F., Hu, R., Neykova, R., Yoshida, N.: Statically verified refinements for multiparty protocols. Proc. ACM Program. Lang. **4**(OOPSLA), 148:1–148:30 (2020). https://doi.org/10.1145/3428216, https://doi.org/10.1145/3428216

Concurrency and Runtime Verification

GPUMC: A Stateless Model Checker for GPU Weak Memory Concurrency

Soham Chakraborty[1,2], S. Krishna[2], Andreas Pavlogiannis[3], and Omkar Tuppe[2(✉)]

[1] TU Delft, Delft, Netherlands
`s.s.chakraborty@tudelft.nl`
[2] IIT Bombay, Mumbai, India
`{krishnas,omkarvtuppe}@cse.iitb.ac.in`
[3] Aarhus University, Aarhus, Denmark
`pavlogiannis@cs.au.dk`

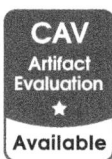

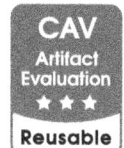

Abstract. GPU computing is embracing weak memory concurrency for performance improvement. However, compared to CPUs, modern GPUs provide more fine-grained concurrency features such as scopes, have additional properties like divergence, and thereby follow different weak memory consistency models. These features and properties make concurrent programming on GPUs more complex and error-prone. To this end, we present GPUMC, a stateless model checker to check the correctness of GPU shared-memory concurrent programs under scoped-RC11 weak memory concurrency model. GPUMC explores all possible executions in GPU programs to reveal various errors - races, barrier divergence, and assertion violations. In addition, GPUMC also automatically repairs these errors in the appropriate cases.

We evaluate GPUMC on benchmarks and real-life GPU programs. GPUMC is efficient both in time and memory in verifying large GPU programs where state-of-the-art tools are timed out. In addition, GPUMC identifies all known errors in these benchmarks compared to the state-of-the-art tools.

1 Introduction

In recent years GPUs have emerged as mainstream processing units, more than just accelerators [29,66,67,73]. Modern GPUs provide support for more fine-grained shared memory access patterns, allowing programmers to optimize performance beyond the traditional lock-step execution model typically associated with SIMT architectures. To this end, GPU programming languages such as CUDA and OpenCL [2,5], as well as libraries [3,4], have adopted C/C++ shared memory concurrency primitives.

Writing correct and highly efficient shared-memory concurrent programs is already a challenging problem, even for CPUs. GPU concurrency poses further challenges. Unlike CPU threads, the threads in a GPU are organized hierarchically and synchronize via barriers during execution. Moreover, shared-memory

ⓒ The Author(s) 2025
R. Piskac and Z. Rakamarić (Eds.): CAV 2025, LNCS 15933, pp. 321–346, 2025.
https://doi.org/10.1007/978-3-031-98682-6_17

accesses are *scoped*, resulting in more fine-grained rules for synchronization, based on the proximity of their threads. Although these primitives and rules play a key role in achieving better performance, they are also complex and prone to errors.

GPU concurrency may result in various types of concurrency bugs – assertion violations, data races, heterogeneous races, and barrier divergence. While assertion violations and data race errors are well-known in CPU concurrency, they manifest in more complicated ways in the context of GPU programs. The other two types of errors, heterogeneous races and barrier divergence, are GPU specific. To catch these errors, it is imperative to explore all possible executions of a program.

The set of possible executions of a GPU concurrent program is determined by its underlying consistency model. State-of-the-art architectures including GPUs follow weak consistency, and as a result a program may exhibit extra behaviors in addition to the interleaving executions or more formally sequential consistency (SC) [49]. However, as the weak memory concurrency models in GPUs differ from the ones in the CPUs, the state-of-the-art analysis and verification approaches for programs written for CPUs do not suffice in identifying these errors under GPU weak memory concurrency. As a result, automated reasoning of GPU concurrency, particularly under weak consistency models, even though a timely and important problem, has remained largely unexplored.

To address this gap, in this paper we develop the GPUMC model checker for a scoped-C/C++ programming languages [61] for GPUs. Scoped-C/C++ has all the shared memory access primitives provided by PTX and Vulkan, and in addition, provide SC memory accesses. The recent work of [61] formalizes the scoped C/C++ concurrency in scoped-RC11 memory model (SRC11), similarly to the formalization of C/C++ concurrency in RC11 [48]. Consequently, GPUMC is developed for the SRC11 model. The consistency properties defined by SRC11, scoped C/C++ programming language follows catch fire semantics similar to traditional C/C++, that is, a program having a SRC11 consistent execution with a data race has undefined behavior. In addition, scoped C/C++ defines *heterogeneous race* [30,35,61,78] based on the scopes of the accesses, and a program having a SRC11-consistent execution with heterogeneous race also has undefined behavior.

Stateless Model Checking (SMC) is a prominent automated verification technique [23] that explores all possible executions of a program in a systematic manner. However, the number of executions can grow exponentially larger in the number of concurrent threads, which poses a key challenge to a model checker. To address this challenge, partial order reduction (POR) [24,32,68] and subsequently dynamic partial order reduction (DPOR) techniques have been proposed [28]. More recently, several DPOR algorithms are proposed for different weak memory consistency models to explore executions in a time and space-efficient manner [6,7,10,43,64,83]. For instance, GenMC-Trust [44] and POP [8] are recently proposed polynomial-space DPOR algorithms. While these techniques are widely applied for programs written for CPUs (weak memory) concurrency models [7, 10, 43–45, 64], to our knowledge, DPOR-based model checking has not been explored for GPU weak memory concurrency.

GPUMC extends the GenMC-TruSt [44] approach to handle the GPU-specific features that the original GenMC lacks. More specifically, GPUMC implements an exploration-optimal, sound, and complete DPOR algorithm with linear memory requirements that is also parallelizable. Besides efficient exploration, GPUMC detects all the errors discussed above and automatically repairs certain errors such as heterogenous races. Thus GPUMC progressively transforms a heterogeneous-racy program to generate a heterogeneous-race-free version. We empirically evaluate GPUMC on several benchmarks to demonstrate its effectiveness. The benchmarks range from small litmus tests to real applications, used in GPU testing [51, 77], bounded model checking [52], and verification under sequential consistency [39, 40]. GPUMC explores the executions of these benchmarks in a scalable manner and identifies the errors. We compare GPUMC with DARTAGNAN [78], a bounded model checker for GPU weak memory concurrency [52]. GPUMC identifies races which are missed by DARTAGNAN in its benchmarks and also outperforms DARTAGNAN significantly in terms of memory and time requirements in identifying concurrency errors.

Contributions and Outline. To summarize, the paper makes the following contributions. Sections 2 and 3 provide an overview of GPU weak memory concurrency and its formal semantics. Next, Sects. 4 and 5 discuss the proposed DPOR algorithm and its experimental evaluation. Finally, we discuss the related work in Sect. 6 and conclude in Sect. 7.

2   Overview of GPU Concurrency

A shared memory GPU program consists of a fixed set of threads with a set of shared memory locations and thread-local variables. Unlike in the CPU, the GPU threads are structured in hierarchies at multiple levels: cooperative thread array(CTA) (cta), GPU (gpu), and system (sys), where cta is a collection of threads and gpu is a group of cta, and finally sys consists of a set of gpus and threads of other devices such as CPUs. Thus, a thread can be identified by its (cta, gpu) identifiers and its thread identifier. The system (sys) is the same for all threads.

Shared memory operations are one of read, write, atomic read-modify-write (RMW), fence (fnc) or barrier (bar). Similar to the C/C++ concurrency [36, 37], these accesses are non-atomic read or write, or atomic accesses with memory orders. Thus accesses are classified as: non-atomic (NA), relaxed (RLX), acquire (ACQ), release (REL), acquire-release (ACQ-REL), or sequentially consistent (SC). In increasing strength, $NA \sqsubseteq RLX \sqsubseteq \{REL, ACQ\} \sqsubseteq ACQ\text{-}REL \sqsubseteq SC$.

The shared memory accesses of the GPU are further parameterized with a scope $sco \in \{cta, gpu, sys\}$. The scope of an operation determines its role in synchronizing with other operations in other threads based on proximity. Thus, shared memory accesses are of the following form where o_r, o_w, o_u, o_f denote the memory orders of the read, write, RMW, and fence accesses respectively.

$$r = X_{o_r}^{\text{sco}} \mid X_{o_w}^{\text{sco}} = E \mid r = \text{RMW}_{o_u}^{\text{sco}}(X, E_r, E_w) \mid \text{fnc}_{o_f}^{\text{sco}} \mid \text{bar}^{\text{sco}}(\text{id})@l@$$

A read access $r = X_{o_r}^{\text{sco}}$ returns the value of shared memory location/-variable X to thread-local variable r with memory order o_r selected from $\{\text{NA}, \text{RLX}, \text{ACQ}, \text{SC}\}$. A write access $X_{o_w}^{\text{sco}} = E$ writes the value of expression E to the location X with memory order o_w selected from $\{\text{NA}, \text{RLX}, \text{REL}, \text{SC}\}$. The superscript sco refers to the scope. An RMW access $r = \text{RMW}_{o_u}^{\text{sco}}(X, E_r, E_w)$, atomically updates the value of location X with the value of E_w if the read value of X is E_r. On failure, it performs only the read operation. The memory order of an RMW is o_u selected from $\{\text{RLX}, \text{REL}, \text{ACQ}, \text{ACQ-REL}, \text{SC}\}$. A fence access fnc is performed with a memory order o_f selected from $\{\text{REL}, \text{ACQ}, \text{ACQ-REL}, \text{SC}\}$. GPUs also provide barrier operations where a set of threads synchronize and therefore affect the behaviors of a program. For a barrier operation $\text{bar}^{\text{sco}}(\text{id})$, sco refers to the scope of the barrier and id denotes the barrier identifier. We model barriers as acquire-release RMWs ($\text{RMW}_{\text{ACQ-REL}}^{\text{sco}}$) parameterized with scope sco on a special auxiliary variable (similar to [46]).

$$X = 0;$$

$$T_1\langle \text{cta}_1, \_\rangle \;\Big|\Big|\; T_2\langle \text{cta}_2, \_\rangle$$

$$X_{\text{REL}}^{\text{cta}} = 1; \quad \begin{array}{l} a = X_{\text{ACQ}}^{\text{cta}}; \\ \text{if}(a == 1) \\ \quad b = X_{\text{NA}}^{\text{cta}}; \end{array}$$

$$\textbf{forall}\ \langle b = 0?\rangle$$

(a)

```
f(tid){
  if(tid%2 == 0){
    S1;
    barcta(1);
  } else {
    S2;
    barcta(2);
  }
}
f(tid); ||... ||f(tid);
```

(b)

Fig. 1. Example of GPU concurrency errors. In (a), we have two threads T_1, T_2 from the CTAs $\text{cta}_1, \text{cta}_2$. In (b) all threads are in the same CTA.

2.1   GPU Concurrency Errors

Traditionally, two key errors in shared memory concurrency are assertion violations and data races. In addition, concurrent programs for GPUs may contain heterogeneous races and barrier divergence errors. The behavior of a program with data race or heterogeneous race is undefined, while divergence errors may lead to deadlocks [2, 61, 78, Section 16.6.2].

Assertion violation: In our benchmarks assertion violations imply weak memory bugs. Assertions verify the values of the variables and memory locations in a program. If the intended values do not match, it results in an assertion violation. Consider the program in Fig. 1a having the assertion **forall** $b = 0$? which checks whether, for all executions, b is 0. If the value of X read into a in T_2 is 1, then b cannot read a stale value 0 from X and the assertion fails.

Data Race: Two operations a and b in an execution are said to be in a data race [61] [78] if (i) a and b are concurrent, that is, not related by *happens-before*, (ii) they access the same memory location, (iii) at least one of the accesses is a write operation, and (iv) at least one of the accesses is a non-atomic operation. In Fig. 1a, if $cta_1 = cta_2$, the threads are in the same cta. In that case, if the acquire-read of X in the second thread reads from the release-write in the first thread, then it establishes synchronization. Hence, the release-write of X *happens-before* the non-atomic read of X, and the program has no data race.

Heterogeneous Race: Two operations a and b in an execution are in a heterogeneous race if (i) a and b are concurrent, (ii) they access the same memory location, (iii) at least one of the accesses is a write operation, and (iv) both accesses are atomic with non-inclusive scope, that is, the scopes of each access includes the thread executing the other access. Note that a heterogeneous race may take place between atomic accesses. In Fig. 1a, if $cta_1 \neq cta_2$ then the acquire-read and release-write do not synchronize and consequently are in a heterogeneous race. Then the program also has a data race between the non-atomic read of X and release-write of X.

Barrier Divergence: Given a barrier, the threads within the given scope of the barrier synchronize. During execution, while a thread reaches the barrier, it waits for all the other threads to reach the barrier before progressing the execution further. Consider the program in Fig. 1b, where all threads execute the function f(). The threads with even thread identifiers synchronize to bar(1) and the thread with odd thread identifiers synchronize to bar(2). Hence the threads are diverging and not synchronizing to a single barrier. Modern GPUs consider it as a divergence error as the non-synchronizing threads may result in a deadlock. Following the definition from [2, Section 16.6.2], we report barrier divergence if at least one of the threads participating in the barrier is blocked at the barrier at the end of execution (no next instruction to execute).

3   Formal Semantics

In this section, we elaborate on the formal semantics of GPU concurrency. A program's semantics is formally represented by a set of *consistent* executions. An execution consists of a set of events and various relations between the events.

Events. An event corresponds to the effect of executing a shared memory or fence access in the program. An event $e = \langle id, \text{tid}, ev, \text{loc}, \text{ord}, \text{sco}, \text{Val} \rangle$ is represented by a tuple where id, tid, ev, loc, ord, sco, Val denote the event identifier, thread identifier, memory operation, memory location accessed, memory order, scope, read or written value. A read, write, or fence access generates a read, write, or fence event. A successful RMW generates a pair of read and write events and a failed RMW generates a read event. A read event $\mathsf{R}_o^{\text{sco}}(X, v)$ reads from location X and returns value v with memory order o and scope sco. A write event $\mathsf{W}_o^{\text{sco}}(X, v)$ writes value v to location X with memory order o and scope sco. A fence event $\mathsf{F}_o^{\text{sco}}$ has memory order o and scope sco. Note that for a fence event, $\text{loc} = \text{Val} = \bot$. The set of read, write, and fence events are denoted by R, W, and F respectively.

Relations. The events of an execution are associated with various relations. The relation program-order (po) denotes the syntactic order among the events. In each thread po is a total order. The relation reads-from (rf) relates a pair of same-location write and read events w and r having the same values to denote that r has read from w. Each read has a unique write to read from (rf^{-1} is a function). The relation coherence order (co) is a total order on the same-location write events. The relation rmw denotes a successful RMW operation that relates a pair of same-location read and write events r and w which are in *immediate-po* relation, that is, no other event a exists such that (r, a) and (a, w) are in po relations. We derive new relations following the notations below.

Notation on Relations. Given a binary relation B, we write $B^{-1}, B^?, B^+, B^*$ to denote its inverse, reflexive, transitive, reflexive-transitive closures respectively. We compose two relations B_1 and B_2 by $B_1; B_2$. Given a set A, $[A]$ denotes the identity relation on the set A. Given a relation B, we write $B_{=\text{loc}}$ and $B_{\neq\text{loc}}$ to denote relation B on same-location and different-location events respectively. For example, $\text{po}_{=\text{loc}}$ relates a pair of same-location events that are po-related. Similarly, $\text{po}_{\neq\text{loc}}$ relates po-related events that access different locations. Relation from-read (fr) relates a pair of same-location read and write events r and w'. If r reads from w and w' is co-after w then r and w' are in fr relation: $\text{fr} \triangleq \text{rf}^{-1}; \text{co}$.

Execution and Consistency. An execution is a tuple *e.g.raph* $= \langle \mathsf{E}, \text{po}, \text{rf}, \text{co}, \text{rmw} \rangle$ consisting of a set of events E, and the sets of po, rf, co, and rmw relations. We represent an execution as a graph where the nodes represent events and different types of edges represent respective relations. A concurrency model defines a set of axioms or constraints based on the events and relations. If an execution satisfies all the axioms of a memory model then the execution is consistent in that memory model.

SRC11 Consistency Model. We first explain the relations of the RC11 model [48] which is extended to SRC11 [61] for GPUs, defined in Fig. 3.

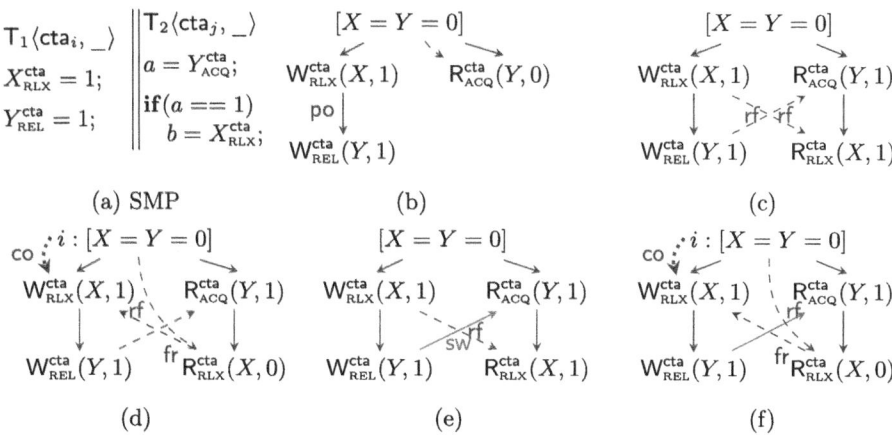

(a) SMP   (b)   (c)

(d)   (e)   (f)

Fig. 2. Executions shown in (b) and (c) are independent of whether $i = j$ or not. (b) shows an execution where Y reads 0 from the initial location. (c) shows an execution where Y and X read 1 in T_2. (d) shows an execution where Y reads 1 from T_1 but cannot synchronize, as T_1 and T_2 are in different CTAs ($i \neq j$). If $i \neq j$, X may read 0 from initialization. (e) is a special case of execution shown in (c) where $i = j$. If $i == j$, then read and write on Y are in synchronization relation because these accesses on Y are scope-inclusive. (f) shows an execution where there is a synchronization on Y with an inclusion relation (so again $i = j$). Hence, X in T_2 cannot read value 0 from initialization, as it violates the coherence axiom; consequently, the execution is forbidden.

RC11 Relations. Relation extended-coherence-order (eco) is a transitive closure of the read-from (rf), coherence order (co), and from read (fr) relations, that is, eco $\triangleq$ (rf $\cup$ co $\cup$ fr)$^{+}$. Note that the eco related events always access the same memory location.

Relation synchronizes-with (sw) relates a release event to an acquire event. For example, when an acquire read reads from a release write then the pair establishes an sw relation. In general, sw uses release-sequence rseq that starts at a release store or fence event and ends at an acquire load or fence event with an intermediate chain of rf-related rmw relations. Finally, relation happens-before (hb) is the transitive closure of the po and sw relations.

To relate the SC memory accesses and fences, the RC11 model defines the scb relation. A pair of events a and b is in scb relation in one of these cases: (1) (a, b) is in po, co, or fr relation. (2) a and b access the same memory location and are in hb relation, that is hb$_{=loc}(a, b)$ holds. (3) a has a different-location po-successor c, and event b has a different-location po-predecessor d, and (c, d) is in happens-before relation.

Based on the scb relation, RC11 defines psc$_{base}$ and psc$_F$. Relation psc$_{base}$ relates a pair of SC (memory access or fence) events and psc$_F$ relates a pair of SC fence events. Finally, RC11 defines psc relation by combining psc$_{base}$ and psc$_F$ relations.

$rseq \triangleq [W]; po_{=loc}^{?}; [W_{\sqsupseteq RLX}]; ((incl \cap rf); rmw)^{*}$

$prel \triangleq [E_{\sqsupseteq REL}]; ([F]; po)^{?}$

$pacq \triangleq (po; [F])^{?}; [E_{\sqsupseteq ACQ}]$

$sw \triangleq prel; rseq; (incl \cap rf); pacq$

$hb \triangleq (po \cup (incl \cap sw))^{+}$

$scb \triangleq po \cup (po_{\neq loc}; hb; po_{\neq loc}) \cup hb_{=loc} \cup co \cup fr$

$pscb_{ase} \triangleq ([E_{SC}] \cup [F_{SC}]; hb^{?}); scb; ([E_{SC}] \cup hb^{?}; [F_{SC}])$

$psc_{F} \triangleq [F_{SC}]; (hb \cup hb; eco; hb); [F_{SC}]$

$psc \triangleq psc_{base} \cup psc_{F}$

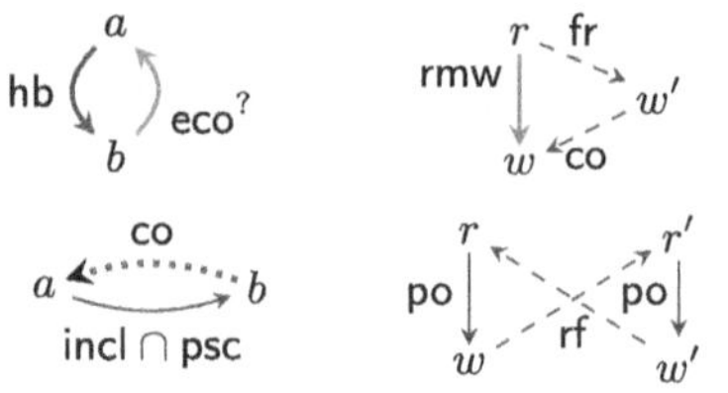

- $hb; eco^{?}$ is irreflexive (Coherence)
- $rmw \cap (fr; co)$ is empty (Atomicity)
- $(incl \cap psc)$ is acyclic   (SC)
- $(po \cup rf)$ is acyclic (No-Thin-Air)

Fig. 3. SRC11 relations and axioms with some violation patterns.

RC11 to SRC11. The SRC11 model refines the RC11 relations with inclusion (incl). Relation $incl(a, b)$ holds when (i) a and b are atomic events, (ii) if the scope of a or b includes the thread of b or a respectively, and (iii) if both a and b access memory then they access the same memory location. Note that the incl relations are non-transitive, that is, $incl(a, b)$ and $incl(b, c)$ *does not* imply an $incl(a, c)$ relation. To see this, consider events a, b, c having scopes cta_1, gpu_1 and cta_2 respectively where cta_1, cta_2 belong to GPU gpu_1. Then we have $incl(a, b)$ and $incl(b, c)$ but not $incl(a, c)$.

Based on the incl relation, the rseq, sw, and hb relations are extended in the SRC11 model. In SRC11, the rf relation in the rseq and sw relations must also be in the incl relation. Note that, even then, the sw related events may not be in the incl relation. Finally, hb in SRC11 is the transitive closure of the po and incl-related sw relations.

SRC11 Axioms. An execution in SRC11 is consistent when it satisfies the axioms in Fig. 3. The (Coherence) axiom ensures that the hb relation or the combination of hb and eco relations is irreflexive and does not create any cycle in the execution graph. The (Atomicity) axiom ensures that there is no intermediate event on the same memory location between a pair of events that are rmw-related. The *SC* axiom forbids any cycle between the SC events which are both in the psc relation and the incl relation. Finally, the (No-Thin-Air) axiom forbids any cycle composed of po and rf relations. These axioms essentially forbid the patterns shown in Fig. 3 in an execution graph. Among these scoped-RC11 axioms, (Atomicity) and (No-Thin-Air) are the same as those of RC11. The (Coherence) and (SC) axioms differ as they use more fine-grained incl relations for the scoped accesses.

Example. Consider the program and its execution graphs in Fig. 2. If $i \neq j$, then the accesses on Y do not synchronize, resulting in Fig. 2d. If $i = j$ then the accesses on Y synchronize which results in Fig. 2c. The execution in Fig. 2f is forbidden as it violates the (Coherence) axiom.

4 GPUMC: Model Checking under SRC11

In this section we discuss the GPUMC approach in Sect. 4.1 followed by a running example in Sect. 4.2. Finally, in Sect. 4.3 we discuss the soundness, completeness, and optimality of the proposed exploration algorithm.

4.1 DPOR Algorithm

GPUMC extends GenMC-TruSt and is in the same spirit as other well known dynamic partial order reduction (DPOR) algorithms [7,10,28,43–45,64].

It verifies a program by exploring all its executions in a systematic manner, ensuring that no execution is visited more than once. Like [44], our algorithm also takes only polynomial space.

Outline Algorithm 1 invokes the EXPLORE procedure to explore the executions of input program under SRC11. The EXPLORE procedure uses Algorithm 2 to enable a read operation to read-from possible writes and thereby explore multiple executions, Algorithm 3 to ensure no execution is explored more than once, and Algorithm 4 to identify and fix errors.

EXPLORE procedure The EXPLORE procedure explores executions $\mathcal{G}$, starting from an empty execution $\mathcal{G}_\emptyset$ where $E = \emptyset$, as long as they are consistent for a given memory model, in this case SRC11 (see Lines 3 to 6 of Algorithm 1). Next, if some of the threads are waiting at a barrier, while all other threads have finished execution, then we observe a barrier divergence, and the execution is said to be Blocked. In a

---

Algorithm 1: DPOR($\mathcal{P}$)

Input: program $\mathcal{P}$
1 EXPLORE($\mathcal{P}, \mathcal{G}_\emptyset$)
2 **Procedure** EXPLORE($\mathcal{P}, \mathcal{G}$)
3   **if** $\neg PoRfAcyclic()$ **then** return
4   **if** $\neg Coherent()$ **then** return
5   **if** $ViolateAtomicity()$ **then** return
6   **if** $\neg InclPscAcyclic()$ **then** return
7   **if** Blocked($\mathcal{G}$) **then** output "divergence in $\mathcal{G}$"
8   **switch** $e \leftarrow NextEvent(\mathcal{P}, \mathcal{G})$ **do**
9   **case** *assertion violation* **do**
10   output "Error in $\mathcal{G}$"
11   **case** $\bot$ **do**
            // no next event
12   output "$\mathcal{G}$"
13   **case** $e = W(x,v)$ **do**
            //add $W(x,v)$ to $\mathcal{G}$
14   CHECKANDREPAIRRACE($\mathcal{G}, e$)
15             $\mathcal{G}' = $ addco($\mathcal{P}, \mathcal{G}, e$)
16   EXPLORE($\mathcal{P}, \mathcal{G}'$)
17   DELAYEDRFS($\mathcal{G}, e$)
18   **case** $e = R(x, \_)$ **do**
19   reversible(e) = true
            //W^x is set of writes on x
20   **for** $w \in W^x$ **do**
                //add rf from $w \in W^x$
21                 $\mathcal{G}' = $ addRF($\mathcal{G}, w, e$)
22   CHECKANDREPAIRRACE($\mathcal{G}', e$)
23   EXPLORE($\mathcal{P}, \mathcal{G}'$)

---

blocked execution, different threads may be waiting at different barriers. In this case (line 7), we report the divergence and terminate. Otherwise, we continue

---

Algorithm 2: DELAYEDRFS($e.g.raph, w$)

---

1   **let R** be set of **reversible** reads in $e.g.raph$
2   **for** *each* $r = R(x, \_) \in R$ *s.t.* $r \notin$ porf.w **do**
3       $Deleted \leftarrow \{e \in E \mid r <_{exe} e \land e \notin$ porf.$w\}$
       //porf.$w=\{e \mid \exists$ a po, rf path in $e.g.raph$ from e to $w\}$
4   **if** CHECKOPTIMAL($e.g.raph, Deleted \cup \{r\}, w, r$) **then**
5         $e.g.raph' \leftarrow$ addRF($e.g.raph|_{E \setminus Deleted}, w, r$),
6   **for** each read $r \in e.g.raph' \cap R \cap$ porf.w set **reversible**$(r) = False$
7   EXPLORE($\mathcal{P}, e.g.raph'$)

---

exploration by picking the next event (line 8). This schedules a thread and the next enabled event of that thread. We use the total order $<_{exe}$ to denote the order in which events are added to the execution.

The exploration stops if an assertion is violated (line 10), or when all events from all threads are explored (line 12). The algorithm reports an error in the first case and in the second case outputs the graph $\mathcal{G}$.

If the exploration is not complete and the current event e is a write (line 13), then the procedure CHECKANDREPAIRRACE detects races due to events conflicting with e (line 14), and also offers to repair them. On detecting a race, the algorithm chooses one of the following based on user choice – (i) announce the race and stop exploration, or (ii) announce the race and continue exploration, or (iii) announce the race and repair the race.

Apart from calling EXPLORE recursively (Line 16) after adding the necessary co edges (line 15) to $\mathcal{G}$, we check if e can be paired with any existing read in $\mathcal{G}$ (line 17). These reads are called "reversible" as we can reverse their order in the execution by placing them after the writes they read from. On a read event r, we consider all possible rfs for r and extend the execution $\mathcal{G}$ to a new execution $\mathcal{G}'$ (addRF, Line 21).

Algorithm 3: CHECKOPTIMAL($e.g.raph, Deleted, w, r$)

---

1   **for** *each event* $e \in Deleted$ **do**
     // $RF(e)$ is the write from which e reads
2   **if** $e = R(x) \land e <_{exe} RF(e) \land RF(e) \in Deleted$ **then return** false
3      $e' \leftarrow$ **if** $e = W(x, v)$ **then** e **else** $RF(e)$
4   **let** Eset $= \{e'' \mid e'' <_{exe} e \lor e'' \in$ porf.$w\}$
5   **if** e' co$_x$ e'' *for some* $e'' \in$ **Eset then return** false
6   **return** true

DELAYEDRFS procedure The procedure pairs all reversible reads r in $\mathcal{G}$ with all same-location write events w (line 1) provided r is not in the po $\cup$ rf prefix of w in $\mathcal{G}$ (line 2), to preserve the (No-Thin-Air) axiom. Moreover, a new execution $\mathcal{G}'$ is obtained from $\mathcal{G}$ where r reads from w (line 5), and all events between r and w which are not po $\cup$ rf before w are deleted (line 3).

CHECKOPTIMAL procedure To ensure that no execution is explored twice, the CHECKOPTIMAL procedure ensures that all writes in the deleted set are co-maximal wrt their location, and all reads in the deleted set read from co-maximal writes. This is done by lines 2 to 5 in CHECKOPTIMAL.

CHECKANDREPAIRRACE procedure We check for races while adding each write w to the execution. For instance, assume that all the reads and writes have been explored (Line 1). For each event e' in this set which is not related to w by hb, we check if any one of them is non-atomic to expose a *data race*. If both have atomic accesses, we check if they are not scope-inclusive to report a *heterogeneous race* (Line 3). Likewise, for each read event added, we consider all explored writes (line 2), and repeat the same check to expose a *data race* or a *heterogeneous race*.

In addition, we also have an option of repair. In Repair (line 6, CHECKANDREPAIRRACE), we either skip and return to EXPLORE, or do the following repairs and terminate. First, if e and e' respectively have atomic and non-atomic accesses with non-inclusive scopes, then we update their scope to make them inclusive: for instance, if e,e' are in different CTAs, we update their scopes to GPU-level. Second, if at least one of e, e' is a non-atomic access, then we update the non-atomic access to relaxed atomic, and update the scopes so that e, e' have the same scope to prevent a heterogeneous race between them later. However, currently, we do not repair on non-atomic location data types.

Algorithm 4: CHECKANDREPAIRRACE($e.g.raph, e$)

---
1 if $e = W(x, v)$ then WR $\leftarrow$ set of seen reads/writes on x
2 if $e = R(x, v)$ then WR $\leftarrow$ set of seen writes on x
3 for *each* $e' \in$ WR *s.t.* $e' \notin$ hb.$e \wedge e \notin$ hb.e' do
4   if $\neg(\text{IsAtomic}(e)) \vee \neg(\text{IsAtomic}(e')) \vee \neg(\text{IsScopeInclusive}(e.g.raph, e, e'))$ then
5   ReportRace(e, e')
6   Repair($\mathcal{P}, e.g.raph, e, e'$)

Comparison with State-of-the-Art. We discuss how our algorithm differs from the existing DPOR algorithms. The first departure comes in the EXPLORE procedure where we perform consistency checking: Lines 3 to 6 are specific to the Scoped RC11 model which is not handled by any of the existing algorithms including the most recent [8,44], since none of them handle scoped models. The DELAYEDRFS procedure is standard in all DPOR algorithms and checks if we can pair reads with eligible writes which have been explored later. Next we have CHECKOPTIMAL, which ensures that we are optimal while exploring executions: here, the optimality check of [8] is tailored for sequential consistency; we extend the optimality checking algorithm for RC11 [44] to SRC11. While optimality is achieved by ensuring co-maximality on writes [44], there could be optimal co orderings that are inconsistent in the non-scoped setting, which are consistent in the scoped case which need to be considered to achieve completeness. This needed careful handling to achieve polynomial space just as [44]. Finally, our CHECKANDREPAIRRACE algorithm is novel and differs from all existing approaches as it reports and also repairs heterogeneous races.

4.2 Exploring the Executions of SEG

We now illustrate the GPUMC algorithm on program SEG as a running example. The assertion violation to check is **exists**$(a = 1 \wedge b = 1)$. This program has 4 consistent executions under SRC11.

The exploration begins with the empty execution, with no events and all relations being empty. As we proceed with the exploration, we use numbers 1, 2, ... to denote the order in which events are added to the execution. Among the enabled events, we have the read from Y, namely, $a = Y_{\mathrm{NA}}$ in thread T_2 and the write to X in T_1. We add two events for these accesses to the execution (lines 18, 21, 13 in EXPLORE). The read on Y has only the initial value 0 to read from; this is depicted by the rf edge to 1, obtaining $\mathcal{G}_1$. On each new call to EXPLORE, the partial execution is checked for consistency (lines 3–6). $\mathcal{G}_1$ is consistent.

$$X = Y = 0;$$

$$\mathsf{T}_1\langle cta_1, \_\rangle \quad \| \quad \mathsf{T}_2\langle cta_1, \_\rangle$$
$$X^{\mathrm{cta}}_{\mathrm{REL}} = 1; \; @l@ \quad \| \quad a = Y^{\mathrm{cta}}_{\mathrm{NA}}; \; @l@ \qquad @c@$$
$$Y^{\mathrm{cta}}_{\mathrm{REL}} = 1; \quad \| \quad b = X^{\mathrm{cta}}_{\mathrm{ACQ}};$$

$$\text{(SEG)}$$

$$\begin{array}{ll} & [init] \qquad\qquad \mathcal{G}_1 \\ 2 : \mathsf{W}^{\mathrm{cta}}_{\mathrm{REL}}(X, 1) & 1 : \mathsf{R}^{\mathrm{cta}}_{\mathrm{NA}}(Y, 0) \end{array}$$

Next, the read event on X from T_2 is added (line 18) having two sources to read from X (line 20): the initial write to X, and the write event 2. This provides two branches to be explored, with consistent executions $\mathcal{G}_2$ and $\mathcal{G}_3$ respectively.

$$\begin{array}{ll} [init] \qquad\quad \mathcal{G}_2 \\ 2 : \mathsf{W}^{\mathrm{cta}}_{\mathrm{REL}}(X, 1) \quad 1 : \mathsf{R}^{\mathrm{cta}}_{\mathrm{NA}}(Y, 0) \\[2ex] \qquad\qquad 3 : \mathsf{R}^{\mathrm{cta}}_{\mathrm{ACQ}}(X, 0) \end{array} \qquad \begin{array}{ll} [init] \qquad\quad \mathcal{G}_3 \\ 2 : \mathsf{W}^{\mathrm{cta}}_{\mathrm{REL}}(X, 1) \quad 1 : \mathsf{R}^{\mathrm{cta}}_{\mathrm{NA}}(Y, 0) \\[2ex] \qquad\qquad 3 : \mathsf{R}^{\mathrm{cta}}_{\mathrm{ACQ}}(X, 1) \end{array}$$

Next, we add write on Y from T_1 to $\mathcal{G}_2, \mathcal{G}_3$ which results in executions $\mathcal{G}_7$ and $\mathcal{G}_4$ respectively. Both $\mathcal{G}_4$ and $\mathcal{G}_7$ are consistent executions.

$$\begin{array}{ll} [init] \qquad\quad \mathcal{G}_7 \\ 2 : \mathsf{W}^{\mathrm{cta}}_{\mathrm{REL}}(X, 1) \quad 1 : \mathsf{R}^{\mathrm{cta}}_{\mathrm{NA}}(Y, 0) \\ \downarrow \qquad\qquad\qquad \downarrow \\ 4 : \mathsf{W}^{\mathrm{cta}}_{\mathrm{REL}}(Y, 1) \quad 3 : \mathsf{R}^{\mathrm{cta}}_{\mathrm{ACQ}}(X, 0) \end{array} \qquad \begin{array}{ll} [init] \qquad\quad \mathcal{G}_4 \\ 2 : \mathsf{W}^{\mathrm{cta}}_{\mathrm{REL}}(X, 1) \quad 1 : \mathsf{R}^{\mathrm{cta}}_{\mathrm{NA}}(Y, 0) \\ \downarrow \qquad\qquad\qquad \downarrow \\ 4 : \mathsf{W}^{\mathrm{cta}}_{\mathrm{REL}}(Y, 1) \quad 3 : \mathsf{R}^{\mathrm{cta}}_{\mathrm{ACQ}}(X, 1) \end{array}$$

Reversible Reads. In $\mathcal{G}_4$, we observe that the read on Y (1) can also read from the write 4 which was added to the execution later. Enabling 1 to read from 4 involves swapping these two events so that the write happens before the corresponding read. Since 2 is po-before 4, both of these events must take place before the read from Y (1) for the rf to be enabled. The read from X (3) however, has no dependence on the events in the first thread and happens after 1 . Therefore, we can delete (line 3 in DELAYEDRFS) 3 , and add the read from X later, after enabling the rf from 4 to 1 (line 5 in DELAYEDRFS). The optimality check (line 4 in DELAYEDRFS) is passed in this case (see also the paragraph on optimality below) and we obtain execution $\mathcal{G}_5$.

We continue exploring from $\mathcal{G}_5$, adding the read on X (Line 18 in EXPLORE) from T_2. Here, X may read from (Line 20, EXPLORE) the initial write or 2 . This results in executions $\mathcal{G}_6$ and $\mathcal{G}_8$ which are both consistent.

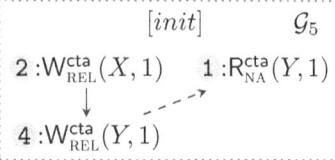

$[init]$ $\mathcal{G}_8$

$2 :\mathsf{W}^{\mathsf{cta}}_{\mathsf{REL}}(X,1)$ $1 :\mathsf{R}^{\mathsf{cta}}_{\mathsf{NA}}(Y,1)$

$4 :\mathsf{W}^{\mathsf{cta}}_{\mathsf{REL}}(Y,1)$ $5 :\mathsf{R}^{\mathsf{cta}}_{\mathsf{ACQ}}(X,0)$

$[init]$ $\mathcal{G}_6$

$2 :\mathsf{W}^{\mathsf{cta}}_{\mathsf{REL}}(X,1)$ $1 :\mathsf{R}^{\mathsf{cta}}_{\mathsf{NA}}(Y,1)$

$4 :\mathsf{W}^{\mathsf{cta}}_{\mathsf{REL}}(Y,1)$ $5 :\mathsf{R}^{\mathsf{cta}}_{\mathsf{ACQ}}(X,1)$

Optimality. From $\mathcal{G}_7$, we do not consider the possibility of Y reading from 4 as it would result in an execution identical to $\mathcal{G}_8$, and consequently violate optimality. The CHECKOPTIMAL procedure checks it to ensure that no execution is explored more than once. This check enforces a "co-maximality" criterion on the events that are deleted while attempting a swap between a read event and a later write event: this is exactly where $\mathcal{G}_4$ and $\mathcal{G}_7$ differ. In $\mathcal{G}_7$, while considering the later write on Y (4) to read from for the read event (1), the deleted (line 3, DELAYEDRFS) read event on X (3) reads from the initial write of X which is not co-maximal since it is co-dominated by 2 (lines 3-5 in CHECKOPTIMAL). Hence, the check-in line 5 of CHECKOPTIMAL fails. In $\mathcal{G}_4$ however, the deleted read on X (3) reads from a co_x-maximal write, and the test passes. Thus, the algorithm only considers the possibility of the Y reading from 4 in $\mathcal{G}_4$, avoiding redundancy.

Program Repair. The exploration algorithm detects the assertion violation in $\mathcal{G}_6$ (since both a, b read values 1) and detects a data race between 1 and 4 .

If GPUMC exploration encounters a heterogeneous race between a pair of accesses then GPUMC automatically repairs the race. To do so, GPUMC changes the scope of the accesses to enforce an inclusion relation. After fixing a heterogeneous race GPUMC terminates its exploration.

Consider a variant of the SEG program where T_1 and T_2 are in different CTAs, GPUMC fixes the heterogeneous race by transforming the scope from cta to gpu.

$$X = Y = 0;$$

$T_1 \langle \text{cta}_1, \_ \rangle$	$T_2 \langle \text{cta}_2, \_ \rangle$
$X_{\text{REL}}^{\text{cta}} = 1; \ @l@$	$a = Y_{\text{NA}}^{\text{cta}}; \ @l@$
$Y_{\text{REL}}^{\text{cta}} = 1;$	$b = X_{\text{ACQ}}^{\text{cta}};$

$@c@$ $\rightsquigarrow$

$$X = Y = 0;$$

$T_1 \langle \text{cta}_1, \_ \rangle$	$T_2 \langle \text{cta}_2, \_ \rangle$
$X_{\text{REL}}^{\text{gpu}} = 1; \ @l@$	$a = Y_{\text{NA}}^{\text{cta}}; \ @l@$
$Y_{\text{REL}}^{\text{cta}} = 1;$	$b = X_{\text{ACQ}}^{\text{gpu}};$

$@c@$

4.3 Soundness, Completeness and Optimality

Theorem 1. *The DPOR algorithm for* SRC11 *is sound, complete and optimal.*

Soundness. The algorithm does not continue exploration from any inconsistent execution as ensured by Lines 3 to 6 in Algorithm 1, and is therefore sound.

Completeness. The DPOR algorithm is complete as it does not miss any consistent and full execution. We prove this in the following steps:

- We first show that starting from any consistent execution $\mathcal{G}$, we can uniquely roll back to obtain the previous execution $\mathcal{G}_p$ (see the supplement for the algorithm to compute $\mathcal{G}_p$ from $\mathcal{G}$). This is proved using the fact that we have a fixed order in exploring the threads, along with the conditions that allow a swap between a read and a later write to take place. To allow a swap of a read r on some variable (say x), all events in *Deleted* respect "co_x-maximality". This is enforced by CHECKOPTIMAL and allows us to uniquely construct the previous execution $\mathcal{G}_p$.
- Second, we show that EXPLORE$(\mathcal{P}, \mathcal{G}_p)$ leads to the call of EXPLORE$(\mathcal{P}, \mathcal{G})$. This shows that if $\mathcal{G}_p$ is reachable by the DPOR algorithm, then $\mathcal{G}$ is also reachable.
- In the final step, we show that walking backward from any consistent $\mathcal{G}$ we have a unique sequence of executions $\mathcal{G}_p, \mathcal{G}_{p-1}, \mathcal{G}_{p-2}, \ldots$, till we obtain the empty execution $\mathcal{G}_\emptyset$. Thus, starting from EXPLORE$(\mathcal{P}, \mathcal{G}_\emptyset)$, we obtain $\mathcal{G}$.

Optimality. The algorithm is optimal as each full, consistent execution $\mathcal{G}$ is generated only once. Lines 23 and 15 of the EXPLORE procedure ensure that each recursive call to EXPLORE generates an execution that has a different rf edge or a different co edge. Also, during the DELAYEDRFS procedure, the swap of a read r with a write w is successful only when the deleted events respect "co_x-maximality". As argued in completeness, for every (partial) consistent execution $\mathcal{G}$, there exists a unique previous consistent execution $\mathcal{G}_p$.

   If the algorithm explores $\mathcal{G}$ twice, it means that there are two different exploration sequences with respective previous executions $\mathcal{G}_p$ and $\mathcal{G}_q$. This is a contradiction as we have a unique previous execution.

Polynomial Space. The DPOR algorithm explores executions recursively in a depth-first manner, with each branch explored independently. Since the recursion depth is bounded by the size of the program, this approach ensures that the algorithm uses only polynomial space.

The proofs and related details are provided in the supplementary material [19].

4.4   Exploring the Reads-From Equivalence

For simplicity, we have focused our presentation on exploring executions that contain the co relation explicitly. However, Algorithm 1 can be easily adapted to explore executions where co is not given explicitly. This corresponds to exploring the reads-from partitioning [22], a setting that is also supported by GenMC [44]. This is often a desirable approach, because it may significantly reduce the search space: there can be exponentially many executions, differing only in their co, all of which collapse to a single class of the reads-from partitioning.

Exploring the reads-from partitioning requires that every time a new execution is explored, the algorithm performs a consistency check to derive a co, so as to guarantee that the execution is consistent. If the program has no SC accesses, this check is known to be efficient for RC11 [10,47], taking essentially linear time [79]. These results easily extend to scoped RC11, by adapting the computation of the happens-before relation so as to take the scope inclusion incl into consideration. On the other hand, the presence of SC accesses makes the problem intractable [31,62], though it remains in polynomial time with a bounded number of threads [9,31].

5   Experimental Evaluation

We implement our approach as a tool (GPU Model Checker GPUMC) capable of handling programs with scopes. GPUMC is implemented in GenMC-Trust [44], and takes scoped C/C++ programs as input and works at the LLVM IR level. Similar to existing approaches, we handle programs with loops by unrolling them by a user-specified number of times. We conduct all our experiments on an Ubuntu 22.04.1 LTS with Intel Core i7-1255U×12 and 16 GiB RAM.

We experiment with GPUMC on a wide variety of programs starting from litmus tests to larger benchmarks. We mainly compare its performance with DARTAGNAN [50,52], a state-of-the-art bounded model checker, which also handles programs with scope [78]. DARTAGNAN has recently integrated the PTX and Vulkan GPU consistency models into its test suite. Even though the consistency model considered by DARTAGNAN are different from SRC11, which GPUMC considers, DARTAGNAN is closest available tool to the kind of work we report in this paper. Two other tools that also handle programs with scopes are iGUARD [39] and SCORD [40]. However, these tools do not reason about weak memory concurrency in GPUs. which makes their benchmarks not directly usable by GPUMC. In order to still experiment with them, we change their shared accesses to atomics.

Table 1. Data race detection: Evaluating on parameterized, single kernel code. Time Out (TO) = 30 min. (Time in Seconds and Memory in MB respectively). The number of events per execution is less than 120. In column Result, R denotes race detected and NR denotes no race. The * on two NR entries shows a wrong result in DARTAGNAN. In Grid column, X,Y represent X CTAs and Y threads per CTA.

Program	Grid	Threads	DARTAGNAN			GPUMC		
			Result	Time	Memory	Result	Time	Memory
caslock	4,2	8	NR	1300	494	NR	50	85
caslock1	4,2	8	R	0.7	304	R	0.1	85
caslock1	6,4	24	R	2.5	670	R	0.1	85
caslock2	4,2	8	R	0.6	270	R	0.1	85
caslock2	6,4	24	R	2.3	680	R	0.1	85
ticketlock	4,2	8	–	TO	1062	NR	320	85
ticketlock1	4,2	8	R	0.7	340	R	0.1	84
ticketlock1	6,4	24	R	965	941	R	0.1	84
ticketlock2	4,2	8	R	0.9	290	R	0.1	84
ticketlock2	6,4	24	R	1020	952	R	0.1	84
ttaslock	3,2	6	–	TO	1116	NR	500	84
ttaslock1	4,2	8	R	0.7	285	R	0.1	84
ttaslock1	6,4	24	R	3.6	321	R	0.1	84
ttaslock2	4,2	8	R	0.7	324	R	0.1	84
ttaslock2	6,4	24	R	4	917	R	0.1	84
XF-Barrier	4,3	12	NR	29	4200	NR	28	85
XF-Barrier1	4,3	12	R	4	1380	R	0.1	85
XF-Barrier1	6,4	24	NR*	190	1476	R	0.2	85
XF-Barrier2	4,3	12	R	9	1399	R	0.1	85
XF-Barrier2	6,4	24	NR*	170	1505	R	0.2	85

5.1   Comparison with DARTAGNAN

We compare the performance of GPUMC with DARTAGNAN [52] on the implementation of four synchronization primitives (caslock, ticketlock, ttaslock, and XF-Barrier), taken from [52,81]. These benchmarks use relaxed atomics, which is a very important feature of real GPU APIs. All the 1 (caslock1, ticketlock1, ttaslock1, and XF-Barrier1) and 2 (caslock2, ticketlock2, ttaslock2, and XF-Barrier2) variants are obtained by transforming the release and acquire accesses to relaxed accesses, respectively. Moreover, the XF-Barrier benchmark uses CTA-level barriers for synchronization. Table 1 shows the results of the evaluation of these applications. We parameterize these applications by increasing the number of threads in the program, the number of CTAs, and the number of threads in a CTA. For comparing with DARTAGNAN, we focus on race detection.

In Table 1 the Grid and Threads columns denote the thread organization, and the total number of threads respectively. The Result column shows the observed result – whether a race was detected (R), or whether the program was declared safe and no race was reported (NR). The Time and Memory columns show the time taken in seconds and the memory consumed in MB taken by DARTAGNAN and GPUMC.

We observe that in all examples except XF-Barrier, GPUMC and DARTAGNAN produce the same results, and GPUMC outperforms DARTAGNAN significantly in time and memory requirements. For the benchmarks XF-Barrier1 and XF-Barrier2 with grid structure (6,4) respectively, GPUMC successfully detects the underlying data race within a fraction of a second. The time and memory requirements we have reported for DARTAGNAN is with loop bound 12 as DARTAGNAN is unable to find the race even after unrolling to loop bound 12. On increasing the loop bound to 13, DARTAGNAN kills the process after showing a heap space error. In conclusion, in all the benchmarks in Table 1, GPUMC significantly outperforms DARTAGNAN.

5.2   Verification of GPU Applications

We evaluate GPUMC on medium to large real GPU applications, particularly for heterogeneous race and barrier divergence errors.

Heterogeneous Races. We experiment with four GPU applications – OneDimensional Convolution (1dconv), Graph Connectivity (GCON), Matrix Multiplication (matmul) and Graph Colouring (GCOL) from [39,40]. Each program has about 250 lines of code. For our experiments, we transform the accesses in these benchmarks with SC memory order and gpu scope. Finally, all these transformed benchmarks have SC accesses except GCON which has only relaxed accesses. We do not execute DARTAGNAN on these programs, as they are multi-kernel and involve CPU-side code, which makes it unclear how to encode them in DARTAGNAN.

Table 2 shows the 4 variants of each program by varying the grid structure. For instance, ldconv12 represents the version having 12 CTAs. The last two columns show the time and memory taken by GPUMC in detecting the first heterogeneous race. The detection of the first heterogeneous races in the ldconv, GCON, GCOL, and matmul benchmarks takes 4, 455, 11, and 18 executions respectively. In all cases, GPUMC detects the first race within 6 min.

Barrier Divergence. Next, we evaluate GPUMC for detecting barrier divergence, with the results shown in Table 3. We consider four GPU applications – histogram [72], XF-Barrier, arrayfire:select-matches (arrayfire-sm) and arrayfire:warp-reduce(arrayfire-wr) [80,82], as well as GkleeTests1 and GkleeTests2 kernels from the GKLEE tests [55,80]. All these benchmarks except Histogram use SC accesses and have barrier divergence. Histogram has a mix

Table 2. Heterogenous race detection using GPUMC on GPU Applications. (Time in Seconds and Memory in MB respectively). Events column represents the maximum number of events across all executions.

Program	Grid	Threads	Events	Memory	Time
1dconv12	12,4	48	1135	85	8.9
1dconv15	15,4	60	1359	85	15.2
1dconv20	20,4	80	1662	85	28.7
1dconv25	25,4	100	1937	85	47.7
GCON4	4,2	8	493	126	2
GCON5	5,2	10	563	150	5
GCON7	7,2	14	697	176	25
GCON10	10,2	20	901	250	75
GCON15	15,2	30	1241	383	295
GCOL4	4,2	8	337	85	0.5
GCOL5	5,2	10	435	85	1.7
GCOL7	7,2	14	643	86	3.6
GCOL10	10,2	20	1000	85	14.5
GCOL15	15,2	30	1051	88	18
matmul4	4,3	12	1036	85	8
matmul5	5,3	15	1054	84	9
matmul7	7,3	21	1424	85	32
matmul10	10,3	30	2556	125	360
matmul15	15,3	45	2154	90	175

of SC and relaxed accesses. In our experiments, we introduce a barrier divergence bug in the original histogram program [72, Chapter 19]. We vary the grid structures, similar to the benchmarks created for experimenting with the heterogeneous race detection.

5.3 Race Repair

Apart from detecting, GPUMC also repairs heterogeneous races as shown in Table 4 on five micro-benchmarks and three GPU applications [39,40]. The #Race column shows the number of races detected and fixed and the #Fix column shows the number of lines of code changes required to fix the detected races. In all cases, GPUMC detects and repairs all races within 3 secs. After repair, we let GPUMC exhaustively explore all executions of corrected programs (bench1, bench2, bench5, matmul finish within 10 min and bench3, bench4, GCOL and 1dconv finish within 6 h). Finally, the Executions column shows the number of executions explored on running the corrected program, and the Events column shows the maximum number of events for all explored executions post-repair.

Table 3. Barrier Divergence using GPUMC on various grid-structured programs (Time in seconds, Memory in MB). Events column represents the maximum number of events seen across executions.

Program	Grid	Threads	Events	Memory	Time
histogram4	4,2	8	144	85	0.1
histogram6	6,4	24	104	85	0.1
XF-Barrier4	4,2	8	132	85	0.1
XF-Barrier6	6,4	24	369	85	0.7
arrayfire-sm	1,16	16	1400	88	13
arrayfire-wr	1,256	256	240	85	0.3
GkleeTests1	2,32	64	700	85	2.5
GkleeTests2	1,64	64	900	86	4

Table 4. Race Repair using GPUMC on various grid-structured programs. #Race denotes the number of races detected and #Fix represents the number of changes made to fix the race. Events column represents the maximum number of events seen across executions.

Program	Grid	Threads	Executions	Events	#Race	#Fix
bench1	2,3	6	720	77	1	2
bench2	2,3	6	205236	83	2	4
bench3	8,1	8	12257280	100	2	4
bench4	4,2	8	12257280	100	2	4
bench5	5,1	5	1200	65	3	3
GCOL	2,1	2	350242	459	3	6
matmul	3,1	3	2409	1153	2	1
1dconv	2,2	4	995328	361	1	1

5.4 Scalability

Figure 4 shows the scalability of GPUMC for increasing number of threads on three benchmarks – SB (store buffer) and two GPU applications 1dconv, GCON. For SB, we create 24 programs with increasing threads from 2 to 25. For 1dconv, we create 30 programs with increasing CTAs from 1 to 30 with four threads per CTA. For GCON, we create 50 programs with increasing threads from 1 to 50. Figure 4 shows the GPUMC execution time and the memory consumed to detect the heterogeneous race for 1dconv and GCON and the assertion violation in SB; the x-axis shows the total number of threads for GCON, SB and CTAs for 1dconv, and the y-axis measures the memory in megabytes (MB) and the time in seconds. We also experiment on the LB (load buffer) benchmark in Table 5. We create 21 programs with increasing threads (LB-2 to LB-22) and exhaustively explore all consistent executions. We observe that in all benchmarks GPUMC exhaustively explores more than 4 million executions within 5500 s.

Table 5. Scalability of GPUMC on safe benchmark LB (Time in Seconds and Memory in MB). Executions column represents the executions explored.

Program	Events	Memory	Executions	Time
LB-3	36	84	7	0.3
LB-7	76	84	127	0.4
LB-12	126	84	4095	1.3
LB-18	186	101	262143	228
LB-22	226	127	4194303	5647

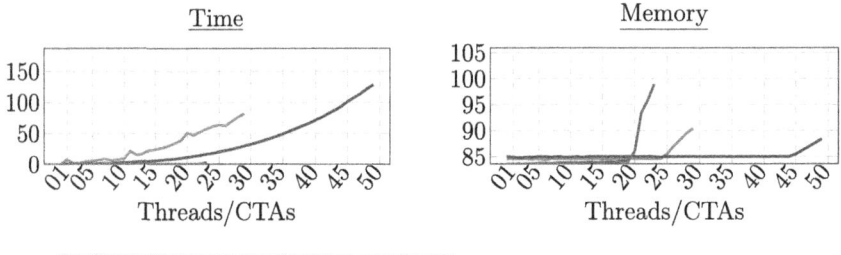

Fig. 4. Scalability: GPUMC execution time and the memory consumed to detect the heterogeneous race for 1dconv and GCON and the assertion violation in SB. The x-axis shows the total number of threads for GCON and SB, and CTAs for 1dconv. The y-axis measures the memory in megabytes (MB) and the time in seconds.

6   Related Work

Semantics. Weak memory concurrency is widely explored in programming languages for CPUs and GPUs [1,15,16,21,35,41,48,65,76], compilers [20,70], and CPU and GPU architectures [12,13,33,60,61,71]. Although GPUMC follows scoped-RC11 semantics [61], it is possible to adapt our approach to several other GPU semantic models. However, developing a DPOR model checker for GPUs with all guarantees that explore executions with po ∪ rf cycle is a nontrivial problem, in general [21,38,41,63], which is future work.

GPU Testing. Testing of GPU litmus programs is used to reason about GPU features [12,74,77], reveal errors [74], weak memory behaviors [12], and various progress properties [42,75–77]. Complementarily, our model checker explores all executions to check the correctness of the GPU weak-memory programs.

Verification and Testing of Weak Memory Concurrency. There are several DPOR algorithms for the verification of shared memory programs under weak memory such as TSO, PSO, release-acquire (RA) and RC11 [6,7,10,18,43,64,83]. DPOR algorithms have also been developed for weak consistency models such as CC, CCv and CM [11]. These are sound, complete, and optimal, although they incur an exponential memory usage. Recently, [44,45] proposed a DPOR algorithm applicable to a range of weak memory models incurring only polynomial space while being also sound, complete and optimal. On the testing front, we have tools such as C11-tester [59], and tsan11rec [58] for several variants of C11 concurrency. However, these tools do not address the verification of programs with scopes.

GPU Analysis and Verification. Several tools propose analysis and verification of GPU programs including GPUVERIFY [17], G-KLEE [55], GPUDrano [14], SCORD [40], IGUARD [39], SIMULEE [80], SESA [56] for checking data races [17,27,34,39,40,57,69,84,85], divergence [17,26,27]. Other relevant GPU tools are PUG [53,54] and FAIAL [25]. However, these do not handle weak memory models.

7 Conclusion

We present GPUMC, a stateless model checker developed on theories of DPOR for GPU weak memory concurrency, which is sound, complete, and optimal, and uses polynomial space. GPUMC scales to several larger benchmarks and applications, detects errors, and automatically fixes them. We compare GPUMC with state-of-the-art tool DARTAGNAN, a bounded model checker for GPU weak memory concurrency. Our experiments on DARTAGNAN benchmarks reveal errors that remained unidentified by DARTAGNAN.

Acknowledgements. This work was partially supported by a research grant (VIL42117) from VILLUM FONDEN.

Disclosure of Interests. The authors have no competing interests to declare that are relevant to the content of this article.

References

1. Vulkan memory model. https://github.com/KhronosGroup/Vulkan-Memory Model
2. Cuda C++ programming guide (2024). https://docs.nvidia.com/cuda/cuda-c-programming-guide/index.html
3. Cuda core compute libraries (CCCL) (2024). https://github.com/NVIDIA/cccl
4. Cutlass 3.6.0 (2024). https://github.com/NVIDIA/cutlass
5. The opencl^{TM} specification (2024). https://registry.khronos.org/OpenCL/specs/3. 0-unified/html/OpenCL_API.html
6. Abdulla, P.A., Aronis, S., Atig, M.F., Jonsson, B., Leonardsson, C., Sagonas, K.: Stateless model checking for TSO and PSO. In: Baier, C., Tinelli, C. (eds.) Tools and Algorithms for the Construction and Analysis of Systems, pp. 353–367. Springer, Heidelberg (2015)
7. Abdulla, P.A., Aronis, S., Jonsson, B., Sagonas, K.: Source sets: a foundation for optimal dynamic partial order reduction. J. ACM **64**(4), 25:1–25:49 (2017). https://doi.org/10.1145/3073408

8. Abdulla, P.A., Atig, M.F., Das, S., Jonsson, B., Sagonas, K.: Parsimonious optimal dynamic partial order reduction. In: International Conference on Computer Aided Verification, pp. 19–43. Springer (2024)

9. Abdulla, P.A., Atig, M.F., Jonsson, B., Lång, M., Ngo, T.P., Sagonas, K.: Optimal stateless model checking for reads-from equivalence under sequential consistency. Proc. ACM Program. Lang. **3**(OOPSLA), 150:1–150:29 (2019). https://doi.org/10.1145/3360576

10. Abdulla, P.A., Atig, M.F., Jonsson, B., Ngo, T.P.: Optimal stateless model checking under the release-acquire semantics. Proc. ACM Program. Lang. **2**(OOPSLA) (2018). https://doi.org/10.1145/3276505

11. Abdulla, P.A., Atig, M.F., Krishna, S., Gupta, A., Tuppe, O.: Optimal stateless model checking for causal consistency. In: Proceedings of TACAS 2023, vol. 13993, pp. 105–125. Springer (2023). https://doi.org/10.1007/978-3-031-30823-9_6

12. Alglave, J., et al.: GPU concurrency: weak behaviours and programming assumptions. In: PASPLOS 2015, pp. 577–591. https://doi.org/10.1145/2694344.2694391

13. Alglave, J., Deacon, W., Grisenthwaite, R., Hacquard, A., Maranget, L.: Armed cats: formal concurrency modelling at arm. ACM Trans. Program. Lang. Syst. **43**(2) (2021). https://doi.org/10.1145/3458926

14. Alur, R., Devietti, J., Navarro Leija, O.S., Singhania, N.: GPUDrano: detecting uncoalesced accesses in GPU programs. In: Majumdar, R., Kunčak, V. (eds.) Computer Aided Verification, pp. 507–525. Springer, Cham (2017)

15. Batty, M., Donaldson, A.F., Wickerson, J.: Overhauling SC atomics in C11 and OpenCL. In: POPL 2016, pp. 634–648. ACM (2016). https://doi.org/10.1145/2837614.2837637

16. Batty, M., Owens, S., Sarkar, S., Sewell, P., Weber, T.: Mathematizing C++ concurrency. In: POPL 2011, pp. 55–66. ACM (2011). https://doi.org/10.1145/1926385.1926394

17. Betts, A., Chong, N., Donaldson, A.F., Qadeer, S., Thomson, P.: GPUverify: a verifier for GPU kernels. In: Leavens, G.T., Dwyer, M.B. (eds.) OOPSLA 2012, pp. 113–132 (2012). https://doi.org/10.1145/2384616.2384625

18. Bui, T.L., Chatterjee, K., Gautam, T., Pavlogiannis, A., Toman, V.: The reads-from equivalence for the TSO and PSO memory models. Proc. ACM Program. Lang. **5**(OOPSLA), 1–30 (2021). https://doi.org/10.1145/3485541

19. Chakraborty, S., Krishna, S., Pavlogiannis, A., Tuppe, O.: Supplementary material for GPUMC (2025). https://doi.org/10.6084/m9.figshare.29143991.v1, https://figshare.com/articles/dataset/Supplementary_material_for_GPUMC/29143991

20. Chakraborty, S., Vafeiadis, V.: Formalizing the concurrency semantics of an LLVM fragment. In: CGO 2017, pp. 100–110 (2017)

21. Chakraborty, S., Vafeiadis, V.: Grounding thin-air reads with event structures **3**(POPL) (2019). https://doi.org/10.1145/3290383

22. Chalupa, M., Chatterjee, K., Pavlogiannis, A., Sinha, N., Vaidya, K.: Data-centric dynamic partial order reduction. Proc. ACM Program. Lang. **2**(POPL) (2017). https://doi.org/10.1145/3158119

23. Clarke, E.M., Emerson, E.A., Sistla, A.P.: Automatic verification of finite state concurrent systems using temporal logic specifications: a practical approach. In: Proceedings of POPL 1983, pp. 117–126. ACM Press (1983)

24. Clarke, E.M., Grumberg, O., Minea, M., Peled, D.A.: State space reduction using partial order techniques. Int. J. Softw. Tools Technol. Transf. **2**(3), 279–287 (1999). https://doi.org/10.1007/s100090050035

25. Cogumbreiro, T., Lange, J., Rong, D., Zicarelli, H.: Checking data-race freedom of GPU kernels, compositionally. In: Silva, A., Leino, K. (eds.) Computer Aided Verification, pp. 403–426. Springer, Cham (2021)
26. Coutinho, B., Sampaio, D., Pereira, F.M., Meira, W., Jr.: Profiling divergences in GPU applications. Concurrency Comput. Pract. Exp. **25**(6), 775–789 (2013)
27. Eizenberg, A., Peng, Y., Pigli, T., Mansky, W., Devietti, J.: Barracuda: binary-level analysis of runtime races in Cuda programs. In: PLDI 2017. Association for Computing Machinery, New York (2017). https://doi.org/10.1145/3062341.3062342
28. Flanagan, C., Godefroid, P.: Dynamic partial-order reduction for model checking software. In: Palsberg, J., Abadi, M. (eds.) POPL 2005, pp. 110–121. ACM (2005). https://doi.org/10.1145/1040305.1040315
29. Francis, E.: Autonomous cars: no longer just science fiction (2014)
30. Gaster, B.R., Hower, D., Howes, L.: HRF-relaxed: adapting HRF to the complexities of industrial heterogeneous memory models. ACM Trans. Arch. Code Optim. (TACO) **12**(1), 1–26 (2015)
31. Gibbons, P.B., Korach, E.: Testing shared memories. SIAM J. Comput. **26**(4), 1208–1244 (1997). https://doi.org/10.1137/S0097539794279614
32. Godefroid, P. (ed.): Partial-Order Methods for the Verification of Concurrent Systems. LNCS, vol. 1032. Springer, Heidelberg (1996). https://doi.org/10.1007/3-540-60761-7
33. Goens, A., Chakraborty, S., Sarkar, S., Agarwal, S., Oswald, N., Nagarajan, V.: Compound memory models. Proc. ACM Program. Lang. **7**(PLDI) (2023). https://doi.org/10.1145/3591267
34. Holey, A., Mekkat, V., Zhai, A.: HAccRG: hardware-accelerated data race detection in GPUs. In: 2013 42nd International Conference on Parallel Processing, pp. 60–69 (2013). https://doi.org/10.1109/ICPP.2013.15
35. Hower, D.R., et al.: Heterogeneous-race-free memory models. In: ASPLOS 2014, pp. 427–440 (2014)
36. ISO/IEC 14882: Programming language C++ (2011)
37. ISO/IEC 9899: Programming language C (2011)
38. Jeffrey, A., Riely, J.: On thin air reads towards an event structures model of relaxed memory. In: LICS 2016, pp. 759–767 (2016). https://doi.org/10.1145/2933575.2934536
39. Kamath, A.K., Basu, A.: Iguard: in-GPU advanced race detection. In: SOSP 2021, pp. 49–65 (2021). https://doi.org/10.1145/3477132.3483545
40. Kamath, A.K., George, A.A., Basu, A.: ScoRD: a scoped race detector for GPUs. In: 2020 ACM/IEEE 47th Annual International Symposium on Computer Architecture (ISCA), pp. 1036–1049 (2020). https://doi.org/10.1109/ISCA45697.2020.00088
41. Kang, J., Hur, C.K., Lahav, O., Vafeiadis, V., Dreyer, D.: A promising semantics for relaxed-memory concurrency. In: POPL 2017, pp. 175–189 (2017). https://doi.org/10.1145/3009837.3009850
42. Ketema, J., Donaldson, A.F.: Termination analysis for GPU kernels. Sci. Comput. Program. **148**, 107–122 (2017). https://doi.org/10.1016/J.SCICO.2017.04.009
43. Kokologiannakis, M., Lahav, O., Sagonas, K., Vafeiadis, V.: Effective stateless model checking for C/C++ concurrency. Proc. ACM Program. Lang. **2**(POPL), 17:1–17:32 (2018). https://doi.org/10.1145/3158105
44. Kokologiannakis, M., Marmanis, I., Gladstein, V., Vafeiadis, V.: Truly stateless, optimal dynamic partial order reduction. Proc. ACM Program. Lang. **6**(POPL), 1–28 (2022). https://doi.org/10.1145/3498711

45. Kokologiannakis, M., Raad, A., Vafeiadis, V.: Model checking for weakly consistent libraries. In: Proceedings of PLDI 2019, pp. 96–110. ACM (2019)
46. Kokologiannakis, M., Vafeiadis, V.: Bam: efficient model checking for barriers. In: International Conference on Networked Systems, pp. 223–239. Springer (2021)
47. Lahav, O., Vafeiadis, V.: Owicki-Gries reasoning for weak memory models. In: ICALP 2015, pp. 311–323 (2015). https://doi.org/10.1007/978-3-662-47666-6_25
48. Lahav, O., Vafeiadis, V., Kang, J., Hur, C.K., Dreyer, D.: Repairing sequential consistency in C/C++11. In: PLDI 2017, pp. 618–632 (2017). https://doi.org/10.1145/3062341.3062352, https://plv.mpi-sws.org/scfix/full.pdf
49. Lamport, L.: How to make a multiprocessor computer that correctly executes multiprocess programs. IEEE Trans. Comput. **28**(9), 690–691 (1979). https://doi.org/10.1109/TC.1979.1675439
50. Ponce-de León, H., Haas, T., Meyer, R.: Dartagnan: SMT-based violation witness validation (competition contribution). In: Fisman, D., Rosu, G. (eds.) Tools and Algorithms for the Construction and Analysis of Systems, pp. 418–423. Springer International Publishing, Cham (2022)
51. Levine, R., Cho, M., McKee, D., Quinn, A., Sorensen, T.: GPUHarbor: testing GPU memory consistency at large (experience paper). In: ISSTA 2023, pp. 779–791 (2023). https://doi.org/10.1145/3597926.3598095
52. Ponce de León, H.: Dat3m (2024). https://github.com/hernanponcedeleon/Dat3M
53. Li, G., Gopalakrishnan, G.: Scalable SMT-based verification of GPU kernel functions. In: FSE 2010, Proceedings of the Eighteenth ACM SIGSOFT International Symposium on Foundations of Software Engineering, pp. 187–196. Association for Computing Machinery, New York (2010). https://doi.org/10.1145/1882291.1882320
54. Li, G., Gopalakrishnan, G.: Parameterized verification of GPU kernel programs. In: 2012 IEEE 26th International Parallel and Distributed Processing Symposium Workshops & PhD Forum, pp. 2450–2459 (2012). https://doi.org/10.1109/IPDPSW.2012.302
55. Li, G., Li, P., Sawaya, G., Gopalakrishnan, G., Ghosh, I., Rajan, S.P.: GKLEE: concolic verification and test generation for GPUs. In: PPOPP 2012, pp. 215–224 (2012). https://doi.org/10.1145/2145816.2145844
56. Li, P., Li, G., Gopalakrishnan, G.: Practical symbolic race checking of GPU programs. In: SC 2014: Proceedings of the International Conference for High Performance Computing, Networking, Storage and Analysis, pp. 179–190 (2014). https://doi.org/10.1109/SC.2014.20
57. Li, P., et al.: LD: low-overhead GPU race detection without access monitoring. ACM Trans. Arch. Code Optim. (TACO) **14**(1), 1–25 (2017)
58. Lidbury, C., Donaldson, A.F.: Dynamic race detection for C++11. In: POPL 2017, pp. 443–457 (2017). https://doi.org/10.1145/3009837.3009857
59. Luo, W., Demsky, B.: C11Tester: A Race Detector for C/C++ Atomics, pp. 630–646. Association for Computing Machinery, New York (2021). https://doi.org/10.1145/3445814.3446711
60. Lustig, D., Cooksey, S., Giroux, O.: Mixed-proxy extensions for the NVIDIA PTX memory consistency model: industrial product. In: ISCA 2022 (2022). https://doi.org/10.1145/3470496.3533045
61. Lustig, D., Sahasrabuddhe, S., Giroux, O.: A formal analysis of the NVIDIA PTX memory consistency model. In: ASPLOS 2019, pp. 257–270. ACM (2019). https://doi.org/10.1145/3297858.3304043

62. Mathur, U., Pavlogiannis, A., Viswanathan, M.: The complexity of dynamic data race prediction. In: LICS 2020, pp. 713–727. Association for Computing Machinery, New York (2020). https://doi.org/10.1145/3373718.3394783

63. Moiseenko, E., Kokologiannakis, M., Vafeiadis, V.: Model checking for a multi-execution memory model. Proc. ACM Program. Lang. **6**(OOPSLA2) (2022). https://doi.org/10.1145/3563315

64. Norris, B., Demsky, B.: A practical approach for model checking C/C++11 code. ACM Trans. Program. Lang. Syst. **38**(3) (2016). https://doi.org/10.1145/2806886

65. Orr, M.S., Che, S., Yilmazer, A., Beckmann, B.M., Hill, M.D., Wood, D.A.: Synchronization using remote-scope promotion. In: ASPLOS 2015, pp. 73–86 (2015). https://doi.org/10.1145/2694344.2694350

66. Özerk, Ö., Elgezen, C., Mert, A.C., Öztürk, E., Savaş, E.: Efficient number theoretic transform implementation on GPU for homomorphic encryption. J. Supercomput. **78**(2), 2840–2872 (2022)

67. Pandey, M., et al.: The transformational role of GPU computing and deep learning in drug discovery. Nat. Mach. Intell. **4**(3), 211–221 (2022)

68. Courcoubetis, C. (ed.): CAV 1993. LNCS, vol. 697. Springer, Heidelberg (1993). https://doi.org/10.1007/3-540-56922-7

69. Peng, Y., Grover, V., Devietti, J.: Curd: a dynamic Cuda race detector. In: PLDI 2018, pp. 390–403. Association for Computing Machinery, New York (2018). https://doi.org/10.1145/3192366.3192368

70. Podkopaev, A., Lahav, O., Vafeiadis, V.: Bridging the gap between programming languages and hardware weak memory models. Proc. ACM Program. Lang. **3**(POPL) (2019). https://doi.org/10.1145/3290382

71. Pulte, C., Flur, S., Deacon, W., French, J., Sarkar, S., Sewell, P.: Simplifying ARM concurrency: multicopy-atomic axiomatic and operational models for ARMv8. PACMPL **2**(POPL), 19:1–19:29 (2018). https://doi.org/10.1145/3158107

72. Reinders, J., Ashbaugh, B., Brodman, J., Kinsner, M., Pennycook, J., Tian, X.: Data Parallel C++: Programming Accelerated Systems Using C++ and SYCL, 2 edn. Apress, Berkeley, CA (2023). https://doi.org/10.1007/978-1-4842-9691-2

73. Reuther, A., Michaleas, P., Jones, M., Gadepally, V., Samsi, S., Kepner, J.: Survey and benchmarking of machine learning accelerators. In: 2019 IEEE High Performance Extreme Computing Conference (HPEC), pp. 1–9 (2019). https://doi.org/10.1109/HPEC.2019.8916327

74. Sorensen, T., Donaldson, A.F.: Exposing errors related to weak memory in GPU applications. In: Krintz, C., Berger, E.D. (eds.) Proceedings of the 37th ACM SIGPLAN Conference on Programming Language Design and Implementation, PLDI 2016, Santa Barbara, CA, USA, June 13–17, 2016, pp. 100–113. ACM (2016). https://doi.org/10.1145/2908080.2908114

75. Sorensen, T., Donaldson, A.F., Batty, M., Gopalakrishnan, G., Rakamarić, Z.: Portable inter-workgroup barrier synchronisation for GPUs. In: OOPSLA 2016, Association for Computing Machinery, pp. 39–58 (2016). https://doi.org/10.1145/2983990.2984032

76. Sorensen, T., Evrard, H., Donaldson, A.F.: GPU schedulers: how fair is fair enough? In: Schewe, S., Zhang, L. (eds.) 29th International Conference on Concurrency Theory, CONCUR 2018, September 4–7, 2018, Beijing, China. LIPIcs, vol. 118, pp. 23:1–23:17 (2018). https://doi.org/10.4230/LIPICS.CONCUR.2018.23

77. Sorensen, T., Salvador, L.F., Raval, H., Evrard, H., Wickerson, J., Martonosi, M., Donaldson, A.F.: Specifying and testing GPU workgroup progress models. Proc. ACM Program. Lang. **5**(OOPSLA), 1–30 (2021). https://doi.org/10.1145/3485508

78. Tong, H., Gavrilenko, N., Ponce de Leon, H., Heljanko, K.: Towards unified analysis of GPU consistency. In: Proceedings of the 29th ACM International Conference on Architectural Support for Programming Languages and Operating Systems, vol. 4, pp. 329–344. ASPLOS 2024, Association for Computing Machinery, New York (2025). https://doi.org/10.1145/3622781.3674174

79. Tunç, H.C., Abdulla, P.A., Chakraborty, S., Krishna, S., Mathur, U., Pavlogiannis, A.: Optimal reads-from consistency checking for C11-style memory models. Proc. ACM Program. Lang. **7**(PLDI), 137:761–137:785 (2023). https://doi.org/10.1145/3591251

80. Wu, M., Ouyang, Y., Zhou, H., Zhang, L., Liu, C., Zhang, Y.: Simulee: detecting Cuda synchronization bugs via memory-access modeling. In: ICSE 2020, pp. 937–948 (2020). https://doi.org/10.1145/3377811.3380358

81. Xiao, S., Feng, W.C.: Inter-block GPU communication via fast barrier synchronization. In: 2010 IEEE International Symposium on Parallel & Distributed Processing (IPDPS), pp. 1–12. IEEE (2010)

82. Yalamanchili, P., et al.: ArrayFire - a high performance software library for parallel computing with an easy-to-use API (2015). https://github.com/arrayfire/arrayfire

83. Zhang, N., Kusano, M., Wang, C.: Dynamic partial order reduction for relaxed memory models. In: PLDI '15, Proceedings of the 36th ACM SIGPLAN Conference on Programming Language Design and Implementation, pp. 250–259. Association for Computing Machinery, New York (2015). https://doi.org/10.1145/2737924.2737956

84. Zheng, M., Ravi, V.T., Qin, F., Agrawal, G.: Grace: a low-overhead mechanism for detecting data races in GPU programs. SIGPLAN Not. **46**(8), 135–146 (2011). https://doi.org/10.1145/2038037.1941574

85. Zheng, M., Ravi, V.T., Qin, F., Agrawal, G.: GMRace: detecting data races in GPU programs via a low-overhead scheme. IEEE Trans. Parallel Distrib. Syst. **25**(1), 104–115 (2014). https://doi.org/10.1109/TPDS.2013.44

Counterexample-Guided Commutativity

Marcel Ebbinghaus$^{(\boxtimes)}$ iD, Dominik Klumpp iD, and Andreas Podelski iD

University of Freiburg, Freiburg im Breisgau, Germany
{ebbima,klumpp,podelski}@informatik.uni-freiburg.de

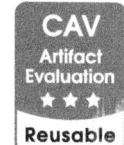

Abstract. We consider the use of commutativity-based reduction for the algorithmic verification of concurrent programs. In existing work, the commutativity relation used for the reduction is mostly fixed statically. In this paper, we propose a *demand-driven* approach to compute the commutativity relation. The approach can be viewed as the direct analogue of the CEGAR approach which uses counterexamples to guide the incremental refinement of the abstraction. Instead of eliminating a counterexample by proving it infeasible and refining the abstraction, we can eliminate a counterexample by proving it *redundant* and expanding the commutativity relation. When we prove a counterexample redundant, we use the proof for a generalization step which allows us to eliminate not just a single counterexample, but a whole infinite set. We present a general scheme where we integrate the new approach with the CEGAR approach. We have implemented an instantiation of the general scheme. An experimental evaluation shows an increase in the number of successfully verified programs by 15% on a challenging benchmark set.

Keywords: verification · concurrent programs · commutativity · reduction · CEGAR

1 Introduction

The benefits of commutativity-based reduction in the verification of concurrent programs are well-established; see e.g. [1,22,27,28]. Commutativity can be employed to simplify programs [12,25], resulting in programs that are easier to verify due to having simpler proofs [13,16,17] and (in algorithmic verification) decreased verification time and space complexity [4,13,30].

The complexity of the control flow of a concurrent program arises from the different possibilities to interleave the executions of the individual threads. Many of the resulting *interleavings* (i.e., sequences of statements from different threads) can be considered *equivalent* because they only differ in the ordering between *commuting* statements. Two statements are said to commute if the order in which they are executed does not matter. The correctness of one interleaving entails the correctness of all interleavings in its equivalence class. Given a program, a

---

The original version of the chapter has been revised. The equations were displayed incorrectly. This has been corrected. A correction to this chapter can be found at https://doi.org/10.1007/978-3-031-98682-6_22

R. Piskac and Z. Rakamarić (Eds.): CAV 2025, LNCS 15933, pp. 347–369, 2025.
https://doi.org/10.1007/978-3-031-98682-6_18

subset of interleavings that covers all equivalence classes is called a *reduction* of the program. Such a reduction can be viewed as another program. It suffices to construct a reduction and prove its correctness in order to prove the correctness of the input program. Since a reduction contains only a subset of interleavings, it can have a simpler proof and may be in the realm of algorithmic verification methods even when the input program is apparently not [13, 15–17].

In model checking of finite-state systems, commutativity-based reductions have been extensively applied under the terminology of *partial-order methods*; see [2]. More recently, they have been used in the fully automated verification of infinite-state systems, particularly concurrent programs over general data structures. Approaches based on CEGAR (Counterexample-Guided Abstraction Refinement) have been successfully combined with commutativity-based reduction [4, 13, 16, 17, 30] to deal with the infinity of the data, i.e., to infer assertions needed in a correctness proof for a reduction of the input program. In existing work, the commutativity relation used in the construction of the reduction is mostly fixed statically, as in [4, 6]. However, it has been recognized that a more dynamic approach can be beneficial where, e.g., the commutativity relation is defined as a function of the candidate proof constructed so far during the CEGAR loop [14], or an *aliasing analysis* derives additional commutativity [30].

In this paper, we propose a *demand-driven* approach to compute the commutativity relation that is needed in the reduction-based verification of the program. The idea is to use counterexamples to guide the incremental construction of the commutativity relation. In each iteration of a CEGAR-style loop, the counterexample under consideration can be used to infer additional commutativity. The new commutativity relation induces a new reduction. The new reduction no longer contains the counterexample. It is now known to be equivalent to more interleavings, one of which remains as a representative in the reduction.

In its use of counterexamples to guide the incremental construction of the commutativity relation, the approach can be viewed as the analogue of the CEGAR approach, which uses counterexamples to guide the incremental construction of the abstraction. Instead of eliminating a counterexample by refining the abstraction, one can eliminate it by expanding the commutativity relation which, in turn, cuts down the reduction further. Just as making the abstraction more precise can eliminate not just one, but a whole set of counterexamples, expanding the commutativity relation can eliminate a whole set of counterexamples. Instead of proving that the counterexamples in the set are infeasible, one proves that the counterexamples in the set are *redundant*, i.e., can be eliminated in favor of another representative through additional commutativity. Redundant counterexamples need no longer to be proven infeasible.

We propose a new scheme called CEGAR+CC, where we apply the new approach of *counterexample-guided commutativity* (CC) on top of the classical approach of counterexample-guided abstraction. That is, in each iteration where a new counterexample is selected, the algorithm decides whether to use the counterexample to make the abstraction more precise, or whether to first try to use the counterexample to make the commutativity relation larger. In our implementation of the scheme, we base the decision of the algorithm on a criterion that indicates when the demand for the new approach counterexample-guided commutativity is the most urgent – namely when the classical approach of counterexample-guided abstraction seems bound to fail.

The contribution of this paper is threefold:

- We introduce the demand-driven approach of counterexample-guided commutativity. CC targets specifically the complex control of a concurrent program. In this sense, CC complements CEGAR, which addresses primarily the complex data. Furthermore, we present a scheme which integrates CC with CEGAR (Sect. 4).
- We present a solution to the very issue that is at the heart of the approach: When we prove a counterexample redundant, we use the proof for a generalization step which allows to eliminate not just a single counterexample, but a whole infinite set (Sect. 5).
- We instantiate the general scheme, where we specifically target those scenarios where pure CEGAR fails to terminate. An experimental evaluation indicates the practical potential of the approach, which increases the number of successfully verified programs by 15% on a challenging benchmark set (Sect. 6).

2   Motivating Example

We demonstrate our approach on the example of the concurrent program shown in Fig. 1, a variation of an example program for the WEAVER verifier [17,29]. In this program, a **Producer** thread and a **Consumer** thread communicate via a shared queue data structure. The queue is modeled by an array `queue` containing the data, an index `front` pointing to the first item in the queue, and a variable `size` for the unbounded number of elements in the queue (initially 0). The **Producer** thread repeatedly calls `add(5)` to insert the number 5 into the queue, while the **Consumer** repeatedly takes an element out of the queue with the statement `x:=take()` and checks that, when it terminates, the assertion x==5 holds (as it does initially). The procedures add and take execute atomically. The code for the procedures uses `assume` statements, which have no effect if the given expression evaluates to **true** and *block* otherwise (see e.g. [26]). In particular, the statement `x:=take()` blocks if the queue is currently empty, due to the line `assume size > 0`. By contrast, the `assert` statement in the **Consumer** thread also has no effect if the given expression evaluates to **true**, but *fails* when x does not have the value 5. We represent such an assertion failure with `x!=5`.

Before proving the correctness of this program, let us determine which pairs of statements from **Producer** and **Consumer** commute. For instance, the statements `add(5)` and `x!=5` commute, since `add(5)` only affects the contents of the queue, and `x!=5` is only concerned with the local variable x in the **Consumer** thread. Hence, the interleavings `add(5)` `x:=take()` `add(5)` `x!=5` and `add(5)` `x:=take()` `x!=5` `add(5)` are *equivalent*: they only differ in the order of commuting statements. It suffices to prove correctness for one of these interleavings; all equivalent interleavings are then also guaranteed to be correct.

Queue data structure

Precondition
$size = 0 \wedge x = 5$

```
1  var queue : [int] int;
2  var front : int;
3  var size  : int;
4
5  atomic add(item : int) {
6      assume queue[front+size] == item;
7      size := size + 1;
8  }
9
10 atomic take() : int {
11     assume size > 0;
12     front := front + 1;
13     size := size - 1;
14     return queue[front-1];
15 }
```

Producer (thread 1)

```
1  while (*) {
2      add(5);
3  }
```

Consumer (thread 2)

```
1  var x : int;
2  while (*) {
3      x := take();
4  }
5  assert x == 5;
```

Fig. 1. Example program.

Unfortunately, that is the extent of commutativity in our example. In particular, the statements `add(5)` and `x:=take()` do not commute: the interleaving `x:=take() add(5)` cannot be executed (it is *infeasible*) due to the fact that `x:=take()` blocks, whereas `add(5) x:=take()` executes without blocking. Consequently, the only benefit of commutativity in our example is that it allows us to choose only representatives where the last occurrence of `x:=take()` (if any) is directly followed by the statement `x!=5`, i.e., interleavings of the form

$$\left(\text{add(5)} + \text{x:=take()} \right)^* \text{x:=take() } \text{x!=5 } \text{add(5)}^* + \text{add(5)}^* \text{x!=5} \quad (R1)$$

If we only consider context-insensitive commutativity, it remains up to a verification algorithm to prove correctness of all such representatives. We show why this is likely to fail, and how counterexample-guided commutativity provides relief.

Abstractly, there are two cases when considering the interleavings in our example: either *(a)* the **Consumer** at some point tries to take an element out of an empty queue (which blocks), or *(b)* the **Consumer** removes elements successfully but, after its loop terminates, the variable x stores the value 5 and the negated assert `x!=5` leads to a contradiction. Suppose a CEGAR-based verification algorithm starts by considering the interleaving

$$\tau_1 = \text{add(5) } \text{x:=take() } \text{x:=take() } \text{x!=5} \,.$$

It determines that this *counterexample* is indeed *infeasible*; it cannot be executed due to reason *(a)*. To prove this, the algorithm computes the sequences of assertions $size \le 0$, $size \le 1$, $size \le 0$, *false*, *false* which hold along the interleaving τ_1 and witness its infeasibility. The CEGAR loop then excludes all interleavings whose infeasibility can be established with these predicates. However, this does not prevent the next iteration of the verification from discovering the interleaving

$$\tau_2 = \boxed{\texttt{add(5)}} \ \boxed{\texttt{add(5)}} \ \boxed{\texttt{x:=take()}} \ \boxed{\texttt{x:=take()}} \ \boxed{\texttt{x:=take()}} \ \boxed{\texttt{x!=5}}$$

and computing the corresponding sequence of assertions $size \leq 0$, $size \leq 1$, $size \leq 2$, $size \leq 1$, $size \leq 0$, *false*, *false*. Note the additional assertion $size \leq 2$ needed to establish the infeasibility. One can imagine how a classical CEGAR loop may proceed: for an ever increasing number of calls to `add(5)`, additional assertions $size \leq 3$, $size \leq 4$, $size \leq 5$, ... are introduced. On an intuitive level, no true progress is being made: the verification examines the same path through the program again and again, each time unrolling the loops further. This is a typical scenario in which CEGAR fails to terminate. And even for a human, it may be challenging to find a proof that covers all these interleavings.

At this point, our proposed CEGAR+CC approach comes to the rescue, an integration of *counterexample-guided commutativity* (CC) and CEGAR. In particular, the instantiation of CEGAR+CC presented in Sect. 6 detects that the verification is not making true progress and failing to find a finite number of assertions that prove infeasibility for all the interleavings with an increasing number of loop unrollings. The key insight behind CEGAR+CC is that such an explicit proof for every counterexample τ encountered by the CEGAR loop is actually not always necessary. Instead, CEGAR+CC infers *additional commutativity* in a way such that the equivalence class of τ is *merged* with the equivalence class of another representative τ' that is preferred (based on criteria we formalize later) over τ. If this is possible, we say that τ is *redundant*. In the next iteration, the set of representatives is refined with the additional inferred commutativity. Consequently, τ no longer appears as a counterexample. The only interleaving in the (newly expanded) equivalence class of τ that may remain is the preferred representative τ'. The presence of τ' depends on whether τ' was previously proven infeasible (in which case it was soundly eliminated) or not. In the latter case, a future iteration may prove that τ' is feasible resp. infeasible, or even detect that τ' itself is also redundant and eliminate it in favor of yet another representative τ'' that is preferred over both τ and τ'.

In our example, the algorithm detects that the second call to `add(5)` and the first call to `x:=take()` in the interleaving τ_2 can indeed be commuted. The only possible obstacle to commutativity for these statements is the case where `x:=take()` blocks on an empty queue. But this case is impossible in τ_2, as the first call to `add(5)` ensures the queue is non-empty. We generalize such an observation of *contextual* commutativity after a specific prefix (here consisting only of the first call to `add(5)`) to a whole set of prefixes. This generalization allows us to show redundancy not only for the current counterexample, but for (ideally) infinitely many other interleavings. Section 5 explains in detail how this generalization works. In our example, the generalization allows us to conclude that after any prefix of the form $\left(\boxed{\texttt{add(5)}} \ \boxed{\texttt{x:=take()}} \right)^{*} \boxed{\texttt{add(5)}}$, the statements `add(5)` and `x:=take()` commute. This drastically shrinks the set of representatives for which we have to explicitly prove infeasibility. In particular, it suffices to consider representatives of the form

$$\left(\boxed{\texttt{add(5)}} \ \boxed{\texttt{x:=take()}} \right)^* \boxed{\texttt{x:=take()}}^+ \boxed{\texttt{x!=5}} \ \boxed{\texttt{add(5)}}^* , \qquad \text{(R2a)}$$

which block on an empty queue and can be proven using only the predicates $size \leq 0$, $size \leq 1$ and *false*, as well as representatives of the form

$$\left(\boxed{\texttt{add(5)}} \ \boxed{\texttt{x:=take()}} \right)^* \boxed{\texttt{x!=5}} \ \boxed{\texttt{add(5)}}^* , \qquad \text{(R2b)}$$

for which the predicates $x = 5 \wedge size \leq 0$, $queue[front] = 5 \wedge size \leq 1$ and *false* are sufficient. These predicates are simple enough that the CEGAR loop discovers them in a few more iterations. The verification thus terminates with the sound verdict that the example program is correct.

3   Preliminaries

We follow the language-theoretic approach in order to introduce concurrent programs. That is, we identify a program $\mathcal{P}$ with a set of traces. A trace τ is a sequence of statements; i.e., $\tau \in \Sigma^*$ where Σ is the finite set of all (atomically executed) statements. As seen in Sect. 2, statements can e.g. be assignments such as $\boxed{\texttt{x:=take()}}$ or assume statements such as $\boxed{\texttt{x!=5}}$.

Intuitively, every trace of $\mathcal{P}$ corresponds to the sequence of edge labels of a path from the initial node to an error location in the control flow graph of $\mathcal{P}$. If such a path does not correspond to an actual execution (because it would be blocked by an assume statement), then the trace is *infeasible*. We define the correctness of $\mathcal{P}$ formally as the infeasibility of all traces in $\mathcal{P}$. Note that we model an **assert** statement through an edge to an error location. The edge is then labeled by an assume statement which uses the negation of the expression in the **assert** statement. Thus, each trace of $\mathcal{P}$ ends with such an assume statement.

If $\mathcal{P}$ is the concurrent program to be verified, then $\mathcal{P}$ consists of all interleavings of traces of the individual threads. We require that this amounts to a regular language over the (finite) alphabet of statements (we consider programs with a finite number of threads). Our model is general enough to accommodate concurrent programs that can dynamically create and join threads [21].

If we assign Hoare triples to statements and, by extension, to sequences of statements, then a trace τ is infeasible if and only if the Hoare triple $\{\top\} \tau \{\bot\}$ is valid. A proof Π is a finite set of Hoare triples for statements. We say that a proof Π is a proof for the trace τ if the Hoare triple $\{\top\} \tau \{\bot\}$ can be derived from Hoare triples in Π by sequential composition. We say that a proof Π is a proof for the program $\mathcal{P}$ if it is a proof for every trace of $\mathcal{P}$, i.e., if $\mathcal{P} \subseteq \Pi$, where we identify Π with the set of traces for which it is a proof. The inclusion can be checked via the inclusion of finite automata which represent $\mathcal{P}$ and Π.

We obtain a finite automaton for $\mathcal{P}$ by taking its control flow graph, where each error location corresponds to an accepting state. We obtain a finite automaton for Π by taking its assertions as states and by adding a transition for each

Hoare triple; we take for the initial state the assertion $\top$ and for the final state the assertion $\bot$.

A *contextual commutativity relation* I [17] is a ternary relation

$$I \subseteq \Sigma^* \times \Sigma \times \Sigma.$$

where a triple $(\tau, a, b) \in I$ signifies that a and b commute *in the context* of τ. We require that $(\tau, b, a) \in I$ whenever $(\tau, a, b) \in I$. Intuitively, a contextual commutativity relation I captures that in some sense (which sense depends precisely on I) the order in which the two statements a and b are executed does not matter, if they are executed directly after the execution of the statements in τ.

Given the semantics of statements and, in extension, of traces (we write $[\![\tau]\!]$ for the semantics of a trace τ, which we can define as a binary relation between program states), the *semantic* contextual commutativity relation $\mathcal{I}$ is defined by

$$\mathcal{I} = \{ (\tau, a, b) \in \Sigma^* \times \Sigma \times \Sigma \mid [\![\tau\, a\, b]\!] = [\![\tau\, b\, a]\!] \}.$$

Unless otherwise stated, we always mean contextual commutativity relations, and thus often omit the adjective *contextual*.

Reduction. Each (contextual) commutativity relation I induces an equivalence relation $\sim_I$ between traces. Intuitively, two traces are equivalent if one can be obtained from the other by successively swapping statements according to the commutativity relation I. Formally, the relation $\sim_I$ is the smallest equivalence relation that contains all pairs of words $(\rho a b \sigma, \rho b a \sigma)$ for $(\rho, a, b) \in I$ and $\rho, \sigma \in \Sigma^*$. The program $\mathcal{P}$ is *closed* under the trace equivalence $\sim_I$ if $\mathcal{P}$ contains the whole equivalence class of each trace $\tau \in \mathcal{P}$; i.e., if $\tau \in \mathcal{P}$ and $\tau \sim_I \tau'$ then $\tau' \in \mathcal{P}$.

Given a commutativity relation I, a *reduction* of a program $\mathcal{P}$ is another program P with $P \subseteq \mathcal{P}$ that contains an equivalent trace τ' for each trace τ in $\mathcal{P}$, i.e.,

$$P \subseteq \mathcal{P} \ \wedge \ \forall \tau \in \mathcal{P} . \exists \tau' \in P . \tau \sim_I \tau'.$$

If the commutativity relation I is sound, i.e., if $I \subseteq \mathcal{I}$ holds, then the correctness of P entails the correctness of $\mathcal{P}$.

We fix a total ordering $\preceq$ over the set of statements Σ and extend it to a lexicographic order $\preceq$ over the set of traces Σ^*, the so-called *preference order* [13]. We say that τ is preferred over τ' if $\tau \preceq \tau'$. Given the commutativity relation I, we define the reduction $reduction_I(\mathcal{P})$ as the (unique) reduction of $\mathcal{P}$ that contains only *minimal* elements with respect to the lexicographic order, i.e.,

$$reduction_I(\mathcal{P}) = \{ \tau' \in \mathcal{P} \mid \forall \tau \in \mathcal{P} . \tau \sim_I \tau' \Rightarrow \tau' \preceq \tau \}$$

Regular commutativity relations I [17] can be defined by requiring that for each pair $(a, b) \in \Sigma^2$, the traces τ with $(\tau, a, b) \in I$ form a regular language. For regular commutativity relations, a reduction that closely over-approximates $reduction_I(\mathcal{P})$ can be constructed effectively and represented by a finite automaton, for every closed program $\mathcal{P}$ represented by a finite automaton; see, e.g., [13]. The fact that we construct an over-approximation is not an issue for soundness; and we come back to this point in Sect. 4.1.

4   CEGAR+CC

This section introduces *counterexample-guided commutativity* (CC). Section 4.1 explains the essential ideas behind CC. Section 4.2 presents CEGAR+CC, a scheme that integrates CC with a CEGAR verification algorithm. A core module of CEGAR+CC is an algorithmic realization of CC, which we detail in Sect. 5.

4.1   Counterexample-Guided Commutativity

Let us fix a concurrent program $\mathcal{P}$, and let τ be a trace of $\mathcal{P}$. As described in Sect. 3, τ corresponds to a path from the initial location to an error location; we thus call τ a *counterexample*. To verify the program $\mathcal{P}$, a verification algorithm typically proves that every such counterexample τ is infeasible. However, CC takes a different approach: building on commutativity-based reduction, we can alternatively determine that the trace τ is *redundant* in the sense that it can soundly be considered equivalent to another trace τ'. If that is the case, it is sound to eliminate τ from the set of counterexamples, as long as τ' remains.

Definition 1. *A trace τ is* redundant *if there exists a trace τ' such that τ' is strictly smaller than τ wrt. the preference order, and τ' is equivalent to τ up to the semantic commutativity relation $\mathcal{I}$, i.e.,*

$$\exists \tau' . \ \tau' \prec \tau \ \wedge \ \tau' \sim_{\mathcal{I}} \tau$$

Requiring the trace τ' to be strictly preferred over τ prevents us from declaring in turn that τ' is redundant due to the existence of τ, as the preference order (like any total order) is acyclic. Observe that redundancy and infeasibility are orthogonal. A redundant trace may be feasible or infeasible, and an infeasible trace may or may not be redundant. The equivalence up to $\mathcal{I}$ however guarantees that τ is feasible if and only if τ' is feasible.

The definition of redundancy is *not* parametric in a commutativity relation, it always refers to the (fixed) semantic commutativity relation $\mathcal{I}$. However, as this relation is not finitely representable, it cannot be used directly in algorithmic verification. Instead, a verification algorithm can work with a different, finitely-representable commutativity relation that soundly under-approximates $\mathcal{I}$ and suffices to establish the redundancy of the trace τ.

Definition 2. *A commutativity relation I_τ* witnesses the redundancy *of a trace τ if I_τ is regular, $I_\tau \subseteq \mathcal{I}$ holds, and τ is equivalent up to I_τ to a trace τ' that is strictly smaller than τ wrt. the preference order, i.e.,*

$$I_\tau \text{ is regular } \wedge \ I_\tau \subseteq \mathcal{I} \ \wedge \ (\exists \tau' . \ \tau' \prec \tau \wedge \tau' \sim_{I_\tau} \tau)$$

Proposition 3. *A trace τ is redundant if and only if there exists a commutativity relation I_τ witnessing the redundancy of τ.*

Proof. Follows directly from the definitions, excepting regularity. For regularity, observe that even a finite subset of $\mathcal{I}$ suffices, as the length of contexts relevant for the equivalence between τ and τ' is bounded by the length of τ.

By the above proposition, checking redundancy of a trace τ boils down to finding a commutativity relation witnessing that redundancy. We discuss a procedure for this task in detail below (Sect. 5). Notably, this procedure generalizes from the redundancy of τ and returns a commutativity relation I_τ which can witnesses the redundancy of a whole infinite set of traces. This capability to go beyond proving redundancy of traces one-by-one is crucial to CC.

Once such a witness I_τ has been found, we can now consider the reduction $reduction_{I_\tau}(\mathcal{P})$. In this reduction, τ is no longer present, as only the most preferred trace in each equivalence class (up to I_τ) is retained. It therefore suffices to prove correctness of this reduction to establish the correctness of $\mathcal{P}$ (by soundness of commutativity-based reduction), without *explicitly* proving the infeasibility of τ; realizing the core idea of CC.

As noted in Sect. 3, we do not generally construct precisely the reduction $reduction_{I_\tau}(\mathcal{P})$, but an over-approximation. This over-approximation is based on the *sleep set algorithm* [18], particularly the form presented in [13]. As such, we must take extra care to ensure that a redundant trace τ is indeed also eliminated from this over-approximation of $reduction_{I_\tau}(\mathcal{P})$. Our procedure for finding a redundancy witness I_τ discussed in Sect. 5 ensures that this is the case.

CC as described up to this point is of interest on its own. One could imagine a preprocessing step before verification that collects a number of sample traces τ from a program $\mathcal{P}$, determines if they are redundant and constructs commutativity relations witnessing this redundancy. The preprocessing could then reduce $\mathcal{P}$ using these commutativity relations and pass the resulting program to a verification engine. The obvious question in this scenario would however be how one selects suitable sample traces, i.e., includes traces τ such that the inferred commutativity relation I_τ is useful to the verification, while avoiding traces τ where inferring I_τ is superfluous and does not aid the verification. The next section addresses these questions by integrating CC with the verification.

4.2 Integrating CEGAR and CC

We propose CEGAR+CC, a scheme that integrates CC with a *counterexample-guided abstraction refinement* (CEGAR) verification algorithm. For the presentation in this section, we choose the *trace abstraction refinement* [19, 20] algorithm. This choice allows us to separate the two approaches by evaluating their effect on either side of an inclusion.

Figure 2 illustrates the CEGAR+CC scheme. For a program $\mathcal{P}$, CEGAR+CC initializes a set of counterexamples P to the set of traces $\mathcal{P}$, and a proof Π as well as a commutativity relation I to the empty set (resp. the empty relation). To establish correctness of $\mathcal{P}$, the inclusion $P \subseteq \Pi$ must hold. As this is typically not the case initially, CEGAR+CC enters a loop. In each iteration, a counterexample $\tau \in P \setminus \Pi$ is selected. At this point, the verification has a choice: It can either

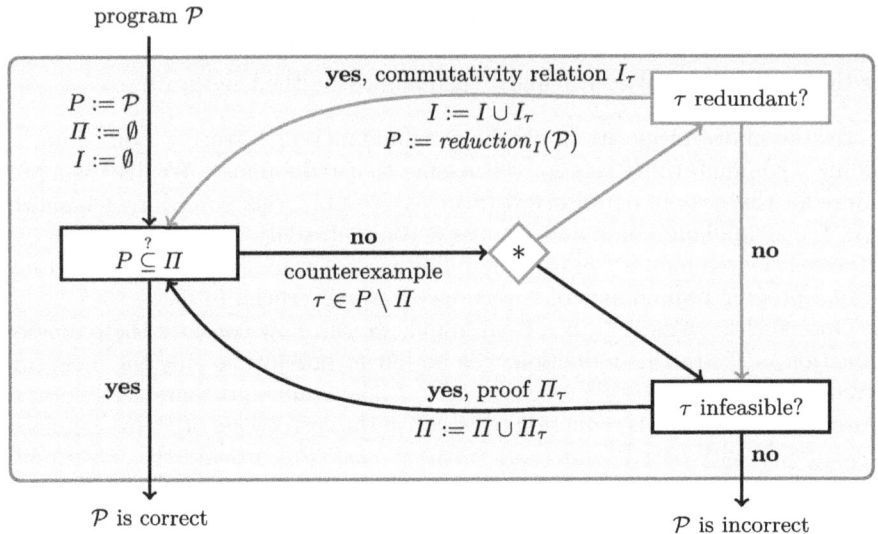

Fig. 2. CEGAR+CC verification scheme. Components highlighted in orange belong to CC. Section 5 discusses details of the redundancy check and inference of the commutativity relation I_τ. As described in Sect. 3, $reduction_I(\mathcal{P})$ denotes the reduction of $\mathcal{P}$ induced by the commutativity relation I.

make an *abstraction refinement* step (as in CEGAR), which will enlarge the proof Π, or it can apply CC in order to shrink the set of counterexamples P.

If the verification chooses to apply CC, it checks if the counterexample τ is redundant and, if so, infers a commutativity relation I_τ witnessing the redundancy. The details of this procedure are explained in Sect. 5, but we emphasize here again that, crucially, the inferred relation I_τ can witness the redundancy for an infinite set of traces, not only for τ itself. CEGAR+CC extends its current commutativity relation I with the inferred I_τ, and then updates P to the reduction of $\mathcal{P}$ induced by the extended commutativity relation. This eliminates τ and other traces whose redundancy is witnessed by I_τ. CEGAR+CC then returns to the beginning of the loop, and again checks if $P \subseteq \Pi$ holds.

In case the verification chooses an abstraction refinement step, or the trace τ is not redundant, CEGAR+CC checks that τ is infeasible, generalizes to a proof Π_τ that can cover a whole infinite set of traces (using standard techniques employed in CEGAR [7]), and extends the set of proven traces Π with Π_τ, before returning to the beginning of the loop. If τ is feasible, the verification terminates immediately, and the program is incorrect.

Theorem 4 (Soundness). *If CEGAR+CC terminates for any resolution of the nondeterminism, the verification verdict (correct resp. incorrect) is sound.*

Proof. Follows from $I \subseteq \mathcal{I}$ and soundness of commutativity-based reduction.

The complementary effect of CC and abstraction refinement can be observed when considering the inclusion $P \subseteq \Pi$. Abstraction refinement *enlargens the right-hand side* Π of the inclusion, whereas CC *shrinks the left-hand side* P of the inclusion. Proofs Π_τ computed by abstraction refinement encode information on the possible *data flow* in the counterexample τ, whereas the additional derived commutativity relation I_τ inferred by CC constrains the possible *(concurrent) control flow* in the reduction. In both cases, progress is made towards finding Π, I and P such that the inclusion holds and the verification terminates.

Theorem 5 (Progress). *Let τ be the counterexample considered in an iteration of CEGAR+CC. Then, in the next and all subsequent iterations, $\tau \notin P \setminus \Pi$ holds.*

Proof. If τ is proven infeasible, $\tau \in \Pi$. If τ is proven redundant, we have $\tau \notin P$. As mentioned in Sect. 4.1, our procedure for finding I_τ ensures that τ is also successfully eliminated from the over-approximation of $reduction_I(\mathcal{P})$ that is constructed in practice.

5   Proving Redundancy and Inferring Commutativity

This section describes a procedure that effectively realizes counterexample-guided commutativity (CC), cf. Sect. 4.1, in the context of the CEGAR+CC verification scheme (Sect. 4.2). That is, given a counterexample trace τ and a current commutativity relation I, we describe an algorithm that, if τ is indeed redundant, attempts to find a commutativity relation I_τ that witnesses the redundancy of the trace τ or even a whole infinite set of traces containing τ.

5.1   Redundancy Checking in Three Easy Steps

Recall that a trace τ is redundant if it is equivalent under the semantic commutativity relation $\mathcal{I}$ to another trace τ' that is strictly smaller than τ wrt. the preference order $\preceq$. Our algorithm proceeds in three steps:

- First, it identifies a commutativity relation under which τ is equivalent to some strictly smaller trace τ'.
- Second, the algorithm proves that the identified commutativity relation is a subset of the semantic commutativity relation $\mathcal{I}$.
- Third, the algorithm generalizes the proof produced by the second step in order to arrive at the final commutativity relation I_τ.

If the commutativity relation chosen in the first step is not a subset of $\mathcal{I}$, the algorithm returns to the first step and chooses another commutativity relation. The overall number of iterations is bounded by the length of the trace τ.

Step I: Points of Potential Redundancy. As we implement CC in the context of CEGAR+CC, our algorithm can benefit from the already-inferred commutativity relation I maintained by CEGAR+CC. It is an invariant of the CEGAR+CC scheme that this commutativity relation I is always regular and included in the semantic commutativity relation $\mathcal{I}$, and that the program $\mathcal{P}$ is closed under I.

We make use of the given relation I by limiting our search (in the first step) to commutativity relations that add a single triple to I. That is, we are interested in triples (ρ, a, b) such that under the commutativity relation $I \cup \{(\rho, a, b)\}$, the counterexample τ is equivalent to a strictly smaller trace. Such triples are identified by what we call *points of potential redundancy* in the counterexample trace τ. Before we give the definition, we revisit the example we discussed in Sect. 2.

Example 6 (continued from Sect. 2). We come back to the trace τ_2 that was discovered in the second iteration of the CEGAR-loop.

$$\tau_2 = \boxed{\texttt{add(5)}} \ \boxed{\texttt{add(5)}} \ \boxed{\texttt{x:=take()}} \ \boxed{\texttt{x:=take()}} \ \boxed{\texttt{x:=take()}} \ \boxed{\texttt{x!=5}}$$

As explained in Sect. 2, instead of checking the infeasibility of τ_2, we check whether τ_2 is redundant. To that end, we observe that τ_2 is equivalent to τ_2', where

$$\tau_2' = \boxed{\texttt{add(5)}} \ \boxed{\texttt{x:=take()}} \ \boxed{\texttt{add(5)}} \ \boxed{\texttt{x:=take()}} \ \boxed{\texttt{x:=take()}} \ \boxed{\texttt{x!=5}} \ ,$$

if the second and third statements in τ_2 commute, which is the case under the commutativity relation $I \cup \{(\boxed{\texttt{add(5)}}, \boxed{\texttt{add(5)}}, \boxed{\texttt{x:=take()}})\}$. In the preference order used in this example, τ_2' is smaller than τ_2. Therefore, the triple $(\boxed{\texttt{add(5)}}, \boxed{\texttt{add(5)}}, \boxed{\texttt{x:=take()}})$ is a point of potential redundancy.

Definition 7. *Let $\tau = x_1 \ldots x_n$. A point of potential redundancy of τ is a triple (ρ, a, b) such that the following conditions hold:*

(i) there exists $k \in \{1, \ldots, n-1\}$ such that $\rho = x_1 \ldots x_{k-1}$, $a = x_k$, and $b = x_{k+1}$;
(ii) there exists $j \in \{1, \ldots, k\}$ such that $b \prec x_j$ and $(x_1 \ldots x_{i-1}, b, x_i) \in I$ for all $i \in \{j, \ldots, k-1\}$; and
(iii) the program $\mathcal{P}$ is closed under the trace equivalence induced by the commutativity relation $\{(\rho, a, b)\}$.

The first condition ensures that $\rho a b$ is a prefix of τ. The second condition identifies an earlier position j in the trace such that commuting the statement $b = x_{k+1}$ just before the statement x_j would result in the smaller trace $\tau' = x_1 \ldots x_{j-1} x_{k+1} x_j \ldots x_k x_{k+2} \ldots x_n$. The condition further requires that I already allows for the necessary commutations, apart from the commutation of $a \ (= x_k)$ and $b \ (= x_{k+1})$. The third condition ensures that the smaller trace τ' is allowed by the control flow of $\mathcal{P}$. If $\mathcal{P}$ is the product of a fixed number of threads (without thread creation or thread joining), this condition is always satisfied when the statements a and b belong to different threads.

Lemma 8. *Let (ρ, a, b) be a point of potential redundancy of τ. If $(\rho, a, b) \in \mathcal{I}$ holds, the commutativity relation $I \cup \{(\rho, a, b)\}$ witnesses the redundancy of τ.*

Step II: Proving Soundness. Given a point of potential redundancy (ρ, a, b), as stated in Lemma 8, it remains to determine whether the commutativity triple (ρ, a, b) is sound, i.e., whether $(\rho, a, b) \in \mathcal{I}$. For this purpose, our algorithm synthesizes a *commutativity condition* φ for (a, b).

Definition 9. *A commutativity condition for a pair of statements (a, b) is an assertion φ such that $(s, s') \in [\![ab]\!]$ iff $(s, s') \in [\![ba]\!]$ for all program states s, s' with $s \models \varphi$. We use $I(\varphi)$ to denote the set of all pairs (a, b) for which φ is a commutativity condition.*

A commutativity condition φ for statements a and b identifies a set of program states such that executing the statement sequence $a\,b$ resp. the statement sequence $b\,a$ in any state satisfying φ exhibits the same behaviour. We discuss strategies for synthesizing commutativity conditions further below in Sect. 5.2.

Lemma 10. *Let ρ be a trace, a, b statements, and φ a commutativity condition for (a, b). If the Hoare triple $\{\top\}\,\rho\,\{\varphi\}$ holds, it follows that $(\rho, a, b) \in \mathcal{I}$.*

Our algorithm uses an SMT solver to check whether the Hoare triple $\{\top\}\,\rho\,\{\varphi\}$ holds. If the SMT solver proves that the triple does hold, it follows that $(\rho, a, b) \in \mathcal{I}$ which in return proves that $I \cup \{(\rho, a, b)\}$ serves as a witness for the redundancy of τ.

Example 11 (continued from Example 6). As explained, the triple (`add(5)` , `add(5)` , `x:=take()`) is a point of potential redundancy of τ_2. The statements `add(5)` and `x:=take()` commute whenever the queue is not empty. This can be expressed by the commutativity condition $size > 0$. Since the Hoare triple $\{\top\}$ `add(5)` $\{size > 0\}$ holds, the augmented commutativity relation $I \cup \{(\,$ `add(5)` , `add(5)` , `x:=take()` $)\}$ is sound and witnesses the redundancy of τ_2.

Step III: Generalizing the Commutativity Relation. In this last step, we generalize from the particular point of redundancy (ρ, a, b) in order to construct a commutativity relation that can witness redundancy for an infinite set of traces. We employ well-known techniques from the repertoire of CEGAR algorithms [7] (e.g. based on *Craig interpolation* and *predicate transformers*) to generalize from the validity of the Hoare triple $\{\top\}\,\rho\,\{\varphi\}$ to a proof Π^{φ} that proves the postcondition φ for an infinite set of traces. This proof induces a new commutativity relation.

Example 12 (continued from Example 11). Taking the Hoare triple $\{\top\}$ `add(5)` $\{size > 0\}$ together with the trivially valid Hoare triple $\{size > 0\}$ `x:=take()` $\{\top\}$, we can show that the commutativity condition $size > 0$ holds after any prefix of the form (`add(5)` `x:=take()`)* `add(5)` . Hence, the commutativity relation

$$I \cup \left\{ \left(\left(\, \texttt{add(5)} \ \texttt{x:=take()} \,\right)^{n} \texttt{add(5)} ,\ \texttt{add(5)} ,\ \texttt{x:=take()} \right) \mid n \in \mathbb{N}_0 \right\}$$

is sound and witnesses the redundancy for an infinite set of traces.

Definition 13. *The* commutativity relation $I(\Pi)$ *induced by a proof* Π *is defined as the relation*

$$I(\Pi) := \big\{ (\rho, a, b) \in \Sigma^* \times \Sigma \times \Sigma \mid (a, b) \in I(\psi) \text{ with } \{\top\}\, \rho\, \{\psi\} \in \Pi \big\},$$

where $\{\top\}\, \rho\, \{\psi\} \in \Pi$ *means that the Hoare triple* $\{\top\}\, \rho\, \{\psi\}$ *can be derived from Hoare triples in* Π *by sequential composition.*

Lemma 14. *For any proof* Π, *it holds that* $I(\Pi) \subseteq \mathcal{I}$.

The commutativity relation $I \cup I(\Pi^\varphi)$ then serves as the witness of redundancy not only for τ, but for all traces τ' that have a prefix $\rho' ab$ with $\{\top\}\, \rho'\, \{\varphi\} \in \Pi^\varphi$.

Proposition 15. *Let* I *be the current commutativity relation of CEGAR+CC, and* τ *a trace. The commutativity relation* $I_\tau := I \cup I(\Pi^\varphi)$, *for a proof* Π^φ *computed as described in this section, witnesses the redundancy of the trace* τ.

Proof. Follows from Lemmas 8, 10 and 14, excepting regularity, which can be shown using the automaton representing Π^φ (see Sect. 3).

By the restriction to witnesses of a certain form, the procedure described in this section may in some cases fail to identify a witness for a redundant trace τ. In this case, the CEGAR+CC algorithm proceeds as if τ was not redundant; this does not impact the soundness of the approach nor its progress.

5.2   Synthesizing Commutativity Conditions

We discuss two strategies to synthesize commutativity conditions for a given pair of statements (a, b). For succinctness, we identify the sequence of statements ab resp. ba with a first-order *transition formula* $ab(\boldsymbol{x}, \boldsymbol{x}')$ resp. $ba(\boldsymbol{x}, \boldsymbol{x}')$ over vectors of primed and unprimed program variables. This transition formula encodes the semantic relation $[\![ab]\!]$ resp. $[\![ba]\!]$. We compute a commutativity condition $\varphi(\boldsymbol{x})$ that ranges only over unprimed program variables.

Necessary and Sufficient Conditions. The most general commutativity condition $\varphi(\boldsymbol{x})$ for a given pair of statements a and b can be expressed directly in terms of their transition formulae:

$$\varphi(\boldsymbol{x}) \quad :\equiv \quad \forall \boldsymbol{x}' \,.\, ab(\boldsymbol{x}, \boldsymbol{x}') \leftrightarrow ba(\boldsymbol{x}, \boldsymbol{x}')$$

Note that in the procedure using these commutativity conditions (Sect. 5.1), the universally quantified variables $\boldsymbol{x}'$ can be replaced by Skolem constants in the SMT encoding for Hoare triple checks with postcondition $\varphi(\boldsymbol{x})$.

Simple Sufficient Conditions with Abduction. Sufficient (though possibly not necessary) commutativity conditions, which may be less complex, can be computed by phrasing the problem as an *abduction* problem [8]:

> **Given:** Formulae α and β such that $\alpha \to \beta$ is not valid.
> **Output:** A formula φ such that $(\alpha \wedge \varphi) \to \beta$ is valid, and $\alpha \wedge \varphi$ is satisfiable.

The second condition on the output rules out trivial solutions such as $\varphi \equiv \bot$. In general, the goal is to get a *simple* formula φ that is as weak as possible.

Dillig et al. [8] describe an SMT-based algorithm to solve the abduction problem. The algorithm computes a maximum set of variables V such that $\alpha \wedge (\forall V . \alpha \to \beta)$ is satisfiable [10]. The solution φ to the abduction problem is derived by applying quantifier elimination to the formula $\forall V . \alpha \to \beta$, and simplifying away any parts of the formula that are already implied by α [9].

$$\varphi := \text{simplifyWithContext}\left(\text{eliminateQuantifiers}(\forall V . \alpha \to \beta), \alpha\right)$$

Let a *semi-commutativity condition* for statements a and b be a formula $\varphi(\boldsymbol{x})$ that makes the implication $ab(\boldsymbol{x}, \boldsymbol{x}') \wedge \varphi(\boldsymbol{x}) \to ba(\boldsymbol{x}, \boldsymbol{x}')$ valid. This resembles an instance of the abduction problem with $\alpha \equiv ab(\boldsymbol{x}, \boldsymbol{x}')$ and $\beta \equiv ba(\boldsymbol{x}, \boldsymbol{x}')$, except for the limitation that the primed variables $\boldsymbol{x}'$ must not occur in $\varphi(\boldsymbol{x})$. To account for this restriction, we modify the algorithm by Dillig et al. [8] by forcing that all primed variables must be in V.

For *commutativity conditions*, we adapt the abduction algorithm further to find an assumption φ that makes an *equivalence* $\alpha \leftrightarrow \beta$ valid. Specifically, we must find $\varphi(\boldsymbol{x})$ such that $\varphi(\boldsymbol{x}) \models ab(\boldsymbol{x}, \boldsymbol{x}') \leftrightarrow ba(\boldsymbol{x}, \boldsymbol{x}')$ holds. In this case, we compute a maximum set V such that $(\alpha \vee \beta) \wedge \forall V . \alpha \leftrightarrow \beta$ is satisfiable, and set

$$\varphi := \text{simplifyWithContext}\left(\text{eliminateQuantifiers}(\forall V . \alpha \leftrightarrow \beta), \alpha \vee \beta\right)$$

6 Instantiating CEGAR+CC

The CEGAR+CC scheme (Sect. 4) has at its core a nondeterministic choice between CEGAR (checking infeasibility of a counterexample and refining the abstraction) and CC (checking redundancy and inferring additional commutativity). Section 6.1 presents an instantiation of the scheme based on the idea that the demand for additional commutativity is greatest whenever CEGAR makes no *true* progress in the verification and seems likely to fail. Section 6.2 empirically evaluates the implementation of the resulting verification algorithm.

6.1 Resolving the Nondeterminism of CEGAR+CC

When a CEGAR-based algorithm fails to verify a program and instead never terminates, a typical reason is that the algorithm is not able to sufficiently generalize from a counterexample. The generalization that we need goes from a counterexample with some number of iterations through a loop in the program $\mathcal{P}$

to the set of all counterexamples with an arbitrary number of iterations through the loop. Such a generalization requires finding an inductive loop invariant. In particular for concurrent programs, the interleaving of multiple loops in different threads leads to an intricate structure that contains nested and interleaved loops. An invariant must account for many cases: the cases where one thread executes an unbounded number of loop iterations before the other thread finishes its first iteration, the case where the loops execute synchronously, and the infinitely many cases in between. Such invariants are often complex (requiring quantification, non-linear arithmetic and other features that fall out of known decidable logic fragments) and out-of-reach for algorithmic verifiers [17].

When CEGAR encounters such a case, it repeatedly considers similar counterexample traces τ that gradually unroll some loops in the program. We use this observation to instantiate CEGAR+CC in a way that strategically employs CC in such cases. If CC shows that such a counterexample τ is redundant, and we infer sufficient commutativity to also witness the redundancy of all similar counterexamples (up to unrolling of loops), the reduction based on this commutativity simplifies the intricate interleaved loop structure. As a consequence, the verification of the new reduction may be able to find an inductive loop invariant.

To formalize the notion of the similarity of two traces up to unrolling of loops, we fix a representation of the current set of counterexamples P as a deterministic finite automaton (think of a control flow graph; see also Sect. 3). We define *path programs* based on this representation of P. We formulate the definition not only for traces τ in P, but also for traces ρ that are prefixes of a trace τ in P. The reason for this will become apparent later.

Definition 16. *Let ρ be a prefix of a trace accepted by the deterministic finite automaton representing P. The* path program *of ρ, denoted pathProgram(ρ), is the automaton formed by the states and edges of P that appear on the (unique) path that is labeled by the prefix ρ.*

The intuition is that traces with the same path program are similar, up to different unrollings of some loops. Path programs are based on the automaton P representing the current set of counterexamples maintained by CEGAR+CC (cf. Sect. 4.2). Previous reductions may have partially unfolded this automaton (relative to the original program $\mathcal{P}$). It suffices to find loop invariants for these partially unfolded loops. We formally state our strategy to resolve the nondeterminism in CEGAR+CC:

> **Instantiation of CEGAR+CC (Sect. 4.2):** Choose the CC branch and check redundancy of the current counterexample τ if and only if another counterexample τ_{old} with pathProgram(τ) = pathProgram(τ_{old}) has been encountered in a previous iteration. Otherwise, check infeasibility of τ.

As stated above, the goal of this strategy is to eliminate all traces in the path program of τ as redundant, based on the indications that CEGAR is failing to suitably generalize and prove the infeasibility of all traces in pathProgram(τ). Recall from Sect. 5 that to derive the commutativity relation I_τ, we identify a prefix ρ of τ, synthesize a commutativity condition φ for the two statements following the prefix ρ in τ, check the validity of the Hoare triple $\{\top\}\,\rho\,\{\varphi\}$, and finally derive the commutativity relation from a proof Π^φ generalized from the proof of said Hoare triple. We adapt this procedure as follows:

Adaptation of CC (Sect. 4.1): For a counterexample trace τ, a prefix ρ and a commutativity condition φ, return a commutativity relation only if for all traces ρ' with $pathProgram(\rho') = pathProgram(\rho)$, the Hoare triple $\{\top\}\,\rho'\,\{\varphi\}$ can be derived by sequential composition of Hoare triples in Π^φ. Otherwise, select another point of potential redundancy and repeat the procedure; or treat τ as non-redundant if no further points of potential redundancy remain.

This ensures that our implementation accepts a commutativity relation I_τ only if that commutativity relation eliminates the entire path program.

6.2   Evaluation

We implemented the described instantiation of CEGAR+CC to evaluate its impact on the verification. Our implementation is based on the open-source[1] commutativity-based software model checker ULTIMATE GEMCUTTER [13,23]. GEMCUTTER verifies reachability properties (and other safety properties) for programs written in C and (a concurrent dialect of) BoogiePL [26].

Implementation Details. As GEMCUTTER operates on a *semi-commutativity* relation (which may allow commuting statements in one direction but not the other), we implemented a straightforward extension of our approach to this setting. Our CEGAR+CC implementation initializes the commutativity relation I to context-insensitive commutativity, i.e. the relation given by the commutativity relation *true*, rather than the empty relation. We do not strictly separate proofs generated for infeasibility checks and proofs backing commutativity relations that witness redundancy of a trace. If a proof Π^φ backing a commutativity relation happens to prove infeasibility of some traces, it is also used to eliminate these traces. Conversely, GEMCUTTER's pre-existing support for proof-sensitive commutativity [13] uses commutativity relations derived from proofs Π_τ generated by infeasibility checks to extend the commutativity relation. We used the *loop lockstep* preference order which prefers traces where a thread-switch occurs before each iteration of a loop in some thread. We implemented an approximation of path programs for the instantiation described in Sect. 6.1, which may cause us to check redundancy more frequently.

The evaluation of our implementation focuses on the following questions:

RQ1: What is the benefit of incorporating redundancy proofs in CEGAR?
RQ2: How much additional commutativity does CEGAR+CC need to infer?
RQ3: What impact does the choice of *sufficient* vs. *necessary and sufficient* commutativity conditions (Sect. 5.2) have on the verification?

---

[1] github.com/ultimate-pa/ultimate

We compared four configurations of GEMCUTTER: *(a)* with *context-insensitive* commutativity, *(b)* with *proof-sensitive commutativity* [13], *(c)* with CEGAR+CC using sufficient commutativity conditions, and *(d)* with CEGAR+CC using necessary and sufficient commutativity conditions. We applied these four variants of GEMCUTTER to the benchmark set [29] of the WEAVER tool [16,17], a benchmark set consisting of 183 (predominantly correct) concurrent programs designed to challenge automated verification tools, in the sense that without sufficient reduction, proving these programs requires complex assertions typically out-of-reach for algorithmic verifiers [17]. Therefore, we do not compare to verification approaches that do not use commutativity-based reduction. We automatically translated the WEAVER benchmarks from their custom format to BoogiePL. All benchmark runs were performed on an AMD Ryzen Threadripper 3970X 32-Core Processor with a memory limit of 16 GB and a timeout of 15 min.

Table 1. Number of successful verification tasks and performance data comparing CEGAR+CC with context-insensitive and proof-sensitive commutativity.

	context-insensitive	proof-sensitive	CEGAR+CC	
			sufficient	nec. & sufficient
# successful tasks	96	99	109	111
CPU time (h:m:s)	0:39:49	0:42:37	0:53:19	0:54:33
memory (GB)	49.2	50.4	57.7	58.5
iterations	925	930	1085	1096
comm. refinements	N/A	N/A	15	19

Table 1 shows the evaluation results. The benefit of counterexample-guided commutativity (**RQ1**) is reflected in the increased number of verified programs. From left to right, each configuration verifies a strict superset of the benchmarks verified by the configurations to its left. The targeted, on-demand inference of additional commutativity provided by CEGAR+CC clearly outperforms the ad-hoc proof-sensitive approach. The increased resource consumption and additional iterations are almost exclusively due to the additionally verified benchmarks. When we only consider the 96 benchmarks solved by all configurations, i.e., where context-insensitive commutativity suffices in principle to verify the programs, CEGAR+CC requires approximately the same amount of resources (± 70 s resp. ± 600 MB across all benchmarks) as context-insensitive commutativity.

The total numbers of commutativity refinements across all benchmarks (cf. Table 1) show that even small amounts of additional commutativity can have significant impact (**RQ2**). A maximum of 2 commutativity refinements per benchmark were sufficient in every case. Finally, constructing necessary and sufficient commutativity conditions shows a small advantage over merely sufficient conditions (**RQ3**) in that two additional programs were successfully analyzed, without significantly increasing resource consumption. Considering all successfully analyzed programs, 41 Hoare triple checks for commutativity conditions *fail* for the configuration with sufficient commutativity conditions in the sense that the computed condition does not hold after the relevant trace prefix, while the configuration with necessary and sufficient (and thus *weaker*) conditions encounters only 29 failing Hoare triple checks for commutativity conditions. As a consequence, more commutativity is inferred for necessary and sufficient conditions than for sufficient conditions. In the two benchmarks that could only be verified with necessary and sufficient conditions, this additional commutativity makes the difference.

7   Related Work

Many works have considered the impact of commutativity in verification, and there has also been research [3,5,24] on commutativity conditions in contexts other than program verification. We focus here on commutativity in *fully automated verification techniques* for concurrent programs over *infinite data domains*.

Among the different combinations and integrations of CEGAR variants with commutativity reasoning, some works consider only context-insensitive, statically fixed commutativity relations, for instance the combination of trace abstraction refinement (also used for the abstraction refinement in CEGAR+CC) with commutativity-based reduction by Cassez and Ziegler [4]. However, various authors have recognized the need for some form of context-sensitive commutativity and introduced different approaches. Wachter et al. [30] integrate commutativity-based reduction with the Impact algorithm, and derive additional so-called *conditional commutativity* for statements manipulating pointers through a separate *aliasing analysis* performed on the abstract reachability tree. Farzan and Vandikas [17] present a CEGAR loop that makes progress on verifying infinitely many reductions at the same time, until one reduction has been proven. This strategy also allows their technique to consider infinitely many contextual commutativity relations, by inserting additional *independence statements* asserting the relevant commutativity conditions in the respective reductions; a violated commutativity simply causes the respective reduction to be excluded and the verification to proceed only on the remaining reductions. Farzan, Klumpp and Podelski [13] also present an integration of commutativity and CEGAR in which *proof-sensitive commutativity* is derived from proofs generated by infeasibility checks (see also the comparison to our approach in Sect. 6.2). All these approaches have in common that they recognize the need for additional commutativity, and draw on various sources to achieve it. Yet, these approaches are not demand-driven, in contrast to CEGAR+CC.

The approach based on *abstract commutativity* presented in [14] initially allows the verification to assume that all statements commute. As the abstraction refinement includes more and more information in the proof, the commutativity relation is refined (and often *restricted*) to ensure that swapping commuting statements preserves the behaviour guaranteed by the proof. By contrast, CEGAR+CC always *extends* the commutativity relation. As the notions of abstract and contextual commutativity are compatible, combining *counterexample-guided* and *abstract* commutativity presents an interesting avenue for future work.

8   Conclusion

In this paper, we present *counterexample-guided commutativity* (CC). The core insight is that commutativity-based reduction enables a verification algorithm to identify *redundant* counterexamples that can be soundly eliminated from the set of counterexamples by inferring additional commutativity. We introduce a new verification scheme called CEGAR+CC that integrates CC with CEGAR, enabling a non-deterministic choice between proving a counterexample infeasible or redundant. When a counterexample is proven redundant, we use the proof for a generalization step that allows us to eliminate not just a single counterexample, but a whole infinite set. We have implemented an algorithm that instantiates CEGAR+CC. We have used our implementation to evaluate the resulting verification algorithm on a challenging benchmark set. The evaluation shows that CC results in a 15% increase in the number of verified programs, and even a small amount of additional commutativity can have a significant impact.

As for future work, the integration with other approaches that adapt the commutativity relation during the verification could be of interest, particularly *abstract commutativity*. Moreover, a key limitation of commutativity-based verification to date is that success crucially depends on the preference order, which determines the representatives of each class, but automatically choosing a suitable order is challenging. In light of this paper, a similarly counterexample-guided approach might also be promising to this end. Finally, while we have integrated CC in one specific CEGAR algorithm, the principles and benefits should also be applicable to many other verification algorithms.

Data Availability Statement. Our implementation of CEGAR+CC and the setup for our evaluation are available on Zenodo [11].

Disclosure of Interests. The authors have no competing interests to declare that are relevant to the content of this article.

References

1. Abdulla, P.A., Jonsson, B., Kindahl, M., Peled, D.A.: A general approach to partial order reductions in symbolic verification (extended abstract). In: Hu, A.J., Vardi, M.Y. (eds.) Computer Aided Verification, 10th International Conference, CAV 1998, Vancouver, BC, Canada, 28 June–2 July 1998, Proceedings. Lecture Notes in Computer Science, vol. 1427, pp. 379–390. Springer (1998). https://doi.org/10.1007/BFB0028760
2. Baier, C., Katoen, J.: Principles of Model Checking. MIT Press (2008)

3. Bansal, K., Koskinen, E., Tripp, O.: Synthesizing precise and useful commutativity conditions. J. Autom. Reason. **64**(7), 1333–1359 (2020). https://doi.org/10.1007/S10817-020-09573-W

4. Cassez, F., Ziegler, F.: Verification of concurrent programs using trace abstraction refinement. In: Davis, M., Fehnker, A., McIver, A., Voronkov, A. (eds.) LPAR 2015. LNCS, vol. 9450, pp. 233–248. Springer, Heidelberg (2015). https://doi.org/10.1007/978-3-662-48899-7_17

5. Chen, A., Fathololumi, P., Nicola, M., Pincus, J., Brennan, T., Koskinen, E.: Better predicates and heuristics for improved commutativity synthesis. In: André, É., Sun, J. (eds.) Automated Technology for Verification and Analysis - 21st International Symposium, ATVA 2023, Singapore, 24–27 October 2023, Proceedings, Part II. Lecture Notes in Computer Science, vol. 14216, pp. 93–113. Springer (2023). https://doi.org/10.1007/978-3-031-45332-8_5

6. Chu, D.-H., Jaffar, J.: A framework to synergize partial order reduction with state interpolation. In: Yahav, E. (ed.) HVC 2014. LNCS, vol. 8855, pp. 171–187. Springer, Cham (2014). https://doi.org/10.1007/978-3-319-13338-6_14

7. Dietsch, D., Heizmann, M., Musa, B., Nutz, A., Podelski, A.: Craig vs. Newton in software model checking. In: Bodden, E., Schäfer, W., van Deursen, A., Zisman, A. (eds.) Proceedings of the 2017 11th Joint Meeting on Foundations of Software Engineering, ESEC/FSE 2017, Paderborn, Germany, 4–8 September 2017, pp. 487–497. ACM (2017). https://doi.org/10.1145/3106237.3106307

8. Dillig, I., Dillig, T.: EXPLAIN: a tool for performing abductive inference. In: Sharygina, N., Veith, H. (eds.) CAV 2013. LNCS, vol. 8044, pp. 684–689. Springer, Heidelberg (2013). https://doi.org/10.1007/978-3-642-39799-8_46

9. Dillig, I., Dillig, T., Aiken, A.: Small formulas for large programs: on-line constraint simplification in scalable static analysis. In: Cousot, R., Martel, M. (eds.) SAS 2010. LNCS, vol. 6337, pp. 236–252. Springer, Heidelberg (2010). https://doi.org/10.1007/978-3-642-15769-1_15

10. Dillig, I., Dillig, T., McMillan, K.L., Aiken, A.: Minimum satisfying assignments for SMT. In: Madhusudan, P., Seshia, S.A. (eds.) CAV 2012. LNCS, vol. 7358, pp. 394–409. Springer, Heidelberg (2012). https://doi.org/10.1007/978-3-642-31424-7_30

11. Ebbinghaus, M., Klumpp, D., Podelski, A.: Artifact for CAV'25 Paper "Counterexample-Guided Commutativity" (2025). https://doi.org/10.5281/zenodo.15198876

12. Elmas, T., Qadeer, S., Tasiran, S.: A calculus of atomic actions. In: Shao, Z., Pierce, B.C. (eds.) Proceedings of the 36th ACM SIGPLAN-SIGACT Symposium on Principles of Programming Languages, POPL 2009, Savannah, GA, USA, 21–23 January 2009, pp. 2–15. ACM (2009). https://doi.org/10.1145/1480881.1480885

13. Farzan, A., Klumpp, D., Podelski, A.: Sound sequentialization for concurrent program verification. In: Jhala, R., Dillig, I. (eds.) PLDI 2022: 43rd ACM SIGPLAN International Conference on Programming Language Design and Implementation, San Diego, CA, USA, 13–17 June 2022, pp. 506–521. ACM (2022). https://doi.org/10.1145/3519939.3523727

14. Farzan, A., Klumpp, D., Podelski, A.: Stratified commutativity in verification algorithms for concurrent programs. Proc. ACM Program. Lang. **7**(POPL), 1426–1453 (2023). https://doi.org/10.1145/3571242

15. Farzan, A., Klumpp, D., Podelski, A.: Commutativity simplifies proofs of parameterized programs. Proc. ACM Program. Lang. **8**(POPL), 2485–2513 (2024). https://doi.org/10.1145/3632925

16. Farzan, A., Vandikas, A.: Automated hypersafety verification. In: Dillig, I., Tasiran, S. (eds.) CAV 2019. LNCS, vol. 11561, pp. 200–218. Springer, Cham (2019). https://doi.org/10.1007/978-3-030-25540-4_11

17. Farzan, A., Vandikas, A.: Reductions for safety proofs. Proc. ACM Program. Lang. 4(POPL), 13:1–13:28 (2020). https://doi.org/10.1145/3371081

18. Godefroid, P.: Partial-Order Methods for the Verification of Concurrent Systems - An Approach to the State-Explosion Problem. Lecture Notes in Computer Science, vol. 1032. Springer (1996). https://doi.org/10.1007/3-540-60761-7

19. Heizmann, M., Hoenicke, J., Podelski, A.: Refinement of trace abstraction. In: Palsberg, J., Su, Z. (eds.) SAS 2009. LNCS, vol. 5673, pp. 69–85. Springer, Heidelberg (2009). https://doi.org/10.1007/978-3-642-03237-0_7

20. Heizmann, M., Hoenicke, J., Podelski, A.: Software model checking for people who love automata. In: Sharygina, N., Veith, H. (eds.) CAV 2013. LNCS, vol. 8044, pp. 36–52. Springer, Heidelberg (2013). https://doi.org/10.1007/978-3-642-39799-8_2

21. Heizmann, M., Klumpp, D., Nitzke, L., Schüssele, F.: Petrification: software model checking for programs with dynamic thread management. In: Dimitrova, R., Lahav, O., Wolff, S. (eds.) Verification, Model Checking, and Abstract Interpretation - 25th International Conference, VMCAI 2024, London, United Kingdom, 15–16 January 2024, Proceedings, Part II. Lecture Notes in Computer Science, vol. 14500, pp. 3–25. Springer (2024). https://doi.org/10.1007/978-3-031-50521-8_1

22. Kahlon, V., Wang, C., Gupta, A.: Monotonic partial order reduction: an optimal symbolic partial order reduction technique. In: Bouajjani, A., Maler, O. (eds.) CAV 2009. LNCS, vol. 5643, pp. 398–413. Springer, Heidelberg (2009). https://doi.org/10.1007/978-3-642-02658-4_31

23. Klumpp, D., et al.: ULTIMATE GEMCUTTER and the axes of generalization. In: Fisman, D., Rosu, G. (eds.) TACAS 2022. LNCS, vol. 13244, pp. 479–483. Springer, Cham (2022). https://doi.org/10.1007/978-3-030-99527-0_35

24. Koskinen, E., Bansal, K.: Decomposing data structure commutativity proofs with mn-differencing. In: Henglein, F., Shoham, S., Vizel, Y. (eds.) VMCAI 2021. LNCS, vol. 12597, pp. 81–103. Springer, Cham (2021). https://doi.org/10.1007/978-3-030-67067-2_5

25. Kragl, B., Qadeer, S.: Layered concurrent programs. In: Chockler, H., Weissenbacher, G. (eds.) CAV 2018. LNCS, vol. 10981, pp. 79–102. Springer, Cham (2018). https://doi.org/10.1007/978-3-319-96145-3_5

26. Leino, K.R.M.: This is Boogie 2 (2008). https://www.microsoft.com/en-us/research/publication/this-is-boogie-2-2/

27. Lipton, R.J.: Reduction: a method of proving properties of parallel programs. Commun. ACM 18(12), 717–721 (1975). https://doi.org/10.1145/361227.361234

28. Peled, D.: Combining partial order reductions with on-the-fly model-checking. In: Dill, D.L. (ed.) CAV 1994. LNCS, vol. 818, pp. 377–390. Springer, Heidelberg (1994). https://doi.org/10.1007/3-540-58179-0_69

29. Vandikas, A., Farzan, A.: Example programs for the Weaver verifier (2021). https://github.com/weaver-verifier/weaver/tree/master/examples

30. Wachter, B., Kroening, D., Ouaknine, J.: Verifying multi-threaded software with Impact. In: Formal Methods in Computer-Aided Design, FMCAD 2013, Portland, OR, USA, 20–23 October 2013, pp. 210–217. IEEE (2013). https://doi.org/10.1109/FMCAD.2013.6679412

Scaling Up Proactive Enforcement

François Hublet[1], Leonardo Lima[2], David Basin[1],
Srđan Krstić[1], and Dmitriy Traytel[2]

[1] ETH Zürich, Zurich, Switzerland
{francois.hublet, basin, srdan.krstic}@inf.ethz.ch
[2] University of Copenhagen, Copenhagen, Denmark
{leonardo, traytel}@di.ku.dk

Abstract. Runtime enforcers receive events from a system and output commands ensuring the system's policy compliance. Proactive enforcers extend traditional (reactive) enforcers by emitting commands at any time, rather only as a response to system actions. However, proactive enforcers have so far lacked support for many useful policy features. This, along with the existing tools' poor performance, hinders their adoption. We present a performance-optimized, proactive enforcement algorithm for a rich policy language: metric first-order temporal logic with function applications, aggregations, and let bindings. We have implemented this algorithm in ENFGUARD, the first proactive enforcer tool that supports the above constructs. We evaluated our tool using a novel set of six benchmarks containing both real-world and synthetic policies and logs, demonstrating that it enforces realistic policies out-of-the-box and achieves the necessary performance to be used in real-time systems.

1 Introduction

Statically certifying the behavior of large, complex systems is often impossible. As an alternative, runtime enforcement [41] has emerged as a family of techniques aimed at observing and correcting the behavior of systems during their execution.

In runtime enforcement, an *enforcer* is a policy enforcement mechanism that observes the real-time execution of a system under enforcement (SuE) through the sequence of *events* that occur in it and sends *commands* to the SuE to ensure policy compliance (Figure 1). These commands instruct the system to suppress, cause, modify, or delay specific events. In *reactive* enforcement, the enforcer emits commands immediately upon receiving events (Figure 1, interactions 1.1–1.2). In *proactive* enforcement [4], the enforcer can additionally give commands at any time, rather than only after SuE events (Figure 1, interactions 2.1–2.2). This is crucial whenever policies require action to be taken before a deadline, even in the absence of SuE actions, as in common, e.g., in privacy regulations [24].

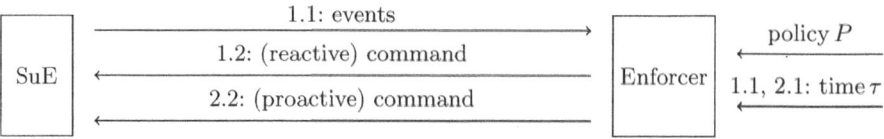

Fig. 1: Communication diagram for enforcement. R-step: 1.1, 1.2; P-step: 2.1, 2.2

© The Author(s) 2025
R. Piskac and Z. Rakamarić (Eds.): CAV 2025, LNCS 15933, pp. 370–392, 2025.
https://doi.org/10.1007/978-3-031-98682-6_19

To be practical, enforcers must be able to process SuE events at high rates. Moreover, they should support policies written in an expressive specification language. As an example, consider the policy stating "an alert must be raised whenever, within a 30-minute window, a data center dc has seen a pattern of unintended reboots of its servers that is classified as an outlier by Grubbs's test [18]:"

let badReboot$(s, dc) = $ reboot$(s, dc) \wedge \neg \bullet (\neg$reboot$(s, dc)$ S intendReboot$(s, dc))$ in

let cntReboots$(dc, c) = c \leftarrow$ CNT$(i; dc)(\blacklozenge_{[0,1800)}($badReboot$(s, dc) \wedge$ tp$(i)))$ in

$\square(\forall dc, l.\ dc, l \leftarrow$ GRUBBS$(dc, c;\ )($cntReboots$(dc, c))) \wedge l \approx 1$

$\longrightarrow$ alert("Data center " ^ int_to_string dc ^ " has rebooted too often"))

In this policy, the user-defined aggregation function GRUBBS takes a finite sequence of pairs (k_i, v_i) with k_i an integer key and v_i a floating-point value, and returns a sequence of pairs (k_i, b_i), where $b_i = 1$ iff the Grubbs test identifies v_i as an outlier in $\{v_1, ..., v_i, ...\}$. A special event tp is used to retrieve the current timepoint. Moreover, this policy contains: *applications of a function* int_to_string and a string concatenation operator (^); *aggregations* that use a user-defined aggregation function GRUBBS and an SQL-style aggregation operator CNT ('count') with grouping, e.g., cntReboots counts the number of reboots in each data center within the last 1800 seconds ($\blacklozenge_{[0,1800)}$ operator); and let *bindings* that define, e.g., an 'unintended reboot' as a reboot event that does not follow (S operator) an announce_reboot event strictly in the past ($\bullet$ operator). To the best of our knowledge, none of the existing proactive enforcement algorithms [4,23,24] supports any of these features. Thus, they cannot enforce policies like the above.

In this paper, we present the first proactive enforcement algorithm that supports metric first-order temporal logic (MFOTL) with function applications, aggregations, and let bindings. We implement this algorithm in ENFGUARD, a new tool building on an existing proactive enforcement algorithm for simple MFOTL policies [24]. The original algorithm works as follows: (1) it maintains a queue of temporal obligations with deadlines (e.g., "fulfill $P(5)$ within three hours"); (2) it checks if newly observed events fulfill pending obligations (e.g., if $P(5)$ occurred), proactively causing events when any deadline risks being missed; and (3) it suppresses and causes events reactively. In addition to supporting a more expressive policy language, ENFGUARD achieves up to 30× speedup over prior work.

We evaluate ENFGUARD on six benchmarks involving a combination of both real-world and synthetic policies and system logs. Our evaluation shows that our tool, unlike previous work [23,24], directly supports all policies from these benchmarks and can enforce them at high event rates (up to 1,000–10,000 events/s).

After reviewing prior work (Section 2), we make the following contributions:

– We extend prior work to support function applications, aggregations, and let bindings (Section 3). This extension fundamentally changes the underlying data structures, the enforcement algorithm, and the enforceable formulae.
– We describe our enforcement algorithm's optimizations (Section 4). These involve the lazy evaluation of Boolean operators, skipping unnecessary subformulae evaluation, and memoization of subformula evaluation results.
– We implement our algorithm in the ENFGUARD enforcer. We validate our

tool's expressiveness and performance on six benchmarks (Section 5), show-
ing that it can be used in real-time and surpasses existing tools' capabilities.
The proofs of all propositions can be found in our technical report [25]. ENF-
GUARD is open source and is publicly available on GitHub [26].

Related Work. Reactive enforcement was introduced by Schneider et al. using
security automata [41,13] that terminate the SuE to prevent violations. Subsequent research supported the suppression [9,17] and causation [31] of individual events by buffering SuE events before making decisions. This (unrealistic)
buffering capability was later dropped [34], and other capabilities, such as delaying events [37,14] and SuE code inspection [38], were considered.

Many enforcers use (timed) automata either as a policy language [15,16] or as
the translation target for logics such as MITL [36,40]. Controller synthesis tools
for LTL [27,12,43], Timed CTL [10,35], and MTL [30,22] also generate enforcers.

Very few works enforce *first-order temporal* policies: Hallé and Villemaire [19]
give an enforcer for LTL-FO$^+$, a first-order variant of future-only LTL. Hublet
et al. [23] reactively enforce a restricted set of MFOTL policies that cannot refer
to the future. Aceto et al. [1,2] consider safety policies in Hennessy-Milner Logic
with recursion; their approach is non-metric and does not support causation.

To the best of our knowledge, only two works study *proactive* enforcement.
Basin et al. [4] describe a proactive enforcer for finite automata and dynamic
condition response graphs [21], which is a propositional formalism. Hublet et
al. [24] provide the only existing proactive first-order enforcement algorithm,
which we substantially extend in this paper.

2   Preliminaries

We now review proactive enforcement (Section 2.1) and metric first-order temporal logic (Section 2.2). We then summarize the relevant data structures (Section 2.3) and the enforcement algorithm (Section 2.4) by Hublet et al [24].

2.1   Proactive runtime enforcement

Let Σ be a signature $(\mathbb{D}, \mathbb{E}, a)$ with an infinite domain $\mathbb{D}$ of values, a finite set
of *event names* $\mathbb{E}$, each with arity $a(e) \in \mathbb{N}, e \in \mathbb{E}$. An *event* $e(d_1, \ldots, d_{a(e)}) \in$
$\mathbb{E} \times \mathbb{D}^{a(e)}$ is a pair of an event name e and its $a(e)$ parameters $d_1, \ldots, d_{a(e)}$.

Events encode system actions that can be observed and controlled by the
enforcer, or only observed. The enforcer can control an event by suppressing or
causing it. We partition $\mathbb{E}$ into *suppressable* event names ($\mathbb{S} \subseteq \mathbb{E}$), *causable* event
names ($\mathbb{C} \subseteq \mathbb{E}$), and *observable* event names ($\mathbb{O} = \mathbb{E} \setminus (\mathbb{S} \cup \mathbb{C})$). The enforcer
can cause all events with names in $\mathbb{C}$ and suppress all events with names in $\mathbb{S}$.
The set $\mathbb{DB}$ of *databases* over Σ is $\mathcal{P}(\{e(\overline{d}) \mid e \in \mathbb{E}, \overline{d} \in \mathbb{D}^{a(e)}\})$ and a *trace*
σ is a sequence $\langle(\tau_i, D_i)\rangle_{0 \le i \le k}, k \in \mathbb{N} \cup \{\infty\}$ of timestamps $\tau_i \in \mathbb{N}$ and finite
databases $D_i \in \mathbb{DB}$, where timestamps grow monotonically ($\forall i < |\sigma|. \ \tau_i \le \tau_{i+1}$)
and progress (if $|\sigma| = \infty$, then $\lim_i \tau_i = \infty$). An index $0 \le i < |\sigma|$ in a trace σ is
called a *time-point*. The empty trace is denoted by ε, the set of all traces by $\mathbb{T}$,

1 $\mathsf{run}(s, \sigma, \sigma', \tau) = \mathbf{case}\ \sigma'\ \mathbf{of}\ \varepsilon \Rightarrow \varepsilon$
2 $|\ (\tau', D) \cdot \sigma''\ \mathbf{when}\ \tau' > \tau \Rightarrow \mathbf{let}\ (o, s') = \mu(\sigma, s, \tau, \mathsf{tick})\ \mathbf{in}$
3      $\mathbf{case}\ o\ \mathbf{of}\ \mathsf{PCom}(D_{\mathbb{C}}) \Rightarrow (\tau, D_{\mathbb{C}}) \cdot \mathsf{run}(s', \sigma \cdot (\tau, D_{\mathbb{C}}), \sigma', \tau + 1)$
4          $|\ \mathsf{NoCom} \Rightarrow \mathsf{run}(s', \sigma, \sigma', \tau + 1)$
5 $|\ (\tau', D) \cdot \sigma''\ \mathbf{when}\ \tau' = \tau \Rightarrow \mathbf{let}\ (o, s') = \mu(\sigma, s, \tau, D); D' = (D \setminus D_{\mathbb{S}}) \cup D_{\mathbb{C}}\ \mathbf{in}$
6      $\mathbf{case}\ o\ \mathbf{of}\ \mathsf{RCom}(D_{\mathbb{C}}, D_{\mathbb{S}}) \Rightarrow (\tau, D') \cdot \mathsf{run}(s', \sigma \cdot (\tau, D'), \sigma'', \tau + 1)$
7 $\mathcal{E}(\sigma) = \mathsf{run}(s_0, \varepsilon, \sigma, \mathbf{case}\ \sigma\ \mathbf{of}\ \varepsilon \Rightarrow 0\ |\ (\tau, D) \cdot \sigma' \Rightarrow \tau)$

Fig. 2: Enforced trace

and the set of finite (resp. infinite) traces by $\mathbb{T}_f$ (resp. $\mathbb{T}_\omega$). For traces $\sigma \in \mathbb{T}_f$ and $\sigma' \in \mathbb{T}$, $\sigma \cdot \sigma'$ denotes their concatenation. A *property* is a subset $P \subseteq \mathbb{T}_\omega$.

Given a prefix of a SuE trace, a *proactive enforcer* can either perform a (re-active) R-step (Figure 1, interactions 1.1 and 1.2), where it reads a new times-tamp τ and database D, or a (proactive) P-step (interactions 2.1 and 2.2) where it reads a τ only. In both cases, it returns an appropriate *command*. In R-steps, a command is of the form $\mathsf{RCom}(D_{\mathbb{C}}, D_{\mathbb{S}})$ where $D_{\mathbb{C}}$ and $D_{\mathbb{S}} \subseteq D$ are databases over the signatures $(\mathbb{D}, \mathbb{C}, a)$ and $(\mathbb{D}, \mathbb{S}, a)$, respectively. Such a command instructs the SuE to cause $D_{\mathbb{C}}$ and suppress a subset $D_{\mathbb{S}}$ of D. In P-steps, a command is of the form $\mathsf{PCom}(D_{\mathbb{C}})$ or NoCom. In the former case, $D_{\mathbb{C}}$ is caused; in the latter, no event is caused or suppressed. Cmd denotes the set of all commands.

Definition 1. *A (proactive) enforcer $\mathcal{E}$ is a triple $(\mathcal{S}, s_0, \mu)$, where $\mathcal{S}$ is a set of states, $s_0 \in \mathcal{S}$ is an initial state, and $\mu : \mathbb{T}_f \times \mathcal{S} \times \mathbb{N} \times (\mathbb{DB} \cup \{\mathsf{tick}\}) \to \mathsf{Cmd} \times \mathcal{S}$ is a computable update function, such that the following two conditions hold:*

$$\forall \sigma, \tau, D \neq \mathsf{tick}, s.\ \exists D_{\mathbb{C}}, D_{\mathbb{S}}, s'.\ \mu(\sigma, s, \tau, D) = (\mathsf{RCom}(D_{\mathbb{C}}, D_{\mathbb{S}}), s') \wedge D_{\mathbb{S}} \subseteq D$$
$$\forall \sigma, s, \tau.\ \exists D_{\mathbb{C}}, s'.\ \mu(\sigma, s, \tau, \mathsf{tick}) \in \{(\mathsf{PCom}(D_{\mathbb{C}}), s'), (\mathsf{NoCom}, s')\}.$$

The first three arguments of μ are the trace prefix σ (containing all of the past excluding the present), the state of the enforcer s, and the current timestamp τ. In R-steps, μ's fourth argument is a new database D and μ returns $\mathsf{RCom}(D_{\mathbb{C}}, D_{\mathbb{S}})$. In P-steps, μ's fourth argument is the special symbol tick and the enforcer can return either $\mathsf{PCom}(D_{\mathbb{C}})$ or NoCom. This induces a trace transduction:

Definition 2. *For any $\sigma \in \mathbb{T}$ and enforcer $\mathcal{E} = (\mathcal{S}, s_0, \mu)$, the enforced trace $\mathcal{E}(\sigma)$ is defined co-recursively in Figure 2.*

To compute the enforced trace $\mathcal{E}(\sigma)$ from the original SuE trace σ, the update function μ is called once on every time-point to generate an R-command (lines 6–7) and once before each clock tick to generate a P-command (lines 3–5).

The enforcer's correctness with respect to a target property P is typically expressed in terms of *soundness* and *transparency* [31]. A sound enforcer ensures that the modified trace always complies with P, while a transparent enforcer modifies the system's behavior *only when necessary* to ensure compliance.

Definition 3. *An enforcer $\mathcal{E}$ is* sound *with respect to a property P iff for any $\sigma \in \mathbb{T}_\omega$, $\mathcal{E}(\sigma) \in P$. An enforcer $\mathcal{E} = (\mathcal{S}, s_0, \mu)$ is* transparent *with respect to a property P iff for any $\sigma \in P$, $\mathcal{E}(\sigma) = \sigma$. A property P (resp. a formula φ) is* enforceable *iff there exists a sound enforcer with respect to P (resp. $\mathcal{L}(\varphi)$).*

2.2 Metric first-order temporal logic

Metric first-order temporal logic (MFOTL) [8,11] is an expressive logic for specifying trace properties. In this paper, we extend MFOTL with function applications in terms, aggregations [7], and non-recursive let bindings [44]. Our MFOTL syntax is defined by the following grammar (extensions highlighted):

$$t ::= c \mid x \mid f(t, \ldots, t)$$

$$\varphi ::= e(t, \ldots, t) \mid t \approx c \mid \neg\varphi \mid \varphi \wedge \varphi \mid \exists x.\ \varphi \mid \bigcirc_I \varphi \mid \bullet_I \varphi \mid \varphi\ \mathsf{U}_I\ \varphi \mid \varphi\ \mathsf{S}_I\ \varphi$$

$$\mid\ x, \ldots, x \leftarrow \omega(t, \ldots, t; x, \ldots, x)\ \varphi\ \mid\ \mathsf{let}\ e(x, \ldots, x) = \varphi\ \mathsf{in}\ \varphi\ .$$

In the above, $e \in \mathbb{E}$, $c \in \mathbb{D}$, $i \in \mathbb{N}$, x ranges over a set $\mathbb{V}$ of variables, f over a set $\mathbb{F}$ of function names, and ω over a set $\Omega \supseteq \{\mathsf{SUM}, \mathsf{AVG}, \mathsf{STD}, \mathsf{MED}, \mathsf{CNT}, \mathsf{MIN}, \mathsf{MAX}\}$ of aggregation operators. In a subformula $\mathsf{let}\ e(\bar{t}) = \varphi_1\ \mathsf{in}\ \varphi_2$, the event e is not allowed to appear in φ_1. We extend the arity function a to functions and aggregation operators so that for any $f \in \mathbb{F}$, $a(f) \in \mathbb{N}$ is the number of arguments of f, and for any $\omega \in \Omega$, $a(\omega)$ is a pair in $\mathbb{N}^2$ such that $a(\omega)_1$ and $a(\omega)_2$ are the input and output arities of ω, respectively. We define the shorthands $\top := p \vee \neg p$, $\bot := \neg\top$, $\varphi \longrightarrow \psi := \neg\varphi \vee \psi$, and the operators "once" ($\blacklozenge_I \varphi := \top\ \mathsf{S}_I\ \varphi$), "eventually" ($\Diamond_I \varphi := \top\ \mathsf{U}_I\ \varphi$), "always" ($\Box_I \varphi := \neg\Diamond_I \neg\varphi$), and "historically" ($\blacksquare_I \varphi := \neg\blacklozenge_I \neg\varphi$). The interval $[0, \infty)$ can be omitted in subscripts.

Next, we present the semantics of MFOTL, deferring the semantics of our extensions to Section 3. A *valuation* $v : \mathbb{V} \to \mathbb{D}$ maps variables to domain elements in $\mathbb{D}$. Under a valuation v, a variable x evaluates to $[\![x]\!]_v = v(x)$ and a constant $c \in \mathbb{D}$ to $[\![c]\!]_v = c$. We write $v[x \mapsto d]$ for the mapping v updated with the assignment $x \mapsto d$, where $x \in \mathbb{V}$ and $d \in \mathbb{D}$. The sequent $v, i \vDash_\sigma \varphi$ (defined in Figure 3 for a fixed, infinite σ) denotes that φ is satisfied at time-point i of trace σ under valuation v (i.e., v is a *satisfaction*). The property induced by a formula φ is $\mathcal{L}(\varphi) = \{\sigma \in \mathbb{T}_\omega \mid \exists v.\ v, 0 \vDash_\sigma \varphi\}$, and we say that a formula φ is *enforceable* when there exists a sound enforcer for $\mathcal{L}(\varphi)$.

We write $\mathsf{fv}(\varphi)$ and $\mathsf{const}(\varphi)$ for the set of free variables and constants of formula φ, respectively. The *active domain* $\mathrm{AD}_{\sigma,E}(\varphi)$ of a formula φ over a finite trace $\sigma = \langle(\tau_i, D_i)_{0 \le i < |\sigma|}\rangle$ and set of event names $E \subseteq \mathbb{E}$ is $\mathsf{const}(\varphi) \cup \left(\bigcup_{0 \le j < |\sigma|}\{d \mid d \text{ is one of } d_k \text{ in } e(d_1, \ldots, d_{a(e)}) \in D_j \text{ and } e \in E\}\right)$. Intuitively, the active domain consists of all domain values present in the trace as well as all constants occurring in the formulae.

2.3 Partitioned decision trees

Let $\mathrm{SAT}_\varphi(v, i, \sigma)$ be a function that returns true iff $v, i \vDash_\sigma \varphi$, i.e., iff a trace σ satisfies φ at i under v, and false otherwise. A *monitor* for a formula φ is an algorithm that computes $\mathrm{SAT}_\varphi(v, i, \sigma)$ by incrementally observing σ's prefixes.

Inspired by binary decision diagrams [33], Lima et al. [32] introduce partitioned decision trees (PDTs) to compactly represent sets of valuations. PDTs

$$
\begin{array}{ll}
v,i \vDash t \approx c & \text{iff } \llbracket t \rrbracket_v = c \quad | \quad v,i \vDash e(t_1, ..., t_{a(e)}) \text{ iff } e(\llbracket t_1 \rrbracket_v, ..., \llbracket t_{a(e)} \rrbracket_v) \in D_i \\
v,i \vDash \exists x.\ \varphi & \text{iff } v[x \mapsto d], i \vDash \varphi \text{ for some } d \in \mathbb{D} \quad | \quad v,i \vDash \neg \varphi \quad \text{iff } v, i \nvDash \varphi \\
v,i \vDash \bigcirc_I \varphi & \text{iff } v, i+1 \vDash \varphi \text{ and } \tau_{i+1} - \tau_i \in I \quad | \quad v,i \vDash \varphi \wedge \psi \text{ iff } v, i \vDash \varphi \text{ and } v, i \vDash \psi \\
v,i \vDash \bullet_I \varphi & \text{iff } i > 0 \text{ and } v, i-1 \vDash \varphi \text{ and } \tau_i - \tau_{i-1} \in I \\
v,i \vDash \varphi \, \mathsf{U}_I \, \psi & \text{iff } v, j \vDash \psi \text{ for some } j \geq i \text{ with } \tau_j - \tau_i \in I \text{ and } v, k \vDash \varphi \text{ for all } i \leq k < j \\
v,i \vDash \varphi \, \mathsf{S}_I \, \psi & \text{iff } v, j \vDash \psi \text{ for some } j \leq i \text{ with } \tau_i - \tau_j \in I \text{ and } v, k \vDash \varphi \text{ for all } j < k \leq i
\end{array}
$$

Fig. 3: MFOTL semantics for a fixed, infinite trace σ

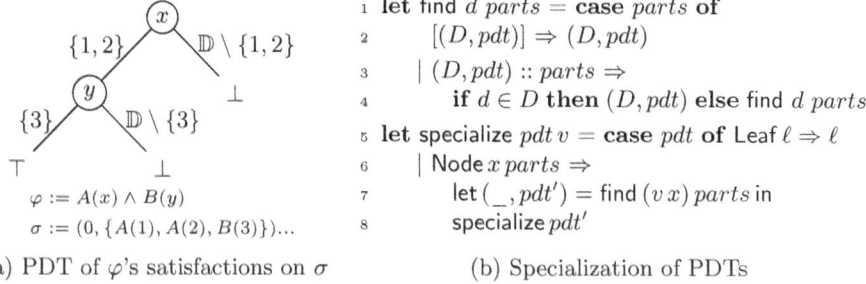

(a) PDT of φ's satisfactions on σ (b) Specialization of PDTs

Fig. 4: Partitioned decision trees (PDTs)

are trees whose internal nodes are labeled with free variables, whose edges are marked with sets of elements that partition $\mathbb{D}$, and whose leaves contain data of interest, e.g., Boolean values. The corresponding algebraic data type is Pdt $a =$ Leaf a | Node $\mathbb{V}$ ($\mathcal{P}_c(\mathbb{D}) \times$ Pdt a)), where $\mathcal{P}_c(X)$ denotes the set of finite or co-finite subsets of X. An example of a PDT storing the satisfactions of the formula $\varphi := A(x) \wedge B(y)$ on a trace $\sigma := (0, \{A(1), A(2), B(3)\})...$ is shown in Figure 4a. Given a specific valuation v, the value $\mathrm{SAT}_\varphi(v, i, \sigma)$ (indicating if v is a satisfaction) can be extracted from a PDT of $\mathrm{SAT}_\varphi(\bullet, i, \sigma)$ using the specialize function shown in Figure 4b: for any leaf, the stored value is immediately returned (l. 8); for any node labeled by a variable x, the child whose edge label contains the value $v(x)$ is selected, and specialization continues from that child (l. 9–10).

Lima et al. [32] describe a monitoring algorithm for MFOTL based on PDTs. They first define a series of functional operations on PDTs, and then describe a monitoring algorithm combining these operations. For example, to compute $\mathrm{SAT}_{\varphi_1 \wedge \varphi_2}(\bullet, i, \sigma)$, they apply a function apply2 $(\lambda b_1\, b_2.\ b_1 \wedge b_2)$ on the PDTs p_1 and p_2 of $\mathrm{SAT}_{\varphi_1}(\bullet, i, \sigma)$ and $\mathrm{SAT}_{\varphi_2}(\bullet, i, \sigma)$. This function is such that

$$\forall f, p_1, p_2, v.\ \mathsf{specialize}\ (\mathsf{apply2}\ f\ p_1\ p_2)\ v = f\ (\mathsf{specialize}\ p_1\ v)\ (\mathsf{specialize}\ p_2\ v).$$

Hence, applying apply2 $(\lambda b_1\, b_2.\ b_1 \wedge b_2)$ correctly evaluates the conjunction. Compared to table-based monitoring algorithms [8], PDT-based algorithms lift many of the restrictions on the supported MFOTL fragment imposed in previous work [8,39], thus significantly increasing expressivity.

2.4   Enforcement algorithm

Not all MFOTL formulae are enforceable, e.g., $\forall x.\ A(x) \longrightarrow B(x)$ is enforceable only if A is suppressable or B is causable. MFOTL enforceability is undecidable [23], yet there are syntactic fragments that guarantee enforceability.

Hublet et al. [24, Section 4] define such an enforceable fragment, called EMFOTL. EMFOTL is defined using type sequents $\Gamma \vdash \varphi : \alpha$, where the context $\Gamma :$ $\mathbb{E} \to \{\mathbb{C}, \mathbb{S}\}$ is a mapping from event names to $\{\mathbb{C}, \mathbb{S}\}$, φ is an MFOTL formula, and $\alpha \in \{\mathbb{C}, \mathbb{S}\}$ is a type. Intuitively, a formula types to $\mathbb{C}$ under Γ ("φ is causable under Γ") if it can be enforced by causing events $e_c(...)$ such that $\Gamma(e_c) = \mathbb{C}$ and suppressing events $e_s(...)$ such that $\Gamma(e_s) = \mathbb{S}$. Conversely, it types to $\mathbb{S}$ under Γ ("φ is suppressable under Γ") if $\neg\varphi$ can be enforced under the same conditions on Γ. EMFOTL is defined as the set of all φ for which $\exists \Gamma.\ \Gamma \vdash \varphi : \mathbb{C}$. The types $\mathbb{C}$ and $\mathbb{S}$ overload the names of the sets of suppressable and causable event names so that only events $e(...)$ with $e \in \mathbb{C}$ (resp. $e \in \mathbb{S}$) can type to $\mathbb{C}$ (resp. $\mathbb{S}$).

Our technical report [25, Appendix A] gives the complete set of typing rules.

Example 1. Consider the formula $\varphi = \Box(\forall x.\ A(x) \longrightarrow \Diamond_{[0,30]} B(x))$ with $A \in \mathbb{O}$ and $B \in \mathbb{C}$. The formula φ can be shown enforceable using the rules

$$\frac{\vdash \varphi : PG(x)^- \quad \Gamma \vdash \varphi : \mathbb{C}}{\Gamma \vdash \forall x.\ \varphi : \mathbb{C}} \forall^{\mathbb{C}} \quad \frac{\Gamma(e) = \mathbb{C} \quad e \in \mathbb{C}}{\Gamma \vdash e(t_1, ..., t_{a(e)}) : \mathbb{C}} \mathbb{E}^{\mathbb{C}} \quad \frac{}{\vdash e(..., x, ...) : PG(x)^+} \mathbb{E}^+_{PG}$$

$$\frac{\Gamma \vdash \varphi : \mathbb{C}}{\Gamma \vdash \Box \varphi : \mathbb{C}} \Box^{\mathbb{C}} \quad \frac{a < \infty \quad \Gamma \vdash \varphi : \mathbb{C}}{\Gamma \vdash \Diamond_{[0,a]} \varphi : \mathbb{C}} \Diamond^{\mathbb{C}} \quad \frac{\Gamma \vdash \psi : \mathbb{C}}{\Gamma \vdash \varphi \longrightarrow \psi : \mathbb{C}} \longrightarrow^{\mathbb{CR}} \quad \frac{\vdash \varphi : PG(x)^+}{\vdash \varphi \longrightarrow \psi : PG(x)^-} \longrightarrow^-_{PG}$$

as follows:

$$\frac{\dfrac{\dfrac{}{\vdash A(x) : PG(x)^+} \mathbb{E}^+_{PG}}{\vdash A(x) \longrightarrow \Diamond_{[0,30]} B(x) : PG(x)^-} \longrightarrow^-_{PG} \quad \dfrac{\dfrac{30 < \infty \quad \dfrac{B \in \mathbb{C} \quad \dfrac{}{B : \mathbb{C} \vdash B(x) : \mathbb{C}} \mathbb{E}^{\mathbb{C}}}{B : \mathbb{C} \vdash \Diamond_{[0,30]} B(x) : \mathbb{C}} \Diamond^{\mathbb{C}}}{B : \mathbb{C} \vdash A(x) \longrightarrow \Diamond_{[0,30]} B(x) : \mathbb{C}} \longrightarrow^{\mathbb{CR}}}{\dfrac{B : \mathbb{C} \vdash \forall x.\ A(x) \longrightarrow \Diamond_{[0,30]} B(x) : \mathbb{C}}{B : \mathbb{C} \vdash \Box(\forall x.\ A(x) \longrightarrow \Diamond_{[0,30]} B(x)) : \mathbb{C}} \Box^{\mathbb{C}}.} \forall^{\mathbb{C}}$$

Each rule shows how to enforce the corresponding MFOTL operator. The $\forall^{\mathbb{C}}$ rule expresses that to cause $\forall x.\ \varphi$ (i.e., $\Gamma \vdash \forall x.\ \varphi : \mathbb{C}$), it is sufficient to (i) cause φ for any valuation (i.e., $\Gamma \vdash \varphi : \mathbb{C}$) and (ii) ensure that all x's values for which φ must be caused can be computed from the arguments of present or past events (i.e., $\vdash \varphi : PG(x)^-$). Condition (ii), called *past-guardedness*, excludes formulas for which an infinite number of events must be caused. It is checked by other past-guardedness rules that derive sequents $\vdash \varphi : PG(x)^+$ (resp. $\vdash \varphi : PG(x)^-$) that mean "whenever φ is true (resp. false) for some valuation v, then $v(x)$ must be the argument of an event in the trace in the past or present". The $\mathbb{E}^+_{PG}$ rule is the base case, whereas the $\longrightarrow^-_{PG}$ rule states that when φ's satisfactions provide such values for x, then $\varphi \longrightarrow \psi$'s violations also do (since $\neg(\varphi \longrightarrow \psi)$ implies φ). The $\Box^{\mathbb{C}}$, $\longrightarrow^{\mathbb{CR}}$, and $\Diamond^{\mathbb{C}}$ rules show how to enforce the other operators: to cause $\Box \varphi$, one must cause φ (at all times); to cause $\varphi \longrightarrow \psi$, one must cause ψ (when φ is false); to cause $\Diamond_{[0,a]} \varphi$ where $a < \infty$, one must cause φ (in at most b time units).

1 **let** enf $(\sigma, X, ts, D) =$
2   **if** $D \neq$ tick **then**   ▷ R-step
3   **let** $\Phi = \bigwedge_{(\xi,v,+)\in X} \xi(ts)[v] \wedge \bigwedge_{(\xi,v,-)\in X} \neg\xi(ts)[v]$ **in**
4   **let** $(D_C, D_S, X') = \text{enf}^+_{ts,\perp}(\Phi, \sigma \cdot (ts, D \cup \{\text{TP}\}), \emptyset, \emptyset)$ **in**
5        $(\text{RCom}(D_C, D_S), X')$
6   **else**   ▷ P-step
7   **let** $\Phi = \bigwedge_{(\xi,v,+)\in X} \xi(ts)[v] \wedge \bigwedge_{(\xi,v,-)\in X} \neg\xi(ts)[v]$ **in**
8   **let** $(D_C, D_S, X') = \text{enf}^+_{ts,\top}(\Phi, \sigma \cdot (ts, \emptyset), \emptyset, \emptyset)$ **in**
9   **if** $\text{TP} \in D_C$ **then** $(\text{PCom}(D_C \setminus \{\text{TP}\}), X')$ **else** (NoCom, X)

10 **let** $\text{enf}^+_{ts,b}(\varphi, \sigma, X, v) = $ **case** φ **of**
11     $e(\bar{t}) \Rightarrow (\{e([\bar{t}]_v)\}, \emptyset, \emptyset)$
12     $\mid \varphi_1 \longrightarrow^{\text{CR}} \varphi_2 \Rightarrow \text{enf}^+_{ts,b}(\varphi_2, \sigma, X, v)$
13     $\mid \forall^C x. \; \varphi_1 \Rightarrow \text{fp}(\sigma, X, \text{enf}^+_{\text{all}, \varphi_1, v, ts, b})$
14     $\mid \Diamond^C_{[0,a]} \varphi_1 \Rightarrow$
15   **if** $a = 0 \wedge b$ **then**
16           $\text{enf}^+_{ts,b}(\varphi_1, \sigma, X, v)$
17   **else**
18           $(\emptyset, \emptyset, \{(\lambda\tau'. \Diamond_{[0, a-(\tau'-\tau)]}$
19           $(\text{TP} \wedge \varphi_1), v, +)\})$
20     $\mid \Box^C \varphi_1 \Rightarrow$
21        $\text{enf}^+_{ts,b}(\varphi_1, \sigma, X, v) \uplus$
22        $(\emptyset, \emptyset, \{(\lambda\tau'. \Box \varphi_1, v, +)\})$
23     $\ldots$
24 **let** $\text{enf}^-_{ts,b}(\varphi, \sigma, X, v) = \ldots$

25 **let** $(\uplus) (D_C, D_S, X) (D'_C, D'_S, X') =$
26     $(D_C \cup D'_C, D_S \cup D'_S, X \cup X')$
27 **let** $\text{fp}(\sigma \cdot (\tau, D), X, f) =$
28     $(D_C, D_S) \leftarrow (\emptyset, \emptyset); \quad r \leftarrow \text{None}$
29   **while** $(D_C, D_S, X) \neq r$ **do**
30        $r \leftarrow (D_S, D_C, X)$
31        $(D_C, D_S, X) \leftarrow r \uplus$
32           $f(\sigma \cdot (\tau, (D \setminus D_S) \cup D_C), X)$
33   (D_C, D_S, X)
34 **let** $\text{enf}^+_{\text{all}, \varphi_1, v, ts, b}(\sigma, X) =$
35     $r \leftarrow (\emptyset, \emptyset, \emptyset)$
36   **for** $d \in \text{AD}_{\sigma, \mathbb{E}}(\varphi_1)$ **do**
37   **if** $\neg\text{SAT}^*_{\neg\varphi_1}(v[d/x], |\sigma| - 1, \sigma, X)$
38   **then** $r \leftarrow r \uplus$
39           $\text{enf}^+_{ts,b}(\varphi_1, \sigma, X, v[d/x])$
40   r

Fig. 5: Proactive real-time first-order enforcement algorithm [24, Algorithm 2]

The EMFOTL enforcement algorithm [24, Algorithm 2] is shown in Figure 5. Its state is a set $X \subseteq$ fo of *future obligations*. The set fo of future obligations contains all triples (ξ, v, p) where ξ is a function $\mathbb{N} \to \text{EMFOTL}$, v a valuation, and $p \in \{+, -\}$. At every time-point i with timestamp ts, the algorithm enforces $\Phi = \bigwedge_{(\xi,v,+)} \xi(ts)[v] \wedge \bigwedge_{(\xi,v,-)} \neg\xi(ts)[v]$ by causing or suppressing events and updating the future obligations to be enforced at $i + 1$.

The algorithm uses a SAT^* monitor extending SAT (Section 2.3) over finite traces in two ways: (1) SAT^* inputs a set X of obligations assumed to hold after the last time-point. For example, $\text{SAT}^*_{\Box A}(v, 0, (0, \{A\}), \{(\lambda\tau. \Box A, \emptyset, +)\})$ holds: if A holds at time-point 0 and $\Box A$ is assumed to hold at time-point 1, then $\Box A$ holds at time-point 0; and (2) SAT^* always returns a conservative evaluation of the formula when future information is lacking. For example, if A occurs at time-point 0, we can conclude that $\Diamond A$ holds $(\text{SAT}^*_{\Diamond A}(v, 0, (0, \{A\}), \emptyset))$, but not necessarily that $\Box A$ holds $(\neg\text{SAT}^*_{\Box A}(v, 0, (0, \{A\}), \emptyset))$ at time-point 0. A fixpoint computation is used in cases that require recursively enforcing multiple subformulae (e.g., causing $\forall x. \; \varphi$ or $\varphi_1 \wedge \varphi_2$). A special causable event TP denotes the *existence of a time-point*. Such an event is always present in R-steps, where a time-point already exists, but not in P-steps. In P-steps, causation of TP leads to the insertion of a time-point (i.e., a PCom).

Example 2. The algorithm from Figure 5 enforces the formula φ in Example 1 over the trace $\sigma = \langle (0, \{A(1)\}), (50, \{B(2)\}) \rangle$ as follows.

Initially, $ts = 0$, $D = \{A(1)\}$, and we have one future obligation corresponding to φ, namely $\mathsf{fo} = (\lambda\tau.\ \varphi, \emptyset, +)$. The algorithm performs an R-step on the first time-point; the formula to be enforced is $\Phi = \varphi$ (l. 3). Since $\varphi = \Box\psi$ with $\psi = \forall x.\ A(x) \longrightarrow \Diamond_{[0,30]} B(x)$, the algorithm generates the same future obligation fo and proceeds with enforcing ψ (l. 20–22). Next, since $\psi = \forall x.\ \chi$ where $\chi = A(x) \longrightarrow \Diamond_{[0,30]} B(x)$, the algorithm performs a fixpoint computation (l. 13; 27–33). In each iteration of this computation, the algorithm enforces χ under all valuations $\{x \mapsto d\}_{d\in\mathbb{D}}$ for which χ is not yet satisfied (l. 34–40). Here, the only such valuation is $v = \{x \mapsto 1\}$. Since $\chi = A(x) \longrightarrow \chi'$ where $\chi' = \Diamond_{[0,30]} B(x)$ and the rule $\longrightarrow^{\mathrm{CR}}$ was used to type χ in Example 1, the algorithm enforces χ' under v (l. 12). It does so by generating the future obligation $\mathsf{fo}' = (\lambda\tau.\ \Diamond_{[0,30-\tau]}(\mathsf{TP} \wedge B(x)), \{x \mapsto 1\}, +)$ (l. 19). After generating fo and fo', the formula Φ holds and the computation terminates, returning $\mathsf{RCom}(\emptyset, \emptyset)$.

Next, the algorithm performs a P-step with $ts = 0$. The formula to be enforced, computed from fo and fo', is $\Phi = \Box\psi \wedge \Diamond_{[0,30]}(\mathsf{TP} \wedge B(1))$ (l. 7). To satisfy Φ's two conjuncts, the future obligations fo and $\mathsf{fo}'' = (\lambda\tau.\ \Diamond_{[0,30-\tau]}(\mathsf{TP} \wedge B(1)), \emptyset, +)$ are generated. The logic used to enforce $\Box$ and $\Diamond$ is the same as above; the enforcement of $\wedge$ uses a fixpoint computation (omitted in Figure 5). As generating fo and fo' suffices to satisfy Φ, the algorithm returns NoCom.

Since there is no time-point with timestamp 1 in the trace, the enforcer then performs a P-step with $ts = 1$. The formula to be enforced is $\Phi = \Box\psi \wedge \Diamond_{[0,29]}(\mathsf{TP} \wedge B(1))$; note the smaller bound on $\Diamond$ due to the new ts. The algorithm again generates the future obligations $\{\mathsf{fo}, \mathsf{fo}''\}$. Similarly, a P-step is performed for $ts = 2, \ldots, 29$, propagating $\{\mathsf{fo}, \mathsf{fo}''\}$. Each of these P-steps returns NoCom.

When ts reaches 30, the algorithm enforces $\Phi = \Box\psi \wedge \Diamond_{[0,0]}(\mathsf{TP} \wedge B(1))$. Since $\Diamond$'s interval is $[0,0]$, this conjunct can only be enforced by causing $\mathsf{TP} \wedge B(1)$ (l. 16), i.e., causing both TP and $B(1)$. The future obligation fo is also generated. The algorithm returns $\mathsf{PCom}(\{B(1)\})$, inserting a time-point $(30, \{B(1)\})$ in σ.

Beyond this time-point, the trace always satisfies ψ and the set of future obligations is just $\{\mathsf{fo}\}$. Therefore, the trace is not further modified.

3   An Extended Enforceable Fragment of MFOTL

We now describe the semantics, typing rules, and monitoring and enforcement algorithms for our three extensions. All proofs of soundness and transparency are given in our technical report [25, Appendix A].

3.1   Function applications

Assume that every function symbol $f \in \mathbb{F}$ is associated with a (terminating) function $\hat{f} : \mathbb{D}^{a(f)} \to \mathbb{D}$. Our semantics of terms is standard:

$$[\![c]\!]_v = c \qquad [\![x]\!]_v = v(x) \qquad [\![f(t_1, \ldots, t_{a(f)})]\!]_v = \hat{f}([\![t_1]\!]_v, \ldots, [\![t_{a(f)}]\!]_v)$$

Monitorability. To ensure that only finitely many function calls are needed to decide whether a given formula is satisfied, restrictions must be imposed. In contrast to classical monitorability which focuses on *informative prefixes* [29], our definition focuses on ensuring finite evaluation steps of first-order formulae.

Example 3. Given a binary function $\mathsf{eq} \in \mathbb{F}$ such that $\mathsf{eq}(x, y) :=$ **if** $x = y$ **then** 1 **else** 0 used to compare two variables, and some $f \in \mathbb{F}$, consider the formulae

$$\varphi_1 := \forall x, y.\ B(x) \wedge B(y) \wedge \neg(\mathsf{eq}(x, y) \approx 1) \longrightarrow A(f(x, y))$$
$$\varphi_2 := \forall x, y.\ A(f(x, y)) \longrightarrow B(x) \wedge B(y) \wedge \neg(\mathsf{eq}(x, y) \approx 1).$$

The formula φ_1 is monitorable: whenever two B events occur for different values of x and y, the event $A(f(x, y))$ also occurs. In contrast, the formula φ_2 cannot be monitored without further assumptions about f: when some $A(z)$ is true, the set of pairs (x, y) such that $z = f(x, y)$ may be neither finite nor co-finite.

The key difference between the formulae is that, when φ_1 is false, there are always events in the present that contain x and y as parameters. There are finitely many such events, and hence the full set of satisfactions can be obtained by filtering satisfactions of $B(x) \wedge B(y) \wedge \neg(\mathsf{eq}(x, y) \approx 1)$ based on the value of $A(f(x, y))$. In contrast, when φ_2 is false, all values of x and y for which $A(f(x, y))$ is true (or, alternatively, $B(x) \wedge B(y) \wedge \neg(\mathsf{eq}(x, y) \approx 1)$ is false) would need to be checked, but the set of such values may be infinite.

Based on these observations, we adopt the following notion of monitorability:

Definition 4. *A closed MFOTL formula φ is monitorable iff for any of its quantified subformulae $Qx.\ \psi$, where $Q \in \{\forall, \exists\}$, either $\vdash \psi : PG^+(x)$, or $\vdash \psi : PG^-(x)$, or x does not appear inside any function argument in ψ.*

Note that the definition of rule $\mathbb{E}_{PG}^+$ shown in Example 1 is unchanged, i.e., a variable is only past-guarded when it occurs directly as an argument of a predicate, and not within a function application.

Monitoring. We now describe how to extend the PDTs from Section 2.3 to efficiently monitor formulae with function applications. Instead of trees labeled by variable names, we consider trees labeled with elements of the type

$$\mathsf{lbl} = \mathsf{LVar}\ ident \mid \mathsf{LEx}\ ident \mid \mathsf{LAll}\ ident \mid \mathsf{LClos}\ ident\ (term\ \mathsf{list}),$$

containing either free variables (LVar), existentially quantified variables (LEx), universally quantified variables (LAll), or closures with a function name and a list of terms (LClos). An example of an extended PDT is shown in Figure 6a.

We call a PDT *well-formed* with respect to a set of variables V iff:

1. Any $\mathsf{LClos}\ f\ \bar{t}$ node with $z \in \mathsf{fv}(\bar{t}) \cap V$ has an $\mathsf{LEx}\ z$ or $\mathsf{LAll}\ z$ node higher up.

This condition ensures that the value of all terms with free variables in V labeling a node can be computed using the knowledge of the value of variables higher up.

Given a PDT representing satisfactions $\mathrm{SAT}_\varphi(\bullet, i, \sigma)$ well-formed with respect to the set of all variables in φ, a valuation v can be checked as in Figure 6b. In our technical report [25, Appendix A], we extend Lima et al.'s [32] algorithm to use the new PDTs and show that it monitors all formulae covered by Definition 4.

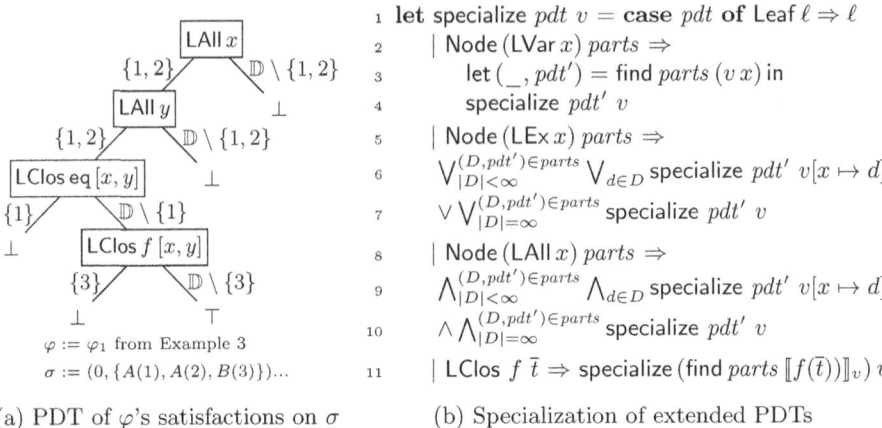

(a) PDT of φ's satisfactions on σ

(b) Specialization of extended PDTs

Fig. 6: Extended PDTs

Example 4. Consider the formula $\varphi_{\mathsf{Grubbs}}$ from Section 1. Let $\varphi'_{\mathsf{Grubbs}} := dc, l \leftarrow$ GRUBBS$(dc, c;)(\mathsf{cntReboots}(dc, c))) \wedge l \approx 1$ and $\varphi''_{\mathsf{Grubbs}} := \varphi'_{\mathsf{Grubbs}} \longrightarrow \mathsf{alert}(\mathsf{msg}(dc))$, where $\mathsf{msg}(dc)$ abbreviates the string term in $\varphi_{\mathsf{Grubbs}}$'s alert event. Note that only variable dc occurs within a function argument. By Definition 4, the formula $\varphi_{\mathsf{Grubbs}}$ is monitorable iff $\forall l.\ \varphi''_{\mathsf{Grubbs}}$ is either PG$^+(dc)$ or PG$^-(dc)$. In Example 7, we will show that $\varphi'_{\mathsf{Grubbs}}$ is PG$^+(dc)$. Using rules $\longrightarrow^-_{\mathrm{PG}}$ and $\forall_{\mathrm{PG}}$ (see (i) below), we show that $\forall l.\ \varphi''_{\mathsf{Grubbs}}$ is also PG$^+(dc)$. Thus, $\varphi_{\mathsf{Grubbs}}$ is monitorable.

Suppose that $\varphi'_{\mathsf{Grubbs}}$ holds for $(dc, l) \in \{(0,1),(1,1)\}$ and $\mathsf{alert}(m)$ holds iff $m = \mathsf{msg}(1)$. Monitoring $\varphi''_{\mathsf{Grubbs}}$, our extended SAT computes the PDT below (ii).

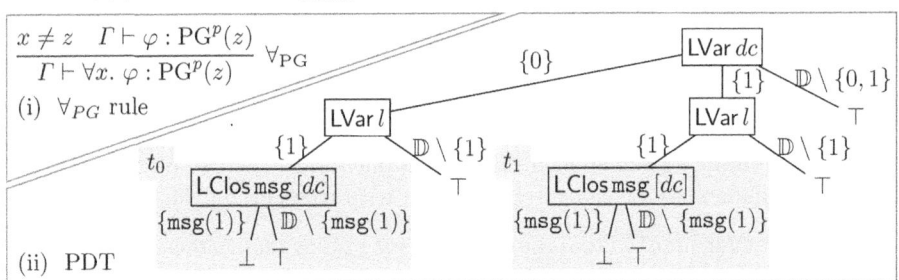

To enumerate the values of dc for which $\varphi''_{\mathsf{Grubbs}}$ is violated, we evaluate the closures. In the subtree marked with t_0, dc is equal to 0. We obtain $\mathsf{msg}(0) \in \mathbb{D} \setminus \{\mathsf{msg}(1)\}$ and t_0 reduces to $\top$. In the subtree marked with t_1, dc is equal to 1 and hence t_1 reduces to $\bot$. The formula is thus violated only for $v = \{dc \mapsto 1, l \mapsto 1\}$.

Enforceability. Our enforcement algorithm (Figure 5) does not terminate in general if functions are naïvely applied. Consider $\Box(\forall x.\ A(x) \longrightarrow A(x+1))$, where A is causable. If $A(i)$ occurs in the present, the algorithm causes $A(i+1)$, then $A(i+2)$, $A(i+3)$, etc. This formula would thus require infinitely many events to be caused once some $A(x)$ occurs. Hence, further restrictions must be introduced to define a fragment of extended EMFOTL that is realistically enforceable.

Key to these restrictions is the notion of a *stable function*:

Definition 5. *Let $\preceq$ be a well-founded relation on $\mathbb{D}$. A function $f : \mathbb{D}^k \to \mathbb{D}$ is $\preceq$-stable iff there exists a finite $C_f \subseteq \mathbb{D}$ such that for any $d_{\mathsf{sup}} \in \mathbb{D}$ and $d_1, \ldots, d_{a(f)} \preceq d_{\mathsf{sup}}$, either $f(d_1, \ldots, d_{a(f)}) \preceq d_{\mathsf{sup}}$ or $f(d_1, \ldots, d_{a(f)}) \in C_f$.*

A $\preceq$-stable function can only produce outputs that are smaller than one of its inputs with respect to some well-founded relation $\preceq$, or are in some finite set C_f. This guarantees that the number of *distinct* domain elements obtainable by repeatedly applying stable functions to an initial, finite set of domain elements is finite. For example, if $\mathbb{D} = \mathbb{N}$, then $f_1 = \lambda x.\ \max(x - 1, 2)$ is $\leq$-stable, but $f_2 = \lambda x.\ x + 1$ is not. Applying f_1 repeatedly to elements in a set $\{d_1, \ldots, d_k\} \subseteq \mathbb{N}$ only produces natural numbers in $\{0, \ldots, \max_{1 \leq i \leq k} d_i\}$ or the natural number 2, while applying f_2 repeatedly to $\{0\}$ reaches all of $\mathbb{N}$.

Formally, for $F \subseteq \mathbb{F}$, $X \subseteq \mathbb{D}$, and $n \geq 0$, define cl^n inductively as follows:

$$\mathsf{cl}^0(F, X) = X \qquad \forall i \geq 0.\ \mathsf{cl}^{i+1}(F, X) = X \cup \bigcup_{f \in F} f((\mathsf{cl}^i(F, X))^{a(f)}).$$

Further, define $\mathsf{cl}(F, X)$ as $\lim_{n \infty} \mathsf{cl}^n(F, X)$. We have:

Lemma 1. $\mathsf{cl}(F, X)$ *is finite for a finite set of stable functions F and a finite X.*

Back to our enforcement setup, if the parameters of all caused events are obtained by applying stable functions to existing domain elements, then only finitely many events may be caused and the enforcement algorithm terminates. In fact, we can be slightly more permissive: causation of events with parameters *not* obtained by applying stable functions is admissible as long as these parameters cannot be further used to derive parameters of caused events. Denoting by $\mathbb{F}_s$ the subset of all stable functions in $\mathbb{F}$, we get our final lemma:

Lemma 2. *Let $\overline{D} \in \mathbb{DB}^\omega$, $k \geq 1$, and disjoint $\mathbb{C}_s, \mathbb{C}_n \subseteq \mathbb{C}$ such that $\forall i \geq 2$,*

$$D_i - D_{i-1} \subseteq \{e(d_1, ..., d_{a(o)}) \mid e \in \mathbb{C} \wedge \forall i \exists f \subset \mathsf{cl}(\mathbb{F}_s, D_{i-1}), \overline{d'} \in \mathsf{AD}_{D_i, \overline{\mathbb{C}_n}}(\varphi)^{a(f)}.\, d_i = \hat{f}(\overline{d'})\}$$

$$\cup \{e(d_1, ..., d_{a(e)}) \mid e \in \mathbb{C}_s \wedge \forall i \exists f \in \mathsf{cl}^k(\mathbb{F}, D_{i-1}), \overline{d'} \in \mathsf{AD}_{D_i, \overline{\mathbb{C}_n}}(\varphi)^{a(f)}.\, d_i = \hat{f}(\overline{d'})\},$$

where $\mathsf{AD}_{D_i, E}(\varphi) := \mathsf{AD}_{\langle(0, D_i)\rangle, E}(\varphi)$, then $\overline{D}$ is eventually constant.

This lemma ensures that if we can (i) partition the set of causable events $\mathbb{C}$ into two sets of *strict causable events* $\mathbb{C}_s$ and *nonstrict causable events* $\mathbb{C}_n$, (ii) ensure that the parameters of existing nonstrict causable events cannot be used to compute the parameters of newly caused events, and (iii) ensure that the parameters of newly caused, strict causable events are obtained from existing domain elements by applying only stable functions, then only finitely many new domain elements can be generated through causation. As a consequence, the enforcement loop $\mathsf{fp}(\sigma, X, \mathsf{enf}^+_{\mathsf{all}, \varphi, v, ts, b})$ in Figure 5 terminates.

To check (i)–(iii), we type event names to elements in $\{\mathbb{C}_n, \mathbb{C}_s, \mathbb{S}_n, \mathbb{S}_s\}$, rather than just $\{\mathbb{C}, \mathbb{S}\}$, and store additional typing judgments $x : \mathsf{PG}^+_E$ if the current value of x is the parameter of some event $e \in E$ in the past or present. The type lattice is modified as shown in Figure 7, with solid lines representing $\sqsubseteq$ (oriented bottom-up) and dotted lines representing an operator $\neg$ that exchanges causability and suppressability. We then replace the rules $\forall^{\mathbb{C}}$ from Example 1 by the rules in Figure 8, where $\mathbb{C}_\alpha$ matches $\mathbb{C}_s$ or $\mathbb{C}_n$ and $\mathsf{fn}(\varphi)$ denotes the set of all functions symbols in φ. All PG rules are updated with the subscript E.

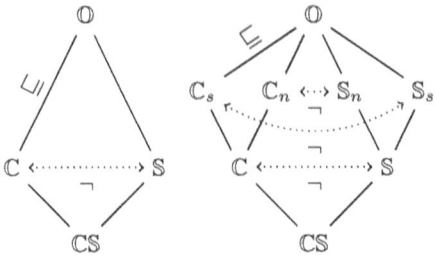

Fig. 7: Hublet et al.'s type lattice [24] (left) and our extended type lattice (right)

$$\frac{\Gamma \vdash \varphi : \tau' \quad \tau \sqsubseteq \tau'}{\Gamma \vdash \varphi : \tau} \; \text{cast} \qquad \frac{\Gamma, x : \text{PG}_E^+ \vdash \varphi : \mathbb{C}_\alpha \quad \vdash \varphi : \text{PG}_E^-(x)}{\Gamma \vdash \forall x. \, \varphi : \mathbb{C}_\alpha} \forall^{\mathbb{C}} \qquad \frac{\bar{t}_i = x}{\vdash e(\bar{t}) : \text{PG}_{\{e\}}^+(x)} \mathbb{E}_{\text{PG}}^+$$

$$\frac{\Gamma \vdash \varphi : \mathbb{C}_\alpha}{\Gamma \vdash \Box \varphi : \mathbb{C}_\alpha} \Box^{\mathbb{C}} \qquad \frac{a < \infty \quad \Gamma \vdash \varphi : \mathbb{C}_\alpha}{\Gamma \vdash \Diamond_{[0,a]} \varphi : \mathbb{C}_\alpha} \Diamond^{\mathbb{C}} \qquad \frac{\Gamma \vdash \psi : \mathbb{C}_\alpha}{\Gamma \vdash \varphi \longrightarrow \psi : \mathbb{C}_\alpha} \longrightarrow^{\text{CR}} \qquad \frac{\vdash \varphi : \text{PG}_E^+(x)}{\vdash \varphi \longrightarrow \psi : \text{PG}_E^-(x)} \longrightarrow_{\text{PG}}^-$$

$$\frac{e \in \mathbb{C} \quad \Gamma(e) = \mathbb{C}_\alpha \quad \forall x \in \bigcup_{i=1}^k \text{fv}(t_i). \, \exists E \subseteq \Gamma^{-1}(\overline{\mathbb{C}_n}). \, \Gamma(x) = \text{PG}_E^+ \quad \bigcup_{i=1}^k \text{fn}(t_i) \subseteq \mathbb{F}_s}{\Gamma \vdash e(t_1, ..., t_k) : \Gamma(e)} \mathbb{E}^{\mathbb{C}_\alpha}$$

$$\frac{e \in \mathbb{C} \quad \Gamma(e) = \mathbb{C}_n \quad \forall x \in \bigcup_{i=1}^k \text{fv}(t_i). \, \exists E \subseteq \Gamma^{-1}(\overline{\mathbb{C}_n}). \, \Gamma(x) = \text{PG}_E^+}{\Gamma \vdash e(t_1, ..., t_k) : \mathbb{C}_n} \mathbb{E}^{\mathbb{C}_n}$$

Fig. 8: Selected modified typing rules for function applications (cf. Example 1)

Example 5. In φ_{Grubbs}, the concatenation function ($\hat{\ }$) within the term in alert is not stable. However, φ_{Grubbs} is still enforceable by causing alert(msg(dc)) whenever φ'_{Grubbs} holds. In our type system, this is reflected by the fact that if alert types to $\mathbb{C}_n$ in Γ, the $\mathbb{E}^{\mathbb{C}_n}$ rule can be applied to derive $\Gamma \vdash$ alert(msg(dc)) : $\mathbb{C}_n$. This rule accepts non-stable functions such as ($\hat{\ }$) in the argument of alert. However, it still requires some non-$\mathbb{C}_n$ event to guard the variable dc in the argument. The non-causable reboot event provides such a guard, as we show in Example 7.

In contrast, a formula such as $\Box(\forall x. \, \text{alert}(x) \longrightarrow \text{alert}(x \,\hat{\ }\, x))$ cannot be typed to $\mathbb{C}$ by causing alert($x \,\hat{\ }\, x$): using alert as a guard for x precludes alert : $\mathbb{C}_n$, but alert : $\mathbb{C}_n$ would be required to cause the right-hand side as it contains ($\hat{\ }$).

Enforcement. With the additional restrictions that we just introduced and our extended monitor, the enforcement algorithm proposed by Hublet et al. [24, Algorithm 2] can be reused when function applications are introduced. The modified termination and correctness proofs rely on Lemma 2 [25, Appendix A].

3.2   Aggregations

Assume that every aggregation operator $\omega \in \Omega$ is associated with a (terminating) function $\hat{\omega} : (\mathbb{D}^{a(\omega)_1})^* \to (\mathbb{D}^{a(\omega)_2})^*$ that maps a multiset of $a(\omega)_1$-tuples into a multiset of $a(\omega)_2$-tuples. Our semantics of MFOTL aggregations is as follows:

$$v, i \vDash_\sigma \bar{x} \leftarrow \omega(\bar{t}; \bar{y}) \, \varphi \text{ iff } v(\bar{x}) \in \omega(M) \text{ where } \bar{z} = \text{fv}(\varphi) \setminus \bar{y} \text{ and}$$

$$M = \left[[\![t]\!]_{v[\bar{z} \mapsto \bar{d}]} \mid v[\bar{z} \mapsto \bar{d}], i \vDash_\sigma \varphi, \bar{d} \in \mathbb{D}^{|\bar{z}|} \right] \text{ and } |\bar{y}| > 0 \text{ implies } M \neq [\,],$$

where $v(\overline{x}) := (v(x_1), \ldots, v(x_{|x|}))$ and $[\![t]\!]_v := ([\![t_1]\!]_v, \ldots, [\![t_{|t|}]\!]_v)$. Note the last condition, which specifies that when there is at least one group variable, the aggregation is only satisfied when at least one valuation satisfies φ. A similar approach is followed in most SQL implementations: aggregation over an empty set without grouping returns a default value (such as 0 for sums), whereas aggregation over an empty set with grouping returns an empty result set. Our definition of aggregation generalizes over that of past monitoring tools [8] by supporting operators that return tuples, rather than a single value. Various algorithms (e.g., clustering algorithms) can thus be implemented as aggregation operators.

Monitorability. Monitoring an aggregation $\overline{x} \leftarrow \omega(\overline{t}; \overline{y}) \; \varphi$, where t is a sequence of terms that may contain function applications, requires that the above set M is finite. Hence, there must exist only finitely many valuations of $\overline{z} := \mathsf{fv}(\varphi) \setminus \overline{y}$ satisfying φ. We modify Definition 4 accordingly.

Definition 6. *An MFOTL formula φ is monitorable iff the condition in Definition 4 holds, and, additionally, for any subformula $\overline{x} \leftarrow \omega(\overline{t}; \overline{y}) \; \psi$ of φ, we have $\vdash \psi : PG^+(z)$ for all variables $z \in \mathsf{fv}(\psi) \setminus \overline{y}$.*

Monitoring. We now show how to transform a PDT of φ into a PDT of $\overline{x} \leftarrow \omega(\overline{t}; \overline{y}) \; \varphi$, imposing the following additional constraint on the PDT of φ:

2. All LVar y nodes with y in $\overline{y}$ appear above all LVar y' nodes with $y' \in \mathsf{fv}(\varphi) \setminus \overline{y}$.

This condition allows collecting values to be placed in the PDT *below* all nodes labeled with the group variables. Our algorithm (Figure 9) inputs $\overline{x}$, $\overline{t}$, and $\overline{y}$, a PDT *pdt* for φ, and a list $\overline{z}$ containing a linearization of the set $\overline{x} \cup \overline{y}$. The variable appearing in nodes of *pdt* are assumed to form, top-down, a subsequence of $\overline{z}$.

The algorithm proceeds in three steps, exemplified in Figure 10. First, the original PDT with Boolean leaves is transformed into a PDT with nodes in $\{\mathsf{LVar}\; y \mid y \in \overline{y}\}$ and leaves containing the multiset M. This is done using the gather function (l. 7–18) that uses standard concat : list list $a \to$ list a and map : $(a \to b) \to$ list $a \to$ list b functions as well as a function applyn that provides an analogue of apply2 for lists of PDTs. The function traverses the tree top-down, collecting constraints on the value of different variables and terms in a list sv. At the leaves, that list is converted into a list of satisfactions vs that are then used to compute all possible evaluations of $\overline{t}$. In a second step, the aggregation operator ω is applied at the leaves using apply to obtain a PDT with leaves carrying $\omega(M)$. The function agg (l. 19) wraps ω to map any empty multiset to None when $|\overline{y}| > 0$. Third and finally, this PDT is transformed into a Boolean PDT, inserting the new variables $\overline{x}$ at their correct position in $\overline{z}$ using insert (l. 20–29), which relies on a function all_leaves [25, Appendix A] that gathers all elements stored in the leaves of a PDT. Being able to insert the $\overline{x}$ at any position is important, since the monitoring algorithm requires free variables in a PDT to be ordered according to their De Bruijn indices in the overall formula. We show:

Lemma 3. *Let $\overline{x} \leftarrow \omega(\overline{t}; \overline{y}) \; \varphi$ be monitorable and $\overline{z} = \mathsf{fv}(\varphi) \setminus \overline{y}$. Let pdt be well-formed with respect to the bound variables in φ. Further assume that condition 2. above holds for pdt and that pdt stores $\mathrm{SAT}_\varphi(\bullet, i, \sigma)$. Then aggregate $\overline{x} \; \overline{t} \; \overline{y} \; \overline{z} \; pdt$ stores $\mathrm{SAT}_{\overline{x} \leftarrow \omega(\overline{t}; \overline{y}) \; \varphi}(\bullet, i, \sigma)$.*

1 **let** distribute $f\,x\,(D, pdt) =$ **if** $|D| < \infty$ **then** $[(\{d\}, f\,d\,pdt) \mid d \in D]$ **else** $[(D, x)]$

2 **let** tabulate $\bar{t}\,sv\,vs =$ **case** sv **of** $[\,] \Rightarrow [\![t]\!]_v \mid v \in vs]$

3     $\mid (x, D) :: sv'$ **where** $x \in \mathbb{V} \Rightarrow$ tabulate $\bar{t}\,sv'\,[v[x \mapsto d] \mid d \in D, v \in vs]$

4     $\mid (t, D) :: sv' \Rightarrow$ tabulate $\bar{t}\,sv'\,[v \mid v \in vs, [\![t]\!]_v \in D]$

5 **let** gather $sv\,\bar{t}\,\bar{y}\,pdt =$ **let** $f\,t\,(D, pdt) = (D, \text{gather}\,(sv \cdot (t, D))\,t\,\bar{y}\,pdt)$ **in**

6   **case** pdt **of** Leaf $\ell \Rightarrow$ **if** $\ell = \top$ **then** Leaf (tabulate $\bar{t}\,sv\,[\emptyset]$) **else** Leaf $[\,]$

7     $\mid$ Node (LVar x) $parts \Rightarrow$ **if** $x \notin \bar{y}$ **then** applyn $(\cup)$ (map $(f\,x)\,parts$) **else**

8   **let** $g\,d\,pdt = $ gather $\{v[x \mapsto d] \mid v \in vs\}\,\bar{t}\,\bar{y}\,pdt$ **in**

9   Node (LVar v) (concat (map (distribute $g\,[\,]$) $parts$))

10    $\mid$ Node (LEx x) $parts \Rightarrow$ applyn $(\cup)$ (map $(f\,x)\,parts$)

11    $\mid$ Node (LAll x) $parts \Rightarrow$ applyn $(\cap)$ (map $(f\,x)\,parts$)

12    $\mid$ Node (LClos $h\,\bar{t}\,\_$) $parts \Rightarrow$ applyn $(\cup)$ (map $(h(\bar{t}))\,parts$)

13 **let** agg $\bar{y}\,\omega\,M =$ **if** $|\bar{y}| > 0 \wedge M = [\,]$ **then** None **else** $\omega\,M$

14 **let** insert $v\,\bar{x}\,\bar{z}\,pdt =$ **case** $\bar{z}, pdt$ **of**

15    $x :: \bar{z}',\_$ **where** $x \in \bar{x} \Rightarrow$ **let** $D = $ map $(\lambda v.\,v\,x)$ (all_leaves pdt) **in**

16   **if** $D = [\,]$ **then** Leaf $\bot$

17   **else** Node (LVar y, distribute $(\lambda d\,pdt.\,\text{insert}\,v[x \mapsto d]\,\bar{x}\,\bar{z}'\,pdt)\,\bot\,(D, pdt))$

18    $\mid y :: \bar{z}',$ Node (LVar $y', parts$) **where** $y = y' \Rightarrow$

19   Node (LVar y', map $(\lambda(D, pdt).\,(D, \text{insert}\,x\,\bar{z}\,pdt)))\,parts$

20    $\mid \_ :: \bar{z}',$ Node $\_ \Rightarrow$ insert $v\,\bar{x}\,\bar{z}'\,pdt$

21    $\mid \_,$ Leaf (Some vs) $\Rightarrow$ **if** $\exists v' \in vs.\,\forall x \in $ dom $v.\,v\,x = v'\,x$ **then** $\top$ **else** $\bot$

22    $\mid \_,$ Leaf None $\Rightarrow \bot$

23 **let** aggregate $\omega\,\bar{x}\,\bar{t}\,\bar{y}\,\bar{z}\,pdt =$ insert $\emptyset\,\bar{x}\,\bar{z}$ (apply (agg $\bar{y}\,\omega$) (gather $[\,]\,\bar{t}\,\bar{y}\,pdt$))

Fig. 9: Computing aggregations in PDTs

Example 6. In φ_{Grubbs}, let cntReboots hold for $(dc, c) \in \{(0, 2), (1, 2), (2, 5), (3, 7)\}$. Assume that the GRUBBS function maps data centers 0 and 1 to cluster $l = 0$ and data centers 2 and 3 (as outliers) to $l = 1$. Our algorithm (Figure 9) computes:

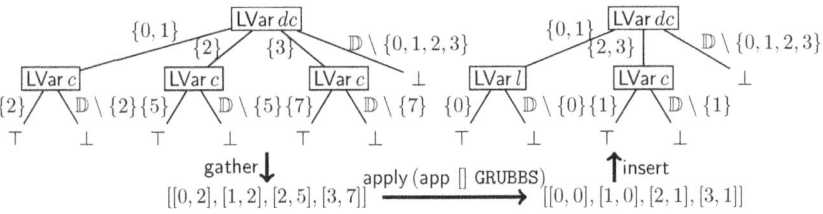

Note that the intermediate PDTs are just leaves as there is no grouping variable.

Enforceability. Aggregations are generally not causable. Formula $\bar{x} \leftarrow \omega(\bar{t}; \bar{y})\,\varphi$ is suppressable iff $\bar{y}$ is non-empty and $\exists z_1, \ldots, z_k.\,\varphi$ is suppressable, where $\bar{z} = \text{fv}(\varphi) \setminus \bar{y}$ (rule agg$^\mathbb{S}$ in Figure 11). Aggregations can provide past-guardedness in two ways: $\bar{x} \leftarrow \omega(\bar{t}; \bar{y})\,\varphi$ types to PG$^p(v)$ iff either (a) $v \in \bar{x}$, $p = +$, all free variables of $\bar{t}$ are past-guarded in φ, and the events used to guard these free variables are not used for causation in Γ (rule agg$_{\text{PG},\bar{x}}$) or (b) $v \in \bar{y}$ and v is past-guarded in f (rule agg$_{\text{PG},\bar{y}}$). The last condition in (a) means that Γ is now relevant for past-guardedness; it excludes non-enforceable formulae (e.g., $\forall x.\,x \leftarrow$

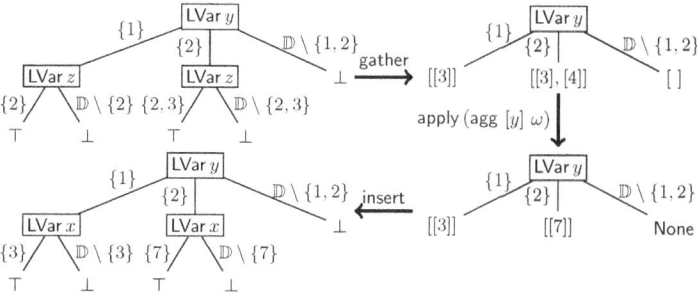

Fig. 10: Formula $x \leftarrow \mathrm{SUM}(z+1; y)\ A(y,z)$ with $D = \{A(1,2), A(2,2), A(2,3)\}$

$$\frac{\forall z \in \mathsf{fv}(\varphi) \setminus \overline{y}. \vdash \varphi : \mathrm{PG}(z)^{+}_{E_z} \quad \Gamma, \forall z.\ z : \mathrm{PG}^{+}_{E_z} \vdash \varphi : \mathbb{S}_{\alpha} \quad |\overline{y}| > 0}{\Gamma \vdash \overline{x} \leftarrow \omega(\overline{t}; \overline{y})\ \varphi : \mathbb{S}_{\alpha}}\ \mathrm{agg}^{\mathbb{S}}$$

$$\frac{v \in \overline{x} \quad \forall u \in \mathsf{fv}(\overline{t}).\ \exists E_u \subseteq \Gamma^{-1}(\overline{\mathbb{C}}).\ \Gamma \vdash \varphi : \mathrm{PG}^{+}_{E_u}(u)}{\Gamma \vdash \overline{x} \leftarrow \omega(\overline{t}; \overline{y})\ \varphi : \mathrm{PG}^{+}_{\bigcup_{u \in \mathsf{fv}(\overline{t})} E_u}}\ \mathrm{agg}_{\mathrm{PG},\overline{x}}$$

$$\frac{v \in \overline{y} \quad \Gamma \vdash \varphi : \mathrm{PG}^{p}_{E}(v)}{\Gamma \vdash \overline{x} \leftarrow \omega(\overline{t}; \overline{y})\ \varphi : \mathrm{PG}^{p}_{E}(v)}\ \mathrm{agg}_{\mathrm{PG},\overline{y}}$$

Fig. 11: Additional typing rules for aggregations

$\mathrm{SUM}(y;)A(y) \longrightarrow A(x))$. Other past-guardedness rules have the same Γ on the LHS of all of their sequents. The rules in Figure 11 are sound [25, Appendix A].

Enforcement. To support the suppression of aggregations as given by rule $\mathrm{agg}^{\mathbb{S}}$ above, an additional case is added to the function enf^{-}:

$$\mid \overline{x} \leftarrow \omega(\overline{t}; \overline{y})\ \varphi_1 \ \Rightarrow\ \mathsf{enf}^{!}_{ts,b}(\neg(\exists z_1, \ldots, z_k.\ \varphi_1), \sigma, X, v).$$

3.3   let bindings

We adopt the semantics of let bindings introduced by Zingg et al. [44]:

$$v, i \vDash_{\sigma} \mathsf{let}\ e(\overline{x}) = \varphi\ \mathsf{in}\ \psi \qquad \text{iff}\quad v, i \vDash_{\sigma[e \Rightarrow (\lambda i. \{\overline{d} \in \mathbb{D}^{|\overline{x}|} \mid v[\overline{x} \mapsto \overline{d}], i \vDash \varphi\})]}\ \psi.$$

where $\sigma[e \Rightarrow R]$ denotes the trace obtained from σ by adding, at each time-point i, all events $e(\overline{d})$ such that $\overline{d} \in R(i)$. With this semantics, let bindings can be soundly unrolled by substituting every occurrence of $e(\overline{t})$ in ψ with $\varphi[\overline{x} \mapsto \overline{t}]$. The enforcement algorithm requires no extension if unrolling is performed prior to typing and enforcement. In fact, with memoization (Section 4) such unrolling should not lead to any significant runtime overhead.

When applied naïvely after unrolling, type inference for the enforcement type system becomes prohibitively slow. To avoid this issue, we introduce the typing rules in Figure 12, proved sound in [25, Appendix A] . The rule let allows φ_1's enforceability type to be reused in φ_2. Additionally, it extends Γ with judgments of the form $\mathsf{let}_e : \bot$ and $\mathsf{let}_{e,i,p} : E$ denoting the existence of a let-bound predicate e and past-guardedness of e's ith argument, respectively. The $\mathsf{let}_{\mathrm{PG}}$ rule extracts past-guardedness information for let-bound predicates from Γ.

$$\frac{\mathsf{let}_e \in \mathsf{dom}\,\Gamma \quad \Gamma(\mathsf{let}_{e,i,p}) = E \quad \bar{t}_i = x}{\Gamma \vdash e(\bar{t}) : \mathrm{PG}_E^p(x)} \; \mathsf{let}_{\mathrm{PG}}$$

$$\frac{\Gamma \vdash \varphi_1 : \tau_1 \quad \Gamma \cup \{\mathsf{let}_{e,i,p} : E \mid \Gamma \vdash \varphi_1 : \mathrm{PG}_E^p(x_i)\}, \mathsf{let}_e : \bot, e : \tau_1 \vdash \varphi_2 : \tau_2}{\Gamma \vdash \mathsf{let}\,e(x_1,\ldots,x_k) = \varphi_1 \,\mathsf{in}\, \varphi_2 : \tau_2} \; \mathsf{let}$$

Fig. 12: Additional typing rules for let bindings

Our report [25, Appendix B] gives the full typing of the formula in Section 1.

Example 7. Rule $\mathsf{agg}_{\mathrm{PG},\overline{x}}$ proves that dc is past-guarded by cntReboots in $\varphi''_{\mathsf{Grubbs}}$ if cntReboots is not in $\mathbb{C}$. It also proves that dc is past-guarded by badReboot in $c \leftarrow \mathtt{CNT}(i; dc)(\blacklozenge_{[0,1800)}(\mathsf{badReboot}(s, dc) \land \mathsf{tp}(i)))$ if badReboot is not in $\mathbb{C}$. Note that dc is past-guarded by reboot in $\mathsf{reboot}(s, dc) \land \neg\,\blacklozenge(\neg\mathsf{reboot}(s, dc) \,\mathsf{S}\,$ $\mathsf{intendReboot}(s, dc))$. We can then use let, $\mathsf{let}_{\mathrm{PG}}$, and the past-guardedness facts established above to show that dc is past-guarded by reboot in $\varphi''_{\mathsf{Grubbs}}$.

Theorem 1. *Let φ be a closed EMFOTL formula with function applications, aggregations, and let bindings. Let enf' be the extended enf function. Denote $\mathsf{unroll}(\varphi)$ the formula obtained by unrolling let in φ. Then the enforcer $\mathcal{E}_\varphi = (\mathcal{P}(\mathsf{fo}), \{(\mathsf{unroll}(\varphi), \emptyset, +)\}, \mathsf{enf}')$ is sound with respect to $\mathcal{L}(\varphi)$.*

We also prove $\mathcal{E}_\varphi$'s transparency for a fragment of EMFOTL [25, Appendix A].

4   Implementation and Optimizations

We have implemented our extensions in an open-source tool, called ENFGUARD (available at [26]), consisting of about 11,000 lines of OCaml code. To ease code reuse, all MFOTL-related function are packaged into a separate library.

ENFGUARD support two types of functions: built-in functions, such as arithmetic operations, and user-defined functions. In addition to SQL-style aggregations, ENFGUARD also supports user-defined aggregations. User-defined functions and aggregations are provided by the user in a Python file. The user must specify each function's signature and whether it is stable, and ensure that it terminates. The enforcer calls Python functions via the `pyml` bindings during monitoring. Support for Python functions makes ENFGUARD more easily extendable.

ENFGUARD's implementation includes three main optimizations:

Associative and commutative (AC) rewriting. Multiple binary conjunctions and disjunctions are replaced by n-ary ones and standard AC-rewriting is applied before enforcement starts. When enforcing an n-ary operator, the enforcement algorithm is called only once on each conjunct or disjunct inside the fixpoint computation, which exponentially reduces the number of calls in the best case.

Memoization. When the trace changes due to causation or suppression, a naïve algorithm drops the previously computed truth values and recomputes new ones. Given φ, we compute the set of *relevant event names* $\mathsf{RE}(\varphi)$ and *relevant future obligations* $\mathsf{RFO}(\varphi)$ that can affect the truth value of φ under assumptions [25, Appendix C]. When enforcement causes new events D^+ or future obligations O, we compute the sets $\{e \mid e(\bar{v}) \in D^+\} \cap \mathsf{RE}(\varphi)$ and $O \cap \mathsf{RFO}(\varphi)$ first. If both are empty, the previous verdict is still valid and can be returned.

Subformulae skipping. Our algorithm does not evaluate subformulae known to be true whenever certain event names do not presently exist. For every subformula φ, we precompute the *present filter* $f_\varphi := \mathfrak{F}_\top(\varphi)$ such that

$$\mathfrak{F}_b(\top) = \lambda D.\ b \qquad\qquad \mathfrak{F}_\top(e(\bar{t})) = \lambda D.\ \exists \bar{t}.\ e(\bar{t}) \in D$$
$$\mathfrak{F}_b(\neg\varphi) = \mathfrak{F}_{\neg b}(\varphi) \qquad \mathfrak{F}_\top(\varphi \wedge \psi) = \lambda D.\ \mathfrak{F}_\top(\varphi)(D) \wedge \mathfrak{F}_\top(\psi)(D)$$
$$\mathfrak{F}_b(\exists x.\ \varphi) = \mathfrak{F}_b(\varphi) \qquad \mathfrak{F}_\perp(\varphi \wedge \psi) = \lambda D.\ \mathfrak{F}_\perp(\varphi)(D) \vee \mathfrak{F}_\perp(\psi)(D)$$
$$\mathfrak{F}_b(\varphi) = \lambda D.\ \top \quad \text{for any } \varphi = \bullet_I \psi, \bigcirc_I \psi, \psi_1 \cup_I \psi_2, \psi_1 \mathsf{S}_I \psi_2.$$

Whenever $f_\varphi(D)$ evaluates to false on the current database, we immediately return without causing or suppressing any events.

5 Evaluation

Our evaluation of ENFGUARD answers the following research questions:
RQ1. Can ENFGUARD's EMFOTL fragment formalize real-world policies?
RQ2. At what event rates can ENFGUARD perform real-time enforcement?
RQ3. Does ENFGUARD's performance improve upon the state-of-the-art?

To evaluate ENFGUARD, we introduce what is, to the best of our knowledge, the largest set of runtime enforcement benchmarks to date. We first present these benchmarks (Section 5.1) and then report on our results (Section 5.2).

5.1 Benchmarks and evaluation setup

We use six benchmarks, each of which pairs a set of policies and a set of logs:
GDPR: 6 formulae encoding privacy policies and a log of a job application system produced over a period of a year [3,24].
GPDR^{FUN}: Variants of the six GDPR formulae that use custom Python functions to store and look up data ownership and consent, with the same log.
NOKIA: 11 formulae encoding data usage policies of a distributed system used in Nokia's mobile data collection campaign [6] and a log of this system [28] spanning one day. The system's original event rate was about 100 events/s.
IC: 8 formulae encoding various policies of a large Web3 distributed platform [42] and 3 platform execution logs [5] having 100–150 events/s.
AGG: 6 fraud detection formulae [7] using aggregations and 2 synthetic logs.
CLUSTER: 2 outlier detection formulae using aggregation operators implemented in Python and 3 synthetic logs.

Figure 13 shows benchmark statistics. For each benchmark, we report the number of formulae and logs, the maximal formula size (defined as its number of operators without unrolling let), the maximal log size (defined as its number of events), and the maximum log event rate (defined as the average number of events per second of real-time execution). We also indicate whether the formulae use let bindings (Let), aggregations (Agg.), and function applications (Fun.), possibly defined in Python (🐍). Our report [25, Appendix D] lists all formulae used.

In this evaluation, we compare ENFGUARD to three tools: ENFPOLY [23] and WHYENF [24], the only existing MFOTL enforcement tools, and MONPOLY [8],

Name	Source	Real	#logs	max |log|	max er	max $\|\varphi\|$	let bindings	Aggreg.	Functions	#formulae	EnfGuard	WhyEnf	EnfPoly	MonPoly
GDPR	[3,24]	✓	1	5,631	10^{-4}	72				6	6	6	2	6
GPDR^{FUN}	[3,24]	✓	1	5,631	10^{-4}	108		✦		6	6			
NOKIA	[28,6]	✓	1	9,458,824	109	44			✓	11	11	11	5	11
IC	[5]	✓	3	634,789	147	179	✓		✓	8	8			8
AGG	[7]		2	100,000		34		✓	✓	6	6			6
CLUSTER	new		1	5,000		42	✓	✦	✓	2	2			

Log statistics (left) · Formulae statistics (middle) · Tool support (right)

Total: 39 · 39 · 17 · 7 · 31
Rewriting required: no · no · yes · yes

Fig. 13: Benchmarks' logs (left), formulae (middle), and tool support (right)

a state-of-the-art MFOTL monitor with aggregations [7], let bindings [44], and built-in functions. As monitoring is a simpler task than enforcement, MonPoly's performance is intended to suggest the likely 'best achievable' results for comparable expressivity, rather than a standard to achieve. All measurements are performed on an AMD Ryzen™ 5 5600X (6 cores) with 16 GB RAM.

5.2   Results

We now present the results of our experiments and answer the research questions.

RQ1: Expressiveness. Figure 13 (right) shows the number of policies each tool supports across all benchmarks. EnfGuard supports all 39 policies, whereas MonPoly supports 31 formulae (all except those containing user-defined constructs), but requires manual rewriting of formulae into its monitorable fragment. WhyEnf and EnfPoly support just 17 and 7 policies, respectively. Both tools cannot enforce formulae with function applications, aggregations, or let bindings. Without let, formulae can become much larger (up to 20 times in practical examples [5]) and difficult to read and maintain. Aggregations strictly increase the policy language's expressiveness [20]: some requirements [5,7] cannot be expressed without them. EnfPoly is additionally restricted to past-only policies.

RQ2: Maximum event rate. Figure 14 shows each tool's average latency ($\text{avg}_\ell(a)$, in ms), maximum latency ($\text{max}_\ell(a)$, in ms) and average event rate avg_{er} for the largest trace acceleration $a \in \{2^0, \ldots, 2^9\}$ such that $\text{max}_\ell(a) \leq \frac{1}{a}$. A trace acceleration is the ratio between the speed that a trace is provided to the enforcer and the trace's real-time behavior (captured by its timestamps). The inequality captures that latency is smaller than the interval between two timestamps in the accelerated trace, i.e., that a tool can process the trace in real time. We report averages over 5 repetitions of each benchmark's largest log.

Except for one formula in IC, EnfGuard can enforce all policies in real time, with event rates ranging from 20–200 events/s when frequent aggregation and causation is involved (AGG, CLUSTER, some of IC) to over 1,000–14,000 events/s in contexts when few commands are emitted and policies are simpler (GDPR, NOKIA). Our experiments show maximum latency values below 20 ms in most cases, and below 100 ms in all but 4 benchmarks using commodity hardware.

	Policy φ	$|\varphi|$	ENFGUARD				WHYENF				ENFPOLY				MONPOLY			
			a	avg$_{er}$	avg$_\ell$	max$_\ell$	a	avg$_{er}$	avg$_\ell$	max$_\ell$	a	avg$_{er}$	avg$_\ell$	max$_\ell$	a	avg$_{er}$	avg$_\ell$	max$_\ell$
GDPR	consent	22	12.8e6	1619	.39	2	.8e6	101	7.6	30	51.2e6	6480	.17	1	51.2e6	6934	.20	1
	deletion	14	25.6e6	3238	.28	2	25.6e6	3238	.20	1					51.2e6	6934	.20	1
	gdpr	72	6.4e6	810	.87	3	.2e6	25	33	110					25.6e6	3465	.13	1
	information	16	12.8e6	1619	.33	2	6.4e6	810	1.1	5.2					51.2e6	6934	.15	1
	lawfulness	17	12.8e6	1619	.35	2	6.4e6	810	1.3	4.4	51.2e6	6480	.17	1	51.2e6	6934	.15	1
	sharing	19	12.8e6	1619	.32	2	3.2e6	405	3.0	15					51.2e6	6934	.20	1
NOKIA	del-1-2	37	32	3503	5	19	not real-time								128	14035	.21	5
	del-2-3	20	128	14013	.58	6	256	28026	.26	2					512	56139	.17	1
	del-3-2	20	128	14013	.55	6	512	56052	.26	2					512	56139	.17	1
	delete	10	128	14013	.54	5	256	28026	.25	2	512	56052	.16	1	512	56138	.17	1
	ins-1-2	25	64	7007	1.1	11	error†								not real-time			
	ins-2-3	20	32	3053	1.5	23	error†								32	3509	2.8	19
	ins-3-2	20	32	3503	5.9	29	256	28026	.28	2					256	28069	.40	3
	insert	10	128	14013	.65	7	256	28026	.26	2	512	56052	.22	2	512	56139	.21	1
	script1	44	128	14013	.64	6	256	28026	.28	2	512	56052	.19	1	512	56139	.24	1
	select	13	128	14013	.54	5	256	28026	.25	2	512	56052	.16	1	512	56139	.16	1
	update	8	128	14013	.53	6	256	28026	.24	2	512	56052	.16	1	512	56139	.16	1

	Policy φ	$|\varphi|$	ENFGUARD				MONPOLY			
			a	avg$_{er}$	avg$_\ell$	max$_\ell$	a	avg$_{er}$	avg$_\ell$	max$_\ell$
IC	validation	166	128	3744	.26	5	256	7489	.36	4
	clean_logs	48	2	59	2.7	281	128	3744	.14	3
	finalization	58	not real-time				128	3744	.14	3
	divergence	50	128	3744	.23	3	128	3744	.19	3
	height	162	128	3744	.24	3	not real-time			
	logging	179	64	1872	.23	10	2	59	.25	381
	reboot	79	2	59	2.4	276	128	3744	.16	3
	unauthorized	64	128	3744	.23	3	2	59	3.0	300
AGG	p1	21	64	640	5.1	9.4	512	5120	.16	1
	p2	22	32	320	13	27	512	5120	.33	1
	p3	27	8	80	44	102	512	5120	.39	1
	p4	31	2	20	54	392	512	5120	.48	1
	p5	32	64	640	6.3	11	512	5120	.25	1
	p6	34	64	640	6.8	12	512	5120	.31	1

	Policy φ	$|\varphi|$	ENFGUARD			
			a	avg$_{er}$	avg$_\ell$	max$_\ell$
GDPR^{FUN}	fconsent	25	12.8e6	1619	.30	2
	fmanagement	22	25.6e6	1619	.31	2
	fdeletion	17	25.6e6	3238	.30	2
	fgdpr	108	6.4e6	3238	.93	4
	finformation	23	12.8e6	1619	.44	3
	fsharing	20	12.8e6	1619	.32	2
CL	dbscan	42	32	160	17	31
	grubbs	42	32	160	14	32

† The tool returns incorrect results on test cases. The formula is not correctly enforced.

Fig. 14: Latency and processing time for the largest a such that $\mathsf{max}_\ell(a) \leq 1/a$.

RQ3: Comparison with the state-of-the-art. Our comparison on the GDPR benchmarks shows ENFGUARD to be 1.5–30× faster than WHYENF and up to 4 times slower than the much less expressive, table-based ENFPOLY. Likely due to its more complex data structures, ENFGUARD is sometimes slower than WHYENF on small formulae (NOKIA), but with a latency still below 10 ms. The large gdpr formula exhibits ENFGUARD's performance advantage over WHYENF: while WHYENF, with an event rate of only 25, suffers a significant slowdown compared to the same benchmark's other formulae, ENFGUARD is still able to process 810 events per second. The comparison with MONPOLY reveals potential for further optimizations, especially for aggregations (AGG). However, the performance gap between ENFGUARD and MONPOLY is smaller for large formulae (IC), with the two tools showing incomparable performance on complex formulae.

Acknowledgments. Hublet is supported by the Swiss National Science Foundation grant "Model-driven Security & Privacy" (204796). Lima and Traytel are supported by a Novo Nordisk Fonden start package grant (NNF20OC0063462). We thank the anonymous CAV reviewers for their insightful feedback.

Disclosure of interests. The authors have no competing interests to declare that are relevant to the content of this article.

References

1. Aceto, L., Cassar, I., Francalanza, A., Ingolfsdottir, A.: Bidirectional runtime enforcement of first-order branching-time properties. Logical Methods in Computer Science **19** (2023)
2. Aceto, L., Cassar, I., Francalanza, A., Ingólfsdóttir, A.: On first-order runtime enforcement of branching-time properties. Acta Informatica pp. 1–67 (2023)
3. Arfelt, E., Basin, D., Debois, S.: Monitoring the GDPR. In: Sako, K., Schneider, S.A., Ryan, P.Y.A. (eds.) 24th European Symposium on Research in Computer Security (ESORICS). LNCS, vol. 11735, pp. 681–699. Springer (2019)
4. Basin, D., Debois, S., Hildebrandt, T.: Proactive enforcement of provisions and obligations. J. Comput. Secur. **32**(3), 247â€"289 (2024)
5. Basin, D., Dietiker, D.S., Krstić, S., Pignolet, Y.A., Raszyk, M., Schneider, J., Ter-Gabrielyan, A.: Monitoring the internet computer. In: International Symposium on Formal Methods. pp. 383–402. Springer (2023)
6. Basin, D., Harvan, M., Klaedtke, F., Zalinescu, E.: Monitoring data usage in distributed systems. IEEE Transactions on Software Engineering **39**(10), 1403–1426 (2013)
7. Basin, D., Klaedtke, F., Marinovic, S., Zălinescu, E.: Monitoring of temporal first-order properties with aggregations. Formal methods in system design **46**, 262–285 (2015)
8. Basin, D., Klaedtke, F., Müller, S., Zălinescu, E.: Monitoring metric first-order temporal properties. Journal of the ACM (JACM) **62**(2), 1–45 (2015)
9. Bauer, L., Ligatti, J., Walker, D.: More enforceable security policies. In: Workshop on Foundations of Computer Security (FCS). Citeseer (2002)
10. Behrmann, G., Cougnard, A., David, A., Fleury, E., Larsen, K., Lime, D.: UPPAAL-Tiga: Time for playing games! In: Damm, W., Hermanns, H. (eds.) International Conference Computer Aided Verification (CAV). LNCS, vol. 4590, pp. 121–125. Springer (2007)
11. Chomicki, J.: Efficient checking of temporal integrity constraints using bounded history encoding. ACM Transactions on Database Systems (TODS) **20**(2), 149–186 (1995)
12. Ehlers, R.: Unbeast: Symbolic bounded synthesis. In: Abdulla, P.A., Leino, K.R.M. (eds.) International Conference on Tools and Algorithms for the Construction and Analysis of Systems (TACAS). LNCS, vol. 6605, pp. 272–275. Springer (2011)
13. Erlingsson, Ú., Schneider, F.: SASI enforcement of security policies: a retrospective. In: Kienzle, D., Zurko, M.E., Greenwald, S., Serbau, C. (eds.) Workshop on New Security Paradigms. pp. 87–95. ACM (1999)
14. Falcone, Y., Jéron, T., Marchand, H., Pinisetty, S.: Runtime enforcement of regular timed properties by suppressing and delaying events. Science of Computer Programming **123**, 2–41 (2016)
15. Falcone, Y., Krstić, S., Reger, G., Traytel, D.: A taxonomy for classifying runtime verification tools. Int. J. Softw. Tools Technol. Transf. **23**(2), 255–284 (2021)
16. Falcone, Y., Pinisetty, S.: On the runtime enforcement of timed properties. In: Finkbeiner, B., Mariani, L. (eds.) 19th International Conference on Runtime Verification, (RV). LNCS, vol. 11757, pp. 48–69. Springer (2019)
17. Fredrikson, M., Joiner, R., Jha, S., Reps, T.W., Porras, P.A., Saïdi, H., Yegneswaran, V.: Efficient runtime policy enforcement using counterexample-guided abstraction refinement. In: Madhusudan, P., Seshia, S.A. (eds.) CAV 2012. LNCS, vol. 7358, pp. 548–563. Springer (2012)

18. Grubbs, F.E.: Sample criteria for testing outlying observations. Ann. Math. Statist. **21**(4), 27–58 (1950)
19. Hallé, S., Villemaire, R.: Runtime enforcement of web service message contracts with data. IEEE Trans. Serv. Comput. **5**(2), 192–206 (2012)
20. Hella, L., Libkin, L., Nurmonen, J., Wong, L.: Logics with aggregate operators. J. ACM **48**(4), 880–907 (2001). https://doi.org/10.1145/502090.502100
21. Hildebrandt, T., Mukkamala, R.R., Slaats, T., Zanitti, F.: Contracts for cross-organizational workflows as timed dynamic condition response graphs. The Journal of Logic and Algebraic Programming **82**(5-7), 164–185 (2013)
22. Hofmann, T., Schupp, S.: TACoS: A tool for MTL controller synthesis. In: Calinescu, R., Pasareanu, C.S. (eds.) International Conference on Software Engineering and Formal Methods (SEFM). LNCS, vol. 13085, pp. 372–379. Springer (2021)
23. Hublet, F., Basin, D., Krstić, S.: Real-time policy enforcement with metric first-order temporal logic. In: European Symposium on Research in Computer Security. pp. 211–232. Springer (2022)
24. Hublet, F., Lima, L., Basin, D., Krstić, S., Traytel, D.: Proactive real-time first-order enforcement. In: International Conference on Computer Aided Verification. pp. 156–181. Springer (2024)
25. Hublet, F., Lima, L., Basin, D., Krstić, S., Traytel, D.: Scaling-up proactive enforcement: Technical report (2025), https://doi.org/10.5281/zenodo.15501642
26. Hublet, François and Lima, Leonardo and Basin, David and Krstić, Srđan and Traytel, Dmitriy: ENFGUARD (2025), https://github.com/runtime-enforcement/enfguard
27. Jobstmann, B., Bloem, R.: Optimizations for LTL synthesis. In: International Conference Formal Methods in Computer-Aided Design (FMCAD). pp. 117–124. IEEE (2006)
28. Kiukkonen, N., Blom, J., Dousse, O., Gatica-Perez, D., Laurila, J.: Towards rich mobile phone datasets: Lausanne data collection campaign. Proc. ICPS, Berlin **68**(7) (2010)
29. Kupferman, O., Vardi, M.Y.: Model checking of safety properties. Formal Methods Syst. Des. **19**(3), 291–314 (2001). https://doi.org/10.1023/A:1011254632723, https://doi.org/10.1023/A:1011254632723
30. Li, G., Jensen, P., Larsen, K., Legay, A., Poulsen, D.: Practical controller synthesis for $MTL_{0,\infty}$. In: Erdogmus, H., Havelund, K. (eds.) ACM SIGSOFT International SPIN Symposium on Model Checking of Software. pp. 102–111. ACM (2017)
31. Ligatti, J., Bauer, L., Walker, D.: Edit automata: Enforcement mechanisms for runtime security policies. International Journal of Information Security **4**, 2–16 (2005)
32. Lima, L., Huerta y Munive, J.J., Traytel, D.: Explainable online monitoring of metric first-order temporal logic. In: International Conference on Tools and Algorithms for the Construction and Analysis of Systems. pp. 288–307. Springer (2024)
33. Minato, S.i.: Binary decision diagrams and applications for VLSI CAD, vol. 342. Springer Science & Business Media (1995)
34. Ngo, M., Massacci, F., Milushev, D., Piessens, F.: Runtime enforcement of security policies on black box reactive programs. In: Rajamani, S.K., Walker, D. (eds.) 42nd ACM SIGPLAN-SIGACT Symposium on Principles of Programming Languages (POPL). pp. 43–54. ACM (2015)
35. Peter, H., Ehlers, R., Mattmüller, R.: Synthia: Verification and synthesis for timed automata. In: Gopalakrishnan, G., Qadeer, S. (eds.) International Conference on Computer Aided Verification (CAV). LNCS, vol. 6806, pp. 649–655. Springer (2011)

36. Pinisetty, S., Falcone, Y., Jéron, T., Marchand, H.: TiPEX: A tool chain for timed property enforcement during execution. In: International Conference on Runtime Verification (RV). pp. 306–320. Springer (2015)
37. Pinisetty, S., Falcone, Y., Jéron, T., Marchand, H., Rollet, A., Nguena Timo, O.: Runtime enforcement of timed properties revisited. Formal Methods Syst. Des. **45**, 381–422 (2014)
38. Pinisetty, S., Preoteasa, V., Tripakis, S., Jéron, T., Falcone, Y., Marchand, H.: Predictive runtime enforcement. Formal Methods Syst. Des. **51**(1), 154–199 (2017)
39. Raszyk, M., Basin, D., Krstić, S., Traytel, D.: Efficient evaluation of arbitrary relational calculus queries. Logical Methods in Computer Science **19** (2023)
40. Renard, M., Rollet, A., Falcone, Y.: GREP: games for the runtime enforcement of properties. In: Yevtushenko, N., Cavalli, A., Yenigün, H. (eds.) International Conference on Testing Software and Systems (ICTSS). LNCS, vol. 10533, pp. 259–275. Springer (2017)
41. Schneider, F.: Enforceable security policies. ACM Trans. Inf. Syst. Secur. **3**(1), 30–50 (2000)
42. The DFINITY Team: The Internet Computer for geeks. Cryptology ePrint Archive, Paper 2022/087 (2022), https://eprint.iacr.org/2022/087
43. Zhu, S., Tabajara, L., Li, J., Pu, G., Vardi, M.: A symbolic approach to safety LTL synthesis. In: Strichman, O., Tzoref-Brill, R. (eds.) International Haifa Verification Conference (HVC). LNCS, vol. 10629, pp. 147–162. Springer (2017)
44. Zingg, S., Krstić, S., Raszyk, M., Schneider, J., Traytel, D.: Verified first-order monitoring with recursive rules. In: International Conference on Tools and Algorithms for the Construction and Analysis of Systems. pp. 236–253. Springer (2022)

An Intermediate Program Representation for Optimizing Stream-Based Languages

Jan Baumeister$^{(\boxtimes)}$ , Arthur Correnson, Bernd Finkbeiner,
and Frederik Scheerer

CISPA Helmholtz Center for Information Security,
Saarbrücken, Germany
{jan.baumeister,arthur.correnson,
finkbeiner,frederik.scheerer}@cispa.de

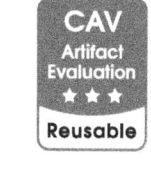

Abstract. Stream-based runtime monitors are safety assurance tools
that check at runtime whether the system's behavior satisfies a formal specification. Specifications consist of stream equations, which relate
input streams, containing sensor readings and other incoming information, to output streams, representing filtered and aggregated data. This
paper presents a framework for the stream-based specification language
RTLola. We introduce a new intermediate representation for stream-
based languages, the StreamIR, which, like the specification language,
operates on streams of unbounded length; while the stream equations
are replaced by imperative programs. We present a set of optimizations
based on static analysis of the specification and have implemented an
interpreter and a compiler for several target languages. In our evaluation, we measure the performance of several real-world case studies. The
results show that the new StreamIR framework reduces the runtime significantly compared to the existing RTLola interpreter. We evaluate the
effect of the optimizations and show that significant performance gains
are possible beyond the optimizations of the target language's compiler.
While our current implementation is limited to RTLola, the StreamIR is
designed to accommodate other stream-based languages, enabling their
interpretation and compilation into all available target languages.

Keywords: Runtime Verification · Stream-based Monitoring ·
Real-time Properties · Intermediate Representation

1 Introduction

Frameworks for runtime monitoring must strike a careful balance between safety
and performance. On the one hand, runtime monitors are responsible for raising
alarms about potential risks and initiating mitigation procedures in real time;
their safety and correctness are, therefore, critical. On the other hand, monitors
are often run on platforms with very limited resources, such as the onboard
computer of an unmanned aircraft, where efficiency is crucial.

© The Author(s) 2025
R. Piskac and Z. Rakamarić (Eds.): CAV 2025, LNCS 15933, pp. 393–407, 2025.
https://doi.org/10.1007/978-3-031-98682-6_20

To ensure the correctness of the monitor, a common approach is to follow the paradigm of *specification-based monitoring*, where the monitor is not programmed in a programming language but rather based on a formal specification. Many frameworks store the specification in memory and then *interpret* the specification against the incoming data at runtime [16]; this, however, causes substantially sub-optimal performance. The alternative approach is to *translate* the specification into a target programming language, such as Rust, and then rely on a standard compiler for the target language to produce executable code [10,18,25]. Even though translated monitors often perform significantly better than an interpreter, compilers for general-purpose programming languages do not optimize based on the specific properties of the specification language. This approach therefore still leaves potential for optimization on the table.

In this paper, we present an optimization framework for the class of stream-based specification languages [13,14,20]. Such specifications consist of stream equations, which relate input streams, containing sensor readings and other incoming information, to output streams, representing filtered and aggregated data. Stream-based monitoring has been applied to the safety assurance of cyber-physical systems, including monitoring of exhaust emissions in cars [11] and the safety of unmanned aircraft [5,9]. Stream-based languages have properties that are relevant for code optimization but are not found in general-purpose programming languages. For example, the value of a particular expression in a given time step of a stream-based monitor is guaranteed to be the same, regardless of other stream evaluations in between. As a result, if-statements can easily be combined or moved outside or inside other statements.

Our framework introduces a new intermediate representation, the StreamIR, specifically designed to represent the relational stream-based specifications in an imperative form and enable optimizations before the code is translated to the target language. We provide an interpreter and a compiler to Rust and Solidity. The optimizations are implemented as a set of rewrite rules that exploit the specific properties of stream-based languages. As the source language, our framework accepts RTLola [6,16] specifications, which is a famous representative of the class of stream-based specification languages, but could easily be extended to support other stream-based languages like TeSSLa [13] or Striver [20].

We evaluate our approach on a set of specifications from RTLola case studies [5,6,8,32]. Interpreting the optimized StreamIR code significantly outperforms the state-of-the-art RTLola interpreter [16]. This is perhaps not surprising, because the RTLola interpreter does not attempt to optimize the specification before the execution. However, our framework also outperforms the direct compilation of RTLola into Rust, demonstrating that the StreamIR optimizations gain an additional speed-up on top of the optimizations already made by the Rust compiler. The situation is similar in our experiments with monitoring smart contracts in Solidity. Here, we assess our compiler by measuring the gas usage. The StreamIR optimizations again achieve substantial performance gains beyond the optimizations of the Solidity compiler.

The rest of this paper is structured as follows: After giving an overview on RTLola in Sect. 2, Sect. 3 introduces the intermediate representation, describes the translation from RTLola specifiations to the StreamIR, and presents the StreamIR optimizations. Section 4 provides details about the implementation and the evaluation of our approach.

Related Work. Runtime monitoring is a dynamic verification approach that has been applied to a variety of domains [22,23], and there are several monitoring tools and case studies [5,9,28]. Monitoring with stream-based specifications was pioneered by Lola [14], which was later extended to Lola2.0 [15] and RTLola [6,16]. Stream-based specification languages are related to synchronous programming languages such as Lustre [21], Esterel [12] and Signal [19]. In contrast to them, stream-based specifications are descriptive languages that use stream equations to describe temporal properties. Other extensions of Lola are TeSSLa [13], Striver [20] or Copilot [29]. Several compilers for stream-based languages exist, including compilers for Lola [18] and TeSSLa [25] to Rust. Other more specific compilers are a compilation [10] from RTLola to the hardware description language VHDL [10] or a compilation from Copilot [30] to the Atom language, a domain-specific language for embedded hard real-time applications. While some of these tools employ an intermediate representation (IR) to support different target languages, all are built for their specific specification language.

The concept of compiler construction through an IR is well-established. The most well-known IR is LLVM, the basis for most modern compilers. However, to the best of our knowledge, a general-purpose IR specifically designed for stream-based specifications does not yet exist. Optimizations of stream based specifications have been studied before. In both RTLola [7] and TeSSLa [24], there exist approaches that describe optimizations specifically designed for their specification language. This paper follows this idea, but, compared to the other approaches, the optimizations are defined on the more general StreamIR, which describes an imperative program, not a set of equations. This approach is complementary to the optimizations based on the specification language.

2   RTLola

An RTLola specification defines a set of streams, each representing an infinite sequence of values. We differentiate between *input streams* which capture external data, and *output streams* that perform computations based on current and past stream values. Consider the specification in Fig. 1 which monitors a waypoint mission of an autonomous drone. The drone is provided with new waypoints through an input stream and must reach each waypoint within 10 s. We have exemplified an evaluation of the specification in Fig. 2.

The specification introduces two input streams: pos, representing the drone's current position, and wp, representing the position of new waypoints. The output stream moving determines whether the drone is currently in motion by comparing its current position to the previous one. This is accomplished using an offset

```
input pos : (UInt64, UInt64)
input wp : (UInt64, UInt64)
output moving
  eval @pos with pos != pos.offset(by: -1, or: pos)
output reached(current)
  spawn @wp with wp
  eval @pos with dist(pos, current) < ε
  close @pos when reached(current)
output missed_wp(current)
  spawn @wp with wp
  eval @Local(10s) with ¬reached(current).aggregate(over: 10s, using: ∃
  close @pos when reached(current)
```

Fig. 1. RTLola specification checking whether a drone reaches new waypoints within 10 s.

lookup – a temporal operator in RTLola that accesses past stream values. The accesses are represented in Fig. 2 through a series of dashed arrows. Since previous values don't exist initially, indicated by the question mark in the top left of the figure, the offset operator requires a default value. The output stream `reached` checks for each waypoint whether it was reached by the drone. In contrast to the previous output stream, this stream is parameterized to describe a set of streams, called *stream instances* – each tracking a specific waypoint.

Instances are created using the *spawn* clause, where the expression computes the *parameter* of the instance. Similarly, the *close* clause defines when instances are removed. In this example, a new instance is spawned for every new waypoint and closed once the corresponding waypoint is reached. The *evaluation* of parameterized streams is applied to every instance, in our example, if the distance between the current position and the waypoint, represented with the instance's parameter, is smaller than a threshold. The figure depicts two instances of the `reached` stream, each respectively monitoring whether waypoint $(5, 3)$ and $(7, 6)$ have been reached. The output stream `missed_wp` tracks whether a waypoint was missed – that is, not reached within a time bound. This stream is also parameterized over the waypoints, but in contrast to the previous streams, the evaluation is applied at a frequency. More precisely, each stream instance is evaluated every 10 s and checks if the waypoint was not reached within the last 10 s.

Note that for each clause – spawn, eval, and close – RTLola has two types of filters: pacings and dynamic filter. The *pacing*, specified with an @-symbol, describes whether the clause is event-based or periodic. For *event-based* clauses, the clause is evaluated when a new input arrives, such as the evaluation of `moving`, which receives new values for every new value of `pos`. *Periodic* clauses are evaluated with a fixed frequency, such as the evaluation of `missed_wp` that is executed every 10 s. *Dynamic filters* are boolean stream expressions and follow after the `when`-keyword. They describe a condition based on stream values; here, we close a stream instance upon reaching the waypoint.

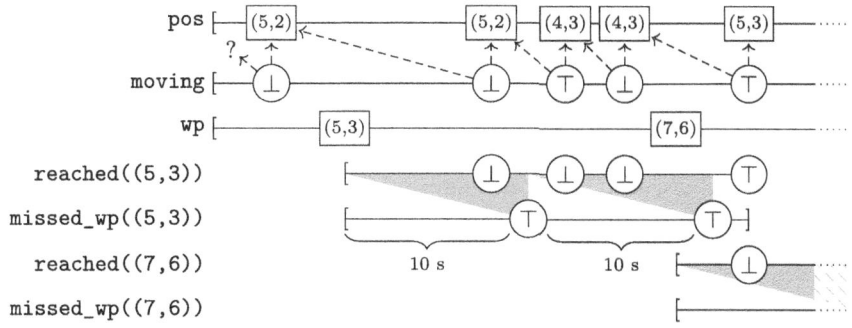

Fig. 2. An evaluation of the RTLola specification from Fig. 1.

From a specification, we can derive a *Dependency Graph* describing the relation between streams. Analysis on this graph returns the required memory and a partial order, indicating which evaluation steps – called *Tasks* – have to be done in which order. These tasks either spawn, shift, evaluate, or close stream instances and correspond to the clauses in the specification. Here, *shifting* an instance reserves space for a new value. The order can be transformed into a list of *layers*, where the layers are evaluated sequentially and all tasks of one layer in parallel. For a more detailed explanation, we refer to the RTLola tutorial [6].

3   Stream Intermediate Representation (StreamIR)

The StreamIR, a new intermediate representation for stream-based specification languages, captures the imperative semantics of those languages and describes operations specific to real-time stream-based monitors, such as spawning, evaluating, and closing a stream instance. Besides typical imperative statements, such as conditionals in the form of if-then-else, it includes stream-based specific statements or expressions. The *guards* in conditions, for example, extend standard logical operators with constructs to check the presence of inputs to model event-based streams or constructs to reason about deadlines of periodic streams. Using this representation, a StreamIR monitor loop{*stmt*} describes a statement that is executed for each input event. The complete syntax, semantics and optimizations are provided in the full version [4] of this paper.

Example 1. The program in Fig. 3 describes a monitor for the specification from Fig. 1. The program is split into three parts following the three pacings of the specification, @pos, @wp, and @Local(10,s). First, the program handles the input wp, and spawns the parameterized output streams. Then, it shifts and evaluates the pos input stream and the non-parameterized moving output stream before iterating over the instances of the reached stream. Since the stream instances of missed_wp are closed with the same condition as the reached stream instances, the monitor handles the closing of these instances in parallel. The last guard iterates over the missed_wp output stream to evaluate its instances. Given

```
if input? wp then
  shift wp ; input wp ; (spawn reached (syn wp) ∥ spawn missed_wp (syn wp)) ;
if input? pos then
  shift pos ; input pos ; shift moving ;
  eval moving (syn pos ≠ get pos −1 (syn pos)) ;
  iterate reached
    shift reached ; eval reached dist(syn pos, self) < ε ;
    if dynamic syn reached self then
      close reached ∥ close missed_wp ;
iterate missed_wp
  if local 10s missed_wp then
    shift missed_wp ; eval missed_wp ¬(window reached self 10s ∃)
```

Fig. 3. A StreamIR program of the example specification in Fig. 1.

that the deadline is local, i.e. relative to the spawn of each instance, the guard checks the deadline of each instance individually.

StreamIR monitors are defined over a sequence of *Memories*. Each memory contains the already computed values – called *prefix* – of each stream instance and the next *deadline* for periodic stream instances, the timestamp of the next stream evaluation according to the frequency. We differentiate between global frequencies that start with the beginning of the monitor and local frequencies that start with the spawn of a stream instance.

Using the memory, we define inference rules to evaluate expressions and guards, i.e., $(M, expr) \Downarrow_t^{inst} val$, and statements, i.e., $(M, stmt) \Downarrow_{I,D,t}^{inst} M'$. A step of the monitor $((M, D), stmt) \Rightarrow_{I,t} (M', D')$ describes a sequence of statement executions, one execution for each passed deadline and one to process the input. For a given input sequence, *a monitor* then describes the sequence of memories according to the inference rules while starting with an initial memory.

Some programs are ill-formed, i.e., the correctness of the program relies on constraints imposed on the input. To avoid such programs, we only consider *well-defined* programs, i.e., each infinite sequence of inputs has a unique output.

3.1   Translation from RTLola to StreamIR

The translation from an RTLola specification to the StreamIR follows the technique illustrated in Fig. 4. Here, each stream in the specification is translated into a set of small StreamIR snippets. Input streams are translated to a statement shifting the stream and writing the new value to memory. Output streams are translated into four statements, one for each task – spawn, shift, eval, and close. The translated statements are then sorted according to their layers, where all statements in a layer are evaluated in parallel while the layers are concatenated sequentially. The translation also generates an initial memory consisting of the prefixes and the deadlines. The initial prefix of every input stream is assigned to an empty list whereas every output stream instance is marked as not-spawned. The initial deadline assigns every global frequency to its first deadline.

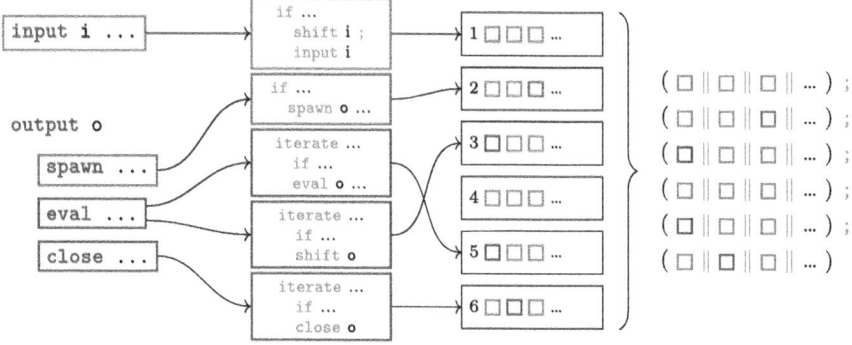

Fig. 4. Overview of the translation from RTLola specifications to StreamIR monitors.

3.2   Optimizations

The translation of the monitors shown in Sect. 3.1 produces specific patterns, allowing for optimizations tailored to these patterns. The StreamIR representation of the monitor, properties of stream-based languages, and the analysis results enable the application of specialized rewriting rules. These rewrite rules follow standard compiler techniques, such as combining if statements or loops. However, since in a correctly constructed StreamIR program, every expression consistently evaluates to the same value regardless of its position, finding these patterns in the StreamIR monitor is simpler than in a general-purpose language. These compilers require complex program analysis which might miss the required assumptions to apply the optimizations.

Example 2. Consider the following snippets. The code on the left is produced by the translation from RTLola and the code on the right is an optimized version:

```
iterate p                                    if schedule global 0.5 then
    if schedule global 0.5                       assign (syn a)
        ∧ dynamic self = syn a then                  eval p ... ;
            eval p ...                               eval q ...
iterate q
    if schedule global 0.5
        ∧ dynamic self = syn a then
            eval q ...
```

First, we assume that the output streams p and q share the same spawn and close clauses, i.e., each clause has the same pacing, **when**-condition, and **with**-expression. This property ensures that the iteration blocks iterate over the same parameters, so the first rewrite rule combines these iterations. A second rule moves the first part of the guards outside the iteration since it is independent of the specific instance. This optimization is possible because the global deadline is parameter-independent, whereas a local deadline would not permit such optimization. Last, the remaining guard uniquely determines one instance, so the

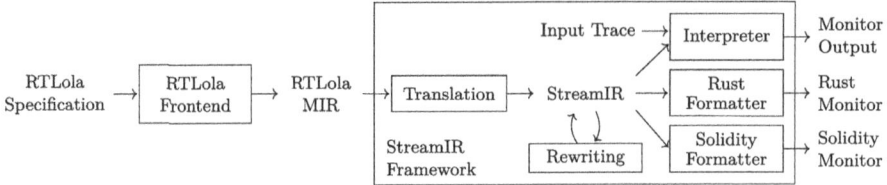

Fig. 5. Overview of the StreamIR framework

next rule replaces the iteration and the if statement with an assign statement directly calculating the parameter.

Memory. Stream-based specification languages operate over an infinite sequence of values. However, an analysis can often determine static memory bounds per stream instance. In RTLola, all temporal accesses are bounded, allowing the dependency analysis to reveal a finite buffer length for all instances. Based on a stream's structure, we can optimize the memory representation using a set of memory rewriting rules analogous to the rewriting rules from the previous paragraph. They include optimizations for non-parameterized streams, instances with a buffer length of 1, and streams that are only accessed synchronously.

Symbolic Execution. The StreamIR enables a partial evaluation of guard conditions. Code blocks surrounded by guards that are never satisfied can be removed, while guard checks can be eliminated if their conditions are never violated. For instance, in RTLola, the evaluation cycle is either completely event- or time-based. By partially evaluating the StreamIR, it is possible to create two versions: one containing event-based streams and one containing time-driven streams.

4   Implementation and Evaluation

Implementation. We extended the RTLola framework [6, 16] with a StreamIR-based interpreter and a compiler to Rust and Solidity. We illustrate our setup in Fig. 5. Our approach uses the existing RTLola frontend for parsing and analyzing specifications. The RTLolaMIR includes all inferred information, such as pacing types or memory bounds. We then apply the translation steps outlined in Sect. 3.1 as well as the rewriting rules introduced in Sect. 3.2. The library outputs the final StreamIR, which is then either interpreted or compiled.

The new *interpretation* uses just-in-time (JIT) compilation for the complete StreamIR while the existing RTLola interpreter [6] only uses JIT compilation for stream expressions. This approach leverages the discussed optimizations, i.e., partial evaluation of the StreamIR to decompose computation in time- and event-driven sections and rewrite rules to optimize control flow and memory.

For the *compiler*, the StreamIR library provides a framework to translate the monitor into different target languages. For each language, a formatter defines the translation of statements and expressions into the corresponding constructs of the target language. Currently, we support the compilation to two programming languages used in different domains. Our Rust formatter generates highly efficient Rust code that can run on microcontrollers. Our second formatter compiles specifications to Solidity, a programming language for smart contracts.

Our artifact is available at Zenodo[1] and our implementation is open-source and available on crates.io[2,3,4,5] and GitHub.[6]

Evaluation. The evaluation was performed on a system with a 13th Gen Intel Core i7-1355U processor. Rust code is compiled using rustc version 1.84.0 with the highest optimization level 3, and Solidity using solc version 0.8.24 optimized for 1000 runs. We evaluate our implementation on three different benchmark sets and exclude the setup phases, such as specification analysis, for the runtime measurements. For the optimizations, we apply the same set of rewriting rules for all specifiations.

Unmanned Aircraft. First, we evaluate our approach using two specifications from the field of monitoring unmanned aircraft. The first specification is a geofencing application [5], where a drone's position is continuously monitored to ensure it remains within a designated geofence. This geofence is defined by a set of polygon lines in which the number of lines is proportional to the number of output streams. The second specification is based on the RTLola tutorial [6], observing the surrounding airspace of a drone to detect potential interference from other drones – called intruders. Unlike the first specification, which we evaluate across varying numbers of polygon lines, this benchmark varies the number of intruders while keeping the specification unchanged. Here, the number of intruders corresponds to the number of stream instances. For both specifications, we measure the execution time over 20 runs, each processing 10,000 input events. We report the runtime of the old interpreter [16], the runtime of the new StreamIR interpreter with and without the optimizations, and the runtime of the optimized and unoptimized monitors compiled using the Rust formatter.

As seen in Fig. 6, the runtime of all monitors increases linearly because the number of stream evaluations increases either with the number of output streams or stream instances. In general, a compilation is much faster than an interpretation. When comparing the interpreter implementation, our new implementation outperforms the old one even without the optimizations by using JIT compilation for the complete StreamIR. After applying the StreamIR rewrite rules, the runtime is significantly reduced. In contrast, the rewrite rules mostly do not affect the runtime for the geofence compilation to Rust, since the Rust compiler

---

[1] https://doi.org/10.5281/zenodo.15222546.

[2] https://crates.io/crates/rtlola-streamir.

[3] https://crates.io/crates/rtlola-streamir-interpreter.

[4] https://crates.io/crates/rtlola2rust.

[5] https://crates.io/crates/rtlola2solidity.

[6] https://github.com/reactive-systems/rtlola-streamir.

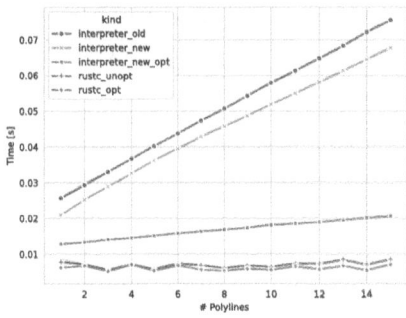 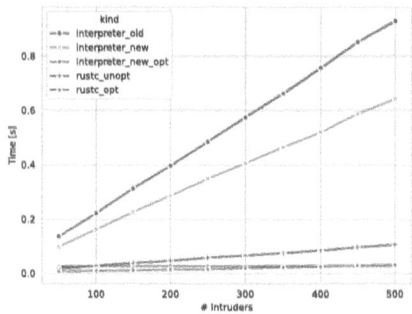

(a) Geofence specification with increasing number of polygon lines.　　(b) Intruder specification with increasing number of intruders.

Fig. 6. Runtime comparison between interpreters and compiled Rust monitors.

is capable of applying most optimizations on its own. For the intruder specification however, StreamIR optimizations are able to significantly optimize the runtime of the compiled monitor. The reason for this are optimizations of parameterized streams, which are easy in the StreamIR representation but hard for a Rust program in general.

Algorithmic Fairness. The second benchmark utilizes the equalized-odds specification [8] for monitoring algorithmic fairness of the COMPAS tool. COMPAS was developed by Northpointe [27] and predicts the recidivism risk of defendants. A retrospective analysis [2] showed the bias of the tool and our recent paper [8] demonstrates the

Table 1. Runtime comparison of the fairness specification.

	Unopt	Opt
Existing Interpreter	17.258	-
StreamIR Interpreter	12.889	7.943
Compilation	3.157	1.443

use of stream-based monitoring to detect such bias. Table 1 depicts the runtime on the COMPAS dataset, using the same evaluation setup described in the previous paragraph. The table reports similar results to the previous benchmark. Optimizations on the StreamIR reduce the runtime of the interpreter and compiler.

Smart Contracts. Efforts have explored monitoring smart contracts [1,3] or expressing them in formal specification languages [17,26,36]. We extend this effort with the compilation to Solidity, so the monitor or smart contract itself can be expressed in RTLola. Since the interpretations can not be executed on the blockchain, our evaluation focuses on the performance benefits of the optimizations when compiling to Solidity.

We extended our framework with a function interface to compile functions describing the contract. The functions set specific input stream values, call the monitor and return new values of output streams. As not all input streams are set by a function, the compiler adapts the StreamIR using partial evaluation.

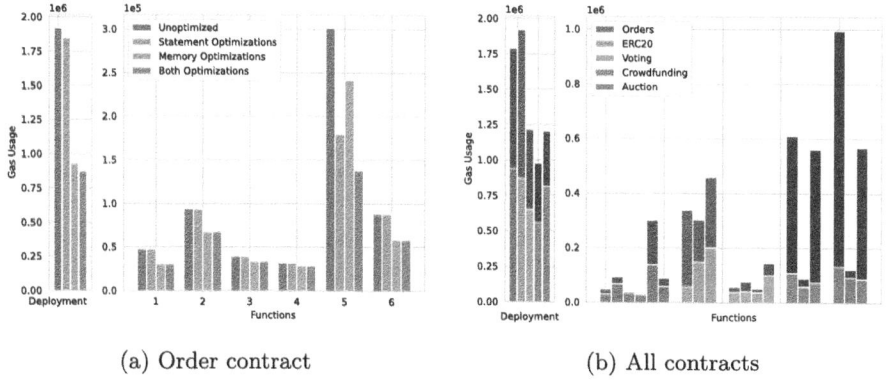

(a) Order contract   (b) All contracts

Fig. 7. Gas usage comparison of the Solidity monitors.

The evaluation uses RTLola specifications that have previously been employed to monitor smart contracts [3,32,35] as well as existing Solidity contracts that we expressed in RTLola [31,33,34]. For the comparison, we assess the required gas, the transaction fee for calling functions on the blockchain, for contract deployment and the average gas consumption per function call over 1000 calls.

Figure 7a displays the average gas consumption per function call when monitoring an ordering system, along with the gas costs for the contracts deployment. The functions allow the interaction with the contract, for example to place a new order, mark an order as delivered or request termination of the contract. The cost of the six functions and the deployment are each represented with four bars, where each bar represents the contract 1. without any optimizations 2. with statement optimizations 3. with memory optimizations, and 4. with both optimizations. The results demonstrate that the deployment costs mostly are reduced by memory optimizations minimizing the use of global variables. Furthermore, the gas reduction of some function calls relies on memory optimizations. By reducing reliance on global storage, these optimizations yield substantial savings in deployment and runtime. Meanwhile, StreamIR optimizations mainly improve function execution costs, especially for functions that update parameterized streams, such as the fifth function for placing a new order. These functions benefit significantly from the iterate-assign optimization, which eliminates unnecessary iterations and removes the need to store activate parameters.

Figure 7b gives an overview of the gas usage across a number of different contracts. In this figure, each bar corresponds to a function in a contract. The top half of the bar illustrates the gas costs for the StreamIR-unoptimized contract, while the lower half shows the reduction obtained by enabling all StreamIR optimizations. For example, the dark blue bars in Fig. 7b correspond with the blue bars in Fig. 7a and the light blue corresponds with the red bars. Figure 7b demonstrate that our optimizations reduce gas usage across all specifications.

Beyond gas usage reduction, the StreamIR optimizations address a fundamental issue of contracts with parameterized output streams. Iteration introduces unbounded gas usage – a highly undesirable property for smart contracts. By applying the optimization that replaces iterations with assignments – feasible for all evaluated specifications – gas usage becomes bounded again.

5   Conclusion

We have presented a new framework for the stream-based specification language RTLola, with an interpretation and a compilation to Rust and Solidity. Our framework uses a new intermediate representation designed for stream-based specifications. Further, we introduced rewrite rules for this representation to optimize the resulting monitors. Even without optimizations, our experiments show that the new interpreter and compiler outperform the existing RTLola interpreter. Additionally, we show the impact of the rewriting rules optimizing the runtime of the monitor. Especially in specifications with parameterized streams, our optimizations speed up the compiled monitor significantly. For the interpretation, our optimizations also have a huge impact for specifications without parameterized streams.

Acknowledgments. This work was partially supported by the Aviation Research Program LuFo of the German Federal Ministry for Economic Affairs and Energy as part of "Volocopter Sicherheitstechnologie zur robusten eVTOL Flugzustandsabsicherung durch formales Monitoring" (No. 20Q1963C), by the German Research Foundation (DFG) as part of TRR 248 (No. 389792660), and by the European Research Council (ERC) Grant HYPER (No. 101055412).

Disclosure of Interests. The authors have no competing interests to declare that are relevant to the content of this article.

References

1. Abraham, M., Jevitha, K.P.: Runtime verification and vulnerability testing of smart contracts. In: Singh, M., Gupta, P.K., Tyagi, V., Flusser, J., Ören, T., Kashyap, R. (eds.) ICACDS 2019. CCIS, vol. 1046, pp. 333–342. Springer, Singapore (2019). https://doi.org/10.1007/978-981-13-9942-8_32
2. Angwin, J., Larson, J., Mattu, S., Kirchner, L.: Machine bias. there's software used across the country to predict future criminals. and it's biased against blacks. ProPublica (2016). https://www.propublica.org/article/machine-bias-risk-assessments-in-criminal-sentencing
3. Azzopardi, S., Ellul, J., Pace, G.J.: Monitoring smart contracts: ContractLarva and open challenges beyond. In: Colombo, C., Leucker, M. (eds.) RV 2018. LNCS, vol. 11237, pp. 113–137. Springer, Cham (2018). https://doi.org/10.1007/978-3-030-03769-7_8
4. Baumeister, J., Correnson, A., Finkbeiner, B., Scheerer, F.: An intermediate program representation for optimizing stream-based languages (2025). https://arxiv.org/abs/2504.21458

5. Baumeister, J., et al.: Monitoring unmanned aircraft: specification, integration, and lessons-learned. In: Gurfinkel, A., Ganesh, V. (eds.) Computer Aided Verification - 36th International Conference, CAV 2024, Montreal, QC, Canada, 24–27 July 2024, Proceedings, Part II. Lecture Notes in Computer Science, vol. 14682, pp. 207–218. Springer (2024). https://doi.org/10.1007/978-3-031-65630-9_10

6. Baumeister, J., Finkbeiner, B., Kohn, F., Scheerer, F.: A tutorial on stream-based monitoring. In: International Symposium on Formal Methods, pp. 624–648. Springer (2024)

7. Baumeister, J., Finkbeiner, B., Kruse, M., Schwenger, M.: Automatic optimizations for stream-based monitoring languages. In: Deshmukh, J., Ničković, D. (eds.) RV 2020. LNCS, vol. 12399, pp. 451–461. Springer, Cham (2020). https://doi.org/10.1007/978-3-030-60508-7_25

8. Baumeister, J., Finkbeiner, B., Scheerer, F., Siber, J., Wagenpfeil, T.: Stream-based monitoring of algorithmic fairness. In: Gurfinkel, A., Heule, M. (eds.) Tools and Algorithms for the Construction and Analysis of Systems, pp. 60–81. Springer, Cham (2025)

9. Baumeister, J., Finkbeiner, B., Schirmer, S., Schwenger, M., Torens, C.: RTLola cleared for take-off: monitoring autonomous aircraft. In: Lahiri, S.K., Wang, C. (eds.) CAV 2020. LNCS, vol. 12225, pp. 28–39. Springer, Cham (2020). https://doi.org/10.1007/978-3-030-53291-8_3

10. Baumeister, J., Finkbeiner, B., Schwenger, M., Torfah, H.: FPGA stream-monitoring of real-time properties. ACM Trans. Embed. Comput. Syst. (TECS) **18**(5s), 1–24 (2019)

11. Biewer, S., Finkbeiner, B., Hermanns, H., Köhl, M.A., Schnitzer, Y., Schwenger, M.: RTLola on board: testing real driving emissions on your phone. In: Groote, J.F., Larsen, K.G. (eds.) TACAS 2021. LNCS, vol. 12652, pp. 365–372. Springer, Cham (2021). https://doi.org/10.1007/978-3-030-72013-1_20

12. Boussinot, F., De Simone, R.: The esterel language. Proc. IEEE **79**(9), 1293–1304 (1991)

13. Convent, L., Hungerecker, S., Leucker, M., Scheffel, T., Schmitz, M., Thoma, D.: TeSSLa: temporal stream-based specification language. In: Massoni, T., Mousavi, M.R. (eds.) SBMF 2018. LNCS, vol. 11254, pp. 144–162. Springer, Cham (2018). https://doi.org/10.1007/978-3-030-03044-5_10

14. d'Angelo, B., et al.: Lola: runtime monitoring of synchronous systems. In: 12th International Symposium on Temporal Representation and Reasoning (TIME 2005), pp. 166–174. IEEE (2005)

15. Faymonville, P., Finkbeiner, B., Schirmer, S., Torfah, H.: A stream-based specification language for network monitoring. In: Falcone, Y., Sánchez, C. (eds.) RV 2016. LNCS, vol. 10012, pp. 152–168. Springer, Cham (2016). https://doi.org/10.1007/978-3-319-46982-9_10

16. Faymonville, P., et al.: StreamLAB: stream-based monitoring of cyber-physical systems. In: Dillig, I., Tasiran, S. (eds.) CAV 2019. LNCS, vol. 11561, pp. 421–431. Springer, Cham (2019). https://doi.org/10.1007/978-3-030-25540-4_24

17. Finkbeiner, B., Hofmann, J., Kohn, F., Passing, N.: Reactive synthesis of smart contract control flows. In: International Symposium on Automated Technology for Verification and Analysis, pp. 248–269. Springer (2023)

18. Finkbeiner, B., Oswald, S., Passing, N., Schwenger, M.: Verified rust monitors for lola specifications. In: Deshmukh, J., Ničković, D. (eds.) RV 2020. LNCS, vol. 12399, pp. 431–450. Springer, Cham (2020). https://doi.org/10.1007/978-3-030-60508-7_24

19. Gautier, T., Le Guernic, P., Besnard, L.: Signal: A Declarative Language for Synchronous Programming of Real-Time Systems. Springer (1987)

20. Gorostiaga, F., Sánchez, C.: Striver: stream runtime verification for real-time event-streams. In: Colombo, C., Leucker, M. (eds.) RV 2018. LNCS, vol. 11237, pp. 282–298. Springer, Cham (2018). https://doi.org/10.1007/978-3-030-03769-7_16

21. Halbwachs, N., Caspi, P., Raymond, P., Pilaud, D.: The synchronous data flow programming language lustre. Proc. IEEE **79**(9), 1305–1320 (1991)

22. Henzinger, T.A., Karimi, M., Kueffner, K., Mallik, K.: Monitoring algorithmic fairness. In: Enea, C., Lal, A. (eds.) Computer Aided Verification, pp. 358–382. Springer, Cham (2023)

23. Junges, S., Torfah, H., Seshia, S.A.: Runtime monitors for Markov decision processes. In: Silva, A., Leino, K. (eds.) CAV 2021. LNCS, vol. 12760, pp. 553–576. Springer, Cham (2021). https://doi.org/10.1007/978-3-030-81688-9_26

24. Kallwies, H., Leucker, M., Prilop, M., Schmitz, M.: Optimizing trans-compilers in runtime verification makes sense–sometimes. In: International Symposium on Theoretical Aspects of Software Engineering, pp. 197–204. Springer (2022)

25. Kallwies, H., Leucker, M., Schmitz, M., Schulz, A., Thoma, D., Weiss, A.: Tessla–an ecosystem for runtime verification. In: International Conference on Runtime Verification, pp. 314–324. Springer (2022)

26. Mavridou, A., Laszka, A.: Designing secure ethereum smart contracts: a finite state machine based approach. In: Meiklejohn, S., Sako, K. (eds.) FC 2018. LNCS, vol. 10957, pp. 523–540. Springer, Heidelberg (2018). https://doi.org/10.1007/978-3-662-58387-6_28

27. Northpoint Inc. d/b/a equivant: Practitioner's guide to compas core (2015). https://archive.epic.org/algorithmic-transparency/crim-justice/EPIC-16-06-23-WI-FOIA-201600805-COMPASPractionerGuide.pdf. Accessed 30 Jan 2025

28. Perez, I., Dedden, F., Goodloe, A.: Copilot 3. Technical report (2020). https://ntrs.nasa.gov/citations/20200003164

29. Perez, I., Goodloe, A.E., Dedden, F.: Runtime verification in real-time with the copilot language: a tutorial. In: Platzer, A., Rozier, K.Y., Pradella, M., Rossi, M. (eds.) Formal Methods - 26th International Symposium, FM 2024, Milan, Italy, 9–13 September 2024, Proceedings, Part II. Lecture Notes in Computer Science, vol. 14934, pp. 469–491. Springer (2024). https://doi.org/10.1007/978-3-031-71177-0_27

30. Pike, L., Goodloe, A., Morisset, R., Niller, S.: Copilot: a hard real-time runtime monitor. In: Barringer, H., et al. (eds.) RV 2010. LNCS, vol. 6418, pp. 345–359. Springer, Heidelberg (2010). https://doi.org/10.1007/978-3-642-16612-9_26

31. Program the Blockchain: Coin funding reference contract (2022). https://programtheblockchain.com/posts/2018/01/19/writing-a-crowdfunding-contract-a-la-kickstarter/. Accessed 30 Jan 2025

32. Scheerer, F.: Monitoring smart contracts with rtlola. Bachelor's thesis, Saarland University (2021)

33. Sudi, A.: Voting reference contract (2021). https://github.com/andresudi/Voting-Smart-Contract/blob/master/Voting.sol. Accessed 30 Jan 2025

34. The Solidity Authors: Simple auction reference contract. https://docs.soliditylang.org/en/latest/solidity-by-example.html#simple-open-auction. Accessed 30 Jan 2025

35. Vogelsteller, F., Buterin, V.: ERC-20: Token standard (2015). https://eips.ethereum.org/EIPS/eip-20. Accessed 30 Jan 2025

36. Zupan, N., Kasinathan, P., Cuellar, J., Sauer, M.: Secure smart contract generation based on petri nets. In: Rosa Righi, R., Alberti, A.M., Singh, M. (eds.) Blockchain Technology for Industry 4.0. BT, pp. 73–98. Springer, Singapore (2020). https:// doi.org/10.1007/978-981-15-1137-0_4

PyCaliper: Python-Embedded Infrastructure for RTL Verification and Specification Synthesis

Adwait Godbole[1]($\boxtimes$) 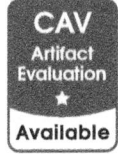, Brian Huffman[2], Fangfei Liu[2],
Carlos V Rozas[2], and Sanjit A. Seshia[1]

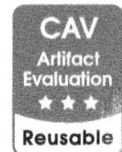

[1] University of California, Berkeley, CA, USA
adwait@berkeley.edu
[2] Intel Labs, Hillsboro, USA

Abstract. We present PyCaliper: a Python-embedded framework
to formulate, verify, and auto-synthesize specifications for hardware
designs at the register transfer level (RTL). By being Python-embedded,
PyCaliper is easy to use and benefits from object-oriented principles
and Python's rich ecosystem. Further, PyCaliper is a common platform
that integrates novel research techniques such as specification synthesis
and mature, industry-scale tooling, thus allowing them to benefit from
each other. We discuss the system and implementation of PyCaliper
and demonstrate its use in two case studies: in the first we compare a
custom verification backend with a commercial tool and gain insights
about the former, and in the second we demonstrate invariant synthesis
for an RTL design.

Keywords: formal specification · hardware verification · invariant
synthesis

1 Introduction

Formal verification of hardware designs provides strong guarantees about correctness and is, thus, a critical step in the chip design process. Verification
accounts for as much as 20% of total development costs [40], which can be
as high as $500M for a modern chip. Industry relies on proprietary verifica-
tion tools such as Cadence/Jasper Proof Apps [13] and Synopsys Formality
[47]. These are mature tools based on decades of research and engineering and
able to handle industry-scale designs. However, as observed more than a decade
ago [42,43], to fully leverage such tools one additionally needs to *synthesize*
high-quality specifications and other proof artifacts. Over the past decade, the
open-source community has seen development of RTL language services, verification infrastructure, novel algorithmic improvements, solver backends (e.g.,
[12,23,29,30,38,53]), and techniques to synthesize proof artifacts such as invari-
ants/abstractions (e.g., [21,56]) that use underlying verification routines. Even

© The Author(s) 2025
R. Piskac and Z. Rakamarić (Eds.): CAV 2025, LNCS 15933, pp. 408–425, 2025.
https://doi.org/10.1007/978-3-031-98682-6_21

so, these have not been widely adopted into industrial flows; industry and open-source tools remain largely disconnected. Importantly, there is a lack of infrastructure to connect tools and techniques that, while complementary in theory, are not integrated in practice. Such infrastructure for cooperating formal methods has several benefits including (a) easier integration of novel research (e.g., specification synthesis and learning) with mature industrial tools, (b) making open-source tools inter-operable with proprietary tools, and (c) enabling comparisons between open-source and proprietary tools.

Desiderata. This suggests developing verification infrastructure that is:

- *Compatible, yet independent.* Given their mainstream acceptance, it should be compatible with industry-standard tools. Simultaneously, it should not be restricted to these tools and should also operate with open-source tooling.
- *Accessible and easy to (re)use.* It should be accessible in a friendly language. Further, it should promote the reuse of artifacts (e.g., specifications, models, and proofs) built in it across proof tasks.
- *Close to the design.* It should operate close to the design implementation making it easier to formulate and debug rich specifications.

This paper presents PYCALIPER, our attempt to build such infrastructure: PYCALIPER is Python-embedded framework that provides a DSL to formulate RTL specifications and verification backends to verify these specifications, and synthesis engines to auto-generate missing parts of specifications.

PYCALIPER **System Overview.** Figure 1 illustrates the PYCALIPER architecture. PYCALIPER specifications (Sect. 2), are formulated by extending the SpecModule abstract class. By being Python-embedded, PYCALIPER leverages Python's rich ecosystem, and promotes reuse by exporting specifications as library modules. Further it allows flexible meta-programming that can be used to build domain-specific invariants targeted to certain kinds of properties. For example, besides generic specifications, we currently support invariants for two-trace security (hyper-)properties [17] (Table 2). Specifications can be complete or "incomplete", i.e., have missing parts, called *holes*.

PYCALIPER is compatible yet independent: it has SVA and BTOR2 verification backends (Sect. 3) that currently interface with both, the commercial Jasper FPV App [13] and a custom BTOR2-based [34] symbolic execution. By closely mirroring the design hierarchy, PYCALIPER allows deep-specification/verification that is close to the RTL implementation. A key component of PYCALIPER are *invariant synthesis engines* (Sect. 4) that leverage automated techniques (e.g., [21,36,45]) to fill holes in incomplete specifications. In this way, PYCALIPER supports *hardware specification engineering*: developing specification formalisms that are amenable to verification and synthesis, and techniques that can operate on these formalisms. PYCALIPER is open-source on GitHub - https://github.com/pycaliper/pycaliper - with a web-page hosted at https://pycaliper.github.io.

Related Work. Formal hardware verification tools such as EBMC [19], the Yosys [53] based SymbiYosys [15], mcy [54], and Pono [29] perform verification by

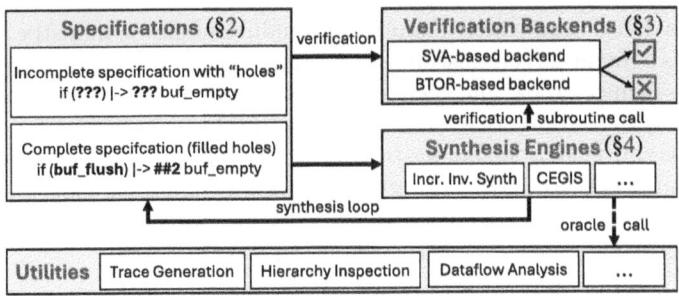

Fig. 1. PYCALIPER System Architecture and Components.

compiling the RTL design and SVA properties to automated (SAT/SMT-based [6]) solvers. Tools based on IC3 and PDR [9,10] (e.g., AVR [23] and Avy [52]) perform unbounded verification of RTL by refinement-based invariant search. PYCALIPER on the other hand, is not a verification tool in itself: our main contribution is Python-embedded infrastructure that enables programmatic RTL specification and interfaces with (SVA and BTOR2)-based verification engines. We use these verifiers as *oracles* to implement invariant synthesis techniques such as syntax-guided synthesis via CEGIS [3] and incremental invariant synthesis [11,36] (the latter itself uses an approach based on PDR).

PYCALIPER draws inspiration from the ease-of-use and flexibility provided by Python-embedded hardware tools: `cocotb` [18] (for test-based validation) and `MyHDL` [31] (for hardware design) and applies these ideas to hardware verification. Its use of *oracle-guided synthesis* [26] *and learning* follows UCLID5 [38,44], which pioneered the use of syntax-guided, oracle-guided, and learning-enabled synthesis in formal verification.

Tooling for hardware verification that leverages programming languages principles has recently seen a lot of interest. The MLIR-based CIRCT [28] infrastructure introduces *verification dialects*, which aim to provide a hardware model-checking tool-friendly intermediate representation (IR). Tools such as Kami [14] also perform hardware verification by formulating a specification language close to the implementation, but they use interactive theorem provers (e.g., Rocq, formerly Coq [7,49]) for verification. Other examples in the PL-for-HW space include design languages such as Clash [5] and Dahlia [35] that are based on HW-specific static types to ensure correctness, e.g., with respect to timing and resource usage. These are design languages, while PYCALIPER is a specification DSL. However, future work can develop new specification constructs in PYCALIPER inspired by the type semantics of these languages.

2   Python-Embedded RTL Specifications

We now describe key PYCALIPER constructs and their semantics.

2.1   PYCALIPER Specifications

Specification Elements. PYCALIPER specifications consist of elements detailed in Table 1. These naturally map to RTL constructs. For example, the `Logic` element is parameterized by its (integer) width and corresponds a reg/wire/logic signal in the Verilog/SystemVerilog design. The abstract `SpecModule` class represents the specification for an RTL module and is inherited by each PYCALIPER specification class.

Figure 2 illustrates such a specification for a `fifo` queue module, with the `__init__` function initializes the module with a set of signals. Note that since these specifications are ordinary Python classes, they can be easily augmented with usual Python code. For example, in the `fifo` module the sizes of the read and write pointers are defined as `Logic` elements with size dependent on the depth of the FIFO queue. The remainder of the class uses these elements to define the specification.

```
module fifo #(                    SV RTL      class fifo(Module):                    def input(self):                      PyCaliper
    parameter DEP=8              module          def __init__(self, cf: config_t):         self.eq(self.reset)             spec. class
) (                                                  super().__init__()                    self.eq(self.push)
    input  logic clk,                                self.DEPTH = cf.depth                 self.eq(self.pop)
    input  logic reset,                              self.DIDX = int(                      self.when(self.push)(self.d_in)
    input  logic push,                                   math.log2(self.DEPTH)+1)          self.inv(~self.empty | ~self.pop)
    input  logic pop,                                self.WIDTH = cf.width
    input  TYPE  d_in,                                                                 def state(self):
    output TYPE  d_out,                              # Input signals                       self.eq(self.rd_ptr)
    output logic empty                               self.reset = Logic()                  self.eq(self.wr_ptr)
);                                                   self.push = Logic()
    logic [$log2(DEP):0] rd_ptr;                     self.pop = Logic()                    for i in range(self.DEPTH):
    logic [$log2(DEP):0] wr_ptr;                     ...                                       self.when(
                                                                                                  self.wr_ptr-self.rd_ptr >
    // FIFO memory                                   # Internal signals                            Const(i,self.DIDX)-self.rd_ptr
    TYPE [DEP-1:0] fifo;                             self.rd_ptr = Logic(self.DIDX)            )(self.fifo_ents[i])
    ...                                              self.wr_ptr = Logic(self.DIDX)
                                                     self.fifo_ents = LogicArray(lambda:  def output(self):
    // FIFO module logic ...                             Logic(self.WIDTH), self.DEPTH)      self.eq(self.avail_entries)
endmodule:fifo                                       ...                                     self.when(~self.empty)(self.d_out)
```

Fig. 2. Left: A `fifo` SystemVerilog RTL module for a FIFO queue. Right: A PYCALIPER `SpecModule` specification corresponding to a no-stale-data property (critical for verifying data-at-rest optimizations against attacks, e.g., [50]) for the `fifo` module.

Inductive Specification. Inductive specifications in PYCALIPER consist of three components: `input`, `state`, and `output` blocks. These correspond to global assumptions, the state invariants, and output assertions, respectively. In general, the `input`, `state`, and `output` functions can be thought of as predicates over the state of the RTL design. With this view, inductive proofs aim to verify the

Table 1. Elements in PYCALIPER specifications and RTL constructs they map to.

Element	Mapping to RTL Construct
SpecModule	An RTL module in the design hierarchy
Struct	A SystemVerilog struct
Group	Bundle of signals under a hierarchical name (e.g., generate block)
Logic	Represents an RTL reg/wire in the design
LogicArray	Represents an (n-D) array of logic signals

following property:

$$T_{\mathrm{RTL}} \models (\mathsf{input}, \mathsf{state}, \mathsf{output}) \overset{\triangle}{=}$$
$$\forall S, S'.\ \mathsf{input}(S) \wedge \mathsf{state}(S) \wedge T_{\mathrm{RTL}}(S, S') \Rightarrow (\mathsf{state}(S') \wedge \mathsf{output}(S'))$$

Invariants. PYCALIPER supports both single trace invariants defined over one design instance as well as two-trace invariants defined over a miter (self-composition) of the design. The latter are used for proofs of security (hyper-)properties [17] such as no-stale-data leakage/observational-determinism [55]. Table 2 (top) illustrates these invariants and their semantics.

Table 2. PYCALIPER invariants (above), synthesis holes (below) and their corresponding semantics. We denote the two module instances in the miter as A and B.

Invariant or Hole	Semantics or Synthesis Spec. (Holes)
self.eq(x: Logic)	A.x = B.x
self.when(expr: Expr)(x: Logic)	expr(A) $\wedge$ expr(B) $\implies$ A.x = B.x
self.inv(expr: Expr)	expr(A)
self.ceqhole(e: Expr, slist: list[Logic])	?$S \subseteq$ slist. $\wedge_{s \in S}$ self.when(e)(s)
self.ctrlhole(ctrl: Logic, dep: Logic)	?LUT. self.inv(dep == LUT(ctrl))

Synthesis Holes. A key feature of PYCALIPER is the ability to synthesize invariants for incomplete specifications. PYCALIPER supports *holes* that identify syntactic templates for the invariant, much like sketching-based synthesis [45,46] or syntax-guided-synthesis (SyGuS) [3]. PYCALIPER currently supports two holes shown in Table 2 (lower half). The first (self.ceqhole(e, slist)) aims to identify a subset of signals from slist that are equal in the two copies of the miter conditional on expression e being true. The second (self.ctrlhole(ctrl, dep)) aims to generate a lookup-table (LUT) of form if (ctrl == X1) Y1 elif (ctrl == X2) Y2 ... provides the value of the dependent signal (dep) as a function of the control signal (ctrl). PYCALIPER implements *synthesis engines* that synthesize a valid solution satisfying the specification. We discuss these in Sect. 4.

Bounded Specifications. In addition to invariant-based unbounded proofs, PYCALIPER also supports bounded verification. A bounded specification can be formulated by defining a function (e.g., f) such that f(i) adds the assumptions and assertions for the i-th cycle. Assumptions and assertions are added by calling pycassume and pycassert respectively with the required property.

```
vals = [randint(0, MAX), randint(0, MAX)]
ins = [Const(val, 32) for val in vals]
expected = Const(sum(vals) % MAX, 32)

class Adder(Module):

  @unroll(2)
  def simstep(self, step: int = 0):
    self.pycassume(self.rst_ni) # active low
    if step == 0:
      self.pycassume(self.a_i == ins[0])
      self.pycassume(self.b_i == ins[1])
    elif step == 1:
      self.pycassert(self.sum_o == expected)
```

Fig. 3. Bounded specification using the unroll(k) construct.

Example 1. Figure 3 provides an example for an Adder module in which the simstep function specifies that the output with two (randomly chosen) inputs a and b equals a + b modulo wrap-around.

Further PYCALIPER provides the unroll(k) function decorator that internally unrolls f for k cycles and verifies the property.

2.2   Keeping Specifications Close to the Implementation

Organizing Specification Using SpecModules. A full design specification often requires multiple properties (e.g., SVA property statements) that complement each other. For instance describing the stage-wise behavior of even a simple pipelined processor requires a collection of properties, one for every pipeline stage. The standard approach to this has been to collect all SVA properties alongside the design module. However, this leads to a large monolithic specification that is hard to maintain and understand. By organizing multiple properties into a SpecModule, PYCALIPER leverages principles of aggregation/-modularity which have been widely adopted in SE/OOP communities [8]. We discuss benefits of this organization in this section and Sect. 2.3.

Mirroring the Design Hierarchy. Since a SpecModule class corresponds to its RTL counterpart and can contain other SpecModule members (corresponding to RTL submodules), PYCALIPER specifications mirror the RTL design hierarchy. Further specification elements (e.g., Logic) within a SpecModule also map to design signals.

The benefits of verification frameworks that operate "close to" the implementation have been demonstrated in previous work [4]. This allows specifications that are easier to formulate (due to low overhead of context-switching between implementation and specification) and more expressive (as the specification can be defined over implementation signals as opposed to some abstraction thereof). PYCALIPER extends these advantages to RTL verification.

Elaboration. PYCALIPER specifications are elaborated before being passed to the verification or synthesis backends. Elaboration uses Python's introspection features (dynamically examining objects in a scope) to traverse the specification hierarchy. A key aspect of elaboration is resolving signal names to their full hierarchical paths in the design. For example, elaboration of a `UART` specification with two (transmit/receive) `fifo` instances, `tx_fifo` and `rx_fifo` respectively will consist of a `tx_fifo.wr_ptr` `Logic` element corresponding to the write pointer of the transmit `fifo`.

2.3   Extensibility and Reuse of Specifications

Software, in particular open-source software, has long benefited from reuse. A key driver of this has been *libraries* that package reusable components. PYCALIPER similarly enables reuse of RTL specifications through parameterization and refinement.

Parameterization. PYCALIPER `SpecModule` can be instantiated with varying arguments. This is useful when formulating parameterized specifications for components such as FIFOs (seen in buffers), and tagged lookup tables (as seen in caches, predictors). For example, in Fig. 2, the `fifo` module is parameterized by the `DEPTH` and element `WIDTH`, passed through the `config` argument. Parameterized specifications of this form can be packaged into Python libraries, much like Verification IPs [41] except being open-source and extensible.

Refinement. PYCALIPER currently supports refinement-based proofs between two specifications under a particular refinement relation. Suppose there are two modules M1 and M2 with inductive specifications (input_1, state_1, output_1) and (input_2, state_2, output_2) respectively. Further suppose that $R(S_1, S_2)$ is a (binary) refinement relation between M1 and M2. Here S_1 and S_2 are states of M1 and M2 respectively. A refinement proof establishes validity of the properties:

$$\Phi_I = \text{input}_1(S_1) \land \text{state}_1(S_1) \land R(S_1, S_2) \Rightarrow \text{input}_2(S_2) \land \text{state}_2(S_2)$$
$$\text{... inputs hold in refinement}$$
$$\Phi_O = \text{state}_2(S_2) \land \text{output}_2(S_2) \land R(S_1, S_2) \Rightarrow \text{state}_1(S_1) \land \text{output}_1(S_1)$$
$$\text{... outputs hold in refinement}$$

Refinement proofs are crucially used in compositional assume-guarantee reasoning [37,51]: they imply that any design that implements M2 also implements specification M1 under the refinement relation R. Symmetrically any proof that holds under the environment of M1 also holds under the environment of M2.

Example 2. Consider the `fifo` buffer from Fig. 2. This `fifo` refines a `Counter` module with a `ctr` signal and increment/decrement (`incdec`) operation (based on example in [14]), with the refinement relation R:

$$R \equiv (\text{ctr} = \text{wr\_ptr} - \text{rd\_ptr}) \land (\text{wr\_ptr} = \text{incdec}) \land (\text{rd\_ptr} = \text{~incdec})$$

PYCALIPER currently supports refinement proofs where both M1 and M2 modules transition synchronously in lock-step. In general, refinement relations may allow one module to *stutter*, i.e., not transition while the other module transitions. Such stuttering refinement [16,32] can be used to relate two modules that have similar functional behaviors but different timing behaviors. For example, Burch-Dill refinement [33] allows verification of a pipelined processor design against its non-pipelined counterpart.

3   Verification Backends

PYCALIPER specifications are elaborated and dispatched to verification backends. We currently support two backends using SVA (SystemVerilog Assertions) [1], and BTOR2 [34] formats. We illustrate these in Fig. 4 and now discuss them.

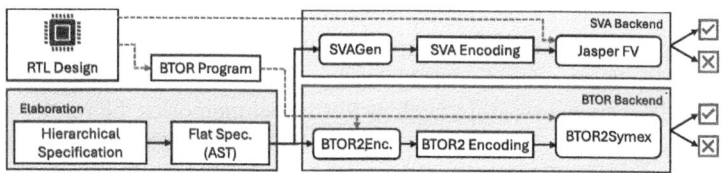

Fig. 4. PYCALIPER Verification Infrastructure: SVA and BTOR2 backends.

3.1   SVA (System Verilog Assertions) Backend

The SVA backend consumes the elaborated PYCALIPER specification and generates a SystemVerilog Assertion (SVA) file which is loaded into the proof engine. It then communicates with the proof engine through an oracle interface while referencing properties from the SVA file.

SVA Generation. The generated SVA file begins with proof harness, which includes clocking/reset assumptions and a counter FSM (used to track steps in a k-inductive proof). Further it compiles the input, state, and output PYCALIPER expressions into SVA properties. Finally, it uses the ctr signal from the FSM to define assumptions and assertions. For example, for a (k-)inductive proof:

```
P_in: assume ctr < k |-> input(...)     P_pre: assume ctr < k |-> state(...)
P_asrt: property ctr == k |-> state(...) && output(...)
```

Oracle-Interface. After loading the above SVA file, PYCALIPER communicates with the proof engine through a query-response interface shown in Table 3. Queries include enabling/disabling assumptions, property checks and trace generation.[1] Thus, the proof engine acts as an oracle for verification/synthesis, similar to the techniques in [25,39].

Table 3. Oracle Action Interface

Actions
enable_assm
disable_assm
cover
check
get_trace

PYCALIPER currently supports the (licensed) Jasper Formal Property Verification (Jasper FPV) App [13] as the proof engine. However, we can enable support for other engines (e.g., open-source tools such as SymbiYosys [15]) by implementing the oracle interface. PYCALIPER interacts with Jasper FPV via a TCP interface which is used to send Tcl commands (e.g., prove P_asrt for a check queries) and receive responses.

3.2 BTOR2 Backend

Yosys-Generated BTOR2 Program. PYCALIPER uses Yosys [53] to convert the (Verilog/SystemVerilog) RTL design into the BTOR2 [34] format. This involves standard synthesis steps such as flattening memories, hierarchy removal, and technology mapping. Importantly, the BTOR2 program preserves signal hierarchy information from the original RTL design which is used to map the PYCALIPER specification signals with their design signal counterparts.

Symbolic Execution. The BTOR2 backend consumes the BTOR2 program and performs symbolic execution. The symbolic execution engine unrolls the BTOR2 program for a certain number of steps (dependent on the k-induction parameter unrolling bound). Further it compiles the (inductive or unroll) specification into BTOR2 expressions and evaluates them on the unrolled symbolic state. The resulting formula is verified using SMT-based verification techniques. While we currently use Boolector as the SMT backend, this can be easily extended to other QFBV solvers [6] by adding appropriate operator mappings.

4   Synthesis Engines

4.1   Background: Formal Synthesis

The problem of formal synthesis of functions can be formulated as follows. Given a target function f to be synthesized, a specification ϕ that f should satisfy, and a concept class $\mathcal{F}$ describing possible function implementations, the synthesis problem aims find $f \in \mathcal{F}$ such that f satisfies ϕ. Different formal synthesis problems formulate ϕ and $\mathcal{F}$ in different ways (e.g., as a set of input-output examples or logical constraints, or a formal language). For example, Syntax-guided synthesis (SyGuS) [3] is a grammar-based approach that uses a syntactic grammar G to induce the space of possible implementations $\mathcal{F}$. In some cases (e.g., Houdini

---

[1] We require dynamically disabling assumptions to perform invariant synthesis (Sect. 4).

[20, 36]) the space of implementations allows for specialized algorithms to search for f.

In the case of PYCALIPER's specification synthesis feature, the synthesis target f corresponds to the `state` invariant function in `SpecModule`. PYCALIPER allows the `state` function to contain holes that act as a templates for missing parts of specifications. PYCALIPER implements synthesis engines that are tailored to the structure of these holes and are based on invariant/abstraction synthesis techniques from literature (e.g., [20, 25, 45]). We now discuss these in more detail.

4.2 Incremental Invariant Synthesis

Recall that `self.ceqhole(e, siglist)` asks to identify signals `s ∈ siglist` such that `self.when(e)(s)` is a valid invariant. PYCALIPER implements a fuel-based variant of the incremental invariant synthesis algorithm [11, 36] for this hole template. It treats the invariants $A = \{$`self.when(e)(s)`$\}_s$ as candidate atoms in a grammar, and searches for a conjunction of a subset of these atoms to form the overall invariant.

The algorithm maintains two subsets of A: `assms` (speculatively guessed assumptions) and `assrts` (assertions). They are always relative inductive, denoted as `assms` ⇀ `assrts`. This means `assms` and the background properties in `input` and (the non-hole part of) `state` imply `assrts` at the next step of execution:

$$\texttt{assms} \rightharpoonup \texttt{assrts} \overset{\triangle}{=}$$
$$\forall S, S'.\texttt{input}(S) \wedge \texttt{state}(S) \wedge \texttt{assms}(S) \wedge T_{RTL}(S, S') \implies \texttt{assrts}(S')$$

The algorithm admits a fuel parameter f^* that imposes an upper bound on $|\texttt{assms}| - |\texttt{assrts}|$ during the search. Intuitively, a higher f^* allows for more speculative guessing (with higher coverage), while a lower f^* forces the algorithm to be more conservative.

$$\text{dive} \ \frac{a = \texttt{strategy}(\texttt{assms}, \texttt{assrts}) \in A \quad |\texttt{assrts}| - |\texttt{assms}| > f^*}{(\texttt{assrts}, \texttt{assms}) \rightarrow (\texttt{assrts}, a :: \texttt{assms})}$$

$$\text{backtrack} \ \frac{\texttt{assms} = a :: \texttt{assms}' \quad \texttt{assms}' \rightharpoonup \texttt{assrts}'}{(\texttt{assrts}, \texttt{assms}) \rightarrow (\texttt{assrts}', \texttt{assms}')} \quad \text{saturate} \ \frac{a \in A \setminus \texttt{assrts} \quad \texttt{assms} \rightharpoonup a}{(\texttt{assrts}, \texttt{assms}) \rightarrow (a :: \texttt{assrts}, \texttt{assms})}$$

$$\text{done} \ \frac{\texttt{assms} \subseteq \texttt{assrts} \quad T_{RTL} \models (\texttt{input}, \texttt{state} \cup \texttt{assrts}, \texttt{output})}{(\texttt{assrts}, \texttt{assms}) \rightarrow \texttt{success}(\texttt{assrts})}$$

Fig. 5. Declarative rules for incremental invariant synthesis.

We present the algorithm as a declarative rule-set in Fig. 5. The algorithm is parameterized by a strategy function that decides what candidate from A to add to the current assms during a *dive* step. Addition is only possible if there is fuel remaining. The *saturate* steps adds all assertions that are relative inductive to the current assms. If the strategy explored bad candidate assumptions, the algorithm may need to *backtrack* (i.e., remove an assumption) and explore other candidates. Once it finds a self inductive assrts that can provide the overall property (output), the concludes with *success*. If *dive* cannot pick a new (unexplored) assumption, or runs out of fuel, synthesis fails.

This algorithm is parameterized by the strategy function (strategy) which has contextual knowledge of assms and assrts as well as possibly other information such as the design hierarchy, signal dependencies, etc. PyCALIPER allows the user to provide a custom strategy (or use one of in-built strategies). We explore two such strategies in our experimental evaluation (Sect. 5.2).

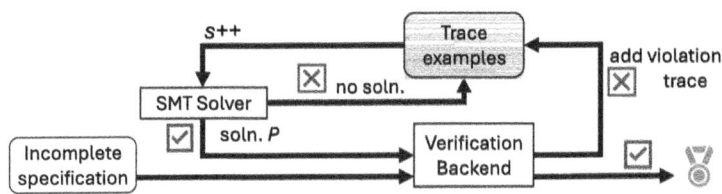

Fig. 6. CEGIS-based routine for synthesizing ctrlhole.

4.3   Counterexample-Guided Inductive Synthesis

The self.ctrlhole(ctrl, dep) hole is synthesized by generating a lookup-table that provides the value of the dep (dependent) signal as a function of the ctrl (controlling) signal. PyCALIPER implements a Counterexample Guided Inductive Synthesis (CEGIS) based synthesis routine illustrated in Fig. 6. The routine starts with a set of traces obtained from the design. Then it searches for a lookup table of size s of the form

```
(ite (= ctrl c_1) d_1 (ite (= ctrl c_2) d_2 ... d_s))
```

that matches the traces. It does so by invoking an SMT solver with c_i and d_i as free variables, and the traces as constraints. If the constraints are unsatisfiable, it means that the current lookup table is too small, and the size of the lookup table s is incremented (up to a bound). Otherwise the satisfying assignment (to c_i and d_i) provides a program P such that $dep = P(ctrl)$ for these traces. This program is checked for inductiveness using a verification backend (Sect. 3). If verification fails, the trace counterexample is added to the set of traces, and the process is repeated again (up to a limit). Adding the trace guarantees that the (incorrect) lookup table candidate will not be produced in a subsequent iteration.

5   Case Studies

We present two case studies that demonstrate PYCALIPER's ability to interface with both open-source and commercial verification backends, as well as its synthesis capabilities to complete missing parts of specifications.

5.1   Mitigating BTI with TAGE-Based Predictor Isolation

In this case study we modify an open-source branch predictor design [2] to mitigate Branch Target Injection (BTI) [24] attacks. We then formally verify the modified design using PYCALIPER's verification backends.

Branch Target Injection (BTI). Indirect branch predictors (IBPs) speculatively predict the targets of indirect branches using lookup tables. The Branch Target Injection (BTI) attack [24] allows a low-privileged (e.g., user-space) process to poison table entries, which allows malicious code execution in high-privileged (e.g., kernel) mode. BTI leverages the shared state maintained by the IBP across different privilege levels.

IsoTAGE: **TAGE-Based Predictor Isolation.** To mitigate BTI, we augment the TAGE-based branch predictor design [2] by adding, to each prediction entry, a `domain` field that matches the privilege level of the process that created that entry. A prediction is only used if the `domain` field matches the current privilege level. This ensures that entries modified in low-privilege mode are not used in high-privilege mode, thus preventing cross-domain poisoning.

Formally Verifying IsoTAGE: **How do the Backends Compare?** We aim to verify the no-poisoning formally using PYCALIPER. We formalize this as a property that says that provided the true branch target in privileged mode (`PRIV`) is in the valid kernel-code segment (less than a boundary `BDRY`), the generated prediction is also in the valid kernel-code segment. Formally, we identify the inductive specification:

$$\texttt{input} \equiv \texttt{mode} = \texttt{PRIV} \implies \texttt{targ\_i} < \texttt{BDRY}$$
$$\texttt{state} \equiv \forall i \in \texttt{IDXSET}.(\texttt{table[i].domain} = \texttt{PRIV} \implies \texttt{table[i].targ} < \texttt{BDRY})$$
$$\texttt{output} \equiv \texttt{prev\_mode} = \texttt{PRIV} \implies \texttt{targ\_o} < \texttt{BDRY}$$

We verify this property using 2-induction with both the SVA and BTOR2 backends and present the results in Table 4.

Interestingly, we observe that the solving times (ST) of the BTOR2 backend (using the Boolector solver [12]) is comparable to SVA backend using the Jasper FPV App. However, the parse time (PT) is where BTOR2 backend falls behind. This is likely due to the fact that we currently use a Python-based `btor2` parsing library - we plan to report this result and improve the parsing performance. This insightful comparison was possible due to PYCALIPER's compatibility with both verification backends.

Table 4. Performance comparison of the SVA and BTOR2 backends on the IsoTAGE benchmark. Legend: TT = total time, ST = solving time, PT = (design) parsing time.

BHT_WIDTH	SVA Backend			BTOR2 Backend				
	TT (s)	ST (s)	PT (s)	TT (s)	ST (s)	PT (s)	Len. (#stmts)	Elems.
4	4.0	**2.6**	1.4	3.6	**2.6**	1	5465	598
5	3.5	**2.5**	1.0	6.2	**2.2**	4	9029	1046
6	3.9	**3.0**	0.9	16.1	**2.1**	14	16142	1942
7	5.1	**4.1**	1.0	55.8	**3.8**	52	30376	3734
8	7.8	**6.9**	0.9	196.1	**6.1**	190	58915	7318
9	12.7	**11.4**	1.3	753.9	**11.9**	742	116186	14486

5.2 Synthesizing Invariants for Dynamic Cache-Partitioning

In the second case study, we perform invariant synthesis for the DAWG (Dynamically Allocated Way Guard) [27] mitigation, that partitions cache ways to ensure that there is no cross-domain information leakage (formulated as a non-interference property [48]). Previous work [22] performs unbounded verification of this property by manually identifying invariants. We apply the incremental invariant synthesis engine (Sect. 4.2) to synthesize k out of 8 cache way invariants for $k = 2, 3, 4$. This is a very challenging problem as the "invariant-width" [36], i.e., the number of invariants that need to be added together to ensure self-inductiveness increases with k.

We attempt two strategies for selecting the invariant candidate order: random (in-built) and a custom (rudimentary) neural strategy. In the latter, we prompt an LLM (gpt-4o) to provide an order of candidates, providing the current set of invariants and the cache partitioning property as context. Implementing this strategy with PyCaliper required $\sim$80 lines of Python code and around 30 min of human effort.

In Table 5, we present the number of verification calls (#VC) and the number of nodes explored (#nodes) in the search as an average computed over 20 runs. We use

Table 5. IIS (Sect. 4.2) with order strategies.

k	Random		Neural	
	#VC ± σ	#nodes ± σ	#VC ± σ	#nodes ± σ
2	16.7 ± 2.3	5.5 ± 0.6	14.3 ± 2.6	4.9 ± 0.9
3	101.6 ± 47.1	13.3 ± 5.5	54.0 ± 21.8	8.5 ± 3.9
4	785.7 ± 91.2	54.3 ± 4.8	163 ± 74.2	11.6 ± 8.6

the SVA-backend with the Jasper FPV App as the verification engine. We see that even our very rudimentary neural strategy outperforms the random strategy, likely by being able to detect a pattern in the invariants using the provided context. The takeaways from this experiment are twofold. Firstly, PYCALIPER allows leveraging industry-scale backends as verification oracles in an invariant synthesis task. Secondly, PYCALIPER uses the Python ecosystem to enable easy prototyping of new ideas.

6   Conclusion

PYCALIPER's ability to leverage Pythonic introspection, meta-programming and object-oriented features enables easy, flexible and reusable (packageable) RTL specification that is close to the implementation. Further, PYCALIPER provides verification backends which can interface both industry-scale tooling as well as custom/open-source verification engines. PYCALIPER uses these verification backends as oracles to implement (parameterizable) synthesis techniques to auto-generate missing parts of specifications. Thus, PYCALIPER supports holistic *hardware specification engineering* as a combination of accessible and flexible hardware specification, verification and synthesis.

Acknowledgments. We thank Federico Mora, Pei-Wei Chen (UC Berkeley), Yatin A. Manerkar (Univ. of Michigan), Elizabeth Polgreen (Univ. of Edinburgh), and Scott Constable (Intel Labs), John Matthews (formerly Intel Labs) for their feedback. This work was supported in part by Intel Corporation under the Scalable Assurance program, DARPA contract FA8750-23-C-0080 (ANSR), and by the iCyPhy center.

Disclosure of Interests. The authors declare that they have no interests other than their affiliations and funding sources mentioned in the acknowledgments.

References

1. IEEE Standard for SystemVerilog–Unified Hardware Design, Specification, and Verification Language. IEEE Std 1800-2017 (Revision of IEEE Std 1800-2012), pp. 1–1315 (2018)
2. Aaron Shappell: tage-predictor (2024). GitHub repository, https://github.com/aaronshappell/tage-predictor
3. Alur, R., et al.: Syntax-guided synthesis. In: Formal Methods in Computer-Aided Design, FMCAD 2013, Portland, OR, USA, 20–23 October 2013, pp. 1–8. IEEE (2013). https://ieeexplore.ieee.org/document/6679385/
4. Appel, A.W., et al.: Position paper: the science of deep specification. Philos. Trans. Roy. Soc. A: Math. Phys. Eng. Sci. **375**(2104), 20160331 (2017). https://royalsocietypublishing.org/doi/abs/10.1098/rsta.2016.0331
5. Baaij, C., Kooijman, M., Kuper, J., Boeijink, A., Gerards, M.: CλaSH: structural descriptions of synchronous hardware using haskell. In: 2010 13th Euromicro Conference on Digital System Design: Architectures, Methods and Tools, pp. 714–721 (2010)
6. Barrett, C., Sebastiani, R., Seshia, S.A., Tinelli, C.: Satisfiability modulo theories. In: Biere, A., van Maaren, H., Walsh, T. (eds.) Handbook of Satisfiability, chap. 26, pp. 825–885. IOS Press (2009)
7. Bertot, Y., Castéran, P.: Interactive Theorem Proving and Program Development: Coq'Art: the Calculus of Inductive Constructions. Springer, Cham (2013)
8. Blume, M., Appel, A.W.: Hierarchical modularity. ACM Trans. Program. Lang. Syst. **21**(4), 813–847 (1999). https://doi.org/10.1145/325478.325518
9. Bradley, A.R.: SAT-based model checking without unrolling. In: Proceedings of the 12th International Conference on Verification, Model Checking, and Abstract Interpretation, VMCAI'11, pp. 70–87. Springer, Heidelberg (2011)

10. Bradley, A.R.: Understanding IC3. In: Cimatti, A., Sebastiani, R. (eds.) SAT 2012. LNCS, vol. 7317, pp. 1–14. Springer, Heidelberg (2012). https://doi.org/10.1007/978-3-642-31612-8_1

11. Bradley, A.R., Manna, Z.: Property-directed incremental invariant generation. Formal Aspects Comput. **20**(4–5), 379–405 (2008). https://doi.org/10.1007/s00165-008-0080-9

12. Brummayer, R., Biere, A.: Boolector: An efficient SMT solver for bit-vectors and arrays. In: Kowalewski, S., Philippou, A. (eds.) TACAS 2009. LNCS, vol. 5505, pp. 174–177. Springer, Heidelberg (2009). https://doi.org/10.1007/978-3-642-00768-2_16

13. Cadence: Jasper FPV App (2024). https://www.cadence.com/en_US/home/tools/system-design-and-verification/formal-and-static-verification/jasper-verification-platform/formal-property-verification-app.html

14. Choi, J., Vijayaraghavan, M., Sherman, B., Chlipala, A., Arvind: Kami: a platform for high-level parametric hardware specification and its modular verification. Proc. ACM Program. Lang. 1(ICFP) (2017). https://doi.org/10.1145/3110268

15. Claire Wolf, et. al.: Symbiyosys (2022). https://github.com/YosysHQ/sby

16. Clarke, E.M., Grumberg, O., Browne, M.C.: Reasoning about networks with many identical finite-state processes. In: Proceedings of the Fifth Annual ACM Symposium on Principles of Distributed Computing. PODC '86, pp. 240–248. Association for Computing Machinery, New York, NY, USA (1986). https://doi.org/10.1145/10590.10611

17. Clarkson, M.R., Schneider, F.B.: Hyperproperties. J. Comput. Secur. **18**(6), 1157–1210 (2010)

18. cocotb: cocotb (2024). https://www.cocotb.org/, https://docs.cocotb.org/en/stable/#

19. diffblue: EBMC: Enhanced Bounded Model Checker (2024). GitHub repository, https://www.cprover.org/ebmc/, https://github.com/diffblue/hw-cbmc

20. Flanagan, C., Leino, K.R.M.: Houdini, an annotation assistant for ESC/Java. In: Proceedings of the International Symposium of Formal Methods Europe on Formal Methods for Increasing Software Productivity. FME '01, pp. 500–517. Springer, Heidelberg (2001)

21. Godbole, A., Cheang, K., Manerkar, Y.A., Seshia, S.A.: Lifting micro-update models from RTL for formal security analysis. In: Proceedings of the 29th ACM International Conference on Architectural Support for Programming Languages and Operating Systems. ASPLOS '24, vol. 2, pp. 631–648. Association for Computing Machinery, New York, NY, USA (2024). https://doi.org/10.1145/3620665.3640418

22. Godbole, A., Ye, L., Manerkar, Y.A., Seshia, S.A.: Modelling and verification of security-oriented resource partitioning schemes. In: Nadel, A., Rozier, K.Y. (eds.) Formal Methods in Computer-Aided Design, FMCAD 2023, Ames, IA, USA, 24–27 October 2023, pp. 268–273. IEEE (2023). https://doi.org/10.34727/2023/isbn.978-3-85448-060-0_35

23. Goel, A., Sakallah, K.A.: AVR: abstractly verifying reachability. In: Biere, A., Parker, D. (eds.) TACAS 2020, Part I. LNCS, vol. 12078, pp. 413–422. Springer, Cham (2020). https://doi.org/10.1007/978-3-030-45190-5_23

24. Intel Corporation: Branch Target Injection / CVE-2017-5715 / INTEL-SA-00088 (2018). Intel Advisory. https://www.intel.com/content/www/us/en/developer/articles/technical/software-security-guidance/advisory-guidance/branch-target-injection.html

25. Jha, S., Gulwani, S., Seshia, S.A., Tiwari, A.: Oracle-guided component-based program synthesis. In: Proceedings of the 32nd ACM/IEEE International Conference on Software Engineering. ICSE '10, vol. 1, pp. 215–224. Association for Computing Machinery, New York, NY, USA (2010). https://doi.org/10.1145/1806799.1806833

26. Jha, S., Seshia, S.A.: A theory of formal synthesis via inductive learning. Acta Informatica **54**(7), 693–726 (2017)

27. Kiriansky, V., Lebedev, I., Amarasinghe, S., Devadas, S., Emer, J.: Dawg: a defense against cache timing attacks in speculative execution processors. In: Proceedings of the 51st Annual IEEE/ACM International Symposium on Microarchitecture. MICRO-51, pp. 974–987. IEEE Press (2018). https://doi.org/10.1109/MICRO.2018.00083

28. Lattner, et. al.: CIRCT: Circuit IR Compilers and Tools (2025). https://circt.llvm.org/, https://github.com/llvm/circt

29. Mann, M., et al.: **Pono**: a flexible and extensible SMT-based model checker. In: Silva, A., Leino, K. (eds.) CAV 2021. LNCS, vol. 12760, pp. 461–474. Springer, Cham (2021). https://doi.org/10.1007/978-3-030-81688-9_22

30. Michael Popoloski: slang (2024). https://sv-lang.com/

31. myhdl: MyHDL (2024), Webpage. https://www.cocotb.org/, https://docs.cocotb.org/en/stable/#

32. Namjoshi, K.S.: A simple characterization of stuttering bisimulation. In: Ramesh, S., Sivakumar, G. (eds.) FSTTCS 1997. LNCS, vol. 1346, pp. 284–296. Springer, Heidelberg (1997). https://doi.org/10.1007/BFb0058037

33. Burch, J.R., Dill, D.L.: Automatic verification of pipelined microprocessor control. In: Dill, D.L. (ed.) CAV 1994. LNCS, vol. 818, pp. 68–80. Springer, Heidelberg (1994). https://doi.org/10.1007/3-540-58179-0_44

34. Niemetz, A., Preiner, M., Wolf, C., Biere, A.: Btor2, BtorMC and Boolector 3.0. In: Chockler, H., Weissenbacher, G. (eds.) CAV 2018, Part I. Lecture Notes in Computer Science, vol. 10981, pp. 587–595. Springer, Cham (2018). https://doi.org/10.1007/978-3-319-96145-3_32

35. Nigam, R., et al.: Predictable accelerator design with time-sensitive affine types. In: Proceedings of the 41st ACM SIGPLAN Conference on Programming Language Design and Implementation. PLDI 2020, pp. 393–407. Association for Computing Machinery, New York, NY, USA (2020). https://doi.org/10.1145/3385412.3385974

36. Padon, O., Wilcox, J.R., Koenig, J.R., McMillan, K.L., Aiken, A.: Induction duality: primal-dual search for invariants. Proc. ACM Program. Lang. 6(POPL) (2022). https://doi.org/10.1145/3498712

37. Pnueli, A.: In transition from global to modular temporal reasoning about programs. In: Apt, K.R. (ed.) Logics and Models of Concurrent Systems - Conference proceedings, Colle-sur-Loup (near Nice), France, 8–19 October 1984. NATO ASI Series, vol. 13, pp. 123–144. Springer, Cham (1984). https://doi.org/10.1007/978-3-642-82453-1_5

38. Polgreen, E., et al.: UCLID5: multi-modal formal modeling, verification, and synthesis. In: 34th International Conference on Computer Aided Verification (CAV). Lecture Notes in Computer Science, vol. 13371, pp. 538–551. Springer, Cham (2022)

39. Polgreen, E., Reynolds, A., Seshia, S.A.: Satisfiability and synthesis modulo oracles. CoRR abs/2107.13477 (2021). https://arxiv.org/abs/2107.13477

40. Semiconductor Engineering: Big Trouble at 3nm (2018). https://semiengineering.com/big-trouble-at-3nm/

41. Semiconductor Engineering: Verification IP (VIP) (2024). https://semiengineering.com/knowledge_centers/intellectual-property/verification-ip-vip/

42. Seshia, S.A.: Sciduction: combining induction, deduction, and structure for verification and synthesis. In: Proceedings of the Design Automation Conference (DAC), pp. 356–365 (2012)
43. Seshia, S.A.: Combining induction, deduction, and structure for verification and synthesis. Proc. IEEE **103**(11), 2036–2051 (2015)
44. Seshia, S.A., Subramanyan, P.: Uclid5: integrating modeling, verification, synthesis, and learning. In: Proceedings of the 15th ACM/IEEE International Conference on Formal Methods and Models for Codesign (MEMOCODE) (2018)
45. Solar-Lezama, A.: The sketching approach to program synthesis. In: Hu, Z. (ed.) APLAS 2009. LNCS, vol. 5904, pp. 4–13. Springer, Heidelberg (2009). https://doi.org/10.1007/978-3-642-10672-9_3
46. Solar-Lezama, A., Tancau, L., Bodik, R., Seshia, S., Saraswat, V.: Combinatorial sketching for finite programs. In: Proceedings of the 12th International Conference on Architectural Support for Programming Languages and Operating Systems. ASPLOS XII, pp. 404–415. Association for Computing Machinery, New York, NY, USA (2006). https://doi.org/10.1145/1168857.1168907
47. Synopsys: Formality Equivalence Checking (2024). https://www.synopsys.com/implementation-and-signoff/signoff/formality-equivalence-checking.html
48. Terauchi, T., Aiken, A.: Secure information flow as a safety problem. In: Hankin, C., Siveroni, I. (eds.) SAS 2005. LNCS, vol. 3672, pp. 352–367. Springer, Heidelberg (2005). https://doi.org/10.1007/11547662_24
49. The Rocq/Coq Development Team: Rocq Prover (2024). https://rocq-prover.org/, https://coq.inria.fr/
50. Vicarte, J.R.S., et al.: Augury: using data memory-dependent prefetchers to leak data at rest. In: 43rd IEEE Symposium on Security and Privacy, SP 2022, San Francisco, CA, USA, 22–26 May 2022, pp. 1491–1505. IEEE (2022). https://doi.org/10.1109/SP46214.2022.9833570
51. Viswanathan, M., Viswanathan, R.: Foundations for circular compositional reasoning. In: Proceedings of the 28th International Colloquium on Automata, Languages and Programming. ICALP '01, pp. 835–847. Springer, Heidelberg (2001)
52. Vizel, Y., Gurfinkel, A.: Interpolating property directed reachability. In: Biere, A., Bloem, R. (eds.) CAV 2014. LNCS, vol. 8559, pp. 260–276. Springer, Cham (2014). https://doi.org/10.1007/978-3-319-08867-9_17
53. Wolf, C., Glaser, J., Kepler, J.: Yosys-A Free Verilog Synthesis Suite (2013)
54. YosysHQ: Mutation Cover with Yosys (2024). GitHub repository, https://github.com/YosysHQ/mcy
55. Zdancewic, S., Myers, A.C.: Observational determinism for concurrent program security. In: 16th IEEE Computer Security Foundations Workshop (CSFW-16 2003), 30 June–2 July 2003, Pacific Grove, CA, USA, p. 29. IEEE Computer Society (2003). https://doi.org/10.1109/CSFW.2003.1212703
56. Zhang, H., Yang, W., Fedyukovich, G., Gupta, A., Malik, S.: Synthesizing environment invariants for modular hardware verification. In: Beyer, D., Zufferey, D. (eds.) VMCAI 2020. LNCS, vol. 11990, pp. 202–225. Springer, Cham (2020). https://doi.org/10.1007/978-3-030-39322-9_10

Correction to: Counterexample-Guided Commutativity

Marcel Ebbinghaus, Dominik Klumpp, and Andreas Podelski

Correction to:
Chapter 18 in: R. Piskac and Z. Rakamarić (Eds.):
Computer Aided Verification, **LNCS 15933,**
https://doi.org/10.1007/978-3-031-98682-6_18

In Chapter 18, several equations were published with incorrect notation. The subscript was either missing or incorrectly updated in multiple occurrences. This was due to a production oversight during typesetting and proofreading.

The corrected equations now display the proper subscript consistently throughout the chapter.

The updated version of this chapter can be found at
https://doi.org/10.1007/978-3-031-98682-6_18

© The Author(s) 2025
R. Piskac and Z. Rakamarić (Eds.): CAV 2025, LNCS 15933, p. C1, 2025.
https://doi.org/10.1007/978-3-031-98682-6_22

Author Index

The manufacturer's authorised representative in the EU is Springer
Nature Customer Service Centre GmbH, Europaplatz 3, 69115 Heidelberg,
Germany. If you have any concerns regarding our products, please
contact ProductSafety@springernature.com

Printed and bound by CPI Group (UK) Ltd, Croydon, CR0 4YY

24/04/2026

02096375-0009